Acclaim for John Minford's translation of t.

"Min ... the r ... idition and scholarship ... y impr ... .iations . . . are excellent. . . . Anyone with a special interest in the *Yi* or a general interest in Chinese culture will find a great deal of value in it. . . . The price is certainly unbeatable."

—*Dao: A Journal of Comparative Philosophy*

"A nicely produced book with an enthusiastic spirit and scholarly credentials . . . [It] has a freshness and clarity about it and reads well [and] has the authority of a solid translator with great scholarly experience. [It] should certainly join the small handful of books that are worthy of consulting time and time again."

—*Yijing Dao*

"[This] new translation . . . explores the multidimensional aspects of this legendary yet largely elusive work in various ways aimed at personalizing it and making it more accessible to the English-speaking world."

—*South China Morning Post*

"Consistently eloquent and erudite, this rendition of the *I Ching* will endure as a classic of the twenty-first century and beyond."

—Anthony C. Yu, Carl Darling Buck Distinguished Service Professor Emeritus in Humanities, University of Chicago

"Readers familiar with the classic Wilhelm/Baynes translation can rest assured that John Minford's new version has surpassed it. . . . It is a work of art. But it is also extremely user-friendly, especially for general readers who wish to consult their fortunes with this book. They will find here, in Minford's many-splendored prose, a largesse of wisdom and sheer mystical power."

—Leo Ou-fan Lee, Sin Wai Kin Professor of Chinese Culture, Chinese University of Hong Kong

"A creative masterpiece in itself, this translation by John Minford—one of the foremost cultural intermediaries of our day—throws fresh light on the great Chinese classic of the occult. It is a kind of unholy resurrection, a cable that disappears into the abyss of a darker time. In it the Bronze Age predicts to the Information Age the shadow of what is to come."

—Timothy Mo, three-time finalist for the Booker Prize

閔福德 譯解

饒宗頤題

I CHING

(YIJING)

The Book of Change

Translated with
an Introduction and Commentary
by

JOHN MINFORD

PENGUIN BOOKS

PENGUIN BOOKS

An imprint of Penguin Random House LLC
375 Hudson Street
New York, New York 10014
penguin.com

First published in the United States of America by Viking Penguin,
a member of Penguin Group (USA) LLC, 2014
Published in Penguin Books 2015

Frontispiece calligraphy by Jao Tsung-yi
Other calligraphy by Liao Hsintien

THE LIBRARY OF CONGRESS HAS CATALOGED THE HARDCOVER EDITION AS FOLLOWS:
Yi jing. English.
I ching = Yijing : the essential translation of the ancient chinese oracle and book of wisdom / translated
by John Minford.
pages cm
ISBN 978-0-670-02469-8 (hc.)
ISBN 978-0-14-310692-0 (pbk.)
I. Minford, John. II. Title. III. Title: Yijing.
PL2478.D49 2014
299'.51282—dc23   2014010101

Printed in the United States of America
1 3 5 7 9 10 8 6 4 2

Designed by Nancy Resnick
Frame art on title page and parts by Nick Misani

In Memory of
Liu Ts'un-yan
(1917–2009)
Teacher and Friend

Contents

Introduction

FROM DIVINATION TO ORACLE

The roots of the Chinese classic the *I Ching*, or the *Book of Change*, lie in ancient practices of Divination. More than three thousand years ago, in the Bronze Age society of the Shang dynasty, the Spirits of Nature and of the Ancestors were regularly questioned and placated by Kings, their Shamans, and their Scribes, through Divination and Sacrifice. These Rituals were accompanied by music and dance, the consumption of fresh and dried meats and cereals, the drinking and libation of alcohol, and perhaps the ingestion of cannabis.[1] The questions posed often concerned the Great Affairs of State. Should the King go to war? Was it going to rain (and would the crops be affected)? Should human prisoners or animals be sacrificed, to bring an end to the drought? Should the King go hunting for elephants? Was the harvest going to be a good one? Sometimes the questions were more personal. Was the King's toothache the result of an offense caused to an Ancestor? What was the significance of the King's dream? In order to elicit answers to such questions, the shoulder bone (scapula) of an ox or the undershell (plastron) of a turtle was ritually prepared and anointed with blood. Carefully placed indentations were made on it, and heat was applied to the indentations with a rod of some sort, producing cracks on the opposite surface. The cracks were then "read" as an oracular response.

The bones and shells were often used several times, and were inscribed with the details of each Divination. They were stored in underground depositories, where they would lie forgotten for thousands of years. Occasionally a farmer might bring one or two to the surface with his plough. These Dragon Bones (as they were known) were ground into powder and used in traditional Chinese medicine. They were especially valued for the healing of wounds. It was only very recently—in the last years of the nineteenth century—that a number of scholars recognized their true nature and began avidly collecting them. The richest trove was discovered (not surprisingly) in and around the ancient Shang-dynasty capital at Anyang, in Henan Province. Since the first extensive excavations of the 1920s, hundreds of thousands of Oracle Bones have been unearthed, and numerous volumes reproducing the inscriptions have been published.[2] Chinese and non-Chinese scholars have engaged in the complex and arduous process of deciphering and interpreting the documentation of this early form of communication with the Other World. Their writings have shed fresh and often startling light on the Shang dynasty, revealing a society greatly at variance with the Way of the Former Kings as it was idealized by sage-philosophers of a later time, such as Confucius. The Shang Priest-Kings seem to have been hugely preoccupied with Warfare and Sacrifice, and in particular with large-scale Human Sacrifice. It was a gruesome business. As the contemporary archaeologist Robert Bagley has coolly observed, "Beheading was the normal method of Sacrifice, but some victims were dismembered or cut in half and a few children seem to have been trussed up and buried alive."[3]

The powerful vassal state of Zhou from the western hinterlands finally conquered its eastern Shang neighbors toward the end of the second millennium BC, and founded its own dynasty. In the period that followed, the earlier shamanistic practices of Divination gradually lost ground to the more "civilized" or "secular" practice of achillomancy—Yarrow Divination—performed by casting the dried stalks of the yarrow, or milfoil, plant, *Achillea millefolium*.[4] Mantic insight into the workings of the Universe and into the dynamic of a situation was provided by the casting of these Stalks.[5] As a nobleman remarks in an entry for the year 644 BC in the early chronicle known as the *Zuo Commentary*, "The Turtle gives Images; the Yarrow gives Numbers."[6] At some point—and here the story becomes obscure—a body of traditional Divination lore seems to have been organized under a series of sixty-four diagrams, or Hexagrams, *gua*, each made up of six Divided (Broken) or Undivided (Unbroken) horizontal Lines. Traditionally the invention of these Hexagrams, or rather of the three-line Trigrams that were thought to constitute them, was ascribed to the legendary Fu Xi, divinely inspired by his observations of the Patterns of the Universe, of Nature, of Heaven and Earth. Some have speculated that it may have been the fall of the Yarrow Stalks themselves that gave rise to these patterns of Divided and Undivided Lines; others trace the Hexagrams back to early patterns scratched on the Oracle Bones.[7] In any event, an oracular text, or "book," became attached to the Hexagrams. This is as much as we can piece together of the hazy early story of the Oracle. There seem to have been several books of a similar nature. One (ours) was known as the *Zhouyi*, the *Change of Zhou*.[8] In those days, it should be remembered, books were bundles of bamboo strips bound together with silk threads or leather thongs.

There have been many different explanations for the term Change itself, today pronounced *yi*, in ancient days closer to *lek*. In the Oracle Bone Inscriptions it is used for a change in the weather: "It will not rain, it will become [*change to*] overcast." "Will it be [*change to*] an overcast day?"[9] Sometimes the change in the weather was the other way round, and the sun came out. But there seems to be no "sun" element in the early graph, which looks more like drops of water (rain or mist) beside the moon.

As the American scholar Donald Harper has observed, there is simply too much that we do not know to permit a precise account of the development of the Hexagrams and of the evolution of the *Zhouyi* from Oracle to what I will refer to loosely as a Book of Wisdom, from achillomancy (Yarrow Divination) to bibliomancy (Divination by the Book known as the *Change of Zhou*).[10] What is indisputable is that several of the early formulae used by the Diviners of the Shang era, as they occur in the surviving Inscriptions, are also found in the Bronze Age text of the Oracle. Richard Kunst has summarized this well: "The divinatory lexicon . . . took up in the late second millennium and early first millennium from where the Oracle Bone Inscriptions left off, then continued to develop through the years of the Zhou dynasty."[11]

This Bronze Age text, which is the basis of Part II of my translation, seems to have gradually stabilized toward the middle of the dynasty (sometime between the ninth and sixth centuries BC). It was widely used by statesmen of the period, as we can read from several episodes in the *Zuo Commentary*. It was canonized as a classic, the *I Ching*, or the *Book [Classic] of Change*, in 136 BC, by which point it had already been provided with a series of commentaries.[12] It has survived through the subsequent two thousand years of Chinese history, the strangest and most incomprehensible item in the Chinese canon, a text central to Confucian orthodoxy, and yet revered by Taoists and Buddhists; the "first of the Confucian Classics" and a pillar of state ideology, and yet at the same time a subtle and powerful vehicle for a wide range of heterodox ideas.

The book we have today, then—new editions of which, serious and not so serious, still appear with regularity in China, Taiwan, and Hong Kong—is the direct descendant of ancient Chinese Divination and Magic. Its core oracular text, the *Change of Zhou*, consisting of the Hexagrams themselves, the Hexagram Judgments, and the Statements attached to each Line, shares many of the preoccupations of Shang-dynasty Divination: the practice of Sacrifice, Ritual, and Warfare; the taking of captives; the activities of a pastoral society (herding, hunting, raising and gelding of livestock); sickness (its cause and cure); astronomical phenomena; and tinglings and other strange premonitions. Its language derives from the earliest known form of Chinese, used to record acts of Divination. If the Oracle Bone Inscriptions (and the later Inscriptions on Bronze Ritual Vessels) are the Chinese language in the making, the *Change of Zhou* is one of the earliest attempts to put that language to a coherent purpose.

In addition to divinatory formulae such as "It is Auspicious," "A Sacrifice was Received," "Supreme Fortune," and "No Harm," the early Oracle incorporated a patchwork of other popular oral materials—fragments of ancestral legend and myth, proverbs, songs, and rhymes—which became attached to a cyclical structure, the series of Sixty-Four Hexagrams. Joseph Needham, the great historian of Chinese science and thought, hazarded a guess as to the process whereby this took place: "First there were the collections of ancient peasant-omens (about birds, insects, weather, subjective feelings, and the like). . . . *Somehow or other these collections coalesced* [my italics] with the books of the professional Diviners, books which preserved traditional lore relating to scapulimancy, Divination by the milfoil sticks [Yarrow Stalks], and other forms of prognostication. . . . They remodelled the text and added elaborate commentaries on it. . . ."[13] Each of the Sixty-Four Hexagrams in the series acquired a Name. The Names were not initially fixed, but varied from one version of the Oracle to another, as did their sequential order and the wording of the text itself—we can see this in the old bamboo-strip or silk transcriptions that have been excavated recently. But the wordless diagrams provided a crystalline structure to which the fluctuating text adhered.[14] However the Hexagrams and their related texts themselves may have evolved, at this early stage in its history the words of the Oracle were linked to no system of ideas, to no Confucian or Taoist philosophy or Yin-Yang cosmology. In other words, the early oracular *Change of Zhou* was not yet a Book of Wisdom. It provided its readers (the kings and aristocrats who consulted it) with glimpses (often puzzling ones) of the workings of the Universe and man's part in it, glimpses descended from the ancient shamanistic dialogue with the unknown. With time these glimpses were to be interpreted in terms of a holistic vision of the Universe, a vision contained in many of the *I Ching* commentaries, a vision associated with the central word Tao.[15] Richard Lynn has summarized this evolution well: "Hexagram Divination . . . changed from a method of consulting and influencing Gods, Spirits and Ancestors—the 'powerful dead'—to a method of penetrating moments of the cosmic order to learn how the Way, or Tao, is configured and what direction it takes at such moments and to determine what one's place is and should be in the scheme of things."[16] Both Oracle and Book of Wisdom put the reader in touch with a greater scheme of things, opening a door to a "larger view" of the world.[17]

FROM ORACLE TO BOOK OF WISDOM

During the two periods of Zhou dynastic decline known as the Spring and Autumn and the Warring States, the text circulated in this early oracular form among the states contending for leadership of the realm and was consulted for advice on pressing matters of state, and sometimes on lesser issues. When the draconian Qin state united the empire, it was one of the few texts to escape the "burning of the books" (in 213 BC), surviving intact, so tradition has it, precisely because it was regarded not as a work of philosophy (and therefore a potential source of dissidence) but "merely" as a useful handbook of Divination.[18] A growing apparatus of quasi-philosophical commentaries was nonetheless already growing up around the urtext of the Oracle. These, known collectively as the Ten Wings and probably dating from the third and second centuries BC, were for many centuries attributed to more or less legendary figures. The Great Treatise (*Dazhuan*), perhaps the most important of these early commentaries, places the origins of the Trigrams in the remote past, setting the superlative tone adopted by many subsequent commentators.

<blockquote>
Of old, when Fu Xi ruled the world,
He gazed upward and observed
Images in the Heavens;
He gazed about him and observed
Patterns upon the Earth.
He observed markings on birds and beasts,
How they were adapted to different regions.
Close at hand, he drew inspiration from within his own person;
Further afield, he drew inspiration from the outside world.
Thus he created the Eight Trigrams,
He made Connection with the Power of Spirit Light,
He distinguished the Myriad Things according to their Essential Nature.[19]
</blockquote>

In a sense, it almost did not matter to whom the Trigrams, the Hexagrams, or the words attached to them were ascribed. In the eloquent words of the American scholar Kidder Smith, the *I Ching* was "the consummate written text, in that nearly every trace of human actors is absent from it. Its language is in this sense disembodied, and, by the same measure, empowered to roam freely throughout the natural world. It is in this sense *shen*, a 'spirit' or 'spiritual,' a text less of culture than of Heaven-and-Earth, of Nature."[20] It continued to occupy this central spiritual space, as Book of Wisdom and Power, for over two thousand years. The central *I Ching* concepts, Yin and Yang, the Tao, Good Faith, and Self-Cultivation, have preoccupied almost every Chinese thinker until the twentieth century.[21] To read or quote from the *I Ching* is to touch the very spiritual heart of things Chinese. Its "quality of mysterious holiness," to quote the American scholar Michael Nylan, "has engaged nearly every major thinker in imperial China."[22] The influential Song-dynasty philosopher Zhou Dunyi considered it to be *the* Spiritual Book par excellence, "the mysterious home of the gods of Heaven and Earth."[23] In 1271, the Mongol ruler Kublai Khan, at the suggestion of a Chinese adviser, named his Chinese dynasty "Yuan," from the opening word of the Judgment for Hexagram I: *yuan*, Supreme or Primordial.[24]

The Classic and Its Many Commentaries

The Ten Wings were the first of many attempts to weave a more sophisticated web of ideas around the basic Oracle, adapting the mantic tradition of the Hexagrams to a philosophical or cosmological scheme. They became an inseparable part of the classic.[25] The layers of text and commentary (and their traditional attributions) are best shown in tabular form.

Layers of Text

The Core Oracular Text

1. The Eight Trigrams (*Ba gua*) and the Sixty-Four Hexagrams (*Liushisi gua*), attributed to Fu Xi.
2. The Hexagram Judgments (*Tuan*), attributed to King Wen, founder of the Zhou dynasty.
3. The Line Statements (*Yaoci*), attributed to the Duke of Zhou, King Wen's son, regent for the second Zhou king.

The Ten Wings (Early Commentaries)

Wings 1–2
On the Judgment (*Tuanzhuan*). This is divided into two parts, Commentary A (Hexagrams 1–30) and Commentary B (Hexagrams 31–64). I give all of this commentary, but do not reproduce this division.
Wings 3–4
On the Image (*Xiangzhuan*). Again divided into two parts, Commentary A (On the Image of the Hexagram) and Commentary B (On the Image of the Lines). In my translation, I place Commentary A immediately beneath the Commentary on the Hexagram Judgment, and Commentary B beneath each relevant Line.
Wings 5–6
The Great Treatise (*Dazhuan; Xici*). Also divided into two parts. This cosmological and metaphysical treatise in rhapsodic form is assembled from various sources. A copy of most of it has been found at the Mawangdui excavations, datable to c. 195 BC. Extracts from this important commentary are scattered throughout my translation.

Wing 7
On the Words (*Wenyan*). A commentary attached to the first two Hexagrams.
Wing 8
The Trigrams Expounded (*Shuo gua*). The origins and symbolism of the Trigrams. I have given samples of this puzzling commentary under the eight Doubled Trigram Hexagrams.
Wing 9
On the Sequence of the Hexagrams (*Xu gua*). Mnemonic verses. I do not include any of this.
Wing 10
Miscellaneous Notes on the Hexagrams (*Za gua*). Rhymed glosses on Hexagram Names. I do not include any of this.

A characteristic passage from the Great Treatise extols the book's Spiritual Power:[26]

The *I Ching* has the measure of Heaven and Earth.
It comprehends the Tao of Heaven and Earth.
Gazing upward, it contemplates the Patterns of Heaven,
Looking down, it scrutinizes the configurations of Earth.
It knows the underlying causes of the occult and the evident.
It traces them back to their origins; it follows them to their ends.
It knows the meaning of birth and death,
How Essence fuses with Energy to form Being,
How the Wandering Soul departs, to be transformed.
It knows the conditions of Spirits and Souls.
It resembles Heaven and Earth; it never transgresses their Tao.
Its knowledge embraces the Myriad Things, its Tao succors All-under-Heaven.
It never goes astray.
It roams widely but is never exhausted.
It rejoices in Heaven, it knows Heaven's Decree.
It is forever free from care.
It is at peace with the land.
It is kind, and can therefore love.
It models itself on the Transformations of Heaven and Earth
And can never go astray.
It follows every twist and turn of the Myriad Things.

It omits nothing.
Its knowledge Connects with the Tao of morning and evening.
Its Spirit knows no boundaries.
The *I Ching* has no form.

The *I Ching* does indeed have "no form" (in the conventional sense), thanks to the unique nonverbal, cyclical device of the Sixty-Four Hexagrams. It neither begins nor ends anywhere. In this it emulates the cyclical movement of the Universe itself. It "has the measure" of Heaven and Earth. It has no date or location other than the moment and place of each reading. It has no story. It has no author. It lives by virtue of the sheer Power that flows from each consultation.

It was widely believed for many centuries that Confucius himself had a hand in some of the *I Ching* commentaries. This belief was already being questioned in the Song dynasty, and is no longer taken seriously. Indeed, the words from the Great Treatise just quoted have more in common with currents of early Taoist thought than they do with Confucius or the Confucian Sage Philosopher Mencius. The practice of writing commentaries in the margins of this powerful text became with the centuries not so much a scholarly pastime as an act of participatory meditation, a therapeutic exercise in its own right, keyed to the Sixty-Four Tarot-like archetypal Hexagrams— Heaven, Earth, The Well, The Cauldron, etc. For the purposes of this new translation, a very few words will have to suffice on the subject of *I Ching* commentary and exegesis. There are literally thousands of such commentaries, and exhaustive studies of some of these are available in English.[27] I give here as an example part of the preface to the influential commentary by the Song-dynasty philosopher Cheng Yi, which harks back to the much earlier Great Treatise. Cheng reflects on the strange properties of this book, on the way it provides the reader with literally "everything":

> The *Book of Change* [*yi*] is Transformation [*bianyi*]. It is the Transformation necessary if we are to be in tune with the Movement of Time, if we are to follow the Flow of the Tao. The Book is grand in its scope; it is all-encompassing. It is attuned to the very principles of Human Nature and Life-Destiny; it penetrates the underlying causes of both the occult and the evident. It exhausts the very Reality of Things; it reveals the Tao of endeavor and completion. . . . The principles governing Fortune and Calamity, the process of waxing and waning, the Tao of Progress and Retreat, of survival and extinction—

these are all to be found in the text of the Book. By delving carefully into it, by investigating the Hexagrams, we can understand the process of Transformation. . . . Its Principles are deep and subtle, its Images crystal clear. In essence and function they share a single source. . . . To those who contemplate this shared depth and connection, and who practice its inherent discipline, the text will provide *everything*.[28]

I have not followed any one of the countless "schools" of exegesis. In the composite running commentary I have created for this translation, I have been unashamedly eclectic, choosing whatever seemed to me most helpful for today's reader. In contrast with this, Richard Lynn's fine translation scrupulously follows one influential interpretation, that of Wang Bi. My selection does, however, include generous extracts from the commentary of the eighteenth-century Taoist Liu Yiming, the Master Awakened to the Primordial (*Wuyuanzi*), which I found to be inspiring. I call him Magister Liu. For Liu, as a Taoist belonging to the lineage of the Complete Reality [Quanzhen] School, the *I Ching* symbols represent phases in the Inner Alchemical Work of Self-Cultivation. To read it is to "study the fundamental principles of Nature, and to arrive at the meaning of life." It is "a basis for living in harmony with existential time."[29] It is a tool for the attainment of a heightened level of consciousness.[30] Magister Liu's vision of the human condition is eloquently expressed in his commentary on Hexagram XLIX, Change:

> To achieve Change is to get rid of something and not use it anymore. . . . This is Illumined Change, achieved through Self-Cultivation. It frees one of Yin Energy, of personal Desire. This is to be rid of Self. Man is born pure, with the True Energies of Yin and Yang intact and unpolluted. True Essence shines within, the Spirit is full of Light. Emotions such as joy, anger, discontent, and happiness have not yet tainted the Heart-and-Mind. Influences such as wealth and poverty have not yet perturbed the Flow of Life. Tiger and rhinoceros can cause no Harm. Swords cannot hurt. Neither Water nor Fire can impinge on Life. Life and Death are of no concern. A child such as this eats when he is hungry and puts on clothes when he is cold. He has no thoughts or cares. His Inner Strength is Illumined. Then, when he reaches the age of sixteen, the Yang cycle comes to a Conclusion, and Yin is born. Conditioned Life begins. A hundred cares confuse the Heart-and-Mind, endless affairs take their toll on

his bodily frame. He comes to think of False as True. As the days and years go by, habit accumulates on habit, estranging him from his True Nature. The Strength of his Inner Light is dimmed. *To undergo Change is to get rid of these habits.* It is to cast aside all this Ignorance and find a way back to Illumination, back to the Primordial Energy of the Tao. In order to do this, one needs first to understand Self. Then the Change will be Sincere. Then there will be Good Faith. With Sincerity and Good Faith, and once the True is distinguished from the False, all human beings are capable of Change. This is indeed their Supreme Fortune! This is the Tao. [My italics.]

THE TAO OF SELF-CULTIVATION

What Magister Liu is proposing is a program of Self-Cultivation. It is, as Joseph Needham remarks of Taoism in general, "a programme for our time as well as theirs."[31] Some readers may already be wondering what the words Tao and Taoism (which will occur countless times in these pages) actually mean. The opening lines of that most venerable of all Taoist classics, *The Tao and the Power*, sound a warning note: "The Tao that can be spoken of is not the true Tao." We speak of it at our peril. The moment we do, it slips through our fingers. Angus Graham has called it a "makeshift name for the unnameable in union with which we are spontaneously on course."[32] Perhaps it is best to say to the inquiring reader, "Words are inadequate for the Tao. But it is nonetheless real. What we can point to are clues left by those who have *experienced* this liberating way of looking at the world." One such man was the poet Tao Yuanming. He wrote:

> I pluck chrysanthemums beneath the eastern hedge,
> And gaze afar at the southern mountains.
> The mountain air is fine at evening of the day
> And flying birds return together homewards.
> Within these things there is a hint of Truth,
> But when I start to tell it, I cannot find the words.[33]

The ancient teacher Master Zhuang, whose brilliant parables pointed to his own experience of the Tao, was more inscrutable: "This is that, that is also this. When this and that are not seen as relative opposites, this is the Axis of the Tao. When the Axis is in the center of the circle, then there is an infinite Resonance."

Taoist Self-Cultivation. An Adept meditating on the Trigrams Kan *and* Li. *In the Taoist alchemical scheme of things, the* Kan *Trigram (one Yang line surrounded by two Yin, Yang within Yin) represents the Yin, or Female, element (Water, Kidneys, White Tiger, Earthly Anima), while the* Li *Trigram (one Yin line surrounded by two Yang, Yin within Yang) represents the Yang, or Male, element (Fire, Heart, Green Dragon, Celestial Animus). In his practice, the Adept extracts True Yang from within Yin (in the* Kan *Trigram), and True Yin from within Yang (in the* Li *Trigram).*

Just as the "true Tao" cannot be spoken, so the *I Ching* achieves something beyond mere words. It gives expression to *pure spirit*. That is why its decoding of the Universe is profoundly liberating. In the words of the Great Treatise, it drums it and dances it!

> The Sages created Images to give full expression to meaning.
> They constructed Hexagrams to give full expression to Reality.
> They attached words to these Images and Hexagrams
>   To give full expression to speech.[34]
>   With all of these Transformations,
>   Communication became possible,
> A full expression of what is beneficial.
>   They drummed it, they danced it,
>   To give expression to Spirit.[35]

The *I Ching* does not think, it is *sine meditatione*.
It does not act, it is *sine actu*.
In its solitude, *in quiete*,
It is motionless, *sine motu*.
In its Resonance, it reaches the core of the World,
It uncovers the *rerum omnium causam*.
In all the World, only the *I Ching* can accomplish this.
It is a most Spiritual Entity, *summus spiritus*!
Through the *I Ching* the Sage plumbs the greatest depths,
Investigates the subtlest Springs of Change.
Its very depth penetrates the Will of the World,
In intima finemque rerum mundi.
Knowledge of the Springs of Change
Enables terrestrial enterprises to be accomplished.
This Spiritual Entity makes speed without haste,
It arrives without traveling.[36]

The poet Ruan Ji echoed this sentiment, this fundamental link between the *I Ching* and the Tao, several hundred years later. "Understand the *I Ching*, and the Tao will remain with you. Its application knows no end. It makes True Connection possible."[37] His life was a "searching out of the truth somewhere between Taoist mysticism and the *I Ching*." The Tang-dynasty poet Meng Jiao described the overwhelming (and wordless) experience of visiting an *I Ching* Recluse by the name of Yin:

My Teacher spoke of Heaven and Earth,
He spoke with the voice of the Spirit Turtle.
Mystery upon mystery, things beyond men's understanding—
One by one, he made all clear.
The autumn moon oozed the whiteness of night,
The cool breeze sang the music of the clear stream.
Listening beside him, I followed deep into Truth,
And suddenly we found ourselves in a distant realm,
Our Spirits Resonating in a Stillness with no need of words.
That moment of enlightenment unravelled a myriad knots.
That evening's thoughts washed away the day's every care.
Now my wanderer's skiff is restless on the moving tide.
My parting horse neighs as the carriage rolls away.
Hermit Yin, in his mountain fastness,
Shared Truth with his newfound friend.[38]

A thousand years later, the poet Qi Biaojia built himself a studio where he contemplated the mysteries of the *I Ching*:

> When the Master becomes wearied of the sights of his garden, he can spend his days with a copy of the *I Ching* in hand, painstakingly working through the text, achieving in the process a sense of release from the vexations of life.[39]

We may not wish to climb a mountain to seek out a Hermit, and we may not have the means to build our own *I Ching* studio. But the path to Self-Cultivation that generations of Chinese readers have found in this book is open to us.

THE *I CHING* IN THE WEST

The *I Ching* first reached the West in the eighteenth century. Ever since that time, Western perceptions of the book have varied greatly, from the highly reverential to the baffled, utterly sceptical, or dismissive. In 1728, the French Jesuit Claude de Visdelou, prevented by blindness from reading or writing himself, dictated the following words from the French Indian enclave of Pondicherry: "It [the *I Ching*] is not strictly speaking a book at all, or anything like it. It is a most obscure enigma, a hundred times more difficult to explain than that of the Sphinx."[40] Hardly encouraging words for today's reader or would-be translator! The British sinologist Herbert Giles referred to "the apparent gibberish of the *Book of Changes*."[41] Bernhard Karlgren, the Swedish philologist, called it a "barely intelligible rigmarole."[42] "It would have been wiser," wrote a frustrated Joseph Needham in 1956, "to tie a millstone about the neck of the *I Ching* and cast it into the sea."[43]

From the Jesuits to James Legge

Three French Jesuits of the early eighteenth century, Jean-Baptiste Régis, Joseph-Anne-Marie de Moyriac de Mailla, and Pierre Vincent de Tartre, produced a complete Latin translation, *Y-King: Antiquissimus Sinarum Liber*, with a highly literate, discursive running commentary.[44] It circulated in manuscript transcriptions for a hundred years, and was published in Germany in two volumes (1834 and 1839).[45] The Jesuits' work presented the book as accurately as any translator has ever done. As the German editor Julius Mohl writes in his preface, it brings out both the work's *auctoritas* and its *obscuritas*. When James Legge, the redoubtable missionary from Aberdeen, began translating the book into English in the nineteenth century, he freely acknowledged his debt to the

Jesuits: "The late M. Mohl said to me once, 'I like it; for I come to it out of a sea of mist, and find solid ground.'"[46] Legge admitted that they had laid the foundation for his own translation: "Their work as a whole, and especially the prolegomena, dissertations, and notes, supply a mass of correct and valuable information. They had nearly succeeded in unravelling the confusion, and solving the [book's] enigma."[47] In his own understanding of the text, Legge essentially followed the Song-dynasty neo-Confucian commentators, while conceding that there were still times when it seemed to mean very little. "If, after all," he pleaded, "there is often 'much ado about nothing,' it is not the translator who should be deemed accountable for that, but his original."[48]

Richard Wilhelm and Carl Jung

By far the most influential version of the twentieth century was Richard Wilhelm's *I Ging: Das Buch der Wandlungen*, first published in 1924. It transformed the book's reception in the modern Western world. Wilhelm had as his guide a remarkable end-of-empire Chinese scholar, Yao Naixuan. But he also had a complex spiritual pedigree of his own. He was a Lutheran missionary working in the German treaty port of Qingdao, but his thinking was also influenced by contemporary currents of thought in his native Germany, such as those of Count Keyserling's Darmstadt School of Wisdom, and the writings of Carl Gustav Jung. Wilhelm died in 1930, not long after his return to Germany. An English version of his translation by Cary F. Baynes was begun before the Second World War while Wilhelm was still alive, but was published only in 1950.[49] Jung wrote a lengthy foreword for it. During the 1960s and 1970s this English version became a cult book. It has continued to be influential, inspiring among many others the novelists Philip K. Dick (*The Man in the High Castle*) and Philip Pullman (*His Dark Materials*), the choreographer Merce Cunningham, the rock band Pink Floyd, and the avant-garde composer John Cage. Delight in the "oracular game" of the *I Ching* runs through Hermann Hesse's great last novel, *The Glass Bead Game* (1943). Both Hesse and Jung found in the *I Ching* the same liberation and enlightenment, the same sense of Resonance and freedom from care, that the Tang poet Meng Jiao described.

A Middle Ground

I myself feel that there is a middle ground somewhere between Meng Jiao, Wilhelm, Hesse, and the Jungians, on the one hand, and the scepticism of the work's many bewildered readers on the other. Even Joseph Needham grudgingly admits that the resolution of doubts through Divination may have some validity: "As a solvent for neuroses of indecision the method [of the *I Ching*] probably paid its way."[50] In so doing, he is merely restating a famous passage from the *Zuo Commentary*, where an officer of the southern realm of Chu argues, "We consult the Oracle in order to *resolve doubts* [my italics]; where we have no doubts, why should we consult it?"⁵¹ This middle, psychological, ground has been well described by Richard Lynn:

> [The reader should] allow the work to address the primary issues with which it is concerned: the interrelatedness of personal character and destiny; how position defines scope of action; how position and circumstances define appropriate modes of behavior; how the individual is always tied to others in a web of interconnected causes and effects; how one set of circumstances inevitably changes into another; and how change itself is the great constant—and flexible response to it the only key to happiness and success. There is a core of insights here concerning the structure of human relationships and individual behavior that can, I believe, speak to this and any other age—if we but allow it to do so.⁵²

The American scholar Michael Nylan echoes this, characterizing the *I Ching* as a book "designed to instill in readers a simultaneous awareness both of the deep significance of ordinary human life and of the ultimately mysterious character of the cosmic process."⁵³ These writers are saying more or less the same thing: that this is a book which when used properly has the ability to open doors, to *reconnect* the individual with the larger Universe and its rhythms. Angus Graham puts it with characteristically cool and dispassionate clarity:

> There is no reason to doubt that Divination systems do help many people to reach appropriate decisions in situations with too many unknown factors, and that the *I Ching* is among the more successful of them. Unless we are to follow Jung in postulating an acausal principle of synchronicity, we must suppose that the *I Ching* serves to break down preconceptions by forcing the Diviner to correlate his situation with a chance set of six prognostications. . . . Since . . . the Hexagrams open up an indefinite range of patterns for correlation, *in the calm of withdrawal into sacred space and time*, the effect is *to free the mind* to take account of all information whether or not it conflicts with preconceptions, *awaken it to unnoticed similarities and connexions*, and guide it to a settled decision adequate to the complexity of factors. This is conceived not as discursive thinking, but as *a synthesizing act* in which the Diviner sees into and responds to everything at once, *with a lucidity mysterious to himself.* The *I Ching* . . . assumes

in the Diviner that kind of intelligence we have discussed in connex-
ion with [the Taoist Master] Zhuangzi, *opening out and responding to*
stimulation in perfect tranquillity, lucidity and flexibility. . . . One consults [the *I Ching*] . . . as though *seeking advice from a daimonic pres-*
ence.[My italics.][54]

Reading the *I Ching* in this way is an interactive process, requiring the
creative participation of the reader. There is ultimately no "book" out there,
no "reader" in here. If there is total Sincerity in the process of consultation,
book and reader come together. They are one. The book *is* you, the reader. It
is your reading of it. No more, no less. It is what you find in yourself, in order
to understand *it*. It is what *you* make of it. In that sense, you *are* the book. The
experience of reading gives you (and any reader) Power. Its/your Power is
limitless.[55]

A Game

Let me put this in another way. The *I Ching* is a game, a most demanding
game. One does not just read it, one does not just translate it. One *plays* it, one
plays *with* it, one interacts with it. It plays too, in deadly earnest. "No two
games are alike. There are only infinite possibilities."[56] The act of reading creates a new dynamic, triggering reflections and conversations that might otherwise never take place. To call this a game is not to be irreverent, it is not to
trivialize it. On the contrary, it is to elevate it. "Games after all are not *only*
games, they are *games*, just as an elephant is not *only* an elephant, it is an *ele-*
phant. Games are also Rituals, Patterns and Symbols of life itself. . . . As Symbols they can at once be rejoiced in and treated with respect as the mysterious
providers of that intense peace which is both action and contemplation."[57] The
game of the *I Ching* constantly urges its readers to attune themselves to the
Resonance of the Tao, to Connect, to tune in to the Springs, or Intimations, of
Change all around them, to see themselves as part of a larger whole. To enter
into a dialogue with the *I Ching* is to enter into a dialogue with the Tao, with
Nature itself, to pass through a "door into the cosmic unity of a Natural
Order."[58] The book's roots in Divination, in the powerful early shamanistic
Rituals and Sacrifices through which Connection was established with the
Other World, are what makes that Connection and Resonance still possible
today. Hexagram XI, *Tai*, Grandeur: "With Communion of Heaven and Earth,
the Myriad Things Connect."

In consultations I have observed that the most important thing is to
approach the reading *with the utmost Sincerity*, to put aside all pretense and
self-deception. Once this premise is established, the book talks back; the

response comes "from the deeper mind." It is (as Angus Graham says) a daimonic presence.

A NEW TRANSLATION?

When I was already well embarked on the enterprise, I asked the *I Ching*, "Is
this an Auspicious moment for a new translation?" It gave a sobering response:
Hexagram I, *Qian*, Heaven, with Unchanging Yang in each of the lowest five
Lines, and a solitary Changing Yang Line in Top Place. "The Dragon *overreaches himself*. There is Regret." [My italics.] Was I engaged in an act of
hubris? Should I commit my manuscript to the flames? But then, with the Top
Yang Line changing to Yin came Hexagram XLIII, *Kuai*, Resolution. "Good
Faith cries Danger. It serves as a Light. . . . The True Gentleman . . . *does not
pride himself* on Inner Strength." My favorite commentator, Magister Liu,
writes, "Good Faith is the means whereby the elimination of Yin will be
achieved, the means whereby the Heart-and-Mind of the Tao can establish
itself and become Master. *Be aware of Danger. Practice Caution and Self-
Cultivation. Let Resolution stem from Good Faith, from Sincerity, not from Pride
or Conceit*." I acknowledged the initial warning, I recognized the Danger of
pride. I also took heart from the encouragement. This Offering—this new version of the most Chinese of all Chinese books—must be made in Good Faith
and Sincerity. I hope my readers will understand this, and forgive the faults
that surely remain, shortcomings in both scholarship and wisdom.

One of the difficulties of translating this work is that there is no author to
be beholden to, and no conventional reader to speak to. The *I Ching* was not
"written" in the normal sense of the word. It came into being through a process of accretion; it is the accumulated residue of generations of Divinations,
wrapped in the wisdom-cocoon of further generations who have consulted its
oracular pages and added their own thoughts in the form of commentaries.
Its Chinese "readers" did not read it like any normal book—they consulted it.
They rarely if ever began at the "beginning" and continued to the "end." The
same will doubtless be true of readers of this translation. They will "read"
according to their individual circumstances. Their expectations will differ
from those of readers of a "normal" work of literature. The relationship
between translator and reader will be correspondingly different. My translation is a spiritual Offering. To translate or to read the *I Ching* is to wrestle with
Spirit, to search for Truth. We are not only gazing into the remote past. We are
also face to face with ourselves and our own age.

The translator's first question must surely be "Which *I Ching*?" Is this to be
a translation of an Oracle (an ancient promptbook for Divination practice,

a series of cryptic, sphinxlike utterances)? Or a translation of a Book of Wisdom (a revered scripture, an elaborate treatise on the nature of the Universe and of human civilization)? I found it more and more impossible to make such a choice. From the first I was drawn to the fresh, enigmatic text revealed by the inspired scholarship and guesswork of Wen Yiduo, Li Jingchi, Arthur Waley, and others in the first half of the twentieth century, and the groundbreaking work done by American scholars in the 1970s and 1980s. I found the scepticism of these scholars refreshing. Clearly many of the old myths surrounding the origins and nature of the text were doubtful at best—including its authorship by a series of Ancient Kings and Sages. But as I studied this "revisionist" material, the newly deciphered Oracle Bone Inscriptions, and the ever more startling archaeological findings, I had a growing feeling that for all the new light being shed, something important was being lost. Where was Fu Xi, the caveman-sage wrapped in his furs, contemplating the origins and mysteries of the Universe, inventing the Eight Trigrams to make some sense of it all? In the words of the Great Treatise already quoted, he "gazed upward and observed Images in the Heavens [the 'night sky'—he was an astronomer]; he gazed about him and observed Patterns upon the Earth [he was a geologist, a geographer, a geomancer]. He observed markings on birds and beasts [he was a naturalist], how they were adapted to different regions [he was an ecologist]. . . . He drew inspiration from within his own person [he was a psychic, a psychologist]; further afield, he drew inspiration from the outside world [he was an empirical scientist]."[59] I missed too the inspired musings of later generations of philosopher-commentators. Modern attempts to divest the original Bronze Age Oracle of all its traditional clutter, despite their brilliance, somehow seemed dry and futile. In short, I missed the essential spiritual quality of the *I Ching*.

So the question "Which *I Ching*?" became less and less simple, and in the end my answer was: "Both. Oracle *and* Book of Wisdom." The Book, to interpret at greater length the shorthand utterances of the Oracle, and give inspirational guidance; the Oracle, to contribute its primitive word-magic to "quicken" the teachings of the Book, and bring them down to earth. I have therefore ended up presenting my *I Ching* in two parts: Book of Wisdom (Part I) and Bronze Age Oracle (Part II). I explain, in the introductory remarks to each Part, how this decision has influenced the way I go about things, the procedures involved. The individual reader will decide which of the two versions to consult first. I have found that some prefer to concentrate on Part I and to read Part II separately, more out of curiosity, and for the light it sheds on early Chinese society and culture. Some have even said that they find Part II completely irrelevant to their purpose.

The Gulf Between Oracle and Book

Three concrete (and well-known) examples may help to illustrate the difference between Oracle and Book more clearly. The Chinese word *fu*, which occurs often (42 times) in the core text of the Oracle, was interpreted by early commentators, and thereafter by virtually all subsequent readers, Chinese and Western, to mean Sincerity (*cheng*). Hence the Name of Hexagram LXI (*Zhong Fu*) was translated by Wilhelm as *Innere Wahrheit* (Inner Truth in Baynes's English version). This is the scriptural understanding, and by and large I have followed it in Part I, the Book of Wisdom, adopting the term Good Faith for this fundamental concept.[60] But in 1928 the young Chinese scholar-poet Guo Moruo was among the first to claim that the word originally referred to captives and booty taken in warfare.[61] This rereading had been made possible by the Oracle Bone Inscriptions, and by other epigraphic and archaeological discoveries of the early twentieth century. In Part II, I have accordingly translated *fu* as Captives. Other frequently occurring characters have been radically reinterpreted in the same light. *Heng/xiang*, which occurs 50 times (see my commentary on the first Hexagram in Part II), seems originally to have meant Sacrifice—the dominant activity in early Chinese society. In Part II, I have translated it accordingly as Sacrifice Received (with minor variations). But in later *I Ching* interpretation, the word gradually came to include in its range of meanings not so much the actual Sacrifice, but the happy results of a Sacrifice *well received* by the Ancestors or Spirits, thus Fortune. This is how I have translated it in Part I.[62] *Zhen* (111 occurrences) seems (again on the basis of Oracle Bone studies) to have originally meant the act of Divination itself, rather than the quality of Steadfastness understood by later commentators (Wilhelm's *Beharrlichkeit*, Baynes's Perseverance). These three examples illustrate the evolution of the core text from Oracle to Book of Wisdom, the way in which "sentences that had been written as pithy Oracles became moralizing statements."[63]

The Name of Hexagram IV, *Meng*, is a fourth and striking example of the gulf separating Oracle and Book. Traditionally it came to be understood as Ignorance or Youthful Folly (Wilhelm's *Die Jugendtorheit*), and this idea permeated the understanding of the entire Hexagram. Arthur Waley, however, writing in 1933 under the influence of the new school of *I Ching* critics, speculated that *meng* was in fact a parasitic mistletoe-like plant, the dodder. This sent him off in a completely new direction. His interpretation, according to which the whole Hexagram is about the qualities and significance of the dodder, is based on a combination of philological and anthropological scholarship, with a substantial dose of his own creative imagination. I have taken up some of Waley's ideas in Part II, while following more traditional readings in Part I.

This is not a translation for sinologists or scholars, although many sinological and scholarly writings have helped in its gestation. I have worked closely with the Chinese text. So far as possible I have kept away from any preconceived Western notions as to its meaning. The discovery of that meaning I leave to each individual reader. My translation strives above all to present this extraordinary Chinese phenomenon in a form that can be *consulted* in the English-speaking world.

The Chinese contains passages of great poetic and numinous beauty. It has exercised an abiding influence on Chinese literati for over two millennia. In addition to being a "spiritual entity," it is also a cultural commonplace book, an encyclopedia of proverb, imagery, and symbolism to which reference has been made throughout the ages. But it is not just a work of literature. It is not just *a* Chinese book. It is *the* Chinese Book, daunting though that may seem.

My translation is "offered" in the awareness that no translation of this awe-inspiring and deeply puzzling book can ever hope to capture more than the faintest echo of the original. These are always going to be "coloured pictures of the wind," as the twelfth-century scholar Qiu Cheng wrote in his poem "On Considering Certain Lines of the *I Ching,* and Showing Them to Zheng Dongqing":[64]

> These Images do but sketch the principles of Change.
> Deepest Tao defies the mind.
> Scholars expound its mysteries in vain,
> Their words but coloured pictures of the wind.

There can never be a definitive version of this book, in any language. Its meaning is simply too elusive. Part of the book's Power and Magic is precisely that. It has over the years meant so many different things to so many different readers, commentators, and translators. It meant one thing for the Jesuits in the eighteenth century, quite another for Richard Wilhelm working with Lao Naixuan in the immediate aftermath of the Chinese revolution of 1911. This chameleon quality was something David Hawkes stressed in our last conversation on this subject, in the summer of 2009, shortly before his death. "Whatever you do," he said, "be sure to let your readers know that every sentence can be read in an almost infinite number of ways! That is the secret of the book. No one will ever know what it *really* means!" Even the most scholarly, even the most spiritually penetrating reading, Chinese or non-Chinese, of this strange book is in the end an act of the Imagination, a search for Truth. It is my belief that if that search is conducted in Good Faith, the book will yield its secrets.

NOTES

1. K. C. Chang made this suggestion about the early Shamans in "The Rise of Kings," in *The Formation of Chinese Civilization: An Archaeological Perspective*, ed. K. C. Chang and Xu Pingfang (2005), p. 129. "When communicating with Heaven, the Shaman was in a trance-like state, which was often drug-induced, particularly through cannabis, or achieved through physical and mental exercises similar to today's *qigong*. . . . [Shamans] often had animal assistants. These included dragons, tigers and deer. Dancing was one of the tasks of the Shaman. The Shaman's paraphernalia included tattoos, plaited hair or a serpent-like head covering, and ring ornaments around the penis." Chang was one of the most exciting scholars working in this area, where anthropology and archaeology meet. See, among his many books, *Art, Myth and Ritual* (1983), especially p. 55.

2. Li Chi, the pioneer Chinese archaeologist, gives an account of this in chapter 1 of *Anyang* (1977). His account is itself based on the classic account by his fellow scholar Tung Tso-pin. The story has been told many times. Peter Hessler's work *Oracle Bones* (London: John Murray, 2006) is a fascinating excursion around the subject. See especially "The Voice of the Turtle," pp. 135–47. One of the most scholarly accounts is by the Jesuit Father Lefeuvre, "Les inscriptions des Shang sur carapaces de tortue et sur os: Aperçu historique et bibliographique de la découverte et des premières études," in *T'oung Pao*, Second Series, vol. 61, livr. 1/3 (1975), pp. 1–82. The Academia Sinica in Taiwan has an attractive Oracle Bone website: http://oraclememory.ihp.sinica.edu.tw/e-collection.htm.

3. See Bagley's long account, "Shang Archaeology," in Michael Loewe and Edward L. Shaughnessy, eds., *The Cambridge History of Ancient China* (1999), pp. 124–231.

4. The yarrow is a plant botanically related to chamomile and tarragon. See Richard Rutt, *The Book of Changes* (1996), p. 151. Yarrow was traditionally used in England for Divination, being placed under the pillow to induce dreams. James Halliwell-Phillipps recorded another mode of Divination with this plant which enabled a person to dream of a future husband: "An ounce of yarrow, sewed up in flannel, must be placed under your pillow when you go to bed, and having repeated the following words, the required dream will be realized: Thou pretty herb of Venus' tree, / Thy true name it is yarrow; / Now who my bosom friend must be, / Pray tell thou me tomorrow. This plant, in the eastern counties, is termed *yarroway*, and there is a curious mode of Divination with its serrated leaf, with which you must tickle the inside of your nose, repeating the following lines. If the operation causes the nose to bleed, it is a certain omen of success." See Halliwell-Phillips's *Popular Rhymes* (1849), p. 223: "Yarroway, yarroway, bear a white blow, / If my love love me, my nose will bleed now." Other European cultures also associated the plant with Divination—and later with forbidden knowledge of other worlds, as suggested by its common names such as Devil's Nettle and Bad Man's Plaything. For interesting information on this subject, see the website greenramblings.blogspot.com.au.

5. I use "mantic" to refer in a broad sense to any method of communication with the "other" world that gives access to hidden knowledge, as in oneiromancy (through dreams), cheiromancy (through observation of the hands), geomancy (through scrutiny of the Earth's configuration).

6. Legge, *Zuo Commentary*, p. 169. This chronicle, nominally attached to the *Spring and Autumn Annals* of the state of Lu, has been tentatively dated to the fourth century BC, although this dating is highly controversial. The authenticity of the *I Ching* "episodes" in the *Zuo Commentary* has also been questioned.

7. See Needham, *Science and Civilisation in China*, vol. 2, p. 347.

8. Bishop Rutt's summary of information on this topic (in his chapter "Divination") is clear and informative.
9. See Liu Zhiji et al., eds., *Hanying duizhao jiaguwen jinyi leijian* (2005), pp. 155 and 428.
10. Loewe and Shaughnessy, *Cambridge History of Ancient China*, p. 859.
11. Richard Kunst, "The Original *Yijing*: A Text, Phonetic Transcription, Translation, and Indexes, with Sample Glosses" (1985), p. 201.
12. Kidder Smith Jr., "*Zhouyi* Interpretations from Accounts in the *Zuozhuan*," *HJAS* 49, no. 2 (December 1989), p. 426.
13. Needham, *Science and Civilisation in China*, vol. 2, p. 311. Here, as throughout this Introduction, all italics are mine.
14. For an explanation of the structure of the Hexagrams, see "How to Consult the *I Ching*," p. xxxvii. For the internal relationships of the Lines, see such entries as "Place" and "Resonance" in the Glossary, p. 795.
15. Tao (or Dao, as it is written in modern Pinyin transcription) was and still is a term shared by all Chinese schools of thought, including that of the Taoists. I continue to spell it in the old way, because it has become so widely used in the English language.
16. Lynn, *The Classic of Changes: A New Translation* (1994), p. 1. Here and elsewhere, for the sake of consistency, I have capitalized words such as "Divination" that are capitalized in my own translation. I have also standardized all references to the book as *I Ching*, so as not to confuse the reader.
17. For the "larger view," see Hexagram XX.
18. Richard Smith, *Fathoming the Cosmos and Ordering the World: The Yijing (I Ching, or Classic of Changes) and Its Evolution in China* (2008), p. 31. For a skeptical view of the "book burning," see Michael Nylan, *The Five "Confucian" Classics* (2001), pp. 29–31 and 204.
19. The Great Treatise, part II, section 2. See Richard Wilhelm and Cary F. Baynes, *The I Ching, or Book of Changes* (1950), pp. 328–9; Chen Guying and Zhao Jianwei, *Zhouyi jinzhu jinyi* (2004), p. 650; James Legge, *The Yi King* (1882), p. 382; Richard Lynn, p. 77; G. W. Swanson, "The Great Treatise: Commentary Tradition to the *Book of Changes*," Ph.D. dissertation, University of Washington (1974), p. 175; Kidder Smith Jr., "The Difficulty of the *Yijing*" (1993), p. 5.
20. Kidder Smith Jr., "The Difficulty of the *Yijing*," p. 5.
21. I refer readers to the entries in my Glossary for further thoughts on the meaning of these terms.
22. Nylan, p. 204.
23. For Zhou Dunyi, see Nylan, p. 204.
24. Liu Ts'un-yan, "The Syncretism of the Three Teachings in Sung-Yuan China," in *New Excursions from the Hall of Harmonious Wind* (Leiden: Brill, 1984), p. 58.
25. Donald Harper, in *New Sources of Early Chinese History: An Introduction to the Reading of Inscriptions and Manuscripts*, ed. Edward L. Shaughnessy (1997), p. 229, fn. 26.
26. The Great Treatise, part I, section 4.
27. One of the most comprehensive book-length surveys is Richard Smith's excellent *Fathoming the Cosmos and Ordering the World* (2008).
28. Cf. Iulian Shchutskii, *Researches on the I Ching* (1979), p. 72; Cheng Yi, *Chengshi yizhuan daodu* (2003), p. 49; and Kidder Smith's Ph.D. dissertation, chapter 5.
29. Thomas Cleary, quoting Liu Yiming in his introduction to *The Taoist I Ching*, pp. 6–7.
30. The words are those of the poet and *I Ching* commentator Yu Yan, quoted by Richard Smith in *Fathoming the Cosmos* (2008), p. 153.
31. Needham, *Science and Civilisation in China*, vol. V: 5, p. 65. Opposite this page, Needham reproduces the picture of the Taoist Adept meditating on the Trigrams *Kan* and *Li*, from the *Xingming guizhi* (Pointer to the Meaning of Human Nature and Life-Destiny), probably of the seventeenth century.
32. A. C. Graham, index to *Disputers of the Tao* (1989), p. 497.

33. Based on William Acker's translation, in *Classical Chinese Literature: An Anthology*, ed. John Minford and Joseph S. M. Lau (2000), pp. 503–4.
34. "Attached Words" was another name for the Great Treatise.
35. Kidder Smith Jr., "The Difficulty of the *Yijing*," p. 7. The Great Treatise, part I, section 12. Cf. Lynn, p. 67; Legge, pp. 376–7; Wilhelm, p. 322.
36. The Great Treatise, part I, section 10. Cf. Lynn, p. 63; Wilhelm, pp. 315–16.
37. These are the concluding words of Ruan Ji's essay on the *I Ching*. Cf. Donald Holzman, *Poetry and Politics: The Life and Works of Juan Chi* (Cambridge: Cambridge University Press, 1976), pp. 98–99, 101, 130–4.
38. For this famous poem, see Richard Smith, *Fortune Tellers*, p. 124; Richard Smith, *Fathoming the Cosmos*, p. 223; also Shchutskii, p. 234.
39. Duncan Campbell's translation, from his forthcoming *Anthology of Garden Literature*.
40. *"Ce n'étoit pas proprement un livre, ni quelque chose d'approchant, c'étoit un énigme très obscure, et plus difficile cent fois à expliquer que celle du sphinx."* This is to be found in his "Notice of the Yi King," sent to the Cardinals of the Congregation for the Propagation of the Faith.
41. Rutt, *Book of Changes*, p. 48; Herbert A. Giles, *History of Chinese Literature* (London: Heinemann, 1901), p. 23.
42. Bernhard Karlgren, "Loan Characters in Pre-Han Texts," *Bulletin of the Museum of Far Eastern Antiquities* (Stockholm) 35 (1963), quoted by Rutt, p. 43.
43. Needham, *Science and Civilisation in China*, vol. 2, p. 311.
44. Dates for these and all historical figures mentioned in this book are given in "Names and Dates," p. 789.
45. It is now available online at Google Books, but unfortunately several pages are missing.
46. Legge, *Yi King*, translator's preface, p. xcvi.
47. Legge, *Yi King*, translator's introduction, p. 9, and fn. 2.
48. Legge, *Yi King*, translator's preface, p. xcvi.
49. Cary Baynes (née Fink) was a seasoned Jungian translator. There is a useful biographical note (written by William McGuire) in the *Journal of Analytical Psychology* 23 (July 1978). She and her second husband, H. G. Baynes, collaborated in translating several of Jung's works. Jung had asked her to translate Wilhelm's German *I Ging* into English before 1930, while Wilhelm was still alive. The translation finally appeared two decades later, after the Second World War, in 1950. Cary Baynes died in October 1977, at the age of ninety-four.
50. Needham, *Science and Civilisation*, vol. 2, p. 347.
51. *Zuo Commentary*, Duke Huan, Year 11; Kidder Smith, "The Difficulty of the *Yijing*," p. 7; Legge, *The Chinese Classics*, vol. 5, pp. 55–7.
52. Lynn, *Classic of Changes*, p. 9.
53. Nylan, *Five "Confucian" Classics*, p. 207.
54. A. C. Graham, *Disputers of the Tao* (1989), pp. 369–70.
55. One perceptive reader found an earlier draft of this paragraph "over the top." I agree. But I have kept it, since after all it is no more "over the top" than the repeated Chinese claims for the *I Ching*! See, for example, the extracts from the Great Treatise and Cheng Yi above.
56. Kidder Smith Jr., "The Difficulty of the *Yijing*," p. 13; Richard Smith, *Fathoming the Cosmos*, p. 1. François Jullien echoes the idea: *"C'est du seul jeu de ses figures [my emphasis], de leurs effets d'opposition et de corrélation, de leurs possibilitiés de transformation . . . que naît du sens."* See his introduction to the 1992 reprint of Philastre's French translation, p. 5. Li Ling's preface to his recent edition of the *I Ching* devotes several pages to the same idea (*Sheng si you ming, fu gui zai tian*, 2013, pp. xxix–xlii).
57. J. B. Pick, *The Phoenix Dictionary of Games* (London: Dent, 1952), introduction, p. 17.
58. Francis Westbrook, "Landscape Transformation in the Poetry of Hsieh Ling-Yün," *Journal of the American Oriental Society* 100, no. 3 (July–October 1980), p. 238.
59. The Great Treatise, part II, section 2. See above.
60. For this and other key words and concepts, see the Glossary.

61. Rutt refers to this early essay by Guo on p. 220. The original (it was many times reprinted) was published in *Eastern Miscellany* (*Dongfang zazhi*) 25, no. 21 (November 10, 1928), pp. 79–93. Kunst gives a very full account of the word *fu* on p. 159ff.
62. See Rutt, p. 127ff.
63. All of this is admirably summarized by Rutt. As usual, he bases his summary on the prior work of Shaughnessy and Kunst.
64. Cf. Shchutskii, p. 235. The original poem can easily be found in the *Tushu jicheng* section on the *I Ching*.

I Ching Diagrams

1. FU XI'S SEQUENCE OF THE EIGHT TRIGRAMS

The generative process of Change, of Nature in Transformation, is represented visually in two traditional diagrams. In Fu Xi's Sequence of the Eight Trigrams (*Fuxi ba gua cixu*), the Eight Trigrams (seen in the top row) are "generated" by the Four Bigrams, which are combinations of Yin and Yang. Yin and Yang proceed from the Supreme Ultimate (*Taiji*), the original state of Non-Being, of undifferentiated, inchoate chaos (*hundun*) that preceded Being (the Phenomenal World of the Myriad Things). This is represented by the famous "gyre within a circle" (sometimes known as the Yin-Yang Fish), which shows in visual terms the all-pervading synergy of Yin and Yang. The whole diagram dates most probably from the Song dynasty and the great neo-Confucian renaissance of *I Ching* studies. Zhou Dunyi, in his "Explanation of the Taiji Diagram," wrote:

> The Supreme Ultimate, in Movement, generates Yang.
> Movement reaches its Ultimate Limit, to become Rest.
> Rest generates Yin.
> Rest in turn reaches its Ultimate Limit,
> And once again there is Movement.
> Thus Movement and Rest alternate.
> They are each other's Source or Root.
> The division into Yin and Yang establishes the Two Bigrams.

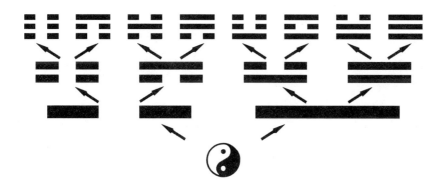

2. FU XI'S COSMIC KEYBOARD

The second diagram, an extension of the first, is known as Fu Xi's Sequence of the Sixty-Four Hexagrams (*Fuxi Liushisi gua cixu*). I like to think of it as an *I Ching* keyboard, the sort of instrument on which the Castalian Master of Music might have improvised in Hermann Hesse's *The Glass Bead Game*. The black "notes" represent Yin, the white "notes" Yang. The various combinations signal the different tonalities or modalities of the Hexagrams. The entire spectrum of Sixty-Four Hexagrams is generated by all the possible sixfold combinations of Yin and Yang. On the extreme right, read vertically from the top, is the First Hexagram, *Qian*, Heaven, made up of six Yang Lines (all white). On the extreme left, again read vertically, is the Second Hexagram, *Kun*, Earth, made up of six Yin Lines (all black). And so forth.

Both of these diagrams, and others, present the reader with vivid visualizations, aids to meditation on Yin and Yang, on the Trigrams, the Hexagrams, and the entire process of Change. Through contemplation of such images, one can be helped to attain a mindful perspective on the world, a calm

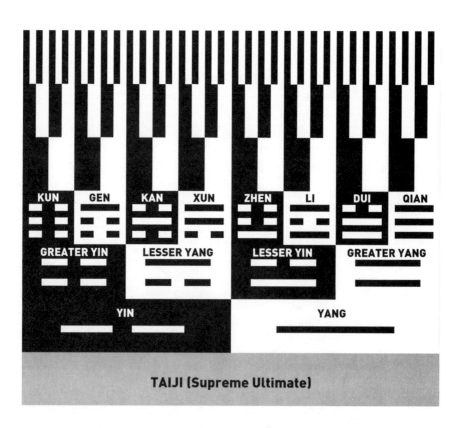

and objective attitude, conducive to a wise response and an appropriate decision. As Zhu Xi himself put it, such diagrams are Images of the Natural Pattern (*ziran zhi li*) of the *I Ching*. They show the Pattern of Change. To meditate on them can therefore be helpful in reaching an understanding of that Pattern and of Change itself.

How to Consult the *I Ching*

DIVINATION PROCEDURES

These are some simple, practical guidelines for Divination with this book.

One should begin in a quiet and receptive state of mind, and approach the Divination with Sincerity and Good Faith. This is important whatever one's actual beliefs. The *I Ching* reflects the state of mind of the Diviner (the person consulting it), providing a glimpse of the Potential Energy of the moment. This reflection, this glimpse, can be true only when the mental state of the Diviner is still.

First, the question is posed. It can be written down, or not. Formulating the question carefully and clearly is a key part of the Divination process. The response, arrived at through one or other of the Divination methods described below, is presented as a six-fold combination of Yin and Yang Lines. Each Line is characterized as either Changing (6 or 9) or Unchanging (7 or 8). When a reading gives Changing Lines, those Lines take on a great significance, since they represent the dynamic forces at work in the evolution from one Hexagram to another.

Yarrow Stalk Method

This traditional method was described in detail by the neo-Confucian philosopher Zhu Xi, whose commentary became standard for many centuries. Arthur Waley and his Bloomsbury friends used matchsticks instead of Yarrow Stalks![1]

The Diviner should choose a clean and quiet place as the place of Divination, with a table in the center of the room, facing south, not too close to a wall. The table should be about five feet long and about three feet wide. Before it is set an incense burner. Fifty Yarrow Stalks are kept wrapped in a length of perfumed silk, and stored in a black cylindrical container. Take them out and place them on the table. The container can be made of bamboo, of hardwood, or of lacquer. The Stalks, once removed and held in both hands, should be ceremonially purified in the smoke rising from the burner. "The incense, the silence and the slow movements indicate that Spirits are being consulted rather than a book."[2] Of the fifty Stalks, one is put aside. This one stalk represents the Supreme Ultimate (*Taiji*), which stands outside the Changes of Yin and Yang.

Next the remaining forty-nine Stalks are divided into two "random" piles, which represent the two poles of Yin and Yang. The two piles are placed one at each end of the divining-table.

A single Stalk is now taken from the right-hand pile and placed between the last two fingers of the left hand. The left-hand pile is then placed in the left hand (some people leave it on the table) and reduced by four Stalks at a time, until there are either one, two, three, or four Stalks left. These are placed between the next two fingers of the left hand (i.e., between the fourth finger and the middle finger). Now the same procedure is applied to the right-hand pile, which is reduced by fours until there are only one, two, three, or four Stalks left in that pile; these are inserted between the middle and index finger of the left hand.

The Diviner now has in the left hand a total of either five or nine Stalks $(1 + 1 + 3,$ or $1 + 2 + 2,$ or $1 + 3 + 1,$ or $1 + 4 + 4)$. He places these five or nine Stalks in a separate pile.

By a process of conversion, 9 is considered to be the equivalent of 2, and 5 the equivalent of 3. If this process is repeated three times, the Diviner will end up with a Line of the Hexagram that is a multiple of 2 and 3. There are four possibilities:

$2 + 2 + 2 = 6,$ or Old Yin, a Changing Line
$2 + 2 + 3 = 7,$ or Young Yang, Yang "at rest," an Unchanging Line
$2 + 3 + 3 = 8,$ or Young Yin, Yin "at rest," an Unchanging Line
$3 + 3 + 3 = 9,$ or Old Yang, a Changing Line

By doing this six times, the Diviner arrives at the composition of a six-line Hexagram. There are sixty-four possible permutations. If the Lines are *all of them Unchanging*—i.e., either 7 or 8—then the Diviner pays attention only to that Hexagram, to its Judgment, to the Commentary on the Judgment, and to the Commentary on the Image of the Hexagram. The Lines and their Statements do not enter into the picture (although some may wish to read them anyway). If, however, there are *Changing Lines* (6 or 9) in the Hexagram, then the Statements attached to those Changing Lines become relevant, and must be consulted. And with the change or changes brought about by the transformation of a Changing Line (or several Lines) into its "opposite" (i.e., when a Yang Line becomes a Yin Line, or vice versa), it becomes necessary to consult the Judgment and Judgment Commentaries of the new Hexagram created as a result.

Here is a hypothetical example. The Divination (whether by Yarrow Stalks or coins) has created the sequence 8/9/7/8/7/8, giving the Lines for Hexagram

XLVIII, The Well. *Do not forget that one always counts up from the base when building a Hexagram.*

9 (Old Yang, a Changing Line) is in the Second Place, and is the only Changing Line in the Divination. The Diviner should first consult the overall Judgment and Commentaries for this Hexagram, and should then pay special attention to the Statement attached to this Changing Line in Second Place. Then, as a result of the dynamic of this Changing Line, the Hexagram evolves into Hexagram XXXIX, Adversity, with Yin in Second Place:

The Diviner should pay attention to the overall Judgment and Commentaries for this second Hexagram.

Coin Method

This method is a lot simpler, and is the most commonly used nowadays, although it lacks the ritual complexity and antiquity of the Yarrow Stalk Method. It may have come into use sometime during or after the Tang dynasty.

Three coins are tossed. Heads counts as 3, Tails as 2. With old Chinese coins from the Manchu, or Qing, dynasty, such as the ones I use, Heads can be the side with Chinese characters, Tails the side with Manchu writing. But one can create one's own conventions.

The possible results are the same as with the Yarrow Stalk Method:

2 + 2 + 2 = 6, or Old Yin, a Changing Line
2 + 2 + 3 = 7, or Young Yang, Yang "at rest," an Unchanging Line
2 + 3 + 3 = 8, or Young Yin, Yin "at rest," an Unchanging Line
3 + 3 + 3 = 9, or Old Yang, a Changing Line

Once the Six Lines have been determined, the rules for the remaining procedures (building the Hexagram, consulting the Judgment and Lines) are the same as those for the Yarrow Stalk Method.

Online Methods

There are many methods available online that simulate the Yarrow Stalk Method or the Coin Method. I personally do not recommend them, since they introduce an element into the process which discourages a thoughtful and calm attitude.

TWO EXAMPLES

In order to help readers with their Divinations, I here present a couple of recent consultations, going through the process step by step. I used the Coin Method.

Consultation 1

Step 1. The Question
The first thing for the reader to do is to formulate a question. In this, as in every subsequent step, the most essential thing is the reader's attitude. For the Divination to "work," this attitude must have the quality of Good Faith and Sincerity, the prime quality stressed throughout the *I Ching*. In other words, the Question must be a truthful expression of the Inner Mind.

The question for this first consultation was as follows: "What can the *I Ching* say to me in this day and age? How can I make sense of it?"

Step 2. Arriving at the Hexagram
The Diviner threw the three coins six times, to arrive at a Hexagram (Heads/Chinese = 3; Tails/Manchu = 2). Each throw of three coins was bound to produce one of the following four numbers:

  6, Divided Line (Old, or Changing, Yin)
  7, Undivided Line (Young, or Unchanging, Yang)
  8, Divided Line (Young, or Unchanging, Yin)
  9, Undivided Line (Old, or Changing, Yang)

The Hexagram was then "built" from the bottom; i.e., the first throw gave the number for the First, or bottom, Line. The last throw gave the Last, or Top, Line.

In this consultation, the six numbers arrived at were, in the following order:

  8 (Young Yin)—Bottom Line
  7 (Young Yang)—Second Line
  8 (Young Yin)—Third Line
  8 (Young Yin)—Fourth Line
  7 (Young Yang)—Fifth Line
  8 (Young Yin)—Top Line

The Diviner inverted the order, since Hexagrams are always built from the bottom.

Next, the two constituent Trigrams were identified, formed by the top three numbers, 8/7/8, and the bottom three numbers, 8/7/8. Using the Finding Table for Hexagrams on pages 856–57, the Diviner found the Trigrams, and then derived from them the resultant Hexagram. The Upper Trigram was *Kan* (third from the left in the Top Line of the Table); the Lower Trigram was also *Kan* (third down on the left-hand side of the Table). These two "met" in the square occupied by Hexagram XXIX.

So the resultant Hexagram was XXIX. The Diviner turned to the relevant page in Part I and found the opening section of the Hexagram organized on the page as follows:

HEXAGRAM XXIX

Kan

The Abyss

Kan/Water

above

Kan/Water

Step 3. What to Notice About the Hexagram and Its Structure
The first thing the Diviner noticed about this Hexagram was that all the Lines were Unchanging. In other words, in this reading there were no Lines with the numbers 6 or 9. (It might not have been so: if the coins had fallen differently,

and the result had been 6/9/6/6/9/6, for example, the Hexagram would still have been XXIX, but every Line would have been Changing.) Since there were no Changing Lines, the Diviner went on to consult only the first section of text—i.e., the Name, the Judgment, and the two Commentaries, On the Judgment and On the Image of the Hexagram. The Diviner did not consult the Line Statements.

The next thing the Diviner paid attention to was the Hexagram structure. There could be lessons to be learned from this. The structure of this Hexagram is formed by the doubling of the same Trigram, *Kan*, Water or The Abyss. That Trigram is made up of two Yin (Divided) Lines around a single Yang (Undivided) Line. The Hexagram Name is also *Kan*. It is *Kan* Doubled. This is significant.

Step 4. What to Read in the Hexagram

After the number of the Hexagram, XXIX, comes the Name. This is the brief "tag" given to each Hexagram, which often, but not always, encapsulates some aspect of the Hexagram's meaning. In my translation, I always provide the Chinese character for the name, in this case坎, followed by its romanization, or spelling in Western letters, in this case *Kan*, and lastly the translation, The Abyss. Many Names are graphic, and in themselves provide clear clues as to a Hexagram's meaning. Good examples of this are The Well, Hexagram XLVIII, and The Cauldron, Hexagram L. Names such as these provide clear Images that dominate the subsequent text. It is not always as simple as this.

In the layout used for my translation, after the Name comes a graph for Turtle, 龜. This is a device I have used throughout my translation to separate sections of the text, for the convenience of the Diviner.

Next the Diviner considered the symbolism or imagery of the Trigram Structure—in this case, Water over Water. What do Water and The Abyss mean in the context of the *I Ching*?

Then the Diviner read the Judgment, the brief mantic Statement that begins the text, followed by the Commentary on the Judgment (under the heading "On the Judgment"), and the Commentary on the Image of the Hexagram (under the heading "On the Image of the Hexagram"). These provide the basic amplification of the Divination response.

In this case, what did the Judgment say? **Good Faith. Fortune in Heart-and-Mind. Actions are honored.** A Diviner new to the *I Ching* might wish at this point to refer to the Glossary, at the back of the book, where there are entries for Good Faith, Fortune, Heart-and-Mind, Act, and Action. This Judgment in effect presented the salient characteristics of the Hexagram response, which was to a great extent positive. The Diviner was being told that the answer to the question was to be found in the basic attitude underlying the whole process of

I Ching Divination: Good Faith. That, in other words, is what it is "saying in this day and age." With Good Faith, the Divination will "make sense." There will be a good result (Fortune) arising from the Diviner's ability to "make sense" of the *I Ching*. This Fortune stems from the Inner Heart-and-Mind. The Fortune in its turn leads to subsequent decisions and Actions being "honored."

Next, in the Commentary on the Judgment (under the heading "On the Judgment"), the Diviner went on to read the first (and oldest) expansion or interpretation of the brief Judgment. This began to explore the symbolism of the Hexagram. The two prominent symbols here were The Abyss and Water. These are linked to the overall idea of Danger or Peril. Often in this Commentary there are remarks about a Line being Centered, True, Firm, or Yielding—these are qualities of Lines and of their interaction, and also of types of response to situations in life. Again, a Diviner may wish to consult the Glossary for these words.

Next the Diviner consulted the Commentary on the Image of the Hexagram (under the heading "On the Image of the Hexagram"). This Commentary often goes one step further in interpreting the symbolism of the Hexagram. **Water flows, in an uninterrupted current. The True Gentleman acts from constancy of Inner Strength.** It stresses two things: the need to emulate the flowing quality of Water, and the importance of cultivating Inner Strength before putting anything into "practice," before teaching, before passing on anything to Others.

Gradually, as the Diviner read these two early Commentaries, it became possible to build up a picture of the Hexagram's meaning. Next, in the Composite Commentary following the graph for Dragon, 𤡑, the Diviner read a series of (hopefully) enlightening comments by later commentators. This was read from beginning to end, but not all of it was immediately or directly relevant to the question. The general message of the Hexagram *Kan*, The Abyss, emerging from the Composite Commentary was that Water flowing through an Abyss or Gorge would bring with it Danger or Peril; that this Danger would need to be faced; and that by facing Danger with Good Faith, one would become stronger, more able to deal with challenges.

This is a Doubled Trigram Hexagram (*Kan* above *Kan*). There are eight such Doubled Trigram Hexagrams in the *I Ching*. For all of these I have translated extracts from an additional early commentary (another of the Ten Wings) known as the Trigrams Expounded, describing a whole list of qualities associated with the Trigram. This Wing may be a little difficult to make sense of; it may seem little more than a sequence of random images, colorful but of little relevance to your question. You may wish to skip it.

Step 5. Contemplation of the Hexagram

Sometimes we may find that at first reading it is indeed hard to make out what the *I Ching* is "saying." To refer back to the wording of the Diviner's Question, it may seem to make little sense, in this or in any day and age. This is where the fifth step, contemplation, becomes so important. In the end, the Book "says" little that is not already in the mind of the Diviner. It draws things out of the Diviner's mind. It functions as a mirror. (See the quotations from Richard Rutt, Angus Graham, and others in my Introduction.) The more you think about the reading, the more you *contemplate* it, the more likely it is that content will come forward from your own consciousness. So even if things appear at first to make little or no sense, persevere. *You* are the one who will ultimately make sense of it all.

It is often necessary to interpret certain words in a broad and figurative sense, not to take them too literally. This is where a commentator like Magister Liu (Liu Yiming) can be most helpful. I quote from him in my commentary to this Hexagram, for example, as saying that "with Good Faith the Auspicious interaction between Yin and Yang can be emulated; the perilous, uninterrupted torrent of Water can be navigated through the Abyss." As a practicing Taoist, Liu is telling the Diviner that the Danger or Peril portrayed in the Hexagram is an Inner Danger; it is the challenge of confronting Self, of exposing and dealing with one's own vulnerability. This Danger can be a positive thing. Liu is tying together aspects of the Hexagram so that they "make sense" in the framework of the Taoist Self-Cultivation that lies at the heart of the *I Ching* (as he sees it).

Throughout this process of reading and contemplation, Good Faith continues to be essential. Cynicism will disconnect the Diviner from meaningful interaction with the text.

Step 6. Conclusions

The Diviner needed to draw the Divination to a conclusion. What did it all amount to, as a response to the question posed? Was there an overriding message in the Hexagram? In order to answer this, it was necessary to synthesize the symbols and mantic statements in such a way that they "made sense." To put it another way, it was necessary for the Diviner to *make* sense of them himself, or herself. In this case, one possible Conclusion might have been as follows:

Life presents us with certain critical passages, seemingly dangerous moments, like the Waters of a torrent rushing through a Gorge. In dealing with such situations, we ourselves must be like Water. We can then turn Danger to our advantage. We can learn from it. In order to succeed in this, we must be adaptable, not aggressive. This is possible only if we have a reservoir of Inner Strength.

Consultation 2

The first Divination arrived at a Hexagram with six Unchanging Lines. This is relatively rare. There are usually one or two Changing Lines. I therefore thought it a good idea to try a second, in the hope that the *I Ching* would present some Changing Lines. Sure enough, it did.

Step 1. The Question

This time, I was the Diviner, and I posed my own question: "Is this new translation timely?" By that I meant, Does it have something to offer its readers that is relevant to this moment in time?

Step 2. Arriving at the Hexagram

I threw three coins six times. The following six Lines resulted:

9 (Old Yang)—Bottom Line
6 (Old Yin)—Second Line
7 (Young Yang)—Third Line
8 (Young Yin)—Fourth Line
9 (Old Yang)—Fifth Line
7 (Young Yang)—Top Line

Inverting the numbers, I arrived at the following Hexagram:

HEXAGRAM XXXVII

Jia Ren

The Family

Xun/Wind

above

Li/Fire

This Hexagram has three Changing Lines (9 in First Place, 6 in Second Place, and 9 in Fifth Place). These Changing Lines and their Statements became important elements in the reading.

Step 3. What to Notice About the Hexagram and Its Structure
The Trigram structure of Family is composed of Wind over Fire. This can be visualized as smoke rising out of the household hearth, an Image evoking the idea of Family.

Step 4. How to Read the Hexagram
At first sight, this Hexagram, Family, is indeed all about the way in which the Family is run—through Discipline, with a focus on what was considered the suitable role for the woman in the traditional Chinese Family, one of docile subservience. Once Discipline is established, the Diviner is told, all is well. **This is the True Tao of the Family. When the Family is True, then the World is settled and at peace.** At first the Diviner might well wonder what all of this has to do with the question, the timeliness or otherwise of a new translation of the *I Ching*. What in this context are we to understand by the Family? With the Changing Line in First Place, Magister Liu begins to explain. Discipline enables order to prevail and prevents things from occurring that would lead to Regret. The first to be disciplined should be Self. For this, the Heart-and-Mind must become Empty, Inner Thoughts must fade away. Liu understands the discipline of the Family in a metaphorical sense, to mean the way one manages Self, the Inner Family made up of all the various thoughts and emotions that drive us on, that cloud the Heart-and-Mind and prevent it from attaining the Heart-and-Mind of the Tao. The Changing Second Line emphasizes the woman's role in the Family. **It is her task to provide food at the Center. To be Steadfast is Auspicious.** Once again Magister Liu interprets

this figuratively. The "woman" is a Yin Image of Yielding and Centered Truth, of the Yielding Tao of Self-Cultivation, of the Calm that governs Movement. The emphasis is on Emptiness and Calm. The new translation that is the subject of the question requires this above all else, if it is to function like a Family, spreading the True Tao. The Changing Fifth Line strikes a new and more positive note. **The King comes to his Family. There is no cause for anxiety. This is Auspicious.** The Yang King is in the Center, writes Magister Liu. The Heart-and-Mind is True. All-under-Heaven is at peace. Love prevails. Again, he interprets this in terms of Self-Cultivation.

Since these three Lines change, the reader is presented with not one but two Hexagrams. When Lines 1, 2, and 5 change, they modify the original Hexagram, to produce a second, Blight.

HEXAGRAM XVIII

Gu

Blight

Gen/Mountain

above

Xun/Wind

Step 5. What to Notice About the Second Hexagram and Its Structure
With this new Hexagram, the emphasis changes yet again. The Mountain of the Upper Trigram now rises above the Wind of the Lower Trigram. The Wind is checked and driven back.

Step 6. How to Read the Second Hexagram
The Diviner is now confronted with Blight, a critical situation, and the enterprise in question (the new translation) is seen in a new light. **Supreme Fortune. It Profits to cross a Great Stream. Three days before, three days after, the first day, *Jia*.** This last sentence is all about timing, about the need for things to happen at an appropriate time. There is Supreme Fortune, and the implication is that the timing is right. On the Judgment: **A Great Stream is crossed, an enterprise of moment undertaken. Each ending is a commencement. This is the Movement of Heaven.** The Great Stream crossed is an Image of embarking on any challenging enterprise, such as a new translation of the *I Ching*. The Movement of Heaven, the cycle of the Tao, is such that each ending is the commencement of something new. Once again Magister Liu is very helpful. This second Hexagram portrays a time of disorder and decay, such as the present. Things are scattered in disarray. This is the idea of Blight, a state in which things are going to ruin, as if through poison or venomous worms. The Hexagram advises how to halt this Blight, how to abandon the False and Return to the True, how to restore soundness and vigor. In the Upper Trigram, the single Yang at the Top signals a Return to the Root, a Return to Life, remedying the harmful, decaying effects of Yin Energy, Cultivating the Tao. This explains the Augury of Supreme Fortune. Great effort will be required, however, as in crossing a Great Stream. Great Danger and Adversity will be confronted. One must temper oneself, in the Dragon's Pool and the Tiger's Cave—in the furnace of the world and its troubles—in order to rediscover True Self. Careful consideration is necessary: of the events that have brought about the Blight, and of the measures required to remedy it.

Step 7. Contemplation of the Hexagrams
From Family to Blight. This is the overall movement of the reading. First the *I Ching* presents a picture of Family and the need for discipline, the need for "womanly" Yielding Calm at the Center—of both Family and Self. Without this, no enterprise (including a new translation) will be True. Then it announces the arrival of the King in his Temple—a major event. In the subsequent Hexagram, Blight, the *I Ching* proposes that the enterprise (the new translation) may indeed be timely, provided it is undertaken in the right spirit.

Then it may make a contribution to halting the decay which blights the modern world.

Step 8. Conclusions

This at least was my understanding of the reading. I should persevere in the undertaking, which has the potential to be helpful in our time, but do so in a spirit of Calm. It is interesting to compare this with the reading in my Introduction, which also had a bearing on the translation, and which gave comparably balanced advice: On the one hand, proceed with Humility. On the other hand, persevere in a worthwhile undertaking.

HOW TO FIND YOUR WAY AROUND IN THIS TRANSLATION

Let us take the third Hexagram as an example.

HEXAGRAM III

Each Hexagram is numbered from 1 to 64.

The Chinese character for the Hexagram Name.

The Hexagram itself, composed of six Lines.

Zhun

The Hexagram Name in the Pinyin system of romanization.

Difficult Birth

Translation of the Hexagram Name.

Early graph for Turtle, used to divide sections of text.

Kan/Abyss

Name of Upper Constituent Trigram.

above

Zhen/Quake

Name of Lower Constituent Trigram.

JUDGMENT

Heading of first section of Core Text, composed of mantic statements.

Supreme Fortune . . .

Text of Judgment itself.

Early graph for Dragon, used as symbol for Composite Commentary, or Digest of Commentaries.

Abyss above Quake. The Chinese graph for *Zhun*, writes Legge . . .

Text of Composite Commentary.

On the Judgment
Difficult Birth . . .

Text of first of the Ten Wings, or early commentaries, relating to Judgment.

On the Image of the Hexagram
Clouds and Thunder,
Nubes et tonitrus . . .

Text of second of the Ten Wings, a commentary relating to Hexagram Name and Hexagram as a whole. Latin is sometimes used for a mantic formula.

This first "mixed" Hexagram of the *I Ching* contains both Yin and Yang Lines . . .

Text of Composite Commentary.

LINES

Section of the Hexagram giving each Line and its Statement.

Yang in First Place

The "quality" of the First Line as reached by the individual Divination, and the "quality" of the place itself. These may coincide, or they may not.

Hesitation . . .

The Statement of this particular Line.

On the Image

Despite hesitation . . .

The part of the Commentary on the Image relating to this particular Line.

Yang Line in Yang Place. This First Line, writes Legge, is Undivided (Yang) and Firm . . .

Text of Composite Commentary.

The remaining text follows the same structure.

The Sixty-Four Hexagrams

Page numbers refer to each Hexagram as it appears in Part I and Part II. Only one Name is given for a Hexagram if the Names are identical in both parts.

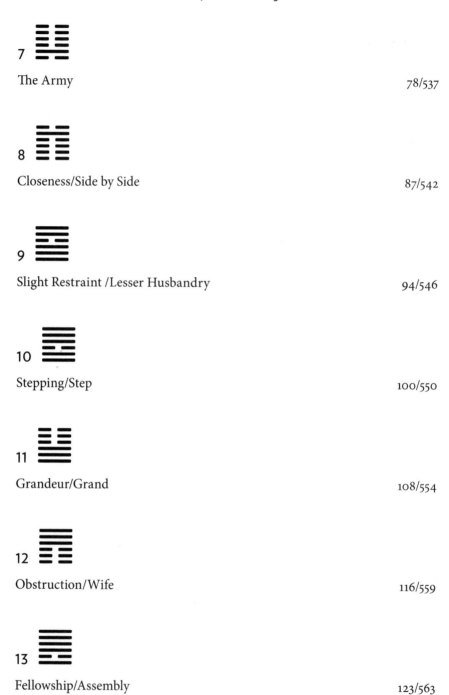

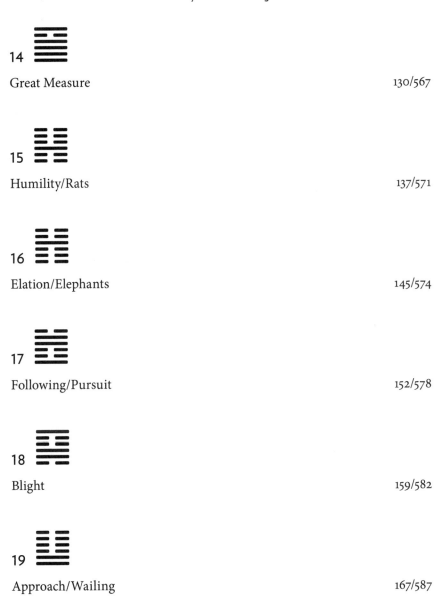

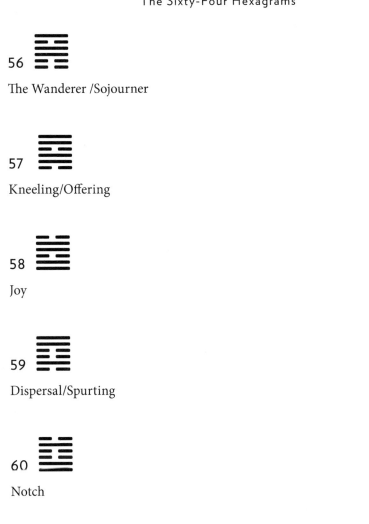

A Note on Pronunciation and Other Conventions

In this book, Chinese names and place names are in general spelled according to the Chinese system known as Hanyu Pinyin, or Pinyin for short. There are one or two exceptions. In the Pinyin system, the names of this book are spelled *Zhouyi* (*Change of Zhou*) and *Yijing* (*I Ching*). I use the old Wade-Giles spelling, *I Ching*, throughout, simply because it has become so familiar to Western readers. Similarly, for the Tao, which is written *dao* in Pinyin, I continue to use the old spelling, again because it is so widely used in English.

The following very short list of approximate equivalents may help readers with some of the more difficult aspects of the Pinyin system:

c = *ts*
q = *ch*
x = *sh*
z = *dz*
zh = *j*

The following rather longer list may also be of some use:

Bang = *Bung*
Bo = *Boar* (wild pig)
Cai = *Ts'eye* ("It's eye," without the first vowel)
Cang = *Ts'arng*
Chen = *Churn*
Cheng = *Churng*
Chong = *Choong* (as in "book")
Chuan = *Chwan*
Dang = *Darng* or *Dung* (as in cow "dung")
Dong = *Doong* (as in "book")
Feng = *Ferng*
Gui = *Gway* (as in "way")
Guo = *Gwore*
Jia = *Jeeyar*
Jiang = *Jee-young*
Kong = *Koong* (as in "book")
Li = *Lee*

Long = *Loong* (as in "book")
Lü = *Lew* (as in the French *tu*)
Mo = *More*
Qi = *Chee*
Qian = *Chee-yenne*
Qing = *Ching*
Rong = *Roong* (as in "book")
Shi = *Shhh*
Shun = *Shoon* (as in "should")
Si = *Szzz*
Song = *Soong* (as in "book")
Sun = *Soon* (as in "book")
Wen = *Wen* (as in "forgotte*n*")
Xi = *Shee*
Xiao = *Shee-ow* (as in "she-cow" without the *c*)
Xin = *Shin*
Xing = *Shing*
Xiong = *Sheeoong*
Xu = *Shyeu* (as in the French *tu*)
Yan = *Yen*
Yi = *Yee*
You = *Yo* [-heave-ho]
Yu = *Yew* (as in the French *tu*)
Yuan = *"You, Anne"*
Zha = *Jar*
Zhe = *Jerrr*
Zhen = *Jurn*
Zhi = *Jirrr*
Zhou = *Joe*
Zhu = *Jew*
Zhuang = *Jwarng*
Zi = *Dzzz*
Zong = *Dzoong* (as in "book")
Zuo = *Dzore*

SOME OTHER CONVENTIONS

I have used capital letters rather liberally to indicate important practices and concepts within the overall scheme of the *I Ching*. I am aware that some readers may find this tiresome. I have found it to be necessary, because the book has more or less invented its own terms and indeed its own language—some would go so far as to call it *I Ching*-speak.

In Part I, capitals are used mostly for terms that became widely accepted in later *I Ching* commentary, such as Self-Cultivation, Stillness, Steadfast, Sincerity, Good Faith, and Illumination. Illustrations of some of these terms are to be found in the Glossary. In Part II, capitals are reserved mainly for terms from the earlier period, such as Divination, Sacrifice, Ritual, Ancestor, and Temple.

Dates for dynasties, people, and books are not given in the main body of the text. They are to be found in the Names and Dates section at the back of the book.

Other information on the traditional ways of arriving at a Hexagram for a consultation, and the particular arrangements of this edition, can be found in "How to Consult the *I Ching*," page xxxvii.

I CHING

THE BOOK OF CHANGE

I Ching

易
经

PART I

Book of Wisdom

With Extracts from Traditional Commentaries

ABOUT PART I

This is the *I Ching*, the *Book*, or *Classic, of Change*, canonized as "first among the Classics" in 136 BC, with extracts from a number of its earliest commentaries, known as the Ten Wings. To these I have added a digest of later Chinese commentaries, from the Han dynasty to the present day, and of a few non-Chinese commentaries, along with my own linking remarks as translator and editor. The aim is to provide the lay reader with a consultable work, a Book of Wisdom that has grown over the centuries, obscuring the original Oracle beneath its accretions.

Readers can, if they wish, turn to Part II for a glimpse of that early Bronze Age Oracle. Here, in Part I, they will find a "received" text that has been used over the past two millennia by the Chinese people, from the poorest peasant trudging to the temple fair to have his or her fortune told, to the general contemplating his next military move; from the most sophisticated poet, the most sensitive landscape painter, to the most arcane philosopher, the most highly skilled physician. Over this long period of time it has been a spiritual resource for men and women from all walks of life. I believe it can serve a similar function today, in its translated form. This is a scriptural translation, a compendium of the perennial philosophy of China through the ages, crystallized around this ancient text. For the British scholar and poet Angus Graham, as I have mentioned in my general Introduction, reading the *I Ching* is "a synthesizing act in which the Diviner sees into and responds to everything at once, with a lucidity mysterious to himself." But while this lucidity may always remain a mystery, it also has discernible benefits. My own teacher and friend Liu Ts'un-yan, to whose memory this translation is dedicated, certainly believed in its practical value. He would push under my door slips of paper inscribed with *I Ching* readings, shorthand encouragements to persevere in my studies—to be Steadfast. In the same spirit, in his last years, more than thirty years later, he insisted in many conversations that simple Good Faith was what mattered most, with the concomitant ability to discriminate between True and False (an emphasis shared by many *I Ching* commentators). "Ah!" he once said with a rueful sigh about a mutual acquaintance, a celebrated colleague. "Completely False!" Brilliant, successful, but False.

I have sought to give each of my two versions a distinctive voice. The Oracle will at times sound brusque. The Book speaks in more deliberate tones—even when the two versions are essentially saying something similar. This is intentional.

The early Jesuit Latin version, to which I have referred in the Introduction, has a peculiar resonance for the contemporary reader. Phrases such as "*Nullum malum*" and "*Nulla est culpa*" still have a powerful ring to them. From time to time I have shamelessly quoted a few Latin tags from the early Jesuits to supplement my English. As Joseph Needham once remarked, Why should we not make use of numinous phrases from our own civilization? (He certainly did!) Sometimes I have modified the Latin slightly, or substituted a Latin version of my own. This may strike some readers as odd. After all, who knows or reads Latin these days? But it is not done out of a perverse desire to obfuscate or impress. I sincerely believe that these occasional Latin snatches, which I have used mainly for the incantatory formulae of the Chinese, can help us relate to this deeply ancient and foreign text, can help create a timeless mood of contemplation, and at the same time can evoke indirect connections between the Chinese tradition of Self-Knowledge and Self-Cultivation on the one hand, at the center of which has always stood the *I Ching*, and, on the other, the long European tradition of Gnosis and spiritual discipline, reaching back as it does to well before the Middle Ages and the Renaissance, to before Ignatius of Loyola and Thomas Aquinas, to Antiquity and beyond. It was the Delphic oracle, after all, that counseled visitors to its shrine to know themselves. We all come to places and books such as this seeking answers to questions that are fundamentally the same. As the Chinese put it, "We humans share the same Heart-and-Mind; that Heart-and-Mind shares the same reasons." This has always been my personal motto as a translator.

But there is another reason for insinuating the odd piece of Latin, a reason that is harder to articulate. Again, as I have stated in the Introduction, over many years I have gradually come to realize (as many others have before me) that there can never be a definitive version of the *I Ching* in any language. Its "meaning" is simply too elusive. All interpretations and translations are works in progress. Part of the book's Power is precisely that it has meant so many different things to so many different readers and commentators over the ages, including its translators. With the passage of time, much of the old accepted understanding fades away. We are bereft of much that was inseparable from the reading of this book, much that gave that reading its Power. In our modern world, the numinous has been for decades in retreat, becoming little more than a faint memory, disappearing with the same alarming rapidity as many natural species. Like the inhabitants of Russell Hoban's visionary postholocaust masterpiece *Riddley Walker* (1980), or of Walter M. Miller Jr.'s equally haunting and prophetic *A Canticle for Leibowitz* (1960), we scavenge for shards of old belief and myth, we piece together whatever fragments we can, from a remote and half-forgotten past. China is no exception. My little scraps of Latin embedded in this *I Ching* are an acknowledgment of this. They serve as slightly subversive reminders that we will never be out of the dark, that we can hope to do little more than clutch at the *disjecta membra* of the past. These half-remembered mumblings (*Non est poenitendi locus!*) are a bit like the dog-Latin and Provençal ravings of Salvatore, the gargoyle vagabond heretic of Umberto Eco's *The Name of the Rose*. "*Penitenziagite!* Watch out for the *draco* who cometh in future to gnaw your *anima!*" He could so easily have been half-remembering Hexagram I, First Line: "The Dragon lies hidden, *Draco est absconditus*. Do not act, *Nole uti.* "

In Part I, the layout is as follows: (1) The core text comes first, centered and in largest type: Hexagram, Hexagram Name, Judgment, and Line Judgments. (2) This is followed, centered on the page again but in slightly smaller type, by a selection from the oldest commentaries, the Ten Wings: On the Judgment, On the Image, On the Words, the Great Treatise, The Trigrams Expounded. These sections are set off from each other by an old graph for Turtle. (3) In smaller type still, following an old graph for Dragon, is my own eclectic digest of later Chinese commentaries and poets, from the Han dynasty onward, together with the thoughts of a few non-Chinese translators and commentators. These I have reworked and often reworded, weaving them together into one collective voice. Where I am adding my own thoughts, I signal this with the initials JM.

In the last years of this long project, I benefited enormously from the work of three commentators in particular. The first is Liu Yiming, a most remarkable individual of the eighteenth century, who brought to his reading of the *I Ching* insights from his lived experience as a Master in the Dragon Gate School of Complete Reality [Quanzhen] Taoism. During his late teens, Liu suffered a nearly fatal illness, and was restored to health by a Taoist monk. (This, incidentally, was also true of my teacher Liu Ts'un-yan. As a youth in Peking he suffered very poor health, which improved only when he received instruction in Self-Cultivation from a monk in the White Cloud Monastery, one of the main centers of Complete Reality Taoism.) Liu Yiming's experience opened his eyes. He set off wandering around remote areas of China, "seeking the Tao," until at the age of twenty-two, in the Northwestern province of Gansu, he encountered a Taoist Master known as the Old Man of Sacred Shrine Valley, who initiated him into the discipline of *neidan*, or Inner Alchemy. This branch of Taoist practice is no mystical mumbo-jumbo, but a carefully thought-out and long-established method of Self-Cultivation. It has been well described by Isabelle Robinet as "a technique of enlightenment, a method of controlling both the world and oneself," a process of "existential and intellectual integration."

Purists may find my exposition of Liu's complex alchemical terminology overly simplistic. To borrow the words of the Canadian novelist Robertson Davies, I do not have "a scholarly understanding of alchemy." Rather I see in Liu's interpretation of the *I Ching* a "lived alchemy," a pointer toward the "transformation of base elements and some sort of union of important elements" in the reader's life.[1]

Inner Alchemy uses the symbolism of the Sixty-Four Hexagrams of the *I Ching* (interpreted within the framework and lexicon of the Alchemical Work) as an aide-mémoire or map for the practice of Cultivating the True Heart-and-Mind of the Tao. This is what makes Liu's *I Ching* commentary so fascinating. For him the book is a Taoist Companion to Life, the Hexagrams themselves becoming aids to visualization, steps on the Path to Self-Knowledge.

After many further years of Self-Cultivation of this sort and more wandering around China's remoter regions, doing all sorts of odd jobs, Liu finally settled in a hermitage in Gansu, offering Taoist teachings and medical advice to all comers. Among his many other writings is a commentary on *The Journey to the West,* which was influential in Anthony C. Yu's monumental translation and interpretation of that great novel. I have found Liu's *I Ching* commentary inspirational, and I quote from it liberally, under the rubric "Magister Liu." I have not attempted to convey in any detail the full intricacy of his *neidan* thinking. Instead I have tried to spell out the broad implications of his Taoist reading of the *I Ching.* The most helpful guide for the modern reader wanting to go further into the subject of Chinese Inner Alchemy is to be found in the two books by Isabelle Robinet listed in my bibliography.

The second commentator whose work I have found most helpful (even if I have not always agreed with his interpretations) is the contemporary Taiwanese philosopher and Taoist scholar Chen Guying. Chen has led a colorful and eventful life. Beginning in the early years of martial law in Taiwan under Chiang Kai-shek, he acquired a reputation as an engaged and controversial political figure, teaching in the Philosophy Department of Taiwan University, and providing outspoken leadership for student protests. He began writing about Existentialism in the 1960s, and went on to rediscover Chinese philosophy and especially Taoism, so he himself says, as the result of his early studies of Nietzsche. His edition of the *I Ching*, with prolific notes and commentary, was done in collaboration with the Beijing scholar Zhao Jianwei. It was first published in Taiwan in the late 1990s, and was reissued in Beijing in 2005. It places the *I Ching* in a proto-Taoist context, and makes important and enlightening connections between it and early Taoist texts such as *The Tao and the Power* and the *Book of Master Zhuang.*

The third of my "late companions" on this journey has been Professor Mun Kin Chok (Cantonese pronunciation of Min Jianshu—we share a surname!),

Professor Emeritus of Marketing at the Chinese University of Hong Kong, member of the National Committee of the Chinese People's Political Consultative Conference, and economic adviser to the Chinese government. Professor Mun, now in his late seventies, is a True Gentleman and a delightful individual. In a 2006 study written in English, he derived a "Chinese leadership wisdom" from the *I Ching*. His commentary is designed for the executive or would-be executive. Since 2006, Professor Mun has gone on to write extensively in Chinese developing the same theme. All of his books are published in Hong Kong. The clarity and practical common sense of his explanations provide a useful counterweight to the Taoist musings of Magister Liu. And yet in a way Magister Liu, Professor Mun, and Professor Chen Guying are all doing the same thing. They are applying the text to life. They are using it to help readers take decisions in their outer and inner lives.

This is not an academic translation, and I have chosen not to clutter the pages with lengthy citations. Instead, I have given further details of sources online on my website, johnminford.com. Interested readers are welcome to visit this website, where they may also find further refinements of this "work-in-progress," and can put their own questions to the translator directly.

I have chosen to follow a format similar to the one I used in my earlier translation of *The Art of War*, breaking the core text into short lines to reflect its pithy, often poetic and parallelistic, nature, at the same time centering it on the page. Commentaries from the Ten Wings are also centered.

NOTE

1. Robertson Davies, *The Cornish Trilogy* (1-vol. ed.) (London: Penguin Books, 1991), vol. 2, *What's Bred in the Bone*, p. 701.

HEXAGRAM I

Qian

Heaven

Qian/Heaven

above

Qian/Heaven

JUDGMENT

Supreme Fortune.

Profitable.

Steadfast.

 Heaven above Heaven. Pure Yang. This is the first of eight Hexagrams formed by doubling a Trigram of the same Name (these are I, II, XXIX, XXX, LI, LII, LVII, and LVIII). The word chosen for the Trigram/Hexagram Name, *Qian*, whatever its original meaning may have been (and there are many understandings of this — see Part II, Hexagram 1), came in later times to be used more and more as a shorthand for Heaven, emblem of Yang Energy and Creativity. The two first Hexagram Names, *Qian* and *Kun*, when joined together into a single word, *qiankun*, came to mean the Universe in its entirety, Heaven and Earth and everything in between. A short poem by the monk-poet Hanshan Deqing begins:

> Snow fills the Universe [*qiankun*],
> The Myriad Things are new.
> My body is wrapped
> In a radiant silver world.

In a verse drama, the Complete Reality Taoist Master Ma Danyang sings of the Spiritual Process, or Work, of Inner Alchemy:

> Achieve purity and tranquillity,
> Retain them within,
> And Heaven-and-Earth will return
> To dwell in the inch-space
> Of your Heart-and-Mind,
> The Universe [*qiankun*]
> In a crucible.
> Then you will know
> The futility of artifice.

Over the years the *I Ching* has provided a compendious ragbag of key words and proverbial expressions; it has been a cultural commonplace book. Joseph Needham called it a "repository of concepts, to which all concrete phenomena in Nature could be referred."

On the Judgment

> *Qian!*
> Grandly Supreme.
> Font of Matter,
> Master of Heaven!
> The clouds pass,
> The rains fall,
> The Array of Matter
> Flows into Form.
> Crystal Comprehension
> Of End and Beginning.
> Each of the Six Places
> Comes in its True Time.
> Each of the Six Dragons
> Rides Heaven in due order.
> The Tao of *Qian*
> Is Transformation,

Change.
To things it gives their True Nature,
Their True Life-Destiny.
It preserves the Great Harmony.
This Profits,
This is Steadfast,
The head raised high
Above the Multitude of Things,
The Myriad Kingdoms
All at Peace.

Grandly Supreme For the often-recurring oracular formula "Supreme Fortune. Profitable. Steadfast," see below, and the discussion of *yuan-heng-li-zhen* in Part II, Commentary to this same Hexagram.

Master of Heaven The Tao of Heaven, writes Zhu Xi, has a Heavenly and Supreme Quality, *yuan*. It has Grandeur, Primordiality. Its Masterly Power is the Font of Creation, of the Myriad Things, of the phenomenal world. Through the Tao of Yin and the Tao of Yang, comments Magister Liu, the Sage Masters both Heaven and Earth. *Qian*, for Zen master Zhixu, is the Buddha Nature.

The clouds pass, the rains fall The Tao of Heaven moves, comments Cheng Yi. It acts and interacts with Earth. In so doing, it creates, it gives birth to all things. This is Fortune, *heng*, writes Yang Wanli; this is the positive manifestation of the *Qian* Hexagram. Clouds and rain are the Energy (*qi*) of that Fortune. Matter is the form into which that Fortune or Energy flows. *Qian* is not just Fortune, adds Yu Yan. It is Supreme in that it lies at the very Origin of Pure Energy, before material distinctions come into play. Its Fortune is to be found in the Flux, in the Flowing into Form, at the point where the Array of Distinctions—those material things that are massive or minute, high or low—becomes manifest. Nothing, comments Jullien, following Wang Fuzhi, illustrates better than clouds the continuous Gestation of Heaven, its continuously evolving Flux, its Movement. Nothing illustrates better than rain Heaven's kindly Enrichment of the Earth, its Fertilization of Life. The positive current of Yang Energy passes through all things, charging and renewing them according to their kind. Through it, the world of Matter "becomes," it constantly realizes itself. JM: The cosmic "mating" of Heaven and Earth during rainstorms, the intercourse of Yang and Yin in Nature, is an ancient Chinese motif. "Clouds-and-Rain" has always been the image par excellence of sexual union and consummation, a reminder that the human microcosm functions like the cosmic macrocosm, that the union of man and woman is simply the interaction of the forces of Nature "writ small." It is an intrinsic part of the intercourse of Heaven and Earth. The two levels interact. They have a Resonance. In an essay entitled "Seeking Rain," the Han-dynasty scholar Dong Zhongshu even proposed that husbands and wives, in order to ensure the timely precipitation of rain, should have sex with each other on every *gengzi* day in the sixty-day cycle. This, wrote an anonymous commentator of the time, would be sure to secure the Harmony of Yin and Yang in the world of Nature—an example of "sexual sympathetic magic." A century earlier, in his preface to a famous poetic rhapsody, the poet Song Yu celebrated sexual ecstasy on a mountaintop, describing the union of a Former King and a Sha-maness. This was the *locus classicus* for the "Clouds-and-Rain":

> The King lay with her,
> And at their parting
> She spoke these words:
> "My home is on the southern slope
> Of Shaman Peak,
> Where from its rounded summit
> A sudden chasm falls.
> At dawn I am the morning clouds,
> At dusk, the driving rain. . . ."

Crystal Comprehension This, writes Zhu Xi, is the Comprehension of the Sage, who "gets" the Tao of *Qian* with crystal clarity, both as to its End and as to its Begin-ning. Hence his Supreme Fortune. Wang Fuzhi understands it to refer to the Tao itself, the all-comprehending, all-knowing Process of *Qian* and of Heaven. The Tao knows all.

Each of the Six Dragons The Six Dragons, writes Zhu Xi, are the Six Lines of this Hexagram, in their respective Places. The Sage comprehends the significance of each—Hidden Dragon, Dragon Seen, Flying Dragon, Dragon Leaping into the deep, etc.—and can therefore act in the appropriate way at the appropriate moment. He rides the Dragons as they progress through the Heavens. In Seclusion, writes Wang Bi, ride the Hidden Dragon. In the Open, ride the Flying Dragon. Ride each of the Six Dragons in due and proper order. Ride the Transformations, take control of the Great Vessel of Heaven. At Rest, be concentrated. In Movement, be straight and true. Never lose sight of the Great Harmony. Is this not the True Essence of Human Nature and Life-Destiny? JM: Again, this passage concerns the Sage, or the Tao, or both. Zen Master Zhixu comments that the Six Places, and hence the Six Dragons, represent stages of Enlightenment, the gradual revelation of the Buddha Nature. They are also, writes Professsor Mun, the six different stages of development in an enterprise. The Lines advise the Leader of an Organization how to adapt to changing conditions.

Profitable and Steadfast We come now to the key "oracular" words Profit/Profit-able, *li*, and Steadfast/Steadfastness, *zhen*, found in this first Judgment, and many times hereafter throughout the *I Ching*. How, asks Zhu Xi, can one ensure that one's actions bring Profit? How and when should one be Steadfast? The answer is to be found in understanding Transformation, the gradual process of Change, the con-stantly shifting situation and its dynamic; and in understanding Change itself, the final outcome of Transformation, the underlying Reality. One must be in tune with that process, with the True Nature of things, with their True Life-Destiny. The Great Harmony that this understanding brings and preserves is the Harmony of Yin and Yang, the creative fusion of their twin Energies through Transformation. The Trans-formations of the Tao of *Qian* Profit all things. Through these Transformations every thing perfects its True and Steadfast Nature and Life-Destiny. Heaven, comments Jullien, following Wang Fuzhi, never deviates from its correct course (visible in the stars and the seasons). Heaven is always True and Steadfast. In the same way, the Sage is judiciously Steadfast in his pursuit of Truth; he is finely attuned to the Inner Logic of the process of Transformation, participating in that process in the appropriate manner at the appropriate stage. Thereby he achieves results that are both Profitable and Steadfast. The Transformation of Reality, the process of Change, is ongoing, constant, and uninterrupted. But each individuation receives from this very process its True individual identity, its True Nature and Life-Destiny. If all beings respect the inner demands of their True Nature, then individual existences and Destinies will be united and reconciled in the Great Harmony.

High above the Multitude Heaven, writes Cheng Yi, is Ancestor of the Myriad Things. The King is Forefather of the Myriad Kingdoms. When the Tao of Heaven, of *Qian*, the Head, "is raised high above the Multitude," then the Myriad Things will all enjoy Fortune together. When the Tao of the Ruler respects the Place of Heaven, then everything within the Four Seas will fall into place. When the King embodies the Tao of Heaven, then the Myriad Kingdoms will be at peace. JM: Again, the Head can be understood as the "head" of the Hexagram *Qian*, the "head" of Heaven and the Tao, the "head" of the Dragon, or the "head" of the King, the Ruler, the Sage, or of all at once.

On the Image of the Hexagram

Strong is the Movement of Heaven.
Tirelessly
The True Gentleman
Tempers himself.

Heaven is the Image of *Qian*, writes Zhu Xi. The Movement of Heaven is strong; it is a powerful "revolution" repeated each day, today's revolving Movement giving way to an identical Movement tomorrow. This celestial phenomenon is fueled by Supreme Cosmic Strength. In the *I Ching*, as Jullien insists, "reality is never the product of creation, always of interaction." Joseph Needham repeatedly emphasizes that the Chinese have no "*spiritus rector.*" The True Gentleman models himself on this, he "works on himself," never allowing petty human desire to harm the Inner Strength of Heaven's Power (the Power of the Tao). The great seventeenth-century painter Shi Tao (Stone Wave), also known as the Bitter Melon Monk, refers to these very words when talking of the artist's training, his quest for Self-Cultivation. The painter must never tire; he must be indefatigable in his application, in his training, in his development as an artist.

The Trigrams Expounded

Qian is Heaven,
Round;
Ruler,
Father.
Qian is

Jade,

Bronze;

Cold,

Ice.

Qian is deep red.

It is head.

Fine horse,

Old horse,

Skinny horse,

Piebald horse.

Fruit of tree.

LINES

Yang in First Place

The Dragon

Lies hidden,

Draco est absconditus.

Do not act,

Nole uti.

On the Image

Yang in lowly Place.

Yang Line in Yang Place. Here Yang Energy occupies a lowly Place, writes Cheng Yi. The True Gentleman abides in that Place. He lies low. His time has not yet come. The Dragon is a strong Yang creature, comments Zhu Xi, but Yang in First occupies the lowest Place of the Hexagram, and must therefore not be drawn into ill-conceived Action. Hence the Image of the Hidden Dragon. Hence the Divination "Do not act." When encountering this Hexagram, and especially if this is a Moving Line, observe this Image well, ponder its significance, writes Zhu Xi. For the Duke of Zhou, brother and adviser to King Wu, and considered by legend to be the author of the Line Statements of the Hexagrams, the Dragon, writes Legge, was symbol of the Superior Man, the True Gentleman, the Great Man, the one who exhibits the virtues or attributes characteristic of Heaven. The creature's proper home is in the water (the word for "hidden" has the water radical), but it can disport itself on the land, and can also fly and soar aloft. The Chinese Dragon has indeed from earliest times been the emblem of the highest dignity and wisdom, of sovereignty and sagehood. Here, in this First Line of the First Hexagram, comments Jullien, following Wang Fuzhi, the Dragon is still hibernating, nourishing his Energy before soaring into the skies. The Vital Force of the Tao continues to irrigate his roots. The Dragon Sage is in Retreat, he rests in obscurity, in anticipation and preparation. He studies but does not teach. He cultivates his moral character in silence, he is content to lead a frugal life, unnoticed. Capacity and Aspiration are there, but the time has not yet come. JM: In the fourteenth chapter of that wonderful Taoist classic the *Book of Master Zhuang*, a story is told of Confucius's having visited the venerable Taoist Laozi (Master Lao, the Old Master, sometimes written Lao Tzu). A disciple asks Confucius about the visit. "I saw a veritable Dragon!" he replies. "A Dragon at one moment coming together into a body, and at the next dispersing to form a colored brilliance. It rides on the clouds of Heaven, it is nourished by Yin and Yang. My mouth fell open in amazement!" The Dragon is the prime image of the *I Ching*, and one of the most powerful. It has been the subject of much rhapsodic speculation. What do we really know about the *long*, the Chinese Dragon, especially in ancient times? As Robert Bagley has remarked, "the literature of Chinese archaeology commonly applies the label Dragon to almost any imaginary animal." The early (c.AD 100) dictionary *Shuowen jiezi* merely says (rather unhelpfully, and clearly itself quoting the early *I Ching* commentaries) that the Dragon "rises up to Heaven in the Spring, and sinks into the Abyss in the Autumn." Today we can see with our own eyes in the museums of the world a rich array of stylized early Chinese Dragons, especially on the extraordinary bronze vessels of the Shang and Zhou dynasties. But do these representations really help? Was this creature in fact no more than a construct, inspired by the discovery of various antediluvian dinosaur remains? Was the Dragon closest to snake, crocodile, or fish? Or are these simply the wrong questions? The chameleon-like Chinese Dragon could change shape at will. It was, and is, an emblem of Change. The contemporary art historian Wu Hung, commenting on the strange animals of hybrid form that pervade Chinese mythology and religion, writes vividly of one surviving bronze Dragon, dating from the Warring States period: "Half-feline and half-reptilian, the Dragon has dorsal spikes and pinioned wings. Its body is covered by linear volutes filled with dots. But its sharp wings, horns, and fins convey a strong sense of three-dimensionality. . . . The mythical animal, bending its cylindrical neck and tightening its sinews and muscles, is about to leap in the air." This is just one among many such Dragon-like creatures. A relatively early, partly Taoistic text, the *Book of Master Guan*, informs us: "The Dragon [like the Turtle] lives in the water. It can acquire the five colors of water, and become a Spirit. If it so wishes it can make itself as small as a silkworm or a caterpillar. Or it can make itself so large as to cover the whole world. If it wishes to rise up, it can fly among the clouds; if it wishes to descend, it can visit the deepest springs. It changes constantly; it can go up or down whenever it so wishes." Clearly this is far from the fire-breathing Western dragon, the evil creature with which St. George (or St. Michael the Archangel, or Cadmus, or Beowulf, or Siegfried) so heroically fought. It is no monster guarding a hoard of treasure, nor is it an archetypal dark shadow against which the Inner Hero must do battle. Far from it. The Chinese Dragon is a creature of light, positive and numinous "symbol of the electrically charged, dynamic, arousing force that manifests itself in the thunderstorm," as Richard Wilhelm puts it so eloquently. It symbolizes the very process of Change itself, disseminating not fire but water, fertilizing the Earth with its Creative Energy. In the Chinese art of geomancy, *fengshui*, the channels in the landscape through which the Energy of the Earth flows are termed Dragon Veins (*longmai*), and the focal points where Positive, or Yang, Energy is concentrated (sites suitable for graves) are termed Dragon Hollows (*longxue*). In astronomy, the Dragon was an important cluster of stars (see Part II). Later, and more generally, the Dragon came to stand for China and for the whole of Chinese culture and history. The Chinese were "Heirs of the Dragon." A song of that name by the contemporary Taiwan singer Hou Dejian became extremely popular among Chinese of all persuasions in the 1980s.

The Chinese Emperor (in later times Prime Dragon), before ascending his throne, was Dragon in Hiding. "Hidden Dragon" indeed became a stock phrase for a man of parts biding his time. The great wizard and strategist of the Three Kingdoms period, Zhuge Liang, when he retreated to the countryside and became a hermit, was known as the Sleeping Dragon. The Leader of an Organization, writes Professor Mun, is advised to keep a low profile, to store Energy for a future move.

On the Words

The Master said:
He possesses Dragon Power,
But stays concealed.
He does not Change
For the World's sake,
Does not crave success or fame.
He eschews the World.
Neither oppressed by solitude,
Nor saddened by neglect,
In Joy he Acts,
In sorrow stands aside.
He is never uprooted.
This is the Hidden Dragon
In lowly place;
This is Yang Energy
Concealed in the deep.
The True Gentleman acts
From Perfection of Inner Strength.
His Actions are then visible daily.
Here he is
Concealed,
He is
Not yet visible,

His conduct is not yet
Perfected.
He does not
Act.

Yang in Second Place

The Dragon

Is seen in the fields,

Draco in campis.

It Profits

To see a Great Man,

Magnum virum.

On the Image

Inner Strength
Spreads its influence far and wide.

On the Words

The Master said:
This is
Dragon Power.
True and Centered,
In daily words
Sincere,
In daily conduct
Earnest.
He guards against depravity;
He preserves
Good Faith.
Good works are done
But never boasted of.
Inner Strength spreads far and wide;
It Transforms.

Yang Line in Yin Place. Centered. The fields lie upon the Earth, writes Cheng Yi. Now the Dragon emerges, visible above the Earth, manifesting Inner Strength, influencing others in a process of universal extension. The Sage Shun cultivated the Earth and caught fish. It Profited him to see a Great Man of Inner Power, the Sage Yao, in order to implement the Tao. Equally it Profited the Sage Yao to see before him a subordinate of Inner Strength, and to enlist his support. The Leader should seek wisdom and advice, writes Professor Mun, from knowledgeable people (Great Men) both inside and outside his Organization. Then he can announce new plans and new products, while maintaining the principles of sincerity, balance, and uprightness. With this Yang Line in Second Place, comments Jullien, following Wang Fuzhi, Dragon Energy becomes manifest; it begins to be openly deployed. Just as in the natural world plants grow and bear fruit, so this Line represents an emergence into the open, above ground. The "fields" can also be seen as the Inner Ground of the Sage's being, a Spiritual Space to be cultivated and made fruitful.

Yang in Third Place

The True Gentleman is vigilant

Throughout the day;

He is

Apprehensive in the evening.

Danger.

No Harm,

Nullum malum.

On the Image

He walks the Way of the Tao,
Back and forth.

On the Words

The Master said:
The True Gentleman
Cultivates Inner Strength,
Fulfills his task,
Through Trustworthiness,

Through Good Faith,

Refining his words,

Building Sincerity.

He knows the limits,

He keeps within them.

He grasps the Spring of the Moment.

He knows Completion,

He perfects Self within it,

He preserves Righteousness.

He occupies height

Without pride,

A lowly place

Without being downcast.

He is vigilant and apprehensive.

He is in tune

With Situation and Time.

Danger.

No Harm,

Nullum malum.

Yang Line in Yang Place. This Third Line, writes Cheng Yi, shows us a person not yet entirely risen from the ranks of the lowly, but whose distinction is already apparent. Such was the case when the subtle Inner Strength of the humble Sage Shun became known. Day and night, without fail, he was vigilant and apprehensive. Although in a dangerous situation, he incurred no Harm. Whether in Advance or in Retreat, whether in motion or at rest, he was always attuned to the ebb and flow of the Tao, always flexible and walking on its path. Only by being conscious of the difficulty of the situation, comments Jullien, following Wang Fuzhi, by not moving too precipitately toward achievement of a goal, can one avoid Harm. The lesson is to persevere, but at the same time to be prudent. The True Gentleman, comments Thomas McClatchie, is the Prince, the *Sapiens* of the Stoics; the Dragon-man, Fu Xi, the human manifestation of *Qian*, or Heaven, the First Man, Sage, and Emperor, rising up out of the Abyss.

Yang in Fourth Place

He leaps

Into the deep,

In profundis.

No Harm,

Nullum malum.

On the Image

In Advancing,
There is
No Harm.

On the Words

The Master said:
High and low
Have no Constant Rule.
Eschew the irregular.
Movement
Knows no Fixed Rule,
Neither Advance
Nor Retreat.
Be not distant from fellow men.
The True Gentleman
Cultivates Inner Strength;
He fulfills his task.
He tunes Self
To the Moment,
And thus incurs
No Harm.

Yang Line in Yin Place. The deep, writes Cheng Yi, is the Dragon's natural place of repose. Leaping into the deep at an opportune moment, the Dragon finds rest. In similar fashion, the Sage always stirs (into Action) at an opportune moment. He calculates before advancing; he judges the moment, and thereby avoids Harm. Advance is possible, comments Zhu Xi, but not necessary. Here a certain hesitation and uncertainty are implied. The leap takes place with no apparent cause, without any sense of urgency or flight. The deep may be the space above, or the caverns beneath—places dark and unfathomable. The Dragon bides his time. He may descend, but he may also leap upward toward Heaven. The Leader, writes Professor Mun, is at a crossroads and needs to make a decision whether he should move forward or not, in a calm and balanced manner, without being impulsive. JM: Tao Yuanming, in his poem "Rhapsody on Scholars out of Their Time," drew on the imagery of these lines:

Hidden Dragon,
Leaping Dragon:
All is
Ordained. . . .
The Enlightened Man's Vision
Bids him eschew office,
Bids him
Retreat to his farm.

Yang in Fifth Place

The Dragon

Flies in Heaven,

Draco volans in coelo.

It Profits

To see a Great Man,

Magnum virum.

On the Image

The Great Man
Sets to work.

On the Words

The Master said:
Sounds of the same sort
Resonate;
Creatures of the same Energy
Congregate.
Water flows to moist ground,
Fire rises to that which is dry.
Clouds follow the Dragon,
Wind follows the Tiger.
The Sage stirs the Myriad Creatures
Into Action.
Pay heed:
Whatsoever derives from Heaven,

The Heaven-bound,
Is drawn to what is above;
Whatsoever derives from Earth,
The Earth-bound,
Is drawn to what is below.
Each follows its kind.

Yang Line in Yang Place. Centered and True. This is the Great Man's Work, writes Cheng Yi, this is the business of the Sage. The Great Man is the Dragon, comments Xu Ji. The Work is the flight. Here, comments Jullien, following Wang Fuzhi, the Yang which has been slowly accumulating is suddenly transformed; it attains perfect freedom of movement (*aisance*). The soaring flight is free progress, effortless and unhampered. Steadfastness has become spontaneity. One day it just happens. The transition to sagehood is like the passage from Apprentice to Master, for aspiring musician, painter, or calligrapher. All the toil of practice is suddenly transformed into an astonishing facility. At this juncture the Sage simply takes off ("leaps"). He follows the Tao as naturally and instinctively as if it were an Edict of Heaven. The Ruler too, thanks to Inner Strength patiently accumulated, at this juncture no longer needs to exert himself in order to be obeyed. The Inner Strength operates of itself; it emanates effortlessly (it is, after all, *mana*) from his Spiritual Ascendance. In business, writes Professor Mun, this is the ideal state. Once an Organization can identify its goals, then its members can apply their expertise appropriately and work with Energy toward those goals.

Yang in Top Place

The Dragon

Overreaches himself.

There is

Regret,

Est quod poeniteat.

On the Image

That which is full
Cannot endure.

On the Words

The Master said:

Be noble,
But hold no position;
Be high,
But have no subordinates
Below.
The worthy hold lower positions
But provide no support.
Movement
Brings Regret.
Things have reached an extremity.
Calamity.
At odds with the moment,
One can Advance
But not Retreat.
One can survive
But not disappear.
One can take hold
But not let go.
Only the Sage can master both
Advance and Retreat;
Only he can survive and disappear,
And never lose his True Nature.

Yang Line in Yin Place. The previous Place (the Flying Dragon) is the highest point in the Hexagram. It is the most opportune moment, writes Cheng Yi, properly Centered and True. To overstep that moment is to go too far, to overreach oneself, with consequent Regret. The Sage knows the limits; he knows when to Advance and when to Retreat; he knows how to survive. He does not overreach himself. He has no pride. He has no Regret. The Sage has already gone through all the spheres in which he is called upon to display his qualities, comments Legge. It is now time for him to let go and relax. The string should not always be pulled taut; the bow should not always be kept drawn. The inflexible use of force will give occasion for Regret. The moral meaning found in the Line is that "the high shall be abased." Here the Dragon is paralyzed (*bloqué*), writes Jullien, following Wang Fuzhi. That which cannot increase, that which is already full, will necessarily decline. But the Dragon is still a Dragon. Its Inner Strength remains intact. The Regret of the Dragon Sage is a stoical Regret. Joseph Needham writes of the "self-regulating Organic System" of the Universe. The Chinese Sage is "only finding out what all natural bodies, celestial and terrestrial, spontaneously know and perform." He quotes Heraclitus: "The Sun will not transgress his measures."

Yang in Final Place

A multitude seen,

Of headless Dragons.

This is

Auspicious,

Bonum.

On the Image

The Power of Heaven
Does not reside
In the head.

On the Words

All-under-Heaven
Is well governed.
The Rule of Heaven
Is made manifest.

 This Final, or Supernumerary, Seventh Line, writers Zhu Xi, refers to the unusual situation where all six Yang Lines of the Hexagram are "changing" to Yin Lines, and where therefore the outcome is Hexagram II, *Kun.* The meaning given to the "Final" Line is essentially the opposite of that of the Sixth, or Top, Line. The Power of Heaven is Yang; it is Firm. But the Yang should not stand at the "head" of things; thus when all six Yang Lines change to Yin, as here, it is considered to be Auspicious. To employ the Firm repeatedly, writes Cheng Yi, to esteem the first (the head) too highly, is excessive. Force gives way to submission, comments Legge, haughtiness to Humility; and the result is Good Fortune. When there are no heads among the Dragons, writes Professor Mun, there is a democratic relationship between the Leader and the members of the group. The situation is close to the Taoist concept of ruling with Non-Action.

The Great Treatise

From Part I, Sections 10 & 1

𥄂 This celebrated treatise, also known as the Great Commentary (*Dazhuan*), or sometimes as the Attached Statements (*Xici*), is one of the earliest, and certainly the most important and eloquent, of the Ten Wings, or classic commentaries on the *I Ching*. It is usually divided into two parts, forming the Fifth and Sixth Wings, the sections of which are numbered in varying ways. It sets out the broad themes and principles of the *I Ching*, and therefore, according to Zhu Xi, cannot be attached to any individual Hexagrams. With all due respect to the great neo-Confucian Master, certain sections *are* especially relevant to particular Hexagrams. This is certainly the case with the opening paragraphs of the Treatise, which I have translated below. In most arrangements of the *I Ching*, the Treatise is printed separately as a self-contained appendix. I have chosen to select only a very few sections and to scatter them among the different Hexagrams, sometimes because of their obvious relevance to a given Hexagram, sometimes in the belief that readers consulting the *I Ching* may find it helpful to pause and reflect on the thoughts of the Treatise, which place the Book's pronouncements in a broader context. Richard Lynn in his translation attaches sections under the Hexagrams, but also gives the Treatise in its entirety. The Jesuits (*Appendix ad Commentarios*), Wilhelm (*The Great Treatise*), and Legge (*The Great Appendix*) all keep it more or less separate. Traditionally it was (yet again!) attributed to Confucius, but was most probably written well after his death, and, as many scholars have pointed out, it contains ideas that are close to the worldview of early Taoism. It is in many ways a work in its own right, expounding at some length, and often poetically, cosmological ideas such as the interplay of Yin and Yang, as well as the general nature of the Tao, ideas that are barely mentioned in the Judgment and Lines of the *I Ching* core text. A large part of the Treatise can be found in the Mawangdui silk manuscript, dated to the early second century BC. Richard Rutt calls it a cosmological and metaphysical treatise, "awkwardly cobbled together from other sources," a "collection of short essays that provide a rationale of the connection between the Hexagrams and the events they predict." In it, "the process began that eventually produced the understanding of the *I Ching* found in most Chinese commentaries, which ultimately received its classic expression in the neo-Confucian synthesis of the Song dynasty."

Principles

𥄂 Before giving the opening words of the Treatise, I give here its grand Statement of Principles from part I, section 10, describing what Wilhelm calls the "psychological basis of the Oracle," the way in which "the conscious and the supraconscious enter into relationship." This passage has already been given in the Introduction, but it deserves to be repeated here.

The *I Ching* does not think,
It is *sine meditatione.*
It does not act,
It is *sine actu.*
In its solitude,
In quiete,
It is motionless,
Sine motu.
In its Resonance,
It reaches
The core of the World,
It uncovers
The *rerum omnium causam.*
In all the World,
Only the *I Ching*
Can accomplish this.
It is a most Spiritual Entity,
Summus spiritus!
Through the *I Ching*
The Sage
Plumbs
The greatest depths,
Investigates
The subtlest Springs of Change.
Its very depth
Penetrates
The Will of the World,
In intima finemque
Rerum mundi.
Knowledge of
The Springs of Change
Enables
Terrestrial Enterprises
To be accomplished.
This Spiritual Entity

Makes speed without haste,
It arrives without traveling.

The "subtlest Springs" (*ji*), the infinitesimally small "germs of Change" (Jullien, "*l'amorce infime de la mutation*"), are the first inklings or stirrings, the faintest hints or suggestions of Movement in the environment. They are triggers, pivots, turning points. In *The Art of War*, in some ways a simplistic (and by no means always benign) strategic application of some of the basic ideas of the *I Ching*, it is the Warrior Adept's awareness of the Springs that brings victory. In a deeper sense, the unique access the *I Ching* provides to the deep inner structure of the present moment, of the "now," the perception it brings of the moment's Inner Dynamic or Potential Energy (*shi*), brings not victory as such, but spiritual and strategic insight, and so Strength or Power. It is in this sense more than a book. It is a Spiritual Entity. This Power of the *I Ching* is intangible and infinite. It mirrors the Power of the Tao itself, as described in the words of the Taoist classic *The Tao and the Power*:

Chapter 42
From the Tao is born the One,
From the One, Two;
From Two, Three;
From Three,
The Myriad Things.

The *I Ching* operates, to quote Legge, like "Spirits, inscrutable, unfathomable, even like that of the Spirit of God." Richard Wilhelm compares it to "an electrical circuit reaching into all situations." He continues: "The circuit only affords the potentiality of lighting; it does not give light. But when contact with a definite situation is established through the questioner, the 'current' is activated, and the given situation is Illumined."

The Opening Remarks of the Great Treatise

Heaven is lofty,
Earth lowly.
These define
Qian and *Kun*.

These opening words of the Treatise announce the grand cosmic architecture of the *I Ching*, built on the twin pillars of *Qian* and *Kun*, the first two Hexagrams, composed as they are of Pure Yang and Pure Yin. Heaven and Earth, writes Zhu Xi, are the substantial manifestations of the Forms and

Energies of Yang and Yin. *Qian* and *Kun*, comments Wang Bi, are the Two Gates of the *I Ching*.

> Lowly and lofty
> Are arrayed,
> Noble and humble
> Have their place.
> Movement and Rest
> Obey Constant Rules,
> Firm and Yielding
> Are defining qualities.
> Tendencies fall into categories,
> Things divide into classes.
> Fortune and Calamity come to pass.
> Heaven engenders images,
> Earth engenders forms.
> Change and Transformation
> Are made manifest.

Lofty and lowly, writes Zhu Xi, are the high and low places of Heaven and Earth and of the Myriad Things. Noble and humble occupy highest and lowest place. Movement is the constant mode of Yang, Stillness the constant mode of Yin. Firm and Yielding are the defining qualities of the Yang and Yin Hexagram Lines. The Heavenly Images referred to here, writes Wang Bi, are the sun, moon, and stars. The Earthly Forms are mountains, lakes, shrubs, and trees. Suspended in the Heavens, the Images revolve to create darkness and light. On the Earth, mountains and lakes circulate Energy, clouds pass by, rains fall. In this way the Process of Transformation is made manifest. Like Nature, comments Richard Wilhelm, the Book itself (in its own internal hierarchy) reflects the differentiation between lowly and lofty. Each Hexagram consists of Six Places, of which the odd-numbered are Firm (Yang) and the even-numbered Yielding (Yin).

> Firm and Yielding
> Press against one another;
> The Eight Trigrams
> Propel each other onward.

Commentators and translators through the ages have had a broadly shared understanding of this important description of the process of Change, the interaction of Yin and Yang, the Dynamic, the sheer Power, of the dual cosmic forces as they perpetuate the Universe in an unending chain of permutations. Firm and Yielding "press against one another," writes Wang Bi, in the interaction of Yin and Yang. They propel each other onward. This is the Transformative Process of the Trigrams and Hexagrams, writes Zhu Xi. The Sixty-Four Hexagrams all derive ultimately from the Two Primal Lines—the Firm or Undivided Line, Yang, and the Yielding or Divided Line, Yin. These Two Primal Lines "press against one another," they interact, they multiply, they generate the Four Bigrams, the fundamental Two-Line permutations of Yang and Yin—halfway between the Primal Lines and the Eight Trigrams. The Four Bigrams then "press against one another" once again to generate the Eight Trigrams, and the Eight Trigrams "propel each other onward" to generate the Sixty-Four Hexagrams. The Eight Trigrams change from one into another in turn, writes Richard Wilhelm, and so the regular alternation of phenomena within the year takes its course. This is the case with all cycles, the life cycle included. What we know as day or night, summer or winter—this, in the life cycle, is life and death.

> Thunder and lightning
> Rouse the Tao.
> Wind and rain
> Nourish it.
> Sun and moon
> Revolve,
> Hot and cold
> Alternate.

All of these Images, writes Zhu Xi, are generated by the process of Transformation. JM: As is so often the case in Classical Chinese, the object of the verbs "rouse" and "nourish" is left unspecified. I take it (as does Richard Lynn) to be the Tao, or the Process of Transformation, as seen throughout the entire cycle of the Sixty-Four Hexagrams.

> The Tao of *Qian*
> Forms Man,
> The Tao of *Kun*
> Forms Woman.

These, writes Zhu Xi, are but two of the Forms generated by the process of Transformation.

> *Qian*
> Masters the Great Beginning,

Kun
Achieves Completion.

The whole Universe, writes Zhu Xi, without exception, consists of combinations of Yin and Yang. In general terms, Yang comes first, Yin follows. Yang dispenses, Yin receives. Yang is light, pure, and formless; Yin is heavy, turbid, and palpable. The Tao of *Qian* creates, writes Chen Guying. The Tao of *Kun* nurtures.

Qian
Masters with ease,
Kun
Acts with simplicity.

The Tao of Heaven and Earth, writes Wang Bi, excels at Beginning, without ever being busy about it (*buwei*). It excels at Becoming, without ever exerting itself. That is its ease, that is its simplicity.

With ease and simplicity
The Principle of the World
Is understood.
Understanding that Principle
Illumines one's place
Within this World.

The Principle of *Qian* and *Kun*, writes Zhu Xi, is seen at work in Heaven and Earth. Humanity is equally shown to be an embodiment of the same Principle. An understanding of that Principle brings with it Illumination, the ability to know one's True Place in the scheme of things.

HEXAGRAM II

Kun

Earth

Kun/Earth

above

Kun/Earth

JUDGMENT

Supreme Fortune.

Steadfastness of a Mare

Profits,

Equae soliditas.

The True Gentleman

Has a Destination,

Sit quo est.

At first he goes astray,

Then finds a Master.

It Profits

To gain friends

In West and South,

To lose friends

In East and North.

It is Auspicious

To rest in Steadfastness,

Bonum est.

Earth above Earth. Pure Yin. This Hexagram, the second composed of a Doubled Trigram, is made up of six Yin Lines. The meaning of *Kun*, writes Zhu Xi, is found in the Tao of Earth. The Tao of Earth is to serve Heaven. Earth is the origin of all things, writes Master Guan. It is the Root and Garden of Life. Earth is the place where all things, beautiful and ugly, good and bad, foolish and clever, come into being. Water is the blood and breath of Earth, flowing through its landscape, connecting through sinews and veins. Chinese Heaven, comments Jullien, following Wang Fuzhi, is always inseparable from Earth. Earth is its true partner. Reality results from the immanent interaction of these two Energizing Breaths (*souffle-énergies*). And yet there is also here a strong emphasis on submission, on the duty of the woman (Yin, Earth) to conform, to serve, an emphasis that has always permeated the feudal value system of China. Earth is a Perfect and Receptive Void, opening herself to the penetrating influence of Heaven, thereby demonstrating her vast capacity. In Earth, Deep Inner Penetration is transformed into Outward-Flowing Radiance. Having taken in the seeds of Heavenly Energy, Earth bestows upon them their Steadfastness and makes them prosper. The Human Heart-and-Mind may indeed "go astray," writes Magister Liu. But eventually it finds tranquillity and submits to the Heart-and-Mind of the Tao. The submissive Yin Energy of Earth finds a Master in the strong Yang Energy of Heaven. A Leader, writes Professor Mun, in addition to being strong, must be open-minded and tolerant. In addition to having Strength and Energy, he must have the ability to be receptive and soft.

On the Judgment

Kun!
Grandly Supreme!
Mother of the Myriad Things,
Willing Servant of Heaven.

Ample is *Kun*,
Sustaining all matter.
Kun's Power
Knows no bounds,
Kun's Capacity
Is vast,
Kun's Radiance
Is great.
Matter in all its variety
Shares in the Fortune of *Kun*.

Qian has the Power, *Kun* the Capacity, writes Legge. *Qian* originates, *Kun* produces. *Kun* gives birth to what has been originated, "sustains matter." The radiance of *Kun* is the beauty that shines forth throughout the vegetable kingdom. JM: Joseph Needham makes the connection between the "germinal ideas" of early Chinese thought and similar ideas of the pre-Socratic philosophers: "The Tao as the Order of Nature, which brought all things into existence and governs their every action, not so much by force as by a kind of natural curvature in space and time, reminds us of the *logos* of Heraclitus of Ephesus, controlling the orderly processes of change." Needham refers to the famous verses from *The Tao and the Power*:

Chapter 25
In the beginning
Was a thing,
Undifferentiated
And yet complete.
Before Heaven and Earth,
There it was,
Silent,
Empty!
Sufficient unto itself!
Unchanging,
Revolving incessantly,
Inexhaustible.
Well was it called Mother
Of All-under-Heaven.
I do not know its name.
We call it the Tao.

Chapter 34
The Great Tao
Floods in every direction!
All things look to it for life,
None are refused.

Chapter 51
The Tao gives birth,
The Power nurtures.

The Mare is of Earth,
Roams the Boundless Earth.

菊 *Qian* rides the Heavens as Dragon, writes Wang Bi, *Kun* roams the Earth as Mare.
The Mare conforms to her Yin position, comments Jullien, following Wang Fuzhi. She
accords with the Yang *élan*. She roams the Earth, thereby asserting herself. The Mare
follows the Stallion, writes Magister Liu. She goes wherever the Stallion goes. She is
gentle but strong. Her Steadfastness is the Steadfastness of Earth.

Kun is soft,
Yielding.
Kun Profits,
Is Steadfast!
The True Gentleman
At first goes astray
And loses the Way;
Later he finds the Flow,
His rightful Place.
Friends are gained
To West and South,
One's own kind
To walk with.
Friends are lost
To East and North.
In the end
There is cause for celebration,
In fine erit gaudium.
Rest in Steadfastness.
This is
Auspicious.
Resonate with
Boundless Earth.

菊 Follow the course of the Tao, writes the Master of Huainan; follow the natural
process of Heaven and Earth. Then it will be easy to manage All-under-Heaven.

On the Image of the Hexagram

Kun,
Potential Energy of Earth.
The True Gentleman
Sustains Matter
Through ample Inner Strength.

Earth is the Prime Image of *Kun*, writes Zhu Xi. They are one and the same. Here we see the pliant, soft Potential Energy of *Kun*. We have seen the heights of Heaven, now we see the depths, the lowliness of Earth. They are infinitely interconnected. *Kun* has utmost Softness, greatest Capacity; there is nothing it cannot contain, nothing it cannot sustain. The Tao of *Kun*, writes Cheng Yi, has as much Grandeur as the Tao of *Qian*. Only the Sage can truly embody this Tao. Earth is broad, its Potential Energy soft and pliant. The True Gentleman contemplates these qualities of *Kun*, Softness and Capacity. As a consequence, his own deep Inner Strength and broad tolerance embrace all things. Inner Emptiness, writes Magister Liu, the Open Space of Heart-and-Mind, enables Outer Acceptance. It enables the Taoist to sustain Others, to accept insult and injury, hardship and sickness, just as the Earth sustains Mountains, just as the Ocean takes into itself the Rivers. JM: *Shi*, Potential Energy, is a key term in *The Art of War*, where it refers to the inherent Power or Dynamic, the Latent Potential, the quality contained in a situation, in a given place or at a given moment in time.

On the Words

Kun
Is most Yielding;
In motion
It is Firm.
It is
Quietest.
Its Power is square.

The whole Hexagram *Kun*, writes Legge, made up as it is of six Divided Lines, expresses the ideal of Yielding, of subordination and docility. The Superior Man, the True Gentleman, does not take the initiative. It is by following that he finds his Lord. The Firmness in motion is that of a mare, docile yet strong, a creature for loyal service to man.

The Trigrams Expounded

Kun
Is Earth,
Mother.
Kun

Stores and serves;
It follows the flow.
It is
Cow and belly.
South-West.
Cloth and cauldron.
Thrifty,
Even.
Large chariot,
Pattern and multitude.
It is handle.
Of soils,
Black.

The Great Treatise

From Part I, Section 11
Closing the Door
Is *Kun.*
Opening the Door
Is *Qian.*
Closing and opening,
These are Change,
Infinite Movement
Back and forth.
Connection.

From Part II, Section 6
The Master said:
Qian and *Kun*
Are the Doors of Change.
Qian is the
Yang Thing,
The penis.
Kun is the
Yin Thing,
The vagina.

When Yin and Yang Energies join,
When Firm and Soft unite,
Then is Substance attained.

丮 One of the first translators to draw attention to this extraordinary passage, and to the sexual dynamic at the very heart of Change, the interplay of Yin and Yang, was the much-reviled (and now largely forgotten) Irish clergyman Thomas McClatchie. McClatchie arrived in the newly established treaty port of Shanghai as a missionary in 1844, and went on to become canon of Shanghai Cathedral. He published his interesting version of the *I Ching* in 1876, much influenced by the new ideas on comparative mythology and religion (Edward B. Tylor's *Primitive Culture* first appeared in 1871). "From the statements of the *I Ching*, and of Confucius in his Commentary, *Qian-Kun* or *Shangdi* [elsewhere McClatchie calls this the Chinese "hermaphroditic deity," and identifies it with Baal of the Chaldeans] is evidently the phallic God of Heathendom represented unmistakably by the usual symbols. *Qian* or his Male portion is the *membrum virile*, and *Kun* or his Female portion is the *pudendum muliebre*; and these two are enclosed in the circle or ring, or *phallos*, the Great Extreme [*Taiji*, the Supreme Ultimate] or Globe of Air [*qi*, Energy], from and by which, as the Great Monad [*Taiyi*], all things are generated. In these two powers of nature we have evidently the Linga and the Yoni of the Hindus." Predictably, McClatchie's contemporary, the prudish Presbyterian James Legge, took great offense at this mention of "sundry things which are not pleasant to look at or dwell upon. Why did he [McClatchie] not dismiss the idea of such conjugal intercourse from his mind altogether? Why make the *I Ching* appear to be gross, when there is not the shadow of grossness in it? It is hardly possible, on reading such a version, to suppress the exclamation *proh pudor*! [For shame!] Can a single passage be adduced in support of it from among all the Chinese critics in the line of centuries? I believe not. The ideas which it expresses are gratuitously and wantonly thrust into this text of the *I Ching*." Canon McClatchie, in his understanding of these Chinese terms (*yangwu* and *yinwu*—literally, Yang Thing and Yin Thing) was well ahead of his time. His rather precise translation is supported by the views of several twentieth-century Chinese intellectuals (e.g., Guo Moruo and Qian Xuantong), and has been vindicated more recently by Edward Shaughnessy in his version of the Mawangdui silk manuscript *I Ching*. It also reflects a pervasive current in early Chinese thought. Douglas Wile writes, "Early texts are marked by the existential loneliness of Yin and Yang for each other, and their union consummates a cosmic synergy." Joseph Needham puts it in his own characteristic fashion: "One notes the solidity of *Qian* as opposed to the cavity in *Kun*, and one can hardly overlook a phallic significance in this, *Qian* as the lance and *Kun* as the grail." *Qian* and *Kun* are two peaks facing each other. From them proceeds the Tao of Change. They are the two leaves of a single entrance, or door, constantly opening onto the Transformation of Things. David Hall and Roger Ames draw attention to the pervasive use of this image in Taoism, the opening and closing

of the Heavenly Gate, moving the leaves of the door back and forth, navigating
between Yin and Yang. As *The Tao and the Power* says:

> *Chapter 6*
> The Gate of the Dark Female
> Is the Root
> Of Heaven and Earth.

> *Chapter 10*
> In opening and closing
> The Gate of Heaven,
> Can you be like a hen?

All of this has deeply sexual implications. The *I Ching* has always been a
source for Chinese ideas of sexuality, often elaborated in alchemical terms. The
mutual physical and psychological benefits of sexual union, the interplay or
intercourse of Yin and Yang, are already referred to in the earliest Chinese sex-
ological texts. Physical intercourse is the Union of Yin and Yang, or the Union
of their Energies (*heqi*, Union of the Breaths of Yin and Yang). Early Taoists
celebrated this Union in collective Sexual Rites. The vagina is the Dark Gate, the
Jade Gate, the Vermilion Gate. In one of the commentaries (the *Xiang'er*) on the
passage just quoted from *The Tao and the Power*, we read:

> The Dark Female
> Is Earth,
> Woman its Image.
> The Yin Cavity
> Is the Gate,
> Office of Life and Death,
> Essence,
> Root.
> The Male Stalk,
> The Penis,
> Is also the Root.

Heaven spreads its influence over Earth, writes Jullien, following Wang Fuzhi.
It penetrates Earth. Earth opens itself to this influence, bringing it to fruition.
This reflects the relationship between Yin and Yang. Yang is firm and solid, Yin
soft and malleable. Yin tends toward condensation of Energy—concentration
and actualization; Yang tends toward deployment of Energy—animation, positive orientation. But there is never Yin without Yang, just as there is never
Heaven without Earth. The Sage gains access to the Power of the Energy that lies
at the base of the world, by himself experiencing this Inner Process of Reality, this

interaction of Yin and Yang. JM: The poet Bo Xingjian uses the same language in his rhapsody "The Great Joy of the Intercourse of Yin and Yang." Young lovers, preparing for the act of love in an upper chamber on a moonlit night, read passages from the *Classic of the Plain Girl*, a sex handbook dating probably from the Sui dynasty. In the handbook, the Plain Girl, immemorial instructress in matters Yin and Yang, gives the Yellow Emperor sensible Taoist advice, advising him not to abstain from sexual intercourse, not to "keep the gates closed," in terms that clearly echo the Great Treatise:

> Heaven and Earth
> Have their Opening and their Closing;
> Yin and Yang
> Have their Transformations.
> Man is modeled on Yin and Yang;
> He follows the Four Seasons.
> Abstain,
> And your Spiritual Energy will not expand,
> Yin and Yang
> Will be blocked.

The Yellow Emperor is advised to keep "opening and closing the doors"—i.e., to make love frequently and thus enjoy health and happiness.

> Between Heaven and Earth,
> All Movement should follow
> The interaction of Yin and Yang.
> Yang attains Yin
> And is thereby Transformed [*hua*];
> Yin attains Yang
> And is thereby Connected [*tong*].
> One Yin,
> One Yang!
> They need each other,
> They work together. . . .
> Know this Tao,
> And you will be happy and strong!
> You will live long
> And be beautiful.

LINES

Yin in First Place

Treading on hoarfrost.

Hard ice

Is on its way,

Fit glacies.

On the Image

Yin solidifies;
In accordance with the Tao,
It becomes
Hard as ice.

On the Words

A family
Accumulating goodness
Enjoys Blessing
In abundance.
A family
Accumulating evil
Knows Misfortune
In abundance.
When a minister
Kills his sovereign,
Or a son
Kills his father:
These are no events
Of a single morning,
Nor of a single evening.
They come to pass gradually.
Matters must be seen clearly
At an early stage.
The Book speaks here
Of the need for vigilance.

Yin Line in Yang Place. Yin is humble and weak in origin, writes Wang Bi, but none-theless accumulates. Be on the lookout at the very outset, advises Magister Liu, for the first signs of negative Yin Energy creeping in. Frost, comments Jullien, following Wang Fuzhi, is a natural Image for the excessive accumulation and condensation of Yin. We must recognize this state of affairs, this Potential Energy in the situation, before it is too far advanced. We need to "read" the minimal degree of freezing present in "hoarfrost," in order to be ready for the really "hard ice" when it comes. In human terms, if we are to act appropriately, we must learn to "read" the undercurrent as it evolves. We must be alert to the Springs of Change, which may presage some spectacular event. JM: This section of the commentary On the Words is quoted in full by the nineteenth-century critic Zhang Xinzhi, in his essay "On Reading *The Story of the Stone*." It is, he says, the underlying theme of that great novel: the Gradual Process of Change (*Jian*, Gradual, is itself the name of Hexagram LIII). Within a family, the accumulation of evil is Gradual, the development of Misfortune is Gradual. There is a need to see things clearly, to nip them in the bud, if one is not to be suddenly confronted with disaster. More recently, in February 2012, these words from the *I Ching* ("A family accumulating goodness . . .") were publicly proposed as a motto to be printed on a new series of Chinese banknotes. The proposal, aimed at raising "awareness of traditional Chinese values," came from the forty-two-year-old "maverick recycling billionaire" Chen Guangbiao, sometimes described as the Warren Buffett of the People's Republic of China. The Leader of an Organization, writes Professor Mun, must keep his eyes open for any changes in both the internal and the external environment. Negative signs of Change to look out for might include a decline in sales, an increase in customer complaints, changes in the prevailing interest rate, or an increase in staff turnover.

Yin in Second Place

Straight,

Square,

Great.

There is neither effort nor practice.

All Profits.

On the Image

This is the Motion of Yin
In Second Place:
Straight and square.

Luminous is the Earth's Tao,
Lex terrae.

On the Words

Straight is true,
Square is righteous.
The True Gentleman
Stays straight within:
This is Reverence.
He remains square without.
This is Righteousness.
When Reverence and Righteousness
Are established,
There is no solitude,
There is Inner Strength.
Actions leave no room for doubt,
Nullus dubitandi locus.

Yin Line in Yin Place. Centered and True. Abiding in Center, writes Wang Bi, in True Place, the True Gentleman here attains the Supreme Quality of Earth. He trusts in the course of Nature. Things are born of themselves. He makes no "effort" to cultivate results; they happen of themselves. He does not rehearse ("practice") matters, and yet everything Profits. This Line presents us with Earth itself, comments Legge, according to the Chinese conception of it, as a Great Cube. Heaven is a Circle or Sphere. In this Hexagram, writes Professor Mun, to be straight is to be honest, to be square is to be upright, to be great is to be large-minded and tolerant. These qualities complement the Strength and Energy of the First Hexagram and create a balanced character in a Leader.

Yin in Third Place

Excellence is

Contained.

Remain Steadfast.

The King's service

May be done,

But without success.

There is a Conclusion,

Finem.

On the Image

Act at the right time.
This is great wisdom,
Claritas magna.

On the Words

The beauty of Yin
Is contained,
In the King's service.
Yin never presumes
To claim success.
This is the Tao of Earth,
The Tao of Wife,
The Tao of Minister.
The Tao of Earth
Knows of no success;
It brings
Conclusion for others,
Finem.

Yin Line in Yang Place. The Tao of Earth, writes Wang Bi, does not initiate; it responds, it awaits orders. This is Excellence Contained, this is Truth. To Contain Excellence, comments Legge, is the part of the Minister or the Officer. He seeks not his own glory, but that of his Ruler. The Leader's Yin character, writes Professor Mun, is projected outward, while his Yang character is "contained" inwardly. His service to the public is done quietly, without claiming any credit for "success."

Yin in Fourth Place

The bag is tied.

Neither Harm,

Nor praise,

Nullum malum,

Nulla gloria.

On the Image

With Caution,
There is no Harm,
Nullum infortunium.

On the Words

In the Transformations
Of Heaven and Earth,
Plants thrive.
In the Closing
Of Heaven and Earth,
Worthy men stay hidden,
Sapientes latent.
The Book of Change speaks
Of Caution.

Yin Line in Yin Place. The "tied bag," coments Jullien, following Wang Fuzhi, signifies a Retreat within oneself, in order to safeguard one's own security. This can be related to the classic situation of the Chinese man of letters during troubled times, choosing retirement, obscurity, and silence in order to escape from tyranny. In such times, it is the height of prudence to "tie the bag." It is indeed the only way to survive with integrity. Remain in softness, writes Magister Liu. Keep inner thoughts within, let not thoughts intrude from without. The Leader keeps a low profile, writes Professor Mun. He restrains his emotions and saves his energies for a better time.

Yin in Fifth Place

A yellow robe.

This is

Greatly Auspicious,

Optimum.

On the Image

Pattern is centered
Within.

On the Properties

Nurture
The Pattern of Culture,
Do not speak out.
The Man of Culture
Contains Radiance
Within;
He manifests the Dragon
Without.

Yin Line in Yang Place. Centered. The fragmentary commentary On the Properties was discovered on a Mawangdui silk manuscript. The Hexagram *Kun*, writes Wang Bi, presents the Tao of the Subject, one whose Excellence is realized in the lowly position of subordinate. He lets his yellow robe hang loosely down, and he secures his Fortune in this way, not by the use of Martial (*wu*) Might. Yellow, comments Jullien, following Wang Fuzhi, is the color of Earth. It represents the perfectly balanced Center, by contrast with dull black and white, or luminous red and green. Here the yellow robe is a lower garment, worn under others; it symbolizes, in addition to the docile submission of Wife or Servant, the Sage's humble self-effacement. The Sage conceals his ability, he does not parade it; he keeps his qualities (his "pattern" or "culture") deep within. JM: Pattern, *wen*, may have once meant a tattoo on the body, then other sorts of pattern in the natural world. It went on to mean patterns of many kinds, on textiles or other stuffs, thence ornamentation, writing, literature, culture, and civilization in general. It was from a very early time contrasted with *wu*, Martial or Warrior. The two founding kings of the Zhou dynasty were King Wen (the Patterned, Civilizing, or Accomplished King) and his son King Wu (the Martial or Warrior King).

Yin in Top Place

Dragons

Battle in the wilds,

Dracones

In desertis pugnant.

Blood flows,

Dark and yellow.

On the Image

The Tao is exhausted,
Lex exhausta.

 Yin Line in Yin Place. This Line, writes Legge, like the Yang in Top Place of the preceding Hexagram ("The Dragon overreaches himself"), points to a time of crisis. The Yin Line is a Dragon doing battle with another Dragon. They bleed, and their blood is of two colors: the color proper to Heaven (dark blue), and the color proper to Earth (yellow). This conflict, writes Magister Liu, stems from an inability to follow Others, a desire to *be followed*, a lack of Harmony and Equilibrium. Yin and Yang are out of tune. The injury is self-inflicted. The "ice" in the First Place and the "blood" in the Sixth, comments Jullien, following Wang Fuzhi, both indicate a crisis, a conflict, a warning that things have reached a critically dangerous turning point. If one can recognize this, if one can acknowledge Life-Destiny and be attentive to the Springs of Change, then the result of this crisis need not be Misfortune. In an Organization, writes Professor Mun, there may be a conflict between old and new visions or policies.

Yin in Final Place

It Profits

To be forever Steadfast,

Oportet ut perpetua sit soliditas.

On the Image

A Grand Conclusion,
Magnus finis.

 As with the Final, or Supernumerary, Line of the First Hexagram, writes Zhu Xi, there is here a general movement from Yin to Yang, hence a Grand Conclusion. Yang is great, Yin is small. Here all Yin elements become Yang; they move from small to great. To reach the Tao, writes Magister Liu, one must know how to be submissive and receptive. One must be forever True and Steadfast.

HEXAGRAM III

Zhun

Difficult Birth

Kan/Abyss

above

Zhen/Quake

JUDGMENT

Supreme Fortune.

Profitable. .

Steadfast.

A Destination

Is of no avail.

It Profits

To establish Lieutenants,

Oportet elevare principes.

Abyss above Quake. The Chinese graph for *Zhun*, writes Legge, shows a plant struggling with difficulty to sprout out of the Earth, to rise gradually above the surface. This difficulty marks the first stages in a plant's growth, its embryonic "growth pains." It also symbolizes the struggles that mark the rise of a state out of a condition of disorder, consequent upon a Great Change, or revolution. "Establishing Lieutenants," writes Chen Guying, can also be understood figuratively to mean adopting good habits, sound principles of conduct; forming good friendships; building a sound basis for one's life. Magister Liu agrees. Once the Heart-and-Mind is True, then the Root is strong and Primal Energy is not dispersed or trapped by Negative Yin Energy.

On the Judgment

Difficult Birth.
First intercourse
Of Firm and Yielding,
Of Yang and Yin.
There is
Movement in Danger,
Great Fortune.
Steadfastness.
Movement
Of Lightning and Rain.
Fullness to the brim,
Heaven's murky brew.
Lieutenants established;
No peace.

On the Image of the Hexagram

Clouds and Thunder,
Nubes et tonitrus.
The True Gentleman
Weaves the Fabric of Order.

This first "mixed" Hexagram of the *I Ching* contains both Yin and Yang Lines, and thus points to "first intercourse of Yin and Yang" and the ensuing pangs of birth. First Intercourse is the Quake, writes Zhu Xi. Difficult Birth takes place in the Abyss, the Place of Peril. The Quake (*Zhen*, Lower Trigram) Moves: that is its mode of Action. The Abyss (*Kan*, Upper Trigram) receives; it is a Place of Danger: that is its Nature. Lightning is an Image associated with Quake, Rain an Image associated with Water in the Abyss. In the Intercourse of Yin and Yang, Lightning and Rain break forth. They move. In this "murky brew," Nature ferments, it gives birth. In this disorder, nothing is fixed, names are as yet undetermined. It is the True Gentleman who instills Order, who weaves its Fabric. He "establishes Lieutenants." But his measures cannot yet bring peace. The Yang Line in First Place is born within the Abyss, writes Magister Liu. At this crucial Intercourse of Yin and Yang, at this Ford between Life and Death, Calamity and Fortune are being determined. The Taoist must be decisive in his Work, must nurture the Sprouts of Spirit, must not allow Yin Energy to invade and cause injury. Ultimately Yang Energy will unfold and prevail, like Thunder in the Clouds. Sweet Dew will descend. The twilight is long, but the dawn is radiant. JM: "Heaven's murky brew," the treacherous but creative Water in which all things are born, is close in meaning to the primordial "chaos" (*hundun*) of the Taoists. (In fact, the character *dun* is very close in form to this Hexagram Name, *Zhun*.) The historian and poet Ban Gu refers to this Hexagram in his "Rhapsody on Connecting with Spirit":

> What confusion lies in *Zhun,*
> In Difficult Birth. . . .

In his concluding words, he summarizes one of the *I Ching*'s main themes, the need to keep an open perception in the Inner Mind of the shifting dynamic of the environment:

> In Heaven's murky brew
> Are forged
> Identity and Life-Destiny.
> A Return to Inner Mind
> Broadens the Tao;
> Only the Sage can achieve this.
> The Primal Force propels all things,
> It flows without ceasing. . . .
> It knows the Springs of Change,
> It enters the Realm of Spirit.

The poet Xie Lingyun, when he sang the praises of his grandfather General Xie Xuan, linked him with this Hexagram. He wrote of the difficulties and dangers Xie Xuan had faced in public life, and of his great victory at the Battle of Fei River (AD 383):

> **In Praise of My Grandfather**
> He left off talking of the Tao
> And donned armor.
> He brought comfort to the world.
> He settled the troubles of Difficult Birth,
> Brought honor to his Lord,
> Prosperity to the Folk.

Xie Xuan did indeed save the fragile southern dynasty that he served. But when the time came, he saw the writing on the wall and was wise enough to retire from public life:

He followed
The Springs of Change;
He knew Truth
And fell silent.

The *Zhun* Hexagram describes the inchoate and messy process of Gestation and Birth, an embryonic process still struggling to find Completion. Yin and Yang have engaged in First Intercourse, and they are in the midst of further Movement, in the midst of Danger, the very process of Birth. (One is tempted to see here a Breaking of the Waters.) The subsequent Lines link the pangs of Birth with Marriage and the Hunt, two different sorts of Chase. At critical points, "horses wheel." Tensions mount. The growing process cannot be hurried, writes Professor Mun. This is true of any Organization in its "start-up" stage, facing difficulties in raising capital, manpower, technology, and networks. The Leader must stay calm. He must not move impulsively. He must be externally flexible and adaptable, like Water, and internally strong and dynamic, like Thunder.

LINES

Yang in First Place

Hesitation.

Caution.

It Profits

To remain Steadfast.

It Profits

To establish Lieutenants.

On the Image

Despite hesitation,
Aspiration
Is set on the True Path.
The noble stoop
To the humble,
Drawing them over in large numbers.

Yang Line in Yang Place. This First Line, writes Legge, is Undivided (Yang) and Firm. Action is possible, but above and ahead (within the Hexagram) lies the Trigram of Danger (*Kan*). Hence the need for Caution and the importance of "establishing Lieutenants" and delegating authority. In this way, writes Magister Liu, Primal Energy can be conserved and nurtured. Confusion must be resolved gradually, writes Richard Wilhelm. To rule by serving, as noble stoops to humble, is the secret of success. Caution and hesitation are advised at this difficult time. The Leader has a strong character (Yang Line), writes Professor Mun, and will not give up his development plan even though he is facing difficulties (he "remains Steadfast"). He should seek assistance from capable people ("Lieutenants").

Yin in Second Place

Difficulty at Birth.

A turning.

Horses wheel,

Pulling at odds.

No brigand this,

But a suitor.

The woman

Stays Steadfast;

She rejects marriage.

She waits ten years to wed.

On the Image

Yin Rides
Firm Yang,
Supra durum.
Difficulty.
Marriage after ten years
Returns all
To its proper state.

Yin Line in Yin Place. Centered and True. A young lady is sought in marriage by a strong suitor, writes Legge. She rejects him, and finally, after ten years, finds a more suitable husband. JM: Marriage does indeed present itself as a resolution of the uncertainties and difficulties that beset this critical juncture. But it must be entered into only with careful deliberation. The horses wheeling, pulling in opposite directions, indicate a difficult relationship. Note that they occur three times in this Hexagram, in Lines 2, 4, and 6. Wait until Yin and Yang are properly matched, writes Magister Liu. Do not act impulsively. The executive, writes Professor Mun, is close to, immediately above, Yang in First Place (he Rides Yang). But clashes may arise between the two. To forge a more productive partnership or alliance with Yang in Fifth Place will take time and requires patience.

Yin in Third Place

There is

No guide.

A deer

Is hunted into the woods.

The True Gentleman,

Understanding

The Springs of the moment,

Abandons the chase.

To continue

Will bring Misfortune,

Poenitebit.

On the Image

One man hunts with no guide,
For the sheer sake of the chase.
The True Gentleman
Abandons the chase,
Seeing trouble ahead,
And Harm.

Yin Line in Yang Place. Pursuit of any goal must be tempered by the wisdom of the True Gentleman, by a cultivated insight into the Springs of Change. The Hunt, writes Chen Guying, is also the quest for a mate, an underlying theme of this Hexagram. Any hasty move will be dangerous, writes Magister Liu. If a weak and incapable Leader (Yin in Yang Place), writes Professor Mun, undertakes a risky venture, then he will suffer a serious setback.

Yin in Fourth Place

Horses wheel;

They pull at odds.

A wife is sought.

A Destination

Is Auspicious,

Hoc bonum.

All things Profit,

In nullo non convenit.

On the Image

Both the seeking and the Destination
Show clarity,
Claritas.

 Yin Line in Yin Place. The bride "goes" with her suitor. All is "clear." This Line Resonates with Yang in First Place. This is the right moment, advises Magister Liu. True Yang Energy is in sight.

Yang in Fifth Place

Fat meat

Is laid in.

To be Steadfast

Is Auspicious

In small matters,

Hoc bonum.

To be Steadfast

In great matters

Brings Disaster,

Hoc infortunium.

On the Image

Generosity
Cannot yet shine.

 Yang Line in Yang Place. Centered and True. This is the Place of Authority (Fifth Place), writes Legge, and the true Ruler should dispense generosity. But at the same time this is the Center of the Upper Trigram, Danger (*Kan*, Abyss), and great things should not be attempted. The Leader, writes Professor Mun, is caught between two Yin Lines, which symbolize difficulties. He should take small steps rather than giant leaps. JM: Go ahead, prepare (as if for the festivities of marriage) in small ways (such as laying in the choicest viands), but resist the temptation to make a big thing, a "great matter," of it.

Yin in Top Place

Horses wheel;

They pull at odds.

Tears of blood

Flow in torrents.

On the Image

This cannot endure.

Yin Line in Yin Place. Do not forget that all may still end in disaster, writes Chen Guying. This Line may describe the "marriage party" and the bride's overwhelming and conflicting emotions on being finally "carried away." JM: The "horses wheeling" may be hesitation, a reluctance or inability to move. Just as Difficulty seems to be over, writes Magister Liu, just as True Yang is in sight, one weeps to see the longed-for goal slip from one's grasp. The Leader, writes Professor Mun, finds himself in extreme difficulty and hesitates. He must be patient and carry on until the breakthrough occurs. The impasse will not last forever.

HEXAGRAM IV

Meng

Youthful Folly

Gen/Mountain

above

Kan/Abyss

JUDGMENT

Fortune.

I seek not

Youthful Folly,

Youthful Folly

Seeks me.

First Divination

Receives a response.

Second and third Divinations,

Importunate questions,

Receive none.

To be Steadfast

Profits,

Necesse est ut sit soliditas.

On the Judgment

Beneath the Mountain,
Danger,
Timendi locus.
A halt.
Fortune lies
In according with Time,
In keeping to Center.
Youthful Folly seeks me out,
Aspirations Resonate.
First Divination,
Strong and Centered,
Receives a response.
Importunate questioning
Is Folly,
Is in need of
Cultivation and guidance,
Work of the Sage.

秀 Mountain above Waters of the Abyss. After the struggles of Hexagram III, *Zhun*, the seed bursting through the soil to be born, here we enter the gushing Waters of the Alpine Abyss, the Spring beneath the Mountain, the wayward Energy of the growing infant, the vagaries of youthful inexperience and Ignorance, Folly groping for Truth. Two Yang Lines confront the Darkness of four Yin Lines. One of the earliest meanings of *meng* is a "covering," a "darkness" (as of the sky), a "blinding" (of the eye). "To open the covering," *qimeng*, is an old term for to "enlighten." Zhu Xi's famous *I Ching Primer* was entitled *Yixue qimeng*, literally "Lifting the Cover from the Study of the *I Ching.*" Richard Wilhelm gives this somewhat enigmatic fourth Hexagram a positive interpretation: intimations of Enlightenment, a dialogue between Youth and Sage, between Wisdom and Folly. The Fool "in his spontaneous and unreflecting attitude, is able to be at the Center, and in accordance with Time." Magister Liu emphasizes that the Darkness can be overcome only through natural innocence. Be open, be still, be sincere, be respectful. This is the path of Non-Action. This nurtures Truth. This makes it possible to tread the path out of Darkness. Professor Mun writes of the need in an Organization for an interactive relationship between Leader and subordinate. One cannot impose Enlightenment, comments Zen Master Zhixu. The Other must be ready and willing to come forward. Danger is inherent in the search for Enlightenment, which leads, after all, through a perilous Abyss.

On the Image of the Hexagram

Beneath the Mountain
Gushes a Spring.
The True Gentleman
Cultivates Spiritual Strength
With determination,
Sapiens virtutem perficit.

The Water of the Spring is pure, comments Zen Master Zhixu. It is fresh, it flows from a deep Source. And just as the Spring must flow, so the Aspiration for Enlightenment cannot be quenched, it can never be destroyed. JM: At the same time, Aspiration and Enthusiasm benefit from the sureness and form of the Mountain. They need guidance and direction. The Mountain, writes Magister Liu, nurtures the Spring. Simplicity and honesty nurture Inner Strength.

LINES

Yin in First Place

Folly

Is dispelled.

It Profits

To punish

With loosened

Manacles and shackles.

Severity

Brings Distress,

Poenitendi locus.

On the Image

Punishment
Strengthens discipline.

Yin Line in Yang Place. Punishment in itself, writes Wang Bi, is abhorred by the Tao. It is contrary to spontaneity (*ziran*). But the *threat* of punishment can have a strengthening effect on discipline. JM: Discipline enables Youth to form mature habits. But to continue too long and too severely in a disciplinarian manner will only have undesirable effects. Punishment must be measured and judicious. Discipline, writes Magister Liu, helps to guard against the debilitating effects of Yin, the stirrings of the Human Heart-and-Mind, in the first stage of Youthful Folly. Any Organization, writes Professor Mun, needs rules and self-discipline.

Yang in Second Place

To tolerate Folly

Is Auspicious,

Hoc bonum.

It is Auspicious

To take a wife,

Optimum.

A child

Sustains the family.

On the Image

The Firm connects
With the Yielding,
With Yin in Fifth Place,
Durum et molle conjugantur.

Yang Line in Yin Place. Centered. The Compliant Master of the household, writes Richard Wilhelm, permits a firm son to take over (and "sustain the family"). JM: One should deal kindly with Folly and Inexperience. Resonance between this Yang Line and Yin in Fifth Place leads naturally to the idea of marriage. The Leader of an Organization, writes Professor Mun, should be patient with those taking on new responsibilities.

Yin in Third Place

Do not marry the woman.

At sight of a man of gold,

She loses control.

No Profit,

Nulla est convenientia.

On the Image

Do not marry the woman.
Her conduct does not follow
The True Flow.

Yin Line in a Yang Place. This, writes Legge, indicates an undesirable character, a woman unable to withstand temptation, one from whom it is wise to keep a distance. The example of a "man of gold" (i.e., a wealthy philanderer) given by Zhu Xi is Lu Qiuhu, famous from the first-century AD *Tales of Virtuous Women*. Returning home from a nine-year absence, he tries to seduce a pretty girl outside his village with the offer of gold and silks, only to discover that she is in fact his own wife. JM: In the story, the wife is a model of Confucian virtue. Her distress at her husband's infidelity drives her to commit suicide. In the Hexagram, things are rather different. A fickle woman throws herself at a rich lover. She loses control. Some commentators take the "woman" as a figurative expression for Foolish Youth, which is too forward in seeking instruction. Magister Liu warns generally against the influence of sensuality and desire. With these, nothing is gained (in terms of the Other). And Self is lost. There is no Profit, simply increased Folly. A Leader, writes Professor Mun, should not use a person who lacks dignity and self-respect.

Yin in Fourth Place

Folly

Is confined.

Distress.

On the Image

Distress is caused
By isolation,
By distance from Firm Yang.

Yin Line in Yin Place. This Yin Line, writes Zhu Xi, is confined in Darkness between two other Yin Lines. Seek out the Power of the Radiant and Firm (Yang), and Distress can be avoided. A senior executive, writes Professor Mun, is weak, unbalanced, and ignorant. He is too stubborn to listen to others. He is "confined" in his own mental cage.

Yin in Fifth Place

Youthful Folly

Is Auspicious,

Hoc bonum.

On the Image

It follows
The True Flow.

Yin Line in Yang Place. Centered. For Chen Guying, there are echoes here of the ancient respect for the innocent wisdom of children and their rhymes. For Magister Liu, this is the True Folly of Youth and Innocence, free of artificial knowledge. It is Folly aware of its own Folly. A wise Leader, writes Professor Mun, is a man with an innocent attitude, modest and open-minded as a child. JM: Children were close to Heaven and Earth and to the world of Spirit. The Taoist classic *The Tao and the Power* and Taoism in general honor the Power of the Inner Child, the Fool, the Babe, the Infant:

Chapter 10
Can you concentrate your breath,
Be soft as an Infant?

Chapter 28
Eternal Power never leaks away.
This is the Return
To Infancy.

Chapter 55
To possess abundant Power
Is to be like a Babe.
Poisonous insects
Will not hurt him,
Fierce beasts
Will not seize him,
Nor birds of prey claw at him.
His bones are weak,
His sinews soft,
But his grip is sure.
He knows no union
Of male and female,
But his penis stirs.
His Essence and Harmony
Are Supreme.

Yang in Top Place

Folly

Is smitten.

Violence

Brings no Profit.

It Profits

To contain violence,

To control brigands.

On the Image

To flow with the Tao,
Above and below.

Yang Line in Yin Place. Never be too severe or aggressive in correcting Others. Make best use of the positive elements in any situation. The Human Heart-and-Mind is the violent brigand, writes Magister Liu. Contain *that* violence. Let go of the Human Heart-and-Mind, quicken the Heart-and-Mind of Tao. This disperses Yin Energy, this makes Yang Energy complete and pure. This is Folly becoming Wisdom.

HEXAGRAM V

Xu

Waiting

Kan/Abyss

above

Qian/Heaven

JUDGMENT

Good Faith.

Luminous Fortune.

This is Auspicious

For the Steadfast,

Hoc bonum.

It Profits

To cross a Great Stream,

Transire magnum fluvium.

On the Judgment

Danger lies ahead,
Periculum.
Firmness and strength
Save from the Pit,
From exhaustion.
Firmness is in
The Seat of Heaven,
True and Centered.
A journey
Brings results.

芽 Waters of the Abyss, above Heaven. The rains have not yet fallen. A strong person might wish to confront Danger boldly, writes Legge, but instead he must be restrained and wait patiently and calmly. In order to nurture the Youthful Folly (of the previous Hexagram), patience and the ability to wait are needed. This is the lesson of the Hexagram: Caution with quiet confidence, Action well considered, plans well matured. "Crossing a Great Stream," an expression frequent in the *I Ching*, can mean the undertaking of any hazardous enterprise, the encountering of any great difficulty, without special reference to Water. But it is also natural to understand the Great Stream as the Yellow River, which the Lords of Zhou were obliged to cross when they rebelled against the dynasty of Shang. The passage of the River by King Wu, the son of King Wen, was certainly one of the greatest deeds in the history of China. It was preceded by a long "waiting," until the time arrived that assured success. JM: "Crossing a Great Stream" should indeed be understood in a more general sense as setting out on any venture into the unknown, going beyond the confines of the familiar, taking a step that could well lead to Danger and should therefore be undertaken only with Caution. It certainly does not refer to the sea, and the time-hallowed translation "Great Water" is therefore a little misleading. The *I Ching*, evolving as it did in the inland Yellow River confines of Shang and Zhou China, had nothing to say about the (ever-changing) ocean, but a lot about Water as observed in other forms. Early Chinese texts, comments Sarah Allan, do not praise the vast "immortal sea." She writes: "The water which most interested Chinese philosophers was that found in the great rivers and the small streams, and in the irrigation ditches which surrounded fields of grain. It was the rain and the pools which form from fallen rain, the ordinary rather than the infinite, that which sustains life and is experienced by all. From the contemplation of this most common and most variable of natural phenomena, the Chinese philosophers sought to understand the fundamental principles of life." To cross the Great Stream, comments Zen Master Zhixu, is to cross the Stream of Life and Death, and ultimately to reach the other shore of Nirvana. With Good Faith, writes Magister Liu, Danger can be managed. Awareness of Danger helps build Inner Strength. Waiting for the right moment, the Taoist enters the Tiger's Lair, suffering no injury from negative Yin Energy. To resolve difficulties in an Organization needs time, writes Professor Mun. Waiting does not mean doing nothing. It means preparing for the future.

On the Image of the Hexagram

Clouds rise up to Heaven,
Nubes sunt in coelo.
The True Gentleman
Takes his ease;
He feasts joyfully.

Qian, the Lower Trigram, Heaven, is Firm and Strong, writes Cheng Yi. It rises upward and moves forward, but runs into the Danger of *Kan*, the Upper Trigram, Water, the Abyss, the Pit. This obstacle obliges it to wait for a later and more Auspicious time. The cloud that has risen up to Heaven has to wait, till it discharges its store of rain, writes Legge, paraphrasing Zhu Xi. This event signals the Harmony of Heaven and Earth, the union of Yin and Yang. The True Gentleman meanwhile enjoys his leisure. He cultivates his Spiritual Strength, he nourishes and harmonizes his Energy, while awaiting the occasion for judicious action.

LINES

Yang in First Place

Waiting

In the meadows,

Sperat in pratis.

It Profits

To persevere.

No Harm,

Nullus error.

On the Image

Do not make a rash move.
Persevere,
Stay with the regular course.

Yang Line in Yang Place. The "regular course," writes Legge, following Cheng Yi, lies in Waiting, at a distance from Danger, for the proper time to Act—working in the meadows, concentrating on daily tasks. Abide in that state of mind. Persevere.

Yang in Second Place

Waiting

On the sandbank.

There is some slight talk.

Ultimately

All is Auspicious,

In fine

Bonum.

On the Image

Taking a stand
On the sandbank,
In the Center,
In medio.
Slight talk
Cannot prevent
An Auspicious issue,
In fine
Optimum.

Yang Line in Yin Place. Centered. The sandbank, writes Legge, is nearer to the Abyss, to *Kan*, Water, Danger. But self-restraint, patience, and forbearance will prevail.

Yang in Third Place

Waiting

In the mud.

Brigands are invited.

On the Image

Calamity
Waits without.
Aggression is invited.
Respect and Caution
Stave off defeat.

 Yang Line in Yang Place. This is the very brink of the Abyss (the last Line before the Upper Trigram), writes Legge. Advance has provoked resistance, which may result in injury. Mud is dangerous, writes Professor Mun. People can be trapped in it. A Leader needs to be particularly cautious.

Yin in Fourth Place

Waiting

In blood.

Leave the Cave.

On the Image

Follow the Flow,
Listen.

 Yin Line in Yin Place. With this Line, writes Legge, the Hexagram passes from the Lower to the Upper Trigram, entering the realm of Danger, of strife and blood-shed. Retreat is essential. One must escape from the Cave, from the Pit, where the enemy threatens such damage. The Cave, comments Zen Master Zhixu, is the world of delusion, from which one now emerges to true perception, listening with compassion (following "the Flow"). Delusion gives way of its own accord to the realization of Enlightenment. The Cave, writes Magister Liu, is a realm of Darkness. To escape from it, the help of Others is needed. Only with that help is it possible to leave the Cave and avoid injury from Yin Energy. The Leader, writes Professor Mun, should stay calm and upright and wait for a chance to escape from a difficult situation.

Yang in Fifth Place

Waiting

With wine and food.

To be Steadfast

Is Auspicious,

Hoc solidum bonum.

On the Image

Centered and True,
In medio et in recto.

Yang Line in Yang Place. Centered and True. This Line is both Strong and Centered, writes Legge. It is in its True Place, the Place of Authority (the Fifth Line is always so). This is a celebration of triumph. With Steadfastness, one will go on from strength to strength.

Yin in Top Place

The Cave

Is entered.

Three uninvited guests

Are treated with honor.

An Auspicious Conclusion,

Finis optimus.

On the Image

This is not in Apt Place.
But there is no great Harm,
Non magnum malum.

Yin Line in Yin Place. One enters deeply into the Abyss, writes Legge. The Yang Third Line below Resonates with this Yin Line. It comes to its aid, with two other

Yang companions. These are the "three guests," the three Yang Lines in the Lower Trigram, who are received "with honor," and whose help proves effectual. The Golden Elixir, writes Magister Liu, is formed. From within the depths of the Cave, where all hope seemed lost, in an empty room, Light is born. Illumination enters the Cave. With the Three Immortal Guests, the Complete and Pure Yang is formed. Yin and Yang are fused as one. JM: Several commentators, incuding Zhu Xi, draw attention to the fact that this Yin Line in Top Place *is* in fact "in Apt Place."

Song

Conflict

Qian/Heaven

above

Kan/Abyss

JUDGMENT

Good Faith.

Caution.

This is Auspicious

Halfway,

In medio

Hoc bonum.

Ultimately

There is Calamity,

In fine

Infortunium.

It Profits

To see a Great Man,

Magnum virum.

There is no Profit

In crossing a Great Stream,

Transire magnum fluvium.

On the Judgment

Firmness above,
Superius durum.
Danger below,
Inferius periculosum.
Strength in the face of Danger.
Conflict.
Good Faith and Caution.
The Firm reaches the Center.
It is Auspicious.
Ultimately there is Calamity.
Conflict
Is unresolved.
It Profits
To see a Great Man.
Center and Truth are valued.
Crossing the Great Stream
Does not Profit,
It leads into the Abyss,
In profundam aquam.

On the Image of the Hexagram

Heaven and Water at odds,
Coelum et aqua in tumultu.
The True Gentleman,
In Action,

Plans first steps
With greatest care.

Heaven above the Waters of the Abyss. The Trigrams of the previous Hexagram are here reversed. Firmness in the Upper Trigram, Qian, seeks to control the Lower Trigram, *Kan*, while the Danger inherent in that Lower Trigram seeks to overwhelm the Upper. They are at odds. The relationship between the two Trigrams is one of Conflict. The three Yang Lines in the Upper Trigram, writes Professor Mun, indicate an Organization dominated by a strong senior management. The lack of Resonance between Yang in Fifth and Yang in Second reveals a poor relationship between the Leader and middle management, leading to serious misunderstanding and Conflict. In business affairs, there is little to be gained from Conflict and confrontation. Compromise is desirable; a meeting "halfway" is Auspicious. JM: The Inner Self also finds itself in Danger when confronted with Strength from Without. This too is Conflict. When the Heart-and-Mind is still obscured with dust, comments Zen Master Zhixu, when Inner Conflict persists, it is dangerous to cross the Great Stream. The single Undivided Line, writes Legge, in the Center of the Lower Trigram, *Kan*, Yang in Second Place, is emblematic of Sincerity, of Good Faith. A sincere individual, a person of Good Faith, will be Cautious, and will enjoy Good Fortune. But, even with such a person, if Conflict continues, the effect will ultimately be undesirable. In the *Analects*, Confucius advises his disciples to "avoid Conflict." The Confucians were, as Simon Leys has remarked, hostile toward the very concept of law and legal argument, advocating instead observance of Rites, or "civilized behaviour." "Laws make people cunning, they foster amorality and cynicism, ruthlessness and a perverse spirit of Strife and Contention." Better by far (than litigation and legal wrangling) is Self-Knowledge, Self-Cultivation. Elsewhere in that strange collection of sayings the *Analects*, the Master, to whom (we should not forget) was attributed for centuries the writing of the first commentaries on the *I Ching*, remarks: "I have never seen a man capable of seeing his own faults, of exposing them in the tribunal of his heart." How rare, in other words, is genuine Self-Knowledge! How common the overly critical judgment of Others and the resultant Conflict and strife! Compare the proverbial saying "He who denounces his own faults is fortunate; he who denounces others is doomed." For Magister Liu, any kind of Conflict with Others—whether it be the quest for power, competition for advancement in the dusty and troublesome world, or mere quarreling about "right and wrong"—is simply a violation of the Harmony of Tao, a departure from the equilibrium of Center. The Taoist deals first with Self, seeks first Inner Balance and Harmony.

LINES

Yin in First Place

The matter

Does not endure,

Non diu durabit.

There is some slight talk.

Ultimately

All is Auspicious,

In fine optimum.

On the Image

Do not prolong
Conflict.
Despite slight talk,
The arguments are clear,
Verba sunt clara.

Yin Line in Yang Place. This Line, writes Legge, is weak, sitting as it does at the bottom of the Hexagram. There is suffering in the early stages of Conflict. Let the matter drop. Be flexible. The result will be Auspicious. Prolonged Conflict can be harmful to both sides, writes Professor Mun. The Leader should carefully examine the situation, estimate the possible outcome, and decide whether or not, on balance, the Conflict is in fact worth it.

Yang in Second Place

Conflict

Fails.

Return home,

Take refuge

In a small town

Of three hundred households.

No Misfortune,

Nullum infortunium.

On the Image

Conflict below
With one above.
Approaching Calamity
Is averted.

Yang Line in Yin Place. Centered. This strong Second Line, writes Zhu Xi, rules the Lower Trigram. One is drawn into Conflict and wishes to engage in it. But Potential Energy is weakened by the Yin Place. One is no Match for Yang in Fifth Place ("one above"). That is why one returns home, to a "small [insignificant] town," proof of Humility. One takes refuge from Calamity. JM: The word *gui* ("return home") has deep undertones. The Taoist "returns" to the place from which he has come, to the place where he should be. He recognizes his Roots. As *The Tao and the Power* puts it:

> Chapter 16
> The Return to the Root
> Is Stillness,
> Recognition
> Of Life-Destiny.

A Chinese official in traditional times, turning his back on public life, "returned" to the fields. This was the cry of the Hermit. As the poet Tao Yuanming wrote:

> I must return!
> Too long has my Heart-and-Mind
> Been my body's slave.
> Why protract
> This melancholy and lonely grief . . . .
> I must return!
> Break off friendships,
> Cease this wandering.
> The world and I
> Must part ways!

Yin in Third Place

Feed

On Ancient Strength.

Steadfast

In face of Danger.

Ultimately,

This is Auspicious,

In fine bonum.

Doing the King's service,

Without success.

On the Image

Follow those above.
This is Auspicious,
Optimum.

 Yin Line in Yang Place. Unequal to Conflict (Yin is here enclosed between two Yang Lines), writes Legge, paraphrasing Zhu Xi, one withdraws from the public arena, endeavoring to keep safely in the background. To "feed on Ancient Strength" is to retain an old position, to live on a modest salary, not to crave promotion, not to venture forth on some dangerous new enterprise. Ancient Strength, writes Professor Mun, is the traditional virtue of non-contention, the avoidance of Conflict.

Yang in Fourth Place

Conflict fails.

Return,

Recognize

Life-Destiny.

There is

A change of course.

Be calmly Steadfast.

This is Auspicious,

Optimum.

On the Image

Do not fall into error.

 Yang Line in Yin Place. To "recognize Life-Destiny," writes Zhu Xi, is to accept calmly that which is True. The executive, writes Professor Mun, should control his temper and cultivate a calm nature. Impulsive action could lead him seriously astray.

Yang in Fifth Place

Conflict.

This is

Supremely Auspicious.

Optimum.

On the Image

Auspicious.
Centered and True,
Medium atque rectum.

 Yang Line in Yang Place. Centered and True. This Fifth Line represents the Great Man, writes Legge, the Man of Good Faith. He can resolve Conflict successfully, impartially. The result is Auspicious. In business, comments Professor Mun, a respected figure, someone balanced, upright, and trustworthy, is called in to moderate the Conflict, to mediate in a just and fair way.

Yang in Top Place

A leather girdle

Is granted.

Ultimately,

Three times in one morning,

It is taken away.

On the Image

To receive a gift of apparel,
In a Conflict,
Merits no respect,
Nulla reverentia.

 Yang Line in Yin Place. Top Place is also Strong, writes Legge, and has two Strong companions. With the Trigram of Heaven riding above the Trigram of Danger (the Waters of the Abyss), Action in any great enterprise is likely to be premature. To gain some trivial honor (such as the "girdle") as a result of Conflict is an unsure victory. JM: In the end what is gained is outweighed by what is lost. Fame and Honor are fickle things.

Shi

The Army

Kun/Earth

above

Kan/Abyss

JUDGMENT

This is Auspicious

For the Steadfast,

For the strong.

No Harm,

Sine malo.

On the Judgment

Steadfast.
True.

Treating the Multitude
With Truth,
Such a one can be King.
The Firm is Centered,
Resonant.
A dangerous Action,
Undertaken,
Meets with compliance.
All-under-Heaven
Is poisoned,
But the Folk follow.
This is Auspicious.
There can be no Harm.

Earth over Waters of the Abyss. Water is stored in the Earth, writes Legge, as an Army is stored "within" the Folk, or Nation. These resources must be properly mobilized and motivated. This Hexagram describes the conduct of military expeditions in a feudal kingdom. The single Yang Line in Second Place is the General, Resonating with the Yin Line in the Fifth Place of Royal Authority. Entire trust is placed in his General by a Compliant King. The General is Strong and True, and his enterprises will be successful. JM: The other four Yin Lines are the Army or Multitude, obedient to their single Leader. Danger is found in *Kan*, the Lower Trigram, the Abyss; and Compliance or Accordance with others, docility, in *Kun*, the Upper Trigram, Earth. War can indeed "poison" All-under-Heaven, threatening devastation and ruin. In the words of *The Tao and the Power*:

Chapter 30
Wheresoever troops are stationed,
Spring up
Briars and thorns.
After long campaigns,
There are sure to be
Years of Calamity.

Chapter 31
War and the weapons of War
Are instruments of Misfortune.
The Man of the Tao
Deals not with them.
They are not
Proper to the True Gentleman.

Just as the previous Hexagram portrayed Conflict as a violation of Harmony, writes Legge, so this Hexagram has little good to say of the extreme case of

Conflict—War. And yet it is a fact that a nation, a Folk, will endure the hardships of War for a Leader whom the People esteem and love. JM: If the result is to be Auspicious and no Harm is to result, this Leader must understand the full Nature (and potential evil) of War. The Upper Trigram, Earth, writes Professor Mun, represents the Army, or the people of an Organization, following their Leader (Second Yang) in an Action that may prove Dangerous. But if the Leader is not sincere and upright, if he is not a person of integrity and vision, then they will take Action against him. Compare *The Art of War*:

Chapter 2
Without a full understanding
Of the Harm caused by War,
It is impossible to understand
The most profitable way
Of conducting it.

Chapter 10
The General
Who Advances
Without seeking fame,
Who Retreats
Without escaping blame,
Whose one aim is
To protect his Folk
And serve his Lord,
This man
Is a Jewel of the Realm.
He treats his troops
As his children;
They will follow him
Into the deepest ravine.
He regards them
As his loved ones;
They will stand by him
Unto death.

There were several military treatises circulating in the second half of the Zhou dynasty, during the two periods known as the Spring and Autumn and the Warring States, when (as the latter name implies) war was the order of the day. Many of the aphorisms in such treatises as *The Art of War* can be applied more broadly to all spheres of life—to any campaign in which strategic decisions have to be made. Within the individual, writes Magister Liu, once the Primal Heart-and-Mind of the Tao is lost, then the Six Thieves (the senses) cause havoc, the Seven Emotions run amok. There is unrest, rebellion, and chaos. These troublemakers must be rooted out, or there will never be peace. This is the only way back to Complete Primal Purity. This is the Precious Tao of the "Army" Hexagram.

On the Image of the Hexagram

Water within Earth,
Aqua sub terra.
The True Gentleman
Cherishes the Folk,
He nurtures the Multitude.

 Just as Water is not outside but within or beneath the Earth, writes Legge, paraphrasing Cheng Yi, just as Water is stored underground, in the same way the Army is not *outside* the nation, it is a part of it. The Ruler must nurture this resource—his Folk, the Multitude—if he is to win their support. JM: To this end, he must educate them, so that they understand the nature of the situation, so that they can share his beliefs. The Master, Confucius, once said: "If a Good Man educates the Folk for seven years, then they can be sent to War. If he fails to teach them to fight, he might as well throw them away." Man's body is a nation, writes Magister Liu. The Heart-and-Mind is the True Gentleman within that nation. The currents of Spirit and Emotion that dwell within the body are the Folk. The values of humane, civilized behavior—righteousness, courtesy, knowledge, and Sincerity—are the Multitude. These—the Folk and the Multitude—are the Root of Life; they must be cherished. These inner resources must be mobilized. The outer Danger must be guarded against. Inner Mastery and Outer Mastery combine in the Tao of the "Army" Hexagram. This is the Tao of the True Gentleman.

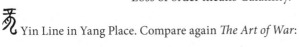

LINES

Yin in First Place

The Army sets out

In orderly fashion.

Without order,

There is Calamity,

Pessimum.

On the Image

Loss of order means Calamity.

 Yin Line in Yang Place. Compare again *The Art of War*:

Chapter 1
Discipline is organization,
Chain of command,
Control of expenditure.

Effective order and discipline depend on the qualities of the General. Julius Caesar's discipline "was truly based on mutual understanding and self-respect, so that his army grew to love him as a man and a soldier, and to believe in him as a Leader." As in War, so in life, comments Zen Master Zhixu. If one cannot lead an orderly life, one's actions, speech, and thoughts will lead to Calamity. In business, comments Professor Mun, know how to define goals and set boundaries, know how to examine resources, at the outset of any undertaking. In the Work, writes Magister Liu, it is essential to follow the right order, the rules of the process. Without that order, impetuous Action will only lead to Calamity.

Yang in Second Place

This is Centered

Within the Army.

All is Auspicious,

Bonum.

No Harm,

Nullum malum.

Three times

The King gives orders.

On the Image

The Favor of Heaven
Is received.
Orders are given.
The King
Cherishes the Myriad States.

Yang Line in Yin Place. Centered. This is the General who "receives the Favour of Heaven," writes Legge. The King (Yin in Fifth Place) rules "by the grace of Heaven," and he delegates power wisely to his trusted General in order to promote the good of all. Chen Guying compares this Line Statement with the famous words from the *Book of Master Zhuang*, chapter 20, "Mountain Tree":

> Now a dragon, now a snake,
> He evolves with Time. . . .
> He goes up, he goes down,
> Making Harmony his rule.
> He floats,
> He wanders
> With the Ancestor of the Myriad Things.

In other words, the King feels free to change his mind, and his orders ("three times"). He "evolves with Time." He is flexible, he makes decisions in Accordance with the changing situation. There is an Auspicious Resonance of mutual trust between this Yang in Second and Yin in Fifth. Yang in Second, writes Professor Mun, is the Action Leader, balanced in the Center, respected. Yin in Fifth is the chief executive, with a soft management style. The Inner Heart-and-Mind, writes Magister Liu, is sincere and has a single purpose. Orders are given and gladly obeyed. With Inner and Outer in mutual support, negative Yin Energy is in Retreat and can cause no Harm.

Yin in Third Place

The Army

Carries corpses.

Calamity,

Infortunium.

On the Image

Great failure.

Yin Line in a Yang Place. This is a great military defeat, caused by an incompetent General. Corpses are being "carried" off the field. Foolish Action, writes Magister Liu, without due consideration of the proper order of the Work of Self-Cultivation, leads not to Long Life but to Calamity. A weak Leader in a strong position (Yin in Yang), writes Professor Mun, makes a rash Advance and causes Calamity.

Yin in Fourth Place

The Army

Retreats.

No Harm,

Nullum malum.

On the Image

No Harm.
No straying
From the True Course.

 Yin Line in Yin Place. A strategic Retreat from this Yin Place of weakness, writes Cheng Yi, is better by far than a foolish Advance, which will only sacrifice troops. This is most humane counsel on the part of the *I Ching*! A cautious Leader, writes Professor Mun, judges it wise to Retreat.

Yin in Fifth Place

There is game

In the fields.

It Profits

To take it.

No Harm,

Nullum malum.

The Elder Son

Commands the Army;

The Younger Son

Carts corpses.

Calamity,

Malum.

On the Image

The Elder Son
Commands,
Acting at Center.
The Younger Son
Carts corpses.
This is an inappropriate delegation.

Yin Line in Yang Place. Centered. In the fields, game birds are doing damage to the crops and must be dealt with. Just so, an invading enemy must be fought. The right people should be put in charge. The entire success of a campaign hinges on such decisions. This Yin Line occupying the key Fifth Place suggests problems of weak leadership. The Elder Son is Yang in Second Place. The Younger Son "carting corpses" is a powerful if somewhat puzzling image of defeat and rout, caused perhaps by the Actions of an inexperienced Leader. An effective Organization, writes Professor Mun, can have only one Leader who has the power to make the final decision. If there is more than one "boss," this will affect the chain of command and lead to disorder and inefficiency.

Yin in Top Place

The Great Ruler

Gives orders,

He founds a nation,

He establishes clans.

There is no room here

For the Small Man.

On the Image

The Great Ruler
Rewards achievement.
The Small Man
Merely brings
Chaos to the land.

Yin Line in Yin Place. In the aftermath of victory, during the period of reconstruction, the King rewards his loyal officers. But he must remain wary of small-minded hangers-on. The Leader of an Organization, writes Professor Mun, rewards those who deserve promotion. He should not use people who lack integrity ("Small Men") even if they have made contributions.

HEXAGRAM VIII

Bi

Closeness

Kan/Abyss

above

Kun/Earth

JUDGMENT

Auspicious.

First Divination

Urges Supreme,

Enduring Steadfastness,

Magna continuitas.

No Harm,

Nullum malum.

Latecomers arrive

From lands not at peace.

Calamity,

Hoc pessimum.

On the Judgment

Closeness,
Mutual Support.
Those below comply;
They obey.
First Divination
Urges Supreme Steadfastness.
The Firm is Centered.
Lands are not at peace.
Upper and Lower
Resonate.
Calamity.
The Tao is exhausted.

On the Image

Water above Earth,
Aqua super terram.
The Former Kings
Established the Myriad States;
They drew Feudal Lords
Close to them.

Water above Earth. The Chinese graph for the Name shows two men (or women), one behind the other. In this Hexagram, writes Kong Yingda, in which the Upper Trigram, *Kan*, Water, the Abyss, is above the Lower Trigram, *Kun*, Earth, Water flows all over the Earth, bringing moisture to all things. Water upon the face of the Earth, writes Chen Guying, is an emblem of Closeness, of Mutual Support, of the relationships among different individuals, the association or familiarity among the different groups that bind society together. The Lower Four Yin Lines Resonate as a "block" with Yang in Fifth. The Yang Line in Fifth Place, writes Legge, is the Ruler, the "Firm Centred," to whom the other five Yin Lines readily submit. Harmonious Closeness is secured by the sovereign authority and Good Faith of one man. His subjects are warned not to be latecomers, not to delay in submitting to him. Spiritually, writes Magister Liu, Yang Energy (in Fifth Place) is in the center of Water. The Tao of Yang, the Creative Energy of the True One, brings about the fusion of Yin and Yang. This can be reached only through a calm state of mind, through Steadfastness. This is how the individual establishes his Inner Realm. With the Yin Line at the Top, the Tao is exhausted. The moment for Closeness has passed. A group of friends gets together to face Danger, writes Professor Mun. The Leader (Yang in Fifth Place) inspires Closeness and obedience. The Organization is in a good position to move forward. Certain elements hesitate. They join late and regret their hesitation.

LINES

Yin in First Place

Good Faith.

Closeness.

No Harm,

Nullum malum.

Good Faith

Fills

The earthen bowl.

Conclusion.

This is Auspicious

For others,

Bonum.

On the Image

It Profits
Others.

 Yin Line in Yang Place. The "earthen bowl," writes Legge, indicates the plain, unadorned character, the Humility and altruism, of Good Faith. A Leader, writes Professor Mun, should be sincere and truthful (he should show Good Faith) with the members of his Organization, like a plain "earthen bowl," filled within and unadorned without.

Yin in Second Place

Closeness

Proceeds from within,

Ex intimo.

This is Auspicious

For the Steadfast.

On the Image

The Self is not lost.

 Yin Line in Yin Place. Centered and True. Closeness, writes Legge, proceeds from the Inward Mind. A Yielding receptivity, writes Magister Liu, going with the Flow, at the very Center—this is Closeness from within. This is Self-Cultivation, Mastery of the Heart-and-Mind, gathering the herbs (Spiritual Medicine) at the right time, receiving from Others, not losing Self. Association with Others, writes Professor Mun, must proceed from Inner Truth, from Sincerity, honesty, dignity, and self-respect.

Yin in Third Place

This is

Closeness

With those

Not one's kind.

On the Image

It will cause
No Harm.

 Yin Line in Yang Place. Closeness with Others who are not of the same way of thinking may cause no obvious Harm, but it is mistaken. It lacks Good Faith. This is merely piling Yin on Yin, writes Magister Liu. Of what value is Closeness of this sort? It is a mistake, writes Professor Mun, to associate closely with a wrong person.

Yin in Fourth Place

Outward

Closeness.

This is Auspicious

For the Steadfast,

Bonum.

On the Image

Outward Closeness
With a Worthy Man,
Following one above.

 Yin Line in Yin Place. This is Outward Closeness with the King, writes Legge, with Yang in Fifth Place, the "one above." Minister and subjects should be Steadfastly Close to their King. With this Closeness, writes Magister Liu, even the foolish can become wise, even the weak can become strong. It is sensible, writes Professor Mun, for Yin in Fourth Place to associate with the Leader, Yang in Fifth Place, who is capable, sincere, and upright.

Yang in Fifth Place

Manifest

Closeness.

The King

Hunts on three sides,

Releasing game ahead.

His men need no prior warning.

This is Auspicious,

Hoc bonum.

On the Image

Auspicious.
In True and Centered Place.
The rebel,
The game,
Is spared.
The receptive
Is embraced.
The one above
Is Centered.

Yang Line in Yang Place. Centered and True. The Ancient Kings, writes Legge, following Zhu Xi, went on great hunting expeditions in the different seasons of the year. But what is described here was common to all. When the beating (the *battue*) was completed, and the shooting ready to commence, one side of the enclosure into which the game had been driven was left open and unguarded—a proof of the Royal Benevolence, which did not seek to slaughter all the game indiscriminately. This Benevolence of the Model King caused his people to follow him of their own accord, with a Manifest, Open Closeness, characterized by Mutual Trust, by Good Faith. The King lets the False go, writes Magister Liu. He spares the rebellious elements. He takes in the Real. His mind is calm and unperturbed. He has entered the Taoist Realm beyond distinctions of Real and False, of rebellion and obedience.

Yin in Top Place

This is

Closeness

That has no head,

Non habet caput.

Calamity.

On the Image

No ultimate
Resolution.

Yin Line in Yin Place. It is too late now, writes Legge. The time for Closeness has passed. There is no proper first step, no first principle, no "head." The Good Faith from which Closeness should properly begin is absent. There is no Tao. The Tao is exhausted. A Closeness without leadership, without basic principle, without the Tao, writes Magister Liu, is a waste of life. To rely on nothing but one's own Yin Energy is a recipe for Disaster. Self-Cultivation requires a Closeness between those who do not yet have the Tao, on the one hand, and those who already have the Tao, on the other; between those who do not have Inner Strength and those who do. It requires gradual practice, step by step, proceeding from a True Heart-and-Mind. Once the Tao and the Inner Strength are where they truly belong, Centered and True, then the Golden Elixir is ready. It can be ingested. Then all negative Yin Energies are transformed. It is as simple as a cat catching a mouse.

HEXAGRAM IX

Xiao Xu

Slight Restraint

Xun/Wind

above

Qian/Heaven

JUDGMENT

Fortune.

Dense clouds,

No rain,

From meadows

To the West.

On the Judgment

A Yielding Line
In Apt Place,
Lines above and below
Resonate.
Restraint,
Strength,
Flexibility.
Firm Lines are Centered,
Aspirations fulfilled.
Fortune.
Clouds but no rain:
Movement
From the West,
No result.

On the Image of the Hexagram

Wind above Heaven,
Ventus supra coelum.
The True Gentleman
Cultivates Inner Refinement,
Spiritual Strength.

秀 Wind above Heaven. "Dense clouds, no rain, from meadows to the West" is also found in Hexagram LXII, Yin in Fifth Place. Yin Energy forms clouds, writes Magister Liu. Yang Energy should bring rain. When there are "clouds but no rain," it means that Yin Energy prevails, and Yang Energy is too weak. Primal Energy must be restored in small steps. The Restraint is slight, writes Legge, paraphrasing Cheng Yi and Zhu Xi, coming as it does from the single Yin Line in Fourth Place (the previous Hexagram had a single Yang Line, in Fifth Place, the General). The Restraint given by that one Yin Line to all the strong Yang Lines can be only Slight. The gentle docility of *Xun*, the Upper Trigram, Wind, cannot long prevail against the sheer Strength of *Qian*, the Lower Trigram, Heaven. Rain falling and moistening the ground should bring beauty and luxuriance to the vegetable world, representing the blessings that flow from good government. The West was the hereditary territory of the house of Zhou, whose blessings should now enrich the whole kingdom, but are somehow "Restrained." The "dense clouds" do not empty their stores. But there will be rain ere long, comment Cheng Yi and Wang Feng. Historically, the Zhou were for a time Restrained, held at bay, by the Shang rulers. But when Zhou finally prevailed, the rain of beneficent government descended on all the kingdom. *Xun*, the organically shaping, gentle Wind, comments Richard Wilhelm, the softest, gentlest force imaginable, passes over *Qian*, the Creative. The rising breath of the Creative is Restrained by means of something "Slight." This is no time for concluding matters, nor is it a time for perfecting. This is a time to attend to lesser things—housekeeping—things on a lesser scale. It is a preparatory time, a time to work at details, not aim for greatness. The time is not ripe for Action, writes Professor Mun, and the Leader must be patient. It would be unwise to make a show of his abilities and strength. Restraint is necessary and beneficial.

LINES

Yang in First Place

A Return,

Following the Tao.

There can be no Harm.

Quodnam est malum?

This is Auspicious,

Hoc bonum.

On the Image

Righteousness
Is Auspicious.

Yang Line in Yang Place. This is a time for judicious and principled Restraint, in tune with the Tao. Veil the Light, writes Magister Liu. Cultivate Self in the Darkness. Embrace the Tao in tranquillity. Returning by small steps along the path of Tao, one can nurture Self. Yang Energy increases daily. For an executive in this difficult position, writes Professor Mun, it is more sensible to stay where he is, to exercise Restraint.

Yang in Second Place

A Return.

He is

Drawn along.

This is Auspicious,

Hoc bonum.

On the Image

Drawn to the Center,
No loss of Self.

Yang in Yin Place. Centered. This is Restraint, secure in Inner Strength. Seek out the True Gentleman, writes Magister Liu. Return to origins. Outwardly things may seem emptier than ever. But within there is more and more substance. The executive, writes Professor Mun, should cooperate with the two Yang Lines, the two capable persons, on either side of him. He should let them "draw him along."

Yang in Third Place

Spokes

Come away from the wheel.

Husband and wife

Eye each other askance.

On the Image

The Family
Is not well regulated.

Yang Line in Yang Place. Progress is impeded by a "mechanical" failure. Harmony is threatened by friction within the Family. A selfish, domineering attitude, writes Magister Liu, erodes Harmony, loses Center. This is a failure of Strength. If a Leader is obstinate or overconfident, writes Professor Mun, he may enter into Conflict with his colleagues, and this will lead to disharmony in the Organization.

Yin in Fourth Place

Good Faith.

Blood departs,

Fear is gone.

No Harm,

Nullum malum.

On the Image

The Line above
Shares
Aspiration.

 Yin Line in Yin Place. Good Faith and Sincerity are needed, writes Richard Wilhelm, in order to be rid of what was previously causing bloodshed (or bad blood), in order to make fear depart. This one Yin Line seeks to Restrain and hold together the entire Hexagram, just as Wind blowing over Heaven seeks to induce the precipitation of rain. The strong Yang Line above, in the Place of the Ruler, provides crucial support. By borrowing Yang Energy from the Line above, writes Magister Liu, one can cultivate Inner Strength and thus escape Harm. This senior executive, writes Professor Mun, needs the trust of the top Leader (Yang in Fifth).

Yang in Fifth Place

Good Faith.

A bond

Of companionship.

Wealth is shared

With neighbors.

On the Image

One is not alone
With wealth.

Yang Line in Yang Place. Centered and True. There is a shared communal blessing, a "bond" of solidarity. Compare this with Hexagram XI, Yin in Fourth Place, where there is no such bond, no such sharing, no wealth shared with neighbors. Here things are far more Auspicious. Good Faith is in the Center, writes Magister Liu. Yin and Yang fuse. The Golden Elixir is formed. There is mutual trust, writes Professor Mun, between Yin in Fourth Place and Yang in Fifth.

Yang in Top Place

Rain falls,

Rain ceases.

Inner Strength

Is esteemed.

It endures.

There is Danger

For a Steadfast woman.

The Moon

Is almost full.

The True Gentleman

Advances.

Calamity,

Hoc malum.

On the Image

Strength
Is fully accumulated.
There is
Misgiving.

Slight Restraint has run its course, writes Legge, paraphrasing Zhu Xi. The Harmony of Nature, of Yin and Yang, is now restored. Restraint is at its height, comments Zen Master Zhixu, and the Restrained must be still for a time. Impediments melt away, they are shed. The rains fall, and the onward movement of the Yang Lines ceases. Caution is urged. Spiritual Self-Cultivation has achieved results. But to pride oneself on having almost reached true sagehood (the moon "almost full") is to court Calamity. Beware! In this unstable situation, writes Professor Mun, any further expansion is definitely ill-advised.

HEXAGRAM X

Lü

Stepping

Qian/Heaven

above

Dui/Lake

JUDGMENT

Stepping

On the Tiger's Tail.

Not bitten.

Fortune.

On the Judgment

The Yielding
Steps on the Firm.
Joy,

Gaudium.
Lake
Resonates with Heaven,
Qian,
Creative Energy.
Stepping on the Tiger's Tail,
Not bitten.
The Fifth Line is Firm,
Centered and True.
It Steps
Into the Place
Of Supreme Sovereign.
There is
No failure,
Nullum malum.
There is
Bright Light.

On the Image of the Hexagram

Heaven above Lake,
Coelum supra lacum.
The True Gentleman
Distinguishes high from low,
Steadies the Aspirations
Of the Folk.

From the Great Treatise

Stepping.
Foundation of Inner Strength,
Perfection of Harmony,
Of a life
Lived in Harmony.

秀 Heaven over Lake. In this Hexagram, Cautious Action is advised. Step forward, but with care. Below *Qian*, Heaven, great Trigram of Strength, writes Legge, is the more gentle Trigram *Dui*, Lake, Image of Joy, with its Yielding Third Line. To "step on the Tiger's Tail" is to engage in something hazardous. See the *Book of History*, chapter 25: "The trembling anxiety of my mind makes me feel as if I were stepping on a Tiger's Tail, or walking upon spring ice." Compare also *Song 195*:

> Never fight a Tiger
> Bare-handed.
> Never cross a river
> Without a boat.
> One thing is known,
> One thing only:
> Caution.
> Take good care.
> Imagine yourself
> On the brink
> Of a deep Abyss,
> Imagine yourself
> Treading on thin ice.

But why does the Tiger not bite? One must first let go of all harmful desire, and then, with the Strength of the Tao, even a hungry Tiger can be taken by the Tail. To emerge unscathed from Danger suggested to some historically minded Confucian commentators King Wen's scrupulous observance of all the rules of Ritual. On these rules, as on so many "stepping-stones," one may safely tread amid scenes of disorder and Danger. In the Taoist view, writes Chen Guying, quoting from the *Book of Master Wen*, one who embodies the Tao is free to "step," is never exhausted. Step forward in Harmony and Joy, with Caution, writes Magister Liu. Then the Tiger "will not bite." Indeed, something of the beast's living and savage Energy can be absorbed. Life and Being in its wholeness can be preserved. Yang of Heaven (in the Upper Trigram) Steps above Yin of Lake (in the Lower Trigram). True Feelings prevail; Random Feelings no longer arise. True Feeling is Feeling-without-Emotion. Controlling Emotion with Feeling-without-Emotion is like a cat catching a mouse; it is like pouring boiling water on snow. In the twinkling of an eye, Disaster is transformed into Blessing. The "Aspirations of the Folk" are steadied. Nothing can defeat the Tao. All tends toward Strength and Center, toward Total Purity. The Tao of Transformation is at work here. The True Path can be trodden. In the Buddhist view, writes Zen Master Zhixu, the Inner Demon (the Tiger) can be taken hold of; it can be dealt with compassionately. Then it "does not bite." Or, as Hellmut Wilhelm paraphrases it, a monstrous, demoniacal, overpowering element is perceived within—a threatening Danger that deprives one of Power—the numinous Tiger Within. To look into the Heart-and-Mind and see the True Face of Buddha is to step on the Tiger's Tail. To be free of pride is to find Fortune "without being bitten." Working under a powerful Leader, writes Professor Mun, is like following a Tiger. As long as the subordinate works properly and does not provoke the superior, he will be safe.

LINES

Yang in First Place

Step

Simply.

Advance.

No Harm,

Nullum malum.

On the Image

Advance alone,
Following one's own Aspirations.

Yang Line in Yang Place. This Line, writes Legge, gives the idea of Action, of firmness and correctness. With a strong Heart-and-Mind and robust Spiritual Energy, writes Magister Liu, "stepping truly and simply" in tune with the Tao, one will surely succeed. One will progress on the path of Self-Cultivation and surely arrive at that place where there is "no Harm." The Organization, writes Professor Mun, is still in the early stage of development (First Place). If the Leader acts according to the true capacity and resources of the Organization, he will make no mistakes.

Yang in Second Place

Step

On a level road.

For the Recluse,

Steadfastness

Is Auspicious.

On the Image

Centered,
Not confused.

Yang Line in Yin Place. Centered. This is a road cut straight along the hillside, writes Legge, a "level road" over difficult ground. Find True Joy, writes Magister Liu. Step forward effortlessly on a "level road," free from all external desire and craving. The Spirit is at peace. Only the Steadfast Recluse can tread this path with Joy, oblivious of Time. JM: The poet Xie Lingyun uses this Line as shorthand for the Recluse (see also Hexagram XVIII, Yang in Top Place):

On Climbing Green Crag
Steadfastness
Is Auspicious.
The Recluse
Steps on a level road,
Lofty minded,
Aloof,
Beyond the scope
Of ordinary mortals.

Yin in Third Place

The blind

See;

The lame

Step

On the Tiger's Tail,

Bitten.

Calamity,

Hoc pessimum.

The Warrior

Acts the Great Ruler.

On the Image

Seeing,
Not clearly.
Treading,

Out of Step.
Calamity arises.
This is not in Proper Place.
He acts the Ruler
Out of ambition.

 Yin Line in Yang Place. This Line, writes Legge, is inappropriately positioned. The excessive strength of will characteristic of a Strong Place brings an impetuous Advance—and the result is Calamity. Confucius did not desire the support of a Warrior who might "attack a Tiger unarmed or cross rivers without a boat," preferring one who would "act with great solicitude, who would think ahead carefully before putting plans into action." Recklessly stepping forward, ignorant of the true details of Self-Cultivation, one mistakes blindness for sight, disability for ability, writes Magister Liu. Stepping boldly on the Tiger's Tail, one is bitten, like a man with one blind eye, like a lame man, foolishly courting Calamity. To parade Warrior-like ability invites Disaster. This is all obstinate Folly. An impulsive Action, writes Professor Mun, leads to Calamity. The Leader of a growing company must not be overconfident in taking Action that would have an influence on the market leader, who might strike back.

Yang in Fourth Place

Stepping

On the Tiger's Tail.

Caution.

An Auspicious Conclusion,

In fine bonum.

On the Image

With Caution,
Aspirations are realized.

 Yang Line in Yang Place. Be firm but not rash, writes Magister Liu. Be honest and clear-sighted, yielding in Action. Prepare for every Danger. If it is necessary to "Step on the Tiger's Tail," do it gingerly, with Caution. Then the Tiger will not bite. Indeed, one can Step onto the Ground of Pure Yang. This is Auspicious. This is to Step firmly but softly. He is in Danger, writes Professor Mun, because he is so close to the Leader (Yang in Fifth). He is vulnerable. He must follow the values and style of the Leader. If a conflict should arise with the "boss," the relationship will be damaged.

Yang in Fifth Place

Step

With resolve.

Steadfast.

There is

Danger,

Periculosum.

On the Image

A True and Proper Place.

 Yang Line in Yang Place. Centered and True. Be strong and in True Center, comments Magister Liu. Follow the heart's wishes, without transgressing the bounds of what is right. Step on the Path of the Tao with resolve. But even when the Golden Elixir is formed, cleave Steadfastly to the One, guard against Danger. Step alone. Thus Calamity is avoided. What has been gained will not be lost. Guard against overconfidence, writes Professor Mun. If a Leader always makes decisions by himself, he walks a dangerous path. He needs to restore his own Inner Balance.

Yang in Top Place

Observe

The Steps.

Examine

The Omens.

Complete

The Cycle.

This is

Supremely Auspicious,

Magna felicitas.

On the Image

This is
Cause for great celebration,
Multum laetari.

 Yang Line in Yin Place. This Line, writes Chen Guying, stresses the constant need for Self-Reflection and Self-Examination. Firmness abides in this Yielding Place (Yang in Yin), writes Magister Liu. "Observe the Steps," proceed in due order, complete the Process, the Work, the full Cycle from Commencement to Conclusion, bringing Commencement to Conclusion. Await the Perfect Unsullied Union of Yin and Yang. To Step on this Way, this Tao of Yang, there must be softness within firmness, there must be firmness within softness. Firmness and softness complement each other. There is neither urgency nor delay. All is Harmony, Joy, and Ease. This is the end of the operation, writes Professor Mun. Review successes and failures. This will provide the Organization with useful insights for future development.

HEXAGRAM XI

Tai

Grandeur

Kun/Earth

above

Qian/Heaven

JUDGMENT

The Small

Depart,

The Great

Arrive.

This is Auspicious.

Fortune.

On the Judgment

With Communion
Of Heaven and Earth,
The Myriad Things
Connect.
There is
Intercourse
Of high and low.
Aspirations
Converge.
Yang within,
Yin without.
Strength within,
Flow without.
The True Gentleman within,
The Small Man without.
The Tao of the True Gentleman
Prevails;
The Tao of the Small Man
Wanes.

On the Image of the Hexagram

Heaven and Earth
Enjoy Communion.
The Ruler accomplishes
The Tao of Heaven and Earth;
He assists Heaven and Earth,
He succors the Folk.

龙 Earth over Heaven. In this Auspicious Hexagram of Connection, writes Zhu Xi, Heaven and Earth enjoy Communion; their Energies connect. JM: The poet Xie Lingyun uses this Hexagram as shorthand for a time of glory, of great prosperity and ease:

In Imitation of Wang Can
. . . The mists have cleared,
Our Master's glory is made manifest;
The clouds have rolled away,
We gaze upon his pure Light. . . .
Grandeur

In its felicity
Is heaped upon us.

The Energy of Heaven rises, writes Magister Liu, the Energy of Earth descends. Yin and Yang Energies fuse. The Myriad Things are born. There is Harmony between Yin (the Small) and Yang (the Great). All Lines Resonate (Yang in First with Yin in Fourth, etc.). Only with this Harmonious Union can matters be properly accomplished. This is the Tao of Grandeur. The Small depart: the Yin without (in the Upper Trigram) submits. The Great arrive: the Yang (in the Lower Trigram) is strong within. The Ruler who understands this is able to rule according to the Tao of Heaven and Earth. The Leader of an Organization, writes Professor Mun, combines the softness of Earth with the strength of Heaven; he achieves Balance and Harmony between his Organization and the public at large. JM: Compare *The Tao and the Power*:

> Chapter 42
> The Myriad Things
> Carry Yin
> On their shoulders;
> They hold Yang
> In their arms.

The Ruler succors the Folk, writes Legge, paraphrasing Cheng Yi, enabling them to Profit from the changing seasons of Heaven and the advantages afforded by Earth. The Energy of Spring calls forth life from the Myriad Things, for the season of sowing and planting; the Energy of Autumn completes all things, makes them solid, to harvest and store. Joseph Needham comments that when Giordano Bruno speaks of sexual intercourse between the Sun and the Earth, whereby all living creatures are brought into being, he is using a characteristic Chinese metaphor. Mystical Enlightenment (Heaven), comments Zen Master Zhixu, and Practical Action (Earth) join together. They are not to be separated. The Inner Demons (the "Small Men") are calmed. They cannot cause Harm; they depart. The perfect power of patience sees the arrival of Grandeur, the Tao of the Great Man.

LINES

Yang in First Place

Reeds are pulled up

By the roots,

In clumps.

It is Auspicious

To set forth,

Si eat, optimum.

On the Image

The Heart-and-Mind
Is on outward things,
Ad extra.

 Yang Line in Yang Place. The True Gentleman's Heart-and-Mind, writes Yang Wanli, is set on the world around him, not on himself. First Yang grows from beneath the soil, comments Magister Liu, and the other Yang Lines are stirred into life. This is like pulling up a reed and bringing the roots with it. The Taoist begins the Work of Self-Cultivation with the appearance of this First Yang, gradually harvesting and refining Energy. As the roots cling together, writes Professor Mun, so the members of an Organization share the same values and follow their Leader out of a sense of solidarity.

Yang in Second Place

Embrace

The wilderness,

Ford

The River.

Do not forsake

Those far away.

Friends depart.

The course is held

At the Center,

In medio.

On the Image

Great Light,
Claritas magna.

Yang Line in Yin Place. Centered. This Great Light is the Light of the Tao, writes Cheng Yi. This Second Line, writes Zhu Xi, balances tolerance ("embracing the wilderness") with courage ("fording the River"). It balances concern for others ("those far away") with impartiality toward factional friends (they "depart"). Balance and objectivity enable a man to hold his course at the Center. The True Gentleman, writes Wang Fuzhi, is not bogged down in cliques of the like-minded ("friends depart"). He goes out to encounter Others. The balance of strength within gentleness, writes Magister Liu, of Yang within Yin, and Yin within Yang, the combination of civilized (soft) and strict (hard) Cultivation—all of this enables one to hold course "at the Center." The Leader is broad-minded, writes Professor Mun. He attracts capable people. He is decisive and courageous in initiating changes. He is balanced in employing people of different abilities.

Yang in Third Place

For every plain

There is

A slope,

For every going

A return.

Be Steadfast

In face of hardship.

Harm

Is averted.

Do not grieve.

Keep Good Faith,

Enjoy the Blessings

Of food and Fortune.

On the Image

This Line is
On the Horizon,

At the Juncture
Of Heaven and Earth.

Yang Line in Yang Place. Everything on Earth is subject to Change, writes Richard Wilhelm, following Cheng Yi. Grandeur is followed by Stagnation. This is the Eternal Terrestrial Law. Evil can be held in check for a while, but it cannot be permanently abolished. It will always return. Sober knowledge of this should keep us from succumbing to illusion when Good Fortune comes our way. Be mindful of Danger, remain Steadfast, and there will be no Harm. As long as Inner Nature and Good Faith remain strong, then there will be Fortune. Nothing lasts forever, writes Professor Mun. Expansion has its limits, as does contraction. Everything has an opposite and moves in a cyclical pattern. Even in a time of Grandeur, a Leader should think of the Danger that may lie ahead. JM: A famous medieval alchemical text echoes this Line:

Unity of the Three, Section 52
For every plain
A slope:
This is the Suchness
Of the Tao,
Of the Tao-as-it-is [*ziran*].
Transformation and Change
Alternate and prosper.
Ebb and flow
Depend on one another.

Yin in Fourth Place

They flutter down.

Wealth

Is not shared

With neighbors.

No need

Of admonition.

Good Faith.

On the Image

Substance is lost.
The Inner Heart-and-Mind
Wills this.

Yin Line in Yin Place. The Yin Lines of the Upper Trigram, *Kun*, Earth, begin here. They all come "fluttering" down, drawn toward the three Yang Lines of the Lower Trigram, *Qian*, Heaven. This Yin Line Resonates with Yang in First Place. There is no need of a financial incentive ("wealth not shared"). Nor is there any need of persuasion ("admonition"). They are drawn by Good Faith. A modern commentator, Yin Meiman, quotes the proverbial saying "When one man achieves the Tao, even fowl and dogs desire to rise with him to Heaven." Weaker brethren (the two neighboring Yin Lines above) flock to the powerful. When this first Yin Line stirs, writes Magister Liu, the other two are set in motion with it. Although the Golden Elixir (the "substance") that was gained has been "lost," this loss can be regained through Good Faith.

Yin in Fifth Place

King Yi

Gave his daughter

In marriage.

Happiness,

Felicitas.

This is

Supremely Auspicious,

Summum bonum.

On the Image

It is Centered.
Inner Aspirations
Are fulfilled.

Yin Line in Yang Place. Centered. King Yi, writes Legge, was the last sovereign but one of the Shang dynasty; according to tradition he married his daughter (or his younger sister) to King Wen of Zhou. See Hexagram LIV/5. This is a marriage, writes Magister Liu, in which Yin loves Yang, and Yang loves Yin. Yin and Yang share one Energy. The True Fire of Nature glows hot in the Alchemical Furnace. Grandeur finds Completion. Gentleness nurtures Inner Strength. In business, writes Professor Mun, this "marriage" resembles a strategic alliance between two companies.

Yin in Top Place

The city wall

Crumbles

Into the moat.

The Army

Is not deployed.

In the hometown,

Orders are issued.

Steadfast.

Distress,

Locus poenitendi.

On the Image

Orders
Are confused.

Yin Line in Yin Place. Grandeur has run its course, writes Legge, following Zhu Xi. It will be followed by Stagnation, a Hexagram of a different and less happy character. The earth dug from the moat, piled up to form a protecting wall, has fallen back into the moat. War only aggravates the evil. The Ruler may issue orders, but Distress cannot be averted altogether. In this Line, writes Magister Liu, weakness prevents one from preserving Grandeur. It is too late for Regret. There is no point in resisting Natural Change, writes Professor Mun. The Leader must accept the end of Grandeur. He can do nothing to stop it. He must make preparations for the bad times to come.

HEXAGRAM XII

Pi

Obstruction

Qian/Heaven

above

Kun/Earth

JUDGMENT

Evil men.

It does not Profit

The True Gentleman

To be Steadfast.

The Great

Depart,

The Small

Arrive.

On the Judgment

There is no Communion
Between Heaven and Earth,
No Connection
Between the Myriad Things.
No Communion
Between high and low.
In All-under-Heaven,
There is no Harmony
Among nations.
Yin within,
Yang without;
Yielding within,
Firm without.
The Small Man within,
The True Gentleman without.
The Tao of the Small Man
Prevails;
The Tao of the True Gentleman
Wanes.

On the Image of the Hexagram

No Communion
Between Heaven and Earth.
The True Gentleman
Guards Spiritual Strength with thrift.
He escapes difficulty,
Seeks neither glory nor reward.

否 Heaven over Earth, the very opposite of *Tai*, Grandeur, the preceding Hexagram. Here, three Yin Lines sit below three Yang Lines. The Upper Trigram, Heaven, isolated in its height, draws upward and away from the Lower Trigram, Earth, which closes in upon itself down below. This leads to a lack of dynamic interaction or Communion, and hence to Obstruction and Stagnation. Negativity prevails. Joseph Needham compares the situation with Shakespeare's "way to dusty death." The Chinese Name, in common usage (modern pronunciation *fou*), signifies, quite simply, Negation. Negative Yin Energy is dominant, comments Magister Liu, Positive Yang Energy is in Retreat. Primal Essence has been lost, and True Yang scattered. All that is left is False Energy. Emotions and desires run riot. This is the Path of Evil. Just as Evil Men cannot profit the True Gentleman, so Bad or Perverse Energy cannot profit True Energy. The Taoist abhors cleverness. He veils his Light and nurtures it in the dark. He conceals his every talent. He does not allow external elements to pollute his Inner Truth. This pollution would be his greatest Obstruction, the hardest Obstacle of all to his Self-Cultivation. He must know how to escape from the pitfall of ambition, from the snare of material desires. *Pi* is a Closing, writes Legge, following Zhu Xi. It is the reverse of *Tai*, the Grand, the Expansive. It is the end of Connection. It is the Hexagram of autumn. The genial influences of Nature have done their work; the processes of growth are at an end. Henceforth increasing Decay must be looked for. Despite the lingering heat, comments Jullien, a chill is already secretly spreading within the natural world. The right way for development is Obstructed, writes Professor Mun. It will not Profit the True Gentleman to be Steadfast in his principles of honesty and integrity. The inferior (Small) man will not let him preserve justice and truth. He should adapt to the conditions of the time, while maintaining his Inner Truth.

LINES

Yin in First Place

Reeds are pulled up

By the roots,

In clumps.

This is Steadfast.

It is

Auspicious,

Hoc bonum.

Fortune.

On the Image

Aspirations
Are set on the Ruler.

Yin Line in Yang Place. First Yin grows from beneath the soil, writes Magister Liu. This is the Root of Obstruction. Once this has stirred, the other two Yin Lines will come up together with it. The Taoist must begin his practice from this first appearance of Yin Energy, before Yang Energy has been harmed. Through Steadfast Self-Cultivation it is still possible to turn from Obstruction and Stagnation to Grandeur and Peace. At the beginning, writes Professor Mun, when confronted with

Obstruction, the Leader should strengthen the teamwork in his Organization. He should improve the spirit of cooperation (as among "reeds in a clump").

Yin in Second Place

Forbearance,

Acceptance.

This is Auspicious

For the Small Man.

For the Great Man,

Obstruction leads to

Fortune.

On the Image

There is no turbulence
Among the Multitude.

Yin Line in Yin Place. Centered and True. In a time of Obstruction, writes Legge, patience and forbearance are proper for the Small Man. The Great Man can have a happy issue out of his distress. Conserve Inner Strength, writes Magister Liu. Avoid difficulty, do not be deluded by Yin Energy. Then, even in the midst of Obstruction, the power of Yin can be guarded against, and Fortune can be achieved.

Yin in Third Place

Shame,

Acceptance.

On the Image

This is not in Proper Place.

Yin Line in Yang Place. Yin Energy is concentrated, writes Magister Liu. Pursuing desire, regarding the False as True, one accepts shame without knowing it to be shame. One follows Yin, not knowing that one is in the very midst of Obstruction. An inferior (Small) man is not ashamed of his incorrect practices, writes Professor Mun. He knows no shame.

Yang in Fourth Place

An order.

No Harm,

Nullum malum.

Companions

Share blessing.

On the Image

Aspirations
Are realized.

Yang Line in Yin Place. The Innate Heart-and-Mind is present and complete in all beings, writes Magister Liu, in the Sage and in every ordinary mortal. It is constrained and veiled by desire. It mistakes pain for pleasure. It does not look back and reflect. Once it does reflect, then Innate Goodness appears, then one good dissolves a hundred ills. In that instant one steps onto the shore of the Tao. JM: Is this "order" the Order or Edict of Heaven, as Zhu Xi thinks? Or the Order of the Innate Heart-and-Mind? Or the orders of the Ruler, as Cheng Yi would have it? Or all three? With this Fourth Line, writes Jullien, following Wang Fuzhi, we see the return of the fruitful, orderly interplay between Yin and Yang. In terms of cyclical change, writes Professor Mun, things now begin to move in a more favorable direction. The "order" is the Order of Heaven.

Yang in Fifth Place

Obstruction

Is ended.

This is Auspicious

For the Great Man.

But what if he should perish?

Then bind him

To the leafy Mulberry Tree.

On the Image

This is the True and Proper Place.

The Great Treatise
From Part II, Section 5

What if he should perish?
The Master said:
Danger arises
From an excessive
Sense of security.
In seeking to preserve existence,
One perishes.
The True Gentleman,
In the midst of security,
Is still mindful of Danger.
There is no threat to his existence,
But he remembers
That he may perish.
In a time of order,
He never forgets
The possibility of turbulence.
In this way
His person is secure,
His nation protected.

禿 Yang Line in Yang Place. Centered and True. This Strong Line in Fifth (its proper, or Apt) Place brings Obstruction to a close. What is in danger of perishing, of being lost? Clearly the Sage, or some quality of his. Hold fast to the Heart-and-Mind of the Tao, writes Magister Liu. Let go of the Human Heart-and-Mind. Do not seek the end of Obstruction. It will end of itself. To be bound to the Mulberry Tree is to forestall Calamity, in such a way that Negative Yin Energy is powerless to infiltrate. The Sage is imperturbable in his Inner Self, writes Jullien. He is bound to the trunk of the tree, to his Center, in order to protect himself from possible destruction by Yin Energy. Even in the face of Danger, he is sheltered by his Steadfastness; he is attached to reality by his indestructible Inner Strength. JM: In early China the Mulberry Tree had sacred associations. It was the Tree of the Suns, the Axis Mundi, the dwelling place of the gods. (See Part II, 12/5.) In the good times, writes Professor Mun, the Leader should never forget the possibility of Obstruction. When he is safe, he should never forget the possibility of Danger.

Yang in Top Place

Obstruction

Is overthrown.

It gives way to

Joy,

Gaudet.

On the Image

Obstruction ends.
It could not long prevail.

 Yang Line in Yin Place. Yin Energy is in Retreat, writes Legge. Distress and Obstruction have come to an end. It is in the order of Change that they should do so, and give place to their opposite. Yang Energy is now in the ascendant. It is a law of Nature, writes Professor Mun, that adversity and felicity follow one another. A Leader who can master this principle will be able to reduce risk in his strategic moves.

HEXAGRAM XIII

Tong Ren

Fellowship

Qian/Heaven

above

Li/Fire

JUDGMENT

Fellowship

In the Wilds.

Fortune.

It Profits

To cross a Great Stream,

Transire magnum flumen.

It Profits

The True Gentleman

To be Steadfast.

On the Judgment

Yielding in Central Place
Resonates with Firm
In Heaven.
Fellowship.
The Action of Heaven:
Strength
Through Pattern and Illumination,
Centered,
True,
Resonant.
The True Gentleman
Connects
The Aspirations of the World.

On the Image of the Hexagram

Heaven and Fire,
Coelum et ignis.
The True Gentleman
Distinguishes kinds and families.

Heaven above Fire. This Hexagram, writes Richard Wilhelm, shows a single Yielding Nature among many Firm persons, a single Yin Line in Second Place, amid five Yang Lines. It embodies the ideal of the Universal Brotherhood of Man. After the negativity of Obstruction in the previous Hexagram, writes Legge, here is Union and Fellowship. The one Yin Line is naturally sought after by all the Yang Lines. The Upper Trigram is that of Heaven; the Lower is that of Fire, whose tendency is to mount upward. Fire ascends, it blazes to the sky and unites with it. The strength of Heaven combines with the Illumination of Fire, writes Magister Liu. All this signals a Union free from selfish motives, free from partiality. It is out in the Wilds. It is based on Truth, on discernment, not on sentiment. In the Wilds, there is no Self, there is no Other. It is a wide-open space devoid of people. Fellowship in this space has shed the ideas of Self and Other. Here the Taoist becomes one with the ordinary world. JM: In the late nineteenth century the Cantonese utopian reformer Kang Youwei called his most important work the *Book of the Great Fellowship*. The expression Great Fellowship is itself taken from the *Book of Rites*, where it describes a golden age "when the Great Tao prevailed, and the whole world was one community. Men of talent were selected, their words were sincere, they cultivated Harmony. . . . Each man had his allotted work, his tasks, and each woman had a home to go to. . . . There was no selfish scheming. Outer doors were left open. This was the Great Fellowship. But now the Great Tao is overshadowed, All-under-Heaven has become like a [closed] family. Selfishness abounds." An Organization in which members have shared values and a common goal, writes Professor Mun, will be able to create a warm atmosphere of Fellowship and will as a consequence be strong. Fire in the Lower Trigram creates warmth. Heaven in the Upper Trigram creates strength. Like-minded people gather round a fire under the sky.

LINES

Yang in First Place

Fellowship

At the gate.

No Harm,

Nullum malum.

On the Image

Beyond the gate,
Fellowship.
There can be no Harm.
Quodnam est malum?

Yang Line in Yang Place. Going out, writes Legge, issuing from the gate, one enters an open space. The whole world is there before one. Selfish thoughts have no place. The mind is not biased, writes Wang Bi. It is at one with the Great Fellowship. At the gate, all are fellows. A Leader should not show personal bias when making Fellowship with others, writes Professor Mun. He should be as if welcoming strangers at the gate of his house, open-minded and generous in spirit.

Yin in Second Place

Fellowship

Within the Clan.

Distress,

Poenitendi locus.

On the Image

This is the way
Of Distress.

 Yin Line in Yin Place. Centered and True. Here, by contrast, writes Richard Wilhelm, the danger is that of forming a closed, claustrophobic Fellowship. This weak Yin Line is hemmed in by the adjacent Yang Lines, by the Clan, which brings Distress. A Leader who creates Fellowship in an exclusive clique, writes Professor Mun, is narrow-minded, driven by insecurity and ego. Confucius said: "The True Gentleman is all-embracing. The Small Man forms cliques."

Yang in Third Place

An ambush

Is laid in a thicket.

A high hill

Is climbed.

For three years one does not rise.

On the Image

The enemy is strong.
One can only wait.

 Yang Line in Yang place. Only by abstaining from rash, impulsive action, writes Legge, can one be saved from Misfortune. Fellowship cannot be created in an instant, writes Professor Mun. It takes time and patience to build the necessary mutual trust.

Yang in Fourth Place

Sitting

Astride a wall.

One cannot attack.

Auspicious,

Hoc bonum.

On the Image

It is right
Not to attack.
Hardship
Is Auspicious.
It sends one back to principle.

 Yang Line in Yin Place. Once more, writes Legge, there is an impulse to attack (Yang Line), but this time, out of fear and a sense of Caution (Yin Place), one does not act. This has fortunate consequences. A Leader, writes Professor Mun, is able to restrain himself; he knows his limits (Yang Line in a Yin Place). He is flexible enough to turn back.

Yang in Fifth Place

Fellowship.

At first a weeping,

Then laughter.

The Great Army

Comes together.

On the Image

From the first,
Fellowship
Is Centered and Forthright.
A coming-together in victory.

The Great Treatise
From Part I, Section 8

With Fellowship,
Weeping turns to
Laughter.

The Master said:

The Tao of the True Gentleman

Is thus.

A going out,

And a staying still;

A silence,

And a speaking.

When two share Heart-and-Mind,

Their strength

Can split bronze asunder.

Words uttered from shared minds

Are fragrant as orchids.

Yang Line in Yang Place. Centered and True. Lines 3 and 4, writes Legge, wish to prevent the Fellowship between this Fifth Yang Line and the Second Yin Line, with which it Resonates. Their opposition at first makes one weep. But when the Army comes together (in Fellowship), it is victorious. This becomes cause for joy and laughter. JM: Sympathy (*tongxin,* sharing a Heart-and-Mind) is the basis for True Fellowship (*Tong Ren*). A shared Heart-and-Mind conquers all obstacles. In the fourth-century *New Tales of the World*, the bond of Fellowship among three members of the bohemian coterie the Seven Sages of the Bamboo Grove was dubbed a friendship "stronger than bronze and fragrant as orchids." A popular Chinese saying echoes the sentiment: "Mankind shares one Heart-and-Mind. That Heart-and-Mind shares one principle." The *lan*, the *cymbidium*, conventionally translated as "orchid," was famed for its fragrance. It was a symbol of the True Gentleman and had a traditional association with Confucius, to whom is attributed a piece of music celebrating the "lone orchid in the hidden vale," symbol of the True Gentleman. Fellowship, writes Magister Liu, comes as one of the fruits of Self-Cultivation. The True Taoist can share these fruits with others. This is open-minded and selfless Fellowship. It is like the victory of a Great Army. Ultimately all will be won over into this Great Fellowship.

Yang in Top Place

Fellowship

In the meadows.

No Regret,

Nullus poenitendi locus.

On the Image

Aspirations
Are not yet achieved.

 Yang Line in Yin Place. Fellowship reaches to all within the meadows. It is not yet universal. It still falls short of the ideal. It is still not out in the Wilds. But there is no cause for Regret.

Da You

Great Measure

Li/Fire

above

Qian/Heaven

JUDGMENT

Supreme Fortune.

On the Judgment

The Yielding
Is in Place of Honor,
In the Great Center.
Above and below
Resonate.
Spiritual Strength

Is strong and refined,
It Resonates
With Heaven;
It accords with Time.
Supreme Fortune.

On the Image of the Hexagram

Fire above Heaven,
Ignis supra coelum.
The True Gentleman
Curbs ill,
He promotes good,
He follows Heaven's Will.

 Fire above Heaven. The Fire and Light of Culture and Refinement in the Upper Trigram, *Li*, writes Legge, shine down above Heaven and Strength in the Lower Trigram, *Qian*. Territory and wealth are both implied in Great Measure. The True Gentleman, in governing his fellow men, especially in a time of prosperity, promotes what is good in them and curbs what is evil, in Accordance with the Will of Heaven. This Hexagram denotes, in a kingdom, a state of Prosperity and Abundance, and in a family or individual, a state of Wealth. There is Danger arising from the pride which it is likely to engender. But the Place of Authority (the Fifth) is occupied by a Yin Line, indicating Humility; and all the other Lines, strong as they are, will act in obedient sympathy. There will be great progress and success. JM: Early manuscripts have *Luo*, Net, as the Name of the Upper Trigram. This Hexagram can then be undersood as Net over Heaven, therefore a "big catch," an Image of Abundance. (See Part II.) Strength is Purity and Truth of Mind, Firm and Unbending, writes Magister Liu. The Sun (Fire) in Heaven shines afar. There is Life in Great Measure. Light Illumines the Myriad Affairs of the World. It is open; there is no Darkness in it. With Inner Mastery, one is strong and Illumined, unmoved by the Myriad Things. Wherever one walks, there is the Tao. This is the Supreme Fortune of Great Measure, unfailing in its far-reaching Action. The Sun at noon Illumines all things, writes Professor Mun. The Lower Trigram, *Qian*, represents resources or wealth, while the Upper Trigram, *Li,* represents a rational senior management. The whole Hexagram signifies an Organization under a soft management (Yin Line in Fifth Place). A modest and open-minded Leader will gain the respect and support of his colleagues, in Great Measure. An arrogant Leader will come to Harm.

LINES

Yang in First Place

No injuries

Are exchanged.

No Harm.

There is hardship.

No Harm,

Nullum malum.

On the Image

No injury.

 Yang Line in Yang Place. No injury is caused, writes Legge. Hardship can be endured without Harm. This is the hardship of Self-Cultivation, writes Magister Liu, the quiet nurturing of Inner Truth. This enables the Taoist to deal with Negative (Yin) Energy, to get rid of the False and embrace the True. A person in this beginning stage of development, writes Professor Mun, should be humble and constantly aware of (and learning from) hardship and difficulties.

Yang in Second Place

A large cart

Is loaded.

There is

A Destination.

No Harm,

Nullum malum.

On the Image

There is accumulation

In the Center.
It will not fail.

Yang Line in Yin Place. Centered. This Strong Yang Line in the Center of the Lower Trigram, writes Legge, Resonates with the Yin Line in Fifth Place, Ruler of the Hexagram. Its accumulated strength is subordinated to the Ruler's Humility. An initiative will succeed. The "large cart," writes Magister Liu, is filled with a Great Measure of Inner Abundance. This protects from Harm. An executive, writes Professor Mun, is assigned a task by his superior (Yin in Fifth Place). With strong Inner Balance, he will master his responsibility, like a large cart able to bear its load.

Yang in Third Place

The Duke serves

The Son of Heaven.

The Small Man fails.

On the Image

The Small Man
Comes to Harm,
Infortunium.

Yang Line in Yang Place. This Strong Line is in its Proper Place, writes Legge. This Top Line of the Lower Trigram (Heaven) is the Proper Place for the Duke, who humbly serves the Yin Ruler, the Son of Heaven, in Line Five. A Small Man occupying this Place, however, without Spiritual Strength, gives himself airs, and he comes to Harm. The Cultivation of the Tao, writes Magister Liu, is the service of Heaven. Its Strength is expressed in firm Action. The Small Man may be strong, but he lacks Truth. He is opposed to Heaven. The dedicated Leader, writes Professor Mun, works for the benefit of his Organization and is welcomed and respected by his colleagues. A mediocre Leader is concerned only with his own personal benefit. He fails as a consequence.

Yang in Fourth Place

No sense of

Self-importance.

No Harm,

Nullum malum.

On the Image

Clear and bright
Discernment.

 Yang Line in Yin Place. Yang Strength is tempered by Position in a Yin Place, writes Legge. By not inflating one's own sense of importance, one does no injury to the mild Ruler, to whom one is so near. This is a sign of insight and intelligence, in the First Line of the Upper Trigram, Fire or Illumination. An outward appearance of insufficiency, writes Magister Liu, is balanced by an Inner Abundance, a Great Measure of Spiritual Strength.

Yin in Fifth Place

Good Faith

Attracts.

It inspires

Obedience.

This is Auspicious,

Hoc bonum.

On the Image

Trust kindles
The Aspiration of Others.
Obedience comes
With ease,
Without premeditation.

Yin Line in Yang Place. Centered. Good Faith, writes Legge, is an "attractive" quality in a Ruler, affecting and "attracting" his ministers and Others. But the Ruler must also possess an obedience-inspiring majesty. JM: The word *wei*, traditionally understood as "awe," is written differently in the Mawangdui manuscript, with the meaning "supple" or "obedient." This obedience is achieved not through planned

Action, but through the charismatic Non-Action of the Taoist Sage. See *The Tao and the Power*:

Chapter 3
He enacts Non-Action,
And all is governed.

Good Faith, writes Magister Liu, proceeds from that openness of Heart-and-Mind where Self does not exist and Others do. The gentleness of Yin and the strength of Yang complement each other. With this Great Measure, one does not need to seek out the obedience of others. It just happens. A good Leader, writes Professor Mun, adopts a soft style of management (Yin in Yang Place) based on mutual trust between himself and members of the Organization.

Yang in Top Place

Heaven's Blessing.

This is Auspicious,

Hoc bonum.

All things

Profit.

On the Image

This is Auspicious
Through Heaven's Blessing.

The Great Treatise
From Part I, Section 12

The Master said:
The Blessing is Heaven's aid.
Heaven aids those
Who live
In the Tao.
Men aid those
Who walk in Trust,
Who tread the Tao of Trust,

Their thoughts
In Accordance with the Tao.
They esteem the Worthy.
Such men receive Heaven's Blessing;
They Profit in all things.

 Yang Line in Yin Place. This is the Top Line of the Upper Trigram, *Li*, Fire, Illumination, Culture. The Strength of Heaven, writes Magister Liu, brings Blessing to the Illumined. When a person is modest and avoids complacency and arrogance, comments Professor Mun, this is Accordance, conformity with the law of Nature, with the Tao. Heaven's Blessing flows.

HEXAGRAM XV

Qian

Humility

Kun/Earth

above

Gen/Mountain

JUDGMENT

Fortune.

The True Gentleman

Has a Conclusion,

Finem habet.

On the Judgment

The radiant Tao of Heaven
Moves downward.
The lowly Tao of Earth

Rises upward.
The Tao of Heaven
Diminishes the full,
Augments the Humble.
The Tao of Earth
Alters the full;
It causes Humility to spread.
Gods and Spirits
Injure the full;
They bless the Humble.
The Tao of Man
Abhors the full;
It loves the Humble.
Humility
Honored
Shines forth;
Humility
Lowly
Cannot be defiled.
This is the Conclusion
Of the True Gentleman.

On the Image of the Hexagram

Mountain within Earth,
In medio terrae mons.
The True Gentleman
Diminishes the many,
Augments the few.
He weighs matters
Impartially.

Earth above Mountain. The Lower Trigram, *Gen*, Mountain, is technically a Yang Trigram, according to the Great Treatise. Thus, in the words of the Judgment, its Yang Energy, the "Tao of Heaven," "moves downward," while the Yin Energy of Earth in the Upper Trigram "rises upward." The single Yang Line in Third Place, amid five Yin Lines, writes Legge, represents Humility, strong but self-effacing. Humility is valued by both Heaven and Earth, by both Spirits and Men. The descent of the Tao of Heaven and the lowly Position of Earth in the First Line are both emblematic of Humility. Here the Mountain has descended beneath the Earth, writes Chen Guying. Two modes of Humility are depicted: in the first three Lines, Internal Self-Cultivation; in the last three Lines, External Application. JM: The Jesuit Claude de Visdelou produced the very first vernacular European translation of this Hexagram, in elegant eighteenth-century French:

> *La Raison du Ciel est éclatante,*
> *et s'abaisse jusqu'à la terre.*
> *La Raison de la Terre est humble,*
> *et s'élève en haut. . . .*

This Hexagram appealed greatly to the China Jesuits, who interpreted its message of Spiritual Humility as support for their policy of Accommodation, of a "humble" acceptance of certain Chinese practices (including the Rites of Ancestor Worship)—a policy that was to attract criticism and eventual condemnation from the Catholic Church. For the small group of Jesuits known as Figurists, especially Joachim Bouvet, this Hexagram represented the Supreme Humility of God. God abhors the Proud; He loves the Humble. God Humbled Himself through the Incarnation of His Son. His Son Humbled Himself and was obedient even unto death. The Mountain buried beneath the Earth is a symbol of God's Divine Majesty, emptied through the Humility of Incarnation. Earth is a symbol of the Redeemer as an incarnated human being. Through His Holy Humility, the righteous persist in holiness till the end ("the True Gentleman has a Conclusion") and in this way gain justice. They are saved (they "cannot be defiled"). All peoples on Earth voluntarily submit to His Divine Example. Richard Wilhelm commented that this Hexagram "offers a number of parallels to the teachings of the Old and New Testament—e.g., Every valley shall be exalted and every mountain and hill shall be made low (Isaiah 40:4)." But there is really no need to seek parallels in the Bible. The dominant Image occurs in the *Book of Songs*:

> *Song 193*
> The high ridges
> Are become valleys,
> The deep vales
> Are become hills.

The qualities of Humility and retiring self-effacement (the courtesy and Self-Knowledge of the True Gentleman, whether Confucian or Taoist) were greatly prized in traditional China. In modern Chinese, the ordinary word for Humility or Modesty is *qian* coupled with *xu*, (literally, "empty"): *qianxu*. Why should Humility be linked to Emptiness? When the Heart-and-Mind is empty (of Self, of desire, of distraction, of prejudice), then it can enter into Harmony with the Tao. Then it can shed any "sense of self-importance." See *The Tao and the Power*:

> *Chapter 5*
> Heaven and Earth
> Are like a bellows,
> Empty
> But never exhausted.
> The more it is used,

The more it produces.
Words
Are soon consumed.
Best hold fast to
The Center.

Chapter 16
Attain
Utmost Emptiness,
Observe Quietness
In earnest.

This is closely linked to the idea of Non-Action, *wuwei*. The Taoist Sage rules through Non-Action. He waits in Emptiness, and everything happens of itself. Compare this with the lines about Non-Action from *The Tao and the Power,* chapter 3, quoted in the previous Hexagram, Yin in Fifth Place. Every Line Statement in this Hexagram XV is unreservedly positive. The Humble, writes Magister Liu, possess but do not depend on, are not attached to, that which they possess. They have talent but do not presume on their talent. For them there is no Self, no Other. These are erased. All pride is gone, the Heart-and-Mind is level. When the Heart-and-Mind is level, then Inner Strength grows daily, Humility grows daily. Outer deficiency is matched by inner sufficiency. The benefits of Humility are many. With Humility, Truth becomes manifest, Life Energy prevails. The Great Tao is attained. True Humility, writes Professor Mun, implies tolerance and open-mindedness. It is one of the important concepts in the Taoist philosophy of Laozi. A truly Humble Leader will be willing to accept different opinions and suggestions raised by his colleagues. Humility strengthens Leadership. Complacency is the beginning of failure.

LINES

Yin in First Place

The True Gentleman

Is Humble.

It avails

To cross a Great Stream.

This is

Auspicious,

Hoc bonum.

On the Image

He is lowly
And nurtures Self.

 Yin Line in Yang Place. This Weak Line, in the Lowest Place of the Hexagram, writes Legge, is a fitting symbol of the True Gentleman, nurturing Spiritual Strength, literally "pasturing," or "shepherding," himself. Humility makes him what he is. JM: Again, to cross a Great Stream is to embark on any undertaking. This will be Auspicious by virtue of its Humility. Humility, writes Magister Liu, is having the flexibility to lower oneself. This is the Humility of the True Gentleman. A Humble Leader, writes Professor Mun, draws others toward himself. They will protect him from Harm.

Yin in Second Place

Humility

Sings.

It is Auspicious

To be Steadfast,

Solidum bonum.

On the Image

The Heart-and-Mind
Is Centered.
Success.

 Yin Line in Yin Place. Centered and True. Humility proclaims itself. Here, writes Chen Guying, in the Center of the Lower Trigram (Mountain), the Humility of the Recluse "sings." His voice is heard in the world. It reverberates. This is Master Zhuang's "Thunder speaking in the silence of the Abyss"; it is Master Guan's "Voice of Silence, heard in the rumbling of Thunder." Humility "singing," writes Magister Liu, is the expression of the Nothing (*wu*) of Self, of the Something (*you*) of Others. It is Yielding and Compliant (Yin in Yin); it is Centered and True (in Apt Place). Outwardly expressed Humility, writes Professor Mun, proceeding from a Steadfast Heart-and-Mind, is Auspicious.

Yang in Third Place

This is

The Diligence,

The Humility,

Of the True Gentleman.

An Auspicious Conclusion,

Hoc bonum.

On the Image

The Myriad Folk
All submit.

Yang Line in Yang Place. Actions carried out with quiet and true Humility, writes Richard Wilhelm, win widespread support. This is the single Yang Line in the Hexagram, writes Magister Liu. It is surrounded by Yin Lines. Humility transforms the Yin Multitude. Humility works with Diligence, growing stronger with each day. The efforts of this capable Leader, writes Professor Mun, will be recognized by the members of his Organization.

Yin in Fourth Place

All things

Profit.

Humility

Is made manifest.

On the Image

Nothing is done
Contrary to principle.

Yin Line in Yin Place. Act in such a way that Humility is made manifest, always keeping principle (the Tao) in mind. The executive in this position, writes Professor Mun, should be particularly cautious in handling delicate relationships with his superior and subordinates.

Yin in Fifth Place

Wealth is not shared

With neighbors.

It Profits

To attack with force.

All things

Profit.

Nihil quod non conveniat.

On the Image

The recalcitrant
Are made to submit.

 Yin Line in Yang Place. Centered. "Recalcitrance" (on the part of a neighbor), writes Legge, sometimes makes force necessary, even for the best and Humblest Ruler. But force must be used with Humility. If soft measures are not effective, writes Professor Mun, then hard measures may need to be applied.

Yin in Top Place

Humility

Sings.

It Profits

To send an Army on the march,

To attack one's own city.

On the Image

Aspirations are not attained.
Military might is resorted to.

秀 Yin Line in Yin Place. With Humility, writes Legge, one takes Action and uses force, but only within one's own sphere, bringing discipline to "one's own city," asserting what is right. "Attacking one's own city" can also be understood, writes Richard Wilhelm, to mean disciplining Self, one's own ego and one's immediate circle. This degree of Humility (which "sings"), writes Professor Mun, may be too extreme. The Leader may need to overcome Self, to show *less* Humility.

Yu

Elation

Zhen/Quake

above

Kun/Earth

JUDGMENT

It Profits

To establish Lieutenants,

To send troops on the march.

On the Judgment

The Firm Resonates;
Aspirations are enacted.
Harmony and Movement prevail.
Heaven and Earth
Move in Harmony.

Sun and moon
Do not stray.
The Four Seasons
Do not exceed their bounds.
The Sage moves in Harmony.
His punishments are clear.
The Folk obey.

On the Image of the Hexagram

Thunder breaks out;
Earth is roused.
The Ancient Kings
Made music
To revere Spiritual Power;
They offered splendor
To the Supreme Deity.
They made Sacrifice
To their Ancestors.

Quake above Earth. The single Yang Line in Fourth Place inspires the other Lines, all of which are Yin. In Elation, Yang Energy breaks forth. Heaven and Earth are in Harmony. Richard Wilhelm translated the Hexagram Name into German as *Die Begeisterung*—"Enthusiasm" in Baynes's English. In one of his lectures from the 1920s, Wilhelm writes lyrically of this Hexagram: "An Image unfolds of Earth, Heaven, and ultimate metaphysical energies, all connected through the spirit of Music. . . . And this brings us to the holy dramatic performances where musical sounds and the dancers' symbolic movements represented cosmic events: the dance of the stars." This apprehends the cosmic law, it represents the Tao of the world and, therefore, the world's mysteries. "Everyone who experiences these is pulled deeply toward the direction of eternity." A thunderstorm clears the air, writes Legge, paraphrasing Cheng Yi, and removes the feeling of oppression. The use of Music at Sacrifices assists the union between the Supreme Deity and his worshippers, creates a link between present and past generations. JM: Ritual and Music were a bridge to the world of the unseen. The *Book of Rites* describes Music as "the Harmony of Heaven and Earth. It is Yang Energy. It is the Image of Spiritual Strength." In the simpler words of a commentary on the *Book of the Huainan Master*, "Music is Life." The Chinese word for Music is the same as the word for Joy, and in Ancient Chinese the two were pronounced in the same way, the sound uncannily resembling the English word "glee." One of the legendary Taoist Recluses of the third century AD, Sun Deng, a mountain-dweller much admired by the Seven Sages of the Bamboo Grove, was both an *I Ching* Adept and a superb musician. In winter he would clothe himself in nothing but his own long, unbound hair. Sun was a Taoist virtuoso of the Art of Transcendental Whistling, a cross between yodeling and *vocalise*—an advanced method of communicating with the Spirits and achieving "immortality." It was almost certainly this same Sun Deng whom the poet Ruan Ji (himself no mean whistler, and something of an *I Ching* expert) went in search of, hiking through the mountains of Henan. After a brief and fruitless verbal exchange with the Recluse, Ruan whistled a little, then took his leave and set off walking back down the mountain. He was about halfway down when he heard a symphonic wave of sound swirling through the hills. An orchestra of flutes and drums seemed to echo through the forests and valleys. This was Taoist Glee, or Elation, the transcendental music of the Recluse, in Harmony with Heaven and Earth. It was the Breath of Nature, the pure Glee of Heaven and Earth. Music is also a perfect metaphor for, and mirror of, the constantly changing improvisatory Nature of all phenomena in the Cosmos. Ge Hong, the Taoist Master of Simplicity, wrote: "By listening to the sound of Music, to its cadences, the wise understand the rise and fall of all things. By watching the world closely, the wise know the meaning of things before they actually appear and take shape." The Yang Energy of Elation, writes Magister Liu, causes all to connect in Harmony. The Myriad Things are all quickened and uplifted by it. In True Glee, Spiritual Strength and Elation complement each other. The music of that Glee is a sufficient "offering" for the Supreme Deity and for the Ancestors. JM: As several of the Line Statements emphasize, True Elation must be distinguished from False Elation.

LINES

Yin in First Place

Elation

Sings.

Calamity,

Hoc pessimum.

On the Image

Aspirations
Are exhausted.
Calamity,
Pessimum.

Yin Line in Yang Place. Do not "sing" Elation, writes Legge, do not proclaim it. This seeking of attention will bring Calamity. Elation should never be an egotistical show of emotion, writes Richard Wilhelm. That is merely foolish Elation. True Elation, writes Magister Liu, is a feeling that unites Self with Others. To "sing" Elation is to think oneself happy when in reality one is not. It is to enter a rigid realm of Folly. It is False Glee. Boasting in public, writes Professor Mun, of the Resonance or special relationship which exists between this Yin Line in First Place and Yang in Fourth is harmful to teamwork. It is shallow.

Yin in Second Place

He is

Firm as a rock.

He does not wait

For day to end.

Steadfast.

This is

Auspicious,

Hoc bonum.

On the Image

Centered and True.

The Great Treatise
From Part II, Section 5

The Master said:
The True Gentleman
In his wisdom
Knows the Springs of Things;
He knows
The tiniest intimations
Of Movement,
The earliest stirrings
Of Fortune.
Seeing these,
He acts,

Not needing to wait for day to end.
Firm as a rock:
He does not need to wait.
The breaking point
Has been perceived;
The tiniest and grandest
Are known,
The Yielding and Firm.
All look up to him.

Yin Line in Yin Place. Centered and True. To abide quietly and firmly in one's station, writes Legge, "like a rock," unaffected by others, not misled by illusion, by greed, by cravings, not letting False externals harm Inner Truth, alert to the slightest signs of Change—this is to be Steadfast. This is Auspicious. JM: Both the formal and informal names of Generalissimo Chiang Kai-shek (*Zhongzheng*, "Centered and True"; *Jieshi*, Cantonese Kai-shek, "Firm as a Rock") were taken from this Line Statement and its Commentary. To "know the Springs of Things" (to be tuned in to the Dynamic of the situation and therefore to be able to predict the movements of the enemy) was a central skill of the Warrior Adept in *The Art of War*:

> *Chapter 6*
> Scrutinize the enemy,
> Know the flaws in his plans.
> Rouse him,
> Discover
> The Springs of his Actions.

Yin in Third Place

Haughty

Elation.

Regret.

Delay brings Regret,

Poenitendi locus.

On the Image

This is not in Proper Place.

Yin Line in Yang Place. Things are out of joint, writes Legge. There is an Excess of Pride ("haughty Elation"). The consequence is Regret. But at the same time, undue delay will also cause Regret. This is a difficult moment. Timing is tricky, and of the essence.

Yang in Fourth Place

From Elation

Comes

Great achievement.

Do not doubt.

Friends rally around.

On the Image

Aspirations are fulfilled.

Yang Line in Yin Place. This is the single Yang Line in the midst of five Yin Lines, writes Legge. Yang is not led astray by Yin. Be confident, and friends will remain loyal. This is Elation inspired by certainty, writes Richard Wilhelm, by freedom from doubt. Confusion becomes unity, writes Magister Liu. Chaos is made stable. Yang Energy prevails, Yin Energy transforms itself. A senior executive, writes Professor Mun, inspires trust by his Sincerity, capability, and strength. The three Yin Lines of the Lower Trigram are the friends who rally around.

Yin in Fifth Place

Steadfastness

In a chronic ailment.

Survival.

On the Image

This Line
Rides

Firm Yang.
The Center is not lost.
Survival.

Yin Line in Yang Place. Centered. The Ruler's Place, writes Legge, paraphrasing Zhu Xi, is occupied by a Weak Yin Line. There is a Danger, of being carried away, literally "submerged," by a False sense of Elation. Despite this, through remaining Steadfast at the Center, one survives. This Yielding Line lacks strength, writes Magister Liu. It is alone and still. It is Empty, with no substance. It is ailing, without Joy. But by holding to the Center, the Yielding can still keep Calamity at bay. This is a soft-style Leader, writes Professor Mun, who relies on his strong assistant (Rides Yang in Fourth Place).

Yin in Top Place

Benighted

Elation.

Change

At Completion.

No Harm,

Nullum malum.

On the Image

Benighted Elation
Cannot long prevail.

Yin Line in Yin Place. One is all but lost in the Dark, writes Legge, in the blind pursuit of pleasure. But a sober awakening from False ("benighted") Elation is still possible, writes Richard Wilhelm. For the Taoist, writes Magister Liu, all Elation, all Glee, when it reaches its height, by its very nature engenders sorrow. It inevitably brings about its own downfall. False Elation comes from the pursuit of objects of desire. True Elation, True Glee, come from Self-Cultivation. This is the Change that comes at Completion. Following the Movement of Yang Energy, Elation bursts out like a clap of thunder ("thunder breaks out"). It rouses Earth and rises up to Heaven, scattering the demons, nurturing the "sprouts" of Inner Life Energy. This is truly Glee beyond compare.

HEXAGRAM XVII

Sui

Following

Dui/Lake

above

Zhen/Quake

JUDGMENT

Supreme Fortune.

To be Steadfast

Profits.

No Harm,

Nullum malum.

On the Judgment

The Firm
Is below the Yielding,

Durum infra molle.
Movement and Delight.
Great Fortune
And Steadfastness.
All-under-Heaven
Follows.

On the Image of the Hexagram

Thunder in the Lake,
Tonitrus in lacu.
Toward evening
The True Gentleman
Goes in to rest.

The Great Treatise
From Part II, Section 2

Oxen are tamed,
Horses yoked;
They carry great loads
Over distances,
They bring Profit
To All-under-Heaven.
This came from
Following.

茆 Lake over Quake. In both Trigrams, the Yang Lines are below the Yin Lines. The Lower Trigram, *Zhen*, Quake or Thunder, writes Legge, is Movement. The Upper Trigram, *Dui*, Lake, is Joy or Delight. The two combined (Movement and Delight) give the sense of a spontaneous Following, the coming together in Harmony of two purposes. Thunder explodes in the Waters of a Lake. This is "followed" by a tremulous agitation, a rippling, a surging of waves. The Movement of the Lower Trigram evokes a response in the Upper. In the Great Treatise, oxen and horses walk on ahead, the wagon "following" behind. Sometimes one Follows Others. Sometimes one is Followed by Others. In both cases the Following must be guided by Steadfastness if it is to be Profitable. I Move, writes Magister Liu, and Others Delight; Others Delight and I Move. We are in accord. We Resonate. True Yin joins with True Yang. Yin Stillness nurtures Yang Energy. In this Hexagram, writes Wang Zongchuan, Firm places itself below Yielding, Yang below Yin, high below low, noble below mean—always esteeming Others to be higher. This gives the idea of Following. To Follow, writes Richard Wilhelm, is to adapt to the True Nature of the situation and to the demands of the time that grow out of that situation. No situation can Profit until one is able to adapt to it ("follow" it, go along with it), instead of wearing oneself out in mistaken resistance to it. Follow the Tao of Stillness and Accord, tune in to the Tao of things as they truly are. See *The Tao and the Power*:

Chapter 16
Each of the Myriad Things
Returns to the Root.
This Return
Is Stillness.

The poet Xie Lingyun uses the Image of the True Gentleman "going in to rest" in his "Rhapsody on Living in the Mountains":

I look up
To the example of the former Sages,
I look within
Into my own Nature,
I go in to rest,
I Cultivate my own Heart-and-Mind,
I live at leisure.

Xie is echoing the great Taoist Master Zhuang:

Cultivate Heart-and-Mind,
Let it be unmoved
By sorrow and joy,
Know that certain things are inevitable.
This is the height
Of Spiritual Strength.

LINES

Yang in First Place

Changes at court.

To be Steadfast

Is Auspicious.

There are exchanges

Beyond the gate;

There is

Success.

On the Image

Follow the true path.
This is Auspicious.
Beyond the gate,
Success.
Things will not fail.

Yang Line in Yang Place. This Strong Line, writes Legge, sits in the Lowest Place of the Quake Trigram, below two Weak Lines. A capable person should mix with people less capable, should adapt to "changes." He should go "beyond the gate" (beyond his immediate inner circle) in search of "exchanges" with Others. This demonstrates a public, "outgoing" spirit, rising above considerations of Self. It will surely succeed. By going "beyond the gate," writes Magister Liu, the Taoist interacts with the material world, borrowing the methods of the world to cultivate the Tao. This is all done with scrupulous care. It will succeed. The capable executive, writes Professor Mun, is willing to listen to the opinions of Others and change his own position if he is wrong.

Yin in Second Place

He is

Bound

To the little boy.

The Great Man

Is lost.

On the Image

One cannot have both.

Yin Line in Yin Place. Centered and True. The "little boy," writes Richard Wilhelm, is the Yin Line in Third Place; the Great Man is the Yang Line in First Place. One cannot "have both" at once. One has to make a choice. Legge quotes the famous lines from Mencius: "I like fish. I also like bear's paw. If I cannot have both, then I will give up the fish and choose the bear's paw. I like life. I also like righteousness. If I cannot have both, then I will give up life and choose righteousness." To be bound to the little boy, writes Magister Liu, is to "follow" Yin, in a spirit of weakness and ignorance. This is a Following that has lost Truth. A Leader, writes Professor Mun, should be careful in choosing his business partner.

Yin in Third Place

He is

Bound

To the Great Man.

The little boy

Is lost.

Following

Achieves its goal.

To remain Steadfast

Profits,

Oportet ut sit soliditas.

On the Image

Let Heart-and-Mind
Abandon
What is below.

 Yin Line in Yang Place. Hold to the Great Man with a strong Will, writes Magister Liu. Steadfastly Follow the Yang of Others, rather than the petty Yin of Self. This may entail a certain loss. But it is the inferior elements ("what is below") that will be lost, and the overall consequences will be Profitable. The Great Man, writes Professor Mun, is Yang in Fourth Place; the "little boy" is Yin in Second Place. The Leader chooses as his business partner someone with good prospects, and gives up someone less promising. He does this in a principled (Steadfast) way.

Yang in Fourth Place

Following

Brings a result.

Steadfastness

Brings

Calamity,

Pessimum.

Good Faith

Lights the way.

There can be no Harm.

Quodnam malum est?

On the Image

Calamity.
With Good Faith along the way,
Success will shine brightly.

Yang Line in Yin Place. There is a certain malaise. An initial Following, though strong, lacks inner conviction. If it is based on personal ambition, it will bring Calamity. But with Good Faith, if trust is placed in the Tao, all can still turn out for the best. This senior executive, writes Professor Mun, is close to the head of the Organization (Yang in Fifth Place). Others Follow him (Yin in Second and Third Places). He must beware of the Danger if his superior is not open-minded. But with Sincerity and respect, there will be no Harm.

Yang in Fifth Place

Good Faith.

Celebration.

Auspicious,

Hoc bonum.

On the Image

Centered and True.

Yang Line in Yang Place. Centered and True. Follow the desire of the Heart-and-Mind, but do not go beyond the limits of propriety. Put Faith in genuine ability, and success is sure. This is Joy, writes Magister Liu. This is a Following with Good Faith, a celebration of the Tao. A Leader with Sincerity and a sense of values, writes Professor Mun, will have a loyal Following.

Yin in Top Place

Grasp.

Bind.

Release.

The King

Sacrifices

On West Mountain.

On the Image

To grasp and bind
Is futile.

 Yin Line in Yin Place. To bind another, writes Magister Liu, to *force* another to Follow (to "grasp"), is contrary to the Spirit of the Tao. In the end it is futile. One must let go ("release"). Others must Follow of their own accord. Qi Mountain, writes Zhu Xi, lies to the West. Here, during the Zhou dynasty, Shamans (Shamanesses, Shaman-Kings) performed Sacrifices to Hills and Streams, ensuring peace and prosperity for the Realm. These religious observances, this powerful example of Following the Potential Dynamic of the Tao, inspired total allegiance.

HEXAGRAM XVIII

Gu

Blight

Gen/Mountain

above

Xun/Wind

JUDGMENT

Supreme Fortune.

It Profits

To cross a Great Stream,

Magnum flumen.

Three days before,

Three days after,

The first day,

Jia.

On the Judgment

The Firm
Is above,
The Yielding
Is below.
Wind is halted.
Supreme Fortune.
All-under-Heaven
Is well governed.
A Great Stream is crossed,
An enterprise of moment
Undertaken.
Each ending is
A commencement.
This is
The Movement of Heaven.

On the Image of the Hexagram

Wind below Mountain,
Ventus sub monte.
The True Gentleman
Cultivates Inner Strength.
He rouses the Folk.

Mountain above Wind. In both Trigrams, the Yin Lines are below the Yang Lines. The single Yin Line in the First Place of the Lower Trigram, writes Legge, paraphrasing Cheng Yi, is the rising force of Yin Energy, which corrupts the Yang Energy of the next two Lines. The entire Lower Trigram, Wind, comes up against the Upper Trigram, Mountain. There it is "halted," driven back. This results in disorder and decay. Things are scattered in disarray. This gives the idea of Blight, a state in which things are going to ruin, as if through poison or venomous worms. (For more detail on the origins of this powerful graph, see Part II.) The Hexagram advises how to halt this Blight, how to abandon the False and Return to the True, how to restore soundness and vigor. In the Upper Trigram, writes Magister Liu, the single Yang at the Top signals a Return to the Root, a Return to Life, remedying the harmful effects of Yin Energy and cultivating the Tao. This explains the Augury of Supreme Fortune. Great effort will be required, however, as in crossing a Great Stream. Great Danger and Adversity will be confronted.

One must temper oneself in the Dragon's Pool and the Tiger's Cave—in the furnace of the world and its troubles—in order to rediscover one's True Self. Careful consideration of the events that have brought about the Blight, and of the measures required to remedy it, is necessary. History is a narrative of constant Change over Time, writes Chen Guying, of "endings" and "commencements," of one condition of affairs giving place to another, and opposite, condition. One must "heed the ending no less than the commencement" (*The Tao and the Power*, chapter 64). This Hexagram deals in particular with "righting the Blight" within a family, cauterizing a decay set in motion over Time by the parents. Before larger affairs of state can be put in order, family affairs must be set to rights. In order to achieve this, "Inner Strength must be cultivated." Blight, writes Professor Mun, or Decay, in an Organization—inefficiency and disorder—can start from either a lower or a higher level. An Organization that has not changed its degenerating structure for some time will gradually stagnate and be consumed by its own rigidity, just as worms breed in a plate of food. To remedy Decay, to check Blight, the Leader must carefully choose the right time ("three days before" or "three days after" *jia*). JM: The Recluse (in the Top Place) deals with this situation in model fashion. He cultivates Inner Strength, "living in solitude," "embracing Unity." In the worldly context, writes Zen Master Zhixu, First Line is the worthy gentleman, Second Line the civilized official, Third Line the wise general, Fourth Line the scheming official, Fifth Line the wise King, and Top Line the principled Recluse.

LINES

Yin in First Place

The father's Blight

Is set right

By a devoted son.

No Harm.

Danger,

Ultimately Auspicious,

In fine optimum.

On the Image

The son
Takes upon himself
The misdeeds
Of the father.

Yin Line in Yang Place. The son sets right the Blight of the father, writes Richard Wilhelm, in its early stages, before the corruption is too deep and advanced. In the end, writes Legge, the father will be seen as having caused no lasting Harm. To check the Blight, writes Magister Liu, more than empty Inaction is called for. What is needed is Caution in the face of Danger. The effects of external Energy must be checked, the Root must be protected from injury. This is to guard against Yin before it has caused Blight. If an executive, writes Professor Mun, can carefully clear up the mistakes made by his predecessor, things will turn out well in the end. The Decay is at an early stage. It should be dealt with now before it spreads.

Yang in Second Place

The mother's Blight

Is set right.

To be Steadfast

Is impossible.

On the Image

The Middle Way
Is attained.

 Yang Line in Yin Place. Centered. In setting things right, writes Richard Wilhelm, paraphrasing Zhu Xi, flexibility and moderation are called for, rather than uncompromising Steadfastness. Do not proceed too drastically, with too great an insistence. Flexibility is the Root, writes Magister Liu, Strength the Branch. When an executive, writes Professor Mun, deals with problems caused by his superior (Yin in Fifth Place), he should be moderate, not rash or harsh. He should be gentle, to avoid any adverse effect on morale or stability in the Organization.

Yang in Third Place

The father's Blight

Is set right.

Slight Regret.

No great Harm,

Non magnum malum.

On the Image

Ultimately no Harm,
In fine nullum malum.

 Yang Line in Yang Place. In being too hard, writes Zhu Xi, one strays from the Middle Way. Absence of moderation causes slight Regret. The Energy of Wind in the Lower Trigram is ultimately gentle and True, so no great Harm is caused. Tough measures, writes Professor Mun, are needed in a time of Decay, but should not be pushed too hard.

Yin in Fourth Place

The father's Blight

Is set right

Leniently.

An Advance brings

Distress.

On the Image

An Advance
Achieves nothing.

 Yin Line in Yin Place. Excessive leniency in this Weak Line, writes Zhu Xi, merely allows the Blight to grow daily more entrenched. Do not proceed in such a slack manner. To cultivate the Tao in this way, writes Magister Liu, to tolerate Blight, can only bring Distress. Weakness and indecision, writes Professor Mun, will cause the situation to deteriorate.

Yin in Fifth Place

The father's Blight

Is set right

Through Praise.

On the Image

Inner Strength
Sets matters right.

Yin Line in Yang Place. Centered. This Yielding Line, writes Zhu Xi, in the Central Yang Place of Honor, acquires (through Resonance) the Inner Strength of the Yang Second Line. Being Yielding and Humble, writes Magister Liu, one praises Others and thereby uses their strength to halt the Blight, to brighten one's own Spiritual Darkness. This is a soft way to halt Blight. The new Leader, writes Professor Mun, uses a balanced approach and earns praise.

Yang in Top Place

Serving

Neither King nor Duke,

He minds

His own affairs,

Aloof.

On the Image

A model sense of
Aspiration.

Yang Line in Yin Place. In the fusion of Yin and Yang, writes Magister Liu, one returns to the highest realm. With the Tao, one becomes one with Truth, one becomes indestructible. With this ultimate Tao, one can halt Blight. The Leader, writes Professor Mun, deals with Blight in his Organization out of his genuine concern for a higher purpose, not out of ambition ("serving neither King nor Duke"), standing aloof. The Recluse lives outside public life, "minding his own affairs," all the while retaining his lofty Aspirations. Xie Lingyun, the mountaineer-poet, avails himself of words from this last Line Statement (together with words from Yang in Second Place in Hexagram X, Stepping):

On Climbing Green Crag
In my confusion,
I sought the new moon
In the west,
The setting sun
In the east.
I walked on till evening,
Rested till dawn;
Shadows shrouded me.
Top Place in Blight:
Best not to serve.
Second Place in Stepping:
Steadfastness
Is Auspicious.
The Recluse
Steps on a level road,
Lofty minded,
Aloof,
Beyond the scope
Of ordinary mortals.

He concludes:

Fain would I live in solitude,
Embrace Unity.
There, in that fusion
Of tranquillity and wisdom,
Inborn Nature will begin to heal.

As his translator John Frodsham points out, "Top Place in Blight" may also have been a dig at the dissolute conduct of the man then "in Top Place"—i.e., Emperor Shao. The last two lines of the poem send the reader to the chapter "Healing Inborn Nature," of *The Book of Master Zhuang*, a work that has provided inspiration for every Chinese Recluse. The poet-alchemist Lu You, who retired from government service at the age of sixty-four, devoted himself thereafter to his preferred mode of Reclusion, the preparation of the Alchemical Elixir. His poem "A Taoist Laboratory" also takes this Top Line as its motto:

Top Place
In the Wind-Mountain Hexagram:
The Recluse.
I shun the world
Of friends and old acquaintances,
The sham of social ways
Which once around me swirled.
A small farm for my livelihood,
Forty acres,
Enough to sustain me,
To let me live as best I can.

HEXAGRAM XIX

Lin

Approach

Kun /Earth

above

Dui/Lake

JUDGMENT

Supreme Fortune.

It Profits

To be Steadfast.

In the eighth month,

Calamity,

Pessimum.

On the Judgment

The Firm penetrates;
It waxes.
Joy
Flows,
Cum gaudio.
Firm is Centered,
Resonant.
There is
Great Fortune in Truth,
In the Tao of Heaven.
Calamity comes
In the eighth month.
Yang wanes;
It is short-lived.

On the Image of the Hexagram

Earth above Lake,
Terra supra lacum.
The True Gentleman
Is limitless
In his teaching and concern;
He is boundless
In nurturing and protecting
The Folk.

Earth above Lake. The two Yang Lines at the base grow upward; they Approach, they Advance into the Hexagram from below, influencing the four Yin Lines above them. From above the waters of the Lake, Earth controls the Danger (of flooding). It oversees and governs. It deals with things. Great Fortune will prevail, writes Legge, paraphrasing Zhu Xi, when an Approach is tempered by Truth, when Caution is grounded in the changing character of conditions and events. Different Approaches, different attitudes, different ways of "governing," of intervening, of dealing with people, are appropriate to different circumstances. Earth above the Lake is symbolic of the Approach of superiors to their inferiors. The "limitless teaching of the True Gentleman," writes Chen Guying, is characteristic of the Lake; the "boundless nurturing" is characteristic of Earth. This Hexagram, writes Magister Liu, is Supremely Fortunate, in that Yang Energy returns, it grows gradually. As the Work progresses, as the Taoist Approaches the Furnace of Self-Cultivation, so Yang is nurtured and Yin is held in check. With the two Yang Lines, Positive Yang Energy expands. But Yin Energy is still strong, while Yang Energy is weak and unsure of itself. Beware of the

Danger that may lie ahead (in the "eighth month"). Earth above Lake, writes Professor Mun, symbolizes the relationship between a Leader and the members of his Organization. He Approaches them in an open-minded fashion, just as Earth accommodates the Water of the Lake. Team spirit and efficiency will be increased. At the same time, the impending Danger represented by the four Yin Lines must be guarded against.

LINES

Yang in First Place

A concerted

Approach.

Steadfast.

Auspicious,

Hoc bonum.

On the Image

Aspirations
Are set on True Conduct.

Yang Line in Yang Place. The first two Lines are both Yang. They act in concert, in unison. At the same time, Yang in First Place has Resonance with Yin in Fourth Place.

Yang in Second Place

A concerted

Approach.

Auspicious.

All things

Profit,

Nihil quod non conveniat.

On the Image

Not yet fully
In accord with orders.

Yang Line in Yin Place. This Line is Centered and Auspicious. But it is not True. One is not yet totally in accord with the "orders" of the day. Options need to be considered carefully and with an open mind.

Yin in Third Place

A complacent

Approach.

Nothing profits.

Remorse,

Tristitia.

No Harm,

Nullum malum.

On the Image

The Place is not Apt.
With remorse,
Harm cannot endure.

Yin Line in Yang Place. This is a weak and ignorant Approach, writes Zhu Xi. It focuses on externals and loses sight of internals. But Remorse can bring a change of Heart-and-Mind, and avert Harm. Urging Others to turn away from a complacent Approach is a profound teaching. This Approach arises out of total Ignorance, writes Magister Liu. It can only evolve from complacency to bitterness and sorrow. Humility (an Approach that rejects the False and holds fast to the True) can, however, save the situation. This, writes Professor Mun, is not a wise Approach. It is the wrong way for the Leader to interact with members of the Organization.

Yin in Fourth Place

A thorough

Approach.

No Harm,

Nullum malum.

On the Image

The Place is Apt.

Yin Line in Yin Place. This Yielding Line in a Yielding Place denotes thoroughness. This Approach, writes Magister Liu, is Yielding but stems from genuine Self-Cultivation, from Mastery of the Heart-and-Mind. The Resonance of this Line with Yang in First Place, writes Professor Mun, creates a Harmony in which the Leader is able to employ capable people.

Yin in Fifth Place

A wise

Approach,

As befits a Great Ruler.

Auspicious,

Hoc bonum.

On the Image

Centered Conduct
Befits a Great Ruler.

Yin Line in a Yang Place. Centered. This is authority that is not overly confident of itself, writes Legge, paraphrasing Zhu Xi, authority that is flexible and employs others judiciously. It is characteristic of the Wise Ruler. It is an Auspicious Tao. Wisdom consists in selecting the right people, writes Richard Wilhelm, and in allowing them to have a free hand without interference. The Taoist acts wisely, writes Magister Liu. The Great Ruler of the Heart-and-Mind is clear and at peace. The Light of Spirit shines within. The Other comes. I await it. Yang comes, Yin receives. It is the ability to move and to be at rest, the flexibility to be fast or slow, depending on circumstances. This involves both fast and slow. It means stopping when one reaches sufficiency. Primal Energy crystallizes out of Emptiness. Yin and Yang fuse into one. A wise Leader, writes Professor Mun, gives capable people the freedom to do their best.

Yin in Top Place

A simple

Approach.

Auspicious.

No Harm,

Nullum malum.

On the Image

Aspiration
Is on inner things,
Mens intus.

 Yin Line in Yin Place. This is a bighearted, honest, unselfish Approach. Here Action enters Non-Action, writes Magister Liu. The Taoist returns to simplicity and purity. Others and Self are both Empty. The original visage manifests itself totally. Beginning and ending are complete.

Guan

Observation

Xun/Wind

above

Kun/Earth

JUDGMENT

Ablution.

No Offering.

Good Faith.

Solemnity.

On the Judgment

Great Observation
From above.
Compliance
Beneath gentleness.

Centered and True,
Observation of
All-under-Heaven.
Observation
From below,
Transformation.
Contemplation of
The Mystic Tao of Heaven,
The unwavering course
Of the Four Seasons.
The Sage bases his teachings
On the Mystic Tao.
All-under-Heaven
Obeys.

On the Image of the Hexagram

Wind moves above Earth,
Ventus super terram.
The Ancient Kings
Inspected the regions,
Observing the Folk.
On this they based their teaching.

Wind above Earth. In the previous Hexagram, Approach, two Yang Lines made their way upward from the base, influencing the four Yin Lines above them, "dealing" with them, whereas here two Yang Lines at the Top above four Yin Lines provide a point (a platform) of Observation. The Hexagram itself has the visual structure of a tower for Observation, an Observatory, which is indeed one of the meanings of the Name, *Guan*. Great Observation (first words of the Commentary on the Judgment— *daguan*) is in that sense the Prospect that opens up before one's eyes, encompassing all, the entire World (All-under-Heaven), a vision that surveys the entire Universe. It is a way of seeing the World. It is the Larger View. This was the name given to the great park, Prospect Garden (Daguanyuan), adjoining the family mansion in the novel *The Story of the Stone*. The park's name symbolized the author's own vision, and the Aspirations of its idealistic young inhabitants. The Larger View stems from the Tao. The poet Jia Yi writes of this in his "Owl Rhapsody:"

Selfish
Is the man of little wisdom,
Scorning Others,
Esteeming Self.

The wise man's is
The Larger View.
For him all is possible. . . .
He lets things go,
Cleaves to the Tao. . . .
His life is a floating,
His death a rest.
Still as the Stillness
Of a deep ravine;
Drifting
Like an unmoored boat. . . .
Feeding and floating
On Emptiness. . . .

In this Hexagram, writes Legge, paraphrasing Cheng Yi, Wind sweeps above Earth. All things dance to its music. Nothing escapes its influence. The wise Ruler exercises a similar influence over his Folk. He is like the Wind, the Folk are like grass. Whichever way the wind blows, the grass bends. The Power (or *mana*) of the Ancient Kings was gained from their Contemplation of the Mystic Tao. Their teachings were adapted to the character and circumstances of the Folk. All-under-Heaven obeyed. The wisdom of the True Gentleman is equally derived from broad Perception and Self-Perception, from his "powers of Observation," or Awareness. JM: The poet Wang Yanshou, in his "Rhapsody on the Hall of Numinous Light," echoes this transformative influence of the Tao:

The Emperors of Old
Harmonized
With the Mystic Tao,
And there was peace.

"Ablution," the first word of the Judgment, writes Chen Guying, represents the deep inner meaning of Sacrifice. It represents Observation, Contemplation, and Self-Reflection at their purest. The physical Offering itself is of lesser significance. The Six Lines of this Hexagram treat different modes of Observation and Contemplation. Practicing the Tao of Cultivating Truth, writes Magister Liu, is like making an Offering to a Spirit. First Sincerity and Trust (Good Faith) should enter the Heart-and-Mind. Action will follow. The Spirit is bright and clear; it moves silently; it is swift but not hasty. It enters with Sincerity; it operates softly. Obstacles separating Yin from Yang are gone; the two connect. White light shines in an Empty Room. Spiritual Observation becomes Great Observation, the Larger View, a Black Pearl suspended in the Great Void, effulgent. Hills and rivers, the great Earth—all lies in the palm of the hand. Every step fuses with the Wondrous Tao. The Taoist understands the Dynamic of this Hexagram. He knows the flowing Advance of Wind, founded upon

Receptivity, upon the acute discernment of True and False that comes from Observation. This is the Tao of Awareness that comes from the Larger View, from the Spiritual View. Active Observation leads to the Larger View. Non-Action deepens the Spiritual View. Observation, writes Professor Mun, enables the Leader to find out (as from the top of a tower) what has been done right or wrong in an Organization in the past, so that he can make timely corrections. The Ablution symbolizes his cleanliness, his dignity and integrity as a Leader.

LINES

Yin in First Place

Youthful

Observation.

For a Small Man,

No Harm,

Nullum malum.

For a True Gentleman,

Distress.

On the Image

The Tao of the Small Man.

Yin Line in Yang Place. This naïve type of Observation, writes Legge, is superficial; it does not reach far. The Small Man, writes Chen Guying, sees things in a shallow way, in a False light. The True Gentleman aspires to see more deeply, to be more sensitive and aware in his Observation. This is the lowest form of Observation, writes Magister Liu, based in inflexible Folly, in the ignorant blindness of an obstinate child. A Leader, writes Professor Mun, needs a deeper and wider perspective, a more long-term vision.

Yin in Second Place

Observation

Through a crack in the door.

It Profits

A woman

To be Steadfast.

On the Image

Shameful Observation.

 Yin Line in Yin Place. Centered and True. A woman, living in retirement, writes Legge, paraphrasing Zhu Xi, peeps furtively through a crack in the door. This may be proper for a woman, but it is a small-minded and shameful way of proceeding for a man. This is short-sighted Observation, writes Magister Liu, the result of cultivating the Yin of Self and neglecting the Yang of Others, not daring to go outside (beyond the "crack in the door") and see the Larger View. This may help a woman to preserve her chastity. But it does not help a man to cultivate Inner Strength. "Woman," writes Professor Mun, here refers to character, not gender. A Leader should be strong and active, observing things in a direct Yang fashion, not in a soft, passive Yin manner.

Yin in Third Place

Observation

Of life.

Choice of

Advance

Or Retreat.

On the Image

He does not stray from the Tao.

 Yin Line in Yang Place. Life's actions have their effects and influences, writes Cheng Yi. Observe and Contemplate life and its actions. In light of that Observation, decide whether this is a time to Advance or Retreat. This may not be the ideal Place (Yin Line in a Yang Place), but it will surely not stray too far from the True Tao. A Leader, writes Professor Mun, needs to Observe the current situation objectively and carefully before making a future move.

Yin in Fourth Place

Observation

Of the Nation's Glory.

It Profits

To be the King's guest.

On the Image

An honored guest.

 Yin Line in Yin Place. A wise man understands how and why a Nation prospers, writes Richard Wilhelm. He understands its path to Glory. He deserves to be given a position of authority, one in which he can exert influence. He should be treated as an honored guest. A Nation's true Glory, writes Legge, lies in the Virtue of its Sovereign, and of his government. As Mencius said, "The True Gentleman does not desire broad territory and numerous subjects. What he truly delights in is to stand at the Center of the World, of All-under-Heaven, bringing tranquillity to the Folk of the Four Seas." Observation of the Nation's Glory, writes Magister Liu, draws one close to Men of the Tao (one becomes the "King's guest"). With their Larger View one's own lesser "powers of Observation" are amplified. A senior executive, writes Professor Mun, must Observe the vision, values, attitude, and behavior of his top Leader (the Nation is the King).

Yang in Fifth Place

Observation

Of life.

For the True Gentleman,

No Harm,

Nullum malum.

On the Image

Observation
Of subjects.

Yang Line in Yang Place. Centered and True. This, writes Chen Guying, is the True Gentleman (Fifth Place is the Place of the Ruler, of Authority), Observing his subjects. Only by so doing, by perceiving Others truthfully, can he see Self in a true light. JM: His is a strong Contemplation, embracing both Self and Others. It is the Larger View. Wind reaches the Centered and True (Yang in Fifth), writes Magister Liu. Firm and Yielding are well matched. The Elixir is only an instant away. But the Work of that final instant is hard to accomplish. Things can so easily come unstuck. The Leader, writes Professor Mun, must constantly review his own conduct.

Yang in Top Place

Observation

Of the Lives of Others.

For the True Gentleman,

No Harm,

Nullum malum.

On the Image

Aspirations
Are not yet settled.

Yang Line in Yin Place. Dissatisfied with the results of mere Self-Reflection, writes Chen Guying, the True Gentleman strengthens himself through objective Contemplation of Others and the external world. The Inner Child is already formed, writes Magister Liu. This is the fruit of Observation. The Larger View has become the Spiritual View. Once Yin Energy has completely withdrawn, and Yang Energy is pure and complete, then the True Person comes into view. The True Gentleman perfects the Work of Self-Cultivation. This is the Spiritual View of Non-Action.

HEXAGRAM XXI

Shi Ke

Biting

Li/Fire

above

Zhen/Quake

JUDGMENT

Fortune.

It Profits

To administer

Punishment.

On the Judgment

An object within the jaw.
Fortune.

Firm and Yielding Lines
Are well apportioned.
Movement combines
With Light.
Thunder and Lightning
Unite in Brilliance.
Yielding Lines in Center
Act upward.
Positions are not Apt.
It Profits
To administer punishment.

On the Image of the Hexagram

Thunder and Lightning,
Tonitrus et fulgur.
Former Kings
Imposed enlightened penalties;
They promulgated strict laws.

Fire over Quake. Yang Lines are in First and Last Place, while between them three Yin Lines surround a single Yang Line in Fourth Place. This can (by a slight stretch of the imagination) be visualized as an open mouth (the "jaw") with an "object" between the teeth, something which must be Bitten through if the mouth is to come together and close, and thus achieve Union. Remove obstacles to Union, writes Legge, summarizing Cheng Yi and Zhu Xi, and high and low will come together. And how are these obstacles to be removed? By decisive action, by clarity of mind, by strength, by Biting—that is, in the social context, through the use and application of legal constraints, through laws and penalties. The rule of law must be respected. A Weak Line is here in the Fifth Place of the Lord of Judgment. Judgment is thus tempered by leniency. There is a "well apportioned" (i.e., equal) number of Firm and Yielding Lines. Thunder/Quake and Lightning/Fire are in Union, they come together in a storm. The Lower Trigram (Quake) symbolizes Majesty, the Upper (Fire) Brilliance or Illumination. The Former Kings modeled themselves on these attributes in their penalties and laws. They were just and impartial, well informed and decisive, judicious and firm. For the individual, writes the Zen Master Zhixu, decisive action is the ordering of inner turmoil, the correction of bad mental habits, prejudices and delusions. Just as criminals may not accept the rule of law, writes Magister Liu, so some people have false ideas about achieving the Tao. They chew but cannot bite. They seek Long Life, but merely hasten the arrival of Death. Just as the Former Kings needed to create justice and impose enlightened laws, so Seekers of the Tao must base their quest on True Principle, on Action within understanding, on discriminating between True and False, not on empty, unreliable images and practices. This Hexagram, writes Professor Mun, emphasizes the importance of law and justice as a guide for conduct. The Quake is the sternness of the law, the Fire is the bright light of understanding. The Leader of an Organization must have strong determination and take decisive Action based on rational understanding. He must insist on the strict rule of law.

LINES

Yang in First Place

The feet are

Shackled.

The toes are

Destroyed.

No Harm,

Nullum malum.

On the Image

It is impossible to move.

Yang Line in Yang Place. Placing someone in shackles, writes Legge, paraphrasing Zhu Xi, is a relatively mild punishment (even though the "toes are destroyed"!). It is suitable for a small offense. It is an effective deterrent, before the crime has progressed far. The shackles, writes Magister Liu, are used to prevent a rash, premature move forward. In traveling the path of the Tao, True Principle must be understood from the very outset. This, writes Professor Mun, is a relatively mild punishment (his translation sees the toes "locked," not "destroyed"). The Leader takes a positive approach; he tries to educate.

Yin in Second Place

The flesh is

Bitten.

The nose is

Destroyed.

No Harm,

Nullum malum.

On the Image

This Rides a Firm Line.

Yin Line in Yin Place. Centered and True. If a hardened offender is to learn a lesson, writes Legge, paraphrasing Cheng Yi, it may be necessary to "Bite his flesh," to "Bite off his nose." Severity may be required. Pain may have to be inflicted. But it must be done fairly (Centered). This is a more severe measure, writes Professor Mun, to deal with an intractable person. The punishment can be strict, so long as it is balanced and correct.

Yin in Third Place

Preserved meat is

Bitten.

Poison is

Encountered.

Slight Distress,

Parvus poenitendi locus.

No Harm,

Nullum malum.

On the Image

The Position is not Apt.

Yin Line in Yang Place. Biting preserved flesh, writes Legge, one may encounter something distasteful and injurious. This may stem from poisoned arrows used to shoot game. The culprit does not submit, writes Richard Wilhelm, paraphrasing Zhu Xi. There is resentment and resistance. The issue is an old one. The ("preserved") meat is tough and spoiled. Punishment is required by the circumstances; if it is meted out fairly, no Harm is caused. Corruption is suspected on the part of an official, who is not in an Apt Position. Perception is slightly higher here than in the Second Line, writes Magister Liu. There has been some progress. But the Truth, the true flavor of the meat, the essence, has not been reached. There has been an error; there is still a serious weakness to overcome. A Leader, writes Professor Mun, in taking decisive Action may meet with resentment and resistance. A Yin Line is not Apt in this Yang Place. One must take care to be impartial and fair.

Yang in Fourth Place

Dried gristle is

Bitten.

A bronze arrow is

Found.

It Profits

To be Steadfast

In face of hardship.

Auspicious,

Hoc bonum.

On the Image

The Light
Does not yet shine.

Yang Line in Yin Place. There are great obstacles to be overcome, writes Richard Wilhelm, powerful and corrupt opponents to be punished. But the "arrow" has not been swallowed. JM: This is the opening Line of the Upper Trigram, *Li*, Fire, or Light. There is further progress, writes Magister Liu. This "dried gristle" is hard to get into. Truth is hard to penetrate, to perceive for what it is. The Work must be Steadfast through hardship. The "bronze arrow," writes Professor Mun, represents the Leader's strength, the Steadfastness of his principles.

Yin in Fifth Place

Dried meat is

Bitten.

Gold is

Found.

Steadfast.

Danger.

No Harm,

Nullum malum.

On the Image

That which is Apt
Is attained.

 Yin Line in Yang Place. Centered. Strive to be like gold, writes Richard Wilhelm, paraphrasing Cheng Yi, true as gold, impartial as yellow (color of the Center). The Work progresses still further, writes Magister Liu. What is clear is made clearer still, until no doubt remains. Gold is Illumination Centered. The Danger indicates the need for Caution. The gold, writes Professor Mun, is both Centered and Strong. The Leader is both tough and gentle; he combines the strength of the Yang Place with the softness of the Yin.

Yang in Top Place

The cangue is

Worn.

The ears are

Destroyed.

Calamity,

Hoc malum.

On the Image

He can hear
But is not enlightened.

Yang Line in Yin Place. The cangue, explains Legge, was the heavy wooden collar or pillory used as a standard punishment in China since ancient times. The same word, *jiao*, is used for foot shackles in the First Line, but here it is "worn" on the shoulders. Some commentators argue (rather unconvincingly) that the cangue referred to here was an excessive punishment, a heavier cangue than usual, damaging the criminal's ears, or making him "deaf to counsel." The Calamity has its Root in the ears, writes Magister Liu, in what one hears and fails to understand. Intelligence is misused; a lifetime is wasted in futile misunderstanding, in random study, placing trust in benighted teachers, failing to discriminate between True and False. What begins within you comes back to you. If the beginning is not clear, the ending will cause injury. The Work of genuine understanding requires the peeling away of layer upon layer, until one reaches the Marrow of the Tao, True Knowledge, Clear Perception. All depends on the considerable effort involved in the proper Work of Self-Cultivation. When a Leader, writes Professor Mun, does not listen to the advice of his colleagues (when he is deaf to their ideas), the result will be Calamity.

HEXAGRAM XXII

Bi

Adornment

Gen/Mountain

above

＇ *Li*/Fire

JUDGMENT

Fortune.

A Destination

Brings Slight Profit.

On the Judgment

Yielding comes,
Giving Pattern
To the Firm.
Firm above

Gives Pattern
To Yielding below.
This is the Slight Profit
Of Destination.
This interplay
Of Firm and Yielding
Is the Pattern
Of Nature.
Pattern and Light
Contained
Is the Pattern of Man.
Observe the Pattern of Nature
In the Changing Seasons.
Observe the Pattern of Man
In the Transformation
Of All-under-Heaven.

On the Image of the Hexagram

Fire beneath Mountain,
Ignis sub montem.
The True Gentleman
Illumines government;
He does not venture
To pass judgment.

Fire beneath Mountain. Fire, writes Legge, casts Light upward, Illuminating and Adorning the Mountain, place of Substance and Truth. *Bi* is Pattern, Adornment. As there is Adornment and Pattern in Nature, so should there be in man and society. But the role of Adornment is secondary to that of Substance. The various small matters of government, adds Legge, paraphrasing Cheng Yi, can be enhanced, graced, by Adornment. But great matters of judgment demand simple, unadorned Truth. JM: Compare *The Tao and the Power*:

Chapter 38
So the Great Man
Cleaves to the Thick,
Not the Thin.
He cleaves to Substance,
Not to Flower.

All beneath the Mountain, writes Magister Liu, is bathed in Light. The Stillness of the Mountain contains the Illumination of Fire. They enhance each other, like a lotus growing in the midst of a conflagration, like a boat being hauled through mud. One Spirit pervades all. Illumination and Stillness, and their interaction, lie at the heart of the Tao of Adornment. Any Organization, writes Professor Mun, needs Adornment for the purpose of establishing or improving its public image. But Adornment without Substance is like a flower which bears no fruit. There must be a balance between the two.

LINES

Yang in First Place

The feet are

Adorned.

The carriage is

Abandoned.

He walks.

On the Image

It is right not to ride.

Yang Line in Yang Place. Attend to Self-Cultivation. Adorn Self in a humble, self-effacing way. If need be, if righteousness requires, abandon every luxury and indulgence (such as the use of a "carriage"). Without these Adornments, one can still "walk" in the way of righteousness. In Adorning the feet, writes Magister Liu, one does not allow False Externals to injure Inner Truth. One is happy to "walk" on one's own two feet. A Leader, writes Professor Mun, is advised to Adorn himself in a plain way.

Yin in Second Place

The beard is an

Adornment.

On the Image

He rises
With those above.

Yin Line in Yin Place. Centered and True. Be roused to Action, writes Legge, by the strong Line above. A young ("bearded") man follows his superior in Third Place. The beard is an Adornment, writes Professor Mun, but it cannot exist without the Substance.

Yang in Third Place

Adorned!

Sleek!

Steadfastness

Is Auspicious

In perpetuity.

On the Image

Be Steadfast
To the very end.
None can hinder you.

 Yang Line in Yang Place. Do not be submerged in ease, writes Legge, paraphrasing Zhu Xi. Be Steadfast. It is not Adornment, but correct firmness, that will secure the respect of others. In the absence of Outward Adornment, writes Magister Liu, one can still have Inner Adornment. This is also an Auspicious Tao. This is the Adornment of Firmness and Illumination.

Yin in Fourth Place

Adornment!

Simple splendor!

A fine white horse!

No robber.

A suitor in marriage.

On the Image

The Position is Apt.
Misgivings.
No Regret.

Yin Line in Yin Place. The horse is splendid, writes Zhu Xi. It has no need of Adornment. It has a simple beauty of its own. True Heart-and-Mind, writes Magister Liu, genuine intention, come from a natural state of being, from Suchness (*ziran*), not from forced effort. They come like "suitors" in quest of marriage. This is Yielding Adornment, in search of Illumination. The fine white horse, writes Professor Mun, is Truth. The Leader should Adorn himself or his Organization with Simplicity and Truth.

Yin in Fifth Place

Adornment

In the park on the hill.

Silk in small bundles.

Distress.

Ultimately Auspicious.

On the Image

There is cause for Joy.

Yin Line in Yang Place. Centered. This Line, writes Legge, paraphrasing Zhu Xi, occupies the Yang Fifth Place of Honor and Authority, and yet it is a Yin Line. It prefers simplicity and economy to extravagance, a small gift to a large one. This transforms manners and customs. It affords occasion for Joy. JM: The "park on the hill" became in later times shorthand for a place of retirement. "The Great Man is off to his park on the hill," wrote the poet Xie Lingyun of an eminent statesman, "doffing his cap of office, and taking farewell of court" in order to retire "to the beach." On another occasion, Xie writes of his own Retreat to an idyllic country estate, to convalesce in the "park on the hill." The earlier poet and astronomer Zhang Heng, in his "Rhapsody on the Eastern Capital," writes of the Emperor luring Hermits from their Retreats:

From their park on the hill,
Offering them
Silk in small bundles.

The "park on the hill," writes Magister Liu, is an expansive space without people, far from worldly concerns. Its remoteness may initially be a cause of Distress for the Taoist. But its tranquillity is a source of Joy. Interestingly, Qiuyuan, "Park on the Hill," is the modern Chinese name for Kew (*qiu*) Gardens, the famous Royal Botanic Gardens in London, with their eighteenth-century Chinese pagoda.

Yang in Top Place

Plain

Adornment.

No Harm,

Nullum malum.

On the Image

The Top Line
Achieves its Aspirations.

 Yang Line in Yin Place. Adornment has run its course, writes Legge. Things return to the plain and pure. Substance is of greater importance than ornament. JM: Adornment must always be kept in a secondary place. *The Tao and the Power*:

> *Chapter 19*
> Display simple,
> Plain silk.
> Embrace the rough,
> The Uncarved Block.

Adornment without color, writes Magister Liu, is Plain Adornment. Illumination and Stillness are as one. Firm and Yielding are merged. This is the right time, writes Professor Mun, for the Leader to return to Simplicity.

Bo

Pulling Apart

Gen/Mountain

above

Kun/Earth

JUDGMENT

No Profit

In a Destination,

Nulla convenientia.

On the Judgment

The Yielding
Is transformed into the Firm.
Small Men prevail.
The Flow is

Halted.
The Image is
Observed.
The True Gentleman
Honors waxing and waning,
Fullness and Emptiness,
The Movement of Heaven,
Actio coeli.

On the Image of the Hexagram

Mountain rests upon Earth.
That which is above
Deals generously
With that which is below.
Peace comes to the dwelling.

Mountain above Earth. Five Yielding (Yin) Lines are below a single Firm (Yang) Line at the very Top. This is a largely negative Hexagram ("No Profit"), dealing with a situation of critical Danger. From First Place, decay sets in—an overthrow, a peeling away, a Pulling Apart. Yin Energy creeps its way steadily up to the Top. Small Men replace Great Men, until only a single one remains. He must wait. The Mountain, which should tower high above, is here "resting" on the Earth. Plainly it has been in some way stripped or overturned. The True Gentleman, writes Yu Fan, should "observe" the dynamic of the Image and learn from it. He must cultivate his Inner Strength and bide his time. He must be "generous" if he is to achieve a "peaceful dwelling." JM: The "bed" Pulled Apart, encountered frequently in the Line Statements of this Hexagram, suggests an "occupant" (Mountain) resting on a "bed" (Earth), a man and his foundation. The Mountain has its foundation in the Earth. The depth of the Earth supports the height of the Mountain. So too, writes Legge, paraphrasing Liu Mu, the Ruler has his foundation in the Folk. By treating them generously, he is able to rule over them peacefully. Yin Energy prevails, writes Magister Liu. Yang Energy, the single Yang Line in Top Place, is threatened. With time, Yin Energy continues to grow, Yang Energy to weaken. Collapse, a Pulling Apart, is imminent. The Taoist can reduce Yin and nurture Yang by successfully discriminating between True and False. He does not allow Negative Yin Energy to dissolve Yang Energy. He follows the Flow and checks the process of dissolution. He rids himself of cleverness; he returns to the Root, to the Primal. The government could collapse, writes Profesor Mun. It could fall apart at any moment, as the result of increasing popular discontent at inefficient administration and poor policies. This is a difficult time, a time of crisis. But if the Leader (Yang in Top Place) is a man of charisma, a man of open-minded tolerance and integrity, he will be able to draw the Folk to him of their own free will.

LINES

Yin in First Place

The bed is

Pulled Apart

By its feet.

It is

Destroyed.

Steadfastness.

Calamity,

Hoc pessimum.

On the Image

That which is below
Is destroyed.

 Yin Line in Yang Place. The first four Lines deal with a bed or couch, and by implication its occupant. The "bed" should probably be understood as a structure or framework affording rest and peace, a foundation underlying the situation. From early times Chinese beds were structured compartments. This structure is being destroyed, beginning at the feet. Yin Energy has gradually begun the process of Pulling Apart, writes Magister Liu. The situation is dangerous for the Leader, writes Professor Mun. He is like a man lying on a bed the feet of which have been destroyed. If capable executives in an Organization (the "feet") have resigned, senior management must discover the reasons for this and take steps to remedy it.

Yin in Second Place

The bed is

Pulled Apart

By its frame.

It is

Destroyed.

Steadfastness.

Calamity,

Hoc pessimum.

On the Image

There is no help forthcoming.

 Yin Line in Yin Place. Centered and True. The destruction gains in intensity, advancing to the frame itself. Yin Energy rises gradually, writes Magister Liu, struggling with Yang Energy. If people begin to criticize the structure ("frame") of an Organization, writes Professor Mun, the Leader should not obstinately ignore their views.

Yin in Third Place

It is

Pulled Apart.

No Harm,

Nullum malum.

On the Image

Upper and lower parts
Are dismantled.

 Yin Line in Yang Place. Despite the Inauspicious situation, writes Zhu Xi, it is still possible to keep a distance and be protected from the other four Yin Lines immediately above and below. Because of the Resonance between this Line and Yang in Top Place, writes Magister Liu, Yin Energy is relatively peaceful. It allows itself to be checked.

Yin in Fourth Place

The bed is

Pulled Apart.

The skin is

Attacked.

Calamity,

Hoc pessimum.

On the Image

Disaster looms.

Yin Line in Yang Place. Gradually, writes Cheng Yi, the assault progresses—from the feet of the bed, to the frame, to the skin of its occupant. Yin is reaching its height. Disaster is imminent. Yang is annihilated. The Tao of Steadfastness is destroyed. Yin Energy Pulls Apart in earnest, writes Magister Liu.

Yin in Fifth Place

Fish are

Strung together.

Palace ladies

Gain favor.

All things

Profit,

Nihil quod non conveniat.

On the Image

Ultimately no Harm.

Yin Line in Yang Place. Centered. Fish are things of a Yin Nature, writes Zhu Xi. Five of them are strung together—the Five Yin Lines. Palace Ladies are persons of Yin beauty; they submit to their Yang Lord in Top Place. This Yin in Fifth Place is their Leader. JM: Yin Energy has reached its culmination. But thanks to the presence of Yang in the next Line, the positive dynamic returns. This, writes Magister Liu, is True Yin, in the Center of the Upper Trigram, Mountain. One fish takes the lead. The Queen gains her King's favor at the head of the palace ladies. True Yin Energy here preserves True Yang Energy. Yin Energy flows with Yang. Pulling Apart is at an end. Yin in Fifth, writes Professor Mun, is the chief of the opposing forces within the

Organization. If the Leader (Top Yang) can get this dissenting chief to stand by his side, he will be out of danger.

Yang in Top Place

The great fruit is

Left uneaten.

The True Gentleman has

A carriage.

The Small Man's house is

Pulled Apart.

On the Image

The Folk
Are his carriage.
The Small Man
Is of no avail.

 Yang Line in Yin Place. The uneaten fruit is the hard kernel, the seed of new Yang life, writes Hu Bingwen. The True Gentleman has survived every attempt made against him, writes Legge, paraphrasing Cheng Yi. He has preserved himself in his integrity, and has accquired fresh vigor. The Folk are his "carriage" and support, they cherish their Sovereign. The plotters, the Small Men, have wrought their own downfall. They no longer prevail; they have dismantled and destroyed their own dwelling. They have "Pulled it Apart." Top Yang is the "uneaten fruit," writes Magister Liu. In its Center is a kernel. Preserve this kernel, and live. Lose it, and die. All depends on the kernel. The True Gentleman preserves it. He cannot be injured by Yin Energy. He uses Yin to perfect Yang. This is his "carriage." He travels in it serenely. Small Men follow their desires; they advance and do not know how to Retreat. They dissolve ("Pull Apart") their entire Yang and ultimately return to the Great Flux. They lose their shelter. Top Yang symbolizes the seed of good, writes Professor Mun. The "great fruit" falls to the ground, uneaten. Good things sprout forth again. The Leader regains the support of the members of his Organization. It is as if he has received a carriage to ride in.

Fu

Return

Kun/Earth

above

Zhen/Quake

JUDGMENT

Fortune.

There is no injury in

Going out or entering.

Friends come.

No Harm,

Nullum malum.

The Tao

Goes round;

It Returns

On the seventh day.

A Destination

Profits,

Convenientia.

On the Judgment

The Firm
Returns;
It moves with the Flow.
There is no injury
In coming or going.
Friends come.
No Harm.
Round and round
Goes the Tao.
This is the Movement of Heaven.
A Destination
Profits;
The Firm prevails.
Return manifests
The Heart-and-Mind
Of Heaven and Earth,
Mentem coeli et terrae.

On the Image of the Hexagram

Thunder within the Earth,
Tonitrus sub terra.
Former Kings
Closed the passes
At the solstice.
Merchants could not travel,
Nor Princes visit the regions.

Quake beneath Earth. The previous Hexagram showed inferior elements prevailing over superior. It showed Destruction, the good elements in Nature and society giving way before the bad. But Change is the law of the Universe. In this Hexagram (the inverse of Pulling Apart), one Firm Yang Line sits beneath five Yielding Yin Lines. The Yang Line is the First of the Lower Trigram, *Zhen*, Quake, Movement, while the three Yin Lines of the Upper Trigram, *Kun*, Earth, denote docility and capacity. This, writes Magister Liu, is the Return of Yang, of the sun which has set only to rise again, which has "gone out" only to "return" and "enter" once more. The Tao moves like this. It recurs in cycles. It moves round, backward, in reverse motion. It "returns" to the primal state of simplicity, to the Root. It revolves, according to the constant Transformations of Change. The Taoist turns away from the world. He Returns to Self, to basic Nature. See *The Tao and the Power*:

> *Chapter 28*
> Return to the state of infancy. . . .
> Return to the Limitless,
> To the Uncarved Block.

> *Chapter 40*
> Return
> Is the movement
> Of the Tao.

As decay reaches its climax, as Yin reaches its extreme, then recovery and renewal can begin to take place. This Return is itself a manifestation of the Heart-and-Mind of the Universe, the Heart-and-Mind of the Tao. The Strong Returning Line in First Place, writes Legge, meets with "no injury," no resistance. The Yin Lines yield before it. They are its "friends." These are the first steps of the Wanderer's Return, of the Return to Roots, to where one should be, a permeating theme in Chinese culture. See the Commentary for Hexagram VI/2. The poet Su Dongpo saw the "closing of the passes" figuratively as an Image of the Non-Action practiced by the True Gentleman. Once the "passes are closed," writes Magister Liu, the attention is more focused and strict. Distracting thoughts no longer arise within. Inimical influences no longer interfere from without. Yang Energy cannot leak or be dissipated. This Return of Yang, of the Pure Perfection of Yang Energy, is indeed a Pass of Life and Death. In a Buddhist perspective, writes Zen Master Zhixu, this Hexagram urges a "closing" of the Six Roots of the senses, the shedding of attachment, a halt to the "traveling" of the six virtues, a simple focus on the Heart-and-Mind of the present moment. All of this is a Return. Yang begins its Return in the cycle, writes Professor Mun. This Return is the initial stage of recovery after a period of stagnation. The Leader of an Organization must be able to anticipate these turning points of the cycle and adapt to them.

LINES

Yang in First Place

Return

From no great distance.

No Regret,

Non est poenitendi locus.

This is

Supremely Auspicious,

Magnum bonum.

On the Image

Cultivate Self.

 Yang Line in Yang Place. This Return is the Way of the True Gentleman, writes Legge, paraphrasing Zhu Xi. Having strayed only a short distance from the Tao, he can still find his way back to the True Path. This is the first stage of individual development, writes Richard Wilhelm, the beginning of Self-Knowledge. True Yang is not yet lost, writes Magister Liu. The Return takes place from no great distance. The Human Heart-and-Mind has not yet been perturbed. The Heart-and-Mind of the Tao is ever-present.

Yin in Second Place

Quiet

Return.

This is

Auspicious,

Hoc bonum.

On the Image

This is close to kindness,
To the humane.

Yin Line in Yin Place. Centered and True. This (in the Commentary on the Image) is a rare use of the Confucian term *ren*, humanity, loving-kindness, fellow feeling. For the quiet Return, compare *The Tao and the Power* (see also Hexagram VI/2):

Chapter 16
I contemplate the Myriad Things
As they Return.

The Return to the Root
Is Stillness,
Recognition of Life-Destiny.

This gentle Return is at the Center of the Lower Trigram, writes Zhu Xi. This is an Auspicious Tao. This Return is Yielding and Flowing, writes Magister Liu. It is the Return of the True Gentleman of the Tao. It borrows the wisdom of the Other to break open the ignorance of Self.

Yin in Third Place

Anxious

Return.

Danger.

No Harm,

Nullum malum.

On the Image

No Harm,
Thanks to righteousness,
Justitia.

 Yin Line in Yang Place. This is at the Top of the Lower Trigram, Quake, Movement, writes Zhu Xi. There is a certain dangerous restlessness and anxiety. But Caution can still enable a Return, and save the situation. This is a repeated Return, writes Magister Liu. With a firm resolve, and with diligence and application, the Return can be accomplished. The Leader, writes Professor Mun, lacks self-confidence and his emotions are unstable. If he changes course too often, he may lose direction altogether.

Yin in Fourth Place

He walks

In the Center.

Solitary

Return.

On the Image

He follows the Tao.

 Yin Line in Yin Place. Keep to the True Path, writes Magister Liu, to the Center. Do not be led astray by Others. This insight is learned; it is attained through practice. The executive, writes Professor Mun, walks alone on his own "middle way."

Yin in Fifth Place

Simple

Return.

No Regret,

Nullus poenitendi locus.

On the Image

Centered,
In medio,
Cultivating Self.

 Yin Line in Yang Place. Centered. This is an easy, spontaneous Return, accomplished with nobility of Spirit (*dun*). It is simple, genuine, honest, and generous. *Dun* describes an essential quality of the Tao. See *The Tao and the Power*:

> *Chapter 15*
> How simple
> Is the Tao,
> Like the Uncarved Block!

This Return, writes Magister Liu, takes place without deliberation, it reaches Center without striving. It comes from Self-Realization. This Return has been known from birth; it is accomplished with ease. For the Leader, writes Professor Mun, this simple Sincerity and Centered Equilibrium enable a Return to the right path.

Yin in Top Place

A Return

Goes astray.

Calamity.

Disaster and Misfortune,

Pessimum infortunium.

Deployment of the Army

Leads to a great defeat,

This is

Misfortune

For the Ruler of the nation.

After ten years,

It is still impossible to march.

On the Image

This is contrary
To the Tao of the Ruler.

Yin Line in Yin Place. This Yin Line at the very Top of the Upper Trigram, writes Zhu Xi, at the very end of Return, indicates that someone has gone seriously astray, is confused and deluded within. No Return is possible. Disaster is inescapable, writes Cheng Yi. Any use of force will simply make matters worse. The Human Heart-and-Mind is at work, writes Magister Liu. The Heart-and-Mind of the Tao is obscured. Outwardly such persons strive for Power, but inwardly they are grievously wounded in Heart-and-Mind. This stems from a failure to understand the True Nature of Return. A Leader, writes Professor Mun, stubbornly insists on going astray. Unless he realizes his True Direction, and Returns to the right path, he will fall into a deep abyss.

HEXAGRAM XXV

Wu Wang

Freedom from Guile

Qian/Heaven

above

Zhen/Quake

JUDGMENT

Supreme Fortune.

It Profits to be

Steadfast.

Absence of

Truth

Leads to

Disaster,

Infortunium.

No Destination

Profits,

Nulla convenientia.

On the Judgment

The Firm
Comes from without,
Is master within.
There is
Movement and Strength.
The Firm is Centered and Resonant.
Great Fortune
Stems from Truth;
This is Life-Destiny,
Decree of Heaven.
Absence of Truth
Brings Disaster.
No Destination Profits.
Without Freedom from Guile,
There can be no Destination.
Without succor of Life-Destiny,
Of Heaven's Decree,
Nothing can be achieved.

On the Image of the Hexagram

Thunder moves beneath Heaven,
Tonitrus sub coelo.
The Former Kings
Were in full accord
With Time,
With the Seasons.
They nurtured the Myriad Things.

禿 Heaven above Quake. The stirring of Primal Energy and Movement in Quake, the Lower Trigram, writes Zhu Xi, joins with Strength in Heaven, the Upper Trigram. The Yin Second Line Resonates with the Yang Fifth Line. But the outcome depends on an underlying Freedom from Guile, on an Innocence resulting from true and unpremeditated simplicity and spontaneity (Suchness, *ziran*). Freedom from Guile, writes Richard Wilhelm, is attained by devotion to Innate Spirit, by cultivating Inner Power, by examining Self deeply and casting aside all wrong thoughts. One does what is right with instinctive sureness and without any ulterior thought of reward or personal advantage. This is what the Former Kings achieved, this Harmony with Life-Destiny, with the Decree of Heaven. *The Tao and the Power* calls this the Return:

Chapter 16
Return to Life-Destiny,
Heaven's Decree,
Is knowledge of Constancy;
Knowledge of Constancy
Is Enlightenment.

Without this Innocent Return, Misfortune is inevitable:

Ignorance of Constancy
Is Guile and Disaster.

In this Hexagram, writes Magister Liu, Movement is within, in the Lower Trigram. Aspiration is set on the Tao. This is the Return of Primal Energy. Strength is in the Upper Trigram, Heaven. The Myriad Things are stirred to Movement. The Tao of Sincerity, of Innocence, causes each and every thing to be True to its Nature, to its Life-Destiny, to Return to a state of Freedom from Guile. Each thing contains its own Truth. Each thing Returns to Freedom from Guile. Heaven and Earth are free. The Former Kings were free. The Tao of Self-Cultivation sets free. The Tao of Freedom from Guile is to be utterly in Accordance with the moment in Time. To attain this Tao it is imperative to seek out the personal teaching of a True Master. Action should follow the law of Nature, writes Professor Mun, the Truth and Innocence of Nature, not personal Will. A Leader should not throw his weight around; he should not behave like a tyrant, or make a display of his bravery. He should not indulge in moments of pleasure or act insincerely. He should be able to listen to the suggestions of others.

LINES

Yang in First Place

Freedom from Guile.

It is Auspicious

To set forth,

Hoc bonum.

On the Image

Setting forth
Realizes Aspiration.

Yang Line in Yang Place. This Yang Line brings with it assurance of success, writes Richard Wilhelm. Aspirations are realized, with intuitive certainty, with the Innocence of a child. If one's thoughts are True, writes Magister Liu, one's Actions will be True. With Innocence and Freedom from Guile within, there will be Freedom without. With Cultivation of the Tao, one is sure to set out on an Auspicious path. A Leader with Integrity and Sincerity, writes Professor Mun, will receive support from within his Organization, and from other institutions.

Yin in Second Place

Harvesting

Without having

Ploughed,

Cultivating

Without having

Broken new ground.

A Destination

Profits,

Est convenientia.

On the Image

Not yet wealthy.

Yin Line in Yin Place. Centered and True. Unexpected Good Fortune comes to the Innocent, write Legge and Wilhelm. One does what one does because it is right, for its own sake, not as the result of some calculation, not for the Profit it will bring. This Line is flexible but lacks Strength, writes Magister Liu. Stillness is advised, not Action. Ploughing and breaking ground require Strength; they require the sowing of seed. Expectation of Profit for no expenditure of effort is unrealistic, writes Professor Mun. One reaps what one sows.

Yin in Third Place

Calamity.

Freedom from Guile.

The ox

Is tied.

A traveler gets it.

Calamity

For local Folk.

On the Image

A traveler
Gets the ox.
For local Folk,
Calamity.

 Yin Line in Yang Place. Calamity may sometimes befall the Innocent, writes Legge. To have great plans but little wisdom, writes Magister Liu, can only bring Harm. This is to be tied rigidly, like an ox, to the artifice of Heart-and-Mind. This is to follow desire, albeit in guileless ignorance.

Yang in Fourth Place

Steadfastness

Is possible.

No Harm,

Nullum malum.

On the Image

Hold fast.

Yang Line in Yin Place. Remain true to your Nature, writes Richard Wilhelm. Do not be led astray by others. Await the time for Movement in Tranquillity, writes Magister Liu. Nurture Yang with Yin. This is a Freedom from Guile that is both Firm and Yielding. If a Leader is True (sincere and fair), writes Professor Mun, he will succeed. But there is an obstruction (Yang in Fifth Place), and he should not move forward at this time.

Yang in Fifth Place

A person

Free from Guile

Falls sick.

He takes no medicine.

Joy.

On the Image

Put medicine aside.

Yang Line in Yang Place. Centered and True. Let Nature take its course, writes Richard Wilhelm. JM: The poet Xie Tiao wrote in reply to a sick friend:

> To take no medicine
> Is a Joy
> Whose fragrance never passes,
> Whose pure taste
> Lingers. . . .

He and his friend were toying with the idea of withdrawing from official life. Just as "non-medication" gives the body a chance to restore its natural balance of Yin and Yang, so retiring from the world (rejecting its "medicine") and becoming a Recluse is a Joy which offers a chance to regain the spiritual balance that has been disturbed by worldly preoccupations. Absolute Sincerity, writes Magister Liu, brings a Return to Innocence, to Freedom from Guile. The Inner Child (the Alchemical Embryo) has been formed. There is no underlying sickness. The condition is caused by Yin Energy that has not yet been transformed. A Leader, writes Professor Mun, should be extremely cautious in taking any Action to remedy an unexpected difficulty (just as an individual should refrain from taking medicine for an illness). He should allow Nature to take its course. The difficulty will then resolve itself of its own accord.

Yang in Top Place

Freedom from Guile.

Action brings

Calamity.

Nothing Profits,

Nihil quod conveniat.

On the Image

Calamity
Arises from exhaustion.

 Yang Line in Yin Place. Despite Freedom from Guile, write Legge and Wilhelm, despite Innocence, the present moment is not right for Action. Everything depends on timing. Be still. Do not initiate any fresh Movement. Calamity comes from not knowing when to stop, writes Magister Liu, from the too-insistent application of strength. Any reckless or excessive move, writes Professor Mun, will lead to Calamity.

Da Xu

Great Restraint

Gen/Mountain

above

Qian/Heaven

JUDGMENT

To be Steadfast

Profits.

It is Auspicious

To eat away from home,

Hoc bonum.

It Profits

To cross a Great Stream,

Transire magnum flumen.

On the Judgment

Firmness and Strength,
Substance and Brilliance.
Daily renewal
Of Inner Strength.
A Firm Line is in Top Place,
The worthy are honored,
Strength is contained.
This is Great Truth.
Not eating at home
Is Auspicious,
It nurtures the worthy.
Crossing the Stream
Resonates with Heaven.

On the Image of the Hexagram

Heaven within the Mountain,
Coelum in medio montis.
The True Gentleman,
With abundant knowledge
Of former words and deeds,
Holds all in Restraint.

Mountain over Heaven. This Hexagram, writes Legge, paraphrasing Cheng Yi, indicates Restraint and Accumulation, strength held in check, the Husbanding of the Creative Power of Nature. The bull and boar in the Fourth and Fifth Lines are beasts requiring "husbandry" (the literal meaning of the Name, *xu*). The "taming" or domestication of these animals is an Image of the Nurturing of Energy. Heaven (Nature) is of all things the greatest. It is being held "within," "contained," by the Restraint of the Mountain, which brings an abundant accumulation of Inner Strength. In a lyrical passage from his book *The Soul of China*, Richard Wilhelm describes a visit to the Buddhist Cave Temples of Yungang in the mountains of Shanxi Province:

> When I had waited for a while quietly and had, as it were, collected myself, the mountain seemed to open its eyes. One image after another stepped out of the night, became alive and began to talk. The large images

uttered deep powerful chords, the small and ever smaller ones resounded with a delicate melody, and eventually the room in the depth of the mountain was filled with a heavenly song of praise, which continued at a greater and greater distance more and more delicately right up to the greatest heights. When I had passed through this inner experience of an inaudible heavenly music, I understood why in the old legends they speak so often of Cave Heavens. . . . I also realized why among the signs of the *I Ching*, in Great Restraint, Heaven within the Mountain, it says "The True Gentleman, with abundant knowledge of former words and deeds, holds all in Restraint." . . . Here in Yungang the stone exhales not only life, but a soul. Hundreds and thousands of human figures and faces, each one of which has a soul, join in harmony in the song of eternity.

The "former words and deeds," writes Magister Liu, are those of the Ancient Sages. By studying these one accumulates Inner Strength, one nurtures the Inner Child, the Alchemical Embryo. This Energy must be "husbanded." To "eat away from home" is not to remove oneself from the world, not to take refuge in solitude, but to face the world, perhaps even to serve at court, to combine Inner and Outer Strength. Then one can cross the Stream and become the companion of ("Resonate with") Heaven. The Strength of Heaven, writes Professor Mun, held within the Mountain, will be released when the time is ripe. The Leader's resources accumulate: his knowledge, experience, friends, special abilities. The Negative Energy of the two Yin Lines is here under the control of the four Yang Lines.

LINES

Yang in First Place

Danger,

Periculum.

It Profits

To desist.

On the Image

Desist.
Do not invite
Disaster.

Yang Line in Yang Place. This Line Resonates with Yin in Fourth Place. Be composed in the early, fragile stages, writes Richard Wilhelm. Wait for an opportunity to release Inner Strength, to let go the Restraint. In the early stages of Great Restraint, writes Magister Liu, any hasty progress is ill-advised. Nurture Inner Strength. The Leader should halt operations, writes Professor Mun, and wait calmly for the appropriate time. He is not yet strong enough to move ahead.

Yang in Second Place

The axle is removed

From the carriage.

On the Image

In the Center
There is
No Harm,
Nullum malum.

Yang Line in Yin Place. Centered. This is a deliberate prevention of Movement in order to nurture Inner Strength. The Taoist must halt the Work, writes Magister Liu, bring the wheels of the "carriage" to a stop, check any onward progress that would cause Harm to Primal Energy. There is a breakdown in relationships, writes Professor Mun. The situation is out of balance. The Leader should call a halt.

Yang in Third Place

A fine horse

Goes in pursuit.

It Profits

To be Steadfast

In hard times.

Daily practice

Of charioteering

And self-defense

Profits.

A Destination

Profits,

Est convenientia.

On the Image

This shares
Aspiration
With Yang in Top Place.

 Yang Line in Yang Place. A forward impetus is waiting to be unleashed. The times are hard. Caution and Steadfastness, single-minded application and preparation are necessary. It is essential, writes Magister Liu, to guard against Danger from the remaining Yin Energy (in Fourth and Fifth Places). A Leader must be strong and decisive, writes Professor Mun, but must also be alert to the obstacle in his path (the Mountain).

Yin in Fourth Place

The horn-guard

Of a young bull is

Supremely Auspicious,

Summum bonum.

On the Image

It is
Cause for joy,
Gaudium.

 Yin Line in Yin Place. The wooden horn-guard attached to the sprouting horns of a young bull prevents him from goring. It forestalls the eruption of force. It tempers Yang with Yin. The young horns, writes Magister Liu, must be protected and nurtured. Primal Energy must not be allowed to dissipate. It must be made firm and strong.

Yin in Fifth Place

The tusks

Of a gelded boar are

Auspicious,

Hoc bonum.

On the Image

This is cause for
Celebration,
Felicitas.

Yin Line in Yang Place. Centered. The gelding of the aggressive boar renders him harmless. The boar is soft, writes Magister Liu, but his tusks are firm (Yin in Yang). Firmness is nurtured by the Yielding softness, by the merging of Yin and Yang. A Leader is in a dangerous situation, writes Professor Mun. He should use an indirect approach to "remove the sting." Gelding tames the boar's aggressive instincts.

Yang in Top Place

The broad highway

Of Heaven,

Via coeli.

Fortune.

On the Image

The grand working
Of the Tao.

Yang Line in Yin Place. The Way is now clear to roam freely in Heaven, writes Zhu Xi. The poet Wang Yanshou, in his "Rhapsody on the Hall of Numinous Brilliance," quotes this Auspicious Line Statement:

The Emperors of Old
Trod the broad highway
Of Heaven;
They enjoyed
Great Fortune.

The Work is complete, writes Magister Liu. With a peal of Thunder the True Man emerges, becomes manifest. The Taoist attains Truth, a body beyond the body, beyond

Heaven and Earth, Completing Self and helping Others to Completion. Great Restraint nurtures Strength. This is a Return to Transformation of the Spirit. Nothing can hold the Leader back now, writes Professor Mun. The resources he has kept in reserve, under his control (Restraint), can be used at last.

Yi

Nourishment

Gen/Mountain

above

Zhen/Quake

JUDGMENT

To be Steadfast

Is Auspicious,

Hoc bonum.

Contemplate

Nourishment,

The quest

To fill the mouth.

On the Judgment

True Nourishment
Is Auspicious.
Contemplate
Nourishment of Self,
Nourishment of Others.
Heaven and Earth
Nourish the Myriad Things.
The Sages
Nourish the worthy;
They Nourish
The Myriad Folk.

On the Image of the Hexagram

Thunder beneath the Mountain,
Sub monte tonitrus.
The True Gentleman
Is circumspect in speech;
He is moderate
In eating and drinking.

Mountain above Quake. The shape of this Hexagram, two outer Yang Lines enclosing four Yin Lines, suggests a mouth (First Line the lower jaw, Top Line the upper jaw, four Inner Lines the cavity). In eating, the upper jaw, like the Trigram Mountain, stays Still, while the lower jaw Moves, like the Trigram Quake. The Hexagram, writes Legge, is concerned with True Nourishment of body and mind, with physical nutrition *and* Spiritual Nutrition, with Self-Fulfillment, Self-Cultivation. *Mencius* 6.1.14: "He that Nourishes nought but the little that is his is a Small Man; he that Cultivates the higher parts of his Nature is a True Gentleman." Throughout the Hexagram, True Nourishment is contrasted with False, with the many ways in which it is possible to stray from the path of Self-Cultivation. JM: This is to be compared with the other "oral" Hexagram, XXI, about biting and decision. The Manchu empress dowager Cixi, when she rebuilt the Peking Summer Palace in the late nineteenth century, named it Yiheyuan, the Garden for the Nourishment of Harmony. Each Line of this Hexagram, writes Magister Liu, treats of True and False Nourishment. Speech is the voice of the Heart-and-Mind. Words uttered should be weighed with care. Food and drink are essential for the body. They should be consumed only after careful scrutiny of their source—and never in excess, always in moderation. If words are circumspect, then the Heart-and-Mind receives Nourishment. When food and drink are consumed in moderation, then the body receives Nourishment. A Leader, writes Professor Mun, should know how to Nourish Self through Self-Development. He should also know how to Nourish Others. In this way, Nourishment will Profit both himself and the Organization.

LINES

Yang in First Place

The Spirit Turtle

Is forsaken.

To contemplate

The open mouth of Others

Is Calamity,

Hoc pessimum.

On the Image

It is ignoble.

 Yang Line in Yang Place. The Turtle and the Spiritual Nourishment it offers, writes Legge, paraphrasing Cheng Yi and Zhu Xi, have been forsaken, and another, baser sort of Nourishment is eyed with envy. This, writes Magister Liu, is to abandon Inner Nourishment and seek External Nourishment, to forsake the True for the False. The Leader of a company, writes Professor Mun, has lost confidence in the well-established policy that has made the company successful in the past (the company's compass, or "Spirit Turtle"). His unstable character and irresolution cause him to envy the success of others, and to lead the company in a dangerous direction.

Yin in Second Place

Nourishment

Is sought.

This is a turning

Away from the path,

And toward the hill.

An Advance

Brings Misfortune,

Hoc pessimum.

On the Image

An Advance
Away from the True Path.

Yin Line in Yin Place. Centered and True. False Nourishment is sought, writes Richard Wilhelm, paraphrasing Zhu Xi, up on "the hill," in begging from others, from superiors (Yang in the First and Top Lines), straying from the True Path of Self-Cultivation, "turning away" from one's True Nature. This is a perverse form of Nourishment, writes Magister Liu. It is based on sheer ignorance and self-conceit. The "hill," writes Professor Mun, refers to the two Yang Lines, in First and Top Places. A Leader should have more self-reliance and self-confidence. He should not need to look to Others to solve his problems.

Yin in Third Place

Nourishment

Fails.

To be Steadfast

Brings Misfortune.

For ten years,

Do not act.

Nothing Profits,

Nihil est quod conveniat.

On the Image

The Tao
Is greatly transgressed.

Yin Line in Yang Place. This is False Nourishment, "feeding" on pleasure and sensual gratification, writes Richard Wilhelm. It is folly. It brings no fulfillment. This is the pursuit of desire, writes Magister Liu, the petty Nourishment of the senses, of the physical self. The Leader, writes Professor Mun, is seeking Nourishment from the wrong source.

Yin in Fourth Place

Nourishment

Is sought.

It is Auspicious,

Hoc bonum.

The Tiger's Eyes

Glare

With eager craving.

No Harm,

Nullum malum.

On the Image

Light spreads from above.

Yin Line in Yin Place. The Tiger's Eyes glare with an insistent desire for Nourishment. Light from a higher Place (from "above") Illumines the quest. This Line, writes Magister Liu, Resonates with First Yang. It seeks Nourishment from Others in a lowly Place, in order to break through the Darkness of Self. There is a Danger of arrogance and insincerity. The Heart-and-Mind must be concentrated and True, with a spontaneous Truth, like the "glaring eyes" of a Tiger. In this Line, writes Professor Mun, the senior executive seeks help from Yang in First Place, to help him through a difficult situation. He is as eager as a Tiger "glaring" at its prey.

Yin in Fifth Place

This is a turning

Away from the path.

To abide in Steadfastness

Is Auspicious,

Hoc bonum.

Do not cross a Great Stream,

Magnum fluvium.

On the Image

Follow the Flow,
Follow
The person above.

 Yin Line in Yang Place. Centered. One is too weak to provide Nourishment one-self, writes Richard Wilhelm, following Zhu Xi. One must rely on the strength of a "person above" (Yang in Top Place). Although one cannot nurture Substance, writes Magister Liu, one can be Steadfast in nurturing Emptiness. One should not undertake anything now in the Work of forming the Elixir, but rather abide in quiet and solitude. The Leader is weak (Yin in Yang), writes Professor Mun. He seeks the help of an able colleague (Yang in Top Place).

Yang in Top Place

Seek the Source

Of Nourishment.

Despite Danger,

This is Auspicious,

Periculosum,

Bonum.

It Profits

To cross a Great Stream,

Magnum fluvium.

On the Image

A great celebration.

Yang Line in Yin Place. True Nourishment is found at the source, in the Tao, writes Richard Wilhelm, following Zhu Xi. To Nourish Others is a grave responsibility, fraught with Danger. It justifies the taking of a bold initiative ("crossing a Great Stream"). Balance Inner and Outer Nourishment, writes Magister Liu. Nourish Others and Self. This is the True Tao of Nourishment.

Da Guo

Great Excess

Dui/Lake

above

Xun/Wind

JUDGMENT

The ridgepole

Sags.

A Destination

Profits.

Fortune.

On the Judgment

Great Excess.
The ridgepole
Sags.
Beginning and Ending
Are weak.
The Firm
Preponderates
In Center.
With gentleness of Wind,
With Joy of Lake,
Success is possible.

On the Image of the Hexagram

Lake submerges Wood.
Lacus lignum extinguit.
The True Gentleman
Stands alone,
Fearless.
He retires from the world,
Without Regret.

Lake above Wind and Wood. In its structure, this Hexagram mirrors Hexagram XXVII, Nourishment. Here two outer Yin Lines enclose four inner Yang Lines. (Compare also Hexagram LXII, Slight Excess.) This suggests a great beam (excessively great; it is too heavy in the middle) unable to support itself on its "props," weak at its "Beginning and Ending." These are extraordinary and testing times. There is an Excess of Yang Energy, writes Magister Liu. Things are out of kilter. The times are out of joint. At any moment, the ridgepole may break, and the whole house may come tumbling down. Isolation ("fearlessly standing alone") may be necessary, write Legge and Richard Wilhelm, in order to safeguard Integrity. The Trigrams, writes Magister Liu, the constructive juxtaposition of Wind and Wood, beneath Lake and Joy, mitigate the difficulty. Progress comes, not fiercely, but like a gentle breeze. It will be harmonious, slow, accomplished with moderation. Adapt to Change, guard against Danger, and success will still be possible. Even within Great Excess there can be a Tao of Moderation, of not going too far. This requires a skillful blending of Yin and Yang, a return to Center and Truth, a freedom from bias and partiality. If a Leader is too aggressive, writes Professor Mun, and undertakes expansion (Yang) in Excess of the resources available (Yin), he will find himself in trouble. By being too arrogant and impulsive, he alienates Others and isolates Self.

LINES

Yin in First Place

A white rush mat

Is spread below.

No Harm,

Nullum malum.

On the Image

The Yielding Line
Is below.

 Yin Line in Yang Place. Extraordinary Caution is needed. There is a need to be Yielding. This is an Excess of weakness, writes Magister Liu. As with a white rush mat spread on the ground, one must be very humble and cautious. This spreading of the rush mat below the Offering, writes Professor Mun, points to the careful preparation needed at the beginning of any new venture.

Yang in Second Place

A withered poplar

Puts forth shoots.

An old man

Takes a young wife.

All things

Profit,

Nihil non convenit.

On the Image

This is an
Extraordinary conjunction.

Yang Line in Yin Place. Centered. In the Lower Trigram, writes Legge, following Zhu Xi, the tree (Wood) growing by the Water's edge has been flooded by the Lake. New shoots sprout from below. They renew the life process, just as, in these extraordinary times, an old man can still succeed in siring offspring. Yin and Yang are matched, writes Magister Liu. The life force is still active. The Yielding quality of the Place prevents this Firm Line from going to Excess. If a declining company, with old-fashioned management and obsolete technology (the "old man"), can merge with a young, dynamic, technologically advanced company (the "young wife"), writes Professor Mun, this merger of Yin and Yang will bring Harmony and Profit.

Yang in Third Place

The ridgepole

Sags.

Calamity,

Hoc malum.

On the Image

Support
Is lacking.

Yang in Yang Place. Unequal to the heavy burden, without support, the structure sags. This is Excessive strength, writes Magister Liu. A stubborn, arrogant Leader, writes Professor Mun, insists on going his own way and plunges blindly ahead. He will isolate himself and collapse in due course.

Yang in Fourth Place

The ridgepole

Curves upward.

This is

Auspicious,

Hoc bonum.

There is unexpected

Distress.

On the Image

It does not sag.

 Yang Line in Yin Place. The ridgepole is braced and equal to the task. The Heart-and-Mind is calm, the Energy harmonious. But strength must be tempered with the Yielding Caution seen in the First Line, with which this Line Resonates. Beware of possible Distress from an "unexpected" quarter. Any Excess will be harmful, writes Magister Liu. It will cause Distress.

Yang in Fifth Place

A withered poplar

Puts forth flowers.

An old woman

Takes a husband.

Neither Harm

Nor praise,

Nullum malum,

Nulla laus.

On the Image

The flowering cannot endure.
The marriage
Is a disgrace.

 Yang Line in Yang Place. Centered and True. The tree flowers, but bears no fruit. It will soon decay. This wanton woman, writes Magister Liu, is excessively pleased with herself. She will bear no children. She will be barren. Truth has been injured by Falsehood. Yin in Top Place is the old woman, writes Professor Mun. Yang in Fifth is her husband. In this case, the merger of a young company with an old company may not meet the needs of the former.

Yin in Top Place

A stream

Is forded.

A head

Is submerged.

Calamity,

Hoc malum.

No Harm,

Nullum malum.

On the Image

The fording
Causes no Harm.

 Yin Line in Yin Place. Pursuing a daring course of Action, writes Legge, without the necessary wisdom and judgment, one goes astray. Unequal to the task, one sinks beneath the water. But no irreparable Harm is done. This is the extremity of Excess, writes Magister Liu. This is reckless folly, and will bring Calamity. A Yin Line in this extreme Place, writes Professor Mun, indicates a weak and dangerous situation. But a Leader can get through it "without Harm" if he behaves sensibly.

Kan

The Abyss

Kan/Water

above

Kan/Water

JUDGMENT

Good Faith.

Fortune

In Heart-and-Mind.

Actions are honored.

On the Judgment

Double Peril.
Water flows,
It does not fill.
Peril is faced,

Faith kept.
Fortune
In Heart-and-Mind.
The Firm occupies Center.
Actions are honored,
Movement brings success.
The hazards of Heaven
Cannot be scaled.
The perils of Earth are
Mountains and rivers,
Hills and precipices.
Kings and Princes
Protect their Realm
With Peril.

On the Image of the Hexagram

Water flows,
In an uninterrupted current.
Aqua continuo veniens.
The True Gentleman acts
From constancy of Inner Strength.
He puts Strength into practice
In his teaching.

The Trigrams Expounded

Kan is Water;
Ditches and channels.
It moistens,
Toils.
It is peril.
Pig.
Second son.
North.
It lies in ambush;
Now straight, now crooked.
Bent bow,
Turning wheel;
Of men,
The melancholic,

An ailing Heart-and-Mind.
Earache.
Blood,
Red.
Of horses,
A strong back,
High spirits,
Hanging head on the move,
Tiny hooves,
Shambling gait.
Of chariots,
Much damaged.
Connection and success,
Moonlight.
Thief.
Of trees,
The hard and firm-hearted.

Abyss above Abyss, Water above Water. *Kan* is a dangerous Abyss, a gorge, and the torrent of Water flowing through it. This Hexagram, formed by doubling the Trigram of the same name, deals with Danger, how Danger is to be encountered, its effect on the Heart-and-Mind, and how to get out of the old habits and delusions in which Heart-and-Mind is trapped. The message is simple: Persevere. Practice Good Faith. Hold fast to the Yang Line in the Center of both Trigrams. Good Faith is the Heart-and-Mind of the Tao, writes Magister Liu. With Good Faith the Auspicious interaction between Yin and Yang can be emulated; the perilous, uninterrupted torrent of Water can be navigated through the Abyss. What is learned through practice, through Self-Development, can then be passed on to Others through teaching. Teaching without Inner Strength, without Good Faith, is worthless. Inner Strength is the only True Source of teaching. It makes Connections. It is the uninterrupted current, one and the same Water, passing from one place to another. It reaches everywhere. JM: In the Taoist sexual-alchemical scheme of things the *Kan* Trigram (one Yang line surrounded by two Yin, Yang within Yin) represents the Female element (Water, Kidneys, White Tiger, Earthly Anima), while the *Li* Trigram (one Yin line surrounded by two Yang, Yin within Yang) represents the Male element (Fire, Heart, Green Dragon, Celestial Animus). This is also true of the two Hexagrams (XXIX, XXX) formed by doubling the two Trigrams. Their Harmony (the Harmony of *Li* and *Kan*) is seen both in sexual intercourse and in advanced meditation practice, where the Inner Yin and Inner Yang of the individual fuse into one whole. (See the illustration of the Taoist Adept in the Introduction, page xix.) Its fruits can be seen in Hexagram LXIII, Complete, where *Li* "sits" under *Kan*. The "empty" center of male *Li* is True (i.e., truly fulfilled) Yin; Outer Yang enfolds Inner Yin. The "full" center of female *Kan* is True Yang; Outer Yin encloses Inner Yang. When *Kan* and *Li* enjoy intercourse, then True Yin is "garnered," it "supplements" True Yang. This produces Pure Essential Yang. This is the Return to

Primordial Undifferentiated Energy. "He puts Strength into practice in his teaching" inevitably brings to mind the opening words of the *Analects* of Confucius: "To learn and to put into practice at the right moment what one has learned—is this not Joy?" The word for "put into practice," *xi*, depicts, as Legge memorably puts it, "the rapid and frequent motion of the wings of a flying bird." A more recent etymology sees the lower part of the graph as "sun," hence "wings in a clear sky." This repeated realization of what has been learned through Self-Cultivation, this "becoming," has its source in Inner Strength and Truth. The poet Xie Lingyun uses the principal Image of this Hexagram (dangerous Water flowing through a Gorge) and that of Hexagram LII, *Gen* (Mountain) as shorthand emblems for his own life's journey. In his poem he sails up a mighty gorge, against the furious waters of the Zhe River:

> **The Island off Fuchun Town**
> Upstream we heave
> Against the raging torrent,
> The rocks keeping us
> Clear of the bank. . . .
> Here lie perils
> Worse than Lüliang Gorge.
> These Flowing Waters
> Teach the meaning of Danger;
> These Serried Mountains
> Teach me to sit
> Still.
> All my life
> I yearned to be a Hermit,
> But was too weak.
> I went astray. . . .
> Now at last I can embrace
> The Light of Innermost Self. . . .

The poet, as his translator John Frodsham comments, has learned from the torrent the lesson of the *Kan* Hexagram: not to shrink from Danger, to "face peril," not to lose his essential Nature, "while the Mountain, the *Gen* Hexagram, has taught him "to sit Still"—in other words, to restrict himself to his limits, to keep the Faith. Lüliang Gorge (a most perilous location) also appears in the *Book of the Taoist Master Lie*. Confucius (in Taoist stories usually a great figure of fun) sees a man swimming down in the swirling waters of the gorge. Thinking that he must surely be in some sort of Danger, and concerned that he may even be trying to put an end to his life, Confucius sends a disciple to the rescue. The man goes on swimming and eventually climbs casually out of the water, singing all the while, his wet hair streaming down his back. To the amazed Confucius he explains that he has no special skill as a swimmer: "I just plunge into the center of the whirlpool and let myself be carried to the bank on the outward movement of the current. I follow the Tao of the Water, rather than some course of my own." In other words, Confucius has completely missed the point! The Taoist swimmer *uses* the Gorge, he "protects his Realm with Peril." Angus Graham's perceptive comment on this chapter from *Master Lie* ("The Yellow Emperor") can be applied to the underlying philosophy of the *I Ching*: "One whose mind is a pure mirror of his situation, unaware of himself and therefore making no distinction between Profit and Danger, will act with absolute assurance, and nothing will stand in his way. . . . Outside things can obstruct and injure us only if we are assertive instead of adaptable. . . . Possession of the Tao is thus a capacity for dealing effortlessly with external things." A capable Leader, writes Professor Mun, prepares against Danger in a timely manner. Danger can sharpen the awareness of a Leader. It can be seen not as an obstruction but as an opportunity to improve the adaptability of the Organization. The poet Mu Hua, in his splendid "Ocean Rhapsody," takes the watery perils of *Kan* to their grandest limits (although the *I Ching* itself never mentions the sea):

What wonders
Does the Ocean not contain?
What marvels
Does it not have in store?
It is the boundless confluence
Of every stream.
It has form,
And yet remains
Empty within.
How vast is the Power of *Kan*!
And yet how lowly its abode.
How grandly it goes forth,
How grandly it takes in!
It is Ancestor,
It is Great Bastion.
Of all things, of all kinds,
What does it contain,
What does it not contain?

LINES

Yin in First Place

Double Abyss.

The Pit

Of the Abyss

Is entered.

Calamity,

Hoc pessimum.

On the Image

The Tao
Is lost.
Calamity.

Yin Line in Yang Place. Misguided efforts, writes Magister Liu, bad habits, repeated folly, drag one ever deeper into Danger. They drill a hole directly into the Pit. One digs oneself further and further into the Abyss.

Yang in Second Place

The Peril

Of the Abyss.

Small gains

Can be sought.

On the Image

One has not yet
Emerged
From the Center.

Yang Line in Yin Place. Centered. Escape from Peril is well nigh impossible. One has not yet emerged from the Pit. One must confine oneself to limited aims. Inner Strength in this Centered Line, writes Magister Liu, preserves the soul from the basest delusions. But the necessary Strength is lacking to see clearly what is good, to be able to Return to the Primal. (That would indeed be a "great" gain!) A step-by-step approach, writes Professor Mun, appears to be more sensible. Such small gains are the basis for larger gains.

Yin in Third Place

There is a

Coming and going.

Abyss

Upon Abyss.

There are

Perilous depths.

The Pit of the Abyss

Is entered.

Do not

Act,

Ne uteris.

On the Image

Ultimately
There can be
No success.

 Yin Line in Yang Place. Do not be drawn into dangerous Action. Do not go deeper into the Pit. Wait for a way out to present itself. Habits of Heart-and-Mind, writes Magister Liu, have become more and more deeply ingrained. This is the Pit of the Abyss. This is the Place of Peril. This is weakness, the inability to renounce habits. Here one is forever a man used by a thing. The Leader, writes Professor Mun, is advised to stay where he is, until conditions change in his favor. Otherwise he will fall into the Abyss.

Yin in Fourth Place

A jug of wine,

Two bowls of rice,

Simple fare

In earthenware vessels,

Offered

Through the window.

Ultimately

No Harm,

Nullum malum.

On the Image

The Firm meets
The Yielding.

Yin Line in Yin Place. At this critical time, Simplicity and Sincerity are urged, not ostentatious ceremony; a simple meal, not a banquet. The "vessels" (or means of communication) are simple and honest, writes Professor Mun, and the "window" through which they are "offered" is a space of openness and light, a clear understanding among executives in an Organization. The Hong Kong poet Leung Ping-kwan pleaded for this sort of "simple fare," for "earthenware vessels," in the summer of 1997, during the ceremonial handover of Hong Kong to the Beijing regime (with all its goose-stepping pomp and circumstance):

> Permit me to abstain
> From the rich banquet.
> Let me eat my simple fare,
> My gruel, wild vegetables,
> Let me cook them,
> Share them with you. . . .

This Yin Fourth Line "meets" the next Yang Line, looking to it for support, humbly offering homage "through the window." This expression is alluded to with ironic wit in the preface to the sixteenth-century pornographic novel *The Lord of Perfect Satisfaction*, as a humorous euphemism for the unorthodox "entry" into the Imperial Palace (a Pit of Danger if ever there was one) of Mr. Xue Aocao, a man endowed with a monumental penis (no humble offering, his). Xue had been summoned to court to please the insatiable Empress Wu Zetian. The *I Ching*, as well as being a Book of Wisdom, could also serve as a Commonplace Book of Mischief!

Yang in Fifth Place

The Abyss

Is not yet full.

It is level.

No Harm,

Nullum malum.

On the Image

The Center is not yet great.

 Yang Line in Yang Place. Centered and True. Deliverance is close at hand. When the Abyss fills with Water, the Danger of the torrent begins to vanish. Here Yang occupies True Center between two Yin Lines, writes Magister Liu. The Abyss is mastered. It is not full to overflowing, but level. Cautious waiting is nonetheless urged. This is only the first stage in breaking through delusion, writes Zen Master Zhixu. The wind may be calm, the waves still. But there are more delusions to be extinguished. The Leader, writes Professor Mun, should not be overly optimistic. There are Dangers ahead.

Yin in Top Place

He is bound

With three strands of cord;

He is caught

In a thicket of thorns.

For three years

There is no success.

Misfortune,

Hoc pessimum.

On the Image

The Tao is lost.

Yin Line in Yin Place. One is deeply entangled in the deepest Pit of the Abyss, obstinately caught up in old habits, bound tight in the "cords" of the world and its troubles. One has "lost" the means to escape from Peril. This thicket of thorns, these cords, writes Magister Liu, are the bad habits of Heart-and-Mind, Vanity and Self-Destruction, the dwelling in Danger's way, the Peril of the Soul. All this will pass in due course. It will be seen to have been nothing but Folly upon Folly. A Leader who has misjudged his direction, writes Professor Mun, now has to pay the price. He has fallen into a deep Pit.

HEXAGRAM XXX

Li

Fire

Li/Fire

above

Li/Fire

JUDGMENT

To be Steadfast

Profits.

Fortune.

A cow is reared.

This is

Auspicious,

Hoc bonum.

On the Judgment

Sun and Moon
Are attached to Heaven.
The Hundred Grains,
The grasses and trees,
Are attached to Earth,
To the soil.
Double Brightness
Is attached to Truth,
Truth
Which transforms and perfects
All-under-Heaven.
The Yielding
Is attached to Center,
To Truth.
Fortune.

On the Image of the Hexagram

Double Brightness,
Duae claritates.
The Great Man
Illumines the Four Quarters
With Continuous Clarity.

The Trigrams Expounded

Li is Fire,
Sun.
It warms,
Makes manifest;
It brightens.
It is South.
Li clings,
Is attached.
It is pheasant,
Eyes,
Second daughter.
It is lightning,

Armor and helmet,

Spear and sword.

Of men,

It is the big-bellied.

It is dry.

It is turtles,

Crabs,

Snails,

Mussels.

Of trees,

It is the hollow,

Rotten at the top.

芚 Fire above Fire. This Hexagram is formed by doubling the *Li* Trigram: Fire, Light, and Sun: also warmth, radiance, and clarity; Outer and Inner Illumination; and Attachment. Inner Illumination, writes Magister Liu, produces Outer Illumination. What is Illumination? It is the ability to see "with continuous clarity" the original Strength or Essence of things. This Vision itself comes from Inner Strength, from Sincerity at the Center of Being, reaching out and connecting with the outside, with "the Four Quarters." Nothing can deceive it. It sees things as they are. It sees that everything, everywhere, to left and right, is the Tao, Connected, Attached. Illumination itself spreads like Fire. It is a chain reaction. Fire is not a substance, it is an event, an interaction. As Professor Mun writes, Fire has no form, it is *given* form by the burning object to which it is "attached." Hence the common interpretation of this Hexagram as Attachment. Fire and Light are "attached to," they rely on, other things. The flame that burns is "attached to" its fuel, to the wood that nourishes it. Fuel generates Radiance. This Synergy, this En-Lightenment, or Illumination, is fed by the Inner Source, or Fuel, of Truth. The Yin Central Line is "attached to" the two Firm Lines on either side of it. This male Trigram (so it is classified) has Yang on its outside, Yin on its inside: Internal Yin within External Yang. The two are interdependent. The Yin in the Center is soft and docile (it is compared to a "cow"); it is gentle understanding and acceptance ("rearing"). In the sexual-alchemical scheme, the combinations of *Li* and *Kan* (the component Trigrams in this and the previous Hexagram) create Hexagrams LXIII and LXIV. Their interaction, to use Joseph Needham's words, extracts "vital" Yang from "seeming" Yin, and "vital" Yin from "seeming" Yang. It ultimately forms the Inner Child, the Primal Unity. Through this process of Transformation, "although belonging to Yin, the woman's body *becomes* male; the Man, though originally Yang, *becomes* female. . . . I am fundamentally Yang, but contain within me the height of Yin; she is fundamentally Yin, but conceals within her the most marvellous True Essence of Yang." The Upper Trigram is the Light of Understanding (Illumination) by which one knows Others, writes Professor Mun. By the Light in the Lower Trigram one comes to know Self, to know one's own strengths and weaknesses. This "continuous clarity," or Illumination (*ming*), was well expressed in *The Tao and the Power*:

Chapter 33
To know Others
Is to be
Wise;
To know Self
Is to be
Illumined.

See also *The Art of War*, chapter 3, "Strategic Offensive":

Know the enemy,
Know yourself,
And victory
Is never in doubt,
Not in a hundred battles.

LINES

Yang in First Place

Tread with care,

With respect.

No Harm,

Nullum malum.

On the Image

With care and respect
Harm is avoided.

历 Yang Line in Yang Place. A humble, gradual approach is commended at the outset of any undertaking, including the quest for Illumination. Illumination, writes Magister Liu, must be nurtured from within. Yang in Yang Place, writes Professor Mun, implies a rash impulse. The Leader should take all risk factors carefully into consideration before taking the first step. Then he will make no mistakes.

Yin in Second Place

Yellow

Fire.

This is

Supremely Auspicious,

Magnum bonum.

On the Image

The Tao of Center
Is reached.

 Yin Line in Yin Place. Centered and True. Yellow is the color of Center, of Harmony and Moderation. The Fire is the Light of Illumination. To reach Center, writes Magister Liu, signifies a humble recognition of one's own lack of Illumination. It means having an "empty" Heart-and-Mind, one that is open to the Illumination of Others. The Leader, writes Professor Mun, is advised not to go to extremes.

Yang in Third Place

Fire

Of the setting sun.

No singing,

No beating

Of earthen pot.

Nought but groans

Of the infirm.

Calamity,

Hoc pessimum.

On the Image

The setting sun
Cannot endure.

Yang Line in Yang Place. This Yang Third Line, writes Legge, sits at the top of the Lower Trigram. The sun is setting. Its Light is exhausted. Regret for the past is futile. It will only lead to further unhappiness. Do not groan. Accept the situation with humble contentment and resignation. Sing and play music (the "pot" was probably a drum of some sort). JM: The Ming-dynasty poet Gao Qi entitled one of his collections *The Earthen Pot Resounds*. His biographer F. W. Mote observes that he may have been alluding to this *I Ching* phrase: "As time passes and the transitoriness of this life comes home, enjoy simple pleasure rather than fruitlessly bewailing fate." Professor Mun echoes this. The sun sets. Life approaches its end. A man's life has an end. This is the Law of Nature. If a man can accept this fact, he will not lament in his old age, but will sing and beat his pot in the light of the setting sun. In an Organization, in desperate times, the Leader must nonetheless encourage his employees; he must maintain enthusiasm and morale.

Yang in Fourth Place

Of a sudden

It flares,

It dies,

It is abandoned.

On the Image

None can abide it!

Yang Line in Yin Place. The Light flares fiercely, writes Richard Wilhelm, like a meteor, like a straw Fire. It is consumed rapidly, it burns out, it has no lasting effect. JM: This is False Illumination, a blaze without Inner Light. The feverish quest for Long Life merely causes injury. This executive, writes Professor Mun, is hot-tempered, like a blazing fire. He forces others to follow him, and blames them if their performance cannot meet his standards. People will eventually abandon him. He burns himself out.

Yin in Fifth Place

There is

Weeping,

There are

Torrents of tears.

Sighing and lamentation.

This is

Auspicious,

Hoc bonum.

On the Image

An Auspicious Line,
Prince of the Hexagram.

 Yin Line in Yang Place. Centered. Genuine sadness and lamentation, writes Richard Wilhelm, are Auspicious proof of Inward Truth and Humility. They are a prelude to Joy. This Leader with Yin characteristics, writes Professor Mun, shows concern and makes the necessary preparations.

Yang in Top Place

The King

Goes to war.

There is

A celebration.

Heads are cut off,

Troops are captured.

No Harm,

Nullum malum.

On the Image

The King brings the regions to order.

Yang Line in Yin Place. A military expedition is conducted with measured severity. The Inner Heart-and-Mind of Truth, writes Magister Liu, the Heart-and-Mind of the Tao, shines brightly, with confidence. This is the "King going to war." Illumination is a campaign. Its mission is to Illumine and make visible the Inner Strength of things. The principal "enemy," the root of the problem, is the Human Heart-and-Mind, the Mundane Mind. Once this "enemy" is captured, and decapitated, then there will be serenity, calm, emotion no sooner felt than connected, Inner and Outer Illumination, and not a speck of Harm! This is the Perfect Illumination, the Best Illumination. The Leader needs strength, writes Professor Mun, if he is to get rid of the weaknesses in the Organization.

Xian

Resonance

Dui/Lake

above

Gen/Mountain

JUDGMENT

Fortune.

To be Steadfast

Profits.

It is Auspicious

To take a wife,

Hoc bonum.

On the Judgment

The Yielding is above,
The Firm below.
Two Energies
Resonate,
They
Connect.
The Mountain calms
The Joy of Lake.
Man is beneath woman.
Heaven and Earth
Resonate,
The Myriad Things
Are transformed,
They are born.
The Sage
Resonates
With the Hearts-and-Minds of men.
The World is at peace.
Observe the Resonance,
The Nature of Heaven and Earth
Made palpable,
The Nature of the Myriad Things,
Rerum omnium naturam.

On the Image of the Hexagram

Lake on Mountain,
Supra montem lacus.
The True Gentleman
Receives others
With Humility.

The Trigrams Expounded

Energies of Mountain and Lake
Connect.

茘 Lake above Mountain. Lake is essentially Yin, a Yielding Trigram; Mountain is Yang and Firm. The Yin Waters of the Lake sit calmly on the Yang Mountain. The Hexagram Name, *Xian*, itself has as one of its original meanings "all," "universal." With the addition of the Heart element, it comes to mean "feeling," "mutual attraction," pronounced *gan* in modern Chinese. (The Ancient Chinese pronunciations were far closer.) *Ganying*, Attraction and Response, thus Resonance or Correspondence, is the way in which things throughout the Universe "connect" (by such qualities as their Yin/Yang polarity). This is a fundamental concept in the *I Ching* commentaries. It is close to what Carl Jung called "synchronicity," the "interdependence of objectives among themselves as well as with the subjective [psychic] states of the observer or observers." The witty fifth-century gallery of miniatures, Liu Yiqing's *New Tales of the World*, tells how a Mr. Yin once asked a monk what was the substance, the most fundamental idea, of the *I Ching*. The monk's reply was short and to the point: "In a single word, Resonance." Mr. Yin went on to ask if the spontaneous ringing of the Magic Bell at the very moment when Bronze Mountain in the west collapsed was a good example of this Resonance. The monk smiled inscrutably and did not reply. In the structure of this Hexagram, each Line is "aligned" with its "Resonant" partner: Yin in First finds Resonance with Yang in Fourth, Yin in Second with Yang in Fifth, Yang in Third with Yin in Top Place. With True Resonance between Yin and Yang, with their "subtle communion," all things are, in principle, possible. Resonance is a prime quality or sensitivity in the mental scheme of the *I Ching*. The reader is constantly urged to be aware of, to be in tune with, at one with, the Resonance around and within. This makes it possible to evolve in Harmony with the Dynamic of life, to adapt to Change, to respond appropriately to circumstances, to be True to Self. In order for Resonance to be effective, it must be True, it must be cleansed of impurities. It must arise spontaneously out of a natural "Self-ness" or "Suchness" (*ziran*). The Line Statements of this Hexagram describe, one after another, differing conditions of pure Resonance, and of impurity, those impediments by which Resonance is limited and hindered. The Hexagram Judgment, writes Jullien, following Wang Fuzhi, offers one of the supreme examples of such Resonance, the Attraction between man and woman, from which flows the continuance of life, a Resonance which is formalized in marriage. "When a woman meets a man, their Resonance, though at first it may lack solidity, can gradually grow more profound day by day, until eventually it becomes a union for life." When a young man and a young woman relate to each other in Truth, writes Magister Liu, then they cease to be conscious of Self and Other as separate entities. Pure Yin and Yang Energies burgeon within them, deeper feelings are aroused, and from this comes a natural and True Resonance, a Resonance of the Tao. The Heart-and-Mind of the Tao is True, the Human Heart-and-Mind is False. False Heart-and-Mind produces a False Resonance, in which Yin and Yang remain separate. True Heart-and-Mind produces a True Resonance, in which Yin and Yang enter deep communion. Yin may Attract and Yang Respond, or vice versa. But True Resonance always stems from the Heart-and-Mind of the Tao. A pure woman is the finest type of this True Resonance. Her Inner Strength lies in her purity and calm. She does not give herself lightly to another, but awaits the right partner and then Responds. Her Response, her Resonance, comes not from her own Heart-and-Mind, but from

Truth itself. Those who genuinely seek to cultivate the Tao, who wish to harmonize Yin and Yang, those who desire the communion and True Resonance of Yin and Yang, would do well to model themselves on the purity and calm of such a woman. JM: An interesting (if less sublime) modern Chinese reading of the Hexagram takes the idea of courtship and wooing more literally and physically, seeing in the Line Statements various stages of sexual foreplay and arousal, beginning with the feet and ending with the mouth. The Commentary on the Image understands the Lake as an emblem of Yielding Humility, literally, Emptiness of Self, the open, hollow mental space that receives and responds, while the Mountain is strong and initiates. Lake and Mountain are interdependent, writes Professor Mun. The Lake rests on the Mountain, the Mountain is nourished by the moisture of the Lake. Just so, the Leader should interact sincerely with his subordinates, helping to obtain a joyful Harmony in the Organization.

LINES

Yin in First Place

The big toe

Resonates.

On the Image

The Heart-and-Mind
Is set on externals.

Yin Line in Yang Place. The Lines of this Hexagram move from one extremity of the body (the big toe) to the other (the mouth), from bodily movements to speech. The big toe, writes Jullien, following Wang Fuzhi, represents a basic, limited response. It can move, but it cannot walk. The overall lesson is to refine and deepen Resonance, to be Steadfast, not be tossed around at the mercy of externals. The big toe, writes Magister Liu, belongs to the Human Realm, the Human Heart-and-Mind. Action based merely on a hunch (like a "feeling" in the big toe), writes Professor Mun, is risky. Intuition alone is not sufficient to justify taking action.

Yin in Second Place

The calf

Resonates.

Calamity,

Hoc pessimum.

It is Auspicious

To abide,

Hoc bonum.

On the Image

Despite Calamity,
It is Auspicious to abide.
Following the Flow
Ensures no injury,
Nullum infortunium.

 Yin Line in Yin Place. Centered and True. The calves cannot move of themselves, writes Legge. They can only follow the feet. Calf Resonance indicates too great an anxiety to Act, at a time when Action and Movement are not appropriate. Be calm. Abide in Truth, free from delusion, until the right moment arrives. Then it will be possible to go with the Flow. In this way, Calamity can be avoided. Calf Resonance lacks the Heart-and-Mind of the Tao, writes Magister Liu. The Calf should be still and not move. Moving will bring Calamity. The executive in this position, writes Professor Mun, should resist the impulse to rush forward. Premature Action may be unfortunate.

Yang in Third Place

The thigh

Resonates,

Blindly following

Others,

Blindly Advancing.

There is

Distress,

Poenitebit.

On the Image

Unsettled.
Aspirations are set on
Following others.

 Yang Line in Yang Place. Neither can the thighs move "of themselves." To attempt to move them in this way is Inauspicious. This Yang Line in a Yang Place is too impulsive. It relies too much on others. It lacks the calm, reflective sense of Truth that should inform Action. This is to let oneself be driven by externals. The Heart-and-Mind is Firm but not Centered. The objective world creates emotion. Dust blows with the wind. This is to lose the Heart-and-Mind of the Tao.

Yang in Fourth Place

It is Auspicious

To be Steadfast.

Regret goes away,

Nullus poenitendi locus.

There is a

Restless

Coming and going.

Friends

Follow.

On the Image

Injury has not yet
Been provoked.
All is
Restless.
The Light is not yet
Sufficiently great,
Claritas nondum magna.

Yang Line in Yin Place. This Line Resonates with Yin in First Place, writes Legge. This may portray uncertain emotional relations between man and wife. Friends merely serve to deepen the restless confusion. One's scope (Light) does not extend far enough. Yin is dragged in by Desire, writes Magister Liu. The Heart-and-Mind of the Tao is tainted by the Human Heart-and-Mind. The "friends" who come are, in fact, emanations of the Human Heart-and-Mind. True Essence is thrown into restless tumult. Being is rocked by the Human Heart-and-Mind. This Resonance arouses the Human Heart-and-Mind and veils the Heart-and-Mind of the Tao. The Leader, writes Professor Mun, must keep his mind sincere and stable, free of restlessness and disturbance. This includes the disturbance arising from personal interests. The "friends" may simply be creating a clique.

Yang in Fifth Place

The back

Resonates.

No Regret,

Nullus poenitendi locus.

On the Image

Aspirations are not effective,
Mens non habet finem.

Yang Line in Yang Place. Centered and True. This Strong Line is said to describe that part of the back above and behind (and so separate from) the heart. It is an objective sounding board of Resonance. This is the True Heart-and-Mind, writes Magister Liu. It has no fixed dwelling place; it is concerned with neither form nor void. It is an open, lively awareness. It is the Heart-and-Mind of the Tao. There is a need, writes Professor Mun, for the Leader to maintain his objectivity and integrity.

Yin in Top Place

The jaw

Resonates,

The cheeks,

The tongue.

On the Image

Speech is voluble.

 Yin Line in Yin Place. The True Gentleman, writes Legge, uses few words. His Resonance is of the Heart-and-Mind. Resonance of speech—empty loquacity and flattery, clever words—lacks substance. This Resonance is False, writes Magister Liu. It is of the Human Heart-and-Mind. Words, movements of the tongue and mouth, laughter—these belong to the body, not to the True Heart-and-Mind. A Leader, writes Professor Mun, cannot persuade people with mere words. Words can be effective only if they are backed up by something solid, by Action.

HEXAGRAM XXXII

Heng

Endurance

Zhen/Quake

above

Xun/Wind

JUDGMENT

Fortune.

No Harm,

Nullum malum.

It Profits

To be Steadfast.

A Destination

Profits.

On the Judgment

Endurance is
Long-lasting.
The Firm is above,
The Yielding below.
Thunder and Wind
Come together.
Movement and Gentleness,
Firm and Yielding,
Resonate.
They are long-lasting
In the Tao.
The Tao of Heaven and Earth
Endures without end.
A Destination Profits.
Each Ending is a Beginning,
Est finis, est initium.
Sun and Moon
Partake of Heaven;
Their radiance
Endures.
The Four Seasons
Are transformed;
Their perfection
Endures.
The Sage
Endures in the Tao.
All-under-Heaven
Is transformed and perfected.
Observe this Endurance,
Observe
The Nature of Heaven and Earth,
The Nature of the Myriad Things,
Rerumque omnium naturam.

On the Image of the Hexagram

Thunder and Wind,
Tonitrus et ventus.
The True Gentleman

Stands firm,

He does not change direction,

Locum non mutat.

 Quake above Wind. From below, a gentle breeze nourishes the Movement of Quake, and its dynamic cycle of Change. As in the previous Hexagram, all Yin and Yang Lines Resonate. But whereas in Hexagram XXXI the concern was with Truth (without which there can be no Resonance), here it is with Spiritual Stamina, Endurance. True Endurance, writes Jullien, following Wang Fuzhi, cannot be achieved through a fixed, obstinate determination to remain unchanged. Life Energy must be regulated *within* Change. Be Centered. Be balanced. Maintain and renew flexible Inner Strength and Integrity through life's vicissitudes. Emulate the Tao of Heaven and Earth, which Endures through the ever-changing cycle of the Seasons. Stand firm, write Legge and Wilhelm, be Steadfast. Persevere in continuous and gentle enactment of the Inner Law, or Tao, of Being. This cannot be achieved in a single day. It requires Endurance, a gradual ascent or a slow descent, depending on the circumstances, reaching ever higher or deeper, step by step on the path of Reality, of the Tao. In a marriage, this is the state of Enduring Union. The husband (above, Thunder, Quake) is the directing and moving force, while the wife (below, Wind) is gentle and submissive. To Endure, writes Magister Liu, Aspiration must be immovable. Endurance must be fierce as Thunder, but at the same time gentle as Wind, growing stronger with time. It is not corrupted by wealth, it is not broken by poverty, it is not crushed by authority. It sees everything as Void. It abides in its True Place. Thus it attains a profound Self-Fulfillment, a Union of Yin and Yang. It Endures, and does not decay. There is an enduring relationship between Thunder and Wind, writes Professor Mun, a balanced relationship between Yin and Yang, a helpful division of labor.

LINES

Yin in First Place

Endurance is

Too deep.

Despite Steadfastness,

Calamity.

Nothing Profits.

On the Image

Premature depth,

Sought at the outset,

Brings
Calamity.

 Yin Line in Yang Place. It is an illusion, writes Jullien, following Wang Fuzhi, to think that one can achieve Endurance in a single short blow. This is like the pseudo-scholars who imagine that from a superficial reading of the Classics they can establish fixed rules for living, and merely create chaos instead. It is like the Zen Buddhists who think they can attain sudden enlightenment, and merely succeed in shackling the Heart-and-Mind all over again. Be quiet, writes Legge. Do not be forward or precipitate in action. Endurance can be created only gradually, by long-continued application and careful reflection. An executive must be patient in developing a long-term relationship, writes Professor Mun. If he wants too much too soon, he may end up empty-handed. He should work step by step toward his objective.

Yang in Second Place

Regret

Goes away,

Nullus poenitendi locus.

On the Image

Abide in the Center
For a long time.

 Yang Line in Yin Place. Centered. In Shang and early Zhou times, to "set up in the Center," to "set up the Center" (*lizhong*), was a cosmological Ritual, which may originally have involved the actual setting up of a flagpole or other device to measure the angle of the sun's shadow. Later, *zhong* came to mean something broader and more philosophical, a balanced (Centered) mode of consciousness and conduct. Here in this Central Line of the Lower Trigram, a Firm Line in a Yielding Place, there is a balanced abiding, an Endurance, in keeping with the Golden Mean. Regret, negative emotion, has been got rid of. Inner Strength is nurtured. An executive, writes Professor Mun, who has a strong character, like this Yang Line in Center, is able to Endure. He will have no reason for Regret.

Yang in Third Place

Inner Strength

Does not Endure.

Disgrace

Is encountered.

Steadfast.

Distress.

On the Image

He is not accepted.

 Yang Line in Yang Place. Moods of hope and fear, writes Richard Wilhelm, drain stamina; they disrupt the Inner Balance necessary for Endurance. Without Inner Strength, writes Magister Liu, without the Endurance necessary to turn Aspiration into Action, the goal has to be abandoned. An executive in this situation, writes Professor Mun, is likely to have a strong but unstable character. He is likely to change his mind often, to be unpredictable. He must learn to control his moods, and not let his moods control him.

Yang in Fourth Place

In the hunt

There is no game.

On the Image

In the wrong Place
For too long,
One cannot hope
To get game.

 Yang Line in Yin Place. This Strong Line in a Weak (and therefore "wrong") Place portrays a mistaken and obstinate illusion, writes Jullien, following Wang Fuzhi, an illusion that Endurance can be attained or "hit upon" by chance, like "game" taken by a hunter. JM: There is nothing gained in this sort of "chase." It is a futile quest, wrong-headed, blind Folly. When one yearns for the Tao, writes Magister Liu, but lacks the Endurance to practice it, this is like getting "no game in the hunt." To Endure in a wrong course of Action, writes Professor Mun, is simply a waste of time. There will be "no game."

Yin in Fifth Place

Inner Strength

Endures.

To be Steadfast

Is Auspicious

For a woman,

Calamity

For a man.

On the Image

The woman
Follows one man
To the very end.
The man acts according to
What he knows to be right.
To obey a wife
Brings Calamity.

Yin Line in Yang Place. Centered. This is the traditional Chinese view of woman's lot: unquestioning docility and obedience, acceptance and devotion, considered right for the cultivation of a peaceful life in the home. The Lady Ban Zhao described this ideal of feminine submission fully in her famous (some would say infamous) *Precepts for Women*: "A woman's duty is to be humble, yielding, respectful and reverential; to put Self after Others. . . . To behave properly and decorously in serving her husband; to be serene and self-possessed, shunning jests and laughter; to be careful with the Sacrificial Offerings for the Ancestors." A man, writes Legge, must be more outward-looking; he must follow what is right. This is his duty. This indicates a flexible, Yin-type Leadership, writes Professor Mun.

Yin in Top Place

Too persistent

An Endurance.

Calamity,

Hoc pessimum.

On the Image

Persistence in Top Place
Brings no success.

Yin Line in Yin Place. Endurance has run its course, writes Legge. The excitement of *Zhen*, the Upper Trigram, Quake, has reached its limit. Strenuous efforts are futile. They will only lead to Calamity. They will end in ruin. The Tao of Endurance, writes Wang Bi, comes from True Calm, not from False Excitement. This extreme Endurance is a failure, writes Magister Liu. The highest must become low. All must Return to Emptiness. Persistent Endurance cheats and invites Calamity. The Leader, writes Professor Mun, should calm down, not stir things up.

Dun

Retreat

Qian/Heaven

above

Gen/Mountain

JUDGMENT

Fortune.

In small things,

To be Steadfast

Profits.

On the Judgment

Fortune lies in
Retreat.
The Firm in Apt Position

Resonates.
It is in Accordance
With Time.
Gradually
The Small
Pervades,
Prevails.

On the Image of the Hexagram

Mountain beneath Heaven,
Mons infra coelum.
The True Gentleman
Distances himself
From the Small Man,
Not in bitterness,
But wishing to
Remain aloof.

Heaven above Mountain. The power of Darkness is in the ascendant. Two Yin Lines encroach upward in the Mountain at the base of the Hexagram. This is the Dynamic, or Potential Energy (*shi*), of the situation. "The Small Man prevails," and the times require the Superior Man, the True Gentleman, to Retreat before him. Through this strategic Retreat, Inner Strength can be nurtured, Steadfast in the Tao. Heaven itself is limitless, it is infinite: the Mountain is high, but it has limits. The two together are an emblem of Retreat. Through Retreat, by being "aloof," by withdrawing into Inner Contemplation, the True Gentleman preserves Inner Strength. Small Men cannot come near him or cause him Harm. Zhang Heng, remarkable mathematician, astronomer, and poet, wrote a "Rhapsody on Contemplating the Mystery," in which he consults various Oracles, including the *I Ching*:

King Wen laid out the Yarrow Stalks.
I received the Hexagram Retreat.
Profit
In a leisurely Retreat,
My fair name preserved.
I traveled to the Mountains,
Into the far distance,
Flying on the swift Wind,
Spreading my fame. . . .
My affinity is with the Dark Bird.
I shall

Return
To the Mother,
I shall find peace.

The Mother he sought was the Tao. The True Gentleman, who practices the Tao, writes Magister Liu, gathers his Vital Spirit, vast as the Heavens. He learns to live in the world without injuring Spirit. He dwells in the dust but is able to rise above the dust. The False Taoist is a Small Man, tiny as a grain of mustard. The slightest thing is more than he can tolerate. A wise Leader, writes Professor Mun, knows when to Retreat, when conditions are not in his favor. He is advised to deal only with small matters. The True Gentleman (Heaven) keeps a distance (Mountain) from the Small Man.

LINES

Yin in First Place

A tail

In Retreat.

Danger,

Periculosum.

A Destination

Is of no avail.

On the Image

Without a Destination,
There will be no Disaster.

 Yin Line in Yang Place. The "tail" in Retreat, writes Legge, suggests a man hurrying away, a precipitate flight, which will only aggravate the Danger of the moment. Disaster can best be avoided by peacefully waiting in obscurity, without a Destination. A late (last-minute) Retreat, writes Professor Mun, will be harmful.

Yin in Second Place

Bind it fast

With thongs

Of yellow oxhide.

None can loosen it.

On the Image

Aspiration is firm.

 Yin Line in Yin Place. Centered and True. With Aspiration, with strength of purpose and conviction, Steadfastness will lead to success, even in Retreat. With the "binding," writes Magister Liu, one holds on to an Empty Void, one maintains Stillness, impervious to external influences and internal thoughts. The bond (Resonance) between this Line and Yang in Fifth Place, writes Professor Mun, should be unshakable.

Yang in Third Place

Bound

In Retreat.

Extreme Danger,

Hoc periculosum.

A servant or concubine

Is nurtured.

Auspicious,

Hoc bonum.

On the Image

Extreme fatigue.
No great affair
Can be accomplished.

Yang Line in Yang Place. This Line is entangled by Small Men, writes Legge, by servants or concubines (the two Yin Lines below it). They must be "nurtured" if their "sting" is to be removed, if they are to be prevented from causing a serious impediment. The Leader, writes Professor Mun, is advised to Retreat in a stately and relaxed way and to restore his Energy for starting a new venture when the right time comes.

Yang in Fourth Place

A well-executed

Retreat.

For the True Gentleman,

This is Auspicious,

Hoc bonum.

For the Small Man,

Misfortune,

Pessimum.

On the Image

The Small Man
Is obstructed.

Yang Line in Yin Place. This is the First Line of the Strong Upper Trigram, *Qian*, Heaven. The Retreat is unhindered. Store True Yang, writes Magister Liu, in a well-executed Retreat, free of personal entanglements. Do not allow the slightest element of Yin Energy to sprout within the Heart-and-Mind. The Small Man, by contrast, is presumptuous. He mistakes False for True. A wise Leader, writes Professor Mun, can control his emotions and desires, while an inferior man cannot. His involvement is with personal interests and motives.

Yang in Fifth Place

A timely

Retreat.

To be Steadfast

Is Auspicious,

Hoc bonum.

On the Image

Auspicious.
Aspirations are set on Truth.

Yang Line in Yang Place. Centered and True. Strength is Centered, writes Magister Liu. Yang is close kin; Yin is distant. This Timely Retreat does not Harm Truth with Falsehood. A wise Leader, writes Professor Mun, knows when and how to Retreat. He does it in a timely fashion.

Yang in Top Place

A Leisurely

Retreat.

All things Profit,

Nihil non conveniat.

On the Image

No misgivings,
Nullus dubitandi locus.

Yang Line in Yin Place. A clear Spirit, one of unfettered detachment, writes Zhu Xi, informs Retreat, free from all doubt or sorrow. The poet Xie Lingyun had this Line in mind when late in life he went on one of his alpine rambles:

> **On Entering the Third Valley of Mayuan**
> This hill was once
> Refuge for a Hermit,
> Leisurely Retreat
> For a Sage. . . .
> Here I may do as I please,
> Wander off alone,
> Enjoy the moonlight,

The plashing of the stream.
Here I may savor
Each moment's pleasure
To the full. . . .

This, writes Magister Liu, is a free and independent Retreat. A serene Retreat, writes Professor Mun.

Da Zhuang

Great Might

Zhen/Quake

above

Qian/Heaven

JUDGMENT

To be Steadfast

Profits.

On the Judgment

Greatness is Might.
Firmness and Movement
Create Might.
The Great is True.

It manifests
The Nature
Of Heaven and Earth,
Coeli et terrae naturam.

On the Image of the Hexagram

Thunder above Heaven,
Tonitrus supra coelum.
The True Gentleman
Does not tread
Where Ritual is absent.

Quake above Heaven. This Hexagram—with its two Yin Lines above a solid body of Four Yang Lines—suggests the shape of a ram with horns, an Image which occurs in four of the Line Statements. The Strong Lines predominate. The Hexagram, writes Legge, suggested to King Wen in his Judgment an abundance of Strength. But Great Might alone is not enough. It must be applied judiciously, held in subordination to the idea of Righteousness, and exerted only in Harmony with Righteousness. Might without Ritual, writes Richard Wilhelm, Strength untempered with Harmony bring Misfortune. JM: For the poet Zuo Si, in his "Rhapsody on the Capital of Wei," the Hexagram has to do with the exercise of Moderation in the construction of a building, the top two Lines resembling the ridgepole of a house. He wrote of Emperor Xuan, who had restored the Zhou dynasty:

He blended ornament and simplicity,
He weighed
Extravagance against frugality,
Striking a middle course,
Adapting dimensions
To the needs of the times.
He consulted the Lines of the *I Ching*,
He modeled himself
On Great Might.

This understanding of the Hexagram goes back to the Great Treatise.

The Great Treatise
From Part II, Section 2

In olden times
Men dwelt in caves,

In the wilderness.
Holy men of later times
Made changes,
Built houses,
With ridgepole and rafters,
Against wind and rain.
This came from Great Might.

Mighty is the Energy of Quake, writes Magister Liu. Thunder rises into the Heavens, spreading a wave of terror and awe. Ritual is the assurance of Moderation in Movement and Stillness. It is the Notch of Regulation. It is Order; it constitutes the rules for Self-Cultivation and for living in the world. Without Ritual, when impulse and desire take over, then there is only False Might. Take one step at a time. All will be merged into the Wondrous Tao. One will become the companion of Heaven, one will work with Thunder. The Tao of Might prizes Truth above all else. Without Truth it is as nothing. Overexpansion, writes Professor Mun, leads to an imbalance between Yin and Yang A Leader must know how to use his Might properly. A wise Leader is the one who has Might but uses it least.

LINES

Yang in First Place

Might

In the toes.

An Advance.

Calamity.

Good Faith.

On the Image

Good Faith
Is surely exhausted.

Yang Line in Yang Place. Advance is too bold, writes Legge, and too lacking in Good Faith, to be wisely undertaken. The toes, writes Magister Liu, may seem to move forward quickly at first, they may seem to wiggle, but they will move backward quickly too. A rash move at the beginning, writes Professor Mun, may be a mistake. Conditions may not be ready.

Yang in Second Place

To be Steadfast

Is Auspicious,

Hoc bonum.

On the Image

It is Centered,
In medio.

 Yang Line in Yin Place. Centered. The fact that this Yang Line is in a Central Yin Place creates a certain balance. This, writes Magister Liu, is Might based on mastery of Self. The combination of Might (a Yang Line) and gentleness (in a Yin Place), writes Professor Mun, is Auspicious. A Leader in this position should avoid overenthusiasm, exuberant self-confidence, impulse, and extreme behavior. He should maintain a modest attitude in a time of Might.

Yang in Third Place

The Small Man

Uses Might.

The True Gentleman

Does not.

He is Steadfast

In face of Danger.

The ram butts the fence;

He snags his horns.

On the Image

The True Gentleman
Refrains.

🦌 Yang Line in Yang Place. The Small Man, writes Legge, exerts Might to the utmost; not so the True Gentleman. His Position is now beyond the safety of the Center, and he will be cautious and refrain from Action. Unlike the ram, he does not injure himself by exerting his Might. Outer Might conceals Inner Weakness, writes Magister Liu. The True Gentleman, the Taoist, perceives that all is Void. The Small Man uses Might for petty gain, and suffers as a consequence. JM: The ram is alluded to by Dong Zhongshu in his "Rhapsody on Scholars out of Their Time":

Strive to

Butt the fence,

And you will merely

Snag a horn.

Do not go out

Through the courtyard door,

And you may stay

Free from Harm.

The last lines of the poem refer to the First Line Statement of Hexagram LX, Notch. A Leader, writes Professor Mun, should think twice before he makes any move, before making a show of his Might.

Yang in Fourth Place

To be Steadfast

Is Auspicious.

Regret goes away,

Nullus poenitendi locus.

The hedge parts.

There is no

Snagging of horns.

A great carriage,

A mighty axle.

On the Image

An Advance is possible.

 Yang Line in Yin Place, as in the Second Line, writes Richard Wilhelm. Might is moderated by flexibility, Yang by Yin. With quiet perseverance and Inner Strength comes success. Obstacles (such as the "hedge"), writes Magister Liu, cease to be a problem (it "parts"). This is the Might of one who knows Self, True Self. The Leader, writes Professor Mun, uses Inner Strength to Advance, like the strong axle of a carriage.

Yin in Fifth Place

The ram is lost

In the borderlands.

No Regret,

Nullus poenitendi locus.

On the Image

The Position is not Apt.

 Yin Line in Yang Place. Centered. Ramlike Might is "lost." This may have its advantages. Aggression is put aside, moderated by a softer attitude. This emptying of Heart-and-Mind, writes Magister Liu, uses knowledge of Others to open up a space for the limitations of Self, to brighten its Light. This Yin Line in a Yang Place, writes Professor Mun, indicates the possibility of using a moderate approach (Yin) to lessen the hard, ramlike character (Yang) of a person's Nature.

Yin in Top Place

The ram

Butts the hedge.

Neither Retreat nor Advance

Is possible.

Nothing Profits,

Nulla convenientia.

Hardship

Is Auspicious,

Hoc bonum.

On the Image

Retreat and Advance
Are both
Inauspicious.
Hardship is
Auspicious;
No Harm endures.

禿 Yin Line in Yin Place. This Line is at the Top of the Upper Trigram, *Zhen*, Quake and Movement. It is also at the Top of the entire Hexagram. Might is actively exerted, writes Legge, but through inherent weakness (this is a Yin Line in Yin Place), the result is a deadlock ("neither Retreat nor Advance is possible"). If, however, one can be aware of this weakness, if one can learn the lessons of hardship, then Good Fortune will result. One can avoid further entanglement by desisting from unwise efforts. JM: For the medieval Taoist Guo Pu, the "ram" butting the "hedge" was an image for the general frustrations and dilemmas of life in the world, especially for one who aspires to a higher level of consciousness:

Poem of a Wandering Immortal
Advance.
The Dragon
Is seen.
Try to Retire.
The ram
Butts the hedge.
Best to flee
Far away
To the mountains,
Beyond wind and dust.

Guo Pu's "Dragon . . . seen" (from Hexagram I/2) is shorthand for entering the "real world," for making one's talent visible and serving at court. Once the courtier (the man of the world) is seen, once he sticks his neck out, if he then refuses to conform and play the game, if he "tries to Retire," he is sure to be caught (in a "hedge"). Better by far to be an outright Hermit, and flee to the mountains. If one indulges in foolish fantasies and weird thoughts, writes Magister Liu, even after a lifetime spent in study, everything will be in vain—like a ram butting the hedge. Better by far to empty the Heart-and-Mind and seek out a good teacher. Better to devote a lifetime to *this* Work. It may not seem like Might from the outside. But in the end it *is* Might, because it is True. The Leader is in a dilemma, writes Professor Mun. He can neither Retreat nor Advance. He must actively seek the proper measures to escape from Adversity.

HEXAGRAM XXXV

Jin

Advance

Li/Fire

above

Kun/Earth

JUDGMENT

Prince Kang

Was given many horses

In a single day.

He was received

Three times

In audience.

On the Judgment

Illumination
Rises above Earth.
Yielding Lines
Advance,
They are Compliant,
They Ascend,
They are attached to
Great Illumination.

On the Image of the Hexagram

Illumination rises above Earth,
Claritas supra terram.
The True Gentleman causes
His Inner Strength
To be
Illumined.

Fire above Earth. According to some, this Prince Kang was the younger brother of King Wu (see Part II). According to others, the name was simply a title for a high noble charged with pacification (*kang*) after the Zhou conquest. Either way, his services earned him favors from the King, who showered him with gifts and personal attention. Advance, writes Legge, should be like the Light of the Sun. The True Gentleman models himself on this. Gently, he lets his Inner Illumination shine; slowly but surely, he manifests his Inner Strength. It is best to continue to seek further Illumination, writes Magister Liu, to explore True Principle, to attain Inner Fulfillment. Thus Illumination increases every day, becoming ever greater and more manifest, until one gradually enters the Realm of the Illumined Vision. The Human Heart-and-Mind has then learned to Flow with Truth, and the Heart-and-Mind of the Tao is Illumined. Three times it receives the Flow. As this practice is repeated, the Flow prevails. It grows stronger. That which is False is dispersed; Truth is preserved. Flow generates Illumination. Illumination generates Flow. Sincerity enhances Illumination. Illumination enhances Sincerity. The rising Sun, writes Professor Mun, as in the Upper Trigram, represents the qualities of brightness and clarity in a Leader, his Illumination. The Yin Lines of Earth are the subordinates who follow him without question.

LINES

Yin in First Place

An Advance

Is held back.

To be Steadfast

Is Auspicious,

Hoc bonum.

Good Faith

Is lacking.

Be tolerant.

No Harm,

Nullum malum.

On the Image

Advance
Alone in Truth.
An Edict
Has not yet been received.

 Yin Line in Yang Place. The trust of the King has not yet been gained. Progress must therefore be gradual and tolerant. At this early stage of Illumination, writes Magister Liu, it is best to be Still, not to Move. Sooner or later, writes Professor Mun, the executive will gain the confidence of others. But for now, Good Faith is lacking. This is not yet the right time to Advance. He must be Steadfast and wait.

Yin in Second Place

Advance.

Grief.

To be Steadfast

Is Auspicious,

Hoc bonum.

Great blessing is received

From the King's Mother.

On the Image

This is Centered and True,
In medio,
In recto.

 Yin Line in Yin Place. Centered and True. In the Darkness made up of three Yin Lines, Illumination is obscured. Advance will only bring grief. Hold Steadfastly to Center. Do not be deluded by False Yin. Then, since there has been no Advance, there can be no grief. Be Steadfast in Emptiness and Stillness. True Yin will appear, False Yin will transform itself and vanish. This is the "great blessing." "The King's Mother," writes Professor Mun, can be understood as those "experienced people" from whom the Leader must seek help.

Yin in Third Place

It is approved by all.

Regret

Goes away,

Nullus poenitendi locus.

On the Image

Aspirations
Move upward.

Yin Line in Yang Place. There is a common trust and purpose, writes Legge. Aspirations are shared. This Line resonates with Yang in Top Place, writes Magister Liu. Self and Others (the two Yin Lines below) all follow the Flow. An Advance meets with general approval. This Line, writes Professor Mun, emphasizes the benefits of a common goal, of Aspirations shared by the Leader with members of his organization (the two Yin Lines below). This creates Good Faith, which will enable him to Advance, and overcome obstacles.

Yang in Fourth Place

Advance

Like a squirrel.

Steadfast.

Danger,

Periculosum.

On the Image

The Position
Is not Apt.

Yang Line in Yin Place. The squirrel's Advance, writes Legge, is stealthy. He scurries forward in little bursts. This Yang Line Resonates with Yin in First Place, writes Magister Liu. But neither Line is in an Apt Position. The Light of Illumination is still veiled by the Yin Lines that surround it. Advance can be only partial, tentative, like a squirrel finding its way in the night, able to see little, and not far ahead. Illumination is weakened by private concerns. The behavior of the squirrel, writes Professor Mun, affects the Harmony of the Organization, and hence its efficiency. The squirrel lacks Ability and Integrity.

Yin in Fifth Place

Regret

Goes away,

Nullus poenitendi locus.

There is no concern

For failure or success.

To Advance

Is Auspicious.

All things Profit,

Nihil est quod non conveniat.

On the Image

An Advance
Is cause for celebration.

Yin Line in Yang Place. Centered. Hold Steadfastly to the right course, indifferent to results, and the enterprise will be crowned with success. This is Illumination that brings Fulfillment out of Emptiness, writes Magister Liu. This Yin Line makes positive use of the two Yang Lines surrounding it. It nurtures itself on the Illumination of Others, recognizing that the Illumination of Self is insufficient. Regret arises from a Heart-and-Mind that is not yet Empty. Once the Heart-and-Mind is Empty, then all concerns for success or failure fall away. A Leader of Yin character, writes Professor Mun, is tolerant and open-minded. He employs capable people in their best roles. He uses the strength of his employees to offset his own weaknesses. He does not care whether the plan will bring him personal gains or losses, so long as it is beneficial to the Organization as a whole.

Yang in Top Place

An Advance

With horns.

A city is attacked.

Despite Danger,

It is Auspicious,

Bonum.

No Harm,

Nullum malum.

Despite Steadfastness,

There is

Humiliation.

On the Image

The Tao
Does not yet shine,
Lex nondum claruit.

Yang Line in Yin Place. The "horns" are an emblem of threatening strength, writes Legge. Even if they are being used against one's own city, against the rebellious elements therein, it is regrettable that the Ruler should have occasion to use force at all. To attack a city, writes Magister Liu, is to conquer Self, to empty the Human Heart-and-Mind. An Advance based on brute Force will simply attract brute Force in return. It will demand absolute Victory. Danger has to be faced before an Auspicious result can occur. A forceful Advance stems from Pride. Self-restraint, writes Professor Mun, may go against one's Nature, but it will prevent one from impulsively going to extremes.

HEXAGRAM XXXVI

Ming Yi

Darkness

Kun/Earth

above

Li/Fire

JUDGMENT

In hard times,

To be Steadfast

Profits,

In adversis

Soliditas.

On the Judgment

Light enters Earth.
Within,
There is Pattern and Light.

Without,
Yielding Compliance.
King Wen lived through Great Adversity.
He was Steadfast in hard times.
His Light was veiled
During Adversity at court.
Viscount Ji maintained
His Aspirations.

On the Image of the Hexagram

Light enters Earth,
Claritas intrat in terram.
The True Gentleman
Governs the Folk.
The Light is veiled,
But it still shines.

Earth above Fire. The Sun (Lower Trigram, *Li*), writes Legge, has sunk beneath the Earth (Upper Trigram, *Kun*) and has therefore plunged into Darkness. The four Yin Lines overshadow the two Yang Lines. The Hexagram Name has traditionally been taken to mean "wounding of the bright," and the individual Lines contain frequent references to wounding and injury, and to the repression of all that is good and bright. JM: The early commentary Sequence of the Hexagrams (one of the Ten Wings) states baldly that *yi* in the Hexagram Name *means* "wounding," and the Tang-dynasty commentator Kong Yingda follows this: "*Yi* means wounding. In this Hexagram, the Sun enters the Earth. In human affairs, there is a Dark Lord above, and a Bright Minister below, one who cannot show his Light. It is a time of great Darkness. One cannot go along with the general trend, which is impure. One must bear with adversity, and remain firm. One must be Steadfast in Inner Strength." The great seventeenth-century scholar Huang Zongxi named his most famous work, *Waiting in Darkness for the Dawn,* after this Hexagram. He saw his own times (the collapse of the Ming dynasty, and the troubles following the Manchu conquest) as a phase in the cosmic cycle during which the forces of Darkness prevailed. In such times the True Gentleman should find a way to preserve his Integrity amid Darkness. A loyal minister is Steadfast, writes Richard Wilhelm, and serves his country, even in hard times under a weak and unsympathetic sovereign. JM: King Wen, whose son King Wu conquered the Shang and founded the Zhou dynasty, was, according to legend, imprisoned by the last Shang ruler, Zhou Xin. It was during the "dark" days of his imprisonment (again according to now largely discredited legend) that he is supposed to have written the Judgments of the *I Ching.* Viscount Ji, uncle of Zhou Xin, offered his debauched nephew sound advice, which went unheeded. Ji is said to have feigned madness in order to withdraw from public life. Some scholars plausibly suggest that the

Hexagram refers to a solar eclipse—for this see Part II. A Leader who is extremely autocratic and incapable, writes Professor Mun, will lead his Organization into bureaucracy, inefficiency, and corruption. A True Leader must be Steadfast in his ideals during a time of Darkness. He must not lose sight of his goal, but must try to pursue it quietly.

LINES

Yang in First Place

Darkness

In flight.

Wings dipped.

The True Gentleman

On his travels

Fasts for three days.

A Destination.

The Master

Is ill spoken of.

On the Image

It is right
To fast.

Yang Line in Yang Place. The True Gentleman endeavors to soar above all obstacles, into the Darkness, writes Richard Wilhelm. But he is wounded and encounters a hostile fate. He Retreats. He fasts for three days. The times are hard. He refuses to make compromises within himself, but remains true to his principles. He has a fixed goal to strive for, even though some speak ill of him. The wings are "dipped," writes Cheng Yi, because they have been wounded. Small Men have injured the True Gentleman in his flight. He perceives the intimations (the Springs) of things, change in the air, and makes a wise decision—to Retreat, to travel elsewhere, even if it means dispensing with official salary and position, and being penniless. This is his "fasting." An upright man, writes Professor Mun, will silently and swiftly leave a corrupt and rotten Organization because he believes the situation will not change. An executive should not be involved in an activity which appears to be dishonest or deceptive. The sooner he gets out of it, the safer he is. JM: Integrity is a lonely choice. Retreat, a Return to True Identity, to True Self, is a hard path, and few are able to take it. Dong Zhongshu writes of this in his "Rhapsody on Scholars out of Their Time," alluding to this very Hexagram:

> My mind wanders back
> To furthest antiquity!
> How remote are my fellow men!
> How overgrown is the path,
> How hard to follow.
> I reflect on the True Gentleman,
> On his plight,
> As he travels,
> Fasting for three days.
> Alas! The World is against me!
> I grieve that none will join me
> In my Return.

Yin in Second Place

Darkness.

The left thigh is

Wounded.

A strong horse

Saves.

Auspicious,

Hoc bonum.

On the Image

This is
Auspicious.
It is in tune
With the Flow
Of the Tao.

Yin Line in Yin Place. Centered and True. The wound is not fatal or disabling. There is still a way to save oneself, and maintain Aspiration. The horse is an Image of Inner Strength. It can rescue from the failure to Retreat in time, writes Magister Liu; it can protect Illumination from any further injury. The "strong horse," writes Professor Mun, is Yang in Third Place, a strong person within the Organization, who comes to the aid of this weak person (Yin Line).

Yang in Third Place

Darkness

In the southern hunt.

A great chief

Is captured.

To be Steadfast

And make haste

Is impossible.

On the Image

The mind is set
On the hunt;
Great gains
Are to be had.

Yang Line in Yang Place. The hunter successfully pursues his game, writes Legge, but he should not be overeager to put things right. The "great chief," writes Magister Liu, is the Human Heart-and-Mind. Its habits are deeply entrenched. To be freed from that Heart-and-Mind (to "capture the chief") requires more than a hasty attempt, which may in fact do more Harm. Gradual Self-Transformation requires the True Fire. No change for the better, writes Professor Mun, will happen overnight. There may be resistance to reform. Hasty actions may result in an unstable situation.

Yin in Fourth Place

It enters the left side

Of the belly.

It reaches

The Heart-and-Mind

Of Injury,

Of Darkness.

It goes out of gate and courtyard.

On the Image

It reaches the thoughts
In the Heart-and-Mind.

 Yin Line in Yin Place. This is a Retreat, writes Legge, following Cheng Yi and Zhu Xi, in order to preserve Integrity. One must leave the scene of Disaster ("go out of gate and courtyard") before the storm breaks. This is to escape from Danger with as little damage as possible. This is to withdraw from False Fire, writes Magister Liu; it is to preserve Illumination from Harm. To "go out of gate and courtyard" is to leave Heart-and-Mind and enter No Heart-and-Mind. To "reach the Heart-and-Mind of Darkness," writes Professor Mun, is to get close to the Leader in Top Place, the man whose actions have brought the Organization into Darkness. This may lead to a decision to leave the Organization, which is too deeply corrupted for any improvement—to "go out of gate and courtyard."

Yin in Fifth Place

Viscount Ji

Is in Darkness.

To be Steadfast

Profits,

Habere soliditatem.

On the Image

Viscount Ji is Steadfast;
His Light
Is not extinguished.

 Yin Line in Yang Place. Centered. This Line is close to the Yin Line in Top Place, the benighted Ruler, the Dark One who is injuring the Light. Viscount Ji (see above under On the Image of the Hexagram) could not formally withdraw from court. He therefore concealed his true sentiments (his Light) in the Darkness and feigned insanity. Although he was imprisoned, he remained Steadfast; he never allowed external hardship to deflect him from his convictions, to dim or extinguish his Light. This is a teaching, writes Richard Wilhelm, for those who are unable to leave their posts in times of Darkness. In order to escape Danger (and preserve their Integrity), they need invincible Steadfastness of Spirit and redoubled Caution in their dealings with the world. The True Fire is within, writes Magister Liu. It glows crimson in the Alchemical Furnace. It Profited Viscount Ji to remain Steadfast in Darkness. Outward Insufficiency veils Inner Abundance. This is to nurture Inner Fire so that Illumination comes to no Harm. Even in Darkness, writes Professor Mun, this senior executive should hold on to his Integrity. He should try to find a good excuse to stay away from the circle of those who make decisions, and so keep his Inner Light bright.

Yin in Top Place

There is no Light,

Only utter Darkness,

Obscuritas.

At first it

Ascends to

Heaven,

Later it

Enters

Earth.

On the Image

At first,
From the heights of Heaven,
The Four Realms are Illumined.
Later, from within Earth,
True principle is lost.

Yin Line in Yin Place. This is the extremity of Darkness, writes Legge, following Cheng Yi. It is the last Line of the Upper Trigram, Earth. The Sun, which should Illumine all from the heights of Heaven, is instead plunged into Darkness; it is hidden in the depths of the Earth. The Sun may well stand for the Ruler, whose evil ways have usurped the place of Principle. The Golden Elixir has been attained, then lost, writes Magister Liu. At first the Work progresses, then it goes to waste. This injury is caused by the failure to understand the process of Illumination. To nurture the Alchemical Fire is to nurture Illumination. To withdraw from the Fire is to conceal Illumination. When the Fire can return to Truth, then the Spirit finds Light; it finds Spiritual Transformation.

Jia Ren

The Family

Xun/Wind

above

Li/Fire

JUDGMENT

To be Steadfast

Profits the woman,

Mulier debet

Habere soliditatem.

On the Judgment

The woman occupies
True Place

Within,
The man
Without.
When man and woman are True,
This is the Great Principle
Of Heaven and Earth,
Coeli magna justitia.
Strict Rulers
Of the Family they are,
Father and Mother.
When fathers are
True Fathers,
And sons
True Sons;
When older brothers are
True Older Brothers,
And younger brothers
True Younger Brothers;
When husbands are
True Husbands,
And wives
True Wives—
This is the True Tao
Of the Family.
When the Family is True,
Then the World is
Settled and at peace.

On the Image of the Hexagram

Wind out of Fire,
Ventus ex igne.
The words of
The True Gentleman
Have substance;
His Actions
Endure.

Wind above Fire. The subject of this Hexagram, writes Legge, is Regulation of the Family and Home, through cooperation of husband and wife in their different spheres. When this becomes universal, it secures the good order of the kingdom. The important place occupied by the wife in the Family is seen in the short sentence of the Judgment: she should be Steadfast, she should occupy her True Position and do her part well. This is the first thing necessary to Regulation of the Family. JM: The laws that operate within the Family also keep the World in order. The Father's words provide fuel for the Fire ("substance"). The constancy and consistency of his Actions cause the Wind to blow (the Upper Trigram). Words are the voice of the Heart-and-Mind, writes Magister Liu. Actions are the melodies of the body. The words of the Taoist have substance, his Actions endure. His Heart-and-Mind is True. All is one in the Heart-and-Mind. The Heart-and-Mind is one Family. The Human Body is a Family. Its various parts—Vitality, Spirit, Soul, Aspiration—are members of one Family. The Human Heart-and-Mind, properly cultivated, gives birth to the Heart-and-Mind of the Tao. Its every emotion—happiness, anger, sorrow, joy—then finds Harmony and Moderation, as in a well-regulated Family. Wood over Fire, writes Professor Mun, is the Family Hearth. Wind over Fire is the Home. Smoke from the chimney blows outside. Each member of a Family has a role to play. The Family is the foundation of society. If a Leader manages his own Family well, then he will be able to manage an Organization, and ultimately a country. Family values bring benefits to any social Organization: group spirit, a mutually supportive and harmonious relationship, close cooperation in hard times. The Hexagram is dominated by its four Yang Lines, just as in traditional Chinese society the male plays the dominant role. The first five Lines are all in Apt Places: all the members of the Family know their proper role. The Yang in Top Place is the Grandfather. Although he is no longer technically in charge, his age gives him a special authority.

LINES

Yang in First Place

The Family

Is disciplined.

Regret

Goes away,

Nullus poenitendi locus.

On the Image

Aspirations
Are unchanged.

Yang Line in Yang Place. Discipline enables order to prevail and prevents things from occurring that would lead to Regret. The first to be disciplined, writes Magister Liu, should be Self. For this, the Heart-and-Mind must become Empty, Inner Thoughts must fade away. Within an Organization, writes Professor Mun, clear rules and definition of responsibilities help maintain order.

Yin in Second Place

It is her task

To provide food

At the Center.

To be Steadfast

Is Auspicious,

Hoc bonum.

On the Image

To follow the Flow,
To be docile,
Obedientia.

Yin Line in Yin Place. Centered and True. This Second Yin Line, writes Legge, fitly represents the wife, her special sphere and duty. She should be unassuming in regard to all and everything beyond her sphere. She should be chaste. She should Resonate and accord with the wishes of Yang in Fifth Place, her husband and lord. JM: The long Chinese tradition of feminine subservience can be seen all too clearly in this Line. Compare *Song 189*:

A daughter is born.
She sleeps on the ground,
Wrapped in swaddling clothes.
She plays with tiles.
Hers to do
Nothing of substance,
But think of wine and food,
And cause no trouble to parents.

With boys it was a different story:

A son is born.
He sleeps in a bed,
Clothed in fine robes.
He plays with a jade scepter. . . .

The "woman," writes Magister Liu, is an Image of Yielding and Centered Truth. This is the Yielding Tao of Self-Cultivation. Calm governs Movement. The Yin character of this Line, writes Professor Mun, indicates a person who is not suitable for external work, but very capable of assuming internal functions.

Yang in Third Place

The Family is managed

With severity.

There is

Regret;

There is

Danger.

This is

Auspicious,

Hoc bonum.

When wife and children

Are frivolous,

Ultimately

There is

Distress,

In fine poenitendi locus.

On the Image

Harsh words do not betoken
Failure.

Frivolity brings
Loss of Family order.

Yang Line in Yang Place. Severity is no bad thing in regulating a Family, writes Legge. It is preferable to frivolity and indulgence. JM: The most famous depiction of a traditional Chinese family is to be found in the eighteenth-century novel *The Story of the Stone*. The father, Jia Zheng (the name means "correct" or "orthodox"), desperately (and ineffectually) strives to impose discipline on his wayward son, for his "riotous and dissipated conduct." Jia Zheng's attempt at "severity" goes a great deal further than "harsh words." In chapter 33, he has the boy brutally beaten. "Gag his mouth!" he shouts to the pages. "Beat him to death." But despite all these efforts, Jia Zheng fails to create order, and his entire family (and especially his "frivolous" son) is caught in a downward spiral of decadence and dissolution. Without severity in the Inner Family (the Spiritual ménage), writes Magister Liu, old thoughts linger, frivolous feelings and desires continue to be felt. This can only lead to Distress. The best approach, writes Professor Mun, is a balance between discipline and leniency. But strictness is preferable to softness.

Yin in Fourth Place

The Family

Is wealthy.

This is

Greatly Auspicious,

Magnum bonum.

On the Image

Follow the Flow.
This is a True Position.

Yin Line in Yin Place. The "wealth" of the wife, writes Legge, is her joyful service as "treasure" of the household, and the affection and harmony that prevail among members of the Family. Spiritual Wealth is renewed daily, writes Magister Liu. Heavenly Treasure is amassed.

Yang in Fifth Place

The King

Comes to his Family.

There is no cause for anxiety.

This is

Auspicious,

Hoc bonum.

On the Image

Mutual love.

 Yang Line in Yang Place. Centered and True. The King is also husband and father, writes Legge, following Cheng Yi. As husband he assists his helpmate in the house. The wife loves her husband. They provide the pattern of mutual love for the family. JM: This rare occurrence of the word "love," *ai*, in the text of the *I Ching* finds an echo in the Great Treatise, from Part I, Section 4:

> The Sage
> Who finds joy in Heaven,
> Who knows Life-Destiny,
> Heaven's Decree,
> Is free from care,
> At peace with his land.
> He is truly kind.
> He is able to love.

The Yang King is in the Center, writes Magister Liu. The Heart-and-Mind is True. All-under-Heaven is at peace. Love prevails.

Yang in Top Place

Good Faith

Inspires awe.

In the end,

This is

Auspicious,

In fine bonum.

On the Image

Self-reflection.

 Yang Line in Yin place. Good Faith, personal character, and Self-Cultivation, writes Legge, inspire respect. Mencius said: "If a man himself does not walk in the True Path, it will not be walked in by his wife and children." The Self-Cultivation of the Taoist, writes Magister Liu, inspires awe. The Alchemical Work begins with Self-Cultivation. When Self no longer exists, Light shines in an Empty Room. Primal Energy comes from Empty Nothingness. The Tiny Pearl Illumines Heaven and Earth. No Evil Spirit can approach it. A Leader, writes Professor Mun, gains trust and respect from the members of his Organization if he is True to himself and has a dignified sternness. Sincerity comes from his Self-Cultivation, dignity from his Sincerity.

HEXAGRAM XXXVIII

Kui

Opposition

Li/Fire

above

Dui/Lake

JUDGMENT

In small matters,

This is

Auspicious,

Bonum.

On the Judgment

Fire rises,
Lake descends.
Two women
Dwell together,

Their Aspirations
Ill-attuned.
Joy
Is attached to
Light.
The Yielding
Progresses,
It moves upward,
It reaches
Center,
Resonating with Firm below.
To undertake small matters
Is Auspicious.
Heaven and Earth
Are in Opposition,
But their enterprise
Is shared.
Man and Woman
Are in Opposition,
But their Aspirations
Still connect.
The Myriad Things
Are in Opposition,
But their enterprise
Is still of the same kind.

On the Image of the Hexagram

Fire above, Lake below,
Ignis supra lacum.
The True Gentleman
Sees difference
Within union.

Fire above Lake. The Hexagram in general, writes Legge, denotes a state in which Opposition and Tension prevail. In the graph, eyes glare at each other. Of the Trigrams, Fire draws upward, Lake sinks downward. When Fire is above, writes Magister Liu, it cannot warm Water. When Water is below, it cannot extinguish Fire. The "small matters" that can and should be dealt with are Yin matters. Great matters are abandoned. The Heart-and-Mind of the Tao is buried and lost. The Human Heart-and-Mind must first be got rid of, before the Heart-and-Mind of the Tao can be recovered. In the Cultivation of the Tao, one must start with small matters. Every Line in this Hexagram except the First is in a "wrong" Place. But progress is still possible—in small matters. Opposition may be healed and surmounted. Enterprises can be shared. There can be "union within difference"; there can be "difference within union." A wise Leader, writes Professor Mun, knows how to integrate differing views into a consensus that can be accepted by the majority. Members of the group should be encouraged to agree on minor issues first.

LINES

Yang in First Place

Regret

Goes away,

Nullus poenitendi locus.

A horse is lost.

Do not go

In pursuit;

It will return

Of its own accord.

An ill-looking person

Is seen.

There is

No Harm,

Nullum malum.

On the Image

Seeing an ill-looking person
Averts Harm.

Yang Line in Yang Place. The situation is compared to a traveler's loss of a horse, which will return of its own accord. Should an ill-looking person be met with, however, one should not shrink from him in fear. Communication with such a person may actually be of benefit. Confucius, writes Zhu Xi, once went reluctantly to "see" an "ill-looking person," the usurper Yang Huo. JM: The scheming Yang Huo had earlier taken Confucius a present of a suckling pig, deliberately choosing a time when he knew Confucius would be out, and thereby obliging Confucius to pay him a "return" call, as the rules of propriety demanded. Confucius for his part deliberately chose a time for his own "visit" when he thought Yang Huo would be out. But as luck would have it, he "bumped into him" on the way, and they had a brief (and inscrutable) exchange. This strange little anecdote occurs both in the Confucian *Analects* (Book 17) and in the later *Book of Mencius* (Book 3). Waley believes it to have been apocryphal. As Zhu Xi points out, it illustrates a cunning way of "seeing" an "ill-looking man" without actually coming to any Harm. The "ill-looking man," writes Magister Liu, is the Human Heart-and-Mind, along with its Five Thieves, which are so often its undoing: joy, anger, happiness, sorrow, and lust. These Thieves must be "seen" for what they are, if Harm is to be averted. The position may return to normal, writes Professor Mun, like a runaway horse that comes back on its own. A premature response could make matters worse.

Yang in Second Place

The Master

Is met with in a lane.

No Harm,

Nullum malum.

On the Image

The Tao
Is not yet lost.

Yang Line in Yin Place. Centered. This could have been a more open encounter, rather than a "meeting in a lane," writes Legge, if it were not for the Opposition and the Tension that mark the time. In the circumstances, a casual, as if it were stolen, interview, as in a lane or an alley, may lead to a better understanding. When Yin and Yang are in Opposition, writes Magister Liu, Perverse Energy prevails, True Energy is weak. The Heart-and-Mind of the Tao can be encountered only in a "small lane," using the Human Heart-and-Mind to produce the Mind of the Tao. An informal approach can be used, writes Professor Mun, to make a connection between a Leader and his colleagues. This may be a way to remove misunderstanding.

Yin in Third Place

A wagon

Is seen.

It is dragged back.

Oxen

Are halted.

A head is

Shaved,

A nose

Cut off.

There is no Beginning,

But a Conclusion,

Nullum est initium,

Est finis.

On the Image

A wagon is dragged.
The Position is not Apt.
No Beginning,
A Conclusion.
A Firm Line
Is encountered.

Yin Line in Yang Place. One may be checked and hindered, writes Legge, insulted and dishonored, even disfigured. But despite Opposition, right will triumph in the end; disorder will in the long run give place to order, disunion to union. The wagon, writes Professor Mun, is blocked by Yang in Fourth Place above (a "Firm Line is encountered"), and "dragged" back by Yang in Second Place below. This is a difficult situation, a dilemma. But this Line Resonates with Yang in Top Place. Help can be sought from a senior colleague who is like-minded, capable, and trustworthy.

Yang in Fourth Place

A lone

Opposition.

A Primal Man

Is encountered.

Good Faith is shared.

There is

Danger.

No Harm,

Nullum malum.

On the Image

Aspirations are at work.

 Yang Line in Yin Place. The Primal Man is a kindred spirit, a charismatic person with whom one can work in Harmony. The Opposition is "lone," writes Magister Liu, because this Yang Line is trapped between Yin Lines. The Heart-and-Mind of Tao is caught in the Human Heart-and-Mind. If a True Gentleman of the Tao (the Primal Man) can be sought out in Good Faith, this will bring Increase, this will unite Yin and Yang. The "lone" will be "lone" no more. The Leader, writes Professor Mun, must seek out a person of like mind, to save him from isolation and build up fellowship.

Yin in Fifth Place

Regret

Goes away,

Nullus poenitendi locus.

There is

An Ancestral Feast.

A Destination.

No Harm,

Nullum malum.

On the Image

A Destination
Is cause for celebration,
Felicitas.

 Yin Line in Yang Place. Centered. The Ancestor is the Heart-and-Mind of the Tao, writes Magister Liu. The False Human Heart-and-Mind is eaten at the feast. This Destination leads to the Tao. This Yin Line, writes Professor Mun, Resonates with Yang in Second Place. They are both Centered. The Yin Leader seeks to complement his weakness with the Yang Strength of a colleague.

Yang in Top Place

Opposition.

Alone.

A pig is seen

Bearing mud;

A cart is

Freighted with ghosts.

A bow is bent,

Then loosened.

This is not an enemy,

But a suitor in marriage.

There is

An Advance.

Rain

Is encountered.

Auspicious,

Hoc bonum.

On the Image

All misgivings
Disappear,
Dubia nulla.

Yang Line in Yin Place. Best friends, writes Richard Wilhelm, are misjudged. They appear to be as dirty as "pigs," as sinister as a "cartload of ghosts." But ultimately the "bow" of hostility is loosened and put aside. The Other is approaching with the best of intentions, for the purpose of a close union (like a "suitor"). The Tension is relieved. Misgivings disappear and misunderstandings are resolved, just as rain relieves the sultriness preceding a thunderstorm. This is the extreme point of Opposition, writes Magister Liu. The Heart-and-Mind of the Tao is buried deep. A hundred doubts and cares have arisen, pollutions of the Human Heart-and-Mind, like "pigs bearing mud," like a "cartload of ghosts." To restore the Heart-and-Mind of the Tao, it is first necessary to understand the Human Heart-and-Mind, to "see" the "pigs" and "ghosts" for what they really are. To use the Human Heart-and-Mind is to "bend the bow." To restore the Heart-and-Mind of the Tao is to "loosen the bow." The encounter with rain is the union of Yin and Yang. It washes away all old pollution. The Leader, writes Professor Mun, gets rid of his suspicions and resolves his doubts. The Resonance between this Line and Yin in Third Place helps to create Harmony, and a Union of Yin and Yang.

Jian

Adversity

Kan/Abyss

above

Gen/Mountain

JUDGMENT

There is

Profit

To West and South.

There is

No Profit

To East and North.

It Profits

To see a Great Man,

Magnum virum.

To be Steadfast

Is Auspicious,

Hoc bonum.

On the Judgment

There is
Difficulty.
Danger lies ahead.
To see Danger,
To know when to halt—
This is wisdom indeed!
There is Profit
To West and South;
A Destination
Reaches Center,
Medium obtinebit.
To East and North,
The Tao is exhausted,
Lex exhausta.
To see a Great Man
Brings success.
Auspicious Steadfastness
In Apt Positions
Brings True Order
To the Realm.

On the Image of the Hexagram

Water on the Mountain,
Supra montem aqua.
The True Gentleman
Reflects on Self,
Cultivates Inner Strength.

Water above Mountain. The graph *Jian*, writes Legge, indicates a stumbling or a difficulty in walking. This Hexagram indicates (among other things) a state of Adversity, which makes government an arduous task. It describes obstructions that appear in the course of time but that can and should be overcome. This may be successfully achieved, now by Activity on the part of the Ruler, and now by a discreet Inactivity. The Judgment seems to require three things: attention to place and direction, the presence of the Great Man, and the firm observance of Truth or Steadfastness. These are needed to cope successfully with the difficulties of Adversity. The South and West represent open country; the North and East represent mountainous regions. Open country is easily traversed and held; mountainous regions are traversed and held only with difficulty. The Hexagram, writes Richard Wilhelm, pictures a dangerous Abyss lying before us in the Upper Trigram and a steep, inaccessible Mountain rising behind in the Lower Trigram. We are surrounded by obstacles. But the Stillness of the Mountain shows how we can extricate ourselves. With Prudence and Caution, writes Legge, we join forces with friends of like mind. We put ourselves under the leadership of a man equal to the situation (the Great Man). In the meantime, we must cultivate Inner Strength. In the words of Mencius, "When we cannot realize what we desire, then we must turn inward and examine ourselves, our True Selves." Lu Ji, general and *I Ching* devotee of the first and second centuries, most famous for having predicted the exact date of his own death, is quoted by the Tang-dynasty commentator Kong Yingda as saying of this Hexagram:

> The Abyss, when it is above the Mountain, loses its capacity to flow and connect. . . . Water, by its original Nature, should be *below* the Mountain. When it is above, it must turn back. There is a need to turn inward, to Return, a need for Self-Reflection. In times of Adversity, one cannot Act. To overcome difficulty, one must reflect on Self, examine and cultivate one's own Inner Strength. In good times, when things connect, when the Tao circulates freely, the True Gentleman can achieve good for the world. But when the times are out of joint, in times of Adversity, he must cultivate his own person.

This Hexagram, writes Magister Liu, is about preserving the Primordial in the midst of the Mundane. Yang is trapped between Yin. The Heart-and-Mind of the Tao is encumbered with the Human Heart-and-Mind. This is an extremely dangerous situation, fraught with Yin Energy. The Danger can be averted by letting the Human Heart-and-Mind gradually fade away. Then the Heart-and-Mind of the Tao can gradually be born. The Great Man is one in whom the Heart-and-Mind of the Child has not been lost. The Child has no knowledge, no greed, no goal. This is the Heart-and-Mind of the Tao, of the Great Man. In a time of Adversity, writes Professor Mun, the Leader should not panic or allow himself to feel too frustrated. He must remain stable and peaceful as a Mountain, while calmly thinking of ways out of the dilemma. He should be Steadfast and seek the help of capable people.

LINES

Yin in First Place

An Advance

Meets with Adversity.

Hold back.

This will be praised.

On the Image

It is right to wait,

Oportet expectare.

 Yin Line in Yang Place. With a rash Advance, writes Legge, the difficulties of Adversity will be overwhelming. Wait for a more favorable time. The Leader should stay where he is, writes Professor Mun, until the time is right for an Advance.

Yin in Second Place

For the King's subject,

Adversity

Follows upon Adversity,

Periculo periculum,

Through no fault of his own.

On the Image

Ultimately there is
No cause for Regret,
Non erit poenitendi locus.

 Yin Line in Yin Place. Centered. The loyal subject, writes Richard Wilhelm, is obliged to confront Adversity. This Line, writes Magister Liu, Resonates with Yang in Fifth Place, the Ruler or King. The Minister or Subject and the King are loyal to one another.

Yang in Third Place

An Advance

Meets with

Adversity,

Si eat,

Erit periculum.

Hold back.

Return.

On the Image

There is Joy
Within the Lower Trigram,
Intus gaudet.

 Yang Line in Yang Place. An Advance will plunge one recklessly into Danger, writes Legge. Withdraw, return, wait for a better time, and one will be received with Joy. Do away with the Human Heart-and-Mind, writes Magister Liu. Hold fast to the Heart-and-Mind of the Tao. The Leader, writes Professor Mun, should return to a more secure place. He should preserve his Strength for the future.

Yin in Fourth Place

An Advance

Meets with

Adversity,

Erit periculum.

Return.

Be united.

On the Image

There is substance here,
In Apt Position.

 Yin Line in Yin Place. JM: Again, it is wiser to hold back, to gather together trusty companions and wait for the right time to act. The Leader, writes Professor Mun, will unite with those below, and will be in a better position to benefit his Organization. The poet Ban Gu, in his "Rhapsody on Communicating with the Hidden," refers to this Hexagram and to Hexagram III, Difficult Birth:

What confusion lies
In Difficult Birth,
And in Adversity!
How much hardship,
How little wisdom!
The Ancient Sages,
In the face of difficulty,
Retreated. . . .
How many are the Changes!
Who can predict
Their Ending or Beginning?

Yang in Fifth Place

Great Adversity,

Magnum periculum.

Friends come,

Amici veniunt.

On the Image

At the Center,
Moderation.

Yang Line in Yang Place. Centered. In Adversity, helpers come to join one. This Line, writes Magister Liu, Resonates with Yin in Second Place, source of friendly aid. It is trapped between two Yin Lines. The Heart-and-Mind of the Tao is obscured by the Human Heart-and-Mind. This is Great Adversity. The "friends who come" are the Heart-and-Mind of the Tao. The Leader, writes Professor Mun, will receive assistance from Yin in Second Place, his "friend," with whom he Resonates. But he should not rely on this. He should also actively seek his own way out.

Yin in Top Place

An Advance

Meets with

Adversity.

Hold back.

This leads to success.

This is

Auspicious.

To see a Great Man

Profits,

Oportet convenire

Magnum virum.

On the Image

Aspirations are within,
Mens est intus.
A Great Man
Should be seen;
The noble
Should be
Followed.

Yin Line in Yin Place. The visit to the Great Man distinguishes this from the advice offered in the previous Lines. The Great Man will help find the way out of Adversity. This points to the end of Adversity, writes Magister Liu. The Human Heart-and-Mind is calmed; the Heart-and-Mind of the Tao comes into view. The Great Man is a True Master of the Tao, a man who has attained Release from Danger, who has completed the Work step by step, in due order. He has reached the Gate of Life, the Door of Death. Success requires the teaching of a True Master. A senior executive in this position, writes Professor Mun, should seek help from the Leader in Fifth Place, who is both capable and upright.

Xie

Release

Zhen/Quake

above

Kan/Abyss

JUDGMENT

There is

Profit

To South and West.

With no Destination,

A coming and a return

Are Auspicious,

Hoc bonum.

With a Destination,

An early start

Is Auspicious,

Hoc bonum.

On the Judgment

Danger leads to
Movement.
Movement averts
Danger.
Release.
Traveling
To South or West
Wins the Folk.
An Auspicious Return
Reaches Center.
An early start
Brings success.
With Release
Of Heaven and Earth,
Thunder and Rain
Arise.
With Thunder and Rain,
The hundred fruits,
The grasses and trees,
Burgeon.

On the Image of the Hexagram

Thunder and Rain,
Tonitrus et pluvia.
The True Gentleman
Forgives errors,
Pardons crimes.

毛 Quake above Water, above the Abyss. Two Yang Lines are surrounded by four Yin Lines. The Hexagram pictures a spontaneous loosening—the untying of a knot, or the unraveling of a complication—a Release, by which the Adversity and Danger of the preceding Hexagram are dissolved and Tensions are eased. Having "no Destination," hesitating, may be Auspicious at first. But in due course a prompt move is indicated, a Release of Positive Yang Energy. Thunder and Rain clear the air. The feeling of oppression is relieved. Thunder moves and rain falls, writes Magister Liu. Yin and Yang Energies connect. This is Release. When Yin Energy is stagnant, the True Gentleman understands the need for an "early start," for appropriate Action. Once Yang Energy returns, then a gentler approach is needed, a more forgiving and tolerant Self-Cultivation. This Release of Yang Energy is like the Gathering of Alchemical Herbs. It must take place at the correct time and in due order. The mountaineer-poet Xie Lingyun is reminded of Release and of Ascent (Hexagram XLVI) as he pushes his way through the undergrowth on one of his alpine hikes:

What I Saw on My Way from South Mountain
Below I spy
The tops of towering trees,
Above I hear
The wild torrent's roar.
Waters part over rocks,
Dense forest paths
Know no footfall.
Release
Resonates.
This is
Ascent
Through Abundance. . . .

LINES

Yin in First Place

No Harm,

Nullum malum.

On the Image

Firm and Yielding
Resonate.
No Harm.

Yin Line in Yang Place. A time for peaceful Reflection and gentle Action. This Yielding Line in a Firm Place finds Resonance (and Strength) in Yang in Fourth Place.

Weakness, writes Magister Liu, can borrow Strength from the Wisdom of the Taoist. Release from Darkness and Danger is possible. A problem should be resolved, writes Professor Mun, by using a moderate approach at an early stage, before it proliferates.

Yang in Second Place

In the hunt,

Three foxes

Are caught.

A yellow arrow

Is obtained.

To be Steadfast

Profits,

Hoc bonum.

On the Image

The Tao of Center
Is reached.

 Yang Line in Yin Place. Centered. Yellow is the color of Center. The "yellow arrow," writes Professor Mun, is a moderate approach. The "three foxes" are evil thoughts, which can be removed by holding Steadfastly to Center. This Yang Line is Central in the Lower Trigram. Inner Strength abides in the Center. Through Centered Steadfastness, the designs of the enemy (the "three cunning foxes," negative thoughts, the three remaining Yin Lines) are gradually overcome. This Release, writes Magister Liu, combines Strength with a Yielding gentleness. It prevents the Human Heart-and-Mind from doing evil. This is "catching three foxes in the hunt." The foxes of the Human Heart-and-Mind are restrained, they are guided on the True Path. Human desires are gently tolerated, and they extinguish themselves. This Release is spontaneous, not premeditated.

Yin in Third Place

The porter

Rides.

Brigands come.

There is

Steadfastness.

Distress,

Poenitendi locus.

On the Image

Vile thing!
He himself
Attracts brigands.
No one else
Can be blamed.

Yin Line in Yang Place. A lowly "porter" rides comfortably in a carriage, making himself vulnerable, attracting Danger. Enticed by his air of apparent ease, brigands attack and plunder him. He is acting above his station and capabilities (Yin in Yang), writes Professor Mun. He should know his own limits. Foolish thoughts of Heavenly Treasure, writes Magister Liu, distract him from the Heart-and-Mind of the Tao. Instead he attracts the Human Heart-and-Mind (the "brigand"). He holds on to the Yin of Self, and does not seek Yang from Others. This is a mistaken Release, a forced attempt to escape Danger, flawed by weakness.

Yang in Fourth Place

The big toe

Is released.

Friends arrive.

Good Faith,

Fides.

On the Image

Not in an Apt Position.

Yang Line in Yin Place. Lesser individuals, Small Men, may try to attach themselves, like a "big toe." Seek Release from such negative attachments. Release them, put them away. Let true "friends" take their place. This Yang Line, writes Magister Liu, Resonates with Yin in First Place (the Small Man). The toe can move but cannot walk. The Human Heart-and-Mind generates Danger. The Heart-and-Mind of the Tao is still weak. Yang Strength is led astray by Weakness (it is in a Yin Place). Trust in the Heart-and-Mind of the Tao. It alone will bring Good Faith and Release from the Human Heart-and-Mind.

Yin in Fifth Place

The Release

Of the True Gentleman

Is Auspicious,

Hoc bonum.

Good Faith is shown

To Small Men.

On the Image

The Small Man
Retreats.

 Yin Line in Yang Place. Centered. All that is contrary to peace and good order has been removed, writes Legge. Even the Small Man can change his ways, inspired by the Good Faith of the True Gentleman. The True Gentleman's Release, writes Magister Liu, comes about by his emptying the Human Heart-and-Mind and seeking out the Heart-and-Mind of the Tao. The Heart-and-Mind of the Small Man is the Human Heart-and-Mind.

Yin in Top Place

The Duke

Shoots at a hawk

On a high wall.

He gets it.

All things

Profit,

Nihil est quod non conveniat.

On the Image

He finds
Release from rebels.

 Yin Line in Yin Place. The "hawk on a high wall" is an inferior in a powerful position, attempting to obstruct Release. He must be "shot down," removed. The "hawk on the wall" is the Human Heart-and-Mind, writes Magister Liu, the Inner Demon of greed and ambition. It must be got rid of. The Heart-and-Mind of the Tao must prevail; it must Release the Human Mind. The Leader, writes Professor Mun, should take this opportunity to remove the inferior man from his Organization.

Sun

Decrease

Gen/Mountain

above

Dui/Lake

JUDGMENT

Good Faith.

This is

Supremely Auspicious,

Magnum bonum.

No Harm,

Nullum malum.

To be Steadfast

Is possible.

A Destination

Profits.

What shall be used?

Two small bowls

Suffice

For the Offering.

On the Judgment

The Lower Trigram
Decreases.
The Upper Trigram
Increases.
The Tao works upward.
Use of two bowls
Accords with Time.
The Firm
Decreases,
The Yielding
Increases.
Each in its Time.
Decrease and Increase,
Fullness and Emptiness:
Each in Harmony
With Time.

On the Image of the Hexagram

Lake beneath Mountain,
Infra montem lacus.
The True Gentleman
Contains anger,
Restrains desire.

Mountain above Lake. Excess of Yang (Firm), writes Jullien, following Wang Fuzhi, produces anger; Excess of Yin (Yielding) produces desire. The two Yang Lines of the Lower Trigram are softened (Decreased) by one Yin Line, giving us Joy or Lake, "containment of anger." The two Yin Lines of the Upper Trigram are contained and strengthened (Increased) by one Yang Line, giving us Mountain, which effectively stops or "restrains" desire. The Mountain-above-Lake configuration of Decrease is the inverse of the Hexagram Resonance (XXXI), where the Lake is *above* the Mountain and attracts Danger. Here, Lake at the foot of the Mountain creates a harmonious interior and exterior landscape. At its core is Good Faith. Excess is reduced; things are brought into Accordance with what is reasonable. This is the Tao of Decrease. Accomplished with Good Faith, it will lead to happiness and success. Decrease, when necessary and gradual, is not to be feared. Two modest "bowls," if part of a sincere Offering, in keeping with the moment in Time, suffice. A Positive Decrease can re-establish equilibrium; it can prevent a blockage; it can enable the evolving process of Change to continue. This is not mystical, but strategic. It flows not from some "higher" level of reality, but from the concrete Nature of the situation. The Tao of Decrease, writes Magister Liu, is not to follow desire but to Decrease desire. Few are capable of being Sincere in this endeavor. They may begin it, but they cannot bring it to a Conclusion. With Sincerity, every thought is True. Wherever the Heart-and-Mind is Sincere, wherever there is Good Faith, it can be seen in one's Actions. The "two small bowls" are the balance of Yang and Yin, of Firm and Yielding, in the Second and Fifth Lines. They Resonate. This Resonance takes one back to the Origin, the Source, the Root. In the business world too, comments Professor Mun, Decrease can sometimes be beneficial—provided it is carried out in Good Faith. In this context, the "two bowls" can be understood as a voluntary reduction in salary, for the good of the enterprise during a bad period. A shift of resources from one sector of a company to another is also an example of Decrease. Gains from a growing sector may offset losses from a declining sector. This will be a "positive sum game." The total gains of the company can still Increase.

LINES

Yang in First Place

A Sacrifice

Is swiftly concluded.

No Harm,

Nullum malum.

A Decrease

Is carefully contemplated.

On the Image

The one above shares
Aspirations.

Yang Line in Yang Place. Respect is paid, support given, to the one above (Yin in Fourth), with which this Line Resonates. But there must be due deliberation. Support given to a weaker unit (Yin in Fourth), writes Professor Mun, could affect the efficiency of the stronger unit (Yang in First). It must be properly thought through. Decrease may be swift, writes Magister Liu, but it must never be rashly undertaken. With proper forethought and care at the outset, it will cause no Harm.

Yang in Second Place

To be Steadfast

Profits.

An Advance

Brings Misfortune.

This is

An Increase

With no Decrease.

On the Image

Stay in the Center.
Aspirations are firm.

Yang Line in Yin Place. Centered. Stay Centered, writes Legge, following Cheng Yi (and the Commentary on the Image). Be cautious. Support others through firmness of Aspiration. (This Yang Line Resonates with Yin in Fifth Place.) The greater whole will Increase, the individual will suffer no Decrease. Yin and Yang combine as one, writes Magister Liu. The Golden Elixir forms. The Heart-and-Mind of the Tao is present, the Human Heart-and-Mind is no longer at work. This is a time for careful consolidation. Any further Decrease will activate the Human Heart-and-Mind once more and obscure the Heart-and-Mind of the Tao. The Leader, writes Professor Mun, should manage the resources under him in a more efficient way (he should be Centered). This will be an Increase (of the whole, of Others) without a Decrease (of Self). In some cases, a person must be careful not to lose his own Strength, if he is to help Others.

Yin in Third Place

Three travel;

Their number

Decreases

By one.

One traveling alone

Gains a friend.

On the Image

Travel alone.
With three,
Doubts arise.

Yin Line in Yang Place. In any group of three, writes Cheng Yi, jealousy and conflict easily arise. One of the group may have to leave ("decrease the number") in order to allow a harmonious relationship, the Harmony of Yin and Yang, to develop. When ignorance and folly generate emotion, writes Magister Liu, then the Human Heart-and-Mind cannot Decrease. Seeking an Increase in the Heart-and-Mind of the Tao, one meets instead with Decrease. This is "three travelers" losing a companion. When, however, there is a Decrease in the dualistic thinking of the Human Heart-and-Mind, and an Increase in the unitary thinking of the Heart-and-Mind of the Tao, then Yin and Yang can join together. Such an Increase comes in the midst of Decrease. This is the "lone traveler gaining a friend."

Yin in Fourth Place

An illness

Decreases.

Joy

Hastens on its way.

No Harm,

Nullum malum.

On the Image

Cause for

Joy.

Yin Line in Yin Place. With Humility, there is healing, a Decrease of illness. Friends and colleagues hasten joyfully to celebrate. This is Pure Yin, unalloyed with Yang, writes Magister Liu. The illness is far advanced. Fortunately this Yielding Line is in its True Place. The Yang of the Other (Yang in First Place, with which this Line Resonates) can be sought out to Decrease (and heal) the illness. A senior executive, writes Professor Mun, knows his weaknesses and corrects them quickly. This enhances the trust of the members of the Organization.

Yin in Fifth Place

Increase.

A Turtle worth

Ten strings of cowries.

A Gift

That cannot be refused.

This is

Greatly Auspicious,

Magnum bonum.

On the Image

Blessings
From above.

Yin Line in Yang Place. Centered. Ten strings would have been one hundred cowrie shells, a small fortune at the time. Such a gift cannot be refused. Nor can the Oracle inscribed on the shell of the Turtle be neglected, revealing as it does the benevolent intent of Heaven. This Yin Line, writes Magister Liu, Resonates with Yang in Second Place. Their Energies form a Wondrous Amalgam, a Priceless Treasure. The "gift that cannot be refused" is the spontaneous Increase that brings a return to the Tao. The Leader, writes Professor Mun, will be Steadfast. He will never abandon his principles, even if he accepts a fortune (a "turtle").

Yang in Top Place

There is no

Decrease.

There is

Increase.

No Harm,

Nullum malum.

To be Steadfast

Is Auspicious,

Hoc bonum.

A Destination

Profits.

The subject

Has no family,

Non habet domum.

On the Image

Aspirations
Are greatly fulfilled.

Yang Line in Yin Place. In this Top Yang line, writes Jullien, following Wang Fuzhi, Decrease begins its transformation into the next Hexagram, Increase. The True Gentleman, in the words of Cheng Yi, gains the devotion and loyalty of his subjects, fulfilling his purpose and dispensing generosity, bringing Increase to those below him. This happens without any Decrease to his own interests. This is the Highest Illumination, writes Magister Liu, the Utmost Excellence. JM: Master Liu often uses this phrase ("the Utmost Excellence") from the opening sentence of the *Great Learning*, one of the Four Books, a short text all educated Chinese of the traditional period knew by heart. It is a classic definition of the Tao of Self-Cultivation, shared by Confucians and Taoists alike. The selfless Leader, writes Professor Mun, will bring no Decrease to his subjects.

HEXAGRAM XLII

Yi

Increase

Xun/Wind

above

Zhen/Quake

JUDGMENT

A Destination

Profits.

It Profits

To cross a Great Stream,

Transire magnum flumen.

On the Judgment

The Upper Trigram
Decreases.
The Lower Trigram
Increases.
The Joy of the Folk
Knows no bounds.
The High
Humbles itself
Beneath the lowly.
Brilliant
Is the Tao of Increase.
A Destination
Profits,
The Centered Lines
Are True.
Blessing,
Gaudium.
Crossing a Great Stream:
The Tao of Wood
Prevails,
Ligni lex.
Increase:
Movement,
And Compliance.
A boundless daily Advance.
Heaven dispenses,
Earth gives birth.
Increase is infinite
It has no fixed place.
The Tao of Increase
Is always attuned to Time.

On the Image of the Hexagram

Wind and Thunder,
Ventus et tonitrus.
This is
Increase.
The True Gentleman,

Seeing goodness,

Moves.

If there is error,

He corrects it.

 Wind above Quake. Wind and Quake enhance each other, writes Magister Liu. The Lower Trigram, Quake, Movement, writes Jullien, combines with the Upper Trigram, Wind/Wood, Gentleness, to form an Image of continuous Propagation and Dissemination. The Tao of Wood makes it possible to cross the stream, on boat or raft. Decrease corrects; Increase fulfills. Heaven (in the Commentary on the Judgment), writes Legge, represents the authority of the Ruler (it "dispenses"); Earth represents the docility of the Folk. The Ruler "softens" his authority, he "humbles himself beneath the lowly," and the Folk benefit. The Ruler causes their resources to Increase. He will be successful in his enterprises; he will overcome great difficulties. All six Lines Resonate, writes Professor Mun. This indicates a good relationship among the respective units of an Organization at the upper level and below. A Leader may Increase the salaries of his employees and Decrease the salaries of his senior executives. This creates a sense of cohesion and cooperation within the whole Organization. Helping Others can be a mutually beneficial act.

LINES

Yang in First Place

It Profits

To embark on a

Great Enterprise.

This is

Supremely Auspicious,

Magnum bonum.

No Harm,

Nullum malum.

On the Image

From this Lowly Place,
A weighty matter

Must never be undertaken

Rashly.

 Yang Line in Yang Place. With this Yang Line at the base of the Hexagram, writes Jullien, Heaven and Earth join together once more. Their interplay begins anew, and the scene is set for a well-founded Increase. It is only natural, comments Legge, to want to make a Move; and great success may well follow. Enterprises of "great moment"—whether they be agricultural, military, or religious—may certainly be considered. But, as the Commentary on the Image reiterates, this must be done with Caution. Here, writes Magister Liu, at the outset of Increase, one may act boldly and with vigor, since initial thoughts are True. An executive, writes Professor Mun, may undertake a big project even though he is in a lower position. He is able to get help from Yin in Fourth Place, with which he Resonates.

Yin in Second Place

Increase.

A Turtle gift,

Worth ten strings of cowries,

Is not to be refused.

To be Steadfast in perpetuity

Is Auspicious,

Hoc bonum.

The King makes Offering

To the High God.

This is

Auspicious,

Hoc bonum.

On the Image

Increase
From without.

Yin Line in Yin Place. Centered. For the Turtle, compare the identical wording in the Fifth Line of the previous Hexagram. The Turtle-Oracle of the Divination is favorable, writes Legge. Men and Spirits bring benefit. The King's Sacrificial Offering to the High God is accepted. Heaven confers benefit from above. The Increase comes from without. JM: Offerings to the High God (*di*) would have included dogs, oxen, and a variety of other animals. This deity (the name is found on the Oracle Bones) was a quasi-Ancestral figure. The word itself was later appropriated for the Emperor, the "thearch," or Son of Heaven. The gift, writes Magister Liu, is the Resonance between this Yin Line and Yang in Fifth Place. Both Yielding (Yin) and Firm (Yang) are Centered and True. Their conjoined Energies are wondrous, like the latent Energy of the Turtle. The birth of the Inner Child is the Offering.

Yin in Third Place

Increase

Through Misfortune.

No Harm,

Nullum malum.

There is

Good Faith;

The Diviner

Instructs the Duke

To offer a *gui*-tablet

Of jade.

On the Image

Increase through Misfortune
Is as it should be.

Yin Line in Yang Place. Even Misfortune can bring Increase, writes Richard Wilhelm. It can quicken the process of Change. There is a potential for good even in those who seem to be entirely evil. JM: The *gui*-tablet (which came in several shapes and sizes) was a numinous talisman, symbol of sovereign power. Here it is used to exorcize Misfortune. Misfortune, writes Magister Liu, can be the means whereby Self-Cultivation progresses. Faith and Caution are the adjuvants. They are the tablet of jade.

Yin in Fourth Place

The Diviner

Instructs the Duke

To obey the Omen.

It Profits

To have support,

To move the nation.

On the Image

Increase of Aspiration.

Yin Line in Yin Place. The Ruler listens to the Diviner's advice in critical initiatives, such as moving the city or capital of a nation. During the Shang dynasty, and indeed throughout Chinese history, this happened several times. In order to "move the nation," writes Magister Liu, in order to move others toward the Tao, one needs the support of a great Inner Strength.

Yang in Fifth Place

Good Faith,

And a kind

Heart-and Mind.

Ask no questions.

This is

Supremely Auspicious,

Magnum bonum.

Good Faith

And Kindness.

Inner Strength.

On the Image

Aspirations are fulfilled.

Yang Line in Yang Place. Centered. Good Faith and Inner Strength prevail. This Yang Line is Centered and True, writes Magister Liu. The Great Tao is complete. With Good Faith and Kindness, one sees the Myriad Things as one great entity; one sees Self and Others as one great Family. It is like the Wind blowing. . . . Everything dances before it. A Leader in this position, writes Professor Mun, has Strength and Balance. He does what is good for Others, even at the expense of Self.

Yang in Top Place

No Increase.

He is struck.

His resolve

Is not constant,

Non perseverat.

Misfortune,

Hoc pessimum.

On the Image

No Increase.
He is rejected,
Struck
From without.

Yang Line in Yin Place. The bad Ruler, writes Jullien, is isolated. None of his subjects brings Increase, no one rallies around him. Rather, they end up attacking him. He is cut off from the Tao of Heaven; he is doomed to Misfortune. This is Strength wrongly applied, writes Magister Liu. No Increase is possible, for Self or Others. Self-Cultivation in the Tao must come first. Only then can one bring Increase to Self and Others.

Kuai

Resolution

Dui/Lake

above

Qian/Heaven

JUDGMENT

There is a proclamation

In the King's court.

Good Faith

Cries Danger,

Periculosum.

A report

To one's own city.

There is no Profit

In making war.

A Destination

Profits.

On the Judgment

Resolute Action.
The Firm
Acts resolutely
Upon the Yielding.
There is
Strength and Joy,
Resolution and Harmony.
The Yielding
Rides
Five Firm Lines.
Good Faith
Cries Danger.
It serves as a Light.
That which one most esteems
Is exhausted.
A Destination
Profits.
The Firm prevails
To the end,
Ad finem.

On the Image of the Hexagram

Lake above Heaven,
Lacus supra coelum.
The True Gentleman
Is generous to those below;
He does not pride himself on
Inner Strength.

Lake above Heaven. The last remnant of winter, cold and dark, can be seen in the solitary Yin Line in Top Place, which disappears as the five Yang Lines, the warm, bright days of approaching summer, mount upward. Corrupt and powerful influences, writes Legge, must be put out of the way. The Yin must be marginalized and eliminated. This elimination of Yin must be achieved by strength of character, by Good Faith, not by force of arms. The True Gentleman must awaken general sympathy, and at the same time go about his enterprise with Resolution, conscious of ("crying") Danger. In his "own city," among his own people, he must make it understood that he takes up arms unwillingly, and that he seeks no personal Profit in War. Then success will attend him. As with the Lake rising above Heaven, there must be both Strength and Joy, there must be both Resolution and Harmony. He must be generous and not isolate himself in the Pride of Self-Cultivation. This Hexagram, writes Magister Liu, shows Yin in Retreat before Yang. The "King's court" is the Heart-and-Mind, where True and False are seen for what they are. "One's own city" is the Self, the place where old habits of thought must be confronted and rooted out. But they have been there for so long, and the Heart-and-Mind has grown deeply attached to them. Wine and carnal pleasure obscure the Light of Truth. They "exhaust" the Tao, that very thing one "most esteems." The lure of Wealth is powerful. Desires and worldly cares proliferate. The Heart-and-Mind is mired in delusion. Good Faith is the means whereby the elimination of Yin will be achieved, the means whereby the Heart-and-Mind of the Tao can establish itself and become Master. Be aware of Danger. Practice Caution and Self-Cultivation. Let Resolution stem from Good Faith, from Sincerity, not from Pride and Conceit. Top Yin is egoism, writes Professor Mun, and the five Yang Lines are determination, Resolution, the desire to remove that egoism. Top Yin is also the senior official whose lack of Integrity threatens the efficiency of the Organization, and who must be removed. JM: In 1688, the thirty-four-year-old Manchu emperor Kangxi consulted the *I Ching* and received this Hexagram. As a result, he decided to purge the entire "Yin" (undoubtedly corrupt) clique around one of his leading Manchu courtiers, Prince Mingju.

LINES

Yang in First Place

There is

Strength

In the toes.

There is no success

In a Destination.

Harm,

Malum.

On the Image

An unsuccessful initiative
Will only bring Harm.

 Yang Line in Yang Place. This is too early a stage in the enterprise, writes Legge. There has not been sufficient preparation to make victory certain. It is best not to take to the field. This "strength in the toes" is impulsive and rash, writes Magister Liu. It will not help to root out the Yin. In fact it may do the very opposite. The Leader, writes Professor Mun, is tempted to act hastily without cautious thinking or planning. He is overconfident, and he overestimates his capabilities.

Yang in Second Place

There are

Cries of alarm.

There is

Armed combat

Evening and night.

Do not fear,

Nullum periculum.

On the Image

Fearlessness comes
From the Tao of Center.

 Yang Line in Yin Place. Centered. When confronted with a crisis, an ambush, an uprising, one must show Resolution, courage, tempered by Caution. No Harm will then ensue. This, writes Magister Liu, is a strong but gentle (because of the Yin Place) way of rooting out the influence of Yin. The Leader, writes Professor Mun, needs to be both confident and cautious when he deals with unforeseen difficulties.

Yang in Third Place

He is strong

In the face.

Misfortune,

Hoc pessimum.

The True Gentleman

Is Resolute;

He walks alone.

He encounters rain.

He is drenched

And angry.

No Harm,

Nullum malum.

On the Image

With Resolution,
Ultimately there can be
No Harm,
In fine
Nullum erit malum.

Yang Line in Yang Place. Here purpose is displayed too openly, too eagerly (Yang in a Yang Place). Strength may be visible "in the face," Resolution may appear "strong," but it is simply not equal to the task. Misfortune will result. Despite the "drenching rain," writes Magister Liu, in the end a gentle Resolution is possible. Despite his isolation (he "walks alone"), writes Professor Mun, he will, once the inferior man has been removed, eventually be understood by Others.

Yang in Fourth Place

His buttocks

Are skinned.

He hobbles.

A sheep

Is dragged.

Regret

Goes away,

Nullus poenitendi locus.

Words heard are

Not believed,

Non creduntur.

On the Image

The Position is not Apt.
Words are heard
But not believed;
They are heard
But not understood.

 Yang Line in a Yin Place. He is beaten till the skin is stripped from the buttocks, like the skin of a sheep dragged along rough ground. He is stubborn and refuses to heed advice (words "not believed"). Like a "dragged sheep," writes Magister Liu, he has difficulty making progress, hampered by the Human Heart-and-Mind. Lack of Faith prevents Resolution. The Leader is in a weak position (Yang in Yin), writes Professor Mun, and if he does not correct his attitude, he will suffer for it. In Liu Xie's *The Literary Mind and the Carving of Dragons*, the words "skinned buttocks" and "hobbling" are used to describe a work of literature that starts with a flourish but ends weakly. "It suffocates; its Energy is trapped."

Yang in Fifth Place

Purslane is weeded

With utter Resolution.

He treads the Center.

No Harm,

Nullum malum.

On the Image

The Center
Does not yet shine.

 Yang Line in Yang Place. Centered. The rooting out of weeds, writes Legge, following Cheng Yi, their total eradication, requires the same Resolution as the removal of evil men in positions of power—indeed, of any evil. The same is true of illicit desires. While a single such desire remains, one cannot "tread" Center, the True Path. These are deep words of admonition. A Leader of an Organization, writes Professor Mun, must be as Resolute in removing an inferior man as he would be in ridding his garden of weeds.

Yin in Top Place

No cries are heard.

Ultimately

There is

Misfortune,

In fine pessimum.

On the Image

Ultimately
One will not prevail,
In fine non durabit.

 Yin Line in Yin Place. Voices of the like-minded ("cries" of Good Faith) cannot be heard, writes Legge, following Hu Bingwen. In this dark extremity, Small Men prevail. Only the Resolution of Inner Strength can extricate one from this predicament. The one inferior man, writes Professor Mun, is about to be replaced by the Yang forces of the group.

Gou

Encounter

Qian/Heaven

above

Xun/Wind

JUDGMENT

A strong woman.

Do not marry the woman.

On the Judgment

The Yielding
Encounters the Firm.
Union with this woman
Will not endure.
When Heaven and Earth meet,
All Matter
Shares their splendor.

Firm Lines are Centered.
All-under-Heaven
Prospers.

On the Image of the Hexagram

Wind beneath Heaven,
Infra coelum ventus.
The Ruler issues orders;
He proclaims them
To the Four Quarters.

Heaven above Wind. Here we have the exact inverse of the previous Hexagram. A single Yin Line is in First Place, beneath five Yang Lines. This is an intrusion, an unexpected Encounter. A bold woman appears suddenly on the scene, writes Legge; she is seeking an Encounter and wishing to subdue all five Yang Lines. No one should become involved with such a woman. An influence such as this, which could penetrate like Wind (the Lower Trigram), must be resisted. By contrast, comments Magister Liu, there is a True Encounter, True Intercourse of Heaven and Earth, between the two Yang Lines (2 and 5) which are both Centered (one in Yin Place, one in Yang). This lies at the root of every prosperous undertaking, in Nature as in the world of men. The Taoist has the Inner Strength to adapt to the Transformations of Yin and Yang. The Taoist can be Yielding within Firmness, can be Firm while also being Yielding, can navigate in and out of Yin and Yang. The Taoist can "encounter" a woman but not "marry" her. Yin Energy will then obey Yang Energy. This is a situation, writes Professor Mun, in which a woman is chased by five men. The woman has a strong desire to dominate. The "strong woman" can also be seen as a strong business partner. If the partner is ambitious for power and domination, the venture may be damaged. A Leader must stay alert and not let business partners become dominant.

LINES

Yin in First Place

It is tied

To a bronze spindle.

To be Steadfast

Is Auspicious,

Hoc bonum.

With a Destination,

Misfortune appears.

A skinny piglet

Capers.

On the Image

Drawn along
By the Yielding Tao.

Yin Line in Yang Place. This First and only Yin Line affects the entire Hexagram and must be checked from the outset. It must be disciplined, like an unruly "piglet." For some commentators the piglet is a promiscuous woman, "capering" with many lovers, who must be held back, "tied to a bronze spindle"—i.e., pinned down to her household duties. Others see not a spindle but the restraining force of a braking device on a carriage, slowing things down. In any event, the force of Yin must be held in check; trouble must be anticipated and prevented in the early stages. A Leader, writes Professor Mun, must not ignore small things which may cause big troubles. A "skinny piglet" could grow into a fat pig. The Leader should also be able to control his own emotions and not let them develop further.

Yang in Second Place

There is fish

In the kitchen.

No Harm,

Nullum malum.

No Profit

For guests.

On the Image

It is right
Not to share the fish
With guests.

Yang Line in Yin Place. Centered. It is best to contain emotions at this time, comments Zhu Xi. It is best not to be overly generous. The Leader, writes Professor Mun, must be able to restrain improper or unethical practices ("fish in the kitchen") in his Organization. He must keep misconduct under control.

Yang in Third Place

Buttocks

Are skinned.

He hobbles.

There is

Danger,

Periculosum.

No great Harm,

Malum non magnum.

On the Image

He walks;
He is not drawn along.

 Yang Line in Yang Place. The opening words are identical to those of Yang in Fourth Place of the preceding Hexagram, describing a sense of unease, of uncertainty, of futility, of great frustration—but no actual Harm. Inner Mastery is unstable, writes Magister Liu. The Human Heart-and-Mind has already polluted the Heart-and-Mind of the Tao (Yin has influenced Yang). This is to "hobble with skinned buttocks." With the Strength of Yang, this can be rectified; the threat of Yin can be averted. The Leader finds himself in a dilemma, writes Professor Mun. He "hobbles." He must stop negative thoughts in the Organization in a timely manner.

Yang in Fourth Place

There is no fish

In the kitchen.

Misfortune commences,

Incipit pessimum.

On the Image

Distance from the Folk
Causes Misfortune.

Yang Line in Yin Place. The Hearts-and-Minds of the Folk (the "fish") have been lost, comments Magister Liu. The Heart-and-Mind of the Tao is obscured, and the Human Heart-and-Mind runs riot. Damage is caused by the unchecked influence of Yin Energy. Misfortune is only to be expected. The Leader has no "fish," writes Professor Mun. His leadership lacks balance (Yang in Yin). This has lost him the support of the people below him.

Yang in Fifth Place

A gourd is wrapped

In purple willow.

Beauty is

Contained.

It descends from Heaven,

Ex coelo venit.

On the Image

Beauty contained
Is Centered and True.
Aspiration has not forsaken
Life-Destiny.

Yang Line in Yang Place. Centered. Yin Energy is held at bay, comments Magister Liu. Yang Energy is not injured. This Firm Line is Centered and True. But the lingering influence of Yin in First Place is still felt. Danger threatens. The Human Heart-and-Mind must be restrained by the Heart-and-Mind of the Tao. Expel cleverness, contain and treasure the Light within. Just as the gourd (*gua*) is "wrapped" in willow leaves, writes Professor Mun, so the Leader surrounds and protects his employees by virtue of his strong and balanced leadership (Yang in Yang). If Inner Beauty is contained, writes Legge, Heaven will send its Blessing.

Yang in Top Place

Horns are

Encountered.

There is

Distress,

Poenitendi locus.

No Harm,

Nullum malum.

On the Image

There is
Exhaustion,
Distress.

 Yang Line in Yin Place. The Encounter, the clashing of "horns," does not augur well. The Golden Elixir, writes Magister Liu, is no sooner gained than lost. This stems from failure to guard against Yin in the early stages. The Leader is arrogant and obstinate (Yang in Yin), writes Professor Mun. This has regrettable consequences.

Cui

Gathering

Dui/Lake

above

Kun/Earth

JUDGMENT

A Sacrifice.

The King

Approaches his Temple.

It Profits

To see a Great Man,

Oportet

Convenire magnum virum.

Fortune.

To be Steadfast

Profits.

It is Auspicious

To make a Great Sacrifice,

Hoc bonum.

A Destination

Profits.

On the Judgment

Gathering.
Compliance and Delight.
The Firm
Is Centered and Resonant.
The King
Approaches his Temple;
He performs
A Filial Sacrifice.
Seeing a Great Man
Brings Fortune.
Gathering in Truth,
Following Heaven's Mandate,
Mandatum coeli.
Observe the Gathering:
The Nature of Heaven and Earth
Is revealed;
The Nature of the Myriad Things
Is revealed.

On the Image of the Hexagram

Lake above Earth,
Lacus supra terram.
The True Gentleman
Keeps his weapons of war prepared,
Against an unforeseen eventuality.

Lake above Earth. Water in the Lake is Gathered above the Earth. It is a time of unity, writes Legge, a joyful Gathering of the like-minded. The King goes to his Ancestral Temple. There he meets with the Spirits of his Ancestors. He returns to his Roots. This is the Great Sacrifice. These are his True Ancestors. The King is in the Centered Fifth Line, with which the Second Yin Line Resonates. He is a charismatic Leader, a man of vision whose qualities inspire respect, writes Professor Mun. His employees (the three Yin Lines of the Lower Trigram Earth) are drawn to him. He is the Great Man. He brings to his Organization Fortune and the Joy of Lake (the Upper Trigram). His Sacrifices are distinguished by their dignity and splendor; his victims are the best that can be obtained. All is in Harmony. But strife (the "unforeseen eventuality") may still be waiting around the corner, and precautions must be taken. Weapons of Wisdom must always be at the ready, writes Magister Liu. Spiritual Awareness must always be silently at work. With weapons such as these one can maintain presence of mind, and the Jewel of Life will not be damaged, even though Water may flood the land (Lake above Earth, another "unforeseen eventuality"). Individuals too must gather together their inner resources; they must harness their Essential Energy in the cause of Spiritual Development. They must respect their true original Nature, their "Ancestor." They must not forsake their Roots. The Ritual of Sacrifice, the attitude of Steadfast reverence, must be followed by commitment, by Action—by setting out toward a Destination. Momentary perceptions of the Void, instants of enlightenment, are not enough. Steps must be taken on solid ground—step after step—if anything real is to be accomplished.

LINES

Yin in First Place

Good Faith.

No Conclusion.

Disorder.

A Gathering.

In an instant,

Weeping turns to

Laughter.

Do not be sad.

A Destination.

No Harm,

Nullum malum.

On the Image

Aspirations
Are confused.

 Yin Line in Yang Place. In the midst of confusion and disorder, writes Magister Liu, when Good Faith has been lost, when Gathering lacks a base in Truth, a cry for help is answered, a Destination—a True Teacher—is found. (This Line has Resonance with Yang in Fourth Place.) The Tao is not far away. Tears then turn to laughter. Indecision is resolved. A vacillating Leader, writes Professor Mun, brings disharmony to the Organization.

Yin in Second Place

It is Auspicious

To be drawn.

No Harm.

Good Faith.

It Profits

To perform the *Yue* Sacrifice.

On the Image

No Harm.
The Center is unchanged,
Nondum mutatum.

 Yin Line in Yin Place. Centered. Intuition, an unchanged sense of Good Faith, draws one forward, to unite with others of like mind. (This Yin Line Resonates with Yang in Fifth.) The *Yue* Sacrifice, offered in the spring, may be of lesser significance; but when performed in Good Faith, with the utmost Sincerity, it draws the Gathering together. Light can be found, writes Magister Liu, even amid the Darkness of the three Yin Lines.

Yin in Third Place

A Gathering,

A Sighing.

No Profit.

No Harm

In a Destination.

Slight Distress.

On the Image

No Harm.
Compliance
With what comes above,
Obediunt.

Yin Line in Yang Place. One yearns to be part of a Gathering, but the times are not propitious. This Yang Place is not Apt for a Yin Line. There is no Resonance. (The Line in Top Place is also Yin.) Attempts to find Resonance close by are less than ideal. Nonetheless, writes Professor Mun, an executive in this position should seek a relationship with Yang in Fourth Place, a person who can play an important role in the decision-making process. Vain fantasies of Attainment in the Tao are hollow, writes Magister Liu. They are insubstantial, they lead to "sighing." One must set forth boldly and seek guidance from the wise. Yin Meiman, in his modern "retelling" of Zhu Xi's classic commentary, quotes a Chinese saying here: "If a boat sets itself against the current, it will not Advance; it can only go backward." He adds, "We Chinese must follow the leadership of the Communist Party if we are ever to be rich as a nation and powerful as a people." These are the new "Great Men"! With these one should "comply"! An extraordinary (and unintentionally very funny) example of the timeless way in which the *I Ching* continues to be ideologically manipulated.

Yang in Fourth Place

Greatly Auspicious.

No Harm.

On the Image

The Position is not Apt.

 Yang Line in Yin Place. The Yin Place softens the Yang Strength of the Line. Only when Yin and Yang are balanced, writes Magister Liu, can the Elixir begin to take form. It is within view. It is Gathering together. The three Yin Lines below this Yang Line, writes Professor Mun, represent the hidden Dangers confronting this executive. He is in the "wrong" position (Yang in Yin). He must exercise great Caution.

Yang in Fifth Place

A Gathering

In Apt Position.

No Harm.

Good Faith

Is absent.

With long-lasting Steadfastness,

Regret goes away.

On the Image

Aspirations
Have not yet shone forth,
Nondum eluscit.

 Yang Line in Yang Place. Centered. Even when others (those who gather round) do not yet share Good Faith, even when they have still not seen the Light, with Steadfastness, Harmony can prevail. A Leader must persevere, writes Professor Mun; he must succeed in inspiring others with his Good Faith if he is to gain their confidence.

Yin in Top Place

A Sighing,

A Weeping,

A Sobbing.

No Harm.

On the Image

Here in Top Place,
There is still no peace,
Nulla est pax.

 Yin Line in Yin Place. The attempted Gathering, the attempt to congregate, has failed. Isolation brings sorrow and lamentation. But if Steadfastness prevails, the final outcome can still be Auspicious. The Leader of an Organization, writes Professor Mun, must examine his past Actions and make the necessary corrections if others are to be willing to associate with him.

HEXAGRAM XLVI

Sheng

Ascent

Kun/Earth

above

Xun/Wind

JUDGMENT

Supreme Fortune.

It Profits

To see a Great Man.

Do not be sad.

A Southern Advance

Is Auspicious,

Hoc bonum.

On the Judgment

The Yielding
Ascends with Time.
There is Compliance,
Flow.
The Firm
Is Centered,
It Resonates.
Great Fortune.
It avails to see a Great Man.
Do not be sad.
There is cause for celebration,
Gaudium.
A Southern Advance
Is Auspicious.
Aspirations are fulfilled.

On the Image of the Hexagram

Wood grows within Earth,
Arbor in terra.
The True Gentleman
Flows with Inner Strength.
The Small
Accumulates
Until it becomes
Tall and Great.

Earth above Wind. The Flowing Energy of the Lower Trigram (*Xun*), writes Legge, following Zhu Xi, combines the qualities of Wind (breeze-like penetration) and Wood (gently thriving vegetation). It rises into and through the Upper Trigram, Earth (*Kun*). Four Yin Lines surround two Yang Lines. Yin dominates. This Ascent is a gradual Advance, like that of a conscientious official who climbs to the highest pinnacle of distinction. Here, the South is a region of brightness and warmth; a Southern Advance will be a joyful progress. This Hexagram, comments Magister Liu, stresses gentle progress, a gradual Ascent into the realm of Truth, requiring long and patient Self-Cultivation. It requires proper teaching from a Master, a Great Man, whose words can open a path leading upward to Wisdom, like an all-penetrating Wind. It is a journey toward the Light—step by step, day by day. Trees grow on the lower slopes of the Earth, writes Professor Mun. As they mature they rise upward. Their Energy Ascends. An enlightened person should follow their example. So should an efficient Organization. It should adopt steady, rather than aggressive, growth.

LINES

Yin in First Place

Sincere

Ascent.

Greatly Auspicious,

Magnum bonum.

On the Image

Those above share
Aspirations.

Yin Line in Yang Place. Good Faith and Sincerity bring about a gentle Ascent, one which is well received by those above. This, writes Magister Liu, requires Humility and an open mind. Men of the Tao must be approached.

Yang in Second Place

Good Faith.

The *Yue* Sacrifice

Profits.

No Harm.

On the Image

Joy,
Gaudium.

Yang Line in Yin Place. Centered. Devotion and Sincerity (Good Faith) are cause for joy. The Sacrifice, writes Magister Liu, is part of the Work. Progress is gradual; it achieves Connection through Sincerity. This Yang Line, writes Professor Mun, Resonates with Yin in Fifth Place. The combination of a strong subordinate (Yang in

Second) and a gentle Leader (Yin in Fifth) results in a Yin-Yang union favorable for an Ascent.

Yang in Third Place

Ascent

Into an empty city.

On the Image

No misgiving,
Nullus dubitandi locus.

Yang Line in Yang Place. This Ascent, writes Legge, is altogether too bold and fearless. One thinks oneself wise and therefore in need of no instruction, comments Magister Liu. But in fact this Ascent leads to a false city, one that contains nothing, no enlightenment, no true knowledge. The executive intending to move forward, writes Professor Mun, should check out the real situation beforehand. There may be obstacles.

Yin in Fourth Place

The King offers a Sacrifice

On Mount Qi.

Auspicious.

No Harm.

On the Image

Caution.

Yin Line in Yin Place. The Zhou kings built their earlier capital at the foot of Mount Qi, to the West, in the region of modern Shaanxi Province. Their Ritual Ascent of the Mountain ensured the Harmony of the Realm. A modest and gradual Ascent through Self-Cultivation, comments Magister Liu, leads to a Higher Realm.

Yin in Fifth Place

To be Steadfast

Profits,

Hoc bonum.

Ascent

Of the terrace.

On the Image

Aspirations
Are greatly attained.

Yin Line in Yang Place. Centered. This Ritual Ascent leads, step by step, to the heights. Gradual Ascent, comments Magister Liu, empties the Human Heart-and-Mind and seeks the Heart-and-Mind of the Tao. When done in this way, climbing the steps of the terrace seems easy and effortless. When the Ascent is complete, it is as if one had been there all along. This, writes Professor Mun, is a "steady rise" for an Organization. It is Steadfast, it is achieved with patience, like climbing the steps of a terrace.

Yin in Top Place

Ascent

Into Darkness.

Unwavering Steadfastness

Profits.

On the Image

Into Darkness at the Top.
Dissolution.
No wealth.

Yin Line in Yin Place. Further Ascent is blind and foolish, writes Legge. Only unwavering Steadfastness can save one from its consequences. The higher the Ascent, the greater the Darkness, comments Magister Liu, if that Ascent is undertaken in folly and selfish vanity. To Ascend *out of* that Darkness, it is essential to find a teacher, it is essential to be Steadfast, to return to Truth. When the future is uncertain and Dark, writes Professor Mun, a Leader should be cautious and avoid any impulsive action.

Kun

Confinement

Dui/Lake

above

Kan/Abyss

JUDGMENT

Fortune.

Steadfast.

This is Auspicious

For a Great Man,

Magnus vir.

No Harm,

Hoc bonum.

There are

Words;

There is no

Belief,

Non credit.

On the Judgment

The Firm is oppressed;
There is Danger,
There is Joy,
Periculosum
Sed laetum.
Only the True Gentleman
Can hold on to Fortune
In Confinement.
This is Auspicious
For a Great Man.
The Firm is Centered.
There is
No belief in words.
Setting store
On talk
Exhausts,
Exhauritur.

On the Image of the Hexagram

No Water in the Lake,
In lacu nulla aqua.
The True Gentleman
Fathoms Life-Destiny,
Holds fast to Aspiration.

Lake above Water. Joy of the Lake is above Danger of the Abyss. Water drains from the Lake, leaving it dry. The graph *kun* in the Hexagram Name has a tree within an enclosure (a completely different word from the *kun* of Hexagram II). The two Yang Lines in Second and Fifth Places, although oppressed and threatened, are Centered, writes Richard Wilhelm. In Second Place, the Confinement is caused by the Yin Lines on either side; in Fifth Place it is caused by the single Yin Line above. All of this indicates Confinement of good men by bad. In hard times such as these, in straitened and distressed times, it is essential to be strong and committed within, and sparing of speech; to hold fast to Aspiration; and not to waste time on words. In both Upper and Lower Trigrams, writes Magister Liu, Yin Energy has affected Yang. Yang Energy cannot connect and circulate. But the Joy of Lake can ultimately emerge from the Danger of the Abyss. There *is* a way out of Confinement. The True Gentleman knows that way. He is Steadfast; he perseveres in Self-Cultivation even in times of Confinement; he finds Joy even when material circumstances are hard, during times of illness, in old age, in the face of psychological obstacles. He holds fast to Aspiration. Confinement and Adversity, writes Professor Mun, can be the source of Fortune.

LINES

Yin in First Place

The buttocks are

Confined

On a tree stump.

He enters

A dark, secluded valley.

For three years

Nothing is seen.

On the Image

All is dark,
Unclear.

Yin Line in Yang Place. The "tree stump" affords no shelter or comfort, writes Legge. The "dark valley" increases distress and gloom. Three years is simply a long time. See also Hexagram LV/6. The "nothing seen" may mean that there is no visible way out of the valley. This Line makes a Great Confinement out of a Small Confinement, writes Magister Liu. It is a weak and self-destructive attitude. It will be hard to emerge from the "dark valley" of gloom. The "stump," writes Professor Mun, is not a proper tree: it provides no shade. Although this Line Resonates with Yang in Fourth Place, neither Line is in Apt Position. This weakens the effectiveness of the Resonance. It is essential to wait with patience and optimism. The way out will eventually show itself.

Yang in Second Place

He is

Confined

Amid food and wine.

Scarlet robes arrive.

A Sacrificial Offering

Profits.

An Advance

Brings Calamity,

Pessimum.

No Harm,

Nullum malum.

On the Image

This is Centered.
There is
Cause for celebration,
Gaudium.

 Yang Line in Yin Place. Centered. Even in the midst of a sumptuous feast, there is a sense of Confinement. The Ruler, clad in scarlet robes, comes to offer support. With the appropriate Ritual Offering, all will be well. This, writes Magister Liu, points to the arrival of Fortune after Confinement, to a time when suffering finally comes to an end and Joy begins. The Great Tao is accomplished. This requires time and patience. Any attempt to achieve a "quick" solution (any "Advance") will merely lead to Calamity.

Yin in Third Place

He is

Confined

On stone,

Held fast

By thorns and thistles.

He enters the Palace;

He does not see

His wife.

Calamity,

Hoc malum.

On the Image

Held by thorns,
He Rides a Firm Line.
Not seeing his wife
Bodes ill.

 Yin Line in Yang Place. This is a comfortless place, writes Legge, a graphic description of the distress and insuperable difficulties brought about by reckless action and reliance ("riding") on others in power (the Yang Line in Fourth Place above). If one does not honor teachers and respect friends, writes Magister Liu, one will be disliked by True Gentlemen. This will be like being Confined "on stone," held fast by "thorns." It is one's own doing. It is to have no knowledge, but to pretend to have attained the Tao. It is to serve the Outer and to lose the Inner; to "enter the Palace and not see one's wife." In the end one will perish.

Yang in Fourth Place

He comes slowly,

Slowly.

He is

Confined

In a bronze carriage.

Distress,

Poenitendi locus.

Conclusion,

Finis.

On the Image

Aspirations are set
On the one below.
This is not Apt,
But it receives support.

Yang Line in Yin Place. This is the first Line of the Upper Trigram, Lake. The Darkness of the Abyss is gradually being left behind. But the "carriage," writes Legge, is not doing its job, it has failed. Too much attention is being paid to the "one below," to the Yin Line in First Place, with which this Line does indeed Resonate. In that Yin Line, all is Dark and unclear. But support now comes from above, from the Yang Line in Fifth Place, and ultimately the good prevails. This must take place "slowly, slowly," writes Magister Liu. There will ultimately be a resolution of Confinement.

Yang in Fifth Place

Nose and feet

Are cut off.

He is

Confined

By crimson robes.

Joy

Comes slowly,

Gaudium.

A Sacrifice

Profits.

On the Image

Nose and feet
Are cut off:
Aspirations

Are not yet attained.
A slow Joy
Is Centered and Straight.
A Sacrifice
Bestows blessing,
Felicitatem.

Yang Line in Yang Place. Centered. The "crimson robes" are those of the nobles, as opposed to the "scarlet robes" of the Ruler in the Second Line. Official life Confines; it brings its troubles, its wounds (to "nose and feet"). But slowly, with a Centered composure (Yang Line in Yang Place), and with the Offering of a Sacrifice, all will turn out for the best. With a long-protracted application to the Work, writes Magister Liu, the Great Tao will be attained. There will be a way out of Confinement.

Yin in Top Place

He is

Confined

Amid creepers and vines,

In fear and peril,

Periculi et timoris locus.

Movement brings

Regret,

Poenitebit.

With Regret,

There will be

An Auspicious Advance,

Hoc bonum.

On the Image

This is not yet Apt.
Regret can still lead to
Auspicious Action.

Yin Line in Yin Place. Here Confinement reaches its extreme. Confined by petty cares and troubles ("creepers and vines"), by the machinations of Small Men, one is perched on a perilous summit. But the extremity is also an opportunity for Change. With genuine Regret, all can still turn out well. With Regret, writes Magister Liu, it will be possible to escape from Confinement, from vain pretension and self-glory.

HEXAGRAM XLVIII

Jing

The Well

Kan/Abyss

above

Xun/Wind

JUDGMENT

Towns change,

But never the Well.

There is neither loss

Nor gain.

There is

Coming and going

At the Well.

The rope fails to raise

Water

From the Well.

The pitcher is broken.

Calamity,

Pessimum.

On the Judgment

Wood within Water,
Lignus infra aquam.
Wood raises Water.
The Well nourishes;
It is never exhausted,
Non exhauritur.
The Well never changes.
The Firm is Centered.
It fails to raise
Water.
No success,
Nulla gloria.
A broken pitcher.
Calamity,
Pessimum.

On the Image of the Hexagram

Water above Wood,
Supra lignum aqua.
The True Gentleman
Comforts the Folk;
He gives encouragement.

Water above Wind, above Wood. The wooden bucket (Lower Trigram) is in the Water (Upper Trigram). The Chinese word for a well was thought of as a simple picture, a plot of land divided into nine parts, a bit like Noughts and Crosses (tic-tac-toe). The central piece of land was public, cultivated jointly by the eight families settled on the other parts. (This traditional etymology has been questioned.) And in the communal Center was the Well, shared by all (see Part II). The Well, writes Legge, is to its neighborhood, and to men in general, what a government is to its people, what a Centered Heart-and-Mind is to an individual. The great principles of Human Nature and good government are unchangeable (and interchangeable). The Wood in the Water is the wooden pole with its bucket, which descends into the "source" and brings the water up from there to the top. The gentle influence of Wind and Wood work together in the Lower Trigram, penetrating upward into the life-giving Water of the Upper Trigram. JM: Just as Water is drawn from the Well, the numinous content deep in the soul is drawn upward into consciousness. This is a powerful Image of the process of Self-Cultivation. To look into the Water of the Well is to adopt the mystic attitude of Contemplation. The Well is indeed a graphic symbol of the soul itself, and of all things feminine. Wood goes down into Water, but emerges out of Water, writes Magister Liu, through the Danger of the Abyss. This Hexagram represents the inexhaustible Nourishment of Water. Those who practice the Self-Cultivation of the Tao are able to nourish Self in this way. They can then nourish Others. This is like the Well. Others and Self are both nourished. Towns (Others; the outside world) may change (men "come and go" at the Well), but not the Well (the Inner Self). To teach Others before one has attained the Tao is to raise Water from the Well with a broken pitcher. One can guide Others only when one has attained the Tao. The Well Hexagram is all about Self-Cultivation.

LINES

Yin in First Place

A muddy

Well,

Not fit for drinking.

There are no birds

At the Ancient Well.

On the Image

Mud has
Sunk to the bottom.
With Time,
The Well is abandoned.

Yin Line in Yang Place. Men in authority, writes Legge, are all too often "muddy" like this Well. They are corrupt and useless. So too are states of Heart-and-Mind. Mud in an old Well, writes Magister Liu, is the silt of Folly and Ignorance. There is no

Water, nothing fit to drink. How can such a person nourish Others? Naturally there are no birds at this Well. If a company can no longer provide the right products, writes Professor Mun, it will be abandoned by the market. Any Organization which neglects self-development or self-preservation will face the danger of elimination.

Yang in Second Place

In the depths

Of the Well,

Fingerlings are shot

With bow and arrow.

The broken pitcher

Leaks.

On the Image

There are no followers.

Yang Line in Yin Place. Centered. Little fish are all that can thrive in this Well, writes Magister Liu. There is not enough Water for anything more substantial. Moreover, the "pitcher" leaks. There is too little moisture. Others cannot benefit, and Self will suffer. There is insufficient Self-Cultivation. The "leaking pitcher," writes Professor Mun, is the Energy wasted by an executive on unworthy pursuits.

Yang in Third Place

A cleansed

Well,

And yet

The Water

Is not fit for drinking.

This pains the heart.

A wise King

Makes the Water fit to draw;

He bestows Blessing,

Felicitatem.

On the Image

Pray for such a wise King.
Pray to receive
Heaven's Blessing.

Yang Line in Yang Place. This is the top of the Lower Trigram, Wood. Self-Cultivation has progressed (Yang in Yang) to the point where one can begin to help Others in their quest, writes Magister Liu. The Well has been cleansed, but the Water is not yet quite "fit for drinking." The influence of the Tao spreads, but one does not yet meet with kindred spirits. The wise King serves as a model. The Well Water is pure, writes Professor Mun, and yet no one draws or drinks from it. Capable people in an Organization have not been used properly by the top management. This is a great loss. Once their worth is recognized (once the Water is "fit to draw"), the whole Organization will benefit. Sima Qian, the Grand Historian, in his biography of the great Chu poet Qu Yuan, quotes the words of this Line (here given in David Hawkes's translation from *The Songs of the South*):

Not to drink when Well is pure
Fills my heart with sorrow sore.
Draw therefrom, if King be wise,
You shall share his blessings too.

The Grand Historian, whose biography damns King Huai for having rejected his loyal minister, comments: "But if the king is *not* wise, what Blessing can there be then?" In his "Rhapsody on Climbing the Tower," the poet Wang Can refers to this same Line, lamenting that his own purity and talent have been neglected:

I wait for the River to run clear,
But it never does.
I long for the day when
The Kingly Way
Will at last be smooth,
When I may take the high road
And try my strength.
I hate to hang
Useless as a gourd,

Undrunk Water
From a Cleansed Well. . . .
My heart is sad,
It bursts with pain. . . .

Yin in Fourth Place

A brick-lined

Well.

No Harm,

Nullum malum.

On the Image

The Well
Has been repaired.

Yin Line in Yin Place. Cultivation of Self, writes Legge, of the deep source of Inner Strength, repairing the Inner Well—these are fundamental both to Self-Knowledge and to the effective government of Others. This is the first Line of the Upper Trigram, Water, writes Magister Liu. One knows how to cultivate Inner Strength ("line" the Well). One can ward off Danger. To reform an Organization, writes Professor Mun, rather than liquidate it, is to repair a Well (to "line it with bricks"), instead of digging a completely new one. Reform is preferable to revolution.

Yang in Fifth Place

The Well

Is fed by a clear, cool spring.

Drink.

On the Image

This is Centered and True,
Medium et rectum.

Yang Line in Yang Place. Centered. The Well, writes Thomas McClatchie, is full of clear water; it does its work, nourishing Inner Life and the life of society, like a good Ruler, a model sovereign. This is Completion of the Great Tao, writes Magister Liu. This is Water with a True Source, deep, nourishing, and inexhaustible. The Leader in this position (Yang in Yang), writes Professor Mun, is a source of strength and wisdom to his Organization, like a "clear, cool spring."

Yin in Top Place

Pull up the rope,

Leave the Well

Open and

Uncovered.

Good Faith.

This is

Supremely Auspicious,

Magnum bonum.

On the Image

Great achievement,
Magnum bonum.

 Yin Line in Yin Place. When the Well is left uncovered, writes Legge, following Zhu Xi, then its use is free to all. All can partake of the inexhaustible life-giving Yin element of Water; in the Top Trigram, they can have access to the Abyss, which is rich in Good Faith. Aspirations have been attained. The work of the Well, of Self-Cultivation, is now completed, writes Magister Liu. There is no need to cover the Well. It can be shared with all. People can finally drink from the Well, writes Professor Mun. The Leader allows them all to use it. His generosity and unselfishness inspire Good Faith.

Ge

Change

Dui/Lake

above

Li/Fire

JUDGMENT

The right day.

Good Faith.

Supreme Fortune.

To be Steadfast

Profits.

Regret

Goes away,

Nullus poenitendi locus.

On the Judgment

Water and Fire
Extinguish one another.
Two women dwell together,
Their Aspirations
Ill-attuned.
Change.
Good Faith
On the right day.
With Change,
Comes belief.
Pattern and Illumination bring
Joy.
Truth brings
Great Fortune.
Change is Apt,
Regret goes away.
Heaven and Earth
Change,
The Four Seasons
Come to pass.
King Tang overthrew Xia;
King Wu overthrew Shang.
This Change of Mandate
Followed
Heaven's Flow;
It Resonated
With fellow men.

On the Image of the Hexagram

Fire in the Lake,
In medio lacus ignis.
The True Gentleman
Regulates the calendar,
Illumines the Seasons.

Lake above Fire. This combination of Trigrams signals Change. Fire and Water (the Lake), writes Richard Wilhelm, are here in conflict; they combat each other, each trying to destroy the other. The situation is more radical here than in Hexagram

XXXVIII, *Kui*, Opposition. There Fire is above Water, and the message is to seek "difference in union," to compromise, to attend to "small matters." The graph for this Hexagram Name, *Ge*, originally depicted the hide or skin of an animal (or the feathers of a bird). It came to mean "Change" very early on, in the sense of a particular Change, an "event" such as the stripping of a hide, an act of human decision and initiative, a turnaround, as opposed to Change, the overall process. Here the Change springs from mutual antagonism within the situation (two women "ill-attuned"). This necessitates the throwing out of the old, and brings renewal. The modern Chinese word for "revolution" was derived (by the Japanese) from the expression *geming*, Change of Mandate, as found in the Judgment of this Hexagram. The Mandate is the Mandate of Heaven. (See the Commentary on the Judgment for Hexagram XLV: "Following Heaven's Mandate.") In modern times to be "counterrevolutionary," *fan geming*, is literally to set oneself against the Change of Mandate (currently defined—until the next Change comes along—as the "socialist revolution," or its protagonist, the Chinese Communist Party). But this Hexagram is far from advocating violent revolution. On the contrary, it argues that Change should not happen hastily. Change should be brought about in a timely fashion, on the "right day," specifically the day *si*, sixth day in the series of Twelve Earthly Branches. (Some read it as *ji*, sixth of the Ten Heavenly Stems.) There are times when Change is needed, and with Good Faith the result can be Supreme Fortune. But Change must above all follow the Flow of Heaven; it must be in Accordance with Nature, in tune with the Aspirations of Man—it must, in other words, accord with the laws of Nature and Society. It must be True. To achieve Change, writes Magister Liu, is to get rid of something and not use it anymore. The Illumination of Fire is within Joy of Lake, they complement one another. This is Illumined Change, achieved through Self-Cultivation. It frees one of Yin Energy, of personal Desire. This is to be rid of Self. Man is born pure, with the True Energies of Yin and Yang intact and unpolluted. True Essence shines within, the Spirit is full of Light. Emotions such as joy, anger, discontent, and happiness have not yet tainted the Heart-and-Mind. Influences such as wealth and poverty have not yet perturbed the Flow of Life. Tiger and rhinoceros can cause no Harm. Swords cannot hurt. Neither Water nor Fire can impinge on Life. Life and Death are of no concern. A child such as this eats when he is hungry and puts on clothes when he is cold. He has no thoughts or cares. His Inner Strength is Illumined. Then, when he reaches the age of sixteen, the Yang cycle comes to a Conclusion, and Yin is born. Conditioned Life begins. A hundred cares confuse the Heart-and-Mind, endless affairs take their toll on his bodily frame. He comes to think of False as True. As the days and years go by, habit accumulates on habit, estranging him from his True Nature. The Strength of his Inner Light is dimmed. To undergo Change is to get rid of these habits. It is to cast aside all this Ignorance and find a way back to Illumination, back to the Primordial Energy of the Tao. In order to do this, one needs first to understand Self. Then the Change will be Sincere. Then there will be Good Faith. With Sincerity and Good Faith, and once the True is distinguished from the False, all human beings are capable of Change. This is indeed their Supreme Fortune! This is the Tao. This Hexagram, writes Professor Mun, is about the incompatibility of Water and Fire, and about the conflicts resulting from this, which lead to Change. Radical Change is sometimes necessary in an organization. But it needs to be handled with care and a sense of order and timing (the "calendar must be regulated"), or it may be resisted fiercely. The Leader must build up his credibility if he is to gain the people's trust and support in achieving Change.

LINES

Yang in First Place

Bind it

With thongs

Of brown oxhide.

On the Image

Do not
Act.

 Yang Line in Yang place. A Change now (a stripping of the "oxhide") would be a Change too soon. Things must be held firmly in place ("bound"). Compare Hexagram XXXIII/2. To be bound like this, writes Magister Liu, interpreting the Line differently, is to be tied to trivialities, following events closely in the external world but paying no attention to the events of the inner world. This is to be unconnected and rigid, and therefore incapable of real Change. Any rash Action now, writes Professor Mun, could bring Danger. This is not the right time to Act. The Leader should stay "bound" where he is, and wait for the moment to present itself.

Yin in Second Place

This is the right day

For Change.

It is Auspicious

To Advance.

No Harm,

Nullum malum.

On the Image

Action

Is cause for felicitation.

 Yin Line in Yin Place. Centered. This Yin Line sits Aptly in the Center of the Lower Trigram, *Li*, Fire, Illumination. Now is the right time for Change, the right time to Act, to Advance. This Change, writes Magister Liu, comes from an Empty Heart-and-Mind, freed of Desire. Freed of Desire, one is freed of Self. Freed of Self, one can realize the existence of Others. This is the Change that seeks Illumination from an Empty Heart-in-Mind. This is a favorable time, writes Professor Mun, for carrying out Radical Change.

Yang in Third Place

Advance

Brings Calamity,

Pessimum.

To be Steadfast

Brings Danger,

Periculosum.

Change is spoken of

Three times.

Good Faith.

On the Image

Why set forth now?

 Yang Line in Yang Place. Real Change may encounter obstacles, ups and downs. But despite the Danger, Steadfastness and Good Faith will eventually win the day. This is an excess of Yang, writes Magister Liu. One thinks one can bring Change to Others, but one is incapable of bringing it to Self. Such an Advance will be Calamitous. The more one insists on it ("three times"), the more this Change, which lacks Sincerity (where is the Good Faith?), will be ineffective.

Yang in Fourth Place

Regret

Goes away,

Nullus poenitendi locus.

Good Faith.

An Auspicious

Change of Mandate,

Hoc bonum.

On the Image

There is Belief
In Aspirations.

 Yang Line in Yin Place. With Good Faith, the greatest Change may be achieved, even something as huge as a Change of Dynasty (or Mandate). If one is strong in one's conduct, but not too insistent, writes Magister Liu, then there will be no Regret. Regret comes when a Change is made without Sincerity. If Change is Sincere, then a Yielding Strength can bring about a Change in Being itself, unconstrained by Yin and Yang. This will be an Auspicious Change, a Great Change, a Change of Mandate, a Change of Life-Destiny.

Yang in Fifth Place

The Great Man

Changes like a Tiger.

Before Divination,

There is

Good Faith.

On the Image

The Pattern
Is resplendent.

🦎 Yang Line in Yang Place. Centered. The Change shines; it is resplendent, like the bright stripes of the Tiger. This Fifth Place is the Place of the Ruler. Yang is Centered and True, writes Magister Liu. The Master is within. He cherishes Yang and eliminates Yin. He opens the Gates of Life. He closes the Doorway of Death. He shuts off the Ghost Road. Alien Energy dissolves. Like a magnificent Tiger, there he stands, immovable! This is Change of the Unchanging! There is no need of Divination here. There is Good Faith. Change has simply taken place. This is the Change of the Great Man; this is his Strength, his assertion of existence. This Leader, writes Professor Mun, has Strength and Sincerity. He is Centered. Others will gladly follow his lead.

Yin in Top Place

The True Gentleman

Changes like a Leopard.

The Small Man

Changes face.

Advance

Is Calamitous,

Hoc pessimum.

It is Auspicious

To abide

Steadfastly,

Hoc bonum.

On the Image

The Pattern of the True Gentleman
Is splendid.
The Small Man
Changes face;
He obeys his Lord.

🦎 Yin Line in Yin Place. The True Gentleman makes a decisive Change (like a Leopard). This is only slightly less substantial than the Change of the Great Man in Fifth

Place. It is decisive, but it is gentle (Yin in Yin). The Small Man, by contrast, is in awe of the True Gentleman's splendor. He is Compliant and submissive. The True Gentleman should be firm and true, but take no overt Action. He should let things happen. He should be Steadfast and Cautious. This, writes Magister Liu, is the Ultimate Change. The Yielding is in True Place, it is True (Yin in Yin). The Work has been accomplished diligently and thoroughly. There is Utmost Emptiness, Total Serenity. This is the awesome Change of the Leopard! Inner Sincerity connects with the Outer World. Essential Being is Transformed, every speck of Mortal Dust is expunged. All is Pure and Bare and Transcendent. Soul and Body are wondrous both. This is the Change of the True Gentleman, achieved through gentle Non-Action. He is at one, at Truth, with the Tao. It takes place because he is utterly Sincere. Small Men, those who do not possess a Heart-and-Mind of Sincerity, are incapable of this. They are capable only of a Face Change, not of a Change of Heart-and-Mind. The Change is complete, writes Professor Mun. Senior employees adapt themselves to new conditions, like a Leopard "changing" its spots. After a Change, the Leader should not push matters too hard, but allow time for consolidation and stability.

HEXAGRAM L

Ding

The Cauldron

Li/Fire

above

Xun/Wind

JUDGMENT

Supremely Auspicious.

Fortune,

Magnum bonum.

On the Judgment

Wood within Fire,
Lignus infra ignem.
Cooked food.
The Sage offers food

To the Supreme Deity.

A great feast

Nourishes

The wise and worthy.

Xun,

Wind and Wood,

Flows.

Ear and eye

Are keen.

The Yielding

Advances upward,

It reaches the Center,

It Resonates with the Firm.

Great Fortune,

Magna convenientia.

On the Image of the Hexagram

Fire above Wood,

Supra lignum ignis.

The True Gentleman

Rectifies Positions;

He strengthens

Life-Destiny.

Fire above Wood. *Xun* in the Lower Trigram is understood as Wood (in addition to its primary meaning of Wind). Within the Cauldron, the Ritual Tripod, food is transformed ("cooked") as a Sacrificial Offering. On the spiritual level, raw psychic material is transformed as Nourishment for the Sage. In the occult language of Taoist sexual alchemy, the Precious Cauldron, *baoding*, is the ideal sexual partner, the female "reaction vessel" for the attainment of perfection through sexual practices. It is the crucible for the *matrimonium alchymicum.* The Cauldron, writes Magister Liu, is the vessel for the process of Self-Cultivation, for the Refinement of the Elixir—the Great Medicine of the Tao. This Work of Refinement dissolves Yin Energy and strengthens Yang Energy; it "cooks" the "raw" and "renews" the "old." It Illumines the Heart-and-Mind; it realizes Life-Destiny. This is Supremely Auspicious. This is the Tao of Great Fortune. The Cauldron, writes Professor Mun, changes things through cooking. The nature and form of the raw is transformed from hard to soft. Old obstructions are removed, new visions are introduced. The members of an Organization feel as if they are reborn. The time to create a new order, a new style of leadership, has begun. It has been pointed out since very early times that this Hexagram itself has a Cauldron-like structure (see Part II).

LINES

Yin in First Place

The Cauldron's legs

Are upturned.

It Profits to remove

Obstruction.

A concubine and son

Are gained.

No Harm,

Nullum malum.

On the Image

The legs are upturned,
But this is not
Contrary to principle.
Obstruction is
Removed.
The Noble Line
Is followed.

Yin Line in Yang Place. The upturned Cauldron, emptied of its accumulated dregs, is Auspicious after all. The concubine, unprepossessing in herself, provides an heir, and through him enjoys her share of honor. This Line Resonates with ("follows") the Noble Yang Line in Fourth Place. The dregs, writes Magister Liu, are the Ignorance and Folly of Petty Men. These cause the Cauldron to be overturned. Once they are removed, then there will be Stability and Truth. The concubine who attains to a higher station by bearing a child is not blamed for her earlier errors. Old food is thrown out, writes Professor Mun, and fresh food is placed in the Cauldron. Inefficient old systems, structures, and practices should be got rid of before one embarks on new plans.

Yang in Second Place

The Cauldron

Is full.

The enemy's hatred

Cannot reach me.

This is

Auspicious,

Hoc bonum.

On the Image

Be careful in deeds.
Ultimately there is
No Distress.

 Yang Line in Yin Place. Centered. If things are done with care, the enemy will be unable to cause Harm. The Cauldron has been emptied of its dregs, and is now full of nourishing food. True Yang has returned, writes Magister Liu. If one cultivates the Heart-and-Mind of the Tao, and is freed of the Human Heart-and-Mind, then even if someone has hateful feelings, one is no longer vulnerable.

Yang in Third Place

The Cauldron's ears

Come away.

Progress is blocked.

The fat meat of the pheasant

Is left uneaten.

Rain falls.

Regret goes away.

An Auspicious Conclusion,

In fine bonum.

On the Image

An untimely loss.

Yang Line in Yang Place. At first, things are looking bad. The "ears" of the Cauldron, its two handles, which should hold the carrying pole, are stripped away (the word used is *ge*, the Name of Hexagram XLIX, Change). They have "come away." Without them, the Cauldron cannot be carried forward, and the choice meat within is left uneaten. There is no Resonance between this Line and Yang in Top Place. But with the continued mingling of Yin and Yang in the Hexagram comes rain, and with it an Auspicious issue. Without the handles, the "ears" of the Cauldron, writes Magister Liu, one may understand one's objective Life-Destiny, but one cannot understand one's Inner Nature. One cannot eat the "fat meat of the pheasant." Nonetheless, with a patient Emptying of Heart-and-Mind, one can "unblock" progress and come to understand one's Inner Nature. With the Heart-and-Mind of the Tao comes an Auspicious Conclusion. Without the handles, writes Professor Mun, the Cauldron cannot be moved. The Leader has difficulty taking Action. Yang in Third Place is capable and energetic, but is not recognized as such by the Yin Leader in Fifth Place ("fat meat is left uneaten"). In due course, the capability will be recognized. In the union of Yin and Yang, "rain falls."

Yang in Fourth Place

The Cauldron's legs

Are broken;

Victuals are spilled,

Appearances spoiled.

Misfortune,

Pessimum.

On the Image

With victuals spilled,
Good Faith
Is absent.

Yang Line in Yin Place. The legs are broken, and the Cauldron cannot perform its function. "A cauldron with broken legs" became in time a cliché for a minister whose incompetence ruins the state. When the legs of the Cauldron are broken, writes Magister Liu, then the Human Heart-and-Mind is stirred into activity, and the

Heart-and-Mind of Tao is injured. The Treasure of Life-Destiny is lost ("spilled vict-uals"). The Heart-and-Mind of Tao has been obscured. The True Fire of Nature must be used to cleanse away all Yin elements. Yang in Fourth Place, writes Professor Mun, Resonates with Yin in First, a weak and incompetent assistant, who makes a mess of things.

Yin in Fifth Place

The Cauldron

Has yellow ears;

It has a

Bronze carrying-bar.

To be Steadfast

Profits.

On the Image

There is substance within.

Yin Line in Yang Place. Centered. "Yellow ears" and "a bronze carrying-bar" sig-nify the Ruler. This Line Resonates with Yang in Second Place, the full Cauldron. There is a Yielding Gentleness in the Center, writes Magister Liu. Fullness and Emp-tiness Resonate. A Steadfast prevention of Danger Profits. This is Cultivation of the Heart-and-Mind of the Tao. The Leader, writes Professor Mun, is the "yellow ears" (handles) of the Cauldron. The soft style of the Leader is strengthened by the strong qualities of the carrying-bar.

Yang in Top Place

The Cauldron has a

Jade carrying-bar.

This is

Greatly Auspicious.

All things

Profit,

Nihil quod non conveniat.

On the Image

The Jade bar
Is in Top Place.
Firm and Yielding
Are well regulated.

 Yang Line in Yin Place. Jade, though a hard substance, has a peculiar softness of its own (Yin in Yang). The great minister here performs for the Ruler in Fifth Place the part which the carrying-bar performs for the Cauldron. The Jade carrying-bar is Total Sincerity, writes Magister Liu. It has the purity of Jade. In it the Firm and the Yielding are as one, fusing with the Reality of the Tao. This is the pinnacle of Cultivation of the Tao, of the Work, of the Complete Capability of the Sage. This is beyond Yin and Yang; it is no longer constrained by Yin and Yang. It is the total integration of the Heart-and-Mind of Man and of the Tao. The Leader, writes Professor Mun, applies firm measures (Yang) in a flexible (Yin) manner. A well-balanced situation brings Harmony and Fortune.

Zhen

Quake

Zhen/Quake

above

Zhen/Quake

JUDGMENT

Fortune.

The Quake

Makes men tremble;

It makes them laugh.

The Quake

Disturbs for a hundred *li*.

Neither ladle nor goblet

Is lost.

On the Judgment

Fear brings Blessing,
Laughter brings Discipline.
The Disturbance
Is felt
Far and near.
Ritual Vessels
Are not lost.
He comes forth,
He preserves the Ancestral Temples,
The Altars of Earth and Grain.
He is
Master of the Sacrifice.

On the Image of the Hexagram

Quake is
Doubled,
Duplex tonitrus.
The True Gentleman,
Through fear,
Reflects on Self.

The Trigrams Expounded

Zhen is
Thunder,
Movement.
A coming forth.
It is Dragon,
Foot.
It is North-East,
Eldest son.
Zhen is
Dark yellow.
It spreads;
It is
A great highway.
Bold decisions.
Green bamboo,

Reed and rush.

Of horses,

It neighs loudly,

Has white hind legs,

Prances,

Has a white star on its forehead.

Of crops,

Legumes,

Strong and prolific.

Quake above Quake. This is another of the eight Hexagrams composed of a Doubled Trigram. The crash or peal of the Quake, Thunder (Heaven's Quake), or Earthquake, its reverberation, its power and movement, the excitation and disturbance it causes—all of these bring fear in their wake, affecting people for many miles around. (The Chinese traditional unit of measurement, the *li*, is approximately half a kilometer. Here, one hundred *li* is just a very great distance.) This Hexagram Name was early on defined by commentators as "Yang Energy, the Energy that sets things moving, that arouses the Earth, especially during the third month of spring—thus Thunder and Lightning." Despite the disturbance, and consequent fear and trembling, Ritual Order is preserved, Vessels are kept safe, Sacrifices are performed. This Hexagram, muses Wilhelm in *The Secret of the Golden Flower*, represents the Life Force breaking out of the depths of the Earth; it is the beginning of all Movement. The compendium of Taoist and other lore, the *Book of the Huainan Master*, describes Thunder as "Yin and Yang hurling themselves upon one another: Lightning occurs when Yin and Yang 'force their way through each other.'" In the *Book of Master Zhuang*, we read: "When Yin and Yang go awry, then Heaven and Earth witness astounding sights. Then we hear the crash and roll of Thunder, and fire comes in a deluge of rain and burns up the great pagoda tree." In the *Historical Records* of Sima Qian, an Earthquake is explained as occurring when "Yang is hidden and cannot come forth, or when Yin bars its way and it cannot rise up." This Dynamic can be seen in the structure of the Trigram *zhen*, where a single Yang Line pushes its way up from beneath two Yin Lines. In an interesting anecdote from the *New Tales of the World*, a certain Chancellor Wang Dao instructs the Taoist Guo Pu to cast him a Hexagram. Guo does so, and announces with some distress: "Your Excellency has received the dangerous Omen Quake." Chancellor Wang asks if it can somehow be modified for the better, to which Guo replies: "Send for your carriage and leave the city. Travel several *li* westward. There you will find a cypress tree. Cut down a length of it the same height as yourself and place it in the bed where you usually sleep. The Calamity will be minimized." Wang follows these instructions, and sure enough, within the space of several days, as predicted, a thunderbolt shatters the "sleeping" cypress. His sons and younger brothers all offer their congratulations. His cousin, Generalissimo Wang Dun, remarks in astonishment: "You actually succeeded in transferring the evil onto a tree!" One Yang Line beneath two Yin Lines, writes Magister Liu, is Movement within Stillness. The Great Tao is lively; it is full of Movement. The Way of the World can be used to Cultivate the Tao; Human Affairs can be used to Cultivate the Inner Strength of Heaven. All of this is Movement. This is Fortune. There is Inner Movement and Outer Movement. If Inner Movement is True, then Outer Movement will also be True. Quake comes as a sudden Movement within Stillness. There may be alarm at first, but this is followed by laughter, because the imperturbable Heart-and-Mind of the Tao is present and serene. Heaven is a good thought in the Mind; Hell is a base thought in the Mind. As base thoughts depart, the Heart-and-Mind of the Tao becomes ever more present. Then the Master dwells in the Center, in serene Stillness. He Resonates and Connects. He greets every eventuality with laughter. Nothing can cause the loss of his "ladle and goblet," not even the most violent Quake that spreads terror for miles around. Cautious as to Inner Movement, he Cultivates his Energy. Fearless as to Outer Movement, he does not allow his Energy to be moved. He is in tune with the Tao of Quake. This Hexagram, writes Professor Mun, represents a dangerous situation in which the pairs of Yin Lines dominate. A Leader faces an intense shock. If he remains Steadfast, he will be able to find a way out without being affected by the Danger. Despite fear, he will be able to take all necessary measures to prepare for the emergency. The shock may even have a positive effect. One who has fear now will not have fear later; one who does not have fear now will have it later.

LINES

Yang in First Place

The Quake

Makes men tremble;

It makes them

Laugh out loud.

It is Auspicious,

Bonum.

On the Image

Fear brings
Blessing,
Felicitatem.
Laughter brings
Discipline.

Yang Line in Yang Place. After the terror and the trembling of the Quake comes a new sense of release, laughter, a new sense of Order and Discipline. This Yang Line in a Yang Place shows a positive response to Quake. Order comes out of Chaos. At the very first sign of Quake, writes Magister Liu, one deals cautiously with what cannot be seen or heard. One "trembles." Later one can "laugh out loud," because the Heart-and-Mind is well prepared, and correct Action can be taken. This is the most Auspicious sort of Movement. The Leader remains Steadfast despite the Danger, writes Professor Mun. The Organization can continue to operate peacefully and smoothly (it can "laugh out loud"), unaffected by the shock.

Yin in Second Place

The Quake

Brings Danger,

Periculum.

Cowrie shells

Are lost.

He climbs the Nine Hills.

He does not go in search.

In seven days

They will be found.

On the Image

Yielding Rides
Firm in First Place,
Supra durum.

Yin Line in Yin Place. Centered. This is a Retreat to the heights in the face of Danger, a temporary acceptance of loss, followed by a spontaneous recovery. There is a predominant weakness in this Line, writes Magister Liu. Vain imaginings have been allowed to soar too high. One attempts what one is not capable of achieving. One loses one's bearings ("cowrie shells") and runs into Danger in the "Nine Hills." With Caution, one can still refrain from unwise Action (a futile "search"). Danger can be averted. If a Leader, writes Professor Mun, discovers financial losses ("lost cowrie shells"), he should take remedial measures ("climb the Nine Hills"). But he should not react rashly ("go in search"). After the shock, the Organization will regain what has been lost ("they will be found").

Yin in Third Place

The Quake

Brings a quivering.

It stirs to

Action.

There is

No Calamity,

Nullum infortunium.

On the Image

The Position is not Apt.

 Yin Line in Yang Place. Fear at the Quake is mitigated by the inherent strength of Third Place. The shock of the Quake quickens resolve. All is aquiver, writes Magister Liu. One fears one's own inability, one fears the difficulty of the task in hand. But since this Yin Line is in a Place of strong Aspiration, one can approach a Man of the Tao and seek assistance. This can strengthen one's own weakness. Then the task will become feasible, and there will be no Calamity. The Leader, writes Professor Mun, is agitated and disturbed by the shock of the Quake. This Danger may cause him to change his mind and adopt a new approach.

Yang in Fourth Place

Quake.

Mud.

On the Image

The Light cannot shine.

 Yang Line in Yin Place. A crippling, disabling Quake is followed by heavy rains. This Yang Line is in the wrong Place, writes Magister Liu. It is hemmed in by two Yin Lines. Every day is spent in the company of Small Men ("mud"). There is the strength

(Yang) to practice the Tao, but not the Inner Aspiration, the Will ("the Light"). One is bogged down, one cannot take a single step forward.

Yin in Fifth Place

The Quake

Comes and goes.

There is

Danger,

Periculum.

No loss.

Work progresses.

On the Image

Despite Danger,
Matters are Centered,
In medio.
There is no loss.

Yin Line in Yang Place. Centered. Repeated aftershocks do not cause Harm for the Centered. Fruitless vacillation without Inner Strength, writes Magister Liu, makes for Movement and Danger. But this Yin Line is Centered, and an inherent Caution saves one from loss. The Centered equilibrium, writes Professor Mun, enables the Leader to survive the threat posed by surrounding Danger.

Yin in Top Place

The Quake

Makes men quail;

It makes them

Stare and tremble.

Advance

Brings Calamity,

Pessimum.

The Quake

Does not strike Self,

It strikes the neighbor.

No Harm,

Nullum malum.

There is trouble

In marriage.

On the Image

They quail with fear.
The Tao of Center
Is not yet attained.
Misfortune,
Pessimum.
No Harm,
Nullum malum.
Fear.
Lessons learned,
Learned from a neighbor's plight.
Caution.

Yin Line in Yin Place. The concluding terrors of the Quake indicate Caution. Here at the Top of Quake, writes Magister Liu, all is fear—quailing and trembling. Nothing can be accomplished. But even in this extremity, one escapes without Harm. Fear itself prevents one from wrongdoing. A True Gentleman guides one in the right direction. There is a popular Chinese belief, writes Chen Guying, that it is Inauspicious to marry during a thunderstorm.

HEXAGRAM LII

Gen

Mountain

Gen/Mountain

above

Gen/Mountain

JUDGMENT

The back

Is still

As a Mountain;

There is no body.

He walks

In the courtyard,

Unseen.

No Harm,

Nullum malum.

On the Judgment

Stillness.
When Time is still,
Be still.
When Time moves,
Move.
In Motion and Stillness,
Be always attuned to Time.
The Tao is bright;
The Tao
Illumines.
Keep the back still,
Still,
In its Proper Place.
Above and below
Lack Resonance;
They do not come together.
The body sustains
No Harm,
Nullum malum.

On the Image of the Hexagram

Double Mountain.
Replicatus mons.
The True Gentleman's thoughts
Never stray
Beyond his proper Position.

Expounding the Trigrams

Gen is mountain,
Stillness,
Completion.
It is
North-East,

Youngest son.
In *Gen*,
The Myriad Things
Are completed;
They have their beginning.
Gen is dog,
Pebble.
Gateway,
Fruits and seeds.
Gatekeeper,
Eunuch.
Gen is finger,
Rat,
Bird with powerful bill.
Of trees,
It is the strong
And many-notched.

Mountain above Mountain. This is another Doubled Trigram. The Trigram *Gen* has traditionally been understood as Mountain, hence Mountain Stillness (as opposed to the dramatic Movement of the previous Hexagram, Quake). One Yang Line above two Yin Lines shows the Firm Substance of Mountain above the Yielding Foundations of Earth. In some early transcriptions, *Gen* is written with the addition of the "tree" element, which extends the meaning to "root." Mountains have been revered in China since earliest times. Confucius himself is supposed to have observed: "The wise find joy in Water, the good find joy in Mountains." Mountains are numinous places, where mortals come close to the world of the Spirits, where they connect with Gods. Mountains mediate between the human world and that of Heaven. The mountaineer-poet Xie Lingyun found a direct path to enlightenment in his alpine excursions:

On Climbing the Highest Peak of Stone Gate Mountain
At dawn with staff
I climb the crags,
At dusk I camp
Among the Mountains. . . .
The high sierra blocks my path,
Dense bamboos veil the track. . . .
Streams tumble through the dusk,
Monkeys shriek in the night.
Deep in meditation,
I will never be parted from Truth.
I cherish the Tao,
I will never abandon it.
My heart is one

With the trees of late autumn,
My eyes delight
In the buds of early spring.
I will remain Steadfast,
Waiting for my end,
Content to find peace
In the natural order of things. . . .

Mountains are the preferred abode of the Taoist and Zen Recluse, as in the famous quatrain by the Tang-dynasty poet Jia Dao:

Seeking the Recluse and Not Finding Him
Beneath the pines,
I ask the boy,
Who tells me,
Master's gone gathering herbs
On the Mountain.
Who knows where?
Somewhere,
Deep in the clouds.

In *The Soul of China*, Richard Wilhelm recalls this Hexagram in connection with Mount Tai, the Eastern Great Mountain of the Five Sacred Mountains (*dongyue*), worshipped as Gateway to the Underworld: "It is always an experience to go up this mountain. You continue to see its cloudy top rise up out of the host of the other hills, and it seems as if it were revealing a secret every time: the secret of the connection between life and death in that great Stillness whose symbol is the Hexagram Mountain." For Chinese writers and painters alike, the Mountain is a place of pilgrimage, a place to be revered, a perpetual source of inspiration and elation, a "place of vision" from which to contemplate the Universe and its mysteries. The scholar and poet Qian Qianyi wrote eloquently of this: "I used to have no understanding of the respect due to that great peak Mount Tai. Now, as I start this journey, I am respectful and pure of mind, I am silent and filled with awe." Mountains are both resting and arresting. They inspire and obstruct. They rise up grandly from the Earth, in quiet and solemn majesty; but they also halt the traveler's onward progress. In this *Gen* Hexagram, Yang reaches upward from the top of each Trigram; the two Yin Lines below move downward. There is both Aspiration and Rest. Movement reaches its natural end in Stillness. The Hexagram points to Stillness and a quiet Heart-and-Mind. It recognizes the need for Movement, but only when the Time is right. The poet Ban Biao paraphrased the words of this Hexagram's Commentary on the Judgment in his "Rhapsody on the Northward Journey":

The Man of True Discernment . . .
Whether Moving or Still,
Whether curved or straight,
Is always in tune with Time.
He treads the path of Sincerity,

He can live in any place,
He fears not the wildest barbarian shore.

Such a person walks quietly "in the courtyard," in the Taoist cloister of the Heart-and-Mind, with back straight and strong, free from selfish thoughts and external desires. To "walk in the courtyard unseen" suggests a person able to Act and Move without being exposed to wayward thoughts, balancing Stillness and Movement. Possibly, muses Richard Wilhelm, the words of this Hexagram embody directions for the practice of yoga. This certainly makes sense of the reference in the Lines to different parts of the body. It also makes a connection with the protomedical reading given in Part II. In *The Secret of the Golden Flower*, Wilhelm expands on this: "The sign *Gen*, Mountain, quietness, represents meditation, which by keeping external things quiescent, quickens the Inner World." See also *The Art of War*:

> Chapter 7
> Be rushing as a wind;
> Be stately as a forest;
> Be ravaging as a fire;
> Be still as a mountain.
> Be inscrutable as night;
> Be swift as thunder or lightning.

Inner and Outer Stillness, writes Magister Liu, are connected. Through Stillness one Cultivates Energy. One discerns that which is good, and holds to it Steadfastly. Outer Stillness is Action that knows its proper time and place; it is True Movement. This too forms part of Stillness. This is "walking in the courtyard unseen"; this is having "no body." There is no Self; there are no Others. These are products of the Human Heart-and-Mind. If the "back is still," then the Human Heart-and-Mind dissolves, and the Heart-and-Mind of the Tao is born. There is only one Tao. Be Still according to that Tao. Move according to that same Tao. Then there can be no Harm. To "walk in the courtyard unseen," writes Professor Mun, is to be without Self. The Leader puts aside his own wishes and desires.

LINES

Yin in First Place

The feet are

Still as a Mountain.

There is

No Harm,

Nullum malum.

Enduring Steadfastness

Profits.

On the Image

The Truth is not lost.

Yin Line in Yang Place. There is Humility inherent in this Yin Line. Nonetheless, the Danger of rash Movement, implied by the Yang Place, must be guarded against. Keep the feet still. Control impulse. Hold fast to the Tao. Still feet, writes Magister Liu, indicate Humility and a reluctance to take random Action, Action that is not proper. If the very first thoughts are True, then Stillness cannot lead to Harm. Weakness and indecision still need to be countered with an Enduring Steadfastness. There are several weaknesses in this Line, writes Professor Mun. It is Yin; it is not in Apt Position; it is not Centered; it is in a low Place in the Hexagram; it is beneath another Yin Line; it has no Resonance with Yin in Fourth Place. A person in this weak position should restrain from impulsive Action. He should control his emotions.

Yin in Second Place

The calves are

Still as a Mountain.

Others

Are not harnessed.

The heart is heavy.

On the Image

There is no
Retreat.
Acceptance.

Yin Line in Yin Place. Centered. There is a potential healing, a Stillness. But the Energy of Others (the Yang Lines above and below) cannot be mastered and harnessed. No Retreat is possible, only a reluctant acceptance. One lacks the foresight for Retreat. Beware. This Yin Line, writes Professor Mun, is obliged to follow Yang in Third Place (the "loins"), even though that person may be wrong. This makes the heart heavy.

Yang in Third Place

The loins are

Still as a Mountain.

The midriff

Is severed.

Danger inflames

The Heart-and-Mind.

On the Image

Peril inflames
The Heart-and-Mind.

 Yang Line in Yang Place. There is Danger in being *too* Still, too stiff. This can damage the flexibility between the upper and lower parts of the body. Discomfort in the midriff generates anger and heat, causing the physical body and the emotions to be "inflamed." An unchecked, rash Movement, writes Magister Liu, will be the undoing of Strength. It will "sever the midriff." This will inflame the Heart-and-Mind with ambition. This is a situation of conflict, writes Professor Mun. An Organization has been "severed" into groups. Action is required from the Leader to reduce the conflict and restore Harmony in the Organization.

Yin in Fourth Place

The body is

Still as a Mountain.

No Harm,

Nullum malum.

On the Image

One does not go
Beyond Self.

Yin Line in Yin Place. One does not go beyond one's own situation and its needs. One exercises self-restraint, keeping one's own counsel, preserving one's own Energy. One does not blame Others, writes Magister Liu. There is no enmity. This is a Yielding Self-Knowledge that leads to Stillness, and that causes no Harm. This senior executive, writes Professor Mun, is in a weak position. He can only restrain Self, he cannot influence Others (there is no Resonance between this Line and Yin in First Place). Self-restraint will protect him from Harm.

Yin in Fifth Place

The jaws are

Still as a Mountain.

Words are measured.

Regret goes away,

Non est quod poenitebit.

On the Image

They are still
Because they are Centered.

Yin Line in Yang Place. Centered. With Stillness, writes Magister Liu, words do not tumble out at random. They are orderly and well considered. This Line is Yielding and Centered. It is a Stillness that benefits Others. A Leader should choose his words with care, writes Professor Mun. He should speak frankly, with substance.

Yang in Top Place

A simple

Stillness.

This is

Auspicious,

Hoc bonum.

On the Image

A Conclusion
Of genuine simplicity.

ͳ Yang Line in Yin Place. Here the Hexagram reaches its final stage. This is the unpremeditated simplicity of the Taoist, the Heart-and-Mind of the Fool, a state of harmonious being in which Action and Non-Action follow a natural rhythm—"simple as an Uncarved Block." See *The Tao and the Power*:

Chapter 15
The wise men of old
Were simple and genuine,
Like an Uncarved Block.

The Tao of being Still at the appropriate time and place, comments Magister Liu, requires both Action and Non-Action, both Movement and Stillness, fusion of Yin and Yang. Those who cultivate the Tao must know where to stop, when to be still. With Tolerance, Caution, and Patience, writes Professor Mun, the Leader will be safe, even at this turning point in a cycle.

HEXAGRAM LIII

Jian

Gradual

Xun/Wind

above

Gen/Mountain

JUDGMENT

A woman weds.

This is

Auspicious,

Hoc bonum.

To be Steadfast

Profits,

Oportet ut sit soliditas.

On the Judgment

There is
Gradual Progress
To an Apt Position;
There is
Success.
An Advance in Truth
Sets the Realm to rights.
A Firm Line is Centered.
There is Stillness,
Gentleness,
And inexhaustible Movement.

On the Image of the Hexagram

Trees on the Mountain,
Supra montem ligni.
The True Gentleman
Abides in Spiritual Strength;
He transforms
The ways of the Common Folk.

Wind and Wood above Mountain. The Upper Trigram, *Xun*, writes Legge, also has, in addition to Wind, the symbolism of Wood. Trees provide shade and protection for the Mountain. The graph for the Hexagram Name contains the element Water. The Hexagram also contains the "hidden" Trigram (Lines 2, 3, and 4) for Water, the Abyss. Progress must be gentle and slow; it must be Gradual, like the infiltration of Water. Decisions must be made carefully in the light of circumstances. Advance must be Gradual, by successive stages. Ascend the Lines by regular steps, to the Top of the Hexagram. The marriage of the woman, literally her Return, *gui*, must likewise proceed in an orderly and correct manner if it is to be Auspicious. This is reflected in the Resonance of Yin in Second with Yang in Fifth. The Work of Self-Realization, writes Magister Liu, is not accomplished in a single morning or evening. The sequence is a subtle one. The Work is of long duration. It requires order, and Gradual Progress. Yin in Second Place and Yang in Fifth, True Yin and True Yang, have a natural Resonance. This is not a contrived union of False Yang and False Yin. This is the Tao of the woman who weds in the proper way. The marriage is not for the sake of a moment's pleasure, which would be Inauspicious and would only lead to failure. Self-Cultivation in the Tao is the same. It must be Gradual. It cannot be quickly attained. The Firm seeks the Yielding, as man seeks woman, without haste, in regular stages. This union grows stronger with time, until finally the Work is completed and effort becomes effortless spontaneity. Yin and Yang are united, Firm and Yielding merge. This produces the seed of the Elixir, a something emerging from nothingness. This is the Path of Self-Cultivation. It is also the Path of Marriage. They must both be founded in Truth. If not, they will not be Auspicious. Without Truth, any amount of striving for perfection—alchemical, sexual, or spiritual—is in vain. The quest must be both Gradual and True. It must plumb the depths of essential Nature, of Life-Destiny. Then all may attain the Great Tao. A lasting relationship does not develop overnight, writes Professor Mun. It is Gradual. It grows with the increase of mutual trust. A person grows slowly, like a tree.

LINES

Yin in First Place

Gradually

Wild geese

Alight on the shore.

Danger

For a young son,

Periculosum.

There are words.

There is

No Harm,

Nullum malum.

On the Image

Righteousness.
No Harm.

Yin Line in Yang Place. The flight of geese across the sky in formation, writes Legge, and their Gradual Descent to the shore, form an image of ordered progress. The "young son" must proceed with Caution. There may be slanderous words, accusations leveled at him. He must stick to his principles. The wild goose was traditionally associated with marriage, and with conjugal fidelity. This beginning of Gradual Progress, writes Magister Liu, is weak and incorrect. The geese, as they descend to the shore, lose the order and symmetry they had when flying in the sky. The wise Leader, writes Professor Mun, is misunderstood by others, who are uncultivated and short-sighted ("there are words").

Yin in Second Place

Gradually

Wild geese

Alight on the rocks.

There is joyous eating and drinking.

Auspicious,

Hoc bonum.

On the Image

There is Joy,
Without excess.

 Yin Line in Yin Place. Centered. Confucius advocated moderation in all things. *Analects* 1.14: "The True Gentleman never seeks to fill himself." The rocks are places of security, writes Magister Liu. But they are not a final resting place. Here one waits, and one practices Self-Cultivation, Emptying the Mind and Filling the Belly. A Leader in this position, writes Professor Mun, is relaxed and optimistic; he shares harmonious delight with his colleagues.

Yang in Third Place

Gradually

Wild geese

Alight on dry land.

A man goes to war

But does not return.

A wife conceives;

She miscarries.

Calamity,

Hoc pessimum.

It Profits

To fight off brigands.

On the Image

He forsakes his fellows.
She miscarries.
The Tao is forsaken.
Fighting off brigands
Brings protection.

Yang Line in Yang Place. The man is ill-considered in his Movements. The husband does not care for his wife, he does not treasure his friends (Yin in First and Second Place). But his strength will nonetheless in the end be useful in protecting his family. The husband goes to war, writes Magister Liu, and does not return. He falls in love with another woman. Meanwhile the wife conceives after a secret affair, but cannot give birth. In this Gradual sequence of events, one is strong (headstrong?) and loses control. The Leader, writes Professor Mun, is obstinate and acts rashly. But he is able to offer protection.

Yin in Fourth Place

Gradually

Wild geese

Alight on a tree.

They roost on a branch.

There is

No Harm,

Nullum malum.

On the Image

Gentleness prevails.

Yin Line in Yin Place. The geese roost on a flat branch, writes Legge, following Zhu Xi. This is the First Line of the Upper Trigram, *Xun*, the ruling image of which is both Wood, in its sense of the permeating force of plant life, and Wind, the gentle breeze whose Gradual influence is so beneficial. Being gentle and obedient helps a man to find sanctuary. The branch provides a temporary roosting place, writes Magister Liu. Here, in Emptiness and Stillness, one waits for the return of Yang. This is Gradual Progress that is Yielding and at the same time holds on to what is True.

Yang in Fifth Place

Gradually

Wild geese

Alight on a hill.

For three years,

The wife fails to conceive.

In the end

Nothing can stand in her way.

It is Auspicious,

Hoc bonum.

On the Image

Nothing can stand in her way.
Her Aspirations are fulfilled.

Yang Line in Yang Place. Centered. She becomes a mother at last. The Harmonious Resonance of this Yang Line with Yin in Second Place ultimately prevails. Strong Yang Gradually occupies Center, writes Magister Liu. True Yin and True Yang unite in Harmony. False Yin and False Yang no longer separate. The Elixir is formed. Difficulties will eventually be resolved, writes Professor Mun, provided the Leader maintains his principles.

Yang in Top Place

Gradually

Wild geese

Alight on the heights.

Feathers serve

For a Ceremony.

This is Auspicious,

Hoc bonum.

On the Image

Disorder
Must not be permitted.

 Yang Line in Yang Place. The culmination of Gradual Progress, writes Legge, must be accompanied by the appropriate Ceremony. The Sacred Embryo is formed, writes Magister Liu. This is like geese alighting on the heights. This is the integrity of the True Gentleman, writes Professor Mun. Ordinary people see it as a model for emulation.

Gui Mei

The Marrying Maiden

Zhen/Quake

above

Dui/Lake

JUDGMENT

Calamitous Advance,

Si eat, hoc pessimum.

Nothing Profits,

Nulla convenientia.

On the Judgment

The Great Righteousness
Of Heaven and Earth

Must be heeded.
Without intercourse
Of Heaven and Earth,
The Myriad Things cannot flourish.
The Marrying Maiden.
An End and a Beginning
For man,
Initium et finem hominis.
There is Joy in Movement.
The Marrying Maiden.
Calamity.
Positions are not Apt.
Nothing Profits.
The Yielding Rides the Firm,
Molle supra durum.

On the Image of the Hexagram

Thunder above Lake,
Supra lacum tonitrus.
The True Gentleman
Sees flaws
In the Conclusion,
In fine.

 Quake above Lake. Thunder above, in the Upper Trigram, rouses Lake below, in the Lower Trigram. Movement disturbs Calm. This Hexagram is generally seen as Inauspicious ("nothing Profits"). The Maiden marries of her own personal initiative, without the "maidenly" reserve or Ritual preliminaries considered proper. When pleasure is the sole goal, writes Magister Liu, when desire and emotion dominate, the union will be Inauspicious. The True Gentleman perceives the flaws; he sees that the union is not harmonious and well founded at the outset. He takes the necessary steps to remedy this.

LINES

Yang in First Place

The Marrying Maiden

Weds as concubine.

The lame

Walk.

An Auspicious Advance,

Si eat, hoc bonum.

On the Image

A secondary marriage
Provides permanence.
The lame walk.
This is
Auspicious.
Support is provided.

Yang Line in Yang Place. Despite the appearance of inferiority, of being "lame," the concubine is strong. She discharges her duties well and serves her lord with modesty. The woman humbles herself, writes Magister Liu. The time is not right, but she does nothing improper. An executive in a junior position, writes Professor Mun, can still make a contribution to the Organization, even though there is no Resonance between this Yang in First Place and Yang in Fourth Place.

Yang in Second Place

The blind

See.

It Profits

A secluded person

To be Steadfast,

Habebit soliditatem.

On the Image

True principle
Is not abandoned.

Yang Line in Yin Place. Centered. Who is the secluded person? A Recluse? A chaste widow? This is a wondrous vision, writes Magister Liu. The Maiden embraces the Tao; she dwells in Seclusion. She seeks True Joy, not False Pleasure. This capable and upright woman, writes Professor Mun, Resonates with Yin in Fifth Place, a weak and not-so-upright husband. In similar fashion, an executive with limited authority can still make contributions to the Organization if he does not cease to be Steadfast.

Yin in Third Place

The Marrying Maiden

Weds as a slave.

She returns,

To wed as concubine.

On the Image

She marries as servant.
The Apt Position
Has not yet been reached.

Yin Line in Yang Place. The Maiden is a mean character, writes Legge, following Zhu Xi. She is a "slave of passion" (Lake, Joy, in the Lower Trigram). No man will wish to marry her as his "proper" wife. If, however, she can "return" and accept the more lowly position of concubine, if (in a broader sense) one can only awaken and humbly accept one's limitations, then all is not lost. She has followed the wrong path, writes Magister Liu. She has mistaken the False for the True. She has debased herself. But she can still find her way back ("return") if she accepts a lesser position. This is not an Apt Place, writes Professor Mun. An executive wants to attain his objective through an irregular process, and may not be able to reach it.

Yang in Fourth Place

The Marrying Maiden

Draws out her time.

She weds late;

She weds

In due course.

On the Image

She waits
For the proper time
To Act.

Yang Line in Yin Place. This woman does not give herself lightly, but waits for the right man, the right time, and the appropriate union. This is to rid oneself of the Human Heart-and-Mind, writes Magister Liu, and to establish the Heart-and-Mind of the Tao. This woman of high status, writes Professor Mun, does not wish to marry a man beneath her expectations, and she postpones the wedding. There is no Resonance with Yang in First Place. In similar fashion, a Leader does not undertake an operation now, believing that the time is not favorable. He postpones his plans until the time is ripe.

Yin in Fifth Place

King Yi

Gave his daughter in marriage.

Her sleeves were less fine

Than those of her serving maid.

The moon near full.

This is

Auspicious,

Hoc bonum.

On the Image

This is
Centered,
In medio.
The Action is noble.

Yin Line in Yang Place. Centered. The King's daughter dressed simply, writes Legge, preferring "the ornament of the hidden man of the heart"—i.e., "inner virtue." This is what she offered her husband. (Legge refers to the First Epistle of Peter.) Like the moon "near full," comments Cheng Yi, the wife should not eclipse her husband. JM: See Hexagram XI/5. King Yi was the penultimate ruler of the Shang; his daughter was perhaps given in marriage to King Wen of the Zhou. The Line praises the admirable Humility and virtue of the princess. It Resonates with Yang in Second Place. A Leader, writes Professor Mun, should avoid competing with others. He does not need to show how strong and powerful he is.

Yin in Top Place

The woman's basket

Contains no fruit.

The man cuts

A sheep.

There is

No blood.

No Profit.

On the Image

No fruit.
An empty basket.

Yin Line in Yin Place. The marriage is broken, writes Legge. It is void. The woman is barren. The Sacrifice is without effect. It bodes ill. This is a selfish union which will fail, writes Magister Liu. Inner Nature and Life-Destiny are injured. There can be no Profit. Neither wife nor husband, writes Professor Mun, can perform a proper function in the Sacrificial Ceremony. In a modern Organization, an executive and his subordinates are incapable of carrying out their duties. This Yin Line is in an Apt Place, but it is weak and it lacks Resonance with Yin in Third Place.

HEXAGRAM LV

Feng

Canopy

Zhen/Quake

above

Li/Fire

JUDGMENT

Fortune.

The King

Approaches,

Rex venit.

He feels no sorrow.

It Profits

To be the Sun at noon,

Sol in meridie.

On the Judgment

Abundant Canopy.
Illumination and
Movement.
The King
Honors the Tao of Yang.
Like the Sun at noon,
He Illumines
All-under-Heaven.
From noon,
The Sun declines.
From full,
The Moon wanes.
Fullness and Emptiness
Of Heaven and Earth
Wax and wane
With Time,
With the Seasons.
How much more so
The affairs of men?
How much more so
The affairs of Spirits?

On the Image of the Hexagram

Thunder and Lightning
Arrive together,
Tonitrus et fulgura.
The True Gentleman
Determines judgments;
He administers punishments.

Quake above Fire. A thunderstorm dispels the Canopy of Darkness. It clears away obstacles and brings Light (Fire). The Ruler must not be sad. He must shine like the Sun at noon, bringing Illumination to all things. This Hexagram indicates the possibility of successful undertakings, of progress and development, despite serious obstacles and frequent references to the surrounding Darkness. (This may be the Darkness of imprisonment or persecution.) The Hexagram sounds a note of Caution, pointing to the cyclic waxing and waning of men's affairs, the rise and fall of Change. The King, writes Professor Mun, is a wise and capable Leader of an Organization, who understands the law of Nature, according to which downward movement will begin once the peak of abundance or prosperity is reached.

LINES

Yang in First Place

A Lord

Of Noble Mind

Is encountered.

For ten days,

No Harm,

Nullum malum.

An Advance

Prospers.

On the Image

After ten days,
Disaster,
Infortunium.

 Yang Line in Yang Place. For a certain length of time, it Profits to collaborate (to Advance) with a kindred spirit, an altruistic King. But this situation will not last forever. There is a limit which cannot be overstepped. The Lord of Noble Mind, writes Magister Liu, is the Sage who shares his Inner Strength. To maintain prosperity, writes Professor Mun, an executive must seek support from someone who shares common values (the "Lord of Noble Mind").

Yin in Second Place

Canopy

Of Darkness!

The Pole Star

Seen at noon.

An Advance.

Doubt and hostility

Are overcome by

Good Faith.

To proceed is

Auspicious,

Hoc bonum.

On the Image

With Good Faith,
Aspirations are attained.

 Yin Line in Yin Place. Centered. In the Canopy of Darkness, only Good Faith, Sincerity based on the Strength of the Tao, can nurture the Light within, can outshine doubt and hostility, bringing Illumination and True Fulfillment. Darkness, writes Magister Liu, hinders the Work. But an Illumined Teacher is at hand, one from whom Strength can be obtained, one who will assist in kindling the Spirit, and in making True Progress. If the Pole Star is seen at noon, writes Professor Mun, then Light has been lost. It is dark as night. The doubt and hostility come from Yin in Fifth Place, with which this Line has no Resonance.

Yang in Third Place

Canopy

Of screens!

The Mei Star

Seen at noon.

The right arm

Is broken.

No Harm.

On the Image

Great undertakings
Are not feasible.

 Yang Line in Yang Place. The Mei Star is a small star near the Pole Star. Darkness has reached its height. The Heavens are obscured. The Light is screened. The "broken arm," writes Magister Liu, is the result of too-insistent Action (Yang in Yang), which is injurious to Illumination. The Darkness grows even greater, writes Professor Mun. This is Darkness at Noon, a solar eclipse. The executive in this position lacks support (his "arm is broken") from his superior, who is weak and incompetent (Yin in Top Place). Although the executive is in a strong position himself (Yang in Yang), any forward Action will be in vain.

Yang in Fourth Place

Canopy

Of darkness!

The Pole Star

Seen at noon.

A Lord of True Mind

Is encountered.

Auspicious,

Hoc bonum.

On the Image

The Position
Is not Apt.
Darkness,
Obscuritas.
No Light,
Non est claritas.
Thanks to a Lord
Of True Mind,
Action
Is Auspicious.

Yang Line in Yin Place. Darkness prevails, but circumstances will improve. A sympathetic Ruler (Yin in Fifth Place) is at hand. The Darkness increases, writes Magister Liu. Cultivate Inner Light, go to meet the Lord of True Mind. He is often hard to see. The True Taoist often conceals his Treasure, he lives hidden in the crowd. Once met, he kindles Light in Others.

Yin in Fifth Place

Illumination

Is at hand,

Claritas.

Celebration,

Praise.

This is

Auspicious,

Hoc bonum.

On the Image

Cause for celebration,
Gaudium.

 Yin Line in Yang Place. Centered. The King approaches. An Auspicious result is assured by the support of the Ruler and his able ministers. Emptiness of Heart-and-Mind, writes Magister Liu, fills the Belly of the Tao. This is the Illumination; this is the Celebration, White Light shining in an Empty Room, the Golden Elixir formed. This is the right time to practice the Tao of Non-Action. With the assistance of capable subordinates, writes Professor Mun, the Leader will be able to enjoy Celebration and praise.

Yin in Top Place

A Canopy

Darkens the dwelling!

It darkens

The Family.

He peers

Through the door.

All is still!

Deserted!

For three years,

Nothing is seen.

Calamity,

Pessimum.

On the Image

He soars
At Heaven's edge.
Concealed.

Yin Line in Yin Place. Everything is unfavorable. The situation is bleak; the Canopy shrouds all in Darkness. The result can only be Inauspicious. The sole recourse lies in escape, to "soar" into the Heavens and become a Recluse. This, however, may bring Calamitous results for Others. The darkened, deserted house, writes Magister Liu, is ignorance of the Great Tao; it is conceit, self-satisfaction, vain embellishment of the façade. This gaudy shrine contains no Buddha.

Lü

The Wanderer

Li/Fire

above

Gen/Mountain

JUDGMENT

Slight Fortune.

For a Traveler,

It is Auspicious

To be Steadfast,

Hoc bonum.

On the Judgment

Yielding Lines
Are Centered;

They flow with the Firm.
The Stillness of Mountain
Is attached to Light.
Slight Fortune.

On the Image of the Hexagram

Fire on the Mountain,
Supra montem ignis.
In administering punishments,
The True Gentleman
Is wise and cautious;
He does not protract litigation.

Fire above Mountain. The Wanderer is a stranger in a strange land. A Wanderer moves on, writes Magister Liu. He does not linger in one place. Fire on the Mountain does not burn for long. It passes through and is quickly gone. This is the Tao of the Wanderer. He passes through and does not linger; he is not attached for long to any country. The Mountain is the substance, the Stillness; the Fire is the application, the Illumination. Like a Wanderer, writes Professor Mun, an international business executive, who makes frequent trips to foreign countries, is exposed to uncertainties and dangers. The local environment may be different from that of his home country. He should adapt to local conditions and respect local laws. A soft style of leadership should be adopted when operating away from home.

LINES

Yin in First Place

The Wanderer's

Anxiety

Attracts

Misfortune.

On the Image

Aspirations
Are exhausted.

Calamity,

Infortunium.

 Yin Line in Yang Place. The preoccupied Heart-and-Mind, writes Legge, is drained of Energy. Unable to see through the things of the world, writes Magister Liu, the Wanderer goes here and there, restless and anxious. He brings about his own Misfortune. An executive, writes Professor Mun, devotes himself to trivial matters and neglects major issues. His competitor may move in a direction that he has ignored, with Calamitous results for the executive's Organization.

Yin in Second Place

The Wanderer

Reaches his lodgings,

Clasps wealth close,

Buys

Young slaves.

On the Image

Ultimately
There is
No Distress,
In fine
Nullum malum.

 Yin Line in Yin Place. Centered. The Wanderer achieves a degree of comfort. He adapts to the situation. He keeps his money in his inner pocket. He is flexible (Yin in Yin) and he mixes with people of a lower class. An executive, writes Professor Mun, wins the trust of the local people and acquires the needed capital and manpower.

Yang in Third Place

The Wanderer's lodgings

Burn;

His servants

Are lost.

Steadfastness.

Danger,

Periculosum.

On the Image

The Traveler's
Arrogance
Causes servants to leave.

Yang Line in Yang Place. The Wanderer's servants (the two previous Yin Lines) are treated with such harshness and arrogance (Yang in Yang) that they decide to leave. He cuts himself off from Others, writes Magister Liu. Excessive firmness leads to the burning of his lodgings and the loss of his servants. An executive in this position, one who is obstinate and reckless, forfeits the trust of the people under him, writes Professor Mun. They leave the Organization.

Yang in Fourth Place

The Wanderer

Seeks a resting place.

He gains

Axe-wealth.

His heart is heavy,

Nullum gaudium.

On the Image

A Place still not found.
Despite gains,
He is still
Melancholy.

Yang Line in Yin Place. This Line is neither Apt nor Centered. Despite material gains (axe-shaped coins), the Heart-and-Mind is still not at peace. The Wanderer, writes Magister Liu, has no close friend ("knower of the sound"); he cannot accomplish his Aspirations. This makes his heart heavy. Since ancient times there have been many who have had the wealth but have lacked the ability to carry out the Tao. This executive, writes Professor Mun, has a good plan and the necessary connections for penetrating the local market of a foreign country. He is a Wanderer who has "gained axe-wealth." But he cannot give full play to his abilities. He is unable to achieve his objective.

Yin in Fifth Place

A pheasant

Is shot,

A second arrow

Lost.

In the end,

He receives

Praise and high office,

In fine,

Laus erit.

On the Image

A height is reached.

Yin Line in Yang Place. Centered. To "shoot the pheasant" is a great achievement; to "lose an arrow" is a slight setback. The gain (pheasant shot) outweighs the loss (arrow lost), writes Professor Mun. The Leader's style is well adapted to local conditions. He cultivates the right contacts with influential people in a foreign country.

Yang in Top Place

The bird's nest

Burns.

The Wanderer

Laughs;

He weeps and wails.

Oxen are lost

In border pasture.

Calamity,

Pessimum.

On the Image

Arrogance
At the Top.
Nest burnt,
Oxen lost:
These Calamities
Are to be expected.

 Yang Line in Yin Place. Violence and arrogance inevitably bring Calamity (the "burnt" nest). To lose oxen is to lose docility and Humility. Conceit and self-importance, writes Magister Liu, eagerness to criticize Others, reluctance to scrutinize Self—these are all symptoms of a falling-off from initial Illumination. The Wanderer abuses his Illumination. The nest is built in a high position, writes Professor Mun. This is overconfidence ("laughter"). But the nest is too high. It burns. He weeps. No one will work for him (his "oxen" are "lost").

Xun

Kneeling

Xun/Wind

above

Xun/Wind

JUDGMENT

Slight Fortune.

A Destination

Profits.

It Profits

To see a Great Man.

On the Judgment

Wind doubled,
Ventus repetitus.

Commands are issued.
Firm Lines are Centered,
In True Place.
Aspirations
Are fulfilled.
The Yielding
Flows with the Firm.
Slight Fortune.

On the Image of the Hexagram

Wind follows Wind,
Ventus ventum sequens.
The True Gentleman
Issues commands
In conducting his affairs.

The Trigrams Expounded

Xun is Wood,
Wind.
It scatters,
Arrays things evenly.
It is South-East,
Eldest daughter.
It enters.
It is cockerel,
Thighs,
Plumb line,
Carpenter's square.
It is white,
Long,
High.
It is Advance,
Retreat.
Xun has no fruit.
It has a strong odor.

Of men, it is

Balding,

Broad of forehead,

Showing the whites of the eyes.

Pursuit of gain,

Seeking threefold profit.

A forceful Trigram.

Wind above Wind. The early graph shows two men Kneeling (see Part II). The Yin Lines in First and Fourth Places "kneel" below the Yang Lines above them. This Hexagram is made up of the Doubled Trigram *Xun*, symbolizing both Wind and Wood (the gentle processes of Infiltration and Vegetation). It is both flexible and penetrating, writes Legge, following Cheng Yi. Wind finds its way into every nook and cranny. Superiors are in Harmony with the needs of inferiors; they "issue" the necessary "commands." Inferiors, for their part, are in Harmony with the wishes of superiors; they obey them. When a Ruler is in tune with what is right, then he is in accord with the Hearts-and-Minds of the Folk. They will obey him and follow ("flow with") him. Superiors and inferiors "kneel" to one another. The Wind blows further and further into the distance, writes Magister Liu, rising ever higher, penetrating everywhere, entering into the Tao. Its Work is unremitting, reaching a deep level of Self-Realization. This is its "Slight Fortune." Some need a "Destination." They need to "see a Great Man," one who considers Inner Nature and Life-Destiny to be of supreme importance, one who values the Tao and the Power above all, one to whom the illusory body is so much dry wood, worldly wealth a mere floating cloud. His Inner Self is rich, although his Outward Appearance may seem insufficient. His Heart-and-Mind is firm; his Aspirations have distant horizons. He never ceases until he reaches the Great Tao. Such is the Great Man. Yang in Second Place and Yang in Fifth Place indicate a strong Leader, writes Professor Mun. Strong Leaders dominate their Organization. They understand the views and needs of their subordinates (the Yin Lines in First and Fourth Places). With a softer approach, the Leader can achieve greater Harmony.

LINES

Yin in First Place

An Advance

Is held back.

Steadfastness

Of a warrior

Profits.

On the Image

Doubt and hesitation
Are resolved by
Steadfastness of a warrior.

Yin Line in Yang Place. Hesitation. A decision is hard to arrive at. It is, however, essential to be Steadfast, to show a warrior's resolve, to be decisive. Everyone has a share of the Tao, writes Magister Liu. The problem is lack of Aspiration, lack of Strength (Yin in Yang). Seek out a teacher; seek personal instruction; be strong and spirited, like "a warrior." This will give access to the Tao. This will bring Profit. A Leader should be decisive, writes Professor Mun. This Yin Line shows indecision and hesitation. There is no Resonance between this Line and Yin in Fourth.

Yang in Second Place

Kneeling

Beneath the bed.

Diviners and sorcerers

Are employed in profusion.

This is

Auspicious.

No Harm.

On the Image

The Center is attained,
Medium obtinet.

Yang Line in Yin Place. Centered. Dark forces strike fear into the heart. But fear is effectively exorcised. To show Humility toward others, writes Magister Liu, is to "kneel beneath the bed." To "employ sorcerers" not only brings oneself under control, it also ensures that others come to "no Harm." When problems are found in an Organization, writes Professor Mun, the Leader should investigate the real root causes, rather than the surface causes. Then he can employ appropriate methods and professionals ("exorcists") to deal with them. The "problem" can also be interpreted as the individual's ego. One should search for this hidden enemy in one's Heart-and-Mind and remove it, like a Shaman exorcising a dark force.

Yang in Third Place

Anxiety.

Discontent.

Distress,

Poenitendi locus.

On the Image

Aspirations are exhausted,
Mens exhausta.

 Yang Line in Yang Place. Anxiety leads to exhaustion and distress, to disenchantment. This distress, writes Magister Liu, comes from an excess of self-satisfaction (Yang in Yang), an obsession with Self as opposed to Others, an inability to have an Empty Heart-and-Mind and to seek improvement. This is Firmness that does not know how to Yield.

Yin in Fourth Place

Regret goes away,

Nullus poenitendi locus.

In the field,

Three kinds of game

Are caught.

On the Image

Success,
Gloria.

Yin Line in Yin Place. Game caught in the hunt was divided into three portions: the first for use in Sacrifice, the second for the entertainment of guests, the third for the kitchen. A hunt providing enough for all three of these purposes was deemed to be successful. A senior executive in this position, writes Professor Mun, is able to develop a good relationship with those above and below him (the "three kinds of game").

Yang in Fifth Place

To be Steadfast

Is Auspicious.

Regret goes away,

Nullus poenitendi locus.

All things

Profit.

No Beginning,

Non habet Initium.

A Conclusion,

Habet finem.

Three days before a *geng* day,

Three days after a *geng* day,

Auspicious,

Hoc bonum.

On the Image

The Position
Is True and Centered,
Sedes recta et media.

Yang Line in Yang Place. Centered. The Tao of the Golden Elixir, writes Magister Liu, at first "kneels" low, thereby attaining depth through being Yielding. This is to have "no Beginning." Then it "kneels" high, and attains full Self-Realization. This is to have a "Conclusion." *Geng* is one of the ancient calendrical cyclic markers.

Yang in Top Place

Kneeling

Beneath the bed.

Axe-wealth

Is lost.

Steadfastness.

Calamity,

Pessimum.

On the Image

Exhaustion at the Top.
Calamity,
Pessimum.

 Yang Line in Yin Place. This is a dark and disturbing situation. One is too fearful to deal with it. Yin Energy has not been transformed, writes Magister Liu. To transform Yin, to attain the Elixir, it is necessary to be Firm, to stand on higher ground (not kneel "beneath the bed"). Otherwise all will be lost, the Work will be wasted. There will be Calamity, despite Steadfastness. The Leader, writes Professor Mun, needs to show greater Strength and creativity if he is to avoid Calamity.

Dui

Joy

Dui/Lake

above

Dui/Lake

JUDGMENT

Fortune.

To be Steadfast

Profits.

On the Judgment

Firm Lines are
Centered,
Yielding
Without.
This Flows

With the Tao of Heaven;
It Resonates with Man.
The Folk are led by Joy;
They forget toil.
Hardship
Is faced with Joy,
Death forgotten.
Great Strength of Joy
Elevates
The spirit of the Folk!

On the Image of the Hexagram

Lake joins with Lake,
Conjunctio lacuum.
The True Gentleman and friends
Converse;
They practice together.

The Trigrams Expounded

Joy is
West,
Autumn.
The Myriad Things
Rejoice.
It is
Sheep,
Mouth.
Youngest daughter.
Marsh,
Lake,
Shamaness.
Tongue.
Destruction,
Bursting open.
Of soils,

Hard and salty.

It is concubine.

The Trigram *Dui*, Lake, is doubled to form this Hexagram. In each Trigram, a single Yin Line sits above two Yang Lines, writes Legge. Water collects in Lake or Marsh. The mood is one of Joy, which inspires the Folk to endure toil and encounter death, led on by the example of their Ruler. They will follow him gladly through any hardship without fear. JM: Compare *The Art of War*:

Chapter 10
The Warrior whose one aim is
To protect his Folk and serve his Lord,
This man is a Jewel of the Realm.
He thinks of his troops as children;
They will follow him into the deepest ravine.
He thinks of them as his loved ones;
They will stand by him unto death.

This Joy is the Joy of Cultivating the Tao, writes Magister Liu. Aspiration is set on the Tao. Joy is in the Tao. To practice the Tao is Joy. This is Fortune. With Inner Joy (in the Lower Trigram) comes Outer Joy (in the Upper Trigram). If Inner Joy is False, so too will be Outer Joy. True Joy is long-lasting. False Joy is short-lived. This is the Profit of Steadfastness. The True Taoist finds no Joy in sensual pleasure or material wealth. His Joy is in the Tao and the Power. The Upper Trigram, writes Professor Mun, is the senior management of the Organization, including its Leader. The Lower Trigram represents the junior employees. The two "Lakes" interconnect; they have a harmonious relationship. The outwardly Yielding character of the two Yin Lines (in Third and Top Places) balances with the Strong character of the Yang Lines, especially in Second and Fifth Places. Both qualities are necessary. A Leader of this type is outwardly soft (friendly, warm, and helpful), and inwardly Firm (abiding by his principles of Sincerity and Balance).

LINES

Yang in First Place

Joy and Harmony.

This is

Auspicious,

Hoc bonum.

On the Image

There is no doubting

In Action,

Nullus est poenitendi locus.

 Yang Line in Yang Place. Inward Harmony brings humble Joy, a simple ability to Act, free from doubt or partiality. This is a natural Joy, writes Magister Liu, an effortless Joy, the Joy of Harmony. This is Auspicious. This is a friendly Leader, writes Professor Mun, open-minded and willing to accept the views of Others. He builds harmonious relationships within the Organization.

Yang in Second Place

Joy

And Good Faith.

This is

Auspicious,

Hoc bonum.

Regret goes away,

Nullus poenitendi locus.

On the Image

Faith in Aspiration,
Mentis soliditas.

 Yang Line in Yin Place. Centered. Joy is tempered by Good Faith. This is Joy in Truth, writes Magister Liu, not in what is False. Illusion fails to move. Joy is Centered. This is Auspicious. This Line is not in an Apt Place, writes Professor Mun. But it is Centered; it is Sincere and fair.

Yin in Third Place

Joy

Comes from without.

Calamity,

Hoc pessimum.

On the Image

The Position is not Apt.

 Yin Line in Yang Place. Joy that comes "from without," idle pleasure, can be misleading and dangerous. This Line is weak, neither Centered nor Apt, writes Magister Liu. This Outer Joy forsakes the True and seeks the False. It hinders Self-Cultivation in the Tao. This is Joy in the service of the Outer World. A Leader, writes Professor Mun, should not seek to achieve Harmony through improper means (Yin in Yang), at the expense of his Integrity. He would be inviting trouble.

Yang in Fourth Place

Joy

Well considered,

Without indulgence.

An ailment

Has a happy resolution,

Gaudium.

On the Image

Cause for celebration,
Felicitas.

 Yang Line in Yin Place. After some hesitation and careful deliberation, a correct decision brings healing and True Joy. Deliberation should precede words and Action, writes Magister Liu. Caution should prevail. An ailment will find a happy Conclusion. An executive must choose, writes Professor Mun, between the Yang Line above (in Fifth Place), the upright Leader, and the Yin Line below (in Third Place), laxity and pleasure.

Yang in Fifth Place

Good Faith

Averts Harm.

Danger,

Periculosum.

On the Image

True Position.

 Yang Line in Yang Place. Centered. Good Faith and Caution, writes Magister Liu, save one from the threat of Harm in the Yin Line in Top Place above. The Danger comes from self-satisfaction and conceit (Yang in Yang), writes Magister Liu. This will inevitably bring failure. Ability can prosper only with Humility and a willingness to learn from Men of the Tao. Those who consort with Small Men and distance themselves from True Gentlemen will surely incur Danger. A Leader, writes Professor Mun, must identify those around him who are sincere, the men of Good Faith.

Yin in Top Place

Seductive

Joy.

On the Image

The True Light
Does not yet shine,
Nondum eluscit.

 Yin Line in Yin Place. Be on guard against the seductive power of pleasure. Beware of clever words and the charming appearance of one who refuses to contemplate faults in Self, who always finds fault in Others, writes Magister Liu. This brings True Joy neither to Self nor to Others. One should never "seduce" Others in order to reach one's own objective, writes Professor Mun.

HEXAGRAM LIX

Huan

Dispersal

Xun/Wind

above

Kan/Abyss

JUDGMENT

Fortune.

The King

Approaches his Temple.

It Profits

To cross a Great Stream,

Transire magnum flumen.

To be Steadfast

Profits.

On the Judgment

The Firm
Comes;
It is not exhausted.
The Yielding
Has its Place
Without;
It is in Harmony
With that which is above.
The King
Approaches his Temple.
He is Centered.
He crosses the Great Stream;
He Rides
Wood.
Success,
Gloria.

On the Image of the Hexagram

Wind moves over Water,
Ventus supra aquam.
The Former Kings
Made Sacrifice to the Deity;
They set up Temples.

The Great Treatise
From Part II Section 2

Tree trunks were hollowed
For boats;
Wood was cut
For oars.
Boats and oars
Connected the unconnected,
They reached distant places.
All-under-Heaven
Profited.

Wind above Water. *Huan* indicates Dispersal from a previous coalescence. It is a melting, a flood, a scattering, a dissipation, leading to a new configuration, a new dynamic. The poet Su Dongpo wrote of this Hexagram: "A well-ordered world is like a great river flowing peacefully downstream in its course. Disorder is like a river flooding in all directions." He went on to draw a lesson for a Ruler presiding over such a state of Dispersal. The Ruler should allow the "river" to find its true course; he should not interfere with the Flux of things; he should not impose a course.

> Water does not act in this way merely for the sake of enjoyment. Something contrary to its Nature is taking place. That is why it bursts its banks and keeps flooding again and again. But things revert to their natural form. Water will eventually recover its peaceful state, of its own accord. The Rulers of Antiquity never struggled with the Folk. They let them find their own course, and then guided them in Accordance with it. . . . In the midst of Dispersal, they remained still and did not struggle. Instead they made plans for the future. They set up Ancestral Temples and determined the place for Sacrifice to the Deity. Then the Hearts-and-Minds of all had somewhere to turn to, something to hold on to.

The word *huan* is also used more positively to describe the "ineffable" and "fluid" quality, the "looseness," possessed by Men of the Tao. See *The Tao and the Power*:

> *Chapter 15*
> In olden times,
> Men of the Tao were
> Wondrously subtle.
> They were
> Mysteriously connected,
> Inscrutable,
> Too deep to fathom. . . .
> Cautious they were,
> As if crossing a stream in winter;
> Circumspect,
> As if sensing peril on every side.
> They were
> Respectful
> Like guests.
> Theirs was
> A Dispersal,
> Like ice melting. . . .

The King Rides Wood (in the Upper Trigram), writes Richard Wilhelm. He crosses the Stream (Lower Trigram, Water of the Abyss). Wind (the alternative Image of the Upper Trigram), the warm breeze of spring, blows over the Water, bringing Dispersal, making waves, thawing ice, breaking down rigidity and separation. The King "approaches his Temple," and there, in the company of the Spirits of his Ancestors, he reunites his subjects in the Ritual of worship. A Temple, writes Zen Master Zhixu, is a sanctuary, a place of safety from the ills of the world. It is also a place in which to accomplish the Dispersal of selfish thoughts. Magister Liu sees Dispersal differently. A man's True Yin and Yang become Dispersed, he writes, when he embraces his Human Heart-and-Mind and abandons the Heart-and-Mind of the Tao. Every step down this path takes him further toward Danger. If he can embrace the Heart-and-Mind of the Tao and abandon the Human Heart-and-Mind, then he can take hold of the Jewel of Life in the Tiger's Lair, he can find the Bright Pearl in the Dragon's Pool (enlightenment in the mundane world). For a Leader, writes Professor Mun, the Wind represents the events around him; the waves in the lake stand for the problems caused by these events. He must reunite the hearts of the people through the values or the culture of his Organization, by emphasizing the contributions of the Ancestors (in the "Temple"). Offering a Sacrifice was a way for a King to build up the group spirit or coherence of his people.

LINES

Yin in First Place

He rides

A strong horse.

Auspicious.

On the Image

Flowing,
Obedientia.

Yin Line in Yang Place. Help and safety, writes Legge, are found in a strong horse, the Yang Line in Second Place immediately above. Here at the very beginning of Dispersal, writes Magister Liu, the Heart-and-Mind of the Tao is not far away. The Human Heart-and-Mind has still not established itself too deeply. A vigorous effort ("a strong horse") can save the situation. The other bank of the river is at hand. The True Treasure is within reach. The Leader, writes Professor Mun, should seek help from a capable person (a "strong horse"). He should act promptly to reduce differences among members of his Organization.

Yang in Second Place

Dispersal.

Seize the moment.

Regret

Goes away,

Nullus poenitendi locus.

On the Image

Aspirations
Are attained.

Yang Line in Yin Place. Centered. This is the moment. Seize it. Do not let it pass by. Yang is trapped within Yin, writes Magister Liu. The Human Heart-and-Mind is at work. But the Heart-and-Mind of the Tao is already well established. Dispersal is here. One should "seize the moment." In order to resolve conflicts effectively in a time of Dispersal, writes Professor Mun, a Leader needs the support of Yin in First Place.

Yin in Third Place

Dispersal

Reaches the person.

No Regret.

On the Image

Aspirations
Are without.

Yin in Yang Place. Dispersal stops short at the individual Self, writes Cheng Yi. It does not reach Others, the greater community. The individual sheds his own selfishness, writes Zhu Xi, and is of service to Others ("without"). This is the extremity of Danger (in the Lower Trigram, Abyss), writes Magister Liu. But there is Resonance between this Line and Yang in Top Place. Follow the Heart-and-Mind of the Tao. This is Dispersal of the person, of the Self, of the Human Heart-and-Mind. The Heart-and-Mind of the Tao is then no longer obscured. A Leader, writes Professor Mun, should put aside Self, personal and selfish desires (Yin in Yang), and concern himself with the problems of Others.

Yin in Fourth Place

The Multitude

Disperses.

This is

Supremely Auspicious,

Magnum bonum.

New heights

Beyond the knowledge

Of ordinary mortals

Are reached

Through Dispersal.

On the Image

Great Light,
Claritas magna.

Yin Line in Yin Place. The Partisanship of the Multitude is brought to an end, writes Legge, following Zhu Xi. After Dispersal, the Multitude can be gathered together again into one great body. This is a new height, or eminence. This is Auspicious and Luminous. This Dispersal of the Yin Multitude, writes Magister Liu, is awaiting the Return of Yang. This is Supremely Auspicious. With Dispersal of False Yin, Return to the True Yang is possible. True Yang and True Yin fuse into one. These are the "new heights." This is "beyond the knowledge of mortals." An executive, writes Professor Mun, should Disperse his own clique and gather together people from the broader community, out of concern for the whole Organization, going along with the Leader (Yang in Fifth Place). He should keep a distance from Yin in Third Place (the ego).

Yang in Fifth Place

A vast

Dispersal.

Great cries

Are uttered.

A Dispersal

From the royal granaries.

No Harm,

Nullum malum.

On the Image

This is in True Position.

Yang Line in Yang Place. Centered. The Ruler takes energetic measures to alleviate the Distress of his Folk. In this Line, writes Magister Liu, Yang is Centered and True. To see through what is False, not to be bound by conditioned ways of thinking and being—this is a Vast Dispersal. "Great cries are uttered" as Falsehood is removed, stripped away. This is the Tao of Dispersal, Mastery of Self, a return to what is proper, to kindness. The Lord of Heart-and-Mind is at one with the Principle of Nature. This is Dispersal of the False and Completion of Reality. A Leader of Integrity, writes Professor Mun, restores healthy order to his Organization.

Yang in Top Place

Dispersal of

Blood.

Departure.

Distance

Is kept.

No Harm,

Nullum malum.

On the Image

Harm
Is kept at a distance.

Yang Line in Yin Place. Danger that might have led to injury and the shedding of blood is averted. In this extremity, writes Magister Liu, Dispersal of blood makes it possible to keep the Human Heart-and-Mind at a distance, preventing it from causing Harm to the Heart-and-Mind of the Tao. The Golden Elixir, the Sacred Embryo, is formed. Finally Yin and Yang fuse as one.

HEXAGRAM LX

Jie

Notch

Kan/Abyss

above

Dui/Lake

JUDGMENT

Fortune.

A Bitter

Notch.

Steadfastness

Does not avail.

On the Judgment

Firm and Yielding
Are equally apportioned.
Firm is in the Center.
The Tao is exhausted,
Lex exhausta.
Danger faces
Joy.
Positions are Apt.
The Notch is
Centered and True;
It is connected.
The Notches of
Heaven and Earth
Bring the Four Seasons
Into being.
When Notches are well regulated,
Wealth
Is not damaged,
The Folk
Are not hurt.

On the Image of the Hexagram

Water above Lake,
Aqua supra lacum.
The True Gentleman calibrates.
He debates virtuous conduct.

Water above Lake. The Lake has a limited capacity, writes Richard Wilhelm, following Cheng Yi. If the water flowing into it exceeds that capacity, the lake will overflow. There must be Regulation, as in the Notches of the bamboo. JM: The graph for the Hexagram Name contains the bamboo "radical element." The Notches, writes Legge, as well as being the bamboo's calibrations, are also the joints of the body. They are the Twenty-Four Turning Points of the Solar Year; they are the details of Regulation and Ritual. The ruling idea of this Hexagram is thus the maintenance of a well-regulated cadence or rhythm, a fine sense of timing. It is essential to be in tune with Time, to be at one with the rhythm of the seasons and the equilibrium of society. JM: Compare *The Art of War*, where I translated *jie* simply as Timing:

Chapter 5
A swooping falcon
Breaks the back of its prey;
Such is the precision of its Timing.
The Warrior Adept's Energy is devastating;
His Timing is taut.
His Energy resembles
A drawn crossbow;
His Timing resembles
The release of a trigger.

But a Notch can be bitter, writes Magister Liu, if one does not adapt to Change, if one is too rigid. This can create Danger. Then even Steadfastness does not avail. The True Gentleman practices the Tao, building Power, taking every step in a measured way, like water flowing easily from one place to another. His every word is well considered. He is at peace, like a Lake on which no wave stirs. When he acts, he never loses touch with his Inner Nature, he never restricts himself to a single Pattern or Notch. He is never restricted by Yin and Yang. Each Notch has its limits. Every Notch connects. That is its Fortune. Water needs to be regulated, writes Professor Mun. An excess causes flooding; a deficiency causes drought. In the same way, conduct should be balanced, neither extravagant nor restricted. A middle way must be found between restraint and freedom. The Leader of an Organization needs to balance corporate responsibility and social responsibility. He should promote diverse or balanced growth, and not concentrate in any one sector. He should not be overly ambitious. He should exercise appropriate restraint. This includes restraint of Self.

LINES

Yang in First Place

Do not go out

Through the courtyard door.

No Harm,

Nullum malum.

On the Image

Recognize both
Connection and Obstruction.

The Great Treatise
From Part I, Section 8

The Master said:
Words are steps to chaos.
If the True Gentleman
Takes no care,
He loses his Minister.
If the Minister
Takes no care,
He loses his life.
Consider with care
The Hinges of Things,
And achievement will not be harmed.
The True Gentleman
Exercises
Caution and care.
He does not go out.

Yang Line in Yang Place. This "door" is the door of the inner apartments, leading out into the courtyard, writes Legge, as opposed to the "gate" of the next Line. Recognize Connection and Obstruction. Act accordingly, regulated by consideration of the Notches, of Time, of the Potential Energy of the moment. Know when not to Act, and at such times be Still. Recognize that seeds of new activity, Triggers of Action, Hinges of Things, have yet to mature. Hold back. This recognition will avert Harm. In his "Rhapsody on Scholars out of Their Time," Dong Zhongshu refers to this Line. The poet is unable to find an ideal community; he refuses to compromise and instead chooses Retirement:

Not going out
Through the courtyard door,
He hopes to be
Free from Harm. . . .
The honest man
Resolutely exercises restraint. . . .
In the clear light of past ages,
Honest men
Were lonely and without resort. . . .

The Notch, "not going out," writes Magister Liu, is the discipline of being Firm at the outset (Yang in Yang), of distinguishing right from wrong before setting out. This

Line is in its True Place. The Leader, writes Professor Mun, should not move forward if there are obstructions ahead (Yang in Second Place). Waiting is the correct decision. Knowing what will succeed and what will be thwarted is wisdom.

Yang in Second Place

Not going out

Through the courtyard gate

Brings

Calamity,

Pessimum.

On the Image

He is utterly out of touch
With Time.

 Yang Line in Yin Place. Centered. Here, by contrast, writes Legge, one knows that one *should* Act, that one *should* "go out"—the gate is open, obstacles are gone—but despite this, one insists on staying still, one hesitates. The moment is missed. The consequences are grave. In the words of the poet Su Dongpo, "The True Gentleman perceives the seeds of good and evil Fortune, and is able to go forth at the proper moment." This Firm Line is weakened by its Yin Place, writes Magister Liu. The Notch of "not going out through the courtyard gate" is solitary and quiet. It has no connection. It is ineffective. It is an obstinate Notch. If the Leader holds back at this time, writes Professor Mun, he will fail to seize an opportunity and will have Regrets.

Yin in Third Place

There is no

Notch.

Lamentation.

On the Image

No other has caused
The lamentation.

Yin Line in Yang Place. "Who else has caused the lamentation but oneself?" comments Legge. The need for Regulation has not been understood. The mistake is one's own. Knowledge comes too late. This Line is neither Centered nor True, writes Magister Liu. The discipline of Notch has been neglected. Pleasure is sought, but no pleasure is gained. The result is self-inflicted pain and lamentation. If a Leader does not know how to exercise self-control, writes Professor Mun, he has no one to blame but himself.

Yin in Fourth Place

The Notch

Of Peace.

Fortune,

Fortunium.

On the Image

The Tao of those above
Is accepted.

 Yin Line in Yin Place. This is a True Line. It has a natural sense of Notch, a calm sense of Regulation. It accords with and supports the next Line, Yang in Fifth Place. This, writes Magister Liu, is a spontaneously peaceful Notch. A senior executive acts in a spontaneous and natural way, writes Professor Mun. He does not need to take orders from his superior (Yang in Fifth Place).

Yang in Fifth Place

A sweet

Notch.

This is

Auspicious.

An Advance

Is highly esteemed.

On the Image

He abides in the Center,
Medium obtinens.

 Yang Line in Yang Place. Centered. A strong Ruler's self-discipline inspires confidence. In the midst of bitterness, writes Magister Liu, one finds sweetness. In the midst of Danger, one achieves Inner Mastery (Yang in Yang, Centered). Any Advance will be highly esteemed. Notches connect. Ultimately, with the Notch that adapts to Change, and connects, one reaches Center and Truth, one attains Spiritual Transformation, the Unfathomable Realm.

Yin in Top Place

A bitter

Notch.

Despite Steadfastness,

Calamity,

Pessimum.

Regret goes away,

Non est poenitendi locus.

On the Image

The Tao is exhausted,
Lex exhauritur.

 Yin in Yin Place. Confucius says in *Analects* 3.4: "Ritual should be sparing, not extravagant." But if "sparing" Regulation is too severe, too spartan, if the Notch is too "bitter," it can lead to Calamity. Restraint and moderation are the remedy for any problem. With these, Regret will disappear. The "bitter Notch," writes Magister Liu, is an obsessive dedication to solitary meditation. This Profits neither Inner Nature nor Life-Destiny. If a Leader persists in exercising excessive Restraint, writes Professor Mun, it may lead to resistance or even rebellion.

Zhong Fu

Good Faith

Xun/Wind

above

Dui/Lake

JUDGMENT

Pigs and fishes.

This is

Auspicious,

Bonum.

It Profits

To cross a Great Stream,

Magnum flumen.

To be Steadfast

Profits,

Soliditas.

On the Judgment

Yielding is within;
Firm is Centered.
Joy and Lake,
A gentle breeze.
Good Faith
Transforms the Realm;
It even transforms
Pigs and fishes.
It Profits
To cross a Great Stream
In an empty wooden boat.
To be Steadfast,
To Resonate with Heaven,
Coelo,
Profits.

On the Image of the Hexagram

Wind above Lake,
Ventus supra lacum.
The True Gentleman
Scrutinizes litigation carefully;
He delays
The sentence of death.

Wind over Lake. The main theme of this Hexagram, writes Legge, is the power of Good Faith, of Sincerity or Truth, emanating from an Inner Void that allows the fullest development of a person's Nature. The two Yin Lines in the Third and Fourth Places, in the Center of the Hexagram, represent that Void, a Heart-and-Mind free from prejudice, open (like an "empty boat"), with no restricting consciousness of Self. The "empty boat" of this Hexagram (Wood over Lake) is Master Zhuang's Image of the Taoist, the "man who wanders in the world, making himself empty: how can anyone harm him?" The Confucian Classic the *Doctrine of the Mean* also speaks of this spontaneous ease of the Center: "Sincerity is the Tao of Heaven. The attainment of Sincerity is the Tao of Man. One who possesses Sincerity attains the Center without effort. He gets there without thought; he reaches the Center of the Tao with ease. This is the Sage." The Yang Lines on each side, above and below the Void, including two in the Center of each Trigram, are the building blocks of Good Faith, of Inner Truth and Sincerity. Sincerity, Good Faith, Trust—these are all connected; they all flow from the Tao; they are the essential qualities of the True Gentleman. When the Heart-and-Mind is filled with Trust, writes Magister Liu, when thoughts are pure, then the myriad worries of the world dissolve. Inner Sincerity radiates outward. This path leads from the lowly to the lofty, from the shallow to the profound, gradually reaching the Place of Profound Fulfillment. The Spiritual Strength of Good Faith is likened to the Wind (Upper Trigram), a gentle breeze blowing over the waters of the Lake (Lower Trigram). "Wind enters into all things," writes Li Guangdi. "The grass, the trees, and the plain—all are stirred by its movement. The highest peaks and the lowest valleys, the deepest caverns and crevasses, all feel its breath. In the depths of Water, in the darkest shade, the Wind blows. It Disperses cold; it thaws ice. Petty Litigation (by contrast) is an area of darkness. The True Gentleman scrutinizes its dark secrets, its detailed minutiae. He investigates each case carefully on its merits, delaying sentence wherever possible. There is nothing his Wisdom and Sincerity cannot reach." He penetrates the Hearts-and-Minds of others with a depth of understanding that knows forgiveness, with a sympathetic appreciation of circumstances, with compassion, writes Richard Wilhelm. The wise Leader, writes Professor Mun, is able to overcome difficulties; he can "cross the Great Stream" in the "boat" of his Sincerity, which will touch others, even the rudest and least intelligent of creatures, "pigs and fishes." JM: The "empty wooden boat" was also present in the mind of the poet Xie Lingyun, as he contemplated the life of a Hermit:

On a Journey to Red Rocks, Sailing out to Sea
Early summer.
The weather is still cool,
The fragrant plants
Have not begun to fade.
I linger in my boat
From dawn to dusk;
Storm clouds
Drift around me. . . .
This immense ocean
Knows no bounds,
My "empty boat"
Skims over it. . . .

Later in life, when he set off into virtual exile, the notion of Good Faith was in the forefront of his mind:

On First Setting out from Shishou City
I hold fast
To the Lines of Good Faith;

I suffer slander
Like the man in the song. . . .
My heart is pure as break of day;
Let me be true to it,
Steadfast,
For all the winter cold.

LINES

Yang in First Place

Preparation

Is Auspicious.

Else

There can be no rest.

On the Image

Aspirations
Are unaltered.

Yang Line in Yang Place. With inward serenity and sincere preparation, writes Richard Wilhelm, Aspirations are not altered or influenced from without. The making of rash and hasty judgments (Yang in Yang), writes Magister Liu, believing first one thing and then another—this is the "else" that brings "no rest." Good Faith, writes Professor Mun, comes from the Leader's Inner World. The Resonance between this Line and Yin in Fourth Place is not helpful in this instance.

Yang in Second Place

The crane

Sings in the shade.

Her chicks

Reply.

Share with me

This beaker of fine wine.

On the Image

This is the innermost wish
Of the Heart-and-Mind.

The Great Treatise,
From Part I, Section 8

The Master said:
The True Gentleman
Dwells in his abode.
When he comes out,
His good words
Resonate for miles around. . . .
Actions near at hand
Are felt far away.
Words and Actions
Are Hinges of the Door,
The Trigger
Of the True Gentleman's
Crossbow,
With which he moves
Heaven and Earth.

Yang Line in Yin Place. Centered. This rhyme of the Singing Crane (no doubt of ancient folk origin) is interpreted allegorically by Legge and Wilhelm, continuing the theme of the Hexagram: the Resonance of Good Faith and Sincerity, in word and deed. It is through Resonance that such qualities work. Just as the young chicks are bound by a deep bond of love, and respond to their mother's song, so too the Heart-and-Mind of man answers to that of another. Such is the Resonance among kindred spirits. They hear one another's music. They are moved from the innermost depths of their being. The circle of Resonance grows ever larger. In his essay "The Pavilion for Releasing Cranes," the poet Su Dongpo quotes this Line, pledging the Hermit who built the pavilion with these words: "Do you, sir, know the pleasure of being a Hermit? It is not to be exchanged even for the throne of a Prince! The I Ching says: 'The crane sings in the shade, Her chicks reply.'" And in the Book of Songs we read:

The crane calls
In the marshes;
Its song is heard
In the Heavens.

The crane is a creature of the utmost purity. It dwells in remote places; it transcends the dusty world. It is extolled in these two Classics. It resembles the Sage Recluse, who takes delight in the company of such birds. This Line forges a Connection between Yin and Yang; it removes the barrier separating them, writes Magister Liu. Spiritual Illumination issues forth of its own accord, like a "crane singing in the shade." Good Faith is darkly concealed within Self-Cultivation (Yang in Yin). The shade, writes Professor Mun, is created by the two Yin Lines immediately above this Centered Line. The Leader's Good Faith is such that the members of his Organization respond to him, like the chicks to their mother crane. The "fine wine" is the fruit of this Good Faith, which can be shared with all. Relationships among people made on the basis of Good Faith will be deep and lasting.

Yin in Third Place

A mate is found.

A drumming,

A stopping.

A weeping,

A singing.

On the Image

The Position is not Apt.

 Yin Line in a Yang Place. This Line Resonates with Yang in Top Place, writes Cheng Yi. Movement and repose, grief and happiness—these are all forms of attachment, of dependence on a person trusted. This is not necessarily either Auspicious or Inauspicious. It is certainly not the way of the Enlightened True Gentleman. No matter how close to others one may be, writes Richard Wilhelm, if one's Center depends on them, one is inevitably tossed to and fro between joy and sorrow. This kind of Faith, writes Magister Liu, mistakes the False for the True. It vacillates between one emotion and another, all of them empty and insubstantial. It Profits a Leader, writes Professor Mun, to be independent and self-reliant.

Yin in Fourth Place

The Moon

Is almost full.

A horse

Has gone astray,

One of a pair.

No Harm,

Nullum malum.

On the Image

He parts with his kind,
He rises upward.

 Yin Line in Yin Place. The horse parts from his mate (Yin in Third Place), writes Richard Wilhelm. He looks upward instead, to a superior (Yang in Fifth Place), for enlightenment, just as the waxing Moon absorbs light from the Sun. Hold firmly to True Direction, to Good Faith, like a horse that gallops straight ahead without looking sideways at its mate (the one that has gone astray).

Yang in Fifth Place

Good Faith

Binds.

There is

No Harm,

Nullum malum.

On the Image

The Position is
True and Apt.

Yang Line in Yang Place. Centered. This Line is the solid heart of the Hexagram, writes Cheng Yi. It is both True and Centered. The Tao of the True Gentleman, his Good Faith, connects ("binds") the world, causes it to Resonate. Inner Strength radiates, it binds the world together. Yin and Yang fuse, writes Magister Liu. When the Work reaches this stage, one is united with the Tao of Nature. All worldly ties are seen to be empty. There can be no Harm. The Leader's Good Faith, writes Professor Mun, has the power to unite. .

Yang in Top Place

Cock's crow

Rises to Heaven,

In coelum ascendit.

Steadfastness.

Calamity,

Hoc pessimum.

On the Image

The cock
Cannot crow for long.

Yang Line in Yin Place. The cock itself cannot rise to Heaven, writes Zhu Xi, but its Aspiration is to do so. The Steadfastness is misplaced; the true situation has not been taken into account. This will lead to Calamity. One should beware of overconfidence such as this, of any inclination to "crow" over good fortune, writes John Blofeld. The intellect is wrongly used, writes Magister Liu. Wishing to climb the heights, one ends up falling. There is a lack of Humility, a random, eclectic "sampling" of faiths—faiths no sooner entered than abandoned. The Leader should not step beyond his ability, writes Professor Mun. He should recognize the limits of his own strength.

HEXAGRAM LXII

Xiao Guo

Slight Excess

Zhen/Quake

above

Gen/Mountain

JUDGMENT

Fortune.

To be Steadfast

Profits.

There is

Success in small matters,

No success in great matters.

A cry uttered

By a bird in flight,

An Ascent,

Bode ill.

A Descent

Bodes well.

This is

Highly Auspicious,

Magnum bonum.

On the Judgment

It Profits
To be Steadfast,
To move in tune with Time.
The Yielding
Occupies the Center.
This is Auspicious
For small matters.
The Firm is out of Position;
It is not Centered.
There is no success
In great matters.
The bird in flight
Utters a cry.
An Ascent
Opposes the Flow,
A Descent
Follows the Flow.

On the Image of the Hexagram

Thunder on the Mountain,
Tonitrus supra montem.
The True Gentleman
In his deeds

May show

Slight Excess

Of reverence,

In his mourning

Slight Excess

Of grief,

In his expenditure,

Slight Excess

Of thrift.

Quake above Mountain. In this Hexagram the four Yin Lines at top and bottom predominate, surrounding the two Yang Lines, whereas in Hexagram XXVIII, *Da Guo,* "Great Excess," four Yang Lines predominate, "sandwiched" between two single Yin Lines in First and Top Places. In both Hexagrams, the Upper Trigram and the Lower Trigram mirror each other. There is an inherent weakness or imbalance. Here, success is feasible only in "small matters." A Slight Excess may even in certain small personal matters be considered Auspicious. *Guo,* the key word in this Hexagram Name, as in the Name of Hexagram XXVIII, has many meanings: "to pass [in space or time]," "to pass by [when visiting someone]," "to pass on," "to pass beyond a frontier," "to go beyond [the Middle Way]," "to exceed [a limit]." Hence it comes to mean Excess in general, transgression or error, a lack of Moderation. The image of a bird in flight is suggested by the shape of the Hexagram. Two wings (four Outer Yin Lines) extend on either side of the body (two Inner Yang Lines). Flight is in itself an image of Slight Excess, just as ascent is seen as opposition to the Flow. Compare this with the sagging ridgepole in Hexagram XXVIII, where two Outer Yin Lines are unable to support the four Inner Yang Lines (the great beam). The need for Humility, writes Legge, is the ruling idea of this Hexagram. It is better by far, more Auspicious, for a bird to descend, to stay near its nest, than to climb into the homeless regions of the air, or to fly rashly up toward the sun. Do not soar too high. Do not go too far. Set modest goals. If necessary, "slighter" things may be a little "overdone" from time to time. This need not affect the overall outcome. A Slight Excess above the norm may be permitted occasionally, writes Professor Mun. As in the Top Line of the previous Hexagram, a Leader should recognize his own limits.

LINES

Yin in First Place

A bird in flight

Brings Calamity,

Pessimum.

On the Image

Nothing can be done.

 Yin Line in Yang Place. This is Flight as Slight Excess. The bird should have stayed in its nest, writes Richard Wilhelm. This is a weak Line, writes Magister Liu. One should abide in one's proper place and concentrate on Self-Cultivation. Any attempt to "fly" will be futile. An executive, writes Professor Mun, should not aim to fly too high. He is not strong or competent enough (Yin in Yang Place), and although the Line Resonates with Yang in Fourth Place, that support may not be adequate.

Yin in Second Place

He passes by

The Ancestor,

He meets

The Ancestress.

He does not reach his Lord,

He meets the Minister.

No Harm,

Nullum malum.

On the Image

The Minister must not be passed by.

 Yin Line in Yin Place. Centered. One has to make do with less than originally intended. The person met with may not be the person originally hoped for. Nonetheless, the encounter is not wholly in vain. This is in keeping with the general tenor of this Hexagram, which is to set modest goals, not to aim too high. Meeting the Ancestress, and not the Ancestor, writes Professor Mun, is an example of Slight Excess. It deviates from the normal practice, but it is justified in a special case. Other examples of Slight Excess might be increasing expenditure over and above a planned budget; giving staff special allowances in an emergency; or hiring extra temporary staff.

Yang in Third Place

Eschew any

Excess.

Beware.

Others approach;

They attack.

Calamity,

Pessimum.

On the Image

Nothing can be done
To avert this Calamity.

 Yang Line in Yang Place. Do not err by being rash. Take care not to be taken unaware by others (the Yang Line above). Danger must be forestalled, writes Magister Liu. In the event of an attack, the Celestial Jewel already gained will be lost. This is Excess of strength (Yang in Yang), writes Professor Mun. An executive in this position should be careful not to be overconfident. He should listen to the advice of others.

Yang in Fourth Place

No Harm,

Nullum malum.

Eschew Excess.

An Encounter,

An Advance,

Will bring Danger.

Caution.

Enduring Steadfastness

Will not avail.

On the Image

The Position is not Apt.
Steadfastness cannot prevail.

Yang Line in Yin Place. This brief encounter cannot be prolonged. It is necessary to adapt to Change, writes Magister Liu. An Excess of Steadfastness will not help. External Energy (Yin in First Place) Resonates. It is attracted and will bring Danger. Exercise Caution. Call a halt when appropriate. Make a move when appropriate. Self-Cultivation in the Tao will bring Release of the Embryo. It will pierce Emptiness and bring Self-Realization. The executive, writes Professor Mun, should keep a distance from the inferior man (Yin in First Place, with which this Line Resonates). He should guard against harmful influence.

Yin in Fifth Place

Dense clouds,

No rain,

From meadows to the West.

The Duke shoots an arrow;

He gets something

In the cave.

On the Image

It is too high above.

Yin Line in Yang Place. Centered. The Duke's arrow has a cord attached to it, to pull in the game. The cave is the Yin Line in Second Place. The first words also occur in the Judgment of Hexagram IX. Clouds are Yin. In the absence of communion with Yang, they cannot discharge their rain. They are futile. The only Profit to be had is down below, in the "cave." The Tao of Self-Cultivation, writes Magister Liu, forms an Elixir compounded of Pure Yin and Yang Energies. "Clouds" from the "meadows" of home are not enough. They produce no rain. "Shooting an arrow" and getting something "in the cave" is another Image of futility. Instead of humbly seeking wisdom from the Sage close at hand (Yang in Fourth Place), one sits idly in the Empty Space of solitary contemplation, using the Void to "shoot" the Void, turning Self and Others all into one Void, "getting" the Other "in the cave." All of this is Void. It achieves nothing. A weak Leader (Yin in Yang), writes Professor Mun, cannot do much for his Organization.

Yin in Top Place

Eschew

Excess.

A bird flies

Into the distance.

Calamity,

Pessimum,

Utter Disaster.

On the Image

This has gone too far.

 Yin Line in Yin Place. An overambitious "flight" leads to complete Disaster. Beware. This is Spiritual Excess, writes Magister Liu. Learning from strange teachers, indulging in outlandish physical practices, gazing into a mirror in order to have out-of-body experiences—all of this is like a "bird flying" too high, unable to stop. It will cause irreparable Harm. JM: A person practicing meditation who does it to Excess, and opens Being to malign influences, may fall prey to the condition known as *zouhuo rumo*, "possession" or "seizure." A classic instance of this is the story of the young Buddhist nun Adamantina, in chapter 87 of *The Story of the Stone*. A Leader in this position, writes Professor Mun, must look downward and seek a connection with those below, especially Yang in Third Place, with which the Line has Resonance. He must not go further and further away "into the distance." Such arrogance will merely forfeit the trust of those beneath him, and will isolate him.

Ji Ji

Complete

Kan/Abyss

above

Li/Fire

JUDGMENT

Fortune in small things.

To be Steadfast

Profits.

An Auspicious Beginning,

A turbulent End.

On the Judgment

Fortune for the Small.
Firm and Yielding are
In True Place;
All Positions are Apt.
An Auspicious Beginning.
Yielding is Centered.
A Turbulent End.
The Tao is exhausted.

On the Image of the Hexagram

Water above Fire,
Aqua supra ignem.
The True Gentleman
Is mindful of
Disaster.
He exercises
Caution.

Water of the Abyss, above Fire. This is the only Hexagram in the entire *I Ching* in which all Firm (Yang) and Yielding (Yin) Lines are in their Proper or True Places: Yang on odd numbers, Yin on even. The Upper Trigram and the Lower Trigram are in perfect alignment. Every Line Resonates. Much of the symbolism stems not just from this balanced Trigram structure, but also from the second word, *ji*, in both this Hexagram Name and the next. This Chinese character, with the water "radical element," has as one of its earliest meanings "to cross a stream" in a boat, or "to cross a ford." Thence it comes to mean "to reach the other bank," a meaning that continued into Buddhist usage, as in the compound *jidu*, "to help mortals cross over the sea of reincarnation," "to help release them from the wheel of samsara and enable them to reach nirvana." In more general terms, *ji* means simply to succeed, to attain a goal, or to help others succeed in attaining theirs. The ruling idea is of arrival at Completion, or Self-Realization. Joseph Needham calls it Consummation, or perfect order. In social terms, the "vessel of the state" is brought safely across a great and dangerous passage. In spiritual terms, the individual reaches a new stage, a new level of Self-Fulfillment. In alchemical terms, the Adept achieves the True Equilibrium of Water and Fire, of Yin and Yang. The Elixir, the Inner Child, is formed. True Yin complements and strengthens True Yang. In the Upper Trigram, *Kan*, Inner Yang is surrounded by two Outer Yin Lines; in the Lower Trigram, *Li*, Inner Yin is surrounded by two Outer Yang Lines. In the traditional terminology of the Chinese sex handbooks, Completion is the climax, the consummation, the final stage of the "battle," the *culmen voluptatis*. Importantly, for the Taoist lover, it is a climax without ejaculation, in which Male (Yang) Energy is stored, not dissipated. This example comes from a Ming dynasty text:

I practice Turtle and Dragon,
Serpent and Tiger.
The enemy surrenders;
I gather the fruits of victory.
Completion.
Withdrawing from the battlefield,
I descend from my horse,
I dismiss my troops.
Quietly resting to regain strength. . . .
I have obtained True Yang.

At postcoital rest, the man, who has absorbed the woman's Yin essence (the "fruits" of sexual "victory"), and has refrained from ejaculation, regulates his breathing and allows his own Vital Essence to be transformed into pure Yang Energy. This is an extension of the cosmic intercourse of Heaven and Earth, as so well stated in the Great Treatise, from Part II, Section 4:

Heaven and Earth
In their intercourse
Give form
To the Myriad Things.
Man and woman
In their sexual congress
Give life
To the Myriad Things.

It is precisely at this point, when this equilibrium has been reached, whether it be social, spiritual, alchemical, or sexual, that any unconsidered movement becomes most perilous. It may cause order to revert to disorder, it may lead to a "turbulent End." The Trigram relationship between Water (Woman), above, and Fire (Man), below, generates Energy like that produced in a boiling kettle. This juncture is hazardous, and it necessitates the utmost Caution. It requires an awareness of possible Disaster. It demands Steadfast Self-Cultivation. When any development reaches its climax, writes Professor Mun, a reverse movement can be expected. Cyclical change is one of the basic concepts of the *I Ching*. This is a warning against complacency.

LINES

Yang in First Place

The wheel

Brakes.

The tail

Is wet.

No Harm,

Nullum malum.

On the Image

This is a righteous course.
No Harm.

 Yang Line in Yang Place. Overcome Danger by holding back firmly, writes Richard Wilhelm. These are Images—the braking of the wheel, the avoidance of wetting the tail—of the Firm held in check. Exercise Caution at the outset and there will be no Harm. Danger is inherent in the strong Nature of the Line (Yang in Yang Place). Danger, writes Professor Mun, is also present in the "hidden" Trigram formed by Lines 2, 3, and 4, *Kan*, the Abyss. Compare this Line with Yang in Second Place in the next Hexagram.

Yin in Second Place

The woman's carriage curtain

Is lost.

Do not search for it.

In seven days

It will be found.

On the Image

The Tao is Centered.

Yin Line in Yin Place. Centered. A woman loses her protection and is exposed, writes Richard Wilhelm. She is weak, but since she is in the correct place (Yin Centered in Second Place), attacks can do her no Harm. Bide time and cultivate Inner Strength, writes Magister Liu. Let distractions pass. Light will then be born in an Empty Room. Spiritual Illumination will come of its own accord. It cannot be hunted down.

Yang in Third Place

The High Ancestor

Attacks

Demon Territory;

He conquers it

In three years.

No room here

For a Small Man.

On the Image

After three years
Comes exhaustion.

Yang Line in Yang Place. Large and bold initiatives may be dauntingly difficult; they may cause extreme stress and fatigue. They are to be undertaken only with Caution, by those properly qualified. Compare Hexagram VII/6. The High Ancestor was probably King Wu Ding of the Shang dynasty. The inhabitants of Demon Territory (*guifang*) were the threatening barbarians on the northwestern frontiers of the Shang realm, the "barbarous hordes of the cold and bleak regions north of the Middle States." Wu Ding's protracted and debilitating campaign against them is seen as the judicious act of a wise but powerful man, succeeding despite the resilience of his enemies. He avoided pitfalls which would certainly have undone a lesser commander. A Leader, writes Professor Mun, must realize that a large and ambitious operation (such as the "attack on Demon Territory") needs not only plentiful resources, but also considerable time. Others see the "conquest" as spiritual victory over the barbarian element within. Compare Yang in Fourth Place, in the next Hexagram.

Yin in Fourth Place

Fine clothes

Turn to rags.

Be cautious

The day long.

On the Image

Hesitation,
Dubitandi locus.

Yin Line in Yin Place. Again, Caution is urged in an uncertain world of Change. Wealth and poverty, finery and rags, can change places with alarming unpredictability and rapidity. The Leader, writes Professor Mun, must prepare against predictable dangers. This Line is the first in the Upper Trigram, *Kan*, the dangerous Abyss. The down-at-heels gentleman Zhen Shiyin, on the verge of Enlightenment, takes up this theme in the opening chapter of Cao Xueqin's *The Story of the Stone*:

> Who shivering once in rags bemoaned his fate,
> Today finds fault with scarlet robes of state.
> In such commotion does the world's theater rage:
> As each one leaves, another takes the stage.
> In vain we roam:
> Each in the end must call a strange land home.

Yang in Fifth Place

Neighbors to the East

Slaughter an ox.

Neighbors to the West

Perform a simple *Yue* Sacrifice.

The Blessing

Is greater,

Felicitas.

On the Image

The Western neighbors
Are more timely.
Great Fortune
Is theirs,
Magnum bonum.

Yang Line in Yang Place. Centered. A simple Offering, such as the *Yue* Sacrifice, writes Legge, made with genuine piety and sincerity, is more acceptable (in the biblical sense); it brings more Blessing than an impressive show laid on without warmth. JM: In other words, a modest effort made at the right time wins more Blessing than an ostentatious effort at the wrong time.

Yin in Top Place

The head is wet.

Danger,

Periculosum.

On the Image

This cannot prevail for long.

Yin Line in Yin Place. This is a violent and perilous Action, a foolish attempt to cross a ford, writes Legge. One ends up plunging headlong into the water. The situation requires great Caution. The Leader, writes Professor Mun, must guard against complacency at the end of a venture. If he lowers his guard, he may suffer defeat when he is on the verge of success. Learn to anticipate dangers such as this, writes Magister Liu. Preserve the fruits of Self-Cultivation. Prevent the unraveling of the hard-won balance of Yin and Yang. The Taoist must combine Action (*youwei*) and Non-Action (*wuwei*) in a timely way, varying them according to the needs of the moment. The Taoist pays attention to both Emptiness (*xu*) and Substance (*shi*), understanding both Inner Essence (*xing*) and Life-Destiny, the objective external Life-Situation (*ming*). JM:This is subtler than, but not ultimately very different from, the excellent advice offered in chapter 3 of *The Art of War*, "Strategic Offensive":

Utimate excellence lies
Not in winning every battle,
But in defeating the enemy
Without ever fighting. . . .

The Skillful Strategist
Defeats the enemy
Without doing battle . . . .
Know when to fight
And when not to fight. . . .
Be ready for the unexpected. . . .
Know the enemy,
Know yourself,
And victory is never in doubt,
Not in a hundred battles.

Wei Ji

Incomplete

Li/Fire

above

Kan/Abyss

JUDGMENT

Fortune.

The little fox,

When almost across,

Gets his tail wet.

There is

No Profit,

Nulla convenientia.

On the Judgment

The Yielding is Centered,
Fortune.
The little fox,
When almost across,
When not quite past Center,
Wets his tail;
He cannot continue to
Completion.
Positions are not Apt,
But Firm and Yielding
Resonate.

On the Image of the Hexagram

Fire above Water,
Ignis supra aquam.
The True Gentleman
Distinguishes things carefully,
Each in its proper abode.

禿 Fire above Water. As in the Name of Hexagram LXIII, the second word, *ji*, Completion, conveys the Image of crossing a ford. Here, however, the attempt is unsuccessful; it remains Incomplete. The relative positions of the Trigrams Water and Fire are reversed. They no longer interact in the same fruitful way, but draw away from each other, Fire upward, Water downward. This time, every Line is technically in the "wrong" Position (Yin is where Yang "should" be, and vice versa). This is a time of instability, a period of transition. Joseph Needham calls it Disorder capable of Consummation and Perfection, the position when all has not yet quite been successfully accomplished. There is a need for Caution, for deliberation, a need to "distinguish things carefully," to put each in its "proper abode," to have a clear discernment of what is what, what is True and what is False. But despite all of this, the Lines do nonetheless Resonate with one another (*ying*). They still offer some hope of Fortune. For the Manager, writes Professor Mun, despite the difficult circumstances, there is still a spirit of cooperation within the Organization. The disorder, as Joseph Needham puts it, is "potentially capable of consummation, perfection and order." JM: The *I Ching* does not conclude neatly with Completion (Hexagram LXIII, Complete). To do so would have been inconsistent with the very idea of Change. The *I Ching* proposes no perfect and abiding state; it offers no permanence other than Change itself. Just as the seasons of the year pursue their ever-recurring round, so it is with human affairs. Completion has come and gone. In this Hexagram, the quest for Self-Realization and the search for order amid signs of disorder begin all over again. The cycle recommences. The "little fox" suggests a lack of Caution on the part of those trying to remedy prevailing disorders. Their attempt is unsuccessful, and they get themselves into trouble. As so often, the Taoist classic *The Tao and the Power* offers counsel similar to that of the *I Ching*. Act in Accordance with the natural course of things. Maintain Caution and be attentive to the smallest detail, the slightest inkling of Change:

> *Chapter 64*
> Deal with things
> In their Non-Being;
> Order things
> Before they reach disorder. . . .
> The tree of great girth
> Began as a sapling.
> The nine-story tower
> Began as a pile of earth.
> The journey of ten thousand *li*
> Began as a single step. . . .
> Life's affairs
> Often fail
> Within close reach of Completion.
> Pay heed to the End
> No less than to the Beginning.
> You will not fail.

As Legge comments, this Hexagram offers advice for a "difficult time." In the poignant concluding lines of his short story "Post-Colonial Affairs of Food and the Heart," the Hong Kong writer Leung Ping-kwan evokes the "difficult time" of 1997, the "return" of Hong Kong to the totalitarian embrace of the Chinese "motherland" (a classically Incomplete moment of Change). Despite the darkness, there is still hope, still a possibility of kindness: "We have differing views on every subject under the sun. We argue endlessly. Sometimes we hurt each other a bit. But somehow we manage to stay together. Maybe in the end we learn to be kind to one another. The present situation is no good for any of us. It's late at night now. Outside the streets are empty and desolate. But we can still linger awhile amid the lights and voices, drunk on the illusion of this warm and joyous moment."

LINES

Yin in First Place

The tail is wet.

Distress,

Poenitebit.

On the Image

Extreme ignorance.

Yin Line in Yang Place. This Yielding Line is the first of the perilous Lower Trigram (*Kan*, Water, Abyss). The young fox runs rashly over ice, only to meet with Distress. The crossing fails. It is Incomplete. The Manager, writes Professor Mun, should assess carefully whether or not there are the resources needed to accomplish a business task. If not, he will surely fail. Do not rush forward in ignorance, writes Magister Liu. Develop Inner Strength gradually, and do not nurse overly ambitious spiritual goals.

Yang in Second Place

The wheels

Brake.

To be Steadfast

Is Auspicious,

Hoc bonum.

On the Image

The Center
Calls for
True Considered Action.

Yang Line in Yin Place. Centered. Hold back, writes Legge, following Zhu Xi. Check onward movement. Yang in a Yin Place, in the Center of the Abyss. Keep the cart from advancing. Apply firmness, writes Magister Liu, but in a yielding manner. Great wisdom may appear foolish; great skill may appear clumsy. Cultivate Self and wait for the timely moment.

Yin in Third Place

Incomplete.

A Calamitous Advance,

Si eat, hoc pessimum.

To cross a Great Stream

Profits,

Oportet transire

Magnum flumen.

On the Image

The Position is not Apt.

 Yin in a Yang Place. Seek out a teacher, writes Magister Liu, in order to achieve Completion. Do not rely on Self alone. Do not embark alone on a foolhardy and dangerous Advance. Seek out Others who possess the Tao. This will help to bring about true Self-Completion. Then even a dangerous crossing, undertaken at the right time, can be decisive and Profitable. It can be Auspicious. When an executive is in a weak and unfavorable position (Yin in Yang Place), writes Professor Mun, and has trouble handling a situation that is beyond his own strength, then he should seek help from a capable person, as represented by Yang in Top Place (with which this Line has Resonance).

Yang in Fourth Place

To be Steadfast

Is Auspicious.

Regret

Goes away,

Nullus poenitendi locus.

Demon Territory

Is shaken with an attack.

After three years

Comes the reward

Of a Great Realm.

On the Image

Aspirations are realized.

Yang Line in Yin Place. Shaking Demon Territory, striking the barbarians, is an example of firm correctness, writes Legge. Spiritually, writes Magister Liu, this Line represents determined and prolonged Self-Cultivation, a triumph over baser elements (the "barbarians within"), in order to achieve one's goal and eventually reach the Great Realm, Completion. A senior executive in Fourth Yang, writes Professor Mun, is close to the Leader in Fifth Yin. He should take advantage of this to undertake an ambitious project, with determination and courage.

Yin in Fifth Place

To be Steadfast

Is Auspicious.

Regret

Goes away.

The True Gentleman

Radiates

Good Faith,

Soliditas.

This is

Auspicious,

Hoc bonum.

On the Image

The Radiance of the True Gentleman
Is Auspicious.

Yin Line in Yang Place. Centered. The Light of the True Gentleman (Fire in the Upper Trigram) shines forth anew, writes Richard Wilhelm. The influence of his Good Faith, its radiance, is felt among men. Empty the Human Heart-and-Mind, writes Magister Liu, and seek the Heart-and-Mind of the Tao. Do not be deluded or led astray by false brilliance. This is the birth of the Light of the True Gentleman. It is quiet and still; it is responsive and connecting. It leads to Completion.

Yang in Top Place

Good Faith

In the drinking of wine,

In bibendo vino

Soliditas.

No Harm,

Nullum malum.

The head is wet.

Good Faith.

The Truth is lost.

On the Image

The head is wet
While drinking.
This shows
A lack of Moderation.

Yang Line in Yin Place. This Hexagram speaks of conviviality, and of the positive Energy that can be shared in the drinking of good wine. But drinking to the point where the "head" gets "wet" shows Excess, a lack of Caution, an unwillingness to moderate impulse with reason and prudence. Convivial gatherings cause no Harm in themselves, but a balance should be sought in them as in all things. "Place a man in peril to judge his integrity, ply him with wine to observe his behavior" (chapter 32 of the *Book of Master Zhuang*). "Contests of skill may start off lightly enough, but they often end darkly, in all sorts of underhand tricks. Drinking on ceremonious occasions may begin in an orderly enough fashion, but often degenerates into chaos. . . . Things may start simply, but they can end up losing all proportion. Words are wind and waves. Actions have consequences, they bring gain and loss. . . . To go beyond the limit, to go to Excess, is dangerous. . . . Completion takes time. A thing poorly Completed cannot be mended. Take constant care! Go along with things, follow the Flow, accept life as it is, and let your mind roam freely. Cultivate the Center, that which is within you" (chapter 4 of the *Book of Master Zhuang*). JM: Or does it simply mean that a fox gets his head wet crossing the ford—in essence a similarly rash situation? (The Chinese text has no fox in either First or Top Place.) Even when a Leader believes that success is in sight, writes Professor Mun, he must still be on his guard against unexpected events. He should not, out of sheer exuberance, place his achievement in peril. JM: The *I Ching* "closes" on this cautiously hopeful note. In truth, it does not close at all, defying all normal notions of Beginning and Ending, all normal expectations of a book. This is a wonderfully open Non-Ending to a wonderfully open Non-Book! It urges (to quote Angus Graham again) an "opening out and responding to stimulation in perfect tranquillity, lucidity and flexibility." It extends an invitation to the free intelligence of the Taoist. True Spiritual Completion, writes Magister Liu, True Realization, results from a natural and gradual process, not from artificial and strenuous effort. Self-Cultivation is the path leading to that goal. The seeker of the Tao Cultivates Self; he guards against Danger. He awaits the timely moment, harmonizing Yin and Yang, balancing Action and Receptivity. In this Tao, it is Yin and Yang that bring about Completion. They Complete each other.

CHANGE
Tiu Lek

PART II
Bronze Age Oracle

With Commentary

ABOUT PART II

Part II of this book presents the *I Ching* as it may possibly have been in the first half of the first millennium BC, during the early Zhou dynasty (the start of which is dated tentatively to 1045 BC) and during that dynasty's later Spring and Autumn and Warring States periods. In this guise, it is normally referred to as the *Zhouyi*, the *Change of Zhou*. This is the Oracle "as it has not existed for nearly 2,500 years."[1] It was then still close to its origins in the ancient practices of Divination by Turtle Shell, Ox Bone, and Yarrow Stalks, merging material from those earlier practices with a hotch-potch of folk rhymes, fragments of myth, proverbs, and other elements. A structure of Sixty-Four Hexagrams had already endowed this motley collection of mantic sayings with an elegant and thought-provoking mathematical order.

My version in this second Part reaches back to this earlier time, before the arrival of the Confucian, Taoist, Buddhist, neo-Confucian, and other more or less philosophical interpretations that are reflected in Part I. It strips that exegesis away from the core text, leaving nothing but the Oracular Judgments (*tuan*) and the Line Statements (*yaoci*). The modern reader can therefore approach the images and symbols directly, in their unadorned state. I have sought (so far as possible) to "respect the original enigma of the symbols," to be "taught by them."[2] This core text comes from a time when Divination, Sacrifice, and Shamanism were still living and direct means of interrogating the Universe. It therefore offers the modern reader-consultant the possibility of a potent encounter with an ancient way of seeing and experiencing the world. I can think of only a few other books that have the potential to do this. I have not attempted to fit this material into any system of ideas, since there was at the time no such system in existence. If Taoism makes an appearance, it is the very early Taoism of such texts as *The Tao and the Power*. When I have referred to other Chinese texts, I have tried to keep mainly to early sources, such as the *Book of Songs* or parts of *Songs of the South*, that pre-date the rationalization and canonization of the *I Ching* in the years before and during the Former Han dynasty.

For each Hexagram entry, my friend Liao Hsintien has written an ancient version of the graph for the Hexagram Name, based on an Oracle Bone Inscription or a Zhou-dynasty Bronze Inscription, or (when these are not available) an early seal-script form. This is followed by a *very* approximate and unscholarly reconstruction of the Early Chinese pronunciation of that character, for the most part based on the *Grammatica Serica Recensa* of the great Swedish scholar Bernhard Karlgren, with reference to Axel Schuessler's more recent *Minimal Old Chinese and Later Chinese*. My approximation should not be taken too seriously. I have not wished to burden readers with unfamiliar phonetic symbols. Early graphs for Turtle (龜) and Dragon (龍) serve again to separate sections of text, and to demarcate commentary.

Nothing I have done is in any way original. I have relied heavily on other scholars, both Chinese and Western, and on recent philological and archaeological discoveries and insights. As a result of these, we are now "in the enviable position of having more of the primary sources of pre-Imperial China at our disposal than any previous generation since at least the Warring States period itself."[3] The scholars include Gao Heng,[4] Li Jingchi,[5] Wen Yiduo,[6] Arthur Waley, and the contemporary American scholars David Keightley, Richard Kunst, and Edward Shaughnessy. Many of their findings were helpfully and intelligently digested by Richard Rutt in *The Book of Changes (Zhouyi): A Bronze Age Document*. Kunst's handwritten notes, available online, have been a huge help.[7] I am also greatly indebted to more general insights into early Chinese culture, society, and Divination found throughout the work of Sarah Allan, K. C. Chang, Stephen Field, Mark Edward Lewis, and Jessica Rawson.

Over the past few decades, the unearthing of an increasing number of early versions of the *I Ching* and associated texts, written on bamboo strips and on silk, has opened the door to ever more radical rereadings of the Oracle and of the society in which it evolved. The most famous of these was the silk manuscript copy unearthed in 1973 at Mawangdui, near Changsha in the southern province of Hunan. This manuscript was buried in the tomb of the Marquis of Dai, chancellor of Changsha, and can be dated to the early years of the second century BC. Discoveries such as this will undoubtedly continue to be made, and more such texts will be deciphered and better understood. In that sense, this version of mine is (as I have already written in my general Introduction) a work in progress, completed (or left incomplete) at a particular moment in time. The *I Ching* will undoubtedly continue to call forth new versions, incorporating new discoveries and insights.

Mine is not a scholarly translation for specialists. It is a plain version for the lay reader. In this second Part, I have used simple, unadorned language, partly out of a desire to capture something of the clipped and sometimes cryptic "Bronze Age" quality of the text, partly to distinguish the material in this Part from the later scriptural commentaries, with their more expansive and wordy style. The American scholar H. G. Creel, writing of the language of the earliest layer of the *I Ching*, wondered "if it was written at a time when the Zhou had not yet learned to write very clear Chinese." He then went on to wonder if there may have been other reasons for its obscurity. "Probably, being a book for wizards, it was intended to be cabalistic."[8]

For both parts I have, in the website created for this translation, johnmin ford.com, pointed to the sources for my own running commentary, not wishing to create yet another sinological maze, or Department of Utter Confusion.[9]

NOTES

1. Kidder Smith Jr., "*Zhouyi* Interpretation," p. 426.
2. "The symbol gives rise to thought," writes Paul Ricoeur in *The Symbolism of Evil*, p. 349; quoted in Franklin M. Doeringer, "The Gate in the Circle," p. 309.
3. Richard Kunst, "The Original *Yijing*," p. 200.
4. Gao Heng was from the Northeast. He studied at Tsinghua University under the great scholars Liang Qichao and Wang Guowei. Later he taught at several universities, specializing in textual studies of early classics, especially the *I Ching* and the *Book of Songs*. In the early 1960s, he enjoyed a brief celebrity as the result of an exchange of poems and letters with Chairman Mao.
5. Li was a Cantonese scholar whose family had emigrated to America. He studied in Beijing under the great "revisionist" historian Gu Jiegang, and later taught at Lingnan University in Canton. He was greatly impressed by Guo Moruo, and in his later work a strong Marxist influence is visible. He died of tuberculosis in 1975. His writings are always stimulating, although Richard Kunst calls him "an interpretation mill, often glossing the same word or phrase in several different ways in different studies published within a short time of each other, while justifying his plurality of views by the indeterminacy in the *Yijing* itself" (p. 403). Li's last work, the little booklet entitled *Zhouyi tongyi*, edited and published posthumously by Cao Chuji in 1981, reflects his final (if not always most level-headed) thoughts.
6. The great poet Wen Yiduo, tragically assassinated in 1946, was one of the most creative of his generation of Chinese men of letters, developing highly original interpretations of several early Chinese texts. As Edward Shaughnessy comments, Wen Yiduo's "level of philological sophistication is matched only by his awe-inspiring imagination" (p. 114). Li Jingchi and Arthur Waley were both heavily influenced by Wen's ideas.
7. At www.humancomp.org/ftp/yijing/yi_hex. I thank my friend Steve Balogh for drawing my attention to this many years ago.
8. Creel, *Birth of China*, p. 268; quoted in S. J. Marshall, *The Mandate of Heaven* (2001), p. 40.
9. This is how the great historian of Chinese scientific thought Joseph Needham characterized Richard Wilhelm's edition, complaining that Wilhelm had "presented the late commentary material as an amorphous mass with no indication of the various authorships and their dates." See *Science and Civilisation in China*, vol. 2 (Cambridge, 1956), p. 308, n.a.

HEXAGRAM 1

Kân

$$\equiv\equiv\equiv$$

Sun Rising

JUDGMENT

Supreme Fortune.

Sacrifice Received.

Profitable Augury.

 Kân is the Name of this first Hexagram. *Kân* has been endlessly discussed over the years. At the very outset it may well have had an astronomical meaning. For the modern scholar-poet Wen Yiduo, it is the Pole Star. Early forms of the graph suggest the grouping of a constellation. For some it is the Sun itself, purest concentration of light and warmth, rising through the morning mist. It may have had these and other meanings. This and the second Hexagram, *K'wen,* are by far the most extensively discussed of the Sixty-Four Hexagrams in the *I Ching,* in both the traditional and modern schools. They are the two Hexagrams made up entirely of Undivided and Divided lines respectively. They are the poles of the entire work, "a microcosm of the entire text, indeed of the entire world."

The four Chinese characters *yuan-heng-li-zhen* used in this first Oracular Judgment recur many times throughout the book, constituting, with a number of other words, a repertoire of formulaic expressions derived from the language of the earlier Oracle Bone Inscriptions. Exactly what they originally meant is obscure. Over the ages they have been extensively philosophized, "invested with a patina of mystic significance."

The first of the four, *yuan,* was a simple early graph depicting a man with a head, hence "great," or Supreme. (Legge: Great and Originating.) Especially controversial is the second, *heng*, which many now believe to have been essentially the same as, or closely linked to, another word, *xiang*, "Sacrificial Offering." (I have already explored some of these terms in the Introduction.) They were graphically the same, apart from the addition of one horizontal stroke. Karlgren believed the two to have been identical, and he speculated that the early graph depicted a Temple (site of both Sacrifice and Divination). The importance of Ritual and Sacrifice in both Shang and Zhou China cannot be overemphasized. Sacrifice, of animals (cattle, sheep, dogs, pigs), of birds of all kinds, and of humans (prisoners of war and slaves), permeated early Chinese society and religion. Sacrificial Ritual and Warfare were the two Great Affairs of the nation. This can be seen throughout the *Book of Songs*:

> *Song 209*
> Stately gestures,
> Purest oxen and sheep,
> For Sacrifice.
> Flayed meat, boiled meat,
> Set out,
> Presented.
> Priestly Offerings
> At Temple Gate,
> Splendid ceremonies.
> August Ancestors,
> Spirits enjoy
> Sacrificial meats. . . .

David Hawkes has drawn attention to "the scale and importance of Animal Sacrifice in Shang Ritual and the use of the symbol for 'sheep' in the characters for 'good,' 'beautiful,' etc., in the Chinese script, which the Shang, presumably, invented." The word *heng/xiang* was later (see Part I) glossed by philosophical commentators (culminating in the Song-dynasty neo-Confucians Cheng Yi and Zhu Xi) as *tong*, "connecting," "getting through," "penetrating," "accomplishing to completion," hence "success," or Fortune. The dimension of Sacrifice and Ritual had faded away. The eighteenth-century Jesuits followed this closely, and they used the Latin *penetrans* as their equivalent of *heng*. From this the nineteenth-century missionary-translator James Legge derived his (otherwise bizarre-seeming) "penetrating." For the whole four-word Judgment, the Lutheran pastor Richard Wilhelm gave "*Wirkt erhabenes Gelingen / Fördernd durch Beharrlichkeit*," which his Jungian English and French translators (Baynes and Perrot) turned respectively into "Works sublime success / Furthering through perseverance" and "*Opère une sublime réussite / Favorisant par la persévérance*." Less and less survived of the text's roots in Sacrifice. I have tried, here in Part II, to suggest something of that earlier level of meaning, to give these terms a more primitive, mantic sense free of the values read into them by later Confucians and neo-Confucians. I have translated *heng/xiang* as Fortune, Sacrifice Received, with certain minor variations. The successful offering of a Sacrifice and its Auspicious reception by the Spirits or Ancestors, its "acceptability in their sight," were closely linked to the benefits, the Fortune, obtained as a result.

The third term, *li*, occurs 119 times in the *I Ching* core text, and it covers a range of related meanings: "profitable," "lucky," "beneficial," "advantageous." In its origins the graph was made up of a knife with grain-in-ear, thus "to reap" or "harvest," the original seed-grain having multiplied many times, hence Profit. (Legge: advantageous.) It comes in expressions such as "Profits" for (1) to see a big man, (2) to cross a big stream, (3) to have a Destination. It also functions in phrases such as "Profitable" for (1) a mare, (2) a woman, (3) a warrior. In other words, it indicates a favorable or positive prognosis.

The fourth term, *zhen*, occurs 111 times in the core text. To quote Richard Kunst: "Its interpretation, which is subject to radical divergence of opinion, is probably the single greatest factor in grasping the meaning of the *I Ching* text overall." *Zhen* was glossed moralistically with the two words *zheng* and *gu*, "upright" and "solid," hence the Jesuit "*solidum*," Legge's "correct and firm," and the Wilhelm/Baynes "Perseverance." The pedigree of interpretation and translation is clear. This "solid" moral virtue was a central theme in the old Confucian reading of the text. In Part I, where I more or less adhere to the traditional way of reading the book, I have translated *zhen* as Steadfast. Modern scholars, however, have traced the word *zhen* back to a graph commonly used in the Oracle Bone Inscriptions, where it seems to mean quite simply "the act of Divination." The resolution of doubt through the practice of Divination thus evolved over the centuries into moral certitude, or Steadfastness. In Part II I have translated *zhen* as Augury or Divination, the process at the heart of the core *I Ching* text, present throughout its entire evolution from ancient times (when it was accompanied by Ritual and Sacrifice) to the present day (with the simple tossing of coins). In Judgments, it often occurs with *li*, "profitable" or "favorable." Thus: "the Divination/Augury is Profitable; it Augurs well."

LINES

Nine in First Place

Sunken Dragon.

Do not act.

Shaughnessy sees the Dragon star-cluster "sinking" into the watery depths beneath the horizon at midwinter. S. J. Marshall, among others, sees the entire Hexagram as a piece of Rain Magic, a relic of ancient practices designed to arouse the Dragon and provide rain. In this first Line, the Dragon is still hibernating at the bottom of a pool, from which it will rise into the Heavens when the time is ripe. The Omen of a Sunken Dragon occurred very early on in a children's song, as recorded in the early historical text the *Zuo Commentary*, Duke Xi, Year 5 (654 BC): "In the eighth month, on the day *jiawu*, the Marquis of Jin laid siege to Shangyang, chief city of [the much smaller state of] Guo. He asked Diviner Yan whether he would prevail. Yan replied in the affirmative. The Marquis then asked when this would happen, to which Yan replied: 'The children have a song:

> At daybreak of day *bing*,
> Tail of Dragon
> Sinks in *chen*.
> They surrender.
> You will capture
> Flags of Guo!

You will prevail at the juncture of the ninth and tenth months.' . . . As it turned out, on the day *bingzi* of the twelfth month, on the first day of the new moon, Jin did indeed destroy Guo, and Duke Chou of Guo had to flee." This is an interesting example of the early popular (and oral) material that may have been incorporated into the Oracle *I Ching*. Some recent commentators see in several of the Line Statements of this Hexagram and the next, with their recurring mention of the Dragon, traces of early astronomy, but vary in their interpretation of details. As early as 1911, the Swiss astronomer Leopold de Saussure (younger brother of the famous linguist Ferdinand) wrote of "the Dragon's spring appearance . . . manifest in the first pages of the *Book of Change*, a book in which the developments of the ethical order always repose *on an astronomical canvas*." [My italics.] The Line Statements of the first Hexagram may represent stages in the yearly passage across the night sky of a star cluster known as the Dragon, echoing or shadowing the daily path of the Sun. Shaughnessy develops this in impressive detail, drawing elaborate astronomical charts, showing the Tail, Heart, Neck, and Horn of the Dragon. "The Chinese have long seen the form of a Dragon in a constellation of stars which becomes visible in the eastern quadrant of the sky in Spring and finally passes out of sight beneath the western horizon in autumn." For Shaughnessy, the Lines of *Kân* use "the image of the Celestial Dragon to characterize the various periods in the growing season of the agricultural year, the time when the crops germinate and grow to maturity." Recent excavations (in Henan Province, 1987) have uncovered what may well be the earliest representation of a Dragon in Chinese history. It is composed of clamshells, and it comes from a neolithic tomb dating to the middle of the fifth millennium BC. This figure too has been tentatively identified with the "macro-constellation" of the Celestial Dragon, symbolizing the East. Kunst goes along with the astro-calendrical reading of this Hexagram, but points also to the more general cultural significance in early China of the actual creature itself, the Dragon: "The sighting of Dragons, as referred to in this Hexagram, made excellent Omens, which needed interpretation. It is natural that when someone spotted a Dragon, he would consult the Oracle to fathom its significance." The *Zuo Commentary*, under the entry for Duke Zhao, Year 29 (513 BC), contains a long digression on the subject of Dragons, their rearing and feeding. One had been sighted near the town of Jiang. The *Commentary* quotes several Line Statements from the first two Hexagrams of the *I Ching*. The Dragon Omens in the Lines of the first Hexagram, with their various prognostications, may represent the distillation of centuries of Divination experience with such phenomena (both celestial and terrestrial) and their aftermath (Fortune or Misfortune). In the earliest *I Ching* commentaries (see Part I), this Hexagram begins to be interpreted more generally as Heaven and Yang, the second Hexagram as Earth and Yin. Chinese Celestial Dragons, unlike their Western counterparts, were "powerful sky and water Spirits, emblematic of Yang power, fertilizing the Earth with rain." They evoke the interplay of sun and cloud in the heavens, the constantly shifting texture and light.

When translating the Hexagram Names, and indeed when translating the entire text, one is brought face to face with the elusive quality inherent in the classical Chinese language itself. The graph for this Name admits of many possibilities. It can point to a number of things: to Asterism, Heaven, Sun. In the Mawangdui silk manuscript, the Name is written quite differently, with a graph pronounced approximately *G'ian*, normally meaning Bolt or Linchpin. Perhaps we are dealing in this Hexagram with the Dragon as Cosmic Linchpin, as the Bolt of Heaven? Who knows? We never even know if the recurring Dragon is singular or plural. This chameleon quality of the *I Ching*, the way it can mean so many different things at one and the same time (a quality surely ideal for an Oracle of Change), is an early manifestation of the powerful ambivalence of the classical Chinese language, which over many centuries informed both the evolution of Chinese philosophy and the Chinese poetic tradition. The Bronze Age *I Ching* captures a moment in Chinese history when language (*wen*), the repertoire of early graphs, first began to evolve from the fragmentary records on Oracle Bones to a more self-conscious vehicle for sustained "writing," whether on bronze, bamboo, or silk. It is language newly minted. It taps into a primitive magico-musical power. It communicates the sheer excitement of the early Chinese written word.

Nine in Second Place

Sighted:

Dragon in a field.

Profits

To see a big man.

The Horn Stars (in the Dragon cluster) became visible above the horizon in early March. "From the perspective of one looking toward the horizon, it would indeed appear as if the Dragon were lurking in the distant fields." Or, according to Marshall's reading, Dragon-like storm clouds are seen to gather over the fields at the time of the Rituals for Spring Rain. "Big man," *daren*, and "little man," *xiaoren*, occur throughout the *I Ching*. "Profits to see a big man" is a recurring formula, like "Profits to cross a big stream." As with the Dragon, we have no way of telling if the "big man" is singular or plural. In Classical Chinese no such distinction was made. Throughout this Hexagram, and throughout the entire *I Ching*, we cannot tell whether we are talking of one Dragon, one field, one man, or several of each. It could just as easily be several Dragons sighted in several fields. The "big man" may have started off as a Soothsayer or Shaman, and later evolved more generally into a person of influence in the community. Kunst compares him with the "influential man" found "in the communities of the Pacific Basin, notably in the South Pacific, but sometimes also in Mesoamerica or the Pacific Northwest." In subsequent tradition, and thus in Part I of this version, the "big man" becomes the Great Man, the Sage, the one endowed with philosophical wisdom, the True Gentleman or Superior Man of Confucianism, the Adept of Taoism.

Nine in Third Place

The noble man is

Busy all day long,

Wary at dusk.

Danger,

No Harm.

 In the *Book of Songs*, some of which dates roughly from the same early Zhou period as the *I Ching* and shares some of the language of the core Oracle, the noble man, the *junzi*, is exactly that, a noble, a member of the ruling class, "my lord" (and hence often "my lover"), or a noble participant in ritual fun and games:

> *Song 67*
> The noble man
> Rejoices,
> Reed-organ
> In left hand. . . .
> The noble man
> Is merry,
> Dance plumes
> In left hand. . . .

Nine in Fourth Place

Leaps

In the deep.

No Harm.

 The Dragon cluster continues its progress across the night sky, its entire torso suddenly "leaping" into view. Kunst draws attention to the repetitive, formulaic nature of Lines such as these, made more visible here by the rhymes (the words for "field," "deep," and "sky" all rhyme in ancient Chinese). There are striking parallels with verses from the *Book of Songs*:

Song 239
Falcons fly
In the sky;
Fish leap
In the deep.

Song 184
Fish sink
In the deep;
They lie
On the shoals.

Song 204
No eagle I,
No hawk,
To soar
In the sky.
No sturgeon,
No snout-fish,
To sink
In the deep.

The poetic aspect of the Oracle has been neglected. The *I Ching* is very much a work of literature, one of the earliest and deepest sources of the Chinese literary tradition, constantly quoted and referred to. As with the *Book of Songs*, its earliest layer contains oral and formulaic material from a time when words, word-magic, and word-music were closely linked.

Nine in Fifth Place

Dragons fly

In the sky.

Profits

To see a big man.

At the midsummer solstice the entire Dragon asterism soars across the sky. Alternatively, the flying, or "moving," Dragon betokens the coming of rain.

Nine in Top Place

Dragon

Gully.

Trouble.

 With the coming of autumn, the star-cluster *Gang*, Gully of the Dragon, sits on the western horizon, poised to sink once again into the depths. The modern scholar Gao Heng takes it more literally as referring to the creature itself: "The Dragon is stuck in a gully or ditch, where the water is shallow and movement cramped, where weeds are many and the mud deep. An image of hardship." Or perhaps the Dragon is simply returning to its pool to hibernate for the winter again, now that the crops have been harvested and rain is no longer needed. Or all of the above.

Nine in Final Place

Sighted:

Headless Dragons,

A host.

Auspicious.

 This Final Place is an extra Seventh Place occurring exclusively in the First and Second Hexagrams. It refers to the unusual case where all six Lines are Changing Lines. The whole Hexagram then evolves into its "opposite." In this case, Hexagram 1 becomes Hexagram 2. The "host" of Dragons may possibly be the Ten Suns and Twelve Moons of early Chinese astro-mythology. Or are the Dragon's "headless" body and tail the only parts visible in the dusk sky, now that its horns and head have sunk below the horizon?

HEXAGRAM 2

K'wen

Earth Flow

JUDGMENT

Supreme Fortune.

Sacrifice Received.

Profitable Augury

For mare.

Destination

For noble man.

Straying at first,

Finding the way.

Profit.

Strings of cowries

Found

West and South,

Strings of cowries

Lost

East and North.

Augury of peace.

Auspicious.

In the Mawangdui silk manuscript, the Name of this Hexagram (there placed not second but thirty-second in the sequence) is written with a different graph, *T'iwen*, "stream," "river," "water" (as in the recurring phrase "Profits to cross big stream"). An early variant form of this graph was used for the word *shun*, "to flow," "to accord with the natural course of things." In *Kân*, the Sun (as Dragon) "rises" up through the mists and into Heaven; here water "flows" down, along the riverbeds and into Earth. The "rising" of the Sun is majestic, an energetic and active process; Earth Flow is quiet and persistent, soft and effortless, but no less powerful. From its earliest origins, long before it was philosophized, the *I Ching* celebrated and promoted "going with the flow," encouraging those who consulted its Hexagrams to yield to the rhythm of the Cosmos, to harness the moment, not to stand against it. How far removed this is from the famous nineteenth-century Darwinian T. H. Huxley's definition of social progress as "a checking of the cosmic process at every step." The yielding (but powerful) softness of Water, of the Feminine, is also celebrated throughout the early Taoist classic *The Tao and the Power*:

> *Chapter 43*
> That which is most yielding
> In the Universe
> Can overwhelm
> That which is most hard. . . .

> *Chapter 6*
> The Valley Spirit
> Never dies.
> It is called
> The Mysterious Feminine [*pin*].

The Mare, the "feminine [*pin*] horse [*ma*]," is the key Image in this Hexagram Judgment, as is the Dragon in the preceding Hexagram. Mares may have been sacrificed (possibly to the Earth), or auspices may have been taken from their behavior. The word *pin* occurs often in the Oracle Bones as a feminine denominator, alongside the graph for "cattle," "sheep," "pig," "horse," or "rhinoceros." In more general terms, the Mare, or Mother Horse, while feminine and docile, is also a powerful and enabling creature. Taoist overtones are strong: the feminine ability to follow and nurture is more highly valued by Taoists than the male ability to lead and act. Another, simpler reading of this entire Hexagram sees it as a Divination by a merchant or prince, as to whether he should use a male or a female horse on a journey. The astro-calendrical reading focuses on the period of the harvest: "*K'wen* marks the culmination of the agricultural and calendrical process (already begun in *Kân*) and the passage into the 'dead' season of winter. . . .

These two months possess an importance . . . for they represent the time of the harvest, certainly the most significant time in the agricultural calendar. . . .Important though *Kân* is, without *K'wen* its promise remains unfulfilled." As in many early societies across the world, in ancient China cowrie shells (*bei*) were treasured, and were used as currency, strung together like beads. Many of them have been found buried in graves (one Shang-dynasty grave contained 3,790 cowries). The mysterious appeal of the cowrie has been attributed to its resemblance to the vulva. It was a symbol of fertility, of life itself. But the word for a string of cowries, *peng*, also meant "friend," in which case the Judgment is about gaining and losing friends, rather than (or as well as) wealth.

LINES

Six in First Place

Frost underfoot.

Hard ice

On its way.

 Perhaps this is an evocation of "the period shortly after the autumnal equinox, when the first frosts of autumn bring a reminder that winter is soon to arrive." In *Song 107*, a man wears "rough shoes" to tread on the "hoarfrost underfoot." Other Songs (lines combined from *Songs 195* and *196*) compare impending danger with treading on ice:

> Tremble,
> Take care;
> As near a deep abyss,
> As near a valley,
> As treading thin ice.

In the *Book of History*, book 25 (a contested, but still interesting, section of that classic), King Mu (fourth King of the Zhou dynasty) describes his sense of anxiety and inadequacy (his inability to live up to the virtue of his Ancestors) as being like "treading on a Tiger's Tail" (compare the Judgment, Hexagram 10) or "treading spring ice."

Six in Second Place

Straight, square, large.

Without practice.

Profit.

㸐 The three adjectives "straight, square, large" may refer to the inspection and sur-veying of the borderlands. "Before winter arrives, there is still much to be done in an agricultural society. The overseers (surveyors) of the land must go out and inspect the harvest." Or perhaps the quality of the Earth itself is so described. In ancient China the sky was thought of as round, the Earth as square. There is a Taoist overtone in the last phrase, "without practice." *Xi* means, literally "the application or practice of knowledge," "repetition," as in the opening sentence of the *Analects of Confucius*: "To learn and to put into practice at the right moment what one has learned—is this not Joy?" (Compare the Commentary to Hexagram XXIX, in Part I.) As Joseph Needham observes, Confucian knowledge, product of a great deal of repetition and application, was "masculine and managing," whereas Taoists sought a "feminine and receptive knowledge, which could arise only as the fruit of a passive and yielding attitude in the observation of Nature." In short, the Taoists did not value knowledge or learning.

> *The Tao and the Power*
> Chapter 19
> Abolish Wisdom,
> Jettison Knowledge.
> The Folk
> Will Profit
> A hundredfold.

Instead of acquiring knowledge, go with the flow. That will Profit. Luck will come. In that sense, luck is a knack; it comes to those who are in tune, not necessarily to those who know and "practice" a great deal.

Six in Third Place

Jade talisman

Contained

Augurs well.

King's service.

No success.

Conclusion.

㸐 The King's service (often in the form of painful and tiresome duties, including military service) is never done, never "successfully concluded," as the *Book of Songs* testifies:

Song 162
King's service
Is never done;
My heart aches.

Song 169
King's service
Is never done;
Day in, day out,
It claims us.

The service is frequently referred to in the Oracle Bone Inscriptions: "Zheng Divined on the *renyin* day: Will he be able to do the King's service?" "Should we call on the army and the chieftain of the Quanfang to attack Zhou and do service to His Majesty?"

Six in Fourth Place

Sack tied.

Neither blame

Nor praise.

 The tied sack may refer to the storing of the harvest.

Six in Fifth Place

Yellow robe.

Supremely Auspicious.

"This may refer to a ritual celebration of the harvest's completion and the continuing preparation for winter." This Line occurs in a Yarrow Stalk *I Ching* Divination recorded in the *Zuo Commentary*, Duke Zhao, Year 12 (530 BC). The whole episode is worth quoting, as an example of the critical early use of the Oracle, showing how already in 530 BC the inherent "goodness" of an intended course of action outweighs the literal, mantic reading of a Line from the *I Ching*. Without goodness, the Hexagram simply "does not apply." The *I Ching* is already beginning the process of transformation from Oracle to Book of Wisdom.

Nankuai, minister of the state of Lu, was plotting rebellion. A man of his village learned of his purpose and sighed as he passed him by. "Alas! Alas!" he said to himself. "What a difficult and hazardous enterprise is this man embarking upon! His thoughts are deep, but his plans shallow. His position is circumscribed, but his aims are ambitious. He is the servant of a family, and yet his schemes affect the Ruler. What kind of a man is this!" Nankuai Divined with the Yarrow Stalks, and received the Changing Line "Yellow robe. Supremely Auspicious." [With this single Line-change, from Divided to Undivided in Fifth Place, Hexagram 2, *K'wen*, becomes Hexagram 8, *Bier*, Side by Side.] He took this reading to be most Auspicious, and he showed it to Zifu Huibo, saying: "If I am contemplating some course of action, what sort of result does this indicate?" To which Huibo replied: "This I have learned—if a project is undertaken in Loyalty and Good Faith, it will prosper. If not, it will fail. The outer part of this Hexagram is strength, the inner part mildness. This is Loyalty. Harmony brings forth purity. This is Fidelity. Hence the words 'Yellow robe. Supremely Auspicious.' Yellow is the color of Center; the robe is the ornament of that which lies beneath. This is Auspicious; it is the height of goodness. But if the Center (heart) has no Loyalty, then there is no color; and if beneath (the robe) there is no Respect, then there can be no ornament. If the enterprise is not a worthy one, there can be no height (of goodness). When outer and inner are in Harmony, then there is Loyalty; when affairs are conducted in Fidelity, then there is Respect; a sincere nourishing of the three virtues makes for goodness. Without these three qualities, this Hexagram *simply does not apply*. This reading from the *I Ching* cannot be taken as a guide for some hazardous enterprise. What are you contemplating that requires ornament? With beauty in the center, *then* you will have the yellow; with beauty above, *then* things will be Auspicious." (My italics.)

As it turned out, Nankuai disregarded this sensible advice and proceeded with his revolt. Within a year he was dead. In the following year, this same chronicle (Duke Zhao, Year 13, 529 BC) records a similar attitude:

At an earlier time, King Ling Divined, saying, "I wish to gain All-under-Heaven." The response was not Auspicious. He threw down the Turtle Shell and cursed Heaven, crying, "Since you will not give me even this little thing, I must needs take it for myself."

Six in Top Place

Dragons fight

In the wilds.

Dark blood,

Yellow blood.

This may be a meteorological Omen. When storm clouds gather against a yellow-tinged sky, accompanied by violent thunder and lightning, the ancient Chinese would sometimes say: "Dragons are fighting; look at their blood spreading over the sky." Some see the struggle among Dragons as a sexual coupling or combat, leading to fertilizing rain. Some see a historical reference to the decisive battle in the Wilds of Mu, when King Wu of Zhou defeated the Shang King, and the Shang people showed their gratitude by offering him baskets full of black and yellow earth.

Six in Final Place

Profitable Divination

In perpetuity.

Final Place is an extra Seventh Place occurring exclusively in the first two Hexagrams. It refers to the unusual case where all six Lines are changing. The Hexagram then evolves into its "opposite." In this case, Hexagram 2 becomes Hexagram 1.

HEXAGRAM 3

D'wen

Sprout

JUDGMENT

Supreme Fortune.

Sacrifice Received.

Profitable Augury.

Destination

Serves no purpose.

Profits

To licence lords.

This Hexagram Name has been understood as Sprout or Sprouting (also Gathering, Storing), whence the extended notion of Growth, and Difficulty in First Growth (see Part I). The earliest Oracle Bone form of the graph does indeed resemble a Sprout pushing its way up through the soil. To "licence lords" (a recurring formula) is to reward loyal ministers with rank and grants of land, thereby strengthening their sense of loyalty—an important consideration in the chaotic times and shifting alliances of the Spring and Autumn and Warring States periods, and during the uncertain postconquest years of the Zhou dynasty, when the *I Ching* became a book. The Lines of this entire Hexagram revolve around two important and connected themes: Marriage and Hunt.

LINES

Nine in First Place

Wheeling.

Augurs well

For a Dwelling.

Profits

To licence lords.

 The *Zuo Commentary*, Duke Zhao, Year 7 (535 BC), records an interesting (and rather complicated) *I Ching* Divination. Zhi, older son of Duke Xiang of Wei, born of a secondary consort, was about to be passed over because of a physical infirmity, in favor of the second son, Yuan. Two of the Duke's ministers were involved in the Divination and the subsequent decision concerning the succession. The *I Ching* first replied with this third Hexagram, appearing to affirm the name of the second son (*yuan*, Supreme, was the first word of the Judgment). On a second consultation, the Oracle replied with the same Hexagram, but this time added "changing to *Bier*, Hexagram 8, Side by Side," i.e., with a Nine in First Place. Attention was thereby focused on this particular Changing Line, which repeats the Judgment's last words, "Profits to licence lords." Minister Kong, Soothsayer, read into this phrase the need to "formally establish" the *second* son (Yuan) as heir, arguing that if the *older* son were destined to succeed, there would be no need to go to all the trouble of "licencing a lord." This reading of the Oracle had, interestingly, already been anticipated in a dream, in which the very first Marquis of Wei, Prince Kang, had appeared to the same Soothsayer-Minister Kong, pointing to Yuan as the new heir designate. Both of the Duke's ministers had a lot to gain from the decision, since in the dream the marquis had also promised promotion to their sons.

Six in Second Place

Sprouting,

Turning.

Riding

A brindled horse.

No bandit.

Marriage.

For woman,

Augurs no conception.

After ten years,

Conception.

 Note the identical wording (about bandit raid and marriage) at Hexagrams 22/4 and 38/6. Chen Guying sums up the current understanding of these "marriage parties": "Marriage was forbidden within the clan, and so men would go out in search of a bride, in mock raids or abductions." The sociologist Wolfram Eberhard describes this "ancient Chinese marital custom," according to which a groom from a poor family disguises himself and a group of his friends as bandits and stages a mock abduction of the bride, to save the bride's family the ignominy of "willingly" giving their daughter to a poor man. Li Jingchi points to similar marriage "abductions" in recent times within the small Ewenke minority in the Chinese Northeast.

Six in Third Place

No guide.

Deer hunter

Enters forest.

Wisely,

Noble man

Abandons chase.

Trouble ahead.

 Any such excursion (into a forest or other untamed space) was fraught with danger, involving exposure to the unknown. Such concerns were frequently recorded in the Oracle Bone Inscriptions.

Six in Fourth Place

Riding

A brindled horse.

Marriage sought.

Auspicious journey.

Profit in all things.

Nine in Fifth Place

Fat meat stored.

Auspicious Augury

In small things.

In great things,

Calamity.

 The "fat meat" (of the pheasant) occurs also in Hexagram 50/3. It may refer to the "choice cuts" presented on festive occasions such as marriage. Or, more prosaically, it may reflect "a concern with having a steady food supply in a hunting-and-fishing-based economy."

Six in Top Place

Riding horse,

A brindled horse.

Streams of tears,

Blood.

 For Li Jingchi, the tears and blood are those of the unfortunate woman who has endured a "marriage raid," during which she may have been subjected to a form of gang rape by the "raiding" party. Arthur Waley follows a completely different line of thinking: "Perhaps the most widespread type of Omen is that which concerns the movements of animals, insects, birds and even plants (apparently uncaused movements of tendrils, twigs and the like). If an animal is of an unusual kind, merely to meet with it is an Omen. To meet a piebald horse is lucky in England." He treats the Fourth Line as an omen taken from the sort of horse on which the new bride arrives on at her husband's house, adding: "The fact that this section refers to primitive marriage institutions has already been recognised." Another view is that the blood is dripping (like tears) from the carcass of the sacrificed (or hunted) deer. The ancient graph for blood is made up of a bowl with blood dripping into it: the blood of a sacrificial beast.

HEXAGRAM 4

Mung

Dodder

JUDGMENT

I seek not

Stripling dodder.

Dodder seeks me.

First Yarrow Divination

Receives response;

Second and third

Are insult.

Insult,

And no response.

Augurs well.

Karlgren points to the range of meanings of the Hexagram Name *Mung*, which include "covered," "ignorant," "to go against with covered eyes," "to brave," and "to deceive." It is a good example of a Chinese word with a "family" of multiple meanings. The two-syllable derivative *tangmeng*, according to Legge, refers to the dodder plant, a "parasite growing on plants and trees, and yielding a seed, like the grub of the silk worm, which is used in medicine." In his ingenious commentary on this Hexagram, which I have largely adopted, Arthur Waley follows the "dodder trail," giving a taste of what our understanding of the *I Ching* might have been if he had ever completed his version. Waley used his imagination, but he also followed closely the writings of the younger "revisionist" generation of Chinese *I Ching* scholars such as Li Jingchi. I give Waley's words at length here, because they demonstrate his extraordinarily wide reading and far-ranging curiosity:

> The *meng* is the dodder (*cuscuta*), an epiphyte which grows on bushes. Now parasitic and epiphyte plants play a very important role in primitive thought, owing to the fact that they seem to be "spontaneously engendered by Nature's breath" (from the *Tushu jicheng* section on the mistletoe). "All parasitic plants are esteemed in a certain sense holy," says a writer on Swiss folklore, quoted by Sir James Frazer. The dodder figures largely in the beliefs of the Thongas. Junod mentions the use of the dodder for augury, and a riddle: "The thing of which the stem is invisible, what is it?" Answer: "The dodder." . . . Twice in this Hexagram the *meng* is called *tongmeng*. *Tong* means "a boy before puberty," "a bull that has not yet grown its horns." As applied to *meng* the term refers to the "incompleteness" of the epiphyte. It is found again in the name which the [ancient dictionary] *Erya* (section on trees) gives to the mistletoe: "twisty boy." . . . The epiphyte, then, which has no roots of its own, is mysteriously nurtured by Heaven, and is therefore in touch with the secrets of Heaven. Hence its importance in rites of Divination. . . . For the connection between dodder and mistletoe, cf. Turner's *Herbal*. Hence the phrase (near the end of the Hexagram) "knocking [beating] the dodder"; whereas *fameng* perhaps refers to the alternative method (Grimm, *radicitus*) of pulling the parasite entirely clear of the tree which harbours it. The opening formula ["I seek not . . ."] is clearly a spell for averting the evil consequences of tampering with the holy plant. Ritual and Divination are closely bound up together. An Omen generally points to the necessity for a Rite. A Rite cannot be performed unless the Omens are favourable.

Kunst also follows Waley, calling this Hexagram "a spell to avert misfortune after accidentally harming dodder." *Song 48* talks of gathering dodder, in a love song of three stanzas, each of which sets out with the gathering of a different plant—dodder, goosefoot, or charlock. It goes on to talk of meeting three young women "in the mulberry grove" (a site for lovers' assignations—see Hexagram 12/5). Another, and rather intriguing, approach to the meaning of this Hexagram could begin with the Shanghai Museum bamboo-strip text, in which the name is written with a different character, *mang*, "shaggy dog," hence perhaps "bad, wild boy." Possibly this was a reference to the last ruler of the Shang dynasty, that notorious "bad boy" Zhou Xin, who in the last years of his fateful rule is supposed to have led a debauched existence. According to legend, "his career was one course of extravagance, lust, and cruelty. To please his infamous concubine he constructed a vast pleasaunce, known as the Deer Terrace, in which there was a lake of wine and a garden with meat hanging on the trees. There all kinds of the wildest orgies were carried on." Zhou Xin may conceivably have insulted the Oracle (by consulting it when drunk, or simply too often?) and therefore received no response. Compare the unsuccessful Divination referred to in the *Book of Songs*, in a song lamenting the times:

Song 195
Turtle tired of me,
Gave me no response.

LINES

Six in First Place

Dodder

Lifted.

Slaves Profit.

Profits

To loosen shackles and fetters.

Journey brings trouble.

Of the pottery figurines excavated in a pit at Xiaotun, the ceremonial precinct at Anyang, the ancient Shang capital, some were shackled and fettered. The men had their hands manacled in front of their bodies, the women behind. Perhaps these shackled slaves were destined for Sacrifice.

Nine in Second Place

Dodder

Bundled.

Auspicious.

Auspicious

To take a wife.

Son

Establishes a family.

Six in Third Place

Do not take a wife.

At sight of bronze man

She loses herself.

No Profit.

 This seems to be a warning against marriage to an untrustworthy woman, who will fall for another man ("lose herself") at the first sight of a muscular competitor. Or it could mean: "Do not take a wife. A bronze *arrow* is sighted, but no bow. No luck." Waley continues his dodder reading, understanding this as a reference to the invisible or absent "stem" or "root" of the golden (or bronze) parasite: "I saw the golden husband; but he had no body."

Six in Fourth Place

Dodder

Bound.

Trouble.

Six in Fifth Place

Stripling

Dodder.

Auspicious.

Nine in Top Place

Dodder

Beaten.

No Profit for marauders.

Profits to quell marauders.

 The dodder has no roots of its own and must be approached with caution. If it is to retain its power, "it must be beaten off the tree," not cut with a knife.

HEXAGRAM 5

Sniu

Cloudburst

JUDGMENT

Captives.

Glory.

Fortune.

Sacrifice Received.

Auspicious Augury.

Profits

To cross a big stream.

The Hexagram Name itself is understood in several ways, including (1) "moist, drenched"; (2) Waley's "some sort of insect or worm"—and its observed behavior; and (3) "stopped by rain," therefore "obliged to delay." The original graph has rain above a large man, perhaps above Heaven. Liu Dajun sees a Ritual Prayer for rain.

LINES

Nine in First Place

Cloudburst

In the meadows.

Profits

To perform *heng* Ritual,

Fixing.

No Harm.

 The "meadows" were open spaces outside the city walls, complete with altars, where crowds could attend Rituals. Waley understands *heng* (written quite differently from the oracular *heng/xiang*) as a special Rite for "fixing" luck. (See Hexagrams 32/1 and 42/6.) Profit or luck would have derived from this Ritual, which may have been something as simple as burying an Oracle Bone or drawing a circle around a certain spot.

Nine in Second Place

Cloudburst

On sand.

Slight complaint.

Auspicious Conclusion.

 Perhaps they (soldiers, captives, or both) are caught in a sudden downpour on the riverbank.

Nine in Third Place

Cloudburst

In mud.

Marauders attracted.

Perhaps soldiers are bogged down on their way back from battle.

Six in Fourth Place

Cloudburst

Of blood.

Coming out of pit.

Is this blood of Sacrifice, or blood of War? Have captives taken refuge in cave dwellings? Have they been held prisoner underground, and are they now escaping? Subterranean or semisubterranean pit-dwellings, pit-stores, even perhaps pit-dungeons, have been identified at many neolithic sites in China, including the famous Banpo Village in Shaanxi Province (fifth to fourth millennium BC). This may, however, possibly refer to the story told to the Viscount of Wu in the *Zuo Commentary*, Duke Ai, Year 1 (493 BC), in which a certain pregnant queen of the Xia dynasty (the dynasty before the Shang), whose husband, Xiang, has been killed in an insurrection, escapes from imprisonment in a pit. Her son subsequently restores the family to power.

Nine in Fifth Place

Cloudburst

Of liquor,

Sated with food.

Auspicious Augury.

Perhaps these were celebrations after battle?

Six in Top Place

Entering a pit.

Three guests arrive

Uninvited.

Beware.

Auspicious Conclusion.

The Pit is both shelter and trap.

HEXAGRAM 6

Dziung

Dispute

JUDGMENT

Captives.

Afraid.

Auspicious to middle.

Calamitous

Conclusion.

Profits

To see a big man.

No Profit

To cross a big stream.

This Hexagram may refer to disagreement over the rights and wrongs of a matter, perhaps involving money, and the consequent airing of grievances. Or it may be about public litigation and denunciation. For Waley, it concerns a dispute over war booty and captives.

LINES

Six in First Place

Service

Cut short.

Slight complaint.

Auspicious Conclusion.

The King's service is cut short before it is too late, before litigation and recrimination can begin in earnest.

Nine in Second Place

Failed Dispute.

A return home,

An escape.

Three hundred households.

No Calamity.

An unsuccessful litigant escapes the consequences and prevents trouble from reaching his extended family and retainers.

Six in Third Place

Old game eaten.

Augury

Of Danger.

Auspicious Conclusion.

King's service

Of no avail.

There is no fresh "catch." One has to resort to eating dried game. This is hazardous, but to throw in one's lot with the King at this stage would achieve nothing.

Nine in Fourth Place

Failed Dispute.

Return to hear

Commands,

Alterations.

Auspicious Augury.

Peace.

Flexibility is shown, an ability to compromise and achieve peace.

Nine in Fifth Place

Auspicious Dispute.

In this case, the Dispute has a good result.

Nine in Top Place

Leather belt granted,

Three times forfeited

In a single morning.

Belts of different materials were traditional emblems of rank and authority. The word for "morning" can also mean "morning audience." The fickleness of the ruler and the transitoriness of honor (which were to be symptoms of the gradual erosion of the Zhou state) provide a discouraging Omen.

HEXAGRAM 7

Sier

Army

JUDGMENT

Auspicious Divination

For a big man.

No Harm.

The graph for the Hexagram Name has a long history, all of it connected with the army, or "host" (in the old sense of an armed multitude, its divisions and camps, its maneuvers and commanders). In the Oracle Bone Inscriptions (where it appears in a simpler form), it sometimes means the place where an army encamps, where it hangs up its weapons, the encampment. One such inscription reads: "On the *yimao* day the King made Divination in the Geng encampment." It can also mean the divisions of the army, as in "On the day *dingyou* it was Divined whether the King should set up three divisions, Left, Center, and Right." In a strangely touching series of four Inscriptions, from Divinations made on four consecutive days, the question is repeatedly asked: "Will the Army be safe from Harm tonight?" This "military" seventh Hexagram seems to refer in part at least to the epic battle in the Wilds of Mu, a tract of open country in what is now Henan Province, in which the Zhou King Wu, carrying the corpse of his father, King Wen, onto the field, attacked and defeated the Shang army.

LINES

Six in First Place

Army

Sets forth,

Pipes arrayed,

Else the strongest

Come to grief.

"Pipes arrayed" is an image of Discipline, one of the Five Fundamentals of War as itemized in *The Art of War*. Much is made in that treatise of the importance of Ritual Preparations for warfare:

> *Chapter 1, Making of Plans*
> Victory belongs to the side
> That scores most
> In the temple calculations
> Before battle.

Discipline, or "proper organization," is visible in a regiment's "flags and insignia, in their drums and gongs," says the great Three Kingdoms general Cao Cao. In the *Zuo Commentary*, Duke Xuan, Year 12 (597 BC), Xian Gu, a general of the state of Jin, leads his troops across the Yellow River against the army of the southern state of Chu, whose power is on the rise. Another Jin officer, Xun Shou, opposes the plan as bound to end in disaster, simply quoting the *I Ching*, without conducting any sort of preliminary Divination. He refers directly (if somewhat arbitrarily and rhetorically) to this very Line. "Our Army is in great peril!" he protests. "In the words of the *I Ching*, where Hexagram 7, *Shi*, changes to Hexagram 19, *Lin* [i.e., at this very Line Statement, Six in the First Place]: 'The Army sets forth, pipes arrayed, else the strongest come to grief.' Troops that proceed in an orderly fashion [with "pipes arrayed"] may perhaps succeed; those that act contrary to this will surely come to grief." He goes on to elaborate on the ways in which Xian Gu's advance will lead to disaster. Ultimately, at the insistence of other officers, his section of the army weakly follows Xian Gu's lead, crosses the Yellow River, and is duly defeated by the assembled forces of Chu at the Battle of Bi.

Nine in Second Place

In the ranks,

All Auspicious.

No Harm.

Three times,

The King

Issues commands.

 These commands may have included rewards and promotions, a bit like the leather belt referred to in the Top Line of the previous Hexagram.

Six in Third Place

Army carries corpse.

Calamity.

 This appears to be another reference to the Battle in the Wilds of Mu, and the carrying onto the battlefield by the Zhou King Wu of the corpse of his father, King Wen. King Wen had, according to venerable tradition, created the Sixty-Four Hexagrams and written the Hexagram Judgments while imprisoned at the Shang court. The early shamanistic catechism *Heavenly Questions* contains a poignant reference to this battle:

> When Wu set out to kill Yin, why was he grieved?
> He went into battle carrying his father's corpse.
> Why was he in such a hurry?

Yin was the other name for Shang, the dynastic house that King Wu was overthrowing. "I suspect," comments the translator David Hawkes, "that in the original version of the story which Qu Yuan is here referring to it was a dead body, as in El Cid's last battle, which led the troops to victory."

Six in Fourth Place

Army camps to left.

No Harm.

 On the left bank of the river?

Six in Fifth Place

Game taken in Hunt.

Profits

To question captives.

No Harm.

Eldest son

Commands the Army,

Younger son

Carts the corpse.

Augury of

Calamity.

Hunting was a well-established ritual celebration of victory. A good catch in the Hunt, with much slaughter of wild beasts, was seen as Auspicious, and these violent conflicts between man and beast were conceived in religious terms. The word for taking game in a Hunt was also the word for getting, or "capturing," a living being for Sacrifice. The *Book of Songs* celebrates the Hunt as one of the great activities of the nobles:

> *Song 180*
> On the lucky day,
> We made Sacrifice;
> We prayed.
> Our hunting carriages
> Were fine,
> Our four stallions
> Strong.
> We climbed the high hill.
> We hunted for game.

The Hunt, Sacrifice, and Warfare were linked. They were all part of the "ritually coded violence" of early Chinese society. So too was the practice of capturing, questioning, and sacrificing the enemy (sometimes cutting off their ears beforehand). Again, the *Book of Songs* celebrates such occasions:

Song 168
We took captives
For questioning.
We came home. . . .
Mighty
Was our General Nanzhong;
The Xianyun barbarians
Were brought to heel.

Song 178
Mighty
Were the plans laid by
Our Great Marshall
Fangshu.
He led his army forth,
Took captives
For questioning.

For other references to War, captives, and Sacrifice, see Hexagram 30. It is possible that the "younger son" is the brother of King Wu most often referred to as the Duke of Zhou, who played such a big part in establishing the Zhou dynasty after the conquest, and to whom tradition later attributed the Line Statements of the *I Ching*. The Augury of Calamity may refer to the Inauspicious Oracle obtained by King Wu before the Battle in the Wilds of Mu. He refused to accept the Oracle, and he went on to defeat the Shang.

Six in Top Place

Mandate of Great Lord,

Kingdom founded,

Inheritance received.

A small man

Is not able.

This again seems to refer to the founding of the Zhou dynasty after the victory over the Shang in the Wilds of Mu.

HEXAGRAM 8

Bier

Side by Side

JUDGMENT

Auspicious.

A Yarrow Divination

Repeated,

Augury in perpetuity.

No Harm.

Arrival

From unsettled borderlands.

Calamity

For a latecomer.

夗 The early graph for this Hexagram Name has two figures, one behind the other—possibly two women (the single element is also used for Female Ancestor). In modern Chinese it means "to compare," i.e., to put two things or two people side by side for the purpose of comparison. It occurs in the Oracle Bone Inscriptions in the sense of "alliance," as, for example: "If the King allies himself with [*bi*] Zhi Guo to attack the Tufang, he will receive abundant assistance." This was certainly a prime consideration in the unsettled times of the Zhou dynasty, when states were constantly forming alliances with one another. With whom should we form an alliance? Whose side should we be on? Which person or group of persons should we be close to ("side by side" with) and support? This Hexagram may, however, be more precisely concerned with the "placing together" side by side of captives prior to their being offered as victims for Human Sacrifice. Archaeologists have remarked on the "groupings" of human skeletons found at different levels of the Shang Sacrificial Pits. The last sentence of the Judgment seems to refer to a story in the *Bamboo Annals*: the Great Yu, mythical founder of the first Xia dynasty, Tamer of the Flood, put to death the chieftain Fangfeng (Protector from the Wind) when he arrived late for an assembly of nobles at Mount Kuaiji.

LINES

Six in First Place

Captives

Side by Side.

No Harm.

Fill the captives' bowl.

Calamitous Conclusion.

Auspicious.

Food and drink are offered to captives destined for Sacrifice. Perhaps their bodies are to be buried side by side. Perhaps they will be mutilated. The Sacrifice, which for them is indeed a Calamity, is nonetheless Auspicious for their captors. According to Waley, the bowl is filled to overflowing with booty taken from the enemy.

Six in Second Place

Side by Side

With those from within.

Auspicious Augury.

"From within" (as opposed to from without—see below) may mean from among those "at court," i.e., within the royal circle, as opposed to from among those "in the countryside," or outside the royal circle. It may also mean from among those "within the country," or "within the realm," as opposed to barbarians. This is advice either on the forming of alliances or on the Ritual placing of Sacrificial Victims.

Six in Third Place

Side by Side

With offenders.

 Place captives side by side with those who have in some way broken the law—i.e., criminals—for the purpose of Sacrifice.

Six in Fourth Place

Side by Side

With those from without.

Auspicious Augury.

 Place them with barbarians, with foreigners; place them side by side with prisoners from beyond the borders, beyond the pale. This will make for an Auspicious Sacrifice.

Nine in Fifth Place

Side by Side,

Made manifest.

On three sides,

King hunts.

Game lost ahead.

Local Folk

Spared.

Auspicious.

In an old tale, found in the *Spring and Autumn Annals of Master Yan*, a certain King is out hunting a bird and fails three times to catch it. In his anger and frustration, he proposes to kill one of the locals for having scared the bird away. But one of his ministers pleads for the man's life and the King ultimately relents. Some readers understand this Line to refer to the practice of hunting with three sides closed, leaving an opening in front as a possible route for escape (see Part I). How this is connected with either the manifest placing side by side of victims or the manifest "forming of alliances" is far from clear. Perhaps this was simply an example of a public act of clemency and generosity, which gained the King the allegiance of the local people.

Six in Top Place

Side by Side,

Headless.

Calamity.

Are these captives taken without their collective head, i.e., their leader or chieftain? Or have they been literally decapitated? In a Shang-dynasty royal tomb at Xibeikang near Anyang, large numbers of human skeletons have been excavated. The bodies were often laid out carefully side by side, indicating large-scale Human Sacrifice. Fifty-nine of the skeletons in one of the principal tomb sections were headless. In other areas, large numbers of human skulls were found (twenty-nine in one, one hundred and eleven in another). In smaller tombs, mutilated or headless skeletons make up a large proportion. Archaeologists have determined that where skulls and skeletons were buried separately, the graves were also sparsely furnished, indicating that the "headless" were probably Human Sacrificial Victims of lesser social rank. Such Victims, whose heads were cut off and presented as Sacrificial Offerings, whether in Royal Tombs or in other places, were either enemies who had invaded the territory ("outsiders") or men who had offended against the Royal Property ("offenders").

HEXAGRAM 9

Siog Xiôk

Lesser Husbandry

JUDGMENT

Fortune.

Sacrifice Received.

Dense clouds,

No rain,

From western meadows.

This is an agricultural Hexagram, as one would expect from the Name. The second graph shows a field and above it a tether or rope. The farmers long for rain. The words "dense clouds, no rain" also occur in Hexagram 62/5. Many Oracle Bone Inscriptions ask about rain: Should we issue a call to dance for rain? Should we dance for rain? Will the rain stop today? Will the rain stop in the early morning? Will it rain tonight? Divined on the day *wuxu*: Will it rain if we make a Human Sacrifice and pray for rain? Should His Majesty not dance for rain? Will there be prompt rain if we play music and dance for rain? Will it rain if we perform a ritual to the River God and the *Yue* God? Will there be rain from the west? Will there be rain from the east? On the third day, in the afternoon it rained from the east; at *xiaocai* [the time of the evening meal?] it stopped [raining]. Despite the agricultural emphasis, Lines Four and Five return to the subject of captives and Sacrifice.

LINES

Nine in First Place

Come back

Down the road.

There will be

No Harm.

Auspicious.

 Return from the fields.

Nine in Second Place

Come back,

Leading.

Auspicious.

 Leading livestock.

Nine in Third Place

Cart sheers away from axle.

Husband and wife

Eye each other

Askance.

 The coming apart of the cart chassis is a token of breakdown in a marriage. Compare Hexagrams 26/2, 34/4, and 44/6. The graph for "cart" is also used for "chariot," and chariots were of enormous importance in the early Zhou—they were the "preeminent symbol of status." Since this is an agricultural context, "cart" seems more appropriate. There is something strangely modern in this connection between a "mechanical" and a matrimonial "breakdown."

Six in Fourth Place

Captives.

A bloody gelding.

Go out warily.

No Harm.

 I follow Kunst in taking this to be a reference to the gelding of farm animals. Gelding also occurs in Hexagram 59/6. Cattle gelded for Sacrifice are here being compared with captives prepared for Human Sacrifice.

Nine in Fifth Place

Captives,

Tightly bound.

Wealth taken from neighbors.

 Wealth and neighbors also appear in Hexagrams 11/4, 15/5, and 63/5. Rutt wonders if the "neighbors" are unfriendly neighboring states.

Nine in Top Place

Rain falls,

Rain ceases.

Still we plant.

Augurs

Danger for wife.

Moon near full.

For noble man,

Calamitous to march.

 Compare Hexagram 26, Greater Husbandry. "Moon near full" also comes in 61/4.

HEXAGRAM 10

Lier

Step

JUDGMENT

Step on Tiger's Tail,

Unbitten.

Sacrifice Received.

Fortune.

This entire Hexagram advises to proceed (to "step") with caution, to distinguish between courage and folly, not to blunder into things recklessly, not to "step on the Tiger's Tail" and get bitten. This is one of the oldest and most central messages of the *I Ching*. It is effectively stated in vivid images such as these, without any of the later philosophizing. According to the *Book of the Huainan Master*, there was once a time of perfect peace when tigers and leopards could be pulled by the tail with impunity. In the Mawangdui silk manuscript, the Hexagram Name is *li*, Ritual, a picture of some ritual object. This could be a phonetic "loan" (the ancient pronunciation of the two was similar), but it could also be an extension of the underlying idea of caution, since Ritual is an important application of "stepping" with care. Li Jingchi sees this as an Augury based on a strange dream. (In his last work, published posthumously in 1981, he frequently puts forward this dream hypothesis to account for otherwise strange and apparently unconnected utterances of the Oracle.)

LINES

Nine in First Place

Step

In plain silk shoes.

Journey brings

No Harm.

Li Jingchi sees this as a Divination for a traveler. To step in plain silk shoes is to do things in a plain, straightforward, unambitious manner.

Nine in Second Place

Step

On the road,

Leisurely.

Auspicious Augury

For the Dark Man.

The "leisurely" (*tantan*) man is the man with a "bigger," more relaxed view. *Tantan* may also describe the road on which he steps, a level road where the going is easy. But the Dark Man (*youren*) may have been a prisoner. He receives an Auspicious response after being unjustly thrown into jail (into the "dark"). We may have here one of many tantalizing *I Ching* fragments of early myth, from the story of Taijia Wei, younger brother of Wang Hai, predynastic Ancestor of the Shang kings. (For Wang Hai, see also my commentary on Hexagram 34/5.) According to the early shamanistic *Heavenly Questions*:

Dark Man Wei
Followed in his brothers' footsteps
And the Lord of Youyi was stirred against him.
Why, when the birds flocked together,
Did she forsake her own son
And give herself to him?
The Dark Man lay with her adulterously
And destroyed his elder brother.

Six in Third Place

Blind see,

Lame walk.

Step

On Tiger's Tail,

Bitten.

Calamity.

The warrior

Acts the great Prince.

 For Li Jingchi, this is a wish from another dream: "If only the blind *could* see!" Then along comes a Tiger and turns it into a nightmare! For the blind and the lame, compare the similar Line Statements in Hexagram 54/1–2. The warrior "steps" beyond the proper domain, like a man with only one eye, or one leg. He is destined for trouble. He is bitten. For the warrior, see also Hexagram 57/1:

Advance.
Retreat.
Profitable Augury
For a warrior.

Nine in Fourth Place

Step

On Tiger's Tail.

Caution.

Auspicious Conclusion.

 Reckless action almost leads to disaster. But caution saves the day.

Nine in Fifth Place

Step

In rough shoes.

Augury of Danger.

 I follow Wen Yiduo. For the rough shoes, made of kudzu, or bast, compare the *Book of Songs*:

> *Song 101*
> [of a wedding trousseau]
> Rough shoes,
> Five pairs;
> Cap pendants,
> One pair. . . .

> *Song 107*
> [a song of courtship]
> Rough shoes,
> Finely plaited,
> Fit for treading on hoarfrost. . . .

Perhaps these "rough" shoes suggest traveling in wintry weather (hence the danger), while the "silk" shoes of the First Line suggest summer.

Nine in Top Place

Watch step,

Examine men.

A return

Is most Auspicious.

 Circumspection enables one to return, to make a turn, at the appropriate time.

T'âd

Grand

JUDGMENT

The little go,

The big come.

Auspicious.

Sacrifice received.

Fortune.

 The Hexagram Name is sometimes explained as an expanded form of the common word *tai*, a large man, "very great," hence Grand. In its seal-script form, however, the graph seems to contain hands and water.

LINES

Nine in First Place

Madder

Root-plucked.

Auspicious to march.

A red dye was extracted from the root of the "earthblood," or madder, *maoru*, a plant related to the French *garance*, the *Rubia tinctorum*. It is also related to the more generic reed *baimao*, white grass, or floss-grass, *Imperata arundinacea*, which symbolized purity and was used for wrapping Sacrificial Offerings and for straining Sacrificial Wine. Compare Hexagram 28/1: "White grass for the mat. No Harm." See also the *Book of Songs*:

> *Song 229*
> Oh!
> The bundles
> Of white madder flower!
> Oh!
> The bundles
> Of madder grass!
> My man has gone far away
> And left me all alone!

If the madder comes up in clumps, roots and all, it is an Auspicious Omen. The stalks were also cut into lengths to use in a form of Divination.

Nine in Second Place

Float across the River

With a big gourd.

No drowning.

Cowries lost.

Reward in mid journey.

Compare the famous Taoist parable in the first chapter of the *Book of Master Zhuang*: Master Hui the Logician has just been complaining of the useless great gourd he has grown from seed. Master Zhuang advises him to make a float out of it, to gird it on and go cruising (like a true Taoist) on the rivers and lakes. Dried gourds were indeed used "as lifebelts" (Arthur Waley). The River (*he*) must be the Yellow River, the Great River of Shang and Zhou times. In Oracle Bone Inscriptions, the Yellow River was the most powerful River Spirit, and Sacrifices, sometimes human, were made to it. See also two passages in the *Book of Songs*, for elements from this Hexagram—Tiger, river, and gourd:

Song 34
Leaves
Of the bitter gourd:
Deep ford
At the crossing. . . .

Song 195
Never fight a Tiger
With bare hands;
Never cross the River
Without a boat.

Nine in Third Place

For every plain

A slope,

For every going

A return.

Divination

For hard times.

No Harm.

Do not be sad.

Captives.

Blessings at the feast.

The "plain/slope" saying is one of several folk proverbs incorporated into the Oracle. It conveys the sense of the constant cyclical process of Change in Nature, observed in such things as the progression of the seasons, the rising and setting of the sun, the alternation of light and darkness, of height and depth. Li Jingchi compares it with the proverbial saying in Hexagram 41/3: "Three travelers . . ." The "hard times" were probably times of dearth or drought. According to Karlgren, the early graph for "hard," *jian*, points to the practice of burning a Human Victim, perhaps a Shaman or a cripple, with his hands tied behind his back, in order to bring rain and alleviate "hardship."

Six in Fourth Place

Fluttering.

No wealth from neighbors.

No caution.

Capture.

For "fluttering," see the *Book of Songs*:

> *Song 162*
> Turtle doves
> Flutter!
> Soaring, diving,
> Settling
> On bushy oaks.
> King's service
> Never ends.
> I cannot tend my father.

> *Song 171*
> Turtle doves
> Flutter!
> They flock together.
> My Lord has wine,
> Fine guests at the feast,
> Goodly company.

> *Song 299*
> Owls
> Flutter!
> Settling in grove by moat,
> Feeding on mulberry trees,
> Comforting with fine song.
> Huai tribes bring tribute from afar,
> Great turtles,
> Elephant tusks,
> And much southern gold.

Birds are a favorite source of omens everywhere in the world, and their "fluttering" seems to signify something, to bring a message. Waley believes the recurring flutter of wings or leaves in the *Book of Songs* to be an Evil Omen for the lover, because *pian* (flutter) sounds like *bian* (change). The ancient Oracle of Dodona in Epirus was an oak tree sacred to Zeus; its whispering leaves and murmuring doves gave omens from the god. The sharing or taking of wealth (see Hexagrams 9/5, 15/5, and 63/5) may have been connected with the taking of booty in war. A military campaign undertaken without sufficient caution may well lead to defeat and capture.

Six in Fifth Place

King Yi

Gives his daughter in marriage.

Joy.

Supremely Auspicious.

 Compare this with Hexagram 54/5: "King Yi gives his daughter in marriage. The bride's sleeves are less fine than her younger sister's. The Moon is almost full. Auspicious." Yi, the penultimate Shang king, father of the last ruler, the "debauched tyrant" King Xin, is supposed to have given his daughter (or possibly his cousin) in marriage to King Wen of Zhou, or (according to another version) to King Ji, King Wen's father (in which case she would have been King Wen's mother). This may explain why King Wen sacrificed to Shang Ancestors as well as to his own, a practice attested to in Oracle Bone Inscriptions. The marriage is celebrated in *Song 236* (see Hexagram 54).

Six in Top Place

City wall

Crumbles into moat.

Troops not deployed.

Proclamation

Issued from city.

Augury of trouble.

 This looks like a Divination conducted during a siege. Despite the collapse of the city wall, the warning is clear: Do not proceed any further with the siege. As Waley notes, "the city wall and its gates are important throughout Zhou civilization." They were a space in which "things often happened and stories began."

HEXAGRAM 12

B'iûg

Wife

JUDGMENT

An offender's wife.

Augurs ill

For a noble man.

The big go,

The little come.

Structurally, this Hexagram and the preceding one, Grand, are exact opposites of each other. I depart from tradition by adopting the graph for the Hexagram Name found in the Mawangdui silk manuscript, *B'iûg*, a "wife" or "married woman," which (if it is indeed not simply a loan for *pi*, the Name in the received text, translated in Part I as Obstruction) changes everything. The focus of the Hexagram then becomes marriage and related Rituals.

LINES

Six in First Place

Madder,

Root-plucked.

Auspicious Divination.

Sacrifice received.

Fortune.

 Madder has already appeared in the previous Hexagram. The first words of the two First Lines are identical.

Six in Second Place

Steamed Offering

Wrapped.

Auspicious

For little men,

Inauspicious

For big men.

Sacrifice received.

Fortune.

 If a big man were to make the offering, it would be in a proper Sacrificial Vessel, not a humble wrapping.

Six in Third Place

Cooked Offerings,

Wrapped.

 The food in both of these Lines is undoubtedly a Sacrificial Offering.

Nine in Fourth Place

Decree.

No Harm.

Orioles

In a ploughed field.

Joy.

It has been suggested that these are not birds, but a harmless dragonlike monster.

Nine in Fifth Place

Wife no more.

Auspicious

For the big man.

All is lost,

Lost!

Tie it to a leafy

Mulberry Tree.

The marriage and the Hexagram are nearing their end. Tie a talisman to a sacred tree as a last resort. This "ancient prophylactic is still used in Siberia and Korea," writes Richard Rutt. JM: In Chinese, "mulberry tree" (modern pronunciation *sang*) rhymes with "lost" (*mang*). This is probably one of several scraps of rhyming folklore incorporated into the *I Ching*. The Mulberry Tree is a recurring motif in early Chinese texts, and is depicted in Oracle Bone script as a tree with many mouths (or suns) among its branches. Ten Suns were supposed to roost in this mythical tree, this World Tree, or Axis Mundi, in the eastern ocean. One of them sets out every morning to journey across the sky. On the colorful Chu silk painted banner from Mawangdui (reproduced in part as the cover of the 1985 edition of the Penguin Classics *Songs of the South*), the Suns are indeed seen "roosting" among the branches of the tree, and within the largest Sun of all stands a bird in silhouette. In more than one poem in *Songs of the South*, the shamanistic "traveler" tethers ("ties") his Dragon-steeds to the Mulberry Tree. Mulberry trees occur frequently in the *Book of Songs*:

Song 121
Bustards flap down,
Settle on leafy mulberries.
The King's service
Is never done. . . .

Silk was already being used for textiles in the Shang dynasty, and silkworms and mulberry trees were considered sacred. They were a subject of Divination. There are Oracle Bone Inscriptions recording Human Sacrifice to the Silkworm Spirit. The Mulberry Grove (*sanglin*) was a sacred precinct, and Mulberry Trees in general were considered numinous. The Mulberry Grove may have been the site of sexual Rites, a place where men and women "intermingled without order." According to one contemporary reading, *Song 111* of the *Book of Songs* describes disorderly conduct occurring between young men and women "rollicking among the mulberry trees." The song, which, incidentally, begins with a line about "gathering dodder" (see Hexagram 4), continues:

She made an assignation
To meet me
In the Mulberry Grove.

Karlgren writes that in the *Book of Songs* the leafy mulberry is a symbol of happy love, of love-trysts and marriage. Sericulture was certainly a woman's affair.

Nine in Top Place

Wife for an instant.

First

Sorrow,

Then Joy.

This follows the text of the Mawangdui silk manuscript, as interpreted by He Xin.

HEXAGRAM 13

D'ung Nien

Assembly

JUDGMENT

Assembly

In the wilds.

Sacrifice Received.

Profits

To cross a big stream.

Profitable Augury

For a noble man.

Both this and the following Hexagram seem to be about military or hunting maneuvers of one sort or another—public assemblies, victory celebrations, or ritual gatherings before and after battle. Mark Edward Lewis comments: "The actions that set the rulers apart from the masses were the 'great services' of the Ancestral Altars, and these services were ritually directed violence in the form of Sacrifices, Warfare and Hunting." The *Book of Songs* records a great Hunt held in preparation for War:

> *Song 154*
> In the second moon
> We held a Great Hunt;
> We practiced for War.
> Young boars we kept,
> Big ones we gave
> To Duke.

LINES

Nine in First Place

Assembly

At the gate.

No Harm.

 This Line and the next seem to refer to ritual gatherings before battle. Men were summoned to the palace or town gate and the Assembly listened to military proclamations.

Six in Second Place

Assembly

In the Ancestral Hall.

Trouble.

Ceremonial Banquets and Sacrifices took place in the Ancestral Hall:

Song 174
Heavy dew dripping
On thick grass;
Peacefully drinking the night away,
Feasting
In the Ancestral Hall.

But why the "trouble"? Did the Oracle, consulted in the Ancestral Hall, predict something Inauspicious?

Nine in Third Place

Rong barbarians

Ambush

In the long grass.

Ascent

Of a high hill.

For three years,

No uprising.

 Rong was a general word for warlike hill tribes from the north and northwest, who spoke a non-Chinese language, and who posed a constant threat during the Zhou dynasty. Sometimes known as Dog Barbarians, they succeeded in taking the Zhou capital Hao in 771 BC and in killing King You—a turning point in the decline of the Zhou dynasty. One interpretation of the "thumbnail story" in this Third Line is that the barbarians are detected in the long grass or on a hill, and are then defeated.

Nine in Fourth Place

Sitting astride

A wall,

Unassailable.

Auspicious.

 Perhaps these are the walls of a besieged city which have been scaled, while the city itself remains untaken. This would be Auspicious for the people astride the wall, the city's inhabitants.

Nine in Fifth Place

Assembly.

Wailing,

Laughter.

The great army

Meets the enemy again.

Victory.

For this juxtaposition of gathering, wailing, and laughter, compare Hexagrams 45/1 and 56/6. Perhaps a defeated army encounters its enemy a second time, and this time is victorious.

Nine in Top Place

Assembly

At Altars

In the meadows.

No Regret.

 The meadows were "without the city walls." Here Sacrifice was offered to the Lord on High at the solstices, and also as part of victory celebrations. In the *Lost Documents of Zhou*, there is a description of such a Sacrifice performed by the Zhou king Wu to celebrate a military victory:

> Infantry and cavalry commanders first attended to the Sacrifice at Altars in the meadows, then captives to be sacrificed flanked the southern gate, all wearing sashes and robes. Ears taken in combat were brought in first. King Wu attended to the Sacrifice, and the Great Master shouldered the white banner from which the head of the Shang King Zhou was suspended, and the red pennant with the heads of his two consorts. Then, with the first scalps, he entered and performed the Burnt Offering Sacrifice in the Zhou Temple.

In the same section of the *Lost Documents*, King Wu is recorded as having taken (Aztec style) a total of 177,779 "scalps" and severed ears, and 310,230 captives. This must surely be a wild exaggeration. The figures given in the Bronze Inscription of the Lesser Yu Cauldron are more likely (see Hexagram 30).

HEXAGRAM 14

D'âd Giug

Great Measure

JUDGMENT

Fortune.

Sacrifice Received.

Great Measure speaks of the benefits enjoyed from the making of Ritual Offerings. These would include a share in the bountiful harvest.

LINES

Nine in First Place

No injury

Exchanged.

No Harm.

Hardship,

No Harm.

For "exchange" (*jiao*), compare Hexagram 38/4. The word may mean something quite different, such as the "crossing" of birds in flight or animals in movement, or something observed "at the crossroads." See Hexagram 17/1. Such phenomena, the flight of crows ("crosswise" or otherwise) and cats "crossing" the road, are still considered significant today. See also in the *Book of Songs*:

Song 215
Crosswise
Flies the mulberry finch
With mottled wings.
My Lord is happy and at ease;
He has
Heaven's Blessing.

Crosswise
Flies the mulberry finch
With mottled throat.
My Lord is happy and at ease;
He gives shelter
To all lands.

Waley takes *jiao* to refer to birdsong. Yet another reading would have it refer to the "crisscross" wooden fetters worn by captives.

Nine in Second Place

A great cart

Is loaded.

Destination.

No Harm.

🦎 Setting out on an expedition.

Song 192
The cart is loaded,
The side-boards thrown away.
My sorrow is everlasting!
Heavy rains oppress;
The load falls.
I beg my Lord for help.

Nine in Third Place

The Duke

Sacrifices

To the Son of Heaven.

Small men

Do not prevail.

Compare the *Zuo Commentary*, Duke Xi, Year 25 (635 BC). Before an important military initiative, Diviner Yan, on behalf of the Marquis of Jin, consults the Turtle Shell, which promises victory; the Marquis himself then consults the *I Ching*, using the Yarrow Stalks, and receives this very Hexagram, with a Changing Third Line (thus forming Hexagram 38, *Kui*). "The Duke Sacrifices to the Son of Heaven" is interpreted to predict victory in battle and a forthcoming royal banquet. "Son of Heaven" as a term for "King" became normal from the reign of King Mu (956–918 BC) onward.

Nine in Fourth Place

A crippled Soothsayer

Scorched by the Sun.

No Harm.

In ancient times, a crippled Soothsayer or Shaman (or Shamaness) was exposed to the blazing sun, to enlist the sympathy of the Spirit World and bring rain during a drought. The poet and Oracle Bone scholar Chen Mengjia drew attention to this practice in his important 1936 article "Myth and Shamanism in the Shang Dynasty." The "scorching" is also mentioned in the *Zuo Commentary*, Duke Xi, Year 21 (638 BC), where the Duke is advised to introduce more moderate measures to induce rain.

Six in Fifth Place

Captives

Are trussed.

Great terror.

Auspicious.

 This is one of several places in the *I Ching* where the terror of captives is described. Why is this Auspicious? Perhaps because the Sacrifice of such captives served the purpose of exorcism, and their terror made it all the more effective.

Nine in Top Place

Blessing from Heaven.

Auspicious.

Profit

In all things.

 See the *Book of Songs*:

> *Song 243*
> May the King receive
> Blessing from Heaven!

HEXAGRAM 15

G'liam

Rats

JUDGMENT

Fortune.

Sacrifice Received.

For a noble man,

Conclusion.

I follow Kunst in reading the Hexagram Name as Rats. Different aspects of the behavior of rats can seem Auspicious or Inauspicious. The Gray Rat, or Great Gray Hamster, was considered a particularly ominous-looking creature, "a solitary, untameable animal that adopts a humanoid stance, standing on its hind legs with its forepaws folded." Rats are frequently mentioned in the *Book of Songs*, and had clearly been seen as a threat since earliest times:

> *Song 113*
> Big rat, big rat,
> Don't gobble our millet!
> Big rat, big rat,
> Don't gobble our corn!
> Big rat, big rat,
> Don't eat our rice-shoots!

LINES

Six in First Place

Rats

Crunch.

Noble man

Crosses big stream.

Auspicious.

Six in Second Place

Rats

Squeal.

Auspicious Augury.

 The Great Gray Hamster "under stress screams loudly."

Nine in Third Place

Rats

At work.

For noble man,

Conclusion.

Auspicious.

 The rats are busy filling their cheek pouches with food to store in their burrows. Kunst makes a comparison with the shrew, which has the highest metabolism of any mammal and is a famous "toiler," never stopping in its efforts to feed itself. It is always "at work."

Six in Fourth Place

Profit in all things.

Rats

Rip.

Six in Fifth Place

Wealth

Not shared by neighbors.

Profits to invade or attack.

Profit in all things.

茐 It is justified to attack a neighboring state that has appropriated wealth and refuses to share it.

Six in Top Place

Rats

Squeal.

Profits to march,

Against town

Or state.

HEXAGRAM 16

Dio

Elephants

JUDGMENT

Profits

To licence lords,

To move troops

Forward.

Elephants were hunted in ancient China, and they were buried sacrificially. Their remains have been found at Yinxu, the Shang-dynasty necropolis. Four thousand years ago, elephants were abundant in the northeast, northwest, and west of China. This is clear from bones and tusks found in Shang and Shu (present-day Sichuan Province) archaeological sites, from the cast-bronze elephants of this period, and from records on Oracle Bones that mention Elephant Sacrifice to the Ancestors. Ivory was worked from very early times, and the word for a "representation" or "image," *xiang*, which forms the right-hand element of this Hexagram Name, was simply a drawing of an elephant. *Xiang* later became a key term in *I Ching* exegesis (one should perhaps say *I Ching* semiotics), meaning not only an Image, but everything contained in, or symbolized by, that Image, everything present in, implied by, or communicated by that "sign." In a sense, the art of reading the *I Ching* is the art of reading these signs or Images. In the Great Treatise, the ancient Sage Fu Xi is said to have devised the Trigrams themselves by looking up and contemplating the Images or signs (*xiang*) of the Heavens, and by looking down and contemplating the patterns (*fa*) of the Earth. The practice of "licencing, establishing, or enfeoffing lords" *jian*, the delegation of authority, the "parceling out of sovereignty among a host of petty princes, or even lords of villages," lay at the heart of feudal Chinese society. The graph for *jian* in its earliest form may have been a picture of a man using both hands to drive a post into the ground, in order to form the structure of a dwelling. It is the second half of the modern word for feudalism, *fengjian*. "Licencing lords" has already occurred in the Judgment for Hexagram 3. The importance of this process for social stability is stressed in the chapter of the *Book of History* entitled "King Kang," which states that "Kings Wen and Wu licenced lords as a wall of protection for us their successors." The chapter "On Music" of the *Book of Rites* contains a detailed account of how King Wu "licenced lords" after his victory over Shang in the Wilds of Mu. Bronze vessels were cast to commemorate such enfeoffments. The inscriptions on these vessels sometimes "narrated the achievement and consequent ceremony of investiture." A famous example of such a ceremony is found on the so-called Qiu Wei *gui*-tureen, one of thirty-seven bronze vessels discovered in 1975 at Mount Qi, the ancient seat of the Zhou before the conquest. This *gui*-tureen is estimated to date from the reign of King Mu (956–918 BC), and it records the ceremony in which the King awarded his subject Qiu Wei various insignia in recognition of his services:

> The King was at Zhou. He approached the Grand Chamber and assumed formal position. Nan Bo came forward, and at the right of Qiu Wei he entered the gate and stood in the center of the hall facing north. The King called out to the Scribe of the Interior to award Wei purple knee pads, a scarlet demi-circlet, and a "jingle-bell." Wei bowed and touched his head to the ground. Venturing in response to extol the Son of Heaven's illustrious beneficence, he herewith makes for his cultured grandfather and his deceased father this treasured *gui*-tureen. May Wei's sons' sons and grandsons' grandsons eternally treasure and use it.

LINES

Six in First Place

Elephants

Sing.

Calamity.

Elephants "sing" (the same word is used for rats squealing in Hexagram 15). They are also known to "dance," probably to dislodge stinging and biting insects from their bodies. Wen Yiduo suggested that "elephants singing"—or Elephant Music—might refer to a martial dance performed by King Wu to celebrate his victory over Shang, which was indeed Calamitous for his enemy.

Six in Second Place

Hemmed in

By rocks.

Not for the entire day.

Auspicious Augury.

 According to Wen Yiduo, to be "hemmed in by rocks" is to be publicly humiliated by exposure on the pillory. Whatever its exact meaning, there is here an Auspicious release from some sort of ordeal. Or are the elephants hemmed in? Do they then break out when they have a fit or frenzy, when they are in "must"?

Six in Third Place

Elephants

Trumpet.

Regret.

Walking slowly

Brings Regret.

 I follow the Fuyang bamboo-strip text. The elephants "trumpet" as they lumber along—their maximum speed being some twenty-five miles per hour, when pressed.

Nine in Fourth Place

Elephants

Ramble.

A great catch.

No hesitation.

Hairpins

Strung with cowries.

An elephant Hunt. A late Shang Oracle Bone Inscription reads: "The King Divined on the day *yihai*. Would there be Misfortune from the Hunt? The Augury was Auspicious. They caught ten elephants and thirty pheasants."

Six in Fifth Place

Augury of illness.

Heng Ritual

Averts death.

Compare Hexagrams 5/1 and 32/3. The *heng* Ritual "fixes" things; it makes them efficacious and permanent.

Six in Top Place

Elephants

In the dark.

Collapsed ramparts.

No Harm.

Elephants may have been used as "primitive tanks" in a night attack on a besieged city, as they were in ancient India.

HEXAGRAM 17

Dzwia

Pursuit

JUDGMENT

Supreme Fortune.

Sacrifice Received.

Profitable Augury.

No Harm.

 This Hexagram may have had something to do with runaway slaves. It certainly concerns Warfare.

LINES

Nine in First Place

Inn collapses.

Auspicious Divination.

A crossing outdoors

Brings success.

The collapse of a building would certainly have been seen as an Omen. But the Divination is Auspicious nonetheless. This "crossing" may possibly refer to Omens observed in the "crossing" flight of birds. Compare the *Book of Songs*:

Song 215
Mulberry birds cross in flight,
Our Lord is blessed by Heaven. . . .
Mulberry birds cross in flight,
Every nation is protected.

It may also be a more ordinary "crossing": crossing paths with another; an encounter.

Six in Second Place

A boy is bound,

A man

Is lost.

Are these captives? Has a boy been pressed into military service, and therefore "lost" as a "man" to his family?

Six in Third Place

A man is bound,

A boy

Is lost.

Pursuit

Brings hope of gain.

Profit

In Divination for a dwelling.

Nine in Fourth Place

Pursuit

Leads to capture,

Augury of Calamity.

Captives on the road.

A covenant.

No Harm.

 The "covenant" may have been a pact between states, a matter involving Sacrifice and the taking or exchange of captives. The captives were probably taken in war, but may possibly have been hunted (pursued).

Nine in Fifth Place

Captives

At a Triumph.

Auspicious.

 The captives are to be sacrificed at a great Ritual of Celebration. For more on the Triumph, see Hexagram 30/6.

Six in Top Place

They are

Grasped,

Tied,

Bound.

The King makes Sacrifice

On West Mountain.

Qu Wanli reads this as human sacrifice, either of captives of war, after the return of King Wen to his home in the west, or else of Shang nobles after the Zhou conquest. There is increasing evidence of this practice in Shang and early Zhou times. Recent archaeological finds provide proof of large-scale decapitation and dismemberment of humans, including young males and sometimes children, prior to their burial in pits. "Often referred to in the Divination Inscriptions as Qiang [barbarians], they were frequently sacrificed to the Shang Ancestors, with the number offered at one time varying from three to four hundred, but usually being about ten."

HEXAGRAM 18

Ko

Blight

JUDGMENT

Fortune.

Sacrifice Received.

Profits

To cross a big stream,

Three days before first day, *jia*,

Three days after.

The graph for this Hexagram Name shows one or more insects in a vessel. The traditional etymology of the graph is as follows: Five poisonous insects are placed in a pot. They consume one another, and the most virulently poisonous insect is left as the survivor. Hence the graph refers to poison. Or it may perhaps have referred to mould (an ominous sign) growing on the wooden tablets of the Ancestors in the Clan Temple, or growing on the sacrificial food set before them; or to mildewed grain from which insects emerged. Arthur Waley sees maggots in the animal flesh sacrificed to the spirits of dead parents. *Gu* is more usually explained as the Blight caused by poison or decay in food. It can also by extension refer to a sinister power causing Blight, in particular the "evil power of woman," that "invisible psychic something, mysteriously generated from sexual indulgence and feminine wiles," visualized as a lascivious worm corrupting man. This is seen in the *Zuo Commentary*, Duke Zhao, Year 1 (541 BC), when a physician sent to examine the Marquis of Jin diagnoses his condition

582

in the following words: "Your illness cannot be cured. As the saying goes, too great an intimacy with womankind brings an affliction, the Blight. This is not ghost-work, nor is it an illness caused by diet. It is a delusion of the mind brought on by debauchery, a disorder consequent upon excessive sexual indulgence. In the *I Ching*, in the Hexagram Blight, this can be seen from the constituent Trigrams: above, *Gen*, Mountain; below, *Xun*, Wind. The Wind blows on the Mountain, just as a woman lays low a young man. The only solution lies in moderation." In the Oracle Bone Inscriptions the word Blight occurs often: Is Mu Bing indeed causing Blight? Does His Majesty's dream of Blight not presage Misfortune? Blight can also be understood as a poison created expressly—perhaps a love charm or philter, "the use of philter-maggots by women desirous of exciting the lusts of men and attracting them into debauchery." As Derk Bodde so perceptively remarks, its "intangible but sexually oriented quality may well be one reason for the deep fear and horror with which the *gu*-Blight has been regarded throughout Chinese history." In 676 BC, in the state of Qin, the *Fu* [Dog Day] Sacrifice was first instituted, in which dismembered dogs were offered to ward off the Blight. From the Han dynasty until the end of the nineteenth century, execution was the legal penalty for the preparation or use of *gu*-poison. *Jia*, in the Judgment, is the first of the ten stems used to count days in the old ten-day calendrical cycle. Three days before *jia* is the day *xin*; three days after *jia* is *ding*. Sacrifices to any given Ancestor were made on the stem day of his birth, and Oracles referring to stem days are a recurrent feature of Turtle Shell and Oracle Bone Inscriptions.

LINES

Six in First Place

Father's Blight

Put to right.

Filial son.

No Harm.

Danger.

Auspicious Conclusion.

"Put it right, Arthur, put it right!" were the last words of the dying Mr. Clennam to his son in Charles Dickens's *Little Dorrit*.

Nine in Second Place

Mother's Blight

Put to right.

No Divination possible.

🦎 Rutt notes the respect accorded here to women Ancestors.

Nine in Third Place

Father's Blight

Put to right.

Small worries.

No great Harm.

Six in Fourth Place

Father's Blight

Washed away.

Going brings Harm.

🦎 This "washing away," or "bathing," of the father's Blight has been linked to the "bathing" of the Ten Suns of early Chinese myth, a myth which itself may be linked to the tribal origins of the Shang dynasty, and ultimately to their totem (and "father"), the Dark Bird (*xuanniao*). The story varies, but it can be tentatively reconstructed as follows: The Ten Suns (also identified with Ten Ravens—they had birds within them, or perhaps they were carried by birds) roosted in the branches of a huge Mulberry Tree, which grew in Warm Water Valley. One of the Ten Suns rose into the sky every morning on its day of the ten-day week, having first been bathed by Xi He, Mother of the Suns, in the Valley. It then journeyed across the sky. In the words of the *Heavenly Questions*:

> Setting out from the Gulf of Brightness
> And going to rest in the Vale of Murk,

From the dawn until the time of darkness,
How many miles is the journey?

This myth was echoed in the (now lost) early oracular precursor of the *I Ching*, the supposedly Shang-dynasty *Guizang*, in a passage quoted by the *Hills and Seas* commentator Guo Pu:

> Behold their ascent!
> A time of brightness,
> Then a time of darkness,
> As the sons of Xi He
> Go out
> From Sun Valley.

Much of the richness of early Chinese myth has been lost, suppressed mainly by Confucian orthodoxy. Much may have lain behind bald phrases such as "Father's Blight washed away" and other enigmatic elements in the early core text of the *I Ching*. Archaeologists may one day uncover more missing pieces of the jigsaw puzzle. Until then we can only point to fragments like this, and hint at their meaning, more or less speculatively.

Six in Fifth Place

Father's Blight

Put to right.

Praise received.

Nine in Top Place

Serving neither King nor nobles.

Aspirations

Are lofty.

Calamity encountered.

The final word, Calamity, is found only in the silk manuscript from Mawangdui. This Line Statement may have referred to Bo Yi and Shu Qi, the princely brothers who withdrew from the service of King Wu when they discovered that he was planning to overthrow the Shang. They starved to death on Mount Shouyang rather than "eat the usurper's food." They eventually died of hunger (Calamity) at the foot of the mountain. Men have praised them through the ages for their uncompromising purity.

HEXAGRAM 19

Bliem

Wailing

JUDGMENT

Supreme Fortune.

Sacrifice Received.

Profitable Augury.

Eighth month,

Calamity.

There are many readings of this Hexagram. Wen Yiduo sees it as a Rain Omen. Others see an eye surveying objects on display at a Sacrifice, and hence attendance at a Ritual. In some versions of the old graph, drops of rain descend from Heaven, hence a long, soaking rain. Li Jingchi, by contrast, sees calamitous drought in the eighth month as a metaphor for poor government, in a strained neo-Marxist political interpretation. Kunst proposes "ceremonial wailing," or "keening," a reading I have followed throughout. Shaughnessy suspects that this Hexagram may have a mythico-astronomical reading, but has "no evidence to justify this suspicion." An early sense of the Hexagram Name was "siege tower," the "overlook" or "overlook-cart" (modern pronunciation *linche* or *linju*) which was rolled on wheels up to a city's walls. The two meanings (siege engine and "overlooking") occur together in *Song 241*:

His Great Majesty,
God on High,

587

Looked down (*lin*);
He surveyed
The four quarters. . . .
He said to King Wen,
"Consult your allies,
Unite with your brothers.
Go forth
With grappling hooks and with ladders,
With overlook-carts and assault engines.
Attack the city of Chong!"

LINES

Nine in First Place

Wailing,

Salt tears.

Auspicious Augury.

 Omens are taken from the wailing of attendants at a Sacrifice. For Wen Yiduo, however, these are various types of rain: deluge, downpour, etc. Others see different sorts of meats laid out for the Sacrifice: salty, sweet, etc.

Nine in Second Place

Wailing,

Salt tears.

Auspicious,

Profit in all things.

 Almost identical to the First Line.

Six in Third Place

Wailing,

Sweet tears.

Nothing Profits.

Grief,

No Harm.

The word translated as "sweet" may also be taken to mean "enough" or "sufficient."

Six in Fourth Place

Violent

Wailing.

No Harm.

Six in Fifth Place

Controlled

Wailing.

Great Ruler

Performs the *Yi* Sacrifice.

Auspicious.

The *Yi* Sacrifice was made to the God of the Soil when an army set out on a campaign. Pieces of flesh were placed before the altar, and drums were smeared with sacrificial blood. The graph for *yi* shows the sacred (phallic) pole of the Altar to the Soil, hung with slices of meat.

Six in Top Place

Intense

Wailing.

Auspicious.

No Harm.

HEXAGRAM 20

Kwân

Observing

JUDGMENT

Ablution.

No Roast Offering.

Captives

With big heads.

For Waley, this Hexagram Name means an "observatory," a place from which to watch for natural signs, to observe the Heavens and to examine Sacrificial Animals, link between Man and Heaven. If the Victims have bruised, swollen heads (from beating), then they are unsuitable for Sacrifice, and need to be observed closely. The graph for "roast offering" has an animal placed on herbs or straw. Perhaps there was no need to roast an animal because there were Human Victims (captives) available instead. The graph for Ablution, or Libation, has a vessel with liquid and two hands. The ground was sprinkled in order to bring down, appease, the Spirits of the Ancestors.

LINES

Six in First Place

Child

Observing.

For a little man,

No Harm;

For a noble man,

Calamity.

 For Waley, the "child observing" refers to the child's intuitive understanding of Omens, and the inspired utterances of young boys approaching puberty, perhaps heard at Initiation Ceremonies: "Their mouths seemed to speak of themselves." In East Asia generally, Waley comments, children's games and songs "were often thought to be mysteriously inspired."

Six in Second Place

Peeping

Observation.

Profitable Augury

For a woman.

 For Chinese women of ancient times, confined as they were to the house, "peeping" was the only means of seeing what was going on around them. A proposed husband might be briefly "sighted" in this way during the procedures of an arranged marriage—perhaps through a screen.

Six in Third Place

Observing

Sacrificial Victims.

Determining

Advance or Retreat.

 Strategic counsel is obtained from the condition of the Victims.

Six in Fourth Place

Observing

The Nation's Glory.

Profits King

To perform

Hosting Ritual.

The graph for "glory" has fire above a kneeling man—perhaps a Sacrificial Ritual. For Waley, the "glory" quite literally consists of "lights," celestial phenomena such as comets and shooting stars, portents indicating the Destiny of the Nation. The important Hosting Ritual (*bin*) also occurs in Hexagram 44/2. *Bin* itself means "to host," or "entertain," a guest—the graph has a house and a man within it, with a cowrie shell, or sometimes the feet of a person arriving. The Priest-King "welcomes" the Spirit of an Ancestor, or of a powerful natural body such as the Sun, and makes him feel "at home." The Ritual or Sacrifice (possibly accompanied by dance) enables the Spirit to be "present," and to enjoy the Sacrifice. One Oracle Bone Inscription reads: "Should the King conduct the Hosting Ritual for Cheng and the Sun?" This Fourth Line was obtained in a Yarrow-Stalk Divination performed in 672 BC (*Zuo Commentary,* Duke Zhuang, Year 22), concerning the future destiny of the young son of a nobleman, the Marquis of the small central state of Chen. Interestingly, in this Divination and its interpretation by the official scribe of the Zhou court, the earlier sense of Hosting Ritual is already gone. It is replaced by the later, more secular, sense of ritualized hospitality, according to which gifts of precious jade and silks are presented to or by the King. As Kidder Smith observes, the seventh-century Zhou scribe is no longer able to read the original *I Ching.*

Nine in Fifth Place

Observing

Our Victims.

No Harm

For our Lord.

Nine in Top Place

Observing

Their Victims.

No Harm

For their Lord.

Diad G'â

Biting

JUDGMENT

Fortune.

Sacrifice Received.

Profits

To mete out punishment.

 Some of the "biting" or "crunching" in this Hexagram may have been carried out in Sacrificial, especially Ancestral, Rites. As for the various foreign bodies (arrows, gold, etc.) that might be "bitten" or"crunched," finding such things in one's food, comments Waley, is considered a lucky or unlucky omen in various regions of Europe. But parts of the Hexagram, he adds, "seem to refer to the feeding behaviour of Sacrificial Animals." Lines 1, 2, and 6 also seem to be about the treatment (or maltreatment) and punishment of slaves or captives.

LINES

Nine in First Place

Ankles fettered,

Feet destroyed.

No Harm.

 Is this a slave or a captive? In any event, there is apparently no *serious* Harm—such as loss of life. Or perhaps the slave *did* no Harm to deserve this unjust punishment?

Six in Second Place

Skin

Bitten,

Nose destroyed.

No Harm.

Six in Third Place

Dried meat

Bitten,

Poison encountered.

Slight trouble,

No Harm.

Nine in Fourth Place

Gristle

Bitten,

Bronze arrow found.

Profit in hard times.

Auspicious.

 The arrowhead suggests that the meat may have come from a beast killed during a Hunt.

Nine in Fifth Place

Dried meat

Bitten,

Gold found.

Augury of Danger.

No Harm.

 To find (and therefore *not* swallow) a piece of gold, or "yellow bronze" (perhaps an arrowhead), in one's food was to be saved from death, since it was considered especially dangerous to swallow gold. The Mawangdui silk manuscript has "poison" in place of "gold."

Nine in Top Place

Fetters worn,

Ears destroyed.

Calamity.

HEXAGRAM 22

Piar

Fine

JUDGMENT

Fortune.

Sacrifice Received.

Slight Profit

In Destination.

 According to Li Jingchi, this entire Hexagram concerns a wedding and the "finery" involved. The bridegroom comes with a wedding party to fetch his betrothed. In the Ewenke hill-dwelling minority people of the Chinese Northeast, the entire clan still goes to the bride's village.

LINES

Nine in First Place

Fine

Feet.

Carriage abandoned.

Walking.

 For Li Jingchi, all the Lines refer to wedding gifts. Are the "fine feet" pigs' trotters? Perhaps, however, it is the young men "walking" with the wedding party who wear "fine" shoes.

Six in Second Place

Fine

Xu-basin.

 The bronze *xu*-basin became current in the early centuries of the Zhou dynasty. It was similar to the *gui*-tureen, but generally rectangular in shape, with rounded corners. It had two handles, usually four feet, and a cover, and it was used for ritual offerings of grain.

Nine in Third Place

Fine,

Sleek.

Auspicious Augury

In perpetuity.

Six in Fourth Place

Fine,

Radiant.

White-plumed horse.

No bandit raid.

A marriage party.

For Li Jingchi, it is the groom who rides a white horse. The "bandit raid" is also mentioned in Hexagrams 3/2 and 38/6.

Six in Fifth Place

Fine

In the hill garden.

Scant silk bundles.

Trouble.

Auspicious Conclusion.

 Is this a parklike setting for Ritual or Sacrifice? In any case, the silk, while fine, seems to have been less in quantity than was expected. Bolts of silk were traditionally presented to the bride's family.

Nine in Top Place

White gelded boar.

No Harm.

 "Pure white" is the perfection of beauty. For Li Jingchi, the "white boar" is another wedding gift. In the Oracle Bone Inscriptions, gelded boars are mentioned as Sacrificial Offerings: "Should we offer ten gelded boars to Shang Jia?"

HEXAGRAM 23

Pûk

Stripped

JUDGMENT

No Profit

In Destination.

 Taken as a whole, this is an Inauspicious Hexagram. The old graph for the Hexagram Name may be a picture of an animal with its skin "stripped" away, and a knife to one side. Most traditional readings translate the key word *chuang* in the Lines (the thing that is "stripped") as a "bed" or "cart." Li Jingchi takes the whole Hexagram to refer to the making of a cart. I have followed Kunst, who (himself following the Japanese scholar Akatsuka Kiyoshi) proposes that *chuang* is a loan or scribal error for the similar word meaning "ewe." Sacrificial Animals were "stripped," or flayed.

LINES

Six in First Place

Ewe

Stripped

From feet.

Augury of Exorcism.

Calamity.

 Compare the following lines from the *Book of Songs*:

Song 209
Pure are
The oxen and sheep
For Autumn and Winter
Sacrifice.
Strip them,
Boil them,
Array them,
Set them out. . . .

The contemporary Islamic festival of Aïd el-Kebir is a good occasion on which to witness the importance attached to the ritual niceties involved in the Sacrifice of sheep: from rearing, purchasing, slaughtering, and butchering to the final family meal.

Six in Second Place

Ewe

Stripped

From hocks.

Augury of Exorcism.

Calamity.

Six in Third Place

Stripped.

No Harm.

Six in Fourth Place

Ewe

Stripped

Of hide.

Calamity.

Six in Fifth Place

Fish strung.

Treat for Palace Folk.

Profit in all things.

 Strings of fish are seen as an Auspicious Omen.

Nine in Top Place

Fine fruit

Not eaten.

Noble man

Gets cart,

Little man

Strips hut.

Several commentators take this as a reference to the disparity between the wealthy nobility and the starving peasantry. Perhaps the peasants "strip" their huts to build a cart for their lord, who then "carts off" their produce (fruit, etc.)?

HEXAGRAM 24

B'iôk

Return

JUDGMENT

Fortune.

Sacrifice Received.

Going and coming.

No urgency.

Friends come.

No Harm.

Back and forth

On the way.

Return in seven days.

Profit in Destination.

The old Oracle Bone graph for the Name has been explained as a picture of an underground dwelling, with steps leading down into and up out of it, and a foot beneath. Hence, "to come and go," "to depart and return." This is a generally positive Hexagram, dealing with various aspects of traveling and the advisability of "returning," or turning back. Only the Top Line is unreservedly ominous.

LINES

Nine in First Place

Return

From no distance.

No great Regret.

Most Auspicious.

 It bodes no ill to Return after a short journey. The actual Destination is not specified.

Six in Second Place

Pause.

Return.

Auspicious.

 Return after a moment's rest and reflection.

Six in Third Place

Return

From the brink.

Danger,

No Harm.

 In translating *bin* as "from the brink," I follow Li Jingchi's 1949 reading. Others qualify the Return as "frowning," which I find obscure.

Six in Fourth Place

Solitary

Return

In mid journey.

 The traveler sets off in company but "returns" alone.

Six in Fifth Place

Hasty

Return.

No Regret.

 I follow Li's 1981 reading. Others qualify the Return as "forced" or "angry," rather than "hasty."

Six in Top Place

Confused

Return.

Disaster.

Calamity.

Troops deployed.

Great defeat.

Ruler of state

Meets with disaster.

For ten years,

No expedition possible.

In the *Zuo Commentary*, Duke Xiang, Year 28 (545 BC), Youji applies this to the Viscount of Chu and his overweening ambition. "The *I Ching* has it, in Top Place of the Hexagram *Fu*: 'Confused Return. Disaster.' So it is with the Viscount of Chu. He wishes to achieve his desires, but has lost the Truth and has no place to which to Return. That is why he is confused. How can he avoid Disaster?"

HEXAGRAM 25

Miwo Miwang

Possession

JUDGMENT

Fortune.

Sacrifice Received.

Profitable Augury.

Matters go astray.

Calamity.

No Profit

In a Destination.

This entire Hexagram deals with Spirit-Possession, its dire consequences and the possibility of being released from them through exorcism. Waley calls it "perhaps the most interesting passage" in the *I Ching*. For him, it deals with "the scape-goat ritual so familiar to us owing to its prevalence among the Semites, and still practised in many parts of the world as a means of ejecting pestilence. Have we any evidence that such a Rite was ever known in China?" he continues. "Certainly we have. In the *Yue Ling* (a section of the ritual classic *Li Ji*), in the passage relating to the last month, we read: 'The officials are ordered to perform the great demon-expulsion and to put out clay bulls in

608

order to send away the Cold Spirit. . . .' Wu Wang (Miwo Miwang) is of course the name of the disease as well as the name of the Spirit which causes it. We may guess that this Spirit was feminine, which is the rule for disease-demons in China as elsewhere." Although this interpretation of Waley's is speculative and has been questioned, I find it rather attractive. As Kunst writes in his notes, "the fact is that there is almost no contextual information here to help us interpret" the Hexagram (as is so often the case). Perhaps the Name represents a transliteration of some expression in an aboriginal language (the modern reconstruction almost sounds like that), possibly part of a secret "priestly language" in which the real names of Spirits were concealed behind special words intelligible only to the initiated. The first syllable of the Hexagram Name came to be understood as a genie, a demon, a ghoul found in deserted tombs, "an old goblin, clad in dark blue and carrying a wooden pestle. Anyone able to call it by its name will have a good harvest." The second syllable has the female radical.

LINES

Nine in First Place

Possession

Departs.

Auspicious.

The exorcism has succeeded.

Six in Second Place

Neither ploughing

Nor harvesting.

Neither breaking of soil

Nor tilling.

Profit in Destination.

For several years, work in the fields is left undone. This is the only clear reference to cultivation in the *I Ching*. Is the implication that under these circumstances, when some kind of Possession, or pestilence, has made cultivation impossible, and has left the fields untended, it is advisable to move to a new place?

Six in Third Place

Bane

Of Possession

Tied to bull.

Travelers acquire

Townsmen's curse.

 "How does one tie a disease to a bull?" asks Waley. "By attaching to it objects (such as herbs or the like) which symbolize the disease. . . . The suggestion that passers-by will pick up the disease and so disburden the locals of it seems to us callous, but it is constantly found in connection with such Rites."

Nine in Fourth Place

Divination possible.

No Harm.

 Divination may suggest a cure for the Possession.

Nine in Fifth Place

Feverish

Possession

Cured with joy,

Not herbs.

 The curse has been lifted not by medicinal means, but by way of Ritual, perhaps an Exorcism. There is no medicine, but there is joy, perhaps the ecstatic joy of the Ritual, with its dancing and shouting.

Nine in Top Place

Possession.

For a traveler,

Calamity.

Nothing Profits.

 The traveler should beware, lest he catch the "townsmen's curse" of Line 3. This is the Calamity first mentioned in the Judgment, *sheng*, a disease of the eye, but apparently also an illness in which the hands, nails, and lips turn green. R. H. Mathews, in his *Chinese-English Dictionary* (Shanghai: Inland Mission and Presbyterian Press, 1931, p. 798), adds that it can also mean "Possession by demons." Compare Hexagram 51/3. The old graph, present in many Oracle Bone and Bronze Inscriptions, seems to show an eye with something above it. The various possible meanings include an affliction of the eye, possibly a cataract, or otherwise an eclipse. It is a Calamity that arises from within; it is a demonic Possession, *yaoxiang*. The fact that *sheng* occurs twice in this Hexagram is further encouragement for those who see this as mainly about exorcism. Exorcism is mentioned in the Oracle Bone Inscriptions: "Should we conduct an Exorcism Ritual for the ailing abdomen of Nan Geng?"

HEXAGRAM 26

D'âd Xiôk

Greater Husbandry

JUDGMENT

Profitable Augury.

Auspicious

To eat away from home.

Profits

To cross a big stream.

Most of this Hexagram is concerned with agriculture, equipment, and livestock: horses, oxen, boars. The old Oracle Bone graph for "husbandry" appears to have some sort of rope or tether above a field or pasture. Perhaps, suggests Li Jingchi, for the peasants or herdsmen to eat "away from home" was to eat in the fields where they worked. In addition to having agricultural value, the animals were essential for Sacrifice. Compare this with its "paired" Hexagram 9, Lesser Husbandry.

LINES

Nine in First Place

Danger.

Sacrifice

Profits.

Nine in Second Place

A cart

Sheers away

From its axle.

 There is some debate as to the exact vehicle part involved in this breakdown. It is probably a piece supporting the axle. Compare Hexagram 9/3.

Nine in Third Place

Fine horses

Gallop in pursuit.

Profitable Augury

In hard times.

Daily practice

As a chariot guard.

A Destination

Profits.

Horses were not used for riding (cavalry) until the fourth century BC. At the time when the *I Ching* came into being, in the Western (i.e., Early) Zhou, they were used to pull carts and chariots.

Six in Fourth Place

Young ox

Wears horn-brace.

Highly Auspicious.

 A wooden brace attached to the forehead of the young ox prevents the frisky animal from causing harm, and from hurting himself.

Six in Fifth Place

A bellowing boar

Is penned.

Auspicious.

 Perhaps the animal has been taken in the Hunt, and is being kept as a Sacrificial Offering.

Nine in Top Place

Bounty of Heaven.

Fortune.

Sacrifice Received.

 Another reading is that Heaven is "not to be feared."

HEXAGRAM 27

Gieg

Breasts

JUDGMENT

Auspicious Augury.

Breasts

Are contemplated;

Substance is sought

For the mouth.

This Hexagram Name has been understood to refer to the jawbones of Sacrificial Animals hung in a Temple and examined for the purposes of Divination, or to the dewlaps (loose folds of skin hanging from the throat) of live animals destined for Sacrifice. In early times, various animals—dogs, pigs, sheep, oxen, buffaloes—and their bones were used for both Sacrifice and Divination. Indeed, their use for Divination may possibly have evolved from accidental cracks caused when they were burned in Sacrifice. Certain commentators concentrate on the condition of the teeth. Others emphasize that which is "within the jaw"—i.e., nourishment. Liu Dajun believes the Hexagram has to do with scrutinizing the face—in other words, Divination through phrenology. The old graph for the Hexagram Name (as found mainly in Bronze Inscriptions) is usually taken to be a picture of the jaw, perhaps with whiskers. A recent reinterpretation, however, which I find most attractive, and which I follow, sees the graph as a picture of a mother's breasts and the head of an infant feeding, suckling. This turns the entire Hexagram into a series of mantic observations of breast-feeding. This admittedly speculative reading also leads very naturally to the later understanding of the Hexagram as "nourishment" (see Part I).

LINES

Nine in First Place

The Magic Turtle

Is forsaken.

Moving breasts

Are contemplated.

Calamity.

 In ancient Divination, a red-hot hardwood poker was applied to the Turtle Shell (plastron), and from the resulting crack was interpreted the Oracular Response. Symbolically, this was Fire applied to Water, the two cosmic forces conjoined. The Turtle was considered sacred, or "magical," from earliest times. In Oracle Bone script, the graph for "magical," *ling*, contains a Turtle beneath rain: there seems to have been an ancient connection made between the appearance of turtles and rain, and turtles may have been involved in Rituals, possibly Sacrifices, to break drought. In addition to being a prime source for Divination, the long-lived turtle, from neolithic times, was seen as a microcosmic symbol of the Universe. The rounded vault of Heaven was seen to resemble a gigantic Turtle's upper shell suspended above the Earth, which in its turn was likened to the Turtle's undershell, or plastron. (See also Hexagram 41/6.) The whole (Heaven and Earth) stood atop four Mountain-like Turtle legs, the corners of the world. In later periods, the Turtle became a common symbol for Longevity and Steadfastness, and is still commonly seen at the foot of inscribed stone steles, binding Heaven and Earth securely together. Here the Oracle may be warning that to abandon the Sacred Ritual of consulting the Turtle, in favor of immediate physical needs (such as were associated with suckling at the breasts), will bring Calamity.

Six in Second Place

Pendant

Breasts,

Empty before long.

Advance brings

Calamity.

 Take heed of the passage of time and the coming of age.

Six in Third Place

Stroked

Breasts.

Augury of Calamity.

For ten years,

No action.

No Profit.

 The Oracle warns of the consequences of a preoccupation with the physical body and the gratification of the senses.

Six in Fourth Place

Pendant

Breasts.

Auspicious.

A glowering Tiger,

A grand aspect.

No Harm.

 Could the Tiger be the Shaman's assistant? Is the Shaman a powerful woman, got up as a Tiger?

Six in Fifth Place

A stroked

Neck.

Auspicious Augury

For dwelling.

Impossible to cross big stream.

Nine in Top Place

Shaken

Breasts.

Danger.

Auspicious.

Profits to cross big stream.

HEXAGRAM 28

D'âd Kwâ

Great Excess

JUDGMENT

Mighty

Ridgepole.

Profit in Destination.

Fortune.

Sacrifice Received.

 Compare this with Hexagram 62, Slight Excess. This Hexagram and its Lines deal with things that have "gone beyond" or "exceeded" their normal limit—partly with the construction of a dwelling and the importance of a sound ridgepole, partly with marriage in later years. It refers to ritual niceties (wrapped offerings), and to a river crossing in appropriate places. I follow the Mawangdui silk manuscript, which qualifies the ridgepole as *long*, "mighty" (the graph has Dragon and chariot).

LINES

Six in First Place

White grass

For a mat.

No Harm.

 White grass mats were used to wrap offerings for Rituals and Sacrifices. See Hexagrams 11/1 and 12/1. See also the *Book of Songs*:

> *Song 23*
> A dead doe
> Lies in the wilds,
> Wrapped in white grass.

Nine in Second Place

A withered willow

Sprouts.

An old man

Gets a young wife.

Profit

In all things.

 This union is something out of the ordinary, but the rejuvenation and renewal are Auspicious.

Nine in Third Place

Sagging

Ridgepole.

Calamity.

The structure cannot support the weight.

Nine in Fourth Place

Mighty

Ridgepole.

Auspicious.

Unforeseen circumstances,

Calamity.

A strikingly ambivalent Omen. The mighty beam seems at first to be Auspicious. But if it weighs *too* "mightily," the roof may suddenly collapse. As Waley points out, the state of beams (sagging, warping, or cracking) is regarded as an omen all over the world. For good reasons!

Nine in Fifth Place

A withered willow

Blooms.

An old woman

Gets a young husband.

Neither Harm

Nor praise.

The Oracle is less enthusiastic (but still not judgmental) about this union, no doubt because the woman can no longer bear children.

Six in Top Place

Crossing a ford.

Getting the head wet.

Calamity.

No Harm.

 Compare Hexagrams 63/6, and 64/6, in both of which the head gets wet—possibly after the immoderate consumption of wine. Going too far. But the Calamity does not have disastrously harmful consequences.

HEXAGRAM 29

K'em

Pit

JUDGMENT

Captives,

Bound.

Fortune.

Sacrifice Received.

Travel brings reward.

This is a consistently Inauspicious Hexagram, about a Pit or Trap, perhaps a burial, a grave, and the Sacrifice of the living (bound victims) on behalf of the dead at Royal Funerals. Wen Yiduo saw in it imprisonment, and the Pit as a dungeon. Waley sees religious Ritual, and refers to a passage in the ancient Chinese Classic the *Book of Rites*: "We Sacrifice to the moon in the Pit." Offerings to the moon, he comments, are still placed by Balkan peasants in holes in the ground. Traditionally, this Hexagram has always been associated with water, often in a dangerous sense—turbulent water gathering in a deep abyss. Its two component and reduplicated Trigrams (as presented in later exegesis; see Part I) represent a Pit within a Pit, or water in an "uninterrupted current," two Divided Lines flowing around a single Undivided Line. Indeed, the Trigram closely resembles the written character for "water." In neolithic China, and well into the Shang dynasty, pit-dwellings, or earth-lodges, subterranean or semisubterranean "constructions" of various shapes and sizes, were commonly used for human habitation, for storage, for animal shelters—and, of course, for burial. These holes in the ground could certainly have served as places of containment for captives. Cave dwellings cut into the loess soil of China's Northwest have continued in use to the present day.

LINES

Six in First Place

Double Pit.

Entering a trap.

Calamity.

 Double Pits were used for Royal Graves. This may also refer to an animal trap used in hunting.

Nine in Second Place

A steep-sided

Pit.

Small gains are sought.

 In a situation fraught with such danger, only modest goals should be set.

Six in Third Place

Thudding

Into the innermost

Pit,

Sheer and deep.

Do not act.

 Darkest depths have been reached.

Six in Fourth Place

A goblet of wine,

Two *gui*-tureens,

Earthenware vessels,

Passed through the window.

Conclusion.

No Harm.

Two *gui*-tureens also occur in the Judgment of Hexagram 41. There are many surviving bronze *gui*-tureens, the word being perhaps more accurately translated as "ritual food basin." They were used for offerings of grain. One of the most famous is the one known as the Kang Hou *gui*, the Basin of Prince Kang, now in the British Museum. This impressive vessel was cast in the early years after the Zhou conquest, to commemorate the appointment of Prince Kang, one of the brothers of King Wu, to the fiefdom of the state of Wei. As with many such bronze vessels, it bears an important Inscription. Jessica Rawson has vividly evoked the function of these bronzes and their Inscriptions, the deciphering of which has provided such insight into the culture and society of Shang and Zhou China: "It is likely that these Inscriptions were intended to be read by both the living and the dead, for it was expected that the Ancestors would be drawn to the feast by the aroma of the food and wine prepared for them in these vessels. The Inscriptions may have been placed inside the vessels so that the Ancestors would read them as they consumed the contents." They were, in other words, a potent means of communication with the world of Ancestors and Spirits. Rows of these bronze vessels must have been "very imposing in the flickering light of a Temple." Early Zhou Bronze Inscriptions, "located at the interstice of material- and text-based history," are perhaps the closest linguistic parallel we have to the earliest layer of the *I Ching* text. The *I Ching* Oracle's divinatory origins are illuminated by some of the fragments preserved in the Oracle Bone Inscriptions, while its use of rhyme and vivid imagery recalls certain poems in the *Book of Songs*. Its repeated reference to concrete details of Ritual, Warfare, Sacrifice, and History (gifts of cowries, propitious moments for an Advance, historical incidents in the Zhou conquest engraved on the collective memory, gruesome records of Human Sacrifice) all find parallels in the carefully composed Bronze Inscriptions. A good example of these Inscriptions can be found in my commentary on the Judgment of Hexagram 16. In the present Hexagram, the *gui*-tureens and the earthenware vessels seem to be being passed down through some sort of skylight or chute ("window") to feed prisoners held underground, to bring them relief. In the *Book of Songs*, Song 15, a dutiful bride sets offerings of boiled water-plants outside the window of the Ancestral Shrine.

Nine in Fifth Place

The Pit

Is not flooded;

Calamity

Is averted.

No Harm.

Six in Top Place

Bound

With threefold braids,

Bound

With double cords.

Set in a thicket of thorns.

For three years,

Not found.

Calamity.

 The late K. C. Chang mentions plaited hair as one of the accoutrements of the dancing Shaman. If there were any doubt that this Hexagram is dealing with a Magic Rite, comments Waley, it would be dispelled by the fact that these phrases all rhyme in the Chinese. The use of thread made of several distinctive strands in connection with magic (for example, to tie lockets, amulets, or charms) is well known, as in the Sumerian incantation "White wool, black wool, a double thread the spindle was spinning: a wondrous thread, a mighty thread, a variegated thread, a thread that does away with the curse." In a footnote, Waley suggests that this is a Rite directed against a pest or disaster. Waley's reading, based on close study of the Chinese text and relevant scholarship, but also on his own poetic intuition and wider reading, gives us an inkling of what may once have been the underlying meaning of some of these Lines, a glimpse through a crack in the door. Too often, alas, we can no longer find the key to open the door itself.

La

Lia

☲

Net,

Oriole

JUDGMENT

Profitable Augury.

Fortune.

Sacrifice Received.

Auspicious

To rear cows.

 This Hexagram, like the preceding one, is a Double Hexagram. The constituent Trigram has traditionally been taken to represent Fire (see Part I). But the Hexagram Name in the Mawangdui silk manuscript is a different graph altogether, *la* (modern pronunciation *luo*), meaning "net," perhaps a bird net, since in certain Oracle Bone Inscriptions the word seems to mean to *catch* a bird in a net. Another old reading interprets the Name *lia* (modern pronunciation *li*) as a bird, one of the many names for the Chinese, or black-naped, oriole, *Oriolus chinensis*. "The body is yellow, the tail and wings have mixed yellow and black colouring. . . . Its call is heard after the opening of spring. When the wheat and mulberries are ripe its call is at its best, with a soft full note like an old cloth-shuttle at work. In winter it hibernates, burying itself in the marshes, covering itself up with mud into an egg-shaped ball. Its flesh is sweet, warming and non-poisonous. It is a stimulant to the spleen, vitalizing and warming. It is specially recommended as a cure for jealousy among women." The Oriole occurs frequently, under a variety of names, in the *Book of Songs*, where its song is often associated with sorrow. Despite its bright yellow plumage, it was sometimes a bird of ill Omen as well as of springtime joy. This may provide a clue to the otherwise incongruous juxtaposition in this Hexagram of bright birds and the gloomy theme of War. Compare the *Book of Songs*:

Song 131
Jiaojiao!
Sang the Oriole,
Alighting on the jujube tree.
Who went with Duke Mu?
Ziju Yanxi was one,
Finest of warriors.
He nears his grave,
He trembles with fear.
Bright Heaven
Has taken our best men. . . .

This song almost certainly refers to a Human Sacrifice at the grave of Duke Mu of Qin (who died in 621 BC), with an oriole, or orioles, singing in the background. The Duke had left instructions that 177 men were to be buried alive (*xunzang*) with him when he died. Other oriole songs have equally dark overtones:

Song 187
Yellow bird, yellow bird!
Don't settle on the oak tree,
Don't eat my millet.
How can I live with
The people of this state?
I must turn back,
I must go home,
To the elders of my clan.

Song 230
How sweetly sings the Oriole
Settling on the mound.
How long the road,
And we so tired. . . .
How sweetly sings the Oriole
Settling on the hill.

I dare not slacken pace,
For fear I will never keep up. . . .

How sweetly sings the Oriole
Settling on the slope.
I dare not slacken pace,
For fear I will never arrive. . . .

This last is a song lamenting the hardship of military service. The cows in the last sentence of the Hexagram Judgment are perhaps being reared for Sacrifice. But they may simply have been for normal procreation. They certainly would have had war-related uses: hide for chariots, horse leathers, skins for drums, straps.

LINES

Nine in First Place

False step.

Be cautious.

No Harm.

Six in Second Place

Yellow Oriole.

Highly Auspicious.

Nine in Third Place

Oriole at sunset.

No drum,

No clay jar,

No chanting.

Elders lament.

Calamity.

Drums and percussive clay jars are still widely used in the Northwest of China to accompany ritual performances. Feathers and masks have traditionally also featured in these performances.

Song 136
Bang!
He beats the drum
On the Hollow Mound!
Winter and summer,
He waves egret feathers
[For the dance]. . . .
He beats the clay jar. . . .
He waves egret plumes
[For the dance].

Gao Heng takes this song as referring to a female Shaman. See also Hexagram 53/6, Alighting: "Wild geese alight on high hill. Feathers used for Ritual Dance. Auspicious." Plumed dancing is mentioned in Oracle Bone Inscriptions. It may have been in origin shamanistic, taking place at Ancestral Shrines and at royal banquets.

Nine in Fourth Place

A sudden arrival.

Burning.

Death.

Abandonment.

Is this a sudden attack by the enemy?

Six in Fifth Place

Tears flow,

Flood.

Grieving,

Lamenting.

Auspicious.

The wording echoes a love song in the *Book of Songs*:

> *Song 145*
> On the marsh shore
> Mid rushes and lilies
> Lies a beautiful lady:
> Waking and asleep,
> Distraught,
> I weep,
> My tears flow in a flood.

Perhaps this Line refers to the helpless aftermath of the sudden attack of Line 4? But why is it Auspicious nonetheless? For whom?

Nine in Top Place

The King

Goes to War.

A Triumph,

A beheading.

Enemy soldiers

Are taken captive.

No Harm.

The Hexagram culminates in a full-scale Triumph. The Oracle Bone Inscriptions refer to the ceremonial beheading of captives of war: "If the King beheads the captives, will it be opposed by Below and Above?" It is fascinating to compare this Hexagram's brief mantic reference to a Military Triumph with the grand ceremony described in an Inscription on the *Duo You Ding* Bronze Cauldron discovered in 1980, dating probably from the reign of the Zhou King Li (857–842 BC). The Inscription mentions 235 captives beheaded and 23 shackled and held for interrogation, and 117 carts (belonging to the Rong barbarians) captured. On another Inscription, probably from the slightly later reign of King Xuan (827–782 BC), the "illustrious Earl Ji" is recorded as having attacked the Xianyun barbarians, beheaded 500, and shackled 50 captives. Compare also two songs from the *Book of Songs*:

> *Song 168*
> Orioles sing in chorus.

In crowds
We gather southernwood,
We take captives
For questioning,
We return home. . . .
Awe-inspiring
Was our General Nanzhong;
The Xianyun barbarians
Were brought to heel.

(Note the orioles again.) According to Legge (following the traditional commentators), this song is "An Ode of Congratulation on the Return of the Troops from Their Expedition against the Xianyun." Captives are being interrogated, or, as Legge speculates, "put to torture," before their ritual beheading.

Song 178
How foolish were those savage tribes
To make enemy of the great state!
Fangshu our Great Marshal
Laid mighty plans,
Led forth his army.
Took captives for questioning.
Many were his war chariots,
Many and ample.
Like claps of thunder they rumbled.
Illustrious was Fangshu,
And true!
He smote the Xianyun barbarians,
He overawed the tribes of Jing.

According to Legge, this song celebrates Fangshu's "successful conduct of a grand expedition against the tribes of the South." Fangshu's victory was also the occasion for a great military Triumph. Both are traditionally said to have taken place in the late ninth century BC. But the most famous early Chinese Triumph recorded on bronze is the one celebrating the earlier success of a campaign against the barbarians led by a certain Officer Yu in 981 BC. Officer Yu commemorated his appointment by casting a great *ding*-cauldron, now referred to as the Great Cauldron of Yu, one of the most impressive bronzes of the entire period. The inscription reads:

In the twenty-third year of his reign, King Kang of Zhou appointed a
man named Yu, grandson of Nangong Kuo, to act as overseer of the
Supervisors of the Military.

Nangong Kuo had been one of the high ministers mentioned by the Duke of Zhou as serving both King Wen and King Wu, founders of the Zhou dynasty (and therefore the immediate Ancestors of King Kang and his father, King Cheng). Two years later, this same Officer Yu had a second bronze cauldron cast, known as the Lesser

Cauldron of Yu, the inscription on which describes in grand detail the Triumph held to celebrate his decisive military victory over a people known as the Guifang (Devil Territory), who most probably lived in the Ordos area of Northwestern China (today's Inner Mongolia and the northern parts of Shaanxi and Shanxi Provinces). Only parts of a single rubbing of this lengthy inscription still survive (the Cauldron itself, probably discovered in the 1840s, was lost shortly thereafter in the chaos of the Taiping Rebellion). It gives fascinating (and gory) details of a Zhou-dynasty military Triumph, and is a vivid record of early Zhou state Ritual, including a striking reference to Divination.

> It was the eighth month, after the full moon, the day *jiashen*; in the morning dusk, the three officials of the left and the three officials of the right and the many rulers entered to serve the wine. When it became light, the King approached the Zhou Temple and performed the *guo*-libation Rite. The King's state guests were in attendance. They presented their travel robes and faced east. Officer Yu, with many flagpoles and with Devil Territory captives suspended from them ... entered through the Southern Gate and reported, saying: "The King commanded Yu ... to attack Devil Territory, to shackle their chiefs and take trophies. [I] shackled two chiefs, took 482 trophies, captured 13,081 men, captured ... horses, took 30 chariots, 355 oxen, and 38 sheep." The King called out to ... command Officer Yu to enter the gate with his trophies and present them in the Western Passageway.... [He] entered and performed a burnt offering in the Zhou Temple.... [He] entered through the Third Gate and assumed a position in the central court, facing north. Officer Yu made his report.... The guests assumed position. [He] served the guests. The King called out: "Serve!" Yu ... presented guests.... At midmorning, three Zhou [officers] ... entered to serve wine. The King entered the Temple. The ... state guests [were] grandly toasted.... [They] offered a victim in Ancestral Sacrifice to the King of Zhou [King Wen], to King [Wu], and to King Cheng.... The Divination cracks had a pattern. The King toasted. Toast followed upon toast, [made by] the King and the state guests. The King called out ... to command Officer Yu to enter with the booty. All of the booty was registered.

It is a powerful scene, well evoked by Herrlee Glessner Creel, who paraphrases the inscription in his own language:

> The effect is one of great spaces, dimmed light, awe-inspiring and sometimes gruesome pageantry. In two campaigns he (Officer Yu) captured many prisoners and much booty, which he enumerates for each campaign. Combining the two, the total is: three chieftains, five thousand and forty-nine severed left ears (or heads) of the slain. More than thirteen thousand and eighty-one men. More than one hundred and four horses. More than one hundred and thirty vehicles (probably carts rather than chariots). Three hundred and fifty-five cattle; thirty-eighty sheep. The King then congratulates Yu. Yu brings forward the three captive

chiefs, and the King orders that they be interrogated as to the reason they have resisted the Zhou. . . . The interrogation being completed, the three chieftains are decapitated. The thousands of severed ears or heads (*guo*) are then offered as a Burnt Sacrifice.

It should not be forgotten that the period in which this Triumph took place is the very period in which the *I Ching* was finding its first form as a text.

HEXAGRAM 31

G'em

Tingling

JUDGMENT

Fortune.

Sacrifice Received.

Profitable Augury.

Auspicious to take a wife.

The early graph for the Hexagram Name had a battle-axe (*yue*) and a mouth. Perhaps this indicated a battle cry, hence an army coming together, an assembly of warriors under one command. I prefer to follow Waley's reading of the Name, which depends on giving the graph an additional "heart" radical, thus a "tingling feeling." (For the derived sense of Resonance, see Part I.) "Feelings are a class of Omen still believed in all over the world. We say in England, I have a 'feeling' in my bones that such and such a thing will happen. A 'feeling' of tingling in the ears means that someone is praising one." The contemporary commentator He Xin understands the Hexagram to be about sexual foreplay: kissing toes, nibbling calves, etc. Others take it to mean "chopping" (of Sacrificial Victims?) or "wounding." An interesting suggestion (which involves adding not the heart radical, but the metal or bamboo radical) is that this refers to the practice of piercing or lancing boils with bone or stone needles, an early form of acupuncture. The Japanese scholar Akatsuka Kiyoshi speculates that the graph as it occurs in the Oracle Bone Inscriptions may have referred to a magical shamanistic Ritual in which the sheer force of the Shaman's voice influenced the Spirits.

LINES

Six in First Place

Tingling

In the big toe.

 The Lines work their way through a series of repetition and variation (toe, calf, thigh, back, mouth), as in Hexagrams 52 (feet, calves, midriff, chest, face, head) and 53 (stream, rocks, shore, tree, mound, hill). This oral-formulaic pattern is one also found throughout the *Book of Songs*. To give a single example:

Song 11
Feet
Of the unicorn!
Forehead
Of the unicorn!
Horns
Of the unicorn!

Six in Second Place

Tingling

In the calf.

Calamity.

Auspicious

For a dwelling.

 In the modern Chinese Almanac, still in use in many parts of the Chinese-speaking world, certain days are marked as being Auspicious for the construction of a house (also for moving house, demolishing a building, having a haircut, getting married, etc.). This Line may reflect a similar custom. Or else perhaps it means that it is Auspicious to stay inside one's dwelling, not to go out of doors.

Nine in Third Place

A Tingling

In the thigh,

A seizing

Of the flesh.

Going brings trouble.

 This is a difficult Line. I follow Li Jingchi in understanding *sui* as "flesh," not "marrow."

Nine in Fourth Place

Auspicious Augury.

Troubles

Are over.

A coming and going,

A restless fidgeting.

Friends follow

One's thoughts.

 This is the "feeling" that friends are thinking (or talking) about you.

Nine in Fifth Place

Tingling

In the back.

No Regrets.

Six in Top Place

Tingling

At the corners

Of the mouth,

In the cheeks,

On the tongue.

HEXAGRAM 32

Geng

Fixing

JUDGMENT

Fortune.

Sacrifice Received.

No Harm.

Profitable Augury.

A Destination

Profits.

Waley understands Fixing to be a Rite for making permanent the good luck of an Omen. It may have been, as he suggests, an action as simple as drawing circles around Omen-objects, or burying them (possibly they were Oracle Bones), perhaps during the new moon, to make things "last all through the month." One of the old graphs for the Hexagram Name may once have been a moon between two horizontal lines (Heaven and Earth).

LINES

Six in First Place

Deep Fixing

Augurs Calamity.

No Profit.

Fixing does not require Omen-objects to be deeply buried, to be "dug deep." To treat them in this way may only bring harm.

Nine in Second Place

Troubles over.

Nine in Third Place

Unless Power be Fixed,

Disgrace will whelm you.

Augury of Distress.

Confucius quotes this Line (or perhaps a popular saying from which it is taken) in *Analects* 13.22: "Southerners say that unless Power is Fixed, a man can be neither Shaman nor Physician. How true! Unless Power be Fixed, disgrace will whelm you."

Nine in Fourth Place

Hunt.

No game.

A fruitless expedition.

Six in Fifth Place

Power Fixed.

Auspicious Augury for woman.

Calamity for man.

For a woman, constant devotion is appropriate (her Energy should be Fixed on her man), whereas a man should be more flexible and independent.

Six in Top Place

Quake Fixed.

Calamity.

 A Quake that persists, with a repeated series of aftershocks, is indeed a Calamity to be dreaded.

HEXAGRAM 33

D'wen

Piglet

JUDGMENT

Fortune.

Sacrifice Received.

Profitable Augury

In small matters.

The graph for the Hexagram Name contains a piglet. The movement of pigs, wild or domesticated, provided common Omens. As Waley comments, "the 'lucky pig' plays an important part in modern New Year observations in Teutonic countries (e.g., Bavaria and Austria), and doubtless elsewhere. The original text beyond doubt concerned Pig-Omens and Pig-Ritual, but has been mutilated beyond possibility of reconstruction. The movements of swine were closely observed by the Chinese. A herd of swine with white trotters crossing a stream is a portent of heavy rain." This is to be seen in the *Book of Songs*:

> *Song 232*
> We met swine
> With white trotters,
> A herd of them,
> Plunging through waves.
> The Moon was caught
> In a Net.

Deluges of rain.
Soldiers fighting east,
No time for rest.

 Waley comments on this song: "The Net, i.e., the Hyades, was connected by the Chinese, as by us, with rain. . . . Rain falling looks like a net cast over the landscape. The characters for 'net' and 'rain' are in their oldest forms very similar."

LINES

Six in First Place

Piglet's

Tail.

Danger.

A Destination

Serves no purpose.

 Gao Heng mentions the modern practice of removing pigs' tails to hasten the fattening process.

Six in Second Place

Tether it with thongs

Of brown oxhide.

No escape.

 The same oxhide occurs in Hexagram 49/1.

Nine in Third Place

Piglet

Bound.

Pain.

Danger.

Auspicious for rearing slaves,

Men and women.

 The piglet is trussed for Sacrifice.

Nine in Fourth Place

Fine Piglet.

Auspicious

For a noble man,

Trouble

For a small man.

 A gift such as this would be appropriate only for someone in a grand position. In *Analects* 17.1, Yang Huo, a powerful minister of the state of Lu, sent Confucius a piglet (the exact same word as this Hexagram Name), thereby embarrassing him greatly, because acceptance of such a generous gift brought with it certain social obligations. See Part I, Hexagram XXXVIII/1.

Nine in Fifth Place

Piglet

For celebration.

Auspicious Augury.

 A pig for Sacrifice at a Triumph, or possibly a gift for a wedding.

Nine in Top Place

Fat Piglet.

Profit in all things.

 An excellent Sacrificial Victim or gift.

HEXAGRAM 34

D'âd Tsiang

Wound

JUDGMENT

Profitable Augury.

 This Hexagram Name has been interpreted in several ways. The left-hand element in the second word (*Tsiang/Zhuang*) may have been used in the Oracle Bone Inscriptions for a Sacrifice, or a Sacrificial Axe. In Lines 3–6, the theme seems to be pastoral: the references are to a ram and its enclosure, perhaps to the domestication of sheep and goats, also perhaps to sheep as Sacrificial Victims. In both agriculture and Sacrificial Ritual, it was of vital importance to determine whether the animal was "wounded" or was strong and healthy. At the same time, the very strength of the beast could lead to violence and injury, to a wounding. Wang Hai, referred to obliquely in Line 5, was the "patron saint" of animal herding and is mentioned several times in the Oracle Bone Inscriptions.

LINES

Nine in First Place

A Wound

In the foot.

Calamitous attack.

Captives are taken.

禿 Perhaps an Augury taken from the condition of the animal. Perhaps a more general reference to "wounded" soldiers.

Nine in Second Place

Auspicious Augury.

禿 This echoes the brevity of the Judgment.

Nine in Third Place

Small men use

Force.

Noble men use

A net.

Augury of Danger.

A ram butts a fence,

Snags his horns.

禿 The Danger is that injury (a "wound") may be caused by force or violence. Compare Line 6 and Hexagram 44/6. For the uses of rams in Sacrifice, see the *Book of Songs*:

Song 211
With vessels full of bright millet,
With pure Sacrificial Rams,
I make Offering
To the Spirit of the Land
And of the Four Quarters.

Song 272
I bring my Sacrifice:
A ram,

A bull.
May Heaven
Be well pleased!

Song 245
We sacrifice a ram
To the Spirit of the Road. . . .

Nine in Fourth Place

Auspicious Augury.

Troubles are over.

The fence is breached,

The ram unharmed.

The axle of the big cart

Is damaged.

The ram breaks through its confinement. Damage to carriages, carts, and chariots is also mentioned in Hexagrams 9/3 and 26/2. Damage to a vehicle, especially when preparing for war, would seem ominous, quite apart from being expensive to repair. Compare *The Art of War*, chapter 2:

Repairs to chariots and armour;
The daily cost of all this
Will exceed
One thousand taels of silver. . . .
Six-tenths of the public coffers
Are spent
On broken chariots,
Worn-out horses,
Armour and helmets. . . .

Six in Fifth Place

Sheep are lost

At Yi.

No Regret.

This is one of the *I Ching*'s fragmentary references to ancient Chinese myth, and to the origins of sheep farming in China. Wang Hai, nomadic Ancestor of the Royal Dynastic House of Shang, took his herds to pasture in a place called Yi (or Youyi). There he was done to death, either because he committed adultery with a local chieftain's wife or because of a dispute over grazing grounds, or both. Compare also Hexagram 56/6.

Six in Top Place

Ram butts fence;

Neither Retreat

Nor Advance is possible.

Nothing Profits.

Auspicious Augury

In hard times.

 The ram is strong and impulsive, and as a result is caught in the fence and wounded.

HEXAGRAM 35

Tsie

Forward

JUDGMENT

Horses are presented

To Prince Kang.

They breed;

They mate

Three times a day.

This Hexagram is concerned mostly with military matters. The early graph for the Hexagram Name shows two arrows, above some sort of container, presented as gifts. Prince Kang was the ninth son of King Wen, and therefore the younger brother of King Wu and also of the Duke of Zhou (regent after King Wu's death, during the early years of King Cheng). In the Inscription on the *gui*-vessel of Prince Kang (now in the British Museum), King Cheng gives orders for Kang to be enfeoffed as the Marquis of Wei, in what had been part of the old territory of the Shang rulers. Horses are believed to have been brought down from the northwestern borderlands, from as early as 1200 BC. Until the fifth or fourth century BC, they were used exclusively to pull chariots for Warfare and Hunting. Chariots were regularly buried in tombs together with horses and sometimes charioteers. Horses were often offered in Sacrifice. The Qiang, traditional enemies of the Shang, were a nomadic people—the early graph of their name (and indeed the modern one) contains the element for "sheep." They were horse breeders, and were also referred to as Duoma Qiang, the "Qiang of many horses." They themselves were often taken captive and offered in Sacrifice. Many Oracle Bone Inscriptions attest to this: "Should we offer Qiang tribesmen in the present Sacrifice?" "Should we conduct the *di*-Sacrifice to the Deities of the Quarters? Should we offer one Qiang tribesman? Should we offer two dogs, split open one ox?"

LINES

Six in First Place

Forward,

Pressing forward.

Auspicious Augury.

No Regret.

Captives abound.

No Harm.

 A military campaign, perhaps against a border tribe, is progressing well. Many captives are taken.

Six in Second Place

Forward,

Onward to victory.

Auspicious Augury.

Great Blessing

From the Royal Grandmother.

 Prince Kang's Royal Grandmother would have been the mother of King Wen; she was probably a Shang princess. This would explain why he was put in charge of an old Shang territory after the conquest.

Six in Third Place

Folk

Advance.

Regrets are over.

 The word for "folk," *zhong*, occurs frequently in the Oracle Bone Inscriptions. The graph shows three men beneath either the sun or an eye, perhaps a group toiling in the heat of the day, or under the watchful eye of an overseer. Ping-ti Ho summarizes the Oracle Bone references to *zhong* as including (1) serfs laboring in the royal fields or fields belonging to lords and officials, (2) retainers participating in the Royal Hunts, and (3) soldiers; but never Sacrificial Victims (this being reserved for barbarian captives).

Nine in Fourth Place

Forward,

Like a large rat.

Augury of Danger.

 Timidity and lack of resolution are dangerous.

Six in Fifth Place

Troubles are over.

Arrows lost,

Found.

No grief.

Destination Auspicious.

Profit in all things.

Nine in Top Place

Probe the enemy,

Then forward!

Attack the city!

Danger.

Auspicious.

No Harm.

Augury of Trouble.

 Compare *The Art of War*, chapter 6:

> Probe him;
> Know his strengths
> And weaknesses.

Despite precautions, all initiatives are fraught with unpredictable Dangers.

HEXAGRAM 36

Miang Dier

Pelican Calling

JUDGMENT

Profitable Augury

In hard times.

It was Li Jingchi who in 1931 first went beyond the "philosophical" reading (Darkness) of this Hexagram and "dredged up" (to use his own words) an earlier and more poetic bird-meaning. There are many early songs that talk of "birds flying" and the movement of their wings.

Song 28
Swallow, swallow,
Flying swallow!
Your wings dip
High and low.
My love is marrying another.
Far across fields
I follow her;
I gaze after her
But cannot see her.
My tears fall
Like rain.

Song 181
The wild geese fly,
Beating their wings.
Our men are on the march,
Toiling in the wilds.
Alas for their sad plight!
And for the widows
Left behind!

This whole Hexagram is laden with undertones of separation, distress, grief, and danger ("hard times"). As in Hexagram 62/1, the bird in flight is Ominous. Hexagram 36 was obtained through Yarrow Stalk Divination in 537 BC, as the *Zuo Commentary* records (Duke Zhao, Year 5). In that instance, in a complex interpretation, the Diviner related the Hexagram to the sun, while implying that there was also a bird lurking somewhere under the name. There is also some speculation that this whole Hexagram, which shows traces of history and myth, may refer to a solar eclipse, and that somehow, at the same time, a bird is implicated, possibly a bird residing in the sun (as in the Chu funeral shroud excavated at Mawangdui). The *Bamboo Annals* contains a record of an eclipse for the year 957 BC which also involves birds: "In the nineteenth year of King Zhao there was a comet in the Lunar Lodge *ziwei*. Duke She and Lord Xin followed the King to attack Chu. The Heavens were greatly obscured, and pheasants and hares were all greatly disturbed. The six armies were lost in the Han River. The King died."

LINES

Nine in First Place

Pelican Calling

In flight,

Left wing dipped.

A noble man travels;

He fasts three days.

A Destination.

The Master

Finds fault.

霓 The graph for *yi*, with the addition of the bird element, is the name for a type of pelican. This magnificent bird has been known in China since ancient times. This is one of several Line Statements (compare Hexagram 61/2, "A crane calls in the shade") that find echoes in the *Book of Songs*.

Song 33
The cock-pheasant flies,
Flapping his wings.
Love has brought me down.
The cock-pheasant flies,
Cries high and low.
My lord has worn away
My heart!

Song 216
The ducks on the dam
Gather in their left wings.
May my lord
Enjoy a long life!

Waley thought the gathering in (and hence "dipping") of wings portended Blessing heaped upon Blessing.

Song 229
Pelicans on the dam,
Cranes in the wood.
That tall man
Vexes me sore.

Ducks on the dam
Gather in their left wings.
My lord is not good;
He chops and changes.

Six in Second Place

Pelican Calling.

His left leg

Is wounded.

A mighty horse

Is gelded.

Auspicious.

 King Mu of Zhou went on a Hunt one day. A black bird fluttered about him and then perched on the yoke of his chariot. The driver lashed out at it with the reins, whereupon the horse bolted, causing the chariot to overturn and injure the King's left leg. Could this legend, the scholar Gao Heng wonders, be somewhere behind this Line? Has the bird been shot? For the horse, which is still mighty though gelded, compare Hexagram 59/1.

Nine in Third Place

Pelican Calling

In the Southern Hunt.

A big head

Is captured.

Haste is not indicated.

 Could this be a reference to King Zhao's disastrous expedition in 957 BC into the southern state of Chu during the solar eclipse already mentioned in relation to the Judgment? In the enigmatic words of the *Heavenly Questions*: "Lord Zhao did much traveling. What did it profit him to meet that white pelican when he went to the Southland?" Could the "big head" have been that of the unfortunate king? Or else possibly that of a large beast captured in the Southern Hunt?

Six in Fourth Place

It enters

The left side of the belly;

It strikes

The Calling Pelican.

Go out of door and courtyard

With care.

The pelican is wounded; the arrow (of the hunter) finds its mark.

Six in Fifth Place

Viscount Ji's

Pelican Call.

Profitable Augury.

Viscount Ji, minister (and uncle) of Zhou Xin, the "wicked" last king of Shang, is often cited as an example of fortitude in adversity. He remonstrated with the King, allowing his hair to become disheveled and feigning madness. As a consequence he was imprisoned and treated as a slave. His admonition of the Shang king is likened to the warning Call of the Pelican. Under the Zhou dynasty, Ji was sent to settle at what is now Pyongyang.

Six in Top Place

No light.

Darkness.

It climbs to Heaven,

It enters Earth.

It has been suggested that this may refer to a meteorite. In one historical source, meteorites are described as falling to Earth with a sound like the cry of a bird. But according to another, simpler understanding, it is an arrow.

HEXAGRAM 37

Ka Niên

Family

JUDGMENT

Profitable Augury

For a woman.

The Hexagram Name is, literally, "family people," hence the various dependent members of the household—women, children, and servants. The graph for "family," from the Oracle Bone script onward, has a roof over a pig. It portrays the individual household, as opposed to the larger collective or clan. The pig was an important source of nourishment and fertilizer, and it was kept enclosed, in or close to the home. Pigpens may have doubled as privies as early as the Shang dynasty. Pigs (along with other domesticated animals—dogs, oxen, horses, and sheep) were also used as Sacrificial Victims to be offered to the Ancestors—the Spirits that bound together the very notion of Family, always at the center of Chinese culture. "The Family is the unit of society, and filial piety is its bulwark," commented Creel in 1936. "This old patriarchal form of Family Life," wrote Richard Wilhelm in 1928, "in which the piously revered Ancestors form a vast community with the living successors, still exists in China in the country, and will continue to do so for a long time; for China is, in the mass, a peasant people, and peasant people have sound and enduring traditions." Derk Bodde comments: "So strong, indeed, was the stress on Family that in later Confucian thinking the state itself was regarded as simply an enlargement of the Family system. . . . The Family was inseparable from the cult of the Ancestors. These Ancestors received regular food offerings from their descendants, by whom they were consulted on all important occasions. They were powerful Spirits capable not only of aiding their own Family, but also of injuring anyone outside the Family who might arouse their ire."

LINES

Nine in First Place

The door of the Family

Is barred.

Troubles are over.

 In Chinese the word for "door" is the same as that for "gate." The graph has "double doors"—like those of a saloon bar in the old American Wild West. In the Mawangdui silk manuscript, we read simply: "The home has a door." In the traditional text, the word for "barred" shows a door with a piece of wood wedged in it—the wooden bolt that keeps the door firmly closed. By making sure the door is well barred, Home and Family (the word is one and the same) are clearly delineated and secured against the outside world. "A Chinese Family house is an entity which can be closed to the outside world by one big door. . . . The securing of that door from the inside is done with a cross-beam, or a pair of wooden bolts, one above the other."

Six in Second Place

Nothing is neglected.

Food is prepared within.

Auspicious Augury.

 This—the preparation of food for consumption and for Sacrifice—is the woman's occupation, and it must be undertaken dutifully. "Food within," *zhongkui*, became a shorthand expression for "wife."

Nine in Third Place

The Family

Wails and moans.

Regret.

Danger.

Auspicious.

Wife and child

Giggle and snigger.

In conclusion,

Trouble.

The contrast is between a Family that suffers, but learns from its suffering, and a spoilt, wealthy Family whose frivolity leads to ruin.

Six in Fourth Place

Family wealth.

Highly Auspicious.

The Chinese words for material "wealth" and for Spiritual Blessing, or "happiness," are closely related. They both derive from a graphic element depicting a full wine vessel, that universal emblem of well-being!

Nine in Fifth Place

The King proceeds

To his Family Home.

No Distress.

Auspicious.

The King's Family Home was the Ancestral Temple, the place where the Ancestral Tablets were kept. If the King is on his way there, then a Sacrifice will be made, and the Ancestors will be propitiated. Compare the Judgments of Hexagrams 45 and 59.

Nine in Top Place

Captives are terrified.

Auspicious Conclusion.

 Compare Hexagram 14/5. Captives are being taken on as household slaves (and therefore part of the Family). At first they are terrified and defiant, but ultimately they submit and all is well.

HEXAGRAM 38

K'iwer

Watching

JUDGMENT

Auspicious

In small matters.

 Waley explains this Hexagram Name as referring to the tenth day, *gui*, of the ten-day cycle; that was the day when Omens were taken during the Shang dynasty. The graph for the Name has two eyes above the cyclical sign.

LINES

Nine in First Place

Troubles

Are over.

A horse

Is lost.

Do not pursue it.

It will return

Of its own accord.

An ill-looking person

Is seen.

No Harm.

 These may all be Images to be seen in, or watched from, the sky. The horse may be the Heavenly Horse, which regularly becomes invisible ("lost") only to be seen again north of the constellation known as the Heavenly Swine—i.e., it is regularly lost and found. It returns. The Chinese of the Zhou dynasty, comments Shaughnessy, were "a society of sky-watchers, who invested the nocturnal luminaries with earthly qualities." They thought it possible to predict the future by observing these. Also, the loss of actual horses was a frequent cause of distress.

> *Song 31*
> Here we stopped;
> Here we stayed.
> Horses were lost
> And found again,
> Down in the woods.

The sighting of an ill-looking or deformed person, Waley comments, can be experienced as an Omen, an "*angang*, or chance meeting." It is still commonly believed by peasants in the remoter parts of Europe, he adds in a footnote, that to meet a priest is unlucky, to meet a prostitute, lucky.

Nine in Second Place

Master

Met in the lane.

No Harm.

 This Omen is connected with meeting an important person in an unlikely place.

Six in Third Place

Seen:

A cart dragged,

An ox resisting,

A man branded,

A nose cut off.

No Beginning,

A Conclusion.

These may all be constellations. The Ox or Dragged Ox is one of the astronomical divisions known as Lunar Mansions, situated opposite the Ghost Cart (*Yugui*). The Ox sets just as the Cart is rising, and could thus be said, in a sense, to "drag" the Cart. The Ghost Cart was said to preside over punishments and executions, acting for the Ancestors as the Sky's Eye. Waley is more literal: "To see a wagon being pulled; the ox, one horn up and one horn down; the man clean-shaven and with his nose cut off." Li Jingchi sees a more political (and cinematic) scenario: A transport-slave drives a cart, viewed by a traveler; the ox, one horn up and one horn down, struggles to pull the cart; the cart is stuck. The slave pushes. At this point the traveler sees the tattoo (brand) on the slave's forehead and notices that his nose is missing. Although at first the cart will not move (there is "no Beginning"), eventually ("a Conclusion") it is released (from the mud).

Nine in Fourth Place

A fox

Is watched.

A legless man

Is met.

Captives are exchanged.

Danger.

No Harm.

The fox may be Sirius, the Dog Star. There is no bad luck in seeing a "legless" man. I follow Wen Yiduo; others think the man was "shaven."

Six in Fifth Place

Troubles

Are over.

In the Ancestral Temple,

Flesh is eaten.

No Harm

In a Destination.

In the Ancestral Temple, flesh offered in Sacrifice is eaten.

Nine in Top Place

A fox

Is watched.

Also seen:

Pigs

Carrying earth,

A cart

Laden with ghosts,

A taut bowstring

Loosed.

No bandit raid,

A marriage party.

Traveling.

Meeting rain.

Auspicious.

禿 This Line also seems filled with astronomical imagery. The Lunar Mansion known as the Ghost Cart corresponds to the constellation known to Western astronomy as Cancer. Immediately south of this, in Canis Major and Puppis, is a Bow and Arrow, pointed at Sirius, the Dog Star (the Heavenly Wolf). According to Wolfram Eberhard, in southern China (Guangdong Province) "ghost cart" was the name of a special kind of owl, an evil bird which attacked children. It also had astrological connections and could appear as a comet in the sky. Waley comments: "The stretching and then loosening of the bowstring was a Ritual for the expulsion of evil influences." The marriage party (mock abduction of a bride) also comes in Hexagrams 3/2 and 22/4.

HEXAGRAM 39

Gân

Stumbling

JUDGMENT

Profit

To West and South,

No Profit

To East and North.

Profit

To see a big man.

Auspicious Augury.

The Hexagram Name is a simple word meaning "to stumble" or "to be lame." Beneath a phonetic element, it has a foot. This Hexagram is mainly about events taking a turn for the better after an initial setback or "stumble." Arthur Waley comments: "Involuntary movements such as stumbling, knocking things over, etc., are extremely familiar as Omens. William the Conqueror is supposed to have stumbled on reaching English soil, and skilfully averted the Omen. In the Pacific stumbling is an Omen of Misfortune or death. . . . The fundamental meaning of the Name is 'foot-impediment.' It will be noticed that here stumbling is a good Omen. To stumble going upstairs means in England that one is going to be married."

LINES

Six in First Place

Stumbling

Forward,

Returning with ease.

 This, according to Li Jingchi, is a simple case of someone (perhaps a merchant) who sets out with difficulty but returns with matters resolved. The "stumbling" is easily corrected.

Six in Second Place

King and servant

Stumble along,

Through no fault of their own.

Nine in Third Place

Stumbling there,

Ambling gently back.

 A correction, a change of heart, brings a favorable turn of events, similar to that of the First Line. For the "gently" ambling, *fan*, see *Song 220*:

> When guests first take their seats,
> How well
> They behave!
> While still sober,
> How gently mannered
> They are!

Six in Fourth Place

Stumbling forward,

Rumbling along in cart.

 A merchant sets out on foot in the face of difficulties; he returns seated in a cart.

Nine in Fifth Place

A big

Stumble.

Friends come.

 Things get off to a bad start, but help is at hand. *Peng,* "friends," can also mean "strings of cowries," and so financial aid.

Six in Top Place

Stumbling forward,

Coming back laden.

Auspicious.

Profits to see big man.

 Again, an expedition starts with difficulty, but ends with great success. The big man would be a person respected in the community, perhaps a Shaman.

HEXAGRAM 40

Kêg

Release

JUDGMENT

Profit

To South and West.

No Destination.

Auspicious

For coming and for return.

Destination.

Auspicious

In early morning.

The graph of the Hexagram Name shows two hands with a knife splitting horns from an ox head. The same word is used (but with a variant pronunciation) in the famous parable of the Taoist Art of Jointing, in the *Book of Master Zhuang*: "Cook Ding was jointing an ox for Lord Wenhui. . . ." Cook Ding carves up the ox "finding his way through the joints by intuition," in such a way that it comes apart without further effort. From the way things come apart or are dismembered, the Name comes to mean the way one thing is "released" or "liberated" from another (see Part I). Similar advice about cardinal directions is offered in Hexagrams 2 and 39. The graph for "early morning," *su*, has a kneeling man and the moon. The overall significance of the whole Hexagram does not (as they say . . .) lend itself easily to interpretation.

LINES

Six in First Place

No Harm.

 One of the shortest and pithiest Line Statements in the *I Ching*.

Nine in Second Place

Taken in Hunt,

Three foxes;

A bronze arrow.

Auspicious Divination.

 For the Shang and Zhou kings, the Hunt was an important Ritual preparation for Warfare. Compare Hexagrams 7/5, 32/4, and 57/4.

Six in Third Place

Baggage and carts

Attract marauders.

Augury of Distress.

 Bandits attack, taking advantage of the fact that the hunters are laden with their catch, or the soldiers are weighed down with their equipment. Compare this with advice given in chapter 2 of *The Art of War* (already quoted in Hexagram 34/4), to avoid being encumbered, with the expense and inconvenience of "broken chariots, worn-out horses, armour and helmets," and instead to travel light. A "wise general feeds off the enemy":

One peck
Of enemy provisions
Is worth twenty

Carried from home;
One picul
Of enemy fodder
Is worth twenty
Carried from home.

Nine in Fourth Place

Thumbs

Are released.

Cowries

Are given.

Captives

Are dismembered.

 "Relax your thumb (on the bowstring)," Waley paraphrases. "A friend (not an enemy) is coming." He takes *peng* as "friends" rather than "cowries." This then becomes a metaphorical instruction to relax unnecessary precautions. In his earlier 1933 study, Waley speculated that this Line Statement might contain a reference to the practice of removing the thumbs of prisoners. I follow Kunst, who suggests that the last two words mean dismembering the captives altogether, prior to Sacrifice.

Six in Fifth Place

A noble man's bonds

Are released.

Auspicious.

Captives

Among small men.

 This seems to be about the conclusion of a war.

Six in Top Place

The Duke

Aims at a hawk

On a high wall.

He gets it.

 A simple incident, whose relevance is, however, obscure.

HEXAGRAM 41

Swêng

Decrease

JUDGMENT

Captives.

Supremely Auspicious.

No Harm.

A Divination

Is possible.

A Destination

Profits.

What shall be used?

Two bronze *gui*-tureens

For the Offering.

This Hexagram forms a pair with the following Hexagram. They deal with the balance in the dynamic of diminution and growth. Both Hexagrams have Line Statements referring to gifts of Turtles. *Gui*-tureens are also mentioned in Hexagram 29/4.

LINES

Nine in First Place

A Sacrifice

Is swiftly accomplished.

No Harm.

A decreased

Libation.

There may be a need to perform the Ritual quickly and to reduce the amount of wine used.

Nine in Second Place

Profitable Augury.

Calamitous Advance.

No Decrease.

Increase.

An Auspicious time for a judicious Increase, but not for a foolhardy Advance.

Six in Third Place

Three travelers

Are decreased by one.

One traveler

Gains a friend.

The first part of this old adage is similar to "Two's company, three's a crowd." A third person interferes with the easy dynamic of two men traveling. The second part refers to the natural tendency of the lone traveler to acquire friends. The advantages of Increase and Decrease are relative to the situation.

Six in Fourth Place

A speedy Sacrifice

Decreases disease,

Hastens

Joy.

No Harm.

 A Ritual can reduce the severity of an illness. Joy as an expression of healing and well-being can also be found in Hexagrams 25/5 and 58/4. Many Oracle Bone Inscriptions ask about illness or disease: "On the evening of the *yi* day, X fell sick. Was there Misfortune?" "Does His Majesty have a disease of the eyes?"

Six in Fifth Place

Increase.

A mighty Turtle gift,

And ten strings

Of cowries.

Not to be refused.

Most Auspicious.

Turtles were presented as Tribute Offerings to the Shang kings, perhaps from as far away as Burma. The turtle, a creature originating in primordial waters, was sacred to the early Chinese, as to many peoples around the world. It was venerated as a receptacle of Vital Force and Longevity, and (perhaps because of its Longevity) as a source of Oracular Knowledge, of insight (through Turtle Shell Divination) into the workings of the Universe, an insight that could not be denied or "refused." The turtle is indeed one of the longest-surviving natural species on the planet, dating back possibly 200 million years. It is also one of the longest-lived. Some extant types of turtle live to beyond a hundred years. The physical shape of the turtle was for the Chinese a representation of the cosmos, the dome of the upper shell, or carapace, resembling Heaven, and the flat undershell, or plastron, resembling Earth. (See also under Hexagram 27/1.) "The vault of the Heavens can be conceived as a gigantic Turtle Shell suspended above the Earth, held up by four mountain-like Turtle legs, at the corners of the world." From late Shang times, the carefully prepared turtle plastron was commonly used for Divination, along with the shoulder bones of the ox. According to an old and no doubt apocryphal legend, the Luo Shu Diagram, the Chinese Magic Square, appeared out of the waters of the Luo River on the back of a turtle. Turtles were a gateway to the supernatural world. They made it possible to know, by Divination, the Mind of Heaven, the judgment of the Sovereign on High. They were most probably sacrificed before being used for Divination, and in this way came to possess a special relationship with the Spirits. It is possible that the shell was still further consecrated by being smeared with the blood of a sacrificed bull. In later times, the Turtle, under its fancy alchemical name Dark Warrior, *xuanwu*, Creature of the North, came to embody the Yin forces of Earth and Winter. It was often pictured coupling with a snake. According to the Han-dynasty dictionary *Shuowen*, the turtle was obliged to mate with a snake in order to reproduce. This has been traced to the Chinese notion that all turtles are female, which view in its turn probably arose from the anatomical fact that the genitals of the turtle are hidden within the cloaca, and there is no visible external organ to mark the sex. "It is a dark, Yin creature, patient, cold-blooded, fond of moisture and prone to hide." Later the word "turtle" became a vulgar term of abuse, partly through the perceived resemblance between the turtle head and the glans penis. For cowries, see Hexagrams 2, 42/2, and 51/2, and the marriage song:

> *Song 176*
> Thick grows the tarragon
> In the center
> Of the mound.
> I have seen my Lord:
> He gave me cowries,
> A hundred strings.

Strings of cowrie shells were often given "as a mark of esteem" by feudal lords to their vassals. A gift of many strings of cowries was important enough to justify a Temple ceremony of presentation by the King.

Nine in Top Place

No Decrease.

Increase.

No Harm.

Auspicious Augury.

Profitable Destination.

A servant is gained,

With no family.

The word for "servant," *chen*, is used for a variety of subordinates, from bonded servants or serfs (bound to the soil, "men of few rights, few opportunities, and few pleasures"), to captives of war, retainers, and ministers of the King. Over the centuries it came to be used as a humble way of referring to oneself ("your humble servant"). "Gifts of slaves, made by the King and others, are very frequent indeed. They are often enumerated, not as so many individuals, but as so many families." Here in the Top Line it is clearly stated that the servant has no family. The original graph for *chen* was a slanting picture of an eye, and it has been suggested that this represents the servant's groveling attitude toward his master. Male servants were *chen*, female servants *qie* (later the term for a concubine). *Zuo Commentary*, Duke Xiang, Year 10: "All the servants, male and female, fled." The relationship between a noble man (*jun*) and his subordinate (*chen*) became one of the five fundamental relationships in the Confucian social order.

HEXAGRAM 42

Iêk

Increase

JUDGMENT

Destination

Profits.

Profits

To cross a big stream.

 This Hexagram forms a pair with the preceding Hexagram. The graph of the Name shows a bowl brimming with liquid, overflowing. Hence Increase. It is interesting that on certain early Oracle Bone Inscriptions this word was sometimes used interchange-ably with the *yi* of *I Ching* (*Yijing*). This may have been related to an Oracle Bone graph for *yi* (Change) in which water is poured from one container into another—hence the associated meanings of a gift offered ("Have a drink!"), of a Change in Nature (liquid decanted), and of "plenitude" (one container filled from another). Such connections are speculative, but they are nonetheless interesting. The Hexagram as a whole seems to be concerned with historical and other situations in which certain elements tend toward "plenitude" or success.

LINES

Nine in First Place

Profits

To embark

On a great enterprise.

Supremely Auspicious.

No Harm.

Great enterprises might have included such projects as the building of new capitals (e.g., the Zhou capitals at Mount Qi and Feng) or the casting of great bronze vessels. Before embarking on any such large-scale works, a Rite of Divination would surely have been performed, and Line Statements such as this may have resulted.

Six in Second Place

Increase.

A Mighty Turtle gift,

Cowries,

Ten strings.

Not to be refused.

An Auspicious Augury

In perpetuity.

The King

Sacrifices

To High God.

Auspicious.

This "gift" may refer to the heavy ransom paid to the Shang by the Zhou for the release of King Wen from prison.

Six in Third Place

Increase.

Calamity.

No Harm

In an enterprise.

Captives are taken.

Report made to the Duke

In the Middle Hall.

A *gui*-tablet,

A tablet of Jade.

 The *gui*-tablet was a scepter of authority.

Six in Fourth Place

A report made

In the Middle Hall.

The Duke acts in accordance.

It Profits the Folk

To migrate.

 This may be a reference to the forced migration of the Shang people after the Zhou conquest.

Nine in Fifth Place

Captives.

A Sacrifice

Of hearts.

No interrogation.

Supremely Auspicious.

A Sacrifice

Of hearts.

Power.

Nine in Top Place

No Increase.

A striking.

Purpose maintained.

A Fixing Ritual

Is not performed.

Calamity.

 Support is not forthcoming. One can only rely on one's own strength of Purpose. For the *heng* Fixing Ritual, see Hexagram 32/1 and Judgment.

HEXAGRAM 43

Kiwet

Tripping

JUDGMENT

Displayed

At the King's court.

Captives cry out.

Danger.

A report from town.

No Profit in battle.

A Destination

Profits.

As with Hexagram 39, here the Hexagram Name refers to an involuntary movement seen as an Omen, and sometimes causing injury.

LINES

Nine in First Place

Toes

Are wounded.

No victory in a Destination.

Harm.

 This injury seriously affects the chances of success.

Nine in Second Place

Fear.

Crying out.

Battle

Evening and night.

No cause for anxiety.

 This nighttime raid by the "enemy" may contain a reference to the *rong* or *quan-rong* (Dog Rong) barbarians, who were a recurring problem during the early Zhou dynasty. The townsfolk are afraid, but all ends well.

Nine in Third Place

Cheekbones

Are wounded.

Calamity.

A noble man trips,

Alone.

He encounters rain,

Drenched and angry.

No Harm.

 Despite the injury and his discomfiture, no irreversible harm is done.

Nine in Fourth Place

Skinless

Buttocks.

Hobbling,

Leading sheep.

Troubles

Are over.

Words

Are heard.

Disbelief.

 It has been suggested that the "hobbling" refers to the Great Yu, mythical tamer of the flood, who according to many legends suffered greatly as a result of his Herculean task. The long immersion in water caused him to have difficulty walking. The Hobbling Steps of Yu later became a shamanistic dance. See Hexagram 44/3. In the *Zuo Commentary*, Duke Xuan, Year 12 (596 BC), the Viscount of Chu lays siege to the capital of the state of Zheng. The Earl of Zheng, realizing that defeat is inevitable, comes out to meet his adversary "stripped bare and leading a sheep," begging for clemency.

Nine in Fifth Place

A goat

Trips

Mid-road.

No Harm.

Apparently an Auspicious sign.

Six in Top Place

Dogs

Bark.

In the end,

Calamity.

 The barking of dogs was considered an ill Omen.

HEXAGRAM 44

Kôh

Encounter

JUDGMENT

A strong woman.

Do not take her

To wife.

 The Hexagram Name refers to a mating. Most of this Hexagram warns of an Inauspicious Encounter. In the Mawangdui silk manuscript, the Name is written with the homophonous word meaning "dog."

LINES

Six in First Place

Silk

Is spooled

On a bronze spindle.

Auspicious Divination.

A Destination

Brings Calamity.

A tethered sow

Is dragged,

Hobbles.

 The sow may be destined for Sacrifice. The connection (if there is one) between the spooled silk and the sow is not clear.

Nine in Second Place

Fish

In the kitchen.

No Harm.

No Profit

In a Hosting Ritual.

 The Hosting Ritual was an important element in early Chinese religion. The simplest early graph has man under roof. It is referred to frequently in the Oracle Bone Inscriptions: "Should His Majesty conduct a Hosting Sacrifice to Shang Jia and the Sun?" See Hexagram 20/4. Through such Sacrificial Offerings, Ancestors (or Kings) were propitiated, made welcome, made to feel at home.

Nine in Third Place

Skinless

Buttocks.

Hobbling.

Danger.

No great Harm.

 See Hexagram 43/4 on the first part of this Line.

Nine in Fourth Place

No fish

In the kitchen.

Augury of Calamity.

 It is impossible to offer even fish as Sacrifice.

Nine in Fifth Place

A gourd

Is bound

With purple willow.

A Jade Talisman

Is contained.

It drops

From Heaven.

 A meteorite? A gourd bound into the shape of a bottle gourd, traditional receptacle for things magical or Taoist?

Nine in Top Place

Encounter

Of horns.

Distress.

No Harm.

 A locking of horns.

HEXAGRAM 45

Dzuts

Deranged

JUDGMENT

Sacrifice received.

The King proceeds

To his Temple.

Profits

To see a big man.

Sacrifice received.

Profitable Augury.

Large Sacrifice

Is Auspicious.

A Destination

Profits.

In the Shanghai Museum bamboo-strip text, the Hexagram Name has a "mouth" radical. In the Mawangdui silk manuscript it has no radical and is simply the word for "soldier." Li Jingchi makes a connection with similar graphs having the "heart" and "sickness" radicals. Soldiers and captives were understandably afflicted in this way, "deranged," traumatized. Where it occurs in the Line Statements, I take it to refer to the distress and agitation of terrified captives (see also Hexagram 37/6). Both this Hexagram and the next refer to the *Yue* Sacrifice (see Second Line). This was a Summer Sacrifice of vegetable offerings to all the Ancestors entitled to special Sacrifices, the number of offerings depending on rank.

LINES

Six in First Place

Captives,

Without success.

Disorderly,

Deranged.

Wailing,

Bursts of laughter.

No cause for anxiety.

No Harm

In a Destination.

 There have been many attempts to reconstruct the meaning of this Line Statement. I maintain the focus on the plight of captives destined for Sacrifice. Li Jingchi thinks the captives have run away.

Six in Second Place

Auspicious,

For a lengthy period.

No Harm.

Profits

To offer captives.

At the *Yue* Sacrifice.

Captives were sacrificed in addition to the vegetable Offerings.

Six in Third Place

Deranged,

Wailing.

No Profit.

No Harm

In a Destination.

Slight Distress.

 As so often, a number of formulaic expressions have attached themselves to the situation, perhaps from a single instance of Divination.

Nine in Fourth Place

Highly Auspicious.

No Harm.

 Perhaps a general comment on the desirability of the Sacrifice.

Nine in Fifth Place

Deranged

At their post.

No Harm.

No captives.

Supreme Augury in perpetuity.

Troubles over.

This Line does not yield a clear meaning. It may be that in the end "booty," rather than captives, was taken and offered.

Six in Top Place

Moaning,

Weeping.

No Harm.

The captives know they are to be sacrificed.

HEXAGRAM 46

Sieng

Ascent

JUDGMENT

Supreme Fortune.

Sacrifice Received.

Profits

To see a big man.

No cause for sorrow.

Auspicious

To march South.

 Ascent is seen as Auspicious in all Line Statements of this Hexagram. The Name was a graph for a unit of measure, probably a container with a handle; it was also used to mean the raising up of something (perhaps in such a container?) in Offering or as Sacrifice, somewhat like the elevation of the Host in Christian worship. More generally, it came to mean to rise upward, as in the Ascent of a Mountain.

LINES

Six in First Place

A highly Auspicious

Ascent.

 This may be the Ascent of smoke from a Sacrifice.

Nine in Second Place

Profits

To offer captives

At the *Yue* Sacrifice.

No Harm.

 This is identical to Hexagram 45/2.

Nine in Third Place

Ascent

To an empty city.

 Perhaps this was the ruined capital of the Shang dynasty, abandoned after the Zhou conquest.

Six in Fourth Place

The King makes Sacrifice

On Mount Qi.

Auspicious.

No Harm.

The Zhou had their capital at Mount Qi before moving east under King Wen, to Feng. In 1977, remains of a Zhou Ancestral Palace were discovered in the vicinity of Mount Qi, in Shaanxi Province, complete with a vault of some seventeen thousand pieces of Turtle Shell, some inscribed with Divination texts.

Six in Fifth Place

Auspicious Augury.

Ascent of the terrace.

 The terrace is stepped. The ascent takes place one level at a time.

Six in Top Place

Ascent

Into darkness.

Profitable Augury,

Unceasing perseverance.

 Perseverance can prevail over darkness.

HEXAGRAM 47

K'wen

Pressed

JUDGMENT

Sacrifice received.

Auspicious Augury

For a big man.

No Harm.

Words.

Disbelief.

The Hexagram Name (the graph has tree within an enclosure, confined, unable to spread naturally) conveys the general idea of suffering and hardship, of oppression and confinement, of being hemmed in and cooped up, of being in dire straits. The "big man" may refer to the Shaman. In the course of this Hexagram, someone suffers imprisonment (perhaps unjustly). He is harshly punished, but somehow is able to escape from confinement.

LINES

Six in First Place

Buttocks

Pressed

By a wooden staff.

A dark valley

Entered.

For three years,

Nothing is seen.

Calamity.

The dark valley may be a prison. The man is beaten with a wooden staff and thrown into prison. He is in the "walled city of gloom," the "slough of despond."

Nine in Second Place

Pressed by

Wine and food.

The Crimson Greaves

Are at hand.

A Sacrificial Offering

Profits.

Calamitous

For Attack.

No Harm.

The first phrase implies overindulgence. Confucius spoke of never being "confined," or overcome, stupefied, by wine—he was, in other words, able to "hold his drink." A lesser man is "mired" in wine and sensual pleasure. The Crimson Greaves may have been a regional barbarian population. This Line Statement may be suggesting that captives from that region be used for Sacrifice.

Six in Third Place

Pressed

By stone.

He grasps a thorny bush.

Enters the Palace.

Does not see his wife.

Calamity.

 A man experiences a testing ordeal (he is imprisoned, made to sit on the "stone of repentance" in a "thorny" enclosure). He returns home, only to discover (unlike Odysseus) that his wife is no longer there to greet him. This Line Statement comes in the *Zuo Commentary*, in an entry for the year 548 BC, when a Yarrow Divination advises a nobleman of the state of Qi (present-day Shandong) not to enter into an Inauspicious marriage with a beautiful widow. The nobleman goes ahead regardless, with disastrous consequences (his whole family is eliminated).

Nine in Fourth Place

Coming slowly,

Pressed

In a bronze chariot.

Distress.

Conclusion.

 Despite "confinement" (the "bronze chariot" is perhaps being used to transport a criminal), he is eventually set free. Or perhaps he is put to death?

Nine in Fifth Place

Nose and feet

Are cut off.

Pressed by

The Scarlet Greaves.

He is gradually released.

Profits

To offer Sacrifice.

 These are the same as the Crimson Greaves. This time it is they who have taken a captive. He is released from captivity, after suffering a gruesome punishment. On his return he should perform a Sacrifice to give thanks.

Six in Top Place

Pressed

By brambles,

By stakes.

There is

Movement.

There is

Regret upon Regret.

Auspicious Advance.

 He is shut up in a prison whose enclosing walls are reinforced with brambles and stakes. Any attempt to escape will only bring Regret. The Auspicious Advance seems incongruous.

HEXAGRAM 48

Tsieng

Well

JUDGMENT

Towns

Change,

Not

Wells.

Neither loss,

Nor gain.

At the Well,

Constant coming and going.

A dry Well.

Water cannot be drawn.

A broken pitcher.

Calamity.

The Well is a source of Water. It was also, according to a much-questioned tradition, greatly favored by the second great Confucian Sage, Mencius (371–289 BC), as a time-honored way of organizing the sharing of agricultural land around a communal plot—the so-called *jingtian*, or well-field, system. (See the Commentary for this Hexagram in Part I.) Four such well-complexes, according to this system, constituted one *yi*—a "town," or district. Some scholars claim it was never more than "a social thought, an aspiration, an ideal." Anyway, people (and animals and birds) came and went at the Well. As an ancient means of drawing Water from the Earth, the Well has always partaken of the power and mystery of that life-giving substance. In normal times, the supply remains constant. There is no Increase or Decrease. Confucius often praised Water, according to one of Mencius's disciples, who famously recorded one of the Master's briefest and most inscrutable remarks: "Water! Ah, water!" The Well, like an acupuncture point on the human body, taps deep into the Earth, into the water table. It is a conduit of Earth Energy. A human settlement, a town, by contrast, is something superficial; it can be moved. Indeed, the Chinese dynasties moved their capitals many times. But the location of the points at which Water can be drawn to the Earth's surface is something that cannot be changed at whim. To try to alter a watercourse can be disastrous. Nature may bring drought. It may, as in the Hexagram Judgment, cause the deep source of the Well's Water to dry up. The means of drawing Water to the surface—pitcher, bucket, the structure of the Well itself—may be damaged, "broken." In either case, the consequences are dire.

LINES

Six in First Place

A muddied

Well,

Not fit for drinking.

No birds

At the old Well.

 The water is polluted. The Well is abandoned, shunned.

Nine in Second Place

Fingerlings shot

With bow and arrow

In the valley

Of the Well.

The broken pitcher

Leaks.

 This activity threatens the functioning of the Well. (Bow and arrow have been added, to avoid any misunderstanding about the method used.) The pitcher is broken and useless.

Nine in Third Place

A tainted

Well.

Not fit for drinking.

Heartache.

Water is drawn.

All can share

A wise King's

Blessing.

 The Well is cleansed, through the Action of a wise Ruler. But in the meantime, it cannot be used.

Six in Fourth Place

A brick-lined

Well.

No Harm.

 The Well is properly maintained, its leaks repaired, and the inside lined with bricks to keep the water pure.

Nine in Fifth Place

A big man,

In a

Tiger Transformation.

Before Divination,

Captives.

Tigers are awe-inspiring creatures and, together with Dragons, seem to have acted as protectors of clans (and their kings and leaders) in ancient China. The Tiger Hunt was an important activity in Shang times, and is mentioned in Oracle Bone Inscriptions: "The King hunted and captured two tigresses, one rhinoceros, twenty-one deer, two boar, one hundred and twenty-seven young deer, two tigers, twenty-three hares, twenty-seven pheasants. In the eleventh month." Rutt suggests for this Line Statement a Ritual in which animals were impersonated. Could the "big man" be a Shaman? Could this be a fragmentary reference to an ancient shamanistic performance, in which the Shaman is possessed by (and dresses up as) a Tiger Spirit? Such a ceremony might have been the prelude to Ritual Sacrifice of human captives, prelude to Divination, with the same big man, the Tiger-Priest, presiding at all stages. Sarah Allan writes of the Man-in-a-Tiger's-Mouth motif found on early bronzes, especially on the *yue*-axes—a man's head flanked by two symmetrical Tigers with encircling maws. These axes (the ancient graph for *yue* was an axe held over a man) may have been used for the ceremonial execution of humans or animals. As K. C. Chang had already observed, the open mouth occurs in many cultures as a symbol of passage to the other world, and the man held in the Tiger's Mouth may indeed have been a *wu*, a Sorcerer or Shaman. Tiger skins are also mentioned in early texts and in a Bronze Inscription, for use in court costume and chariot canopies.

Six in Top Place

A noble man,

In a

Leopard Transformation.

A small man,

In a

Mask of Hide.

Calamitous Advance.

Auspicious Augury

For a dwelling.

In the *Zuo Commentary,* a king wears leopard-skin shoes. Is this another shaman-istic persona? Is one of the king's nobles playing the role of Leopard-Priest? Tigers and Leopards guard the Gates of Heaven on the famous Mawangdui silk banner, from the southern state of Chu. They are also mentioned in the shamanistic poem "Summons of the Soul," from *Songs of the South*:

> Tigers and Leopards guard the nine gates,
> Their jaws ever ready to rend up mortal men. . . .
> The Earth God lies, nine-coiled,
> With dreadful horns on his forehead,
> And a great humped back and bloody thumbs,
> Pursuing men, swift-footed:
> Three eyes he has in his Tiger's Head,
> And his body is like a bull's.

But what is the "small man" doing with the leather mask?

HEXAGRAM 50

Tieng

Cauldron

JUDGMENT

Supremely Auspicious.

Sacrifice Received.

The Hexagram Name evokes in a single powerful syllable the extraordinary world of the early Chinese bronze vessels, imposing masterpieces of bronze casting, examples of which can be seen in many of the world's major museums. Probably the finest collection of all (the old Chinese Imperial Collection) is housed in the National Palace Museum in Taipei. Herrlee Glessner Creel, the great American historian of early China, once described the Shang Bronzes as "probably the most exquisite objects which men have ever created from metal, regardless of time and place." These vessels—some made for the storing and warming of "wine" (an aromatic grain-based brew), for the pouring of libations, some for the preparing and cooking of sacrificial grains and meats—were part of the elaborate ritual culture of the Shang and Early Zhou. They evoke the grand Sacrificial Banquets in which food and drink were offered to the Spirits of the Ancestors. These Rituals "bound together not just the whole living world but the whole known Universe." They were closely related to Divination, the central practice from which the *I Ching* itself is descended. It is indeed appropriate that one of the Hexagrams should be named after this Ritual vessel. Shang and Zhou bronze vessels were often decorated with stylized Dragons or Tigers, or with the imposing and often enigmatic *taotie* mask, the face of a mythical creature whose meaning still eludes archaeologists and historians of art. The bronze *ding* (one of many fundamental vessel forms) was usually a tripod, its three legs allowing the placing of the vessel directly into a bed of hot charcoal or some other fuel. It evolved from the simpler pottery Cauldron used for household cooking (a *tajine* on legs). There were also square, four-legged *ding*, or *fangding*, which may have been reserved for royalty. The *Zuo Commentary*, Duke Xuan, Year 3, refers to the casting of the Nine Cauldrons by Yu, founder of the Xia dynasty, and their "transfer," legitimizing each change of dynasty:

> The distant regions sent pictures of various objects, and tribute of metal was submitted from the governors of the Nine Provinces. This was used to cast Cauldrons with various objects depicted on them. All the hundreds of kinds of objects were to be found on them, so that the people could learn about the Gods and the malevolent Spirits. . . . The last ruler of the Xia was a dark man lacking in virtue, and the Cauldrons were transferred to the Shang, who ruled for six hundred years. The last ruler of Shang was a cruel and oppressive tyrant, and the Cauldrons were transferred to Zhou.

The Nine Cauldrons became symbols of legitimate power. It has been pointed out since very early times that this Hexagram itself has a Cauldron-like structure. The First Divided Line represents the legs or feet; Lines 2, 3, and 4, all Undivided, represent the solid body, the belly of the Cauldron; Line 5, Divided, represents the two "ears," or handles; and Line 6, Undivided, is the rod inserted through these handles, by which the Cauldron is lifted and carried or suspended from a hook over the fire.

LINES

Six in First Place

The Cauldron

Is upturned.

Profits

To tip out dross.

A slave is taken,

A woman and child.

No Harm.

 What is the dross? Dregs of Sacrificial Wine? It may also refer to a wife's failure to bear children, which leads to the taking of another woman (a slave).

Nine in Second Place

The Cauldron

Is full.

A companion

Is ill.

No Harm.

Auspicious.

Nine in Third Place

The ears

Of the Cauldron

Are broken.

Movement

Is blocked.

Pheasant fat meat

Is left uneaten.

Rain falls.

Regret

Goes away.

Auspicious Conclusion.

 Perhaps, suggests Li Jingchi, a Hunt has to be canceled because of bad weather. The weather improves, and all is well.

Nine in Fourth Place

The legs

Of the Cauldron

Are broken;

The Duke's stew

Is spilled.

Severe punishment.

Calamity.

 Whoever has caused the breakage (and consequent upset) pays for it heavily.

Six in Fifth Place

Yellow ears

Of the Cauldron.

Bronze carrying-bar.

Profitable Divination.

 The "ears" were the carrying-rings on the top edge of the Cauldron.

Nine in Top Place

Jade carrying-bar

Of the Cauldron.

Highly Auspicious.

Profit in all things.

 The carrying-bar was most probably made of bronze and inlaid with jade, not made of solid Jade. Jade has occupied a very special place in Chinese culture ever since the Stone Age, as the most precious and mysterious of stones, a most Auspicious substance. The earliest Jade objects date to the early neolithic period (from approximately the seventh millennium BC). Many early pieces have been unearthed, and their extreme simplicity and beauty still inspire a deep sense of awe. The eminent Chinese archaeologist K. C. Chang has written: "The most common Ritual Jades, the *bi* and *cong*, are now regarded by many scholars as shamanic paraphernalia endowing the bearer with the power to ascend from Earth (the square *cong*) to Heaven (the round *bi*), with the assistance of the Shaman's animals (which are engraved on all kinds of Ritual Jades)." The Taoist alchemist Ge Hong in his work *The Master Who Embraces Simplicity* praised Jade in ecstatic terms, as a "unique and consecrated substance, purest and most divine of natural treasures, vehicle of communication with the unseen powers of the Universe."

HEXAGRAM 51

T'ien

Quake

JUDGMENT

Sacrifice Received.

Quake

Rumbles!

Laughter

Resounds!

Quake stirs

For a hundred *li*.

No ladle is dropped,

No wine spilled.

In the Mawangdui silk manuscript, the Name is written as *chen*, signifying the fifth of the Twelve Earthly Branches—a related word with early calendrical and astronomical meaning. The great French sinologist and sociologist Marcel Granet points to the way in which Quake evokes "the intimate correspondence between the actions of Nature and human behaviour. . . . Thunder opens and shakes the soil, releasing the Dragon, which escapes from the subterranean retreat where winter has confined it; men hereafter can open the ground and cultivate it through fruitful labor." The Name can mean both Quake and Thunder—the first becoming early on more specific as *dizhen*, Earth Quake, whereas Thunder was Heaven's Quake. The Hexagram contains in its Judgment and Line Statements a series of onomatopoeic expressions, two-syllable words conveying either the impressive sound made by the Thunder/Quake or the trembling and fear they cause, or both. (Such expressions were common in early poetry, e.g., in the *Book of Songs*.) Thunder and Quake, and associated phenomena such as Lightning, represent Nature at its most violent and frightening, but also at its most awe-inspiring and powerful. In the *Book of Songs* the awe-inspiring quality of the King is several times described as Quake-like, like a clap of Thunder:

> *Song 263*
> Shaken as by Quake
> Was the land of Xu.
> Like a roll of Thunder,
> Like a Thunder clap,
> Xu quaked
> And was stirred.
> The King spread his War Might,
> He thundered,
> He raged. . . .

The Thunder of this Hexagram also suggests the overpowering War Might of the Zhou conquest. Despite the awe-inspiring sound of the Thunder, which can be felt for miles around, a joyous Sacrificial Ceremony (perhaps a spring Fertility Rite?) proceeds without mishap. In the *Songs*, the word for "quake" is also used to refer to that other awe-inspiring stirring, the birth of an infant. "The natural phenomenon of Thunder serves throughout the entire text of the Hexagram first as a portent of the beginning of Spring, and more important, as a symbol for the rebirth of all things."

LINES

Nine in First Place

Quake

Rumbles!

Laughter

Resounds!

Auspicious.

This is almost identical to the wording of the Judgment. The connection between rumbling Thunder and resounding Laughter is obscure. For some reason, fear turns to joyous laughter. Unless of course it is nervous relief at Thunder rumbling away into the distance after a storm.

Six in Second Place

Quake comes.

Danger.

Cowries are lost.

Climb the Nine Mounds,

Do not search.

In seven days

They are found.

This Line seems to be talking of a traveler or merchant who loses his money. The mysterious appeal of the cowrie shell is attributed to its resemblance to the vulva (see Hexagram 2). Like Thunder, it was a symbol of fertility. Strings of cowries were widely used as a form of currency during the Shang dynasty. At a single Shang-dynasty site in Shandong Province, 3,790 cowries were found. (See again the Commentary to Hexagram 2.) Cowries were transported with some difficulty to Anyang and the Central Plain: "Before reaching Anyang these shells had to be traded or carried over at least five hundred miles of territory peopled by fierce barbarians, across mighty rivers, and through forests full of ferocious beasts." Their loss would have been a great blow.

Six in Third Place

Quake,

Quivering.

For a traveler,

No Calamity.

One of many Divinations that refer to the making of a journey.

Nine in Fourth Place

Quake.

Mud.

 In a thunderstorm, men prostrate themselves on the ground, they fall in the mud. Or is this the softening of the earth in Spring? Or deteriorating conditions for travel, brought on by a storm?

Six in Fifth Place

Quake

Comes and goes.

Danger.

No loss.

Work progresses.

 Despite the dangerous aspect of the Thunder, all is well. During the Spring, there is much work to be done in the fields.

Six in Top Place

Quake.

Quailing,

Staring and trembling.

Calamitous Advance.

The Quake

Does not strike the person,

It strikes the neighbor.

No Harm.

Trouble in marriage.

 An obscure Line. The Quake, whether an Earth Quake, or Thunder, or Lightning strike, does not cause loss of life.

HEXAGRAM 52

Ken

Tending

JUDGMENT

The back

Is tended,

The body

Unprotected.

He walks

In an empty courtyard.

No Harm.

This whole Hexagram is puzzling. Gao Heng suggested Tending for the Name. I mainly follow Li Jingchi, who reads the Hexagram in terms of traditional Chinese medicine, and the need to "tend," or take care of, the whole body, from feet to head. That medical tradition and this Hexagram urge a more preventive attitude toward health, an awareness of the first intimations of illness. Partial "tending of the back" is not sufficient. The "empty courtyard" then becomes a metaphor for the body as a whole, left "untended." Waley reads it quite differently. According to his reading, the Hexagram refers to "Omen-taking according to the way in which rats, mice or the like" gnaw the body of the Sacrificial Victim exposed as "bait" to the Ancestral Spirit. Kunst reads the Name as "to cleave," and understands the Hexagram to be about the cutting up of Sacrificial Victims. Karlgren sees in the early form of the graph a "man with a (big) staring eye."

LINES

Six in First Place

The feet

Are tended.

No Harm.

Profitable Augury

In perpetuity.

 Pay attention to the smallest foot injury or ailment. This is preventive medicine.

Six in Second Place

The calves

Are tended.

There is

No strength

In the flesh.

The heart

Is sad.

 There is not enough flesh on the calves. Loss of weight is a concern, and it directly affects the emotions.

Nine in Third Place

The loins

Are tended;

The midriff

Is split.

Illness.

The heart

Is inflamed.

Injury to the midriff causes pain in the heart.

Six in Fourth Place

The chest

Is tended.

No Harm.

Chest and abdomen are each a "seat" of vital organs.

Six in Fifth Place

The face

Is tended.

Measured words

Are spoken.

Troubles

Are over.

The manner of speaking is an integral component of, and sign of, health.

Nine in Top Place

The brow

Is tended.

Auspicious.

HEXAGRAM 53

Tsiam

Alighting

JUDGMENT

A woman

Weds.

Auspicious.

Profitable Augury.

The Hexagram Name implies a gradual movement forward, a gliding, a skimming over water, a gentle "alighting" on dry land. The verbal structure of this Hexagram is close to that of several poems in the *Book of Songs*, where a formulaic image is repeated with variations in each stanza:

Song 248
Wild ducks
On the River Jing:
Our Ancestors
Are at peace.
The wine is clear,
The food is fragrant. . . .

Wild ducks
On the sand:
Our Ancestors

Are tranquil.
The wine is plentiful,
The food is fine. . . .

Wild ducks
On the island:
Our Ancestors
Are at rest.
The wine is well strained,
The food well sliced. . . .

Wild ducks
Where streams meet . . .

Wild ducks
In the gorge . . .

Song 181
Wild geese
Fly;
They flap their wings.
Our men
Are on the march;
They toil
In the wilds.
Wretched
Is their plight,
Wretched
The plight of the widows.

Wild geese
Fly;
They gather on the marshes.
Our men build the fort,
Wall after wall.
They toil.
Finally
They find a home.

Song 159
Wild geese
Fly past the island.
My lord cannot return.
Where can he stay?
Wild geese
Fly past the shore.

My lord will not return.
Where can he stay?

In the *Songs*, the wild goose, or wild duck, is a symbol of marital separation, the separation of man and wife during wartime, of lovers during peacetime. Wild geese migrating in autumn "automatically evoked the association of soldiers on the march, and consequently, women left to cope by themselves." They are also a poetic commonplace for melancholy. S. J. Marshall weaves an imaginative and convincing story out of the Line Statements of this Hexagram, describing it as the "other half" of *Song 181*, expressing the lonely anguish of the wife of a young soldier who has gone away to fight with King Wu against the Shang. According to this reconstructed narrative, in the First Line the geese reach the bank, and the villagers are concerned for the safety of their children. In the Second Line, the geese reach the rocks, a place of relative safety, and there is cause for celebration. In the Third Line, the woman's husband has not returned from the campaign; she is pregnant but miscarries when brigands (possibly deserters from the campaign) try to rob her. In the Fifth Line, the geese are seen alighting on the village burial ground. The woman finally gives up hope of her husband's return. It remains a mystery why the Hexagram Judgment is nonetheless so positive about a woman's marriage.

LINES

Six in First Place

Wild geese

Alight

On mountain stream.

Danger for children.

Words of Caution.

No Harm.

 Children might fall into the rushing water. They must be warned not to go too close to the water.

Six in Second Place

Wild geese

Alight

On rocks.

Good cheer.

Wine and food.

Auspicious.

 Rocks are a place of relative safety.

Nine in Third Place

Wild geese

Alight

On dry land.

A man

Goes to war,

Does not return.

A wife conceives,

Miscarries.

Calamity.

Profits to ward off brigands.

It is prudent to protect the village against intruders during the chaos of war.

Six in Fourth Place

Wild geese

Alight

On tree;

They perch

On branch.

No Harm.

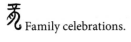 A danger is averted. Some read "branch" as "beam."

Nine in Fifth Place

Wild geese

Alight

On mound.

For three years

The wife

Fails to conceive.

Finally there is

No shame.

Auspicious.

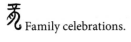 The sight of geese settling on the (burial) mound would be naturally seen as Ominous. But the wife finally gives birth.

Nine in Top Place

Wild geese

Alight

On high hill.

Feathers

For Ritual Dance.

Auspicious.

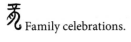 Family celebrations.

HEXAGRAM 54

Kiwer Mwed

Marrying Maiden

JUDGMENT

Calamitous Advance.

No Profit.

A marriage Hexagram, this time concerned with a match among royals, and the problems encountered. *Kiwer* (modern *Gui*) means, literally, "returning," and occurs frequently in this sense in the Oracle Bone Inscriptions. The bridegroom comes to collect the bride, who "returns" with him. According to some scholars, the early graph contains a simple element for "breasts" (compare Hexagram 27), and the whole refers to the prominent breasts of a fully mature but as yet unmarried woman. *Mwed* (modern *Mei*) can mean "younger sister" or female cousin. This Hexagram has been understood to refer to the ill-fated "diplomatic" marriage of Chang, Earl of Zhou, later known as King Wen, the Accomplished King, to a princess of the Shang dynastic house—the "maiden." She was not able to bear him children (see the Top Line), whereas his union with a secondary wife, Lady Shen, produced a son and heir, Fa, the future King Wu, the Warrior King. It is not clear who Lady Shen was, whether she was a sister of the Princess, or someone totally unconnected. The story is told in *Song 236*:

> A bride came
> From Shang's great nation,
> Younger cousin of Heaven.

King Wen fixed a lucky day;
He met her at the River Wei.
They joined the boats;
They made
A bridge of them,
Dazzling in their splendor.

A command came
From Heaven
Ordering King Wen of Zhou,
In his capital,
To give succession to Lady Shen,
Eldest daughter of her line.
Bravely she bore King Wu. . . .

The Advance in the Judgment (where it is Calamitous) and in the First Line (where it is Auspicious) is either a military campaign or a figurative description of a marriage "expedition," or both. Often military and amorous adventure, military treatises and sex handbooks, shared a common language. Take, for example, this passage from a Late Ming sex treatise of the sixteenth century AD: "A superior general when engaging the enemy first concentrates on drawing out his opponent." On which the commentator observes: "The superior general refers to the Taoist Adept. To engage means to engage in the act of love. The enemy is the woman." The origins of both types of "strategic" discourse—warfare and sexual relations—go back to very early times, framed in arcane dialogues between the Dark Girl and the Yellow Emperor.

LINES

Nine in First Place

The Marrying Maiden

Brings

Younger sisters.

The lame

Walk.

Auspicious Advance.

This is "sororal polygamy": younger sisters or cousins are taken along with the bride as secondary wives or concubines. See *Song 22*, in which (according to one reading) the bride's sisters lament their ill fortune at not being allowed to be part of their sister's marriage:

> The Great River
> Divides and joins again.
> Our bride went to marry.
> She did not take us,
> Did not take us.
> Later she changed her mind.

Song 261 celebrates the splendor of such a marriage:

> A hundred carriages rumbled,
> Eight bridle-bells tinkled;
> Incomparable was their splendor.
> Her younger sisters
> Went with her;
> They thronged like clouds.

The practice tacitly underlying this whole Hexagram emphasizes the benefits to the man (in this case the King) of intercourse with several young women, "younger sisters" of the bride. That intercourse with several younger women enhanced the Energy of the man was an accepted part of traditional Chinese thinking. It is interesting to note in passing that King Wen's marital life became the subject of the orthodox Confucian reading of the first (and most famous) song of the *Book of Songs*, "The Ospreys" (in fact a popular love song in folk mode, dealing with, among other things, lovers and their riverside rendezvous; the gathering of herbs; sleeplessness; and music). The unfortunate *Book of Songs*, like its near contemporary the *I Ching*, acquired an all-but-impenetrable patina (one is tempted to say fog) of Confucian dogma over the course of two millennia. "The Ospreys" became a song in praise of King Wen's principal queen, who (to quote the Han-dynasty commentator Zheng Xuan), "in her virtue and jealousy-free seclusion, sought additional mates for the King, tossing and turning until she found them." The number of these royal mates (i.e., occupants of the Zhou king's harem) has been variously computed, but one Chinese commentator reckons there would have been about one hundred twenty-three secondary wives, nine ladies of the third rank, twenty-seven of the fourth rank, and eighty-one of the fifth. According to later commentators, King Wen's virtuous queen wisely accepted the traditional wisdom that (in the words of the Sui dynasty *Secrets of the Jade Chamber*) "those who seek to practice the Tao of uniting Yin and Yang for the purpose of gaining Energy (*qi*) and cultivating life must not limit themselves to just one woman. They should get three or nine or eleven, the more the better." The lame walking and the blind seeing also appear in Hexagram 10/3. It has been suggested that their appearance here is a figurative expression of the reversal of fortune, by which the junior bride becomes the mother of the heir, in an Auspicious union.

Nine in Second Place

The blind

See.

Profitable Augury

For the Dark One.

 The Dark One also appears in Hexagram 10/2, where it may have been a fleeting reference to the brother of the pre-dynastic Shang herdsman Wang Hai. It has also been read more generally as "a prisoner." Is this perhaps King Wen imprisoned at Youli, by the last king of Shang? When he lay in his prison cell composing the Judgments of the *I Ching*, was he "seeing in the dark"?

Six in Third Place

The Marrying Maiden

Brings her sister;

She returns

To her old home.

 The Princess is sent back to her parental home. Has she been rejected? Has her sister (or cousin, the one who conceived) been kept on in her place?

Nine in Fourth Place

The Marrying Maiden

Misses her time,

She arrives late.

Delay.

 The Shang princess fails to conceive. This is why she is sent home.

Six in Fifth Place

King Yi

Gives his daughter in marriage.

The bride's sleeves

Are less fine

Than her younger sister's.

The Moon

Is almost full.

Auspicious.

🦎 This summarizes the historical vignette. Yi was the penultimate ruler of the Shang dynasty, father of the disastrous King Xin. The "daughter" he gives in marriage is the Princess, the Marrying Maiden. The opening words of this Line Statement have already come in Hexagram 11/5. The remainder may describe the success of the second wife. Perhaps there is here a reference to the traditional view that the King should have physical intercourse with his women only during a full moon.

Six in Top Place

The woman's basket

Has no fruit.

The man

Slaughters a sheep.

There is

No blood.

No Profit.

🦎 These are vivid images of the failure of the Princess to conceive and bear a son. They are the Inauspicious culmination of what is in general an unfavorable Hexagram. This Top Line was received by the Marquis Xian of Jin, in the year 645 BC, when he divined with Yarrow Stalks as to the advisability of marrying his elder daughter to Earl Mu of Qin (in a diplomatic initiative). With this last Line changing from Divided to Undivided, Hexagram 54 "evolves" into Hexagram 38, *K'iwer*, Watching. The words clearly point to an Inauspicious Union, and Scribe Su interpreted the Divination as unfavorable. The Marquis went ahead with the marriage anyway, with disastrous consequences (see Hexagram 47/3). A modern reading of this Line takes the first two words (*cheng kuang*) to refer to the woman's "receiving canister"—the "basket," or pelvic region, containing her sexual organs. In other words, her womb is barren; it bears no fruit. This is in keeping with the use of the phrase in an early sex manual from the Mawangdui excavations, where the man is urged to "touch the receiving canister" during foreplay. The term subsequently made its way into the amorous lexicon, and it is to be found in later erotic verse.

HEXAGRAM 55

P'iông

Citadel

JUDGMENT

Fortune.

Sacrifice Received.

The King

Is present.

There is

No sadness.

Noon is a suitable time

For Sacrifice.

In the Oracle Bone and Bronze Inscriptions, the graph for this Hexagram Name was a Ritual Vessel filled with grain—and hence, in later texts, "plenty." It was also a place-name. The Citadel P'iông (modern Feng) was a name for the old capital, Chong, northwest of present-day Chang'an and west of the river Feng, which flows north into the river Wei. It became the temporary capital of the Zhou people when they moved east from Mount Qi. They moved again soon afterward to Hao, a few miles away, on the other side of the river. King Wen (the Accomplished) laid siege to the Citadel, as celebrated in the *Songs*:

Song 241
King Wen
Received a Mandate.
He did battle;
He attacked Chong.
He made his capital
At Feng.
Glorious King Wen!
He built
His moated citadel;
He built Feng. . . .

Song 244
The siege-platforms trembled;
The walls of Chong
Towered high.
Culprits were quietly bound;
Ears were cut off
In great numbers.
He made Sacrifice to Heaven,
Sacrifice of Propitiation.
He annexed
The Spirits of the Land;
He perpetuated
The Ancestral Sacrifices.
None dared affront him.

Siege-platforms shook;
High rose the walls of Chong.
He attacked,
Harried;
He cut off and destroyed.
None dared oppose him.

According to the *Historical Records* of Sima Qian, it was Hu, Earl of Chong, whose calumny had caused King Wen (or the Western Duke, as he was then called) to be imprisoned at Youli by the last Shang king, the debauched Zhou Xin. According to legend, it was during this seven-year imprisonment that King Wen wrote the Hexagram Judgments. So all of this is closely linked to our text and its legendary origins. Later, King Wen's son Fa, King Wu, the Warrior King, finally defeated the Shang at a decisive battle in the Wilds of Mu. In an absorbing study of this Hexagram, S. J. Marshall points to a total solar eclipse on June 20, 1070 BC, at which time King Wu and the people of Feng may have been preparing to mourn the death of King Wen. Wen's own "name," Chang, means Solar Radiance (double sun). The eclipse was seen as an Omen of the fall of the Shang dynasty. King Wu consulted the Turtle Oracle and decided to launch his invasion of Shang shortly after this eclipse. As the *Heavenly Questions* puts it:

> When Wu set out to kill the Shang,
> Why was he grieved?
> He went into battle carrying his father's corpse:
> Why was he in such a hurry?

David Hawkes believes that in the original version of the story, King Wu did in fact carry his father's dead body into battle. See Hexagram 7/3. According to Marshall, this Hexagram is all about the eclipse, as observed at the Citadel of Feng, which preceded, and foretold, the subsequent conquest of Shang. It is "a web of sparsely-worded seemingly disconnected political events . . . woven around the Omen of the Dipper being seen at noon." I find his interpretation (presented at great length in his book *The Mandate of Heaven*) both intriguing and convincing, and I have largely followed it. But much of this is controversial, and other scholars give widely differing accounts. The *Bamboo Annals* refers to a conjunction of five planets some two years prior to the attack on Chong, coinciding with the ominous appearance of a Red Crow on the Zhou altars. As with so many of the new readings of the *I Ching*, we await conclusive archaeological or palaeographic evidence.

LINES

Nine in First Place

A Lord of noble mind

Is encountered.

For ten days

There is

No Harm.

Going brings a reward.

This prognostication, that the next ten-day week would see nothing untoward happen, occurred routinely in Oracle Bone Inscriptions.

Six in Second Place

The Light

Is obscured

In the Citadel;

The Dipper

Is seen

At noon.

An uncertain Advance.

Captives are taken.

The King

Complies.

Auspicious.

This, according to Marshall, is the eclipse of June 20, 1070 BC. I follow him in identifying *fa* as Fa, the name of the future Warrior King. Fa hesitates, but finally decides to launch his attack.

Nine in Third Place

Darkness falls

On the Citadel.

Stars are seen

At noon.

The right arm

Is broken,

No Harm.

Why was the right arm broken?

Nine in Fourth Place

Light is obscured

In the Citadel.

The Dipper is seen

At noon.

A Lord of true mind

Is encountered.

Auspicious.

Six in Fifth Place

Joy

At the Light's Return.

Praise.

Auspicious.

 The eclipse has passed.

Six in Top Place

Dwelling

In the Citadel.

The family is screened.

He glances through the door

At desolation,

At a place deserted.

Three years,

And no audience.

Calamity.

 King Wu proposes to spend three years alone in a Ritual Hut, in the Citadel, mourning the death of his father, King Wen. But Divination predicts that this will only lead to Calamity. So instead he launches his attack on the Shang dynasty.

HEXAGRAM 56

Gli

Sojourner

JUDGMENT

Small Sacrifice

Received.

Auspicious Augury

For a Sojourner.

In the Bronze Inscriptions, the graph shows men beneath a flag or standard. It seems to have meant (among other things) a cohort, or unit of an army (some sources say five hundred men). Other Inscriptions also show a chariot in the graph. Troops were often stationed on the frontier or sent to fight in some distant place, hence the more generalized idea of a person away from home, a "sojourner." In *Song 227*, the word is used of foot soldiers sent on a campaign to the south:

> Foot soldiers,
> Chariot drivers,
> Legions,
> Cohorts!
> Marching!
> Soon we'll go home!

Perhaps the original "sojourners" were early Zhou nomadic herdsmen, or traveling merchants. Rutt finds traces in this Hexagram of Fire Oracles, but this is speculative. Others treat the whole Hexagram as a series of vignettes from the old tale of Wang Hai, pre-dynastic Shang Ancestor, First Herdsman, and archetypal Nomad-Sojourner. This tale occurs elsewhere in the *I Ching*, and there are fragmentary references to it in other early texts. Wang Hai reaches the way station or marketplace where he buys slaves (Line 2), only to lose them as the result of a fire (Line 3); he then recovers his wealth (Line 4) and rejoices (in an adulterous affair?), only to suffer Calamity, i.e., death (Top Line), at the hands of the local chieftain. This reading is in my opinion a little contrived, but is certainly another example of imaginative *I Ching* reconstruction.

LINES

Six in First Place

In his lodgings,

The Sojourner

Jingles cowrie shells;

He invites Disaster.

 The traveler invites trouble by making his wealth audible.

Six in Second Place

The Sojourner

Reaches his lodgings.

He clasps wealth close;

He gets young slaves.

Augury.

 So far, so good.

Nine in Third Place

The Sojourner's lodgings

Catch fire.

Slaves are lost.

Augury of Danger.

Things begin to go badly wrong.

Nine in Fourth Place

The Sojourner

Seeks a resting place.

He gains axe-wealth.

His heart is sad.

Axe-shaped ingots were used as currency at least from the seventh century BC. Despite the partial turn for the better, the Sojourner still feels a sense of restlessness and gloom.

Six in Fifth Place

A pheasant

Is shot

With a single arrow.

The bird vanishes.

It lives.

Nine in Top Place

The bird's nest

Burns.

The Sojourner

Laughs.

He weeps and wails.

Oxen are lost at Yi.

Calamity.

It does seem likely that this refers to Wang Hai, whose name is frequently found in the Oracle Bone Inscriptions, including one hundred instances of Sacrificial Offerings made to him, sometimes of as many as three hundred oxen. The name *hai* was sometimes written with the addition of the graph for "bird." The Shang "totem" was the Dark Bird (thought by some to have been a swallow).

> *Song 303*
> Heaven ordered
> The Dark Bird
> To descend,
> To give birth
> To Shang.

In other early sources, the Shang people are born from a swallow's egg. In Hexagram 34/5, Wang Hai loses his sheep at Yi. In this Hexagram, it is his oxen that go missing. He laughs (perhaps at the pleasure of sleeping with the chieftain's wife, "she of the smooth sides and lovely skin"), then weeps and wails at his subsequent Misfortune. The chieftain of Yi or Youyi orders his men to set fire to Wang Hai's "nest," then steals his oxen and ultimately puts him to death. In the *Book of Hills and Seas*, there is a very brief mention of the episode, specifically mentioning the killing. The modern scholar Yuan Ke expands the story as follows: "There was a man called Wang Hai, who held a bird in each hand, and ate the heads of the birds. He was a sovereign of the Shang. He once took his fat oxen and sheep to Youyi, and entrusted them to the Youyi chieftain and to the River Chief. The chieftain of the Youyi resented the fact that Wang Hai had made love to his wife. He killed him, and stole his oxen and sheep."

HEXAGRAM 57

Swen

Offering

JUDGMENT

Small Sacrifice

Received.

A Destination

Profits.

Profits

To see a big man.

 This Hexagram seems to concern a Sacrificial Offering. An Oracle Bone graph similar to the Hexagram Name shows two men kneeling, while a similar seal-script graph shows them kneeling at an altar.

LINES

Six in First Place

Advance.

Retreat.

Profitable Augury

For a warrior.

𣎴 A simple Wartime Divination.

Nine in Second Place

An Offering is laid

Before the Altar.

Diviners,

Shamans

Smear blood.

Auspicious.

No Harm.

𣎴 I read *fen* as "smearing blood," a Ritual of Exorcism or, when followed by Ablution, a form of Ritual Purification.

Nine in Third Place

A grudging

Offering.

Distress.

𣎴 The Sacrifice is made with an ill grace (literally "with a frown"), and therefore fails.

Six in Fourth Place

Troubles

Are over.

In the Hunt

Game of three kinds

Is taken.

 An Auspicious success in the Hunt. The game could be used for Ceremonial Feasting, or for Sacrificial Offerings.

Nine in Fifth Place

Auspicious Augury.

Troubles

Are over.

Profit in all things.

No Beginning.

Conclusion.

Auspicious

Three days before a *geng* day,

Three days after a *geng* day.

 After an Inauspicious start, matters improve. *Geng* is the seventh day of the ancient cycle of Ten Heavenly Stems. The graph for Conclusion depicted the end of a silk thread. Perhaps early Omens were taken from silk reeling. Compare Hexagrams 2/3, 5/1, and 6.

Nine in Top Place

An Offering is laid

Before the Altar.

Wealth is lost.

Augury of Calamity.

 Despite the Offering, things end badly.

HEXAGRAM 58

D'wâd

Joy

JUDGMENT

Sacrifice Received.

Divination Profits.

 The text of this Hexagram (Judgment and Line Statements) is one of the briefest and most enigmatic in the *I Ching*. There are many differing interpretations of the Name itself. I have followed one of the more widely accepted, and I treat the whole Hexagram as a series of observations on the various types of Joy. One explanation of the early graph is that it represents *qi*, Energy or vapor, emerging from the mouth, or head, of a man, becoming manifest; hence laughter or mirth. I am by no means confident. Another sense of the word *dui* was "exchange," "barter."

LINES

Nine in First Place

Joy.

Harmony.

Auspicious.

 Joy is tempered by a sense of balance and proportion.

Nine in Second Place

Joy.

Capture.

Auspicious.

Troubles are over.

 The natural joy of victory.

Six in Third Place

Forced

Joy.

Calamity.

 Forcing another to come to one, subjugating another, can only have bad consequences.

Nine in Fourth Place

Well considered

Joy.

No peace.

Containment of disease.

Contentment.

 A negotiated settlement, an end to "dis-ease," may not bring the most intense Joy. It may not be perfect or conclusive, it may not cure completely; but it is nonetheless a step in the right direction, something to be pleased about.

Nine in Fifth Place

Captive in Bo.

Danger.

 Li Jingchi claims that Bo was the name of an ancient state. A military expedition to the state of Bo ends badly.

Six in Top Place

Protracted

Joy.

 There is no mantic prognostication here.

HEXAGRAM 59

Xwân

Spurting

JUDGMENT

Sacrifice Received.

The King

Proceeds to his Temple.

Profits

To cross a big stream.

Profitable Augury.

This Hexagram may concern the "spurting" of blood during the gelding of a stallion, an important and sometimes dramatic and risky operation. The various ways in which blood "spurts" are seen as more or less Auspicious. Horses played an important part in early Chinese warfare. Recent studies have established that most of the life-size clay horses unearthed from the mausoleum (the "buried army") of Qinshihuang, the first emperor of a united China, were castrated. Every one of the 520 chariot-pulling horses in the terra-cotta army has a penis but no testes, while of the 116 cavalry horses studied, some are castrated, but many are not. The archaeologist making the study observed that written references to castrated pigs had previously been found on shells and bones at least three thousand years old. According to some commentators, the "spurting" of blood in this Hexagram has a more general medical meaning. It is possibly a primitive form of bloodletting, using stone needles in an acupuncture-like fashion. Still others take the "spurting" as a reference to mounting floodwater.

LINES

Six in First Place

A mighty horse

Is gelded.

Auspicious.

The same words occur in Hexagram 36/2.

Nine in Second Place

Blood

Spurts;

It gushes over the table.

Troubles are over.

The table may be an altar on which the Sacrifice or gelding is performed.

Six in Third Place

It spurts

Over the body.

No Regret.

Six in Fourth Place

It spurts

On the multitude.

Supremely Auspicious.

It spurts

On the mound.

Unexpected.

Nine in Fifth Place

It spurts

From the liver.

A mighty neighing.

It spurts

In a royal dwelling.

No Harm.

 The word for "liver" is found in the Mawangdui silk manuscript.

Nine in Top Place

Blood

Spurts.

The gelding

Is complete.

No Harm.

Tsiet

Notch

JUDGMENT

Sacrifice Received.

Bitter Notch.

No Divination possible.

The bamboo Notch, or joint, spaced at regular intervals along the stem of the plant, is an image of moderation and thrift. Kunst speculates that when Yarrow Stalks were prepared for Divination, the leaves, which had to be stripped off at the Notches, were tasted to see if they were sweet or bitter (Lines 5 and 6). This may have indicated how suitable or propitious the Stalks would be for Divination. He quotes Western herbalist Sarah Garland's observation that young yarrow leaves taste sweet, and older ones "peppery." Otherwise "thrift" is the dominant theme of the Hexagram. "If you regard thrift as something bitter, then Divination is not possible."

LINES

Nine in First Place

Do not go out

By the courtyard door.

No Harm.

 Compare this, says Gao, with the modern fortune-teller's saying "It profits nothing to go out by the gate." Better stay at home and lie low. In the Oracle Bone Inscriptions, "going out," "going in," and "returning" were often the subject of Divination: "Should His Majesty go out to Dun?" "Should His Majesty go in? Will it be Inauspicious?" "Should His Majesty return?"

Nine in Second Place

If you do not leave home,

Calamity.

 Compare this, says Gao, with the modern proverb "It profits not to stay at home." In stark contrast with the previous Line, it is now advisable to stir abroad, to act.

Six in Third Place

No Notch.

Weeping.

No Harm.

 Unrestrained weeping, but with no dire consequences.

Six in Fourth Place

Notch of Peace.

Sacrifice Received.

 Unlike the bitterness of the Judgment, this is moderation or thrift practiced with a sense of detachment and serenity.

Nine in Fifth Place

Sweet Notch.

Auspicious.

Going brings a reward.

The message of the previous Line is taken one step further. Pleasure is taken in thrift.

Six in Top Place

Bitter Notch.

Augury of Calamity.

Troubles

Are over.

Despite the initial prognostication, which is unfavorable, a change of heart can lead to eventual relief.

HEXAGRAM 61

Tiông P'iug

Captives Taken

JUDGMENT

Pigs and fishes.

Profits

To cross a big stream.

Profitable Augury.

These may be sucking pigs and fishes, relatively ordinary Sacrificial Offerings (when compared to larger animals, or humans). The Hexagram Name itself has also been interpreted as "hitting" or "getting" captives, perhaps shooting them with an arrow. The Sacrifice of pigs and fishes may itself have been performed to mark a victory and the taking of captives. There are several references to Sacrificial Ritual in the Lines.

LINES

Nine in First Place

Auspicious

For a burial.

Or else no peace.

 This Line has been interpreted in many different ways.

Nine in Second Place

A crane calls

In the shade.

Its mate responds

In harmony.

Share this beaker

Of fine wine

With me.

 An old rhyming song, in which male and female birds harmonize. Perhaps this is a pair of young lovers drinking freely together—in anticipation of the Ritual of Marriage. Compare *Song 165*, where the search for a mate is echoed in birdsong and celebrated in the drinking of wine:

> *Ding-ding*
> Goes the woodman's axe.
> *Ying-ying*
> Call the birds,
> Leaving the dark valley,
> Moving to the treetops.
> Their song seeks
> A friend's voice. . . .
> They beat the drum,
> They dance!
> We drink
> Clear wine!

Six in Third Place

Enemy soldiers

Are taken.

Drumming,

Resting,

Weeping,

Singing.

 Are these emotionally charged celebrations after a victorious campaign?

Six in Fourth Place

The Moon

Is almost full.

A horse

Is lost,

One of a pair.

No Harm.

 The "Moon almost full" also comes in Hexagram 9/6. Is this a Ritual Hunt by moonlight?

Nine in Fifth Place

Captives

Are taken,

Tightly bound.

No Harm.

"Captives . . . tightly bound" also occurs in Hexagram 9/5. They may be destined for Human Sacrifice. This widespread practice is also referred to in Hexagrams 45/2 and 46/2.

Nine in Top Place

The sound of wings

Rising to Heaven.

Calamitous Augury.

 Waley finds this Line "particularly intriguing" but does not say why, calling the whole Hexagram "obscure and corrupt." The "sound of wings" may be the sound of a chicken destined for Sacrifice. It may, however, simply be the Inauspicious sound of a humble bird trying to fly too high—which would anticipate the next Hexagram.

HEXAGRAM 62

Siog Kwâ

Slight Excess

JUDGMENT

Sacrifice Received.

Profitable Augury.

Success in small matters,

Not in great.

The call of a bird

In flight.

Ascent

Bodes ill;

Descent

Bodes well.

Greatly Auspicious.

Compare this with Hexagram 28, *D'âd Kwâ*, Great Excess. The main word in both Hexagrams, *kwâ* (modern *guo*), combines the related ideas of "passing" and "going too far." (See Part I.) "Great matters" (as opposed to "small matters") are those connected with War and Ritual. This is stated plainly in the *Zuo Commentary*, Duke Cheng, 13th Year: "The two Great Matters of State are Sacrifice and War." It is wise not to embark on such things; it is wise not to "fly" too high, not to go too far, even to the "slightest" degree. Eschew Excess. Adopt a cautious attitude, in order to avoid the Calamity consequent on any Excess. The cry of the bird (heard as it flies into the distance) is an Omen.

LINES

Six in First Place

A bird

In flight.

Calamity.

This takes up the theme of "flying too high." For the Omen of the bird in flight, compare *Song 224*:

A bird
Flies high,
Into the sky.
Where is that man's heart
Going?
Will loyalty bring
Anything but Calamity?

Six in Second Place

Passing by

The Ancestor,

Meeting

The Ancestress.

Meeting

The Minister,

Not reaching

The Lord.

No Harm.

 The "lesser" encounters are free from Harm.

Nine in Third Place

Eschew Excess.

Beware.

Another approaches,

Attacks.

Calamity.

 Check impulse, hold back, be cautious.

Nine in Fourth Place

No Harm.

Eschew Excess.

An encounter

Brings Danger.

Caution.

Do not act.

No Augury in perpetuity.

 Constant Caution is the recurring message of this Hexagram.

Six in Fifth Place

Dense clouds,

No rain,

From meadows

To the West.

The Duke

Shoots a bird

With a corded arrow;

He takes it

From the hollow.

Looming clouds are also to be found in Hexagram 9. This was surely an old proverbial saying, arising out of the experience of protracted drought, and the refusal of clouds to shed longed-for rain. As for the Duke, he may originally have intended to shoot the bird down from the sky (from on high), but he ends up getting it from a hole in the ground (from below). This illustrates the Hexagram theme of not aiming too high, of sticking to small affairs, to more modest goals.

Six in Top Place

Eschew Excess.

A bird in flight

Is caught

In a net.

Calamity.

Disaster.

In this final Line, the harmful consequences of Excess and the fate of the bird in flight are linked again.

HEXAGRAM 63

Kied Tsier

Completion

JUDGMENT

Sacrifice Received.

Profitable Augury

In small things.

Auspicious Beginning,

Turbulent Conclusion.

The underlying Image in this Hexagram and the next is the crossing or fording of a river. In getting across, despite all the Danger involved, one "completes" an important task, one succeeds, one is victorious. But this is no permanent state of affairs; it is not just a Conclusion. It is also a Beginning, which may lead to a subsequent phase of turbulence (*luan*), another Conclusion, and yet another Beginning. Some commentators see this Hexagram as referring to the "completion" of the Shang dynasty (its Conclusion), and the next Hexagram as referring to the glorious but as yet "incomplete" future of the newly ascendant Zhou dynasty (its Beginning). As so often, the Lines have a shifting subject: fox, man, general, King, cart driver, young woman. All have to make strategic decisions.

LINES

Nine in First Place

The wheels

Brake,

The tail is wet.

No Harm.

 The cart's onward momentum is checked. But the crossing is successful. No one actually falls into the water. Compare Hexagrams 5/3 and 38/3.

Six in Second Place

The lady

Loses her hairpiece.

Seek it not.

It will be found

On the seventh day.

 All may seem "lost." But with patience a solution will present itself.

Nine in Third Place

The High Ancestor

Attacks

Demon Territory.

He conquers it

In three years.

No room here

For small men.

The Shang High Ancestor Wu Ding reigned from about 1200 to 1181 BC. He put down the troublesome barbarian tribes of the Northwest (Demon Territory) in a major military expedition. Exploits on this scale are not for ordinary (small) men to emulate. In one of the Zhou Dynastic Odes from the *Book of Songs*, King Wen refers to Demon Territory as he laments the decline of the last Shang kings:

Song 255
Said King Wen:
You Shang
Are like grasshoppers,
Like cicadas,
Like bubbling water,
Like boiling soup!
Small and great
Go to ruin,
While you persist in this course,
Raging
Across the Middle Kingdom,
As far as Demon Territory.

Six in Fourth Place

Padded clothes

Are wet.

Exercise Caution

The day long.

 Despite a mishap, Patience and Caution make it possible to Complete the crossing.

Nine in Fifth Place

Neighbors to the East

Slaughter an ox.

Neighbors to the West

Offer a simple

Yue Sacrifice.

A greater

Blessing.

Auspicious.

 The Shang were to the east, the Zhou to the west. This Line points to the evolution from the more primitive sacrificial practices of the Shang to the simpler and milder practices of the Zhou.

Six in Top Place

The head

Is wet.

Danger.

 This may be a man's head, a fox's head, a horse's head, or even the "head" of a cart. Whichever it is, the Line Statement warns that at this late stage of affairs, Danger is still lurking. Even when one is "across," all may still go badly wrong. "Head . . . wet" may also refer to the immoderate consumption of wine in celebration of victory. Compare Hexagram 64/6.

HEXAGRAM 64

Miwed Tsier

Incomplete

JUDGMENT

Sacrifice Received.

The little fox

Almost across

Gets his tail wet.

No Profit.

The fox, fording a river, occurs in the *Book of Songs*:

> *Song 63*
> Fox drags,
> Fording River Qi.
> My heart aches.
> My man has no robe. . . .

This is the second one of the final pair of Hexagrams. At this stage, before "completing" the crossing, before Completion, Danger should be anticipated. Caution should be exercised to avoid Calamity at the last moment, even as the other side of the stream comes within reach.

LINES

Six in First Place

The tail

Is wet.

Trouble.

Nine in Second Place

Wheels

Are braked.

Auspicious Divination.

 The cart driver fords the stream slowly, as in the First Line of the previous Hexagram.

Six in Third Place

Incomplete.

Calamitous Advance.

Profits

To cross a big stream.

 The apparent contradiction here (should one cross, take an initiative, or not?) may stem from a corrupt text. Or it may point to a more subtle distinction, implying that there are different kinds of Advance, the first more overtly military, and therefore tending to Disaster, the second a more strategic and careful move across water into new territory.

Nine in Fourth Place

Auspicious Divination.

Troubles

Are over.

Zhen attacks

Demon Territory.

After three years

He is rewarded

With a great Realm.

This Zhen, according to some, was a Zhou general granted great honors by the ruling Shang for his successful campaign against the Northern Barbarians. This may have taken place as part of the grand expedition already referred to (in the Third Line of the previous Hexagram), led by the Shang High Ancestor, King Wu Ding.

Six in Fifth Place

Auspicious Divination.

No Regret.

A noble man's

Light.

Captives.

Auspicious.

The victory over Demon Territory would certainly have led to the taking of a large number of captives. See the inscription on the Lesser Yu Cauldron, Hexagram 30/6, for details of a similar expedition several hundred years later.

Nine in Top Place

Captives.

Wine is drunk.

No Harm.

Captives.

The head

Is wet.

The ladle

Is lost.

This last Line Statement of the *I Ching* has provoked many a conjecture. There is No Harm in celebrating victory, but festivities can get out of control and have disastrous consequences. One is not wholly "across."

Works Consulted and
Suggestions for Further Reading

The literature on the *I Ching* both in Chinese and in Western languages is overwhelming. I list here, under author, editor, or translator, a few works that have been directly relevant to this translation and that might provide readers with ideas for further reading. For more detail, the reader can consult one of the full bibliographies available, both in print and online.

General Reference in Western Languages

Allan, Sarah. *The Shape of the Turtle: Myth, Art and Cosmos in Early China.* Albany: State University of New York Press, 1991.

———. *The Way of Water and Sprouts of Virtue.* Albany: State University of New York Press, 1997.

Imaginative investigations of early Chinese ways of thinking.

Bodde, Derk. *Essays on Chinese Civilization.* Princeton: Princeton University Press, 1981.

Chan, Wing-tsit, trans. *A Source Book in Chinese Philosophy.* Princeton: Princeton University Press, 1963.

Chang, K. C. *Shang Civilization.* New Haven: Yale University Press, 1980.

———. *Art, Myth and Ritual: The Path to Political Authority in Ancient China.* Cambridge, MA: Harvard University Press, 1983.

Chang, K. C., and Xu Pingfang, eds. *The Formation of Chinese Civilization: An Archaeological Perspective.* New Haven and Beijing: Yale University Press and New World Press, 2005.

These are just three of Professor Chang's many deeply illuminating and imaginative studies of early Chinese society. Chapter 5 and the epilogue of the last book contain some of his final thoughts before his death in 2001.

Creel, Herrlee Glessner. *The Birth of China: A Survey of the Formative Period of Chinese Civilization.* London: Jonathan Cape, 1936.

———. *The Origins of Statecraft in China.* Vol. 1: *The Western Chou Empire.* Chicago: University of Chicago Press, 1970.

These two books by the grand old man of American sinology are still essential reading for their clear understanding of this period.

Eberhard, Wolfram. *A Dictionary of Chinese Symbols.* London and New York: Routledge, 1986.

Field, Stephen L. *Ancient Chinese Divination.* Honolulu: University of Hawai'i Press, 2008.

A clearly written treatment of Divination, from ancient to modern times.

Fung Yu-lan (Feng Youlan). *A History of Chinese Philosophy.* Translated by Derk Bodde. 2 vols. Princeton: Princeton University Press, 1952–1953.

Still one of the best all-purpose surveys of Chinese thought through the ages, excellently translated from the Chinese original of the 1930s.

Graham, A. C. *Disputers of the Tao: Philosophical Argument in Ancient China*. La Salle, IL: Open Court, 1989.

Always thought-provoking and inspiring in its fresh approach to ancient Chinese philosophy.

Grand Dictionnaire Ricci de la Langue Chinoise. 7 vols. Paris and Taipei: Instituts Ricci, Desclée de Brouwer, 2001.

This encyclopedia (it is so much more than a dictionary) benefited from the participation over many years of the Jesuit Jean Lefeuvre, an authority on Oracle Bone script, whose hand can be seen in many of the entries.

Hawkes, David, trans. *The Songs of the South: An Ancient Chinese Anthology of Poems*. Rev. ed. London: Penguin, 1985.

The classic translation of the early shamanistic poetic anthology, a book that sheds much light on the southern regions of the early Chinese world. This revised edition contains much new commentary.

Karlgren, Bernhard. *Grammata Serica Recensa*. Stockholm: Museum of Far Eastern Antiquities, 1957.

Despite more recent scholarship, still the most usable, and widely used, reference for early Chinese graphs. I have used Karlgren's Early Chinese phonetic reconstructions as the basis for the Hexagram Names in Part II.

Lee, Thomas H. C., ed. *China and Europe: Images and Influences in Sixteenth to Eighteenth Centuries*. Hong Kong: Chinese University Press, 1991.

Contains a good introduction to the early translations of the Jesuits.

Legge, James, trans. *The Chinese Classics*. 5 vols. London: Trübner, 1861–1872.

Legge's Victorian versions of the basic Classics and his digests of the orthodox commentaries remain indispensable for their thoroughness and erudition. His *I Ching* appeared later (1882) in a different series (see "Translations into Western Languages," below).

Lewis, Mark Edward. *Sanctioned Violence in Early China*. Albany: State University of New York Press, 1990.

The first in a series of studies of early Chinese society, based on extensive and intelligent reading of primary texts of the period.

Li Chi. *Anyang*. Seattle: University of Washington Press, 1977.

Indispensable study of the Anyang excavations, and of Shang society.

Loewe, Michael, and Edward L. Shaughnessy, eds. *The Cambridge History of Ancient China: From the Origins of Civilization to 221 B.C.* Cambridge: Cambridge University Press, 1999.

This bulky compendium brings together historical and archaeological scholarship of the late twentieth century.

Major, John S., et al., ed. and trans. *The Huainanzi: A Guide to the Theory and Practice of Government in Early Han China.* New York: Columbia University Press, 2010.

Maspero, Henri. *La Chine Antique.* New ed. Paris: Presses Universitaires de France, 1965. Translated into English by Frank A. Kierman Jr. as *China in Antiquity* (Boston: University of Massachusetts Press, 1978).

A classic study of China until the third century BC, still impressive for its broad sweep and telling detail. The English translation has a useful index.

Minford, John, and Joseph S. M. Lau, eds. *Classical Chinese Literature: An Anthology of Translations.* New York and Hong Kong: Columbia University Press and Chinese University Press, 2000.

A handy compendium for general reference, with a companion volume providing Chinese texts.

Needham, Joseph, et al. *Science and Civilisation in China.* Many vols., ongoing. Cambridge, MA: Cambridge University Press, 1956–.

Since its inception, this mammoth series of tomes (translated more than once into Chinese, so highly was it valued in China) has provided the world with a broad and enlightened survey not just of Chinese science, but of the Chinese mind.

Nylan, Michael. *The Five "Confucian" Classics.* New Haven and London: Yale University Press, 2001.

A refreshing look at the Classics, including a long chapter on the *I Ching* ("The *Changes*," pp. 202–52).

Pregadio, Fabrizio, ed. *Routledge Encyclopedia of Taoism.* 2 vols. London: Routledge, 2008.

A wonderful treasure trove of short essays by a host of Taoist scholars from all over the world. Includes several illuminating essays by the late Isabelle Robinet.

Rawson, Jessica, ed. *Mysteries of Ancient China.* London: British Museum, 1996.

A popular work (catalog for a major exhibition) edited by one of the authorities on early China.

Robinet, Isabelle. *Taoism: Growth of a Religion.* Translated by Phyllis Brooks. Stanford: Stanford University Press, 1997.

———. *The World Upside Down: Essays on Taoist Internal Alchemy.* Translated by Fabrizio Pregadio. Mountain View, CA: Golden Elixir Press, 2011.

I have found these to be some of the most inspired expositions of Taoism and Taoist alchemy.

Rule, Paul A. *K'ung-tzu or Confucius? The Jesuit Interpretation of Confucianism.* Sydney: Allen & Unwin, 1986.

Intelligent introduction to this absorbing topic, with much detail about the Figurists and their obsession with the *I Ching*, written by a meticulous scholar with a strong Jesuit background and knowledge of Vatican archives. Excellent bibliography.

Schuessler, Axel. *Minimal Old Chinese and Later Han Chinese: A Companion to Grammata Serica Recensa.* Honolulu: University of Hawai'i Press, 2009.

Schwartz, Benjamin I. *The World of Thought in Ancient China.* Cambridge, MA: Harvard University Press, 1985.

Van Gulik, Robert. *Sexual Life in Ancient China: A Preliminary Study of Chinese Sex and Society from ca. 1500 B.C. till 1644 A.D.* Leiden: Brill, 1961.

> Essential reading for anyone interested in traditional China. The new editions have even put the Latin passages into English.

Wilhelm, Richard. *The Soul of China.* Translated by John Holroyd Reece and Arthur Waley. London: Butler & Tanner, 1928.

> This fine English translation of *Die Seele Chinas* (1926) includes Waley's versions of the poems. The book provides fascinating insights into Chinese culture, and into the mind of the great German sinologist and translator of the *I Ching*.

———. *The Secret of the Golden Flower: A Chinese Book of Life.* Translated by Cary F. Baynes. London: Kegan Paul, 1931.

> Translated by Baynes from the 1929 German version of this alchemical work of uncertain date. With a lengthy commentary and a moving appendix, "In Memory of Richard Wilhelm," both by Carl Gustav Jung.

Wilkinson, Endymion. *Chinese History: A Manual.* Rev. and enl. ed. Cambridge, MA: Harvard–Yenching Institute, 2000.

> Indispensable and reliable source for factual information, dates, etc.

Yang Xiaoneng, ed. *The Golden Age of Chinese Archaeology: Celebrated Discoveries from the People's Republic of China.* New Haven: Yale University Press, 1999.

> Contains contributions from many of the leading scholars in the field of early Chinese history and archaeology, including Keightley, Shaughnessy, and Rawson.

Oracle Bone and Bronze Inscriptions

Keightley, David N. *Sources of Shang History: The Oracle-Bone Inscriptions of Bronze Age China.* Berkeley: University of California Press, 1978.

———. "Akatsuka Kiyoshi and the Culture of Early China: A Study in Historical Method." *Harvard Journal of Asiatic Studies* 42, no. 1 (June 1982), pp. 267–320.

———. *The Ancestral Landscape: Time, Space, and Community in Late Shang China.* Berkeley: Center for Chinese Studies, University of California, 2000.

> Three of Professor Keightley's many brilliant studies of the Oracle Bones and of Shang society. Everything he writes combines rigorous textual and epigraphic scholarship with elegance and an intense historical imagination.

Shaughnessy, Edward L. *Sources of Western Zhou History: Inscribed Bronze Vessels.* Berkeley: University of California Press, 1991.

———, ed. *New Sources of Early Chinese History: An Introduction to the Reading of Inscriptions and Manuscripts.* Berkeley: Society for the Study of Early China and the Institute of East Asian Studies, University of California Press, 1997.

> Two of Professor Shaughnessy's many essential works.

Early Inscriptions and Etymology: General Reference in Chinese

Chen Chusheng. *Jinwen changyong zidian*. Xi'an: Shaanxi People's Press, 2004.

   Handy dictionary of characters in Bronze Inscriptions.

He Jinsong. *Hanzi wenhua jiedu*. Wuhan: Hubei People's Press, 2004.

   Interesting if sometimes controversial explanations of the origins of Chinese characters.

Li Pu et al. *Guwenzi gulin*. 12. vols. Shanghai: Shanghai Educational Press, 2004.

   Monumental compilation of Oracle Bone graphs, with comprehensive exegesis from a wide range of sources.

Liu Zhiji, Zhang Deshao, Takashima Ken-ichi, and Zang Kehe, eds. *Hanying duizhao jiaguwen jinyi leijian*. Nanning: Guangxi Educational Press, 2005.

   A useful sampling of Oracle Bone Inscriptions, complete with English translations, well indexed.

Xu Zhongshu. *Jiaguwen zidian*. Chengdu: Sichuan Reference Press, 1989.

   Standard dictionary of Oracle Bone characters, reprinted many times.

General Studies of the I Ching *in Western Languages*

Collani, Claudia von. "The First Encounter of the West with the *Yijing*: Introduction to an Edition of Letters and Latin Translations by French Jesuits from the 18th Century." *Monumenta Serica* 65 (2007), pp. 227–387.

   A superb essay, delving deep into rare Italian archives to reveal the true nature of the interaction between the early Jesuits and their Chinese contemporaries.

Doeringer, Franklin M. "The Gate in the Circle: A Paradigmatic Symbol in Early Chinese Cosmology." *Philosophy East and West* 32, no. 3 (1982), pp. 309–24.

Gernet, Jacques. *La raison des choses: Essai sur la Philosophie de Wang Fuzhi (1619–1692)*. Paris: Gallimard, 2005.

   Gernet is awe-inspiring in the range and depth of his thinking, and in his detailed command of this difficult Ming/Qing philosopher and *I Ching* commentator.

Jullien, François. *Figures de l'Immanence: Pour une lecture philosophique du Yi King*. Paris: Grasset, 1993.

   Fascinating and provocative study, inspired by Jacques Gernet's lectures on the great Ming/Qing philosopher Wang Fuzhi.

Marshall, S. J. *The Mandate of Heaven: Hidden History in the Book of Changes*. Richmond: Curzon, 2001.

   A brilliant new look at the *I Ching*, challenging many traditional readings.

Nielsen, Bent. *A Companion to Yi Jing Numerology and Cosmology: Chinese Studies of Images and Numbers from Han to Song*. London: RoutledgeCurzon, 2003.

   A thorough introduction to the obsessive world of *I Ching* numerology. Not for the fainthearted, but fascinating.

Peterson, Willard J. "Making Connections: 'Commmentary on the Attached Verbaliza-tions' of the *Book of Change*." *Harvard Journal of Asiatic Studies* 42, no. 1 (1982), pp. 67–116.

One of the most helpful scholarly studies of the Great Treatise.

Shaughnessy, Edward. "The Composition of the *Zhouyi*." Ph.D. dissertation, Stanford University, 1983.

Together with the work of Richard Kunst, this changed the course of Western *I Ching* studies.

Shchutskii, Iulian. *Researches on the I Ching*. Princeton: Princeton University Press, 1979.

This study, originally a Ph.D. thesis completed in 1935 at the Russian Institute of Oriental Studies, was rewritten and first published after the author's death. It is now rather dated, and largely superseded by the works of Smith and Nielsen, but still of considerable interest. Shchutskii was arrested in 1937, as a suspect anthroposophist, and died in one of Stalin's prison camps in 1960.

Smith, Kidder, Jr. "*Zhouyi* Interpretation from Accounts in the *Zuozhuan*." *Harvard Journal of Asiatic Studies* 49, no. 2 (1989), pp. 421–63.

———. "The Difficulty of the *Yijing*." *Chinese Literature: Essays, Articles, Reviews* 15 (1993), pp. 1–15.

Two of the very best short essays of their kind.

Smith, Kidder, Jr., et al., eds. *Sung Dynasty Uses of the I Ching*. Princeton: Princeton University Press, 1990.

An excellent study of the rediscovery of the *I Ching* by the Song-dynasty neo-Confucians.

Smith, Richard J. *Fathoming the Cosmos and Ordering the World: The Yijing (I Ching, or Classic of Changes) and Its Evolution in China* (Charlottesville: University Press of Virginia, 2008).

Wonderfully exhaustive and well-organized survey of *I Ching* studies in China.

———. *The I Ching: A Biography*. Princeton: Princeton University Press, 2012.

Especially interesting for its fourth chapter, on the *I Ching* in a broader East Asian context.

Visdelou, Claude de [known in Chinese as Liu Ying]. "Notice du livre Chinois nommé Y-king, ou Livre Canonique des Changements, avec des notes, par M. Claude Vis-delou, Evêque de Claudiopolis." Included in Antoine Gaubil's *Le Chou-king: Un des livres sacrés de la Chine* (Paris: Panthéon Littéraire, 1843), pp. 137–49.

One of the very first European introductions to the *I Ching*, written in the form of a letter to the Cardinals of the Propagation of the Faith in Rome by the blind renegade Jesuit priest Claude de Visdelou, who dictated it from the French Indian colony of Pondicherry in January 1728.

Waley, Arthur. "The Book of Changes." *Bulletin of the Museum of Far Eastern Antiquities* (Stockholm) 5 (1933), pp. 121–42.

This gives a taste of what might have been if Arthur Waley had ever gone ahead and completed his promised version of the *I Ching*: iconoclastic, highly speculative, but always scholarly and poetic, and always expressed in the impeccable English that was the hallmark of this great translator.

————. Review of *Change: Eight Lectures*, by Hellmut Wilhelm. *The Listener* (London), March 30, 1961, pp. 579–80.

Wilhelm, Hellmut. *Heaven, Earth, and Man in the Book of Changes: Seven Eranos Lectures.* Seattle: University of Washington Press, 1977.

Inspirational essays by the son of the translator Richard Wilhelm, himself a distinguished sinologist.

Wilhelm, Richard, and Hellmut Wilhelm. *Understanding the I Ching: The Wilhelm Lectures on The Book of Changes.* Princeton: Princeton University Press, 1995.

Includes Irene Eber's translation of Richard Wilhelm's *Wandlungen und Dauer* (Lectures on the *I Ching*: Constancy and Change) and Hellmut Wilhelm's "*Change*: Eight Lectures on the *I Ching*."

General Studies in Chinese

These are so numerous, I list only a few of the most interesting.

Guo Wenyou. *Zhouyi cihai.* Chengdu: Sichuan Press, 2005.

Comprehensive and scholarly index to all the words used in the text and the Ten Wings.

Li Jingchi. "*Zhouyi* jiaoshi." *Lingnan xuebao* 9, no. 2 (1949), pp. 51–148.

Interesting early thoughts from one of the leading *I Ching* revisionists, not included in later collections.

————. *Zhouyi tanyuan.* Beijing: Zhonghua, 1978; reprinted 2007.

Collected essays, the earliest dating from the 1930s, the latest from the 1960s.

Li Xueqin. *Zhouyi suyuan.* Chengdu: Sichuan, 2006.

Liao Mingchun. *Zhouyi jingzhuan shiwu jiang.* Beijing: Beijing University Press, 2004.

Wen Yiduo. "*Zhouyi* yizheng leizuan" and "Putang zashi." Essays included in *Wen Yiduo quanji* (1948).

Selected Chinese Editions and Commentaries

Before the Qin Dynasty

Shanghai Museum bamboo-strip version.

Dating from c. 300 BC. Illegally excavated by tomb robbers in the early 1990s in Hubei Province, then acquired in Hong Kong by the Shanghai Museum. The best version is that contained in the lavishly produced publication edited by Pu Maozuo (see below).

Mawangdui silk version.

> Dating from c. 195 BC, excavated in Hunan Province in 1973. There are now many published versions of this important early text.

Fuyang bamboo-strip version.

> Dating from c. 165 BC, excavated in Anhui Province in 1977. Reproduced in Han Ziqiang, *Fuyang Hanjian Zhouyi yanjiu* (Shanghai: Guji, 2004).

Pu Maozuo, ed. *Chuzhushu Zhouyi yanjiu*. 2 vols. Shanghai: Guji, 2006.

> A comprehensive compendium (1,045 pp.) of many of these early materials.

Chen Renren. *Zhanguo Chuzhushu Zhouyi yanjiu*. Wuhan: Wuhan University Press, 2010.

> Full study of the Shanghai Museum bamboo-strip text.

After the Han Dynasty

Wang Bi and Han Kangbo. *Zhouyi zhu*.

> Their commentary on the *I Ching*. Included in *Wang Bi ji jiaoshi*, edited by Lou Yulie. 2 vols. Beijing: Zhonghua, 1980. This is the edition followed by Richard Lynn in his translation.

Kong Yingda. *Zhouyi zhengyi*.

> The True Meaning of the *I Ching*. Largely based on the above, this became the standard edition for many centuries.

Cheng Yi. *Chengshi Yizhuan*.

> Mr. Cheng's Commentary on the *I Ching*. Along with Zhu Xi's *Zhouyi benyi* (see below), one of the two key Song-dynasty commentaries. Incorporated into the 1715 *Zhouyi zhezhong*. Reissued recently (2003) by (among others) Qilu Press in Jinan, as *Chengshi yizhuan daozhu*.

Zhu Xi. *Zhouyi benyi*.

> The Original Meaning of the *I Ching*. The classic Song-dynasty edition with Zhu Xi's commentary, which became the indispensable guide to the reading of the *I Ching* for Chinese students, and continues to be read today. A useful modern punctuated edition was issued by Qilu Press, Jinan, in 2003, and in 2007 the Dangdai Shijie Press testified to the continuing relevance of Zhu Xi by issuing a 550-page edition complete with explication in vernacular Chinese (*baihua*) by Yin Meiman. The Shanghai Guji Press brought out a handy small-format reproduction of the old 1936 Shijie Press edition, which was itself based on the Imperial Printery (Wuyingdian) Thirteen Classics edition of 1739. In 2008 the Fujian People's Press issued a facsimile of a Southern Song–dynasty edition of 1265. Zhu Xi's work is also incorporated into the 1715 *Zhouyi zhezhong*.

———. *Yixue qimeng*.

> A Primer of *I Ching* Studies. Zhu Xi's second exposition of the *I Ching*, this deals mainly with details of Divination procedure and the various diagrams

associated with the book. Joseph Adler published a translation in 2002 (Global Scholarly Publications, New York).

Ouyi Zhixu. *Zhouyi chanjie.*

A Zen Exposition of the *Change of Zhou*. Reprinted in 2004, and again in a new improved edition in 2011, by Jiuzhou Press, Beijing. The basis for Cleary's *Buddhist I Ching.*

Niu Niu et al., eds. *Rijiang Yijing jieyi.*

Daily Lessons in the *I Ching*. A primer compiled by a team of more then seventy eminent scholars (including the Manchu Fulata) in the early years of the Kangxi reign, at the young Manchu emperor's request, for his edification, and to guide him as a ruler. He was already fond of citing the *I Ching*. "In 1680 I had begun a preliminary reading of the *Book of Changes* . . . taking three days over each Hexagram. Four years later we began to go through it again." (See Jonathan D. Spence, *Emperor of China* [London: Alfred A. Knopf, 1974], p. 44.) "In 1683, after Taiwan had been captured, the court lecturers and I discussed the image of the fifty-sixth Hexagram in the *Book of Changes*, Fire on the Mountain": the calm of the Mountain signifies the care that must be used in imposing penalties. . . . My reading of this was that the Ruler needs both clarity and care in punishing. . . ." (See Spence, p. 29.) The Emperor wanted more than a simple understanding. "I told my court lecturers not to make the book appear simple. There are meanings here that lie beyond words." (See Spence, p. 59.) There is a modern reprint, 2011, by Chinese Medical Classics Press, Beijing.

Li Guangdi et al., eds. *Zhouyi zhezhong.*

A Balanced Edition of the *I Ching*. The Imperial Compendium of 1715, commissioned by the Kangxi emperor in the later years of his reign from a team of scholars headed by Grand Secretary Li Guangdi, collating many of the standard commentaries, including those of Zhu Xi and Cheng Yi, and adding a commentary of its own. Conveniently punctuated and reissued in 2003 by Jiuzhou Press, Beijing, as part of their series *Yixue jingdian*, a new edition itself based on the Taiwan 1983 reprint of the Imperial Wenyuange Siku edition of 1782. The 1715 Imperial Compendium became the "standard" edition of the *I Ching* for over two centuries, and was the one used by Régis, Legge, Philastre, and Wilhelm. I have also referred to the Taiwan reprint of 1971, taken by Zhenshanmei Press from an edition of 1868, originally published by Ma Xinyi, Governor of Zhejiang.

Liu Yiming. *Zhouyi chanzhen.*

Exposition of the Truth of the *I Ching*. Included in Magister Liu's *Twelve Works on the Tao* (*Daoshu shi'er zhong*). There is a lithographic reprint of this dated 1913. A useful punctuated edition entitled *Liushisi gua yu yangsheng* (The Sixty-Four Hexagrams and Self-Cultivation) appeared in China as early as 1990 (Shanxi People's Press). In 2011 Jiuzhou Press in Beijing issued a superior reprint edited by Zhong Youwen. This is a fascinating Quanzhen Taoist interpretation, from which I have greatly benefited. It is the basis for Cleary's *Taoist I Ching*. All of Magister Liu's *Twelve Works on the Tao* are available online, at the following website: www.wenhuacn.com/zhexue/daojiao/dianji/daoshu12.

Modern Editions

Gao Heng. *Zhouyi dazhuan jinzhu*. Shandong: Qilu, 1979.
———. *Zhouyi gujing jinzhu*. Rev. ed. Beijing: Zhonghua, 1984.

> All of Gao's work on the *I Ching* is essential reading, for his encyclopedic knowledge of other contemporary texts, such as the *Book of Songs* (his 1980 edition of this other Classic should be read alongside his *I Ching*) and the *Zuo Commentary*.

Li Jingchi. *Zhouyi tongyi*. Edited by Cao Chuji. Beijing: Zhonghua, 1981.

> This was Li's last short work, compiled before his death in 1975, and edited and published posthumously. It relies heavily on the insights of Wen Yiduo, but with a distinct (and sometimes facile) Marxist veneer. As Kunst has commented (p. 403), Li was "an interpretation mill, often glossing the same word in several different ways in different studies published within a short time of each other, while justifying his plurality of views by the indeterminacy inherent in the *Yijing* itself." Most of Li's other studies are included in his *Zhouyi tanyuan* (1978), with the exception of his long 1949 essay "*Zhouyi jiaoshi*" (see under "General Studies in Chinese," above), which was already much influenced by Wen Yiduo, and was his final study before Marxist orthodoxy set in after "liberation." I have always found Li's work useful.

Zhao Jianwei. *Chutu jianbo Zhou Yi shuzheng*. Rev. ed. Taibei: Wanjianlou, 2000.

> A useful compilation of bamboo-strip and Mawangdui silk manuscript materials.

Chen Guying and Zhao Jianwei. *Zhouyi jinzhu jinyi*. Rev. ed. Beijing: Shangwu, 2005.

> Chen, a Western-trained philosopher from Taiwan, who subsequently moved to Mainland China, has a very particular, and often highly convincing, interpretation of the *I Ching*, seeing it not as a Confucian Classic, but as one of the three texts that make up the early Taoist wisdom literature of China, the other two being *The Tao and the Power* and the *Book of Master Zhuang*. I have found this edition extremely useful.

Liu Dajun and Lin Zhongjun. *Zhouyi jingzhuan baihua jie*. Shanghai: Guji, 2006.

> Complete translation into modern Chinese, by two of China's leading *I Ching* scholars.

He Xin. *Tianxingjian: Yijing xinkao*. Beijing: Zhongguo minzhu fazhi, 2008.

> An occasionally stimulating, often frustrating, "new investigation" and commentary by this prolific and controversial contemporary intellectual.

Zhang Liwen. *Boshu Zhouyi zhuyi*. Zhengzhou: Zhongzhou guji, 2008.

> A very useful commentary and translation of the Mawangdui silk manuscript, extensively revised, incorporating many readings from recently excavated *I Ching* texts.

Translations into Western Languages

Blofeld, John, trans. *I Ching: The Book of Change*. New York: Dutton, 1968.

A very readable translation, often based on Blofeld's own personal understanding, assisted by a number of his Chinese friends.

Cleary, Thomas, trans. *The Taoist I Ching*. Boston: Shambhala, 1986.

Translated from Liu Yiming's *Zhouyi chanzhen*. I have benefited greatly from Cleary's translation of the Liu commentary, though differing from it from time to time. Readers with an interest in Taoism and Taoist alchemy will find much fascinating reading in Cleary's three-volume collection *The Taoist Classics* (Boston: Shambhala, 2003).

———, trans. *The Buddhist I Ching*. Boston: Shambhala, 1987.

Translated from Ouyi Zhixu's *Zhouyi chanjie*.

———, trans. *The Tao of Organization*. Boston: Shambhala, 1988.

Translated from Cheng Yi's *Chengshi Yizhuan*.

Gotshalk, Richard. *Divination, Order, and the Zhou yi*. Lanham, MD: University Press of America, 1996.

A valuable reconstruction of the early Bronze Age Oracle text.

Harlez, Charles de, trans. *Le Yih-King: texte primitif, rétabli, traduit et commenté*. Brussels: Mémoires de l'Académie Royale 47 (1889).

Republished in garbled form, with new commentary, as *Livre des Mutations. Texte primitif traduit du Chinois, présenté et annoté par Raymond de Becker* (Paris: Denoël, 1959).

Huang, Kerson, and Rosemary Huang, trans. *I Ching*. New York: Workman, 1987.

A refreshing look at the classic from a Chinese professor of particle physics at MIT and his wife.

I Ching, The. New Lanark, South Lanarkshire, UK: Geddes & Grosset, 1998.

An anonymous, and by and large sensible, translation in the popular pocket series Fate and Fortune.

Javary, Cyrille J. D., and Pierre Faure, trans. *Yi Jing, le Livre des changements*. Paris: Albin Michel, 2002.

Javary, an inspirational French *I Ching* guru, is president of the Paris-based group Djohi: Association pour l'étude et l'usage du Yi Jing.

Karcher, Stephen, trans. *Total I Ching: Myths for Change*. London: Sphere, 2008.

A free, poetic reading.

Kunst, Richard. "The Original *Yijing*: A Text, Phonetic Transcription, Translation, and Indexes, with Sample Glosses." Ph.D. dissertation, University of California, Berkeley, 1985.

A brilliant rereading of the *I Ching* in the light of modern scholarship and archaeology. Kunst's exhaustive handwritten notes, from which I have benefited hugely, are available online at http://research.humancomp.org/ftp/yijing/yi_hex.htm.

Legge, James, trans. *The Yi King*. Sacred Books of China, part 2. Oxford: Clarendon Press, 1882.

> One of Legge's last works, for Max Müller's series. It would have been even more useful if Legge had followed the format of his earlier *Chinese Classics*, with full Chinese text and apparatus. Still of great value, if missionary-biased, as an accurate digest of the traditional reading.

Lynn, Richard John, trans. *The Classic of Changes: A New Translation of the I Ching as Interpreted by Wang Bi*. New York: Columbia University Press, 1994.

> This scrupulous version follows the early and precocious commentator Wang Bi, but also contains a great deal of other translated material.

McClatchie, Thomas, trans. *A Translation of the Confucian Yih King, or the Classic of Change*. Shanghai: American Presbyterian Mission Press, 1876.

> Wonderfully adventurous, if often crazy, version by the Dean of Shanghai, much derided by Legge.

Mun Kin Chok, trans. *Chinese Leadership Wisdom from the Book of Change*. Hong Kong: Chinese University Press, 2006.

> By one of the founders of the Chinese University of Hong Kong Business School, this is a sensitive application of classic Chinese philosophy to modern management studies. I have benefited greatly from Professor Mun's down-to-earth approach.

Palmer, Martin, and Jay Ramsay, with Zhao Xiaomin, trans. *I Ching: The Shamanic Oracle of Change*. London: Thorsons, 1995.

Pearson, Margaret J., trans. *The Original I Ching: An Authentic Translation of the Book of Changes*. Rutland, VT: Tuttle, 2011.

> Pearson believes that "all women who read the *Changes* deserve at least one translation by a woman scholar."

Philastre, Paul-Louis-Félix, trans. *Tscheou-Yi: Le Yi King ou livre de changements de la dynastie de Tscheou*. Paris: Annales du Musée Guimet, 1885–1893.

> Reprinted in Paris by Zulma in 1992, with introduction by François Jullien. Useful because it follows almost word for word the 1715 compendium, and gives the Cheng Yi and Zhu Xi commentaries pretty much in their entirety, with an admixture of others. An abbreviated version (the main text, without commentaries, but with Chinese original text and *baihua* translation) has also been issued in China, by the Yuelu Press (Changsha, 2009).

Régis, Jean-Baptiste, Joseph de Mailla, and Pierre du Tartre, trans. *Y-King: Antiquissimus Sinarum Liber*. 2 vols. Edited by Julius Mohl. Stuttgart: J. G. Gotta, 1834–1849.

> Translation by a group of French Jesuits completed in the first quarter of the eighteenth century, but not printed for over a hundred years. Now available on Google Books, imperfectly scanned. Sometimes I have used the text of de Mailla's earlier manuscript draft, reproduced in Claudia von Collani's extraordinary study (see "General Studies of the *I Ching* in Western Languages," above).

Ritsema, Rudolf, and Shantena Augusto Sabbadini, trans. *The Original I Ching Oracle: The Pure and Complete Texts with Concordance*. London: Watkins, 2005.

> Translated under the auspices of the Eranos Foundation.

Rutt, Richard, trans. *The Book of Changes (Zhouyi): A Bronze Age Document, Translated with Introduction and Notes*. Durham East-Asia Series, no. 1. Richmond, Surrey, UK: Curzon Press, 1996.

An intelligent study by a former British missionary in Korea who went on to become Anglican bishop of Leicester before converting to Catholicism. Much is based on the work of Kunst and Shaughnessy, but Rutt also provides well-written surveys of much background information.

Shaughnessy, Edward L., trans. *I Ching: The Classic of Changes; The First English Translation of the Newly Discovered Second-Century BC Mawangdui Texts*. New York: Ballantine Books, 1996.

An important translation done from the recently excavated silk manuscript (including material not found in the "received text"), by one of the world's foremost scholars of early Chinese texts.

Terrien de Lacouperie and Albert Etienne Jean-Baptiste. *The Oldest Book of the Chinese: The Yh-king and Its Authors*. Vol. 1: *History and Method*. London: D. Nutt, 1892. Originally published in the *Journal of the Royal Asiatic Society* 14 (1882) and 15, no. 2 (1883).

Vilified by Legge. Prime example of the bizarre theory that the *I Ching* and the Chinese language derived from ancient Akkadian.

Wang Dongliang, trans. *Les signes et les mutations: une approche nouvelle du Yi King, histoire, pratique et texte*. Paris: Asiathèque, 1995.

Based on the work of the Shandong University scholar Liu Dajun.

Wilhelm, Richard, trans. *I Ging: Das Buch der Wandlungen*. Jena: Diederichs, 1924.

Wilhelm, a Lutheran missionary in China, devoted many years of his life to this work, guided by Lao Naixuan, a great *I Ching* exponent of the old school. The English translation by Cary F. Baynes, one of Jung's translators, with foreword by C. G. Jung himself, *The I Ching, or Book of Changes*, became a cult book in the 1960s (Princeton: Princeton University Press, 1950). The French translation, *Yi King: Le Livre des Transformations* (Paris: Librairie de Médicis, 1973), was by another Jungian, Etienne Perrot.

Wu Chung, trans. *The Essentials of the Yi Jing*. St. Paul, MN: Paragon House, 2003.

A complete, intelligent, relatively traditional version.

Zottoli, Angelo, S. J. *Mutationum Liber*. In *Cursus Litteraturae Sinicae*. Vol. 3: *Studium Canonicorum*. Shanghai: Ex Typographia Missionis Catholicae in Orphanotrophio Tou-Sè-Wè, 1880.

Partial Latin translation and summary of high quality by a late-nineteenth-century Italian Jesuit.

Bibliographies

Hacker, Edward, Steve Moore, and Lorraine Patsco, eds. *I Ching: An Annotated Bibliography*. New York: Routledge, 2002.

Shaughnessy, Edward L. "I Ching (Chou I)." In *Early Chinese Texts: A Bibliographical Guide,* edited by Michael Loewe. Berkeley: University of California Press, 1993, pp. 216–28.

Smith, Richard. "The *Yijing* (Classic of Changes) in Global Perspective: Some Pedagogical Reflections." *Education About Asia* 8, no. 2 (Fall 2003).

A topically organized bibliography, a study guide, and other related materials. Consult also Smith's excellent bibliography in *Fathoming the Cosmos* (see "General Studies of the *I Ching* in Western Languages" above).

Wilhelm, Hellmut. *The Book of Changes in the Western Tradition: A Selective Bibliography.* Seattle: Institute for Comparative and Foreign Area Studies, 1975.

Websites

biroco.com

The excellent Yijing Dao section of this website was created by S. J. Marshall, author of *The Mandate of Heaven.*

The I Ching on the Net. pages.pacificcoast.net/~wh/Index.html.

A good collection of links.

Djohi.org

The French Djohi group's site includes a useful guide to other *I Ching* sites.

zhouyi.sdu.edu.cn

An active, if often poorly presented, Chinese site, based at the Centre for *I Ching* Studies of Shandong University.

jianbo.org

An excellent Chinese website for recently discovered texts.

chineseetymology.org

A useful website for ancient graphs, compiled by the indefatigable Richard Sears.

johnminford.com

A substantial part of this website is devoted to the *I Ching.*

Names and Dates

Legendary Figures

Fu Xi, legendary figure associated with the invention of the Trigrams, and of fire, nets for hunting and fishing, musical instruments, and knotted cords for calculating time.

Yellow Emperor, legendary figure who became the supreme figure in the Taoist pantheon. For the historian Sima Qian, he was the "fountainhead of Chinese civilization."

Wang Hai, mythical Ancestor of the Shang rulers, and first herdsman.

The Sage Emperors

Yao, first of the Sage Emperors, associated with agriculture and the calendar.

Shun, minister under Yao, whom he succeeded after Yao's abdication, reluctantly supplanting Yao's son Dan Zhu, and marrying two of Yao's daughters.

Great Yu, an official under Yao, who succeeded Shun. He drained and tamed the floodwaters, where his father, Gun, failed. His son Qi founded the Xia, the first hereditary dynasty.

Dates of Historical Dynasties and Kings

Xia Dynasty (2100?–1700? BC)

Shang Dynasty (c. 1700–1045)

Later Shang Kings (approximate dates of reign)

Wu Ding (1200–1181)
Zu Geng (1180–1171)
Zu Jia (1170–1151)
Geng Ding (1150–1131)
Wu Yi (1130–1119)
Wen Wu Ding (1118–1106)
Di Yi (1105–1086)
Di Xin or **Zhou Xin,** last ruler of Shang (1085–1045)

Zhou Dynasty (c. 1045–221)

Founders of the Zhou Dynasty

King Wen (1099–1050), the Accomplished King, founder of Zhou, long-suffering vassal of Zhou Xin. He died before the overthrow of Shang was complete. According to legend, he wrote the Judgments for the Hexagrams while imprisoned by the Shang.

King Wu (1049–1043), the Warrior King, King Wen's son, first king of the Zhou dynasty.

Duke of Zhou (1042–1036), son of King Wen, brother of King Wu, regent after Wu's death.

Early Zhou Kings

Cheng (1036–1006)
Kang (1005–978)
Zhao (977–957)
Mu (956–918)
Gong (917–900)
Yih (899–873)
Xiao (872–866)
Yi (865–858)
Li (857–842)
Gong He (841–828)
Xuan (827–782)
You (781–771)

Later Zhou Periods

Spring and Autumn (770–476)
Warring States (475–221)

Subsequent Dynasties

Qin (221–206)
Han, Former (202 BC–AD 23)
Xin (interregnum) (AD 9–23)
Han, Later (25–220)
Three Kingdoms (220–280)
Period of Division / Six Dynasties (220–589)
Sui (581–618)
Tang (618–907)
Five Dynasties (902–960)
Song, Northern (960–1127)
Song, Southern (1127–1279)
Liao (Khitan) (916–1125)
Jin (Jurchen) (1115–1234)
Yuan (Mongol) (1279–1368)
Ming (1368–1644)
Qing (Manchu) (1644–1911)

Modern Era

Republic (1912–1949)
People's Republic (1949–)

Dates of Historical Figures and Books

Akatsuka Kiyoshi, contemporary Japanese sinologist.
Allan, Sarah, contemporary American sinologist.
Ames, Roger T., contemporary American philosopher and sinologist.
Analects of Confucius (fifth century BC?), sayings of Confucius.
Art of War, The (fifth–fourth century BC?), early strategic and military treatise.

Bamboo Annals (Warring States?), early historical text.

Ban Biao (3–54), historian and poet of the Later Han dynasty.

Ban Gu (32–92), son of Ban Biao, and also a historian and poet of the Later Han.

Baynes, Cary F. (1883–1977), translator from German of Richard Wilhelm and Carl Gustav Jung.

Blofeld, John (1913–1987), longtime resident of Peking; translator of *I Ching*.

Bo Xingjian (775–826), Tang-dynasty poet; brother of famous poet Bo Juyi.

Bodde, Derk (1909–2003), American sinologist.

Bouvet, Joachim (1656–1730), Jesuit China-missionary and Figurist.

Chang, K. C. (1931–2001), archaeologist and anthropologist.

Charme, Alexandre de la (1695–1767), Jesuit China-missionary.

Chen Guying, contemporary philosophical scholar.

Chen Mengjia (1911–1966), poet and scholar.

Cheng, François, contemporary writer and scholar, resident in France.

Cheng Yi (1033–1107), Northern Song–dynasty philosopher and *I Ching* commentator.

Chiang Kai-shek (1887–1975), the Kuomintang Generalissimo.

Confucius (Kongzi, 551–479 BC), the Great Sage.

Creel, Herrlee Glessner (1905–1994), American sinologist.

Doctrine of the Mean (first century BC?), early Confucian text, one of the Four Books, taken from the *Book of Rites* (*Liji*).

Dong Zhongshu (179?–104? BC), Han-dynasty philosopher and poet.

Dong Zuobin (1895–1963), Oracle Bone scholar and historian.

Eberhard, Wolfram (1909–1989), German-American sinologist and folklorist.

Foucquet, Jean-François (1665–1741), Jesuit China-missionary and Figurist.

Gao Heng (1900–1986), Chinese scholar of early texts, especially the *I Ching*.

Gao Qi (1336–1374), Ming-dynasty poet.

Ge Hong (250–330), Taoist Master "Who Embraces Simplicity."

Graham, A. C. (1919–1991), British sinologist, philosopher, and translator.

Granet, Marcel (1884–1940), French sociologist and sinologist.

Gu Jiegang (1893–1980), revisionist historian.

Guan, Master (fourth century BC?), Taoist Master.

Guo Moruo (1892–1978), poet, scholar, cultural commissar.

Guo Pu (276-324), Six Dynasties Taoist, Diviner, and man of letters.

Halliwell-Phillipps, James (1820–1889), Victorian antiquarian.

Han Kangbo (c. 332–385), *I Ching* commentator of the Eastern Jin dynasty.

Hanshan Deqing (1546–1623), Ming-dynasty poet.

Hawkes, David (1923–2009), British sinologist and translator.

He Xin, contemporary intellectual.

Hesse, Hermann (1877–1962), author of *The Glass Bead Game*.

Hu Bingwen (1250–1333), Mongol-dynasty *I Ching* commentator.

Jao Tsung-yi, contemporary Hong Kong man of letters and calligrapher.

Jia Dao (779–843), Tang-dynasty poet.

Jia Yi (200–168 BC), Han-dynasty poet.

Jullien, François, contemporary French philosopher and sinologist.

Jung, Carl Gustav (1875–1961), Swiss psychotherapist and philosopher.

Kang Youwei (1858–1927), reformist thinker.

Kangxi, Emperor (1654–1722), second Manchu emperor.

Karlgren, Bernhard (1889–1978), Swedish sinologist.

Keightley, David, contemporary American sinologist; Oracle Bone expert.

Keyserling, Hermann Alexander von (1880–1946), German philosopher.

Kong Yingda (574–648), Tang-dynasty commentator on the Classics, including *I Ching*.

Kunst, Richard, contemporary American sinologist; *I Ching* scholar.

Legge, James (1815–1897), Scottish missionary and sinologist; translator of *I Ching*.

Leung Ping-kwan (1949–2013), Hong Kong poet, novelist, and essayist.

Lewis, Mark Edward, contemporary American sinologist.

Li Chi (1896–1979), Chinese archaeologist.

Li Guangdi (1642–1718), editor of "Imperial" *I Ching* of 1715.

Li Jingchi (1902–1975), *I Ching* scholar.

Liang Qichao (1873–1929), intellectual and reformer.

Lie, Master (fourth century BC?), early Taoist Master.

Liu An (179–122 BC), Prince of Huainan, patron of Taoist learning.

Liu Dajun, contemporary Chinese *I Ching* scholar.

Liu Mu (1011–1064), Song-dynasty *I Ching* commentator.

Liu Xie (fifth century), author of *Carving Dragons and the Mind of Literature*.

Liu Yiming (1734–1821), Taoist Master; *I Ching* commentator (Magister Liu).

Liu Yiqing (403–444), prince of the Liu Song dynasty; author of *New Tales of the World*.

Lost Documents of Zhou, a compilation dating probably from the Warring States period.

Lu Ji (187–219), general and *I Ching* commentator of the Later Han dynasty.

Lu You (1125–1209), Song-dynasty poet.

Lynn, Richard, contemporary American sinologist.

Ma Danyang (born c. 1123), early Master of the Complete Reality School of Taoism.

Mailla, Joseph-Anne-Marie de Moyriac de (1669–1748), Jesuit China-missionary.

Marshall, S. J., contemporary British *I Ching* scholar; creator of the *I Ching* site biroco.com.

McClatchie, Thomas (1814–1885), China-missionary and translator of *I Ching*.

Mencius (Mengzi, 371–289 BC), second Confucian Sage.

Meng Jiao (751–814), Tang-dynasty poet.

Mohl, Julius (1800–1876), German editor of printed Jesuit translation of *I Ching*.

Mote, F. (1922–2005), American sinologist.

Mu Hua (fl. 300), poet of Western Jin dynasty.

Mun Kin Chok, Hong Kong–based professor of business studies; *I Ching* commentator.

Needham, Joseph (1900–1995), British sinologist; historian of Chinese science.

New Tales of the World (*Shishuo xinyu*), collection of pithy anecdotes by Liu Yiqing.

Nylan, Michael, contemporary American sinologist.

Ouyi Zhixu (1599–1655), Zen Master and *I Ching* commentator of Ming–Qing transition.

Pan Yue (247–300), poet of Western Jin dynasty.

Philastre, Paul-Louis-Félix (1837–1902), French translator of *I Ching*.

Prémare, Joseph-Henri de (1666–1736), Jesuit China-missionary.

Qi Biaojia (1602–1645), man of letters of the Late Ming dynasty.

Qian Qianyi (1582–1664), man of letters of the Ming–Qing transition.

Qu Wanli (1907–1979), Taiwan scholar and academician.

Qu Yuan (c. 340–278 BC), poet and statesman of the southern state of Chu.

Régis, Jean-Baptiste (1664–1738), Jesuit China-missionary.

Rutt, Richard (1925–2011), Korea missionary and *I Ching* scholar.

Secret of the Golden Flower, Taoist alchemical classic, translated by Richard Wilhelm.

Shaughnessy, Edward, contemporary American sinologist.

Shi Tao (1642–1707), painter of early Qing dynasty.

Smith, Kidder, Jr., contemporary American sinologist and *I Ching* scholar.

Smith, Richard, contemporary American sinologist and *I Ching* scholar.

Song Yu (c. 290–223 BC), poet, from the state of Chu, during the late Zhou period.

Spring and Autumn Annals of Master Yan, state of Qi chronicle, Warring States period.

Story of the Stone, The (eighteenth century), novel by Cao Xueqin and Gao E.

Su Dongpo (1037–1101), Song-dynasty poet and man of letters.

Sun, Master (fourth century BC?), credited with strategic treatise *The Art of War.*
Swanson, Gerald, contemporary American sinologist.
Tao and the Power, The, early Taoist classic of uncertain date.
Tao Yuanming (365–427), poet of the Eastern Jin dynasty.
Tartre, Pierre Vincent de (1669–1724), Jesuit China-missionary.
Unity of the Three (Zhouyi cantongqi), classic of Taoist alchemical thinking, originating
    probably in the Later Han.
Visdelou, Claude de (1656–1737), Jesuit China-missionary.
Waley, Arthur (1889–1966), British man of letters, translator, and sinologist.
Wang Bi (226–249), Three Kingdoms philosopher and commentator on *I Ching.*
Wang Chong (27–c. 100), philosopher of the Later Han dynasty.
Wang Feng (Mongol dynasty), *I Ching* commentator.
Wang Fuzhi (1619–1692), philosopher, man of letters, and *I Ching* commentator.
Wang Guowei (1877–1927), many-talented scholar and man of letters.
Wang Tao (1828–1897), late-Qing-dynasty man of letters; assistant to James Legge.
Wang Yanshou (c. 124–c. 148), poet of the Later Han dynasty.
Wang Zongchuan (fl. 1186), *I Ching* commentator of the Southern Song dynasty.
Wen Yiduo (1899–1946), poet and scholar.
Wilhelm, Richard (1873–1930), German China-missionary, sinologist, and translator.
Wilhelm, Hellmut (1905–1990), son of Richard Wilhelm; German-American sinologist.
Wu Zetian (reigned 690–705), empress who usurped the Tang throne.
Xie Lingyun (385–433), poet and mountaineer of the Six Dynasties period.
Xie Xuan (343–388), general; grandfather of Xie Lingyun.
Xu Ji (Mongol dynasty), *I Ching* commentator.
Xue Aocao (late seventh century?), legendary lover of Empress Wu.
Yang Wanli (1127–1206), Southern Song–dynasty poet and *I Ching* commentator.
Yao Naixuan (1843–1921), late Qing / Republican scholar; Richard Wilhelm's guide to the
    I Ching.
Yin Meiman, contemporary editor of Zhu Xi's *I Ching* commentary.
Yu Fan (164–233), Han-dynasty *I Ching* commentator.
Yu Xingwu (1896–1984), scholar; Oracle Bone expert.
Yu Yan (1258–1314), poet and *I Ching* commentator of the Mongol dynasty.
Zan Ning (919–1001), Buddhist monk.
Zhang Heng (78–139), poet and astronomer of the Later Han dynasty.
Zhang Liwen, contemporary *I Ching* scholar.
Zhou Dunyi (1017–1073), philosopher of the Northern Song dynasty.
Zhu Xi (1130–1200), Southern Song philosopher and *I Ching* commentator.
Zhuang Zhou (c. fourth century BC), early Taoist Master.
Zhuge Liang (181–234), strategist and wizard of the Three Kingdoms period.
Zuo Commentary (c. fifth century BC), early historical classic.
Zuo Si (250?–305), poet of the Western Jin dynasty.

Glossary

In this Glossary, I include a number of entries from across the range of Chinese thought and *I Ching* interpretation—from earliest times, and through the various schools, including (and especially) Liu Yiming's Taoist commentary. The purpose is to make the ideas accessible to readers with little prior knowledge of Chinese thought. As can be readily seen, most of the ideas are interconnected, and all of them relate to the central idea of Self-Cultivation. Often, especially in the second section, "Fundamental Concepts," I have taken phrases from the *I Ching* itself and the various Commentaries in order to illustrate a given term. These phrases are prefaced by the Hexagram number and Name, e.g., XXV, *Freedom from Guile*.

Terms and References

This first section brings together some frequently occurring structural terms and references relevant to the complex evolution of the text. Readers are also advised to see the section "How to Consult the *I Ching*" (page xxxvii) and the table entitled "Layers of Text" (page xiv).

Oracle Bone Inscriptions, *jiaguwen*
Inscriptions found on the ox bones and turtle shells used in Divination, excavated over the past century. These have shed light on early Chinese society and the practices of Sacrifice and Divination, and are sometimes helpful in understanding *I Ching* formulae.

Bronze Inscriptions, *jinwen*
Inscriptions from bronze vessels cast during the Shang and Zhou dynasties to commemorate significant events. Their language is often close to that of the *I Ching*.

Bamboo-Strip Manuscript
An incomplete early transcript of the *I Ching* on bamboo strips, dated to around 300 BC, now in the Shanghai Museum.

Mawangdui Silk Manuscript
One of the earliest handwritten transcriptions of the *I Ching*, dated to around 195 BC. The Mawangdui excavations in Hunan Province (1972–1974) yielded many handwritten copies of early philosophical and medical texts, including the *I Ching* and *The Tao and the Power*.

Oracle, or Core Text
This is the bare text of the *Zhouyi* (the *Change of Zhou*), in other words, the *I Ching* without any of its commentaries (Ten Wings or later).

Book of Wisdom, or Classic
I use the term Book of Wisdom to refer to the *I Ching* from the time it became a canonized classic, in the Former Han dynasty, and during the subsequent two millennia, when commentaries grew up around it and readers consulted it for insight into their lives.

Yarrow Stalks
Yarrow Divination was performed by casting the dried stalks of the yarrow, or milfoil plant. For details, see the Introduction and "How to Consult the *I Ching*" (page xxxvii).

Trigram, *gua*
One of eight diagrams that together make up all the possible threefold combinations of Divided and Undivided Lines. (See "*I Ching* Diagrams," page xxiii.) Legend ascribed their invention to the mythical sage Fu Xi, who is said to have derived them from Patterns observed in Nature. Particular Images are attached to each of the Eight Trigrams (e.g., *Gen*/Mountain; Kan/Abyss, etc.).

Hexagram, *gua*
One of sixty-four six-line diagrams, each one analyzed traditionally in terms of an Upper and a Lower component Trigram. Together they make up all the possible sixfold combinations of the Divided and Undivided Lines. These are the structural units of the *I Ching*. Each Hexagram has a Name, and gives rise to a text.

Judgment, *tuan*
This first section in the core text of the *I Ching* gives the initial response, often in terms of whether the Divination is Auspicious or Inauspicious, and what is the most appropriate Action, and sometimes giving the Hexagram's central Image or Images. For example, for Hexagram II, *Earth*, the Judgment gives considerable detail: "Supreme Fortune. Steadfastness of a Mare Profits. The True Gentleman has a Destination. At first he goes astray, then finds a Master. It Profits to gain friends in West and South, to lose friends in East and North. It is Auspicious to rest in Steadfastness." Some Judgments are a great deal shorter than this.

Image, *xiang*
The Image is the nonverbal language of the *I Ching*. As the commentator Wang Bi wrote, "When one has attained the Image, one can forget the word." Particular Images are attached to each of the Eight Trigrams (*Gen*/Mountain, *Li*/Fire, etc.). From the Han dynasty, the Images came to include the whole range of symbolic associations for each Trigram and Hexagram. For Zhu Xi, they are the prelinguistic expression of Fu Xi's insight into Heaven-and-Earth. They are (1) the actual *objects* after which Fu Xi modeled the Hexagrams, (2) the Hexagrams and Trigrams *themselves* as diagrams, (3) their Yin-Yang configuration and meaning, and (4) the various symbolic correlations elaborated in the commentary The Trigrams Expounded.

Ten Wings, *shiyi*
Traditional term for the earliest commentaries, dating from the years immediately before and during the Former Han dynasty. See the table "Layers of Text" (page xiv).

On the Judgment, *tuanzhuan*
An early commentary, one of the Ten Wings, expounding the meaning of the (often brief and cryptic) Judgment.

On the Image, *xiangzhuan*
Another early commentary, one of the Ten Wings, expounding the basic symbolism of the Hexagram's Trigram structure and general imagery. It often refers to the Places occupied by certain Lines, and their dynamic relationship.

The Great Treatise, *dazhuan; xici zhuan; xixi*
A lengthy early commentary, another of the Ten Wings, of a rhapsodic nature, Greating basic underlying principles of the *I Ching*. In the present edition, sections of the Great Treatise are quoted under different Hexagrams. See also the Introduction for lengthy extracts.

On the Words, *wenyan*
An early commentary attached to the first two Hexagrams, another of the Ten Wings.

The Trigrams Expounded, *shuogua*
Another early commentary, one of the Ten Wings, dealing with the Trigrams and their symbolism.

Lines, *yao*; **Line Statements,** *yaoci*
Each of the six Lines making up a Hexagram has certain qualities, and from these are derived Statements. They are part of the core text. For example, in Hexagram II, *Earth*, the First Line Statement reads: "Treading on hoarfrost. Hard ice is on its way." This is then interpreted, in the early commentary On the Words, to counsel vigilance and Caution. When consulting the *I Ching*, special attention is paid to Statements for Changing Lines. These have a value of either 6 (Old Yin) or 9 (Old Yang). They generate a new Hexagram.

Divided and Undivided Lines
Yin Lines are Divided, and are represented visually by a broken line. Yang Lines are Undivided, and are represented by an unbroken line.

Place, *wei*
Places within a Hexagram are significant. Every Hexagram has Six Places, counting from the base. Odd Places (1, 3, and 5) are intrinsically Yang. Even Places (2, 4, and 6) are intrinsically Yin. Lines in certain Places should ideally have Resonance with Lines in certain other Places: 1 with 4; 2 with 5; 3 with 6. For example, a Yang Line in First and a Yin Line in Fourth have Resonance, whereas a Yang Line in First and a Yang Line in Fourth do not. When a Yang Line occurs in a Yin Place (as is often the case), then it is not Apt. The Fifth Place is the Place of the Ruler (Professor Mun's Leader), and frequently dominates the Hexagram. The Fourth Place is the Minister (Professor Mun's "executive"). There are many other hierarchical ways of describing the qualities of the various Places, but I have not touched upon these in my translation.

Changing and Unchanging Lines
Every Line of a Hexagram is either Yang or Yin. Depending on the fall of the Yarrow Stalks or the Coins, a Yang Line may be either Young Yang (*Shao Yang*, with the value of 7) and Unchanging, or Old Yang (*Lao Yang*, with the value of 9) and Changing. Similarly, a Yin Line may be either Young Yin (*Shao Yin*, with the value of 8) and Unchanging, or Old Yin (*Lao Yin*, with the value of 6) and Changing. If a Line is Changing, it becomes its "opposite" (i.e., Yang turns into Yin and vice versa) and generates a new Hexagram structure.

Apt, *dang*
In the Chinese commentaries (especially in the Commentary on the Image), emphasis is laid on whether or not a certain Line (*yao*) is Apt or True (*dang; zheng*) in (or for) a certain Place (*wei*) within the Hexagram. Each of the Six Places in the structure of a Hexagram

has an inherently Yin or Yang quality. The Odd Places (Lines 1, 3, and 5) are inherently Yang, the Even Places (Lines 2, 4, and 6) inherently Yin. The presence of a Line in a Place to which it is not attuned (e.g., a Yin Line in a Yang Place) becomes an element in the reading of the Hexagram. It may reflect an imbalance or tension in the dynamic at the moment of Divination. Conversely, if the Line-Place combination is Apt (i.e., Yang in First, Third, or Fifth; Yin in Second, Fourth, or Top), this is more likely to be Auspicious. This is one of the preoccupations of the early Commentary on the Image. Closely connected are the concepts of Resonance (*ying*) and Centrality, or being Centered (*zhong*). Some later commentators took this aspect of *I Ching* Divination to great lengths and engaged in extremely complex considerations of the interrelationship between Places. I have only touched on it lightly. An excellent and detailed study of all this is contained in Bent Nielsen's book *A Companion to Yi Jing Numerology and Cosmology: Chinese Studies of Images and Numbers from Han to Song.*

Center, Centered, *zhong*
In any *I Ching* Hexagram structure, the Lines which are Centered and True or Apt are Yin in Second Place and Yang in Fifth Place. But even if a Second or Fifth Line is *not* True (e.g., Yang in Second), it is still considered Centered. This (as with everything in the *I Ching*) is both a technical quality of a Hexagram and a reflection of the dynamic at the moment of Divination. Often a commentary (e.g., the Commentary on the Image) will draw attention to the fact that a Line is Centered but *not* True, and will explain the resultant tension. "Center" also has a more general meaning. It is the Mean, the Middle Way of proper and balanced behavior, and is closely linked to Harmony. The Center is also a point of origin, to which one returns once one has achieved a degree of Self-Knowledge. The *Doctrine of the Mean* (or *Central Pivot*) 1:4; 2:1: "When there are no stirrings of contentment and anger, of sorrow and joy, this is to be Centered, this is to be 'in the axis'; when once those feelings have issued forth, if they are in Centered Moderation, that is Harmony. To be Centered is the Great Root of the World; Harmony is the fulfillment of the World's Tao. The True Gentleman is Centered." XXXII / 2, *Endurance:* "In Shang and early Zhou times, to 'set up the Center,' *lizhong*, was a cosmological Ritual, which may have originally involved the literal setting up of a flagpole or other device to measure the angle of the sun's shadow. Later, *zhong* came to mean something broader and more philosophical, a balanced (Centered) mode of consciousness and conduct. Here in this Central Line of the Lower Trigram, a Firm Line in a Yielding Place; there is a balanced abiding, an Endurance, in keeping with the Golden Mean. Regret, negative emotion, has been got rid of. Inner Strength is nurtured." XVIII / 2–3, *Blight:* "In setting things right, flexibility and Moderation are called for, rather than uncompromising Steadfastness. Do not proceed too drastically, with too great an insistence. In being too hard, one strays from the Middle Way. Absence of Moderation causes slight Regret." LXI, *Good Faith:* The *Doctrine of the Mean* also speaks of the *spontaneous ease* of the Center: "Sincerity is the Tao of Heaven. The attainment of Sincerity is the Tao of Man. One who possesses Sincerity attains the Center without effort. He gets there without thought; he reaches the Center of the Tao with ease. This is the Sage."

True, *zhen; zheng*
This has several meanings. Things and people can be True (*zhen*) as opposed to False (*jia*). More specifically to the *I Ching*, a Line can be True (*zheng*) to its Place in the Hexagram; it can be Apt. This normally refers to a Yang Line in a Yang (or odd) Place, a Yin Line in a Yin (or even) Place.

Centered and True, *zhongzheng*
When a Yin Line is in Second Place, or a Yang Line is in Fifth Place, this is Centered and True. It is often Auspicious.

Resonance, *ying*
Sometimes this has been translated as "correspondence," sometimes as "responsiveness." It is Resonance that produces Movement and Change. From it one can know the innate tendencies of things, "where they are going." As a technical term, this is the Harmonious Resonance between two Lines in a Hexagram, in particular between two Lines in equivalent Places in the two constituent Trigrams, i.e., between Lines 1 and 4, 2 and 5, and 3 and 6. If the two are of the same "polarity" (i.e., both Yin or both Yang), then there is strictly speaking *no Resonance*. This is by and large Inauspicious. If one is Yin and the other Yang, then *they Resonate*. This is Auspicious. When two Lines Resonate, they share Aspiration. As well as being a technical feature of a Hexagram, Resonance is also a desirable quality in the overall environment, and in the individual's relationship with that environment. When things or people Resonate, they also Connect. They are in tune with each other, with the Cosmos, with Change; they are in Harmony with the Tao. This is Auspicious. XXXI, *Resonance*: "Attraction and Response, Resonance or Correspondence, is the way in which things throughout the Universe Connect (by such qualities as their Yin/Yang polarity). This is a fundamental concept in the *I Ching* commentaries. It is close to what Carl Jung called 'synchronicity,' the 'interdependence of objectives among themselves as well as with the subjective (psychic) states of the observer or observers.'" With True Resonance between Yin and Yang, with their "subtle communion,'" all things are in principle possible. Resonance is a prime quality or sensitivity in the mental scheme of the *I Ching*. The reader is constantly urged to be aware of it, to be in tune with it, to be at one with the Resonance around and within. This makes it possible to evolve in Harmony with the Dynamic of life, to adapt to Change, to respond appropriately to circumstances, to be True to Self. In order for Resonance to be effective, it must be True, it must be cleansed of impurities. It must arise spontaneously out of a natural "Self-ness" (*ziran*). "When a young man and a young woman relate to each other in Truth," writes Magister Liu (XXXI, *Resonance*), "then they cease to be conscious of Self and Other as separate entities. Pure Yin and Yang Energies burgeon within them, deeper feelings are aroused, and from this comes a natural and True Resonance, a Resonance of the Tao. The Heart-and-Mind of the Tao is True, the Human Heart-and-Mind is False. False Heart-and-Mind produces a False Resonance, in which Yin and Yang remain separate. True Heart-and-Mind produces a True Resonance, in which Yin and Yang enter deep communion. Yin may Attract and Yang Respond, or vice versa. But True Resonance always stems from the Heart-and-Mind of the Tao."

Fundamental Concepts

Act, Action, *wei*
This is conscious, purposeful, decisive Action, as opposed to the spontaneous Non-Action of the Taoist.

Advance, *zheng*
Also "to attack," "to march," "to set out on an expedition." Essentially this is a military term, which comes to mean any initiative, as in a campaign. This may or may not be Auspicious, depending on the surrounding circumstances. XXXV, *Advance* 1 and 2: "Advance

is too bold, too lacking in Good Faith, to be wisely undertaken. Advance will only bring grief. Hold Steadfastly to Center. Do not be deluded by False Yin. Then, since there has been no Advance, there can be no grief. Be Steadfast in Emptiness and Stillness." Good Faith enables one to Advance and overcome obstacles.

All-under-Heaven, *tianxia*
From earliest times, this expression was used for the Empire, the whole world known to the Chinese, everything that exists "under the Heavens."

Aspiration, *zhi*
Sometimes translated as Will, Intention, or Purpose, this word implies sustained attention to something and orientation of Action toward it. It is what one is "intent" on. To hold on to this, to be Steadfast in realizing one's Aspirations, is the sign of the True Gentleman. Aspiration is often mentioned in the Commentary on the Image: "Set your Aspirations on the Tao." Let the Heart-and-Mind be completely directed toward that goal. To endure, Aspiration must be immoveable. XXXII/3, *Endurance*: "It requires Inner Strength to turn Aspiration into Action."

Auspicious, *ji*
An Auspicious (or lucky) situation, and the Hexagram associated with that situation, is one that is likely to lead to Fortune or Success. Cf. the French *faste*. One recent etymology, based on Oracle Bone graphs, sees in the early graph the penis of a male child—boys were considered more Auspicious than girls. This is very speculative.

Calamity, *xiong*
An extremely ominous or unlucky situation or outcome. Cf. the French *néfaste*. XLII/3, *Increase*: "Calamity, or Misfortune, can also be the means whereby Self-Cultivation progresses."

Change, *yi*; *bian*; *hua*
These three words are significantly different in meaning. Change (*yi*) is when X replaces or changes places with Y, through exchange or substitution, as with the Hexagrams of the *I Ching*, when Changing Lines cause one Hexagram to Change into another. Change (*bian*) is when X changes but remains X (alteration). Change (*hua*) is when X changes into Y (transformation).

Complete Reality School of Taoism, *quanzhen*
This important Taoist lineage, which emphasized Internal Alchemy, was founded in the twelfth century by Wang Zhe and his disciple Ma Danyang. The eighteenth-century *I Ching* commentator Liu Yiming was a prominent figure in the Dragon Gate branch of this school.

Compliance, Accordance with, going with the Flow, *shun*
This is to Flow, to follow the course of Water, as opposed to going contrary to it, *ni*. This is a Yin quality, closely linked to Yielding. It is to be in Accordance with the Will of Heaven. Heaven aids those who live in Accordance with the Tao. When a person is modest and avoids complacency and arrogance, this is Accordance, conformity with the law of Nature, with the Tao, with the Flow of Heaven's Blessing. XXV, *Freedom from Guile*: The Tao of Freedom from Guile is to be utterly in Accordance with the moment in Time. But Change must above all follow the Flow of Heaven; it must be in Accordance with Nature, in tune with the Aspirations of Man—it must, in other words, accord with the laws of Nature and

Society. It must be True. The Rulers of Antiquity never struggled with the Folk. They let them find their own course, and then guided them in Accordance with it.

Connection, *tong*

This is a key term in the traditional understanding of the *I Ching*. When things and people Connect, the situation becomes Auspicious. XXIX, *The Abyss*: Inner Strength is the only True Source of teaching. It makes Connections. It is the uninterrupted current, one and the same water, passing from one place to another. It reaches everywhere. XXXIX, *Adversity*: In good times, when things Connect, when the Tao circulates freely, the True Gentleman can achieve good for the world. When the times are out of joint, he must cultivate his own person. XLVI/2, *Ascent*: Progress is gradual; it achieves Connection through Sincerity. LX, *Notch*: Notches Connect. Ultimately, with the Notch that adapts to Change and Connects, one reaches Center and Truth; one attains Spiritual Transformation, the Unfathomable Realm.

Danger, *li*

This is the threat or menace looming in the situation; it indicates the need for Caution. When a Dangerous Situation is approached correctly, there will be No Harm. Danger is often pictured as present in Yin Lines. XXIX, The *Abyss*: The Danger lies in the torrent of Water flowing through the Gorge. This Hexagram deals with Danger, how Danger is to be encountered, its effect on the Heart-and-Mind, and how to get out of the old habits and delusions in which Heart-and-Mind is trapped. The message is simple: Persevere. Be True. Practice Good Faith.

Decree of Heaven, *tianming*

This is Fate, Destiny, the mission of Self-Perfection that Heaven has given a person. On a broader scale, it is the Fate of a nation.

Destination, *youwang*

A "place to go," hence a direction for an initiative or Action. Such a direction may be Auspicious or Inauspicious. XLII/1, *Increase*: There is no success in a Destination. Harm. On the Image: An unsuccessful initiative will only bring Harm.

Distress, *lin*

Sometimes translated as Misfortune, or Trouble. A negative result, milder than Calamity.

Divination, *zhen*

This was the early meaning of this term, the resolution of doubt through Divination. In the later, more philosophical interpretation of the *I Ching*, it came to mean Steadfast.

Elixir, Golden Elixir of Immortality, *jindan*

This is the alchemical term for the ultimate result of Self-Cultivation, the Holy Embryo, the Immortal Fetus, the Inner Child. It is central to Magister Liu's interpretation of the *I Ching*: "The union of White and Golden Light produces the Holy Embryo from which Spirit will emerge to become Immortal." XXX, *Fire*: In the sexual-alchemical scheme, the combinations of *Li* and *Kan* (the component Trigrams in this and the previous Doubled Trigram Hexagram) create Hexagrams LXIII, *Complete*, and LXIV, *Incomplete*. Their interaction, to use Joseph Needham's words, extracts "vital" Yang from "seeming" Yin, and "vital" Yin from "seeming" Yang. This is what ultimately forms the Inner Child, the Primal Unity. Through this process of Transformation, "although belonging to Yin, the woman's body *becomes* male; the Man, though originally Yang, *becomes* female. . . . I am fundamentally Yang, but contain within me the height of Yin; she is fundamentally Yin, but conceals within her the most marvellous True Essence of Yang." L, *The Cauldron*: The Cauldron, writes Magister Liu, is the vessel for the process of Self-Cultivation, for the Refinement of the Elixir—the Great Medicine of the Tao. This Work of Refinement dissolves Yin Energy and strengthens Yang Energy; it "cooks" the "raw" and "renews" the "old." It Illumines the Heart-and-Mind; it realizes Life-Destiny. This is Supremely Auspicious. This is the Tao of Great Fortune. LIII, *Gradual*: This union grows stronger with time, until finally the Work is completed and effort becomes effortless spontaneity. Yin and Yang are united, Firm and Yielding merge. This produces the seed of the Elixir, a something emerging from nothingness. This is the Path of Self-Cultivation. It is also the Path of Marriage. They must both be founded in Truth. If not, they will not be Auspicious. Without Truth, any amount of striving for perfection—alchemical, sexual, or spiritual—is vain. The quest must be both Gradual and True. It must plumb the depths of essential Nature, of Life-Destiny. Then all may attain the Great Tao. LV/5, *Canopy*: Emptiness of Heart-and-Mind, writes Magister Liu, fills the Belly of the Tao. This is Illumination, this is Celebration, White Light shining in an Empty Room, the Golden Elixir formed. This is the right time to practice the Tao of Non-Action.

Emptiness, Emptying the Mind, *xu; xuxin*
The Tao gathers in Emptiness, in Quietude, in the Empty Room, in the Void of a Heart-and-Mind emptied of feeling and passion. XXXV, *Advance*: Regret arises from a Heart-and-Mind that is not yet Empty. II, *Earth*, On the Image: Inner Emptiness, writes Magister Liu, the Open Space of Heart-and-Mind, enables Outer Acceptance. It enables the Taoist to sustain Others, to accept insult and injury, hardship and sickness, just as the Earth sustains Mountains, just as the Ocean takes into itself the Rivers. XX, *Observation*, On the Image: Jia Yi's poem—"The wise man's is / the Larger View. / For him all is possible. . . . / He lets things go, / Cleaves to the Tao. . . . / His life is a floating, / His death a rest. / Still as the Stillness / Of a deep ravine; / Drifting like an unmoored boat. . . . / Feeding and floating / On Emptiness." XXXIV/5, *Great Might*: This gentle emptying of Heart-and-Mind uses knowledge of Others to open up a space within the limitations of Self, to brighten its Light. XXXV/2, *Advance*: In the Darkness made up of three Yin Lines, Illumination is obscured. Advance will only bring grief. Hold Steadfastly to Center. Do not be deluded by False Yin. Then, since there has been no Advance, there can be no grief. Be Steadfast in Emptiness and Stillness. True Yin will appear, False Yin will transform itself and vanish. XXXV/5: This is Illumination that brings Fulfillment out of Emptiness, writes Magister Liu. This Yin Line makes positive use of the two Yang Lines surrounding it. It nurtures itself on the Illumination of Others, recognizing that the Illumination of Self is insufficient. Regret arises from a Heart-and-Mind that is not yet Empty. Once the Heart-and-Mind is Empty, then all concerns for success or failure fall away. L/3, *The Cauldron*: Nonetheless, with a patient Emptying of Heart-and-Mind, one can come to understand one's Inner Nature. LXI, *Good Faith*: That Void, a Heart-and-Mind free from prejudice, open (like an "empty boat"), with no restricting consciousness of Self. The "empty boat" of this Hexagram (Wood over Lake) is Master Zhuang's Image of the Taoist, the "man who wanders in the world, making himself empty: how can anyone cause him Harm?" LXIV/5, *Incomplete*: Empty the Human Heart-and-Mind, writes Magister Liu, and seek the Heart-and-Mind of the Tao. Do not be deluded or led astray by false brilliance. This is the birth of the Light of the True Gentleman. It is quiet and still; it is responsive and connecting. It leads to Completion.

Energy, *qi*
Also translated as "vitality," "life breath," or "vital breath." One of the most fundamental concepts in the whole of Chinese traditional thinking. It is the basic substance out of which the entire Universe is composed. In the words of the Confucian Sage Mencius: "The way to make *qi* is to nourish it with Integrity." Human beings have some measure of control over the rate at which their original *qi* stagnates or is depleted. Balance in the mental and emotional spheres can be induced by Self-Cultivation. Various techniques designed to retain (and, ideally, augment) the *qi*'s activity include both moral and physical arts: moderation in daily habits, adjustment of posture, meditation, habituation to goodness, and a calm acceptance of fate. *Qi* is a force that expands and animates the world in a turning motion, the revolutions by which it spreads and distributes itself into every corner of Space and Time. In modern Chinese, the word for "weather" is *tianqi*, the Energy of Heaven.

Fill the Belly, *shifu*
This is to empty the Human Heart-and-Mind and to fill, or fulfill, the Heart-and-Mind of Tao. It is to Cultivate Life, to refrain from arbitrary Patterns of thought and Actions in order to accumulate Energy. For the origin of the phrase, see *The Tao and the Power*, chapter 3: "Therefore the Sage rules by emptying their hearts and filling their bellies. . . ."

Firm, *gang*
A quality of Yang. Firmness often needs to be modified, or tempered, by the Yielding gentleness of Yin.

Folk, *zhong*
The word for Folk, *zhong*, occurs frequently in the Oracle Bone Inscriptions. The graph shows three men beneath either the sun or an eye, perhaps a group toiling in the heat of the day, or under the watchful eye of an overseer. Ping-ti Ho summarizes the Oracle Bone references to *zhong* as including (1) serfs laboring in the royal fields or fields belonging to lords and officials, (2) retainers participating in the royal hunts, and (3) soldiers; but never Sacrificial Victims (this being reserved for barbarian captives).

Fortune, *heng*
The word was in its earliest usage closely linked to the word for Sacrifice, and meant the "fortunate" state of affairs resulting from a Sacrifice well received.

Good Faith, *fu*
The French *bonne foi*, used by Philastre to translate *fu*, suggested to me Good Faith. Others translate it as Sincerity (Legge), Inner Truth (Richard Wilhelm), Trust (Lynn), and Inward Confidence and Sincerity (Blofeld). "This Hexagram is the Energy of Inner Truth," wrote Richard Wilhelm. "Truth understood here in it deepest meaning, Truth as Harmony with Heaven." All of these ideas—Sincerity, Inner Truth, Harmony, Good Faith—are closely linked. It is through Inner Truth, through open candor, through Good Faith, that "a man does justice to his own essence and remains true to his vocation." Good Faith is one of the underlying principles of the *I Ching*. Indeed, it is an absolute condition of the very process of *I Ching* consultation that it should be done in Good Faith, with Sincerity and Honesty. Only then, when every pretense, every ripple of confused consciousness, has settled into a state of quiet and receptivity, is the Oracle able to function as a mirror. XXXVII/6, *The Family*: Good Faith, personal character, and Self-Cultivation inspire respect. XLII/5, *Increase*: With Good Faith and Kindness one sees the Myriad

Things as one great entity, one sees Self and Other as one great Family. It is like the Wind blowing. . . . Everything dances before it. LXI, *Good Faith*: The Power of Good Faith, of Sincerity or Truth, emanates from an Inner Void that allows the fullest development of a person's Nature. LX, *Notch*: The Tao of the True Gentleman, his *Good Faith*, Connects the world. XXIX, *The Abyss*: Persevere. Practice Good Faith. Hold fast to the Yang Line in the Center of both Trigrams. Good Faith is the Heart-and-Mind of the Tao, writes Magister Liu. With Good Faith, the Auspicious interaction between Yin and Yang can be emulated.

Great Man, *daren*
This may originally have referred to a Shaman or Priest-King. With time it came to mean a person of stature, a Man of the Tao, a Teacher, someone whose wisdom would benefit the individual consulting the *I Ching*. Personal Transmission through Teachers is a recurring theme throughout Chinese thinking. XXXIX, *Adversity*: The Great Man is one in whom the Heart-and-Mind of the Child has not been lost. This is the Heart-and-Mind of the Tao. The Great Man is a True Master of the Tao, a man who has attained Release from Danger, who has completed the Work step by step, in due order. He has reached the Gate of Life, the Door of Death. XLVI, *Ascent*: The Great Man's words can open up a path leading upward toward Wisdom, like an all-penetrating wind. LVII, *Kneeling*: The Wind blows further and further into the distance, writes Magister Liu, rising ever higher, penetrating everywhere, entering into the Tao. Its Work is unremitting, reaching a deep level of Self-Realization. This is its Slight Fortune. Some need a Destination. They need to "see a Great Man," one who considers Inner Nature and Life-Destiny to be of supreme importance, one who values the Tao and the Power above all, one to whom the illusory body is so much dry wood, worldly wealth a mere floating cloud. His Inner Self is rich, although his Outward Appearance may seem insufficient. His Heart-and-Mind is firm, his Aspirations have distant horizons. He never ceases until he reaches the Great Tao. Such is the Great Man.

Harm, *jiu*
This occurs most often in the phrase "No Harm," meaning that whatever the other qualities of a situation and a decision may be, there will be no *serious* negative consequences. Nothing *really untoward* will happen, no Misfortune. It is closely related to the term Danger, which indicates the threat of potentially negative consequences (Harm) in a situation. L/2, *The Cauldron*: Cultivate the Heart-and-Mind of the Tao, free it from the Human Heart-and-Mind. Then even hatred can cause no Harm. LVIII/5, *Joy*: Good Faith and Caution, writes Magister Liu, save one from the threat of Harm in the Yin Line in Top Place above. The Danger comes from self-satisfaction and conceit (Yang in Yang). This will inevitably bring failure. Ability can prosper only with Humility, and a willingness to learn from Men of the Tao. Those who consort with Small Men and distance themselves from True Gentlemen will surely incur Danger.

Harmony, *he*
Harmony is linked to Centrality, Sincerity, and Good Faith. The opening words of the *Doctrine of the Mean* (*Zhongyong*) bring this out (see the section "Terms and References," above, under "Center"). XX, *Observation*: Wang Yanshou's poem—"The Emperors of Old / Harmonized / With the Mystic Tao, / And there was peace."

Heart-and-Mind, *xin*
This translation (rather than either "heart" or "mind") "reflects the blending of belief and desire (thought and feeling, ideas and emotions)" in the Chinese word. This compound

English word is singular ("The Heart-and-Mind *is* set on externals. . . .") and has nothing whatsoever to do with winning over "hearts and minds." XL, *Release*: The Human Heart-and-Mind generates Danger. The Heart-and-Mind of the Tao is still weak. Yang Strength is led astray by Weakness (this is a Yin Place). Trust in the Heart-and-Mind of the Tao. It alone will bring Good Faith and Release from the Human Heart-and-Mind. XLI, *Decrease*: When Ignorance and Folly generate emotion, writes Magister Liu, then the Human Heart-and-Mind cannot Decrease. Seeking an Increase in the Heart-and-Mind of the Tao, one meets instead with Decrease. This is "three travelers" losing a companion. When, however, there is a Decrease in the dualistic thinking of the Human Heart-and-Mind, and an Increase in the unitary thinking of the Heart-and-Mind of the Tao, then Yin and Yang can join together. Such an Increase comes in the midst of Decrease. This is the "lone traveler gaining a friend." XLIV/4, *Encounter*: The Heart-and-Mind of the Tao is obscured; the Human Heart-and-Mind runs riot. Damage is caused by the unchecked influence of Yin Energy. Calamity is only to be expected. XLIV/5: But the lingering influence of Yin in First Place is still felt, the threat of Danger. The Human Heart-and-Mind must be restrained by the Heart-and-Mind of the Tao. Expel cleverness, contain and treasure the Light within. L/4, *The Cauldron*: When the legs of the Cauldron are broken, writes Magister Liu, then the Heart-and-Mind of the Tao is injured, and the Human Heart-and-Mind is stirred into activity. The Treasure of Life-Destiny is lost ("spilled victuals"). The Heart-and-Mind of the Tao has been obscured. The True Fire of Nature must be used to cleanse away all Yin elements. LIX, *Dispersal*: A man's True Yin and Yang become Dispersed, Magister Liu writes, when the man clings to his Human Heart-and-Mind and abandons the Heart-and-Mind of the Tao. Every step down this path takes him further toward Danger. If he can only embrace the Heart-and-Mind of the Tao and abandon the Human Heart-and-Mind, then he can take hold of the Jewel of Life in the Tiger's Lair, he can find the Bright Pearl in the Dragon's Pool (enlightenment in the mundane world).

Humility, *qian*

XIX/3, *Approach*: Humility (an Approach that rejects the False and holds fast to the True) can save the situation.

Illumination, *ming*

This is the Light of Spirit, the Tao shining in an Empty Room. XXXV, *Advance*: When the Human Heart-and-Mind has learned to Flow with Truth, then the Heart-and-Mind of the Tao is Illumined. Flow generates Illumination. Illumination generates Flow. Sincerity enhances Illumination. Illumination enhances Sincerity. XXXVI, *Darkness*: To nurture the Alchemical Fire is to nurture Illumination. XXX, *Fire*: Inner Illumination, writes Magister Liu, produces Outer Illumination. What is Illumination? It is the ability to see *with continuous clarity* the original Strength or Essence of things. This Vision itself comes from Inner Strength, from Sincerity at the Center of Being, reaching out and connecting with the outside, with the Four Quarters. Nothing can deceive it. It sees things as they are. It sees that everything, everywhere, to left and right, is the Tao, Connected, Attached. Illumination itself spreads like Fire. It is a chain reaction. Fire is not a substance, it is an event, an interaction. As Professor Mun writes, Fire has no form, it is *given* form by the burning object to which it is "attached."

Inner Alchemy, *neidan*

This is a general term for the "inward turning" tradition of Self-Cultivation, whereby the Adept achieves existential and intellectual integration. It makes use of the symbolism of the *I Ching* for this inner journey, and, while fundamentally Taoist, it includes elements from Confucianism and Buddhism. The ultimate goal is to return to Unity with the Tao, to create or rather re-create the Inner Child, the "new man," the Golden Elixir.

Inner Strength, Inner Power, *de*
This is the fruit of Self-Cultivation. It is the manifestation or *mana* of the Tao, operating in the human sphere. It is the personal capacity to carry out the most Harmonious course of Action, or Non-Action, which is the Way or Tao. XVII, *Following*: In the words of Taoist Master Zhuang, "Cultivate Heart-and-Mind, / Let it be unmoved / By sorrow and joy, / Know that certain things are inevitable. / This is the height of Spiritual Strength." XX, *Observation*, On the Image of the Hexagram: The Power (or *mana*) of the Ancient Kings was gained from their Contemplation of the Mystic Tao. Their teachings were adapted to the character and circumstances of the Folk. All-under-Heaven obeyed. The wisdom of the True Gentleman is equally derived from broad Perception and Self-Perception, from his "powers of Observation" or Awareness. XXIX, *The Abyss*: Inner Strength is the only True Source of teaching. It makes Connections. It is the uninterrupted current, one and the same water, passing from one place to another. It reaches everywhere. XLIV, *Encounter*: By contrast, comments Magister Liu, there is a True Encounter, True Intercourse of Heaven and Earth, between the two Yang Lines (Second and Fifth), which are both Centered (one in Yin Place, one in Yang). This lies at the root of every prosperous undertaking, in Nature as in the world of men. The Taoist has the Inner Strength to adapt to the Transformations of Yin and Yang. The Taoist can be Yielding within Firmness, can be Firm while also being Yielding, can navigate in and out of Yin and Yang. The Taoist can "encounter" a woman but not "marry" her. Yin Energy will then obey Yang Energy. XLV, *Gathering*: Weapons of Wisdom must always be at the ready, writes Magister Liu. Spiritual Awareness must always be silently at work. With weapons such as these one can maintain presence of mind, and the Jewel of Life will not be damaged, even though Water may flood the land (Lake above Earth, another "unforeseen eventuality"). Individuals too must gather together their inner resources; they must harness their Essential Energy in the cause of Spiritual Development. They must respect their true original Nature, their "Ancestor." They must not forsake their Roots. The Ritual of Sacrifice, the attitude of Steadfast reverence, must be followed by commitment, by Action—by setting out toward a Destination. Momentary perceptions of the Void, instants of enlightenment, are not enough. Steps must be taken on solid ground—step after step—if anything real is to be accomplished. LX, *Notch*: The True Gentleman practices the Tao, building Power, Inner Strength, taking every step in a measured way, like Water flowing easily from one place to another. His every word is well considered. He is at peace, like a Lake on which no wave stirs. When he acts, he never loses touch with his Inner Nature, he never restricts himself to a single Pattern or Notch. He is never restricted by Yin and Yang. Each Notch has its limits. Every Notch Connects. That is its Fortune.

Life-Destiny, *ming*
This is the self-perfection that Heaven has given a person, to accomplish which is the consummation of Taoist practice. It can also be translated as Life-Store, the font of vitality, or, as the Taoist Adept would put it, the store of "vital forces of a human being that are wasted in sex, violent emotions, and desires, all of which cause the vital fluids (sexual fluids, sweat, saliva, moist breath) to drain away. When this Life-Store is exhausted, the result is death."

Movement, *dong*
This is contrasted with Stillness. Hexagram I, *Heaven*: As Zhu Xi comments on the opening of the Great Treatise, "Movement is the constant mode of Yang, Stillness the constant mode of Yin."

Myriad Things, *wanwu*
Everything that exists, all external phenomena.

Nature, *tian*
Literally, Heaven. The course of Heaven which things follow or should follow—the recurrence of the Seasons, the cycles of the Heavenly Bodies, the customs of men—is the Tao of Heaven. Everything which man cannot alter—his Nature, his Destiny—is due to the Decree of Heaven.

Non-Action, *wuwei*
This is not idly "doing nothing," the attitude of a *fait néant*, but the relaxed, effortless attitude of the Taoist, who *seems* to *do* nothing, but actually does a great deal, because he is naturally in Harmony with the Tao. Things just happen. IV, *Youthful Folly*: Magister Liu emphasizes that the Darkness can only be overcome through natural innocence. Be open, be still, be sincere, be respectful. This is the path of Non-Action.

Non-Being, Nothing, *wu*
This is the opposite of Being. It is the formless, undifferentiated Void or Chaos out of which Being comes. It is in returning to that Non-Being, in the Return to that Root, that the Taoist (and the well-attuned consultant of the *I Ching*) seeks his or her Destiny. *The Tao and the Power*, chapter 64: "Deal with things in their Non-Being; / Order things before they reach disorder."

Pattern, *wen*
The word may have once meant a tattoo on the body, then other sorts of pattern in the natural world. It went on to mean patterns of many kinds, on textiles or other stuffs, thence ornamentation, writing, literature, culture, and civilization in general. See commentary on II/5, *Earth*.

Potential Energy, *shi*
This is the Inner Dynamic, the Latent Potential, contained in a situation, in a given place or moment in time. Act accordingly, regulated by consideration of the Notches, of Time, of the Potential Energy of the moment. LX, *Notch*: Know when *not* to Act, and at such times be Still. Recognize that seeds of new activity, Triggers of Action, hinges of Things, have yet to mature further. It is also a key word in *The Art of War*.

Power, *de*
See Inner Strength.

Profit, *li*
This is the positive or lucky outcome, as opposed to Harm. Also translated as Beneficial or Favorable.

Recluse, *yinshi*
The Hermit. XXIX, *The Abyss*: Xie Lingyun's poem—"All my life / I yearned to be a Hermit, / But was too weak. / I went astray. . . . / Now at last I can embrace / The Light of Innermost Self. . . . "XVIII, *Blight*: The Recluse deals with the situation in model fashion. He cultivates Inner Strength, "living in solitude," "embracing Unity." XXV/5, *Freedom from Guile*: Just as "non-medication" gives the body a chance to restore its natural balance of Yin and Yang, so retiring from the world (rejecting its "medicine") and becoming a

Recluse is a Joy which offers a chance to regain the spiritual balance that has been disturbed by worldly preoccupations.

Regret, *hui*
The fundamental negative emotion. Often, when the situation improves, this is described as "going away."

Retreat, *dun*
The times may require the True Gentleman to retreat. XXXIII, *Retreat*: Through strategic Retreat, Inner Strength can be nurtured, Steadfast in the Tao. Heaven itself is limitless, it is infinite; the Mountain is high, but has limits. The two together are an emblem of Retreat. Through Retreat, by being "aloof," by withdrawing into Inner Contemplation, the True Gentleman preserves Inner Strength. Small Men cannot come near him or cause him Harm. Zhang Heng's poem—"King Wen laid out the Yarrow Stalks. / I received the Hexagram Retreat. / Profit / In a leisurely Retreat, / My fair name preserved. / I traveled to the Mountains, / Into the far distance, / Flying on the swift Wind, / Spreading my fame. . . . / My affinity is with the Dark Bird. / I shall / Return / To the Mother. / I shall find peace." The Mother he sought was the Tao. The True Gentleman, who practices the Tao, writes Magister Liu, gathers his Vital Spirit, vast as the Heavens. He learns to live in the world without injuring Spirit. He dwells in the dust but is able to rise above the dust. The False Taoist is a Small Man, tiny as a grain of mustard. The slightest thing is more than he can tolerate. A wise Leader, writes Professor Mun, knows when to Retreat, when conditions are not in his favor. XXXIII/6, *Retreat*: Xie Lingyun's poem—"This hill was once / Refuge for a Hermit, / Leisurely Retreat for a Sage. . . . / Here I may do as I please, / Wander off alone, / Enjoy the moonlight, / The plashing of the stream. / Here I may savor each moment's pleasure / To the full. . . ."

Return, *fan*; *gui*; *fu*
Return is the Movement of the Tao. XVIII, *Blight*: In the Upper Trigram, writes Magister Liu, the single Yang at the Top signals a Return to the Root, a Return to Life, remedying the harmful effects of Yin Energy, cultivating the Tao. LIX/4, *Dispersal*: With Dispersal of False Yin, Return to True Yang is possible. XXIV, *Return*: This, writes Magister Liu, is the Return of Yang, of the sun which has set only to rise again, which has "gone out" only to "return" and "enter" once more. The Tao moves like this. It recurs in cycles. It moves around, backward, in reverse motion. It "returns" to the primal state of simplicity, to the Root. It revolves, according to the constant Transformations of Change. The Taoist *turns away* from the world. He Returns to Self, to basic Nature. XXV, *Freedom from Guile*: *The Tao and the Power*, chapter 16—"Return to Life-Destiny, Heaven's Decree, / Is knowledge of Constancy; / Knowledge of Constancy is Enlightenment." XXXVI / 1, *Darkness*: In the words of Dong Zhongshu, "Alas! The World is against me! / I Grieve that none will join me / In my Return." XXXIX, *Adversity*: Lu Ji—There is a need to turn inward, to Return; there is a need for Self-Reflection. In times of Adversity, one cannot Act. To overcome difficulty, one must reflect on Self, examine and cultivate one's own Inner Strength. In good times, when things Connect, when the Tao circulates freely, the True Gentleman can achieve good for the world. But when the times are out of joint, in times of Adversity, he must cultivate his own person. This Hexagram, writes Magister Liu, is about preserving the Primordial in the midst of the Mundane. Yang is trapped between Yin. The Heart-and-Mind of the Tao is encumbered with the Human Heart-and-Mind. This is an extremely dangerous situation, fraught with Yin Energy. The Danger can be averted by letting the Human Heart-and-Mind gradually fade away. Then the Heart-and-Mind of the Tao can

gradually be born. The Great Man is one in whom the Heart-and-Mind of the Child has not been lost. The Child has no knowledge, no greed, no goal. This is the Heart-and-Mind of the Tao, of the Great Man.

Ride, *cheng*
This is used in the Commentary on the Image to describe the relationship between a Yin Line and the one immediately "below" it, on which it relies, or "rides." XLVII/3, *Confinement*, On the Image: Held by thorns, he Rides a Firm Line (Yang in Second Place). XVI/5, *Elation*, On the Image: This Line Rides Firm Yang (Yang in Fourth Place).

Ritual, *li*
Originally, this referred to religious Ritual, or Rites, and Ceremony. "Sacrificing to the Ancestors at the right time and place and with the proper deportment and attitude is Ritual. So is the proper performance of Divination. In a broader sense, it covers the entire gamut of ceremonial or polite behaviour, secular as well as religious." This extended idea in the Confucian worldview (sometimes translated "propriety") included "the full panoply of appropriate and thus mutually satisfying behaviours built upon emotional insights . . . encompassing circumspect behaviour, considerate acts, and exquisite courtesy. . . . An all-embracing system whereby to join Heaven and Earth in Harmony . . . to moderate human likes and dislikes and to adjust joy and anger." XXXIV, *Great Might*: Ritual is the assurance of Moderation in Movement and Stillness. It is the Notch of Regulation. It is Order; it constitutes the rules for Self-Cultivation and for living in the world. Without Ritual, when impulse and desire take over, then there is only False Might. Take one step at a time. All will be merged into the Wondrous Tao.

Sage, *sheng*; *shengren*
XXXII, *Endurance*: The Sage endures in the Tao. XXXVII, *The Family*: The Sage who finds Joy in Heaven, who knows Life-Destiny, Heaven's decree, is free from care, at peace with his land. He is truly kind. He can love.

Self, *ji*
XXXVII/6, *The Family*: When Self no longer exists, Light shines in an Empty Room.

Self-Cultivation, *yangsheng*; *yangxing*; *xiuyang*; *xiudao*
This is possibly the most important single expression in the traditional understanding of the *I Ching*. It is the means by which the individual can reach the Tao. XIX/4, *Approach*: Genuine Self-Cultivation is Mastery of the Heart-and-Mind. Self-Cultivation is a term that covers a wide range of practices crossing over many borders in Chinese ways of thinking and living. These can be physical or psychological (various forms of yoga, including elements such as breathing and massage, or plain "sitting" and still meditation); they can be sexual or dietetic (including the ingestion of various drugs); they can be simple ethical principles, such as living according to Moderation and Harmony. Self-Cultivation in the broad sense also includes such activities as calligraphy, painting, music, and all of the arts, when carried out in Harmony with the Tao. XXXVII/6, *The Family*: The Alchemical Work begins with Self-Cultivation. Krishnamurti wrote: Self-Knowledge has no end, it is an endless river. Only when the mind is tranquil—through Self-Knowledge and not through imposed Self-Discipline—only then, in that tranquillity, in that silence, can reality come into being. It is only then that there can be bliss, that there can be creative action. XXI/6, *Biting*: The Work of genuine understanding requires the peeling away of layer upon layer, until one reaches the Marrow of the Tao, True Knowledge, Clear

Perception. All depends on the considerable effort involved in the proper Work of Self-Cultivation. XXV, *Freedom from Guile*: The Tao of Self-Cultivation sets free. The Tao of Freedom from Guile is to be utterly in Accordance with the moment in Time. To attain this Tao, it is imperative to seek out the personal teaching of a True Master. XXIX, *The Abyss*: This repeated realization of what has been learned through Self-Cultivation, this "becoming," has its source in Inner Strength and Truth. XLI, *Decrease*: Magister Liu often uses the phrase "the Utmost Excellence" from the opening of *The Great Learning*, one of the Four Books, a short text all educated Chinese of the traditional period knew by heart. The phrase itself forms part of the classic definition of the Tao of Self-Cultivation, shared by Confucians and Taoists alike. "From the Son of Heaven down to the common people everyone should regard Self-Cultivation as the Root." XLVIII, *The Well*: JM—Just as Water is drawn from the Well, the numinous content deep in the soul is drawn upward into consciousness. This is a powerful Image of the process of Self-Cultivation. To look into the Water of the Well is the mystic attitude of Contemplation. The Well is indeed a graphic symbol of the soul itself, and of all things feminine. Wood goes down into Water, but emerges out of Water, writes Magister Liu, through the Danger of the Abyss. This Hexagram represents the inexhaustible Nourishment of Water. Those who practice the Self-Cultivation of the Tao are able to nourish Self in this way. They can then nourish Others. This is like the Well. Others and Self are both nourished. Towns (Others, the outside world) may change (men "come and go" at the Well), but not the Well (the Inner Self). To teach Others before one has attained the Tao is to raise Water from the Well with a broken pitcher. One can guide Others only when one has attained the Tao. The Well Hexagram is all about Self-Cultivation. LVIII/3, *Joy*: Outer Joy forsakes the True and seeks the False. It hinders Self-Cultivation in the Tao. This is Joy in the service of the Outer World.

Sincerity, *cheng*
Also translated as Integrity. The wholeness or completeness of a person displayed in the authenticity of his words. Being true to oneself. Being Real and True. Good Faith. Refusing to deceive oneself. Major et al. write in *The Huainanzi* (page 871): "Complete, uninhibited integration between a person's most basic, spontaneous impulses and his or her expressed words and actions. . . . When stimulated by external phenomena, consciousness moves within the mind-body matrix as a wave of *qi* [Energy] that culminates in feeling or thought or sound or motion or some combination of them. Most of these expressions emerge depleted of the potency and dynamism intrinsic to the field from which they have arisen, because they are refracted through the prisms of self-consciousness, preconception, and insecurity that obstruct the ordinary human mind [Heart-and-Mind]. In the rare instances that (or among the rare individuals for whom) an internal response evolves from baseline to full expression totally unimpeded, it produces a moment imbued with extraordinary power. Such sincerity can evoke a response in the minds and bodies of others or paranormal phenomena such as telekinesis." This is a high-flown explanation. But it comes near to evoking the sheer Power of Sincerity. That same Power enables readings of the *I Ching* to "speak" with Truth. That Power of Sincerity is an indispensable and underlying condition of any effective consultation. Honesty, seriousness, being true to one's True Self, true to the Nature of being, Actuality, Realness. XLI, *Decrease*: With Sincerity every thought is True. Wherever the Heart-and-Mind is sincere, wherever there is Good Faith, it can be seen in one's Actions. Sincerity is the Tao of Heaven. The attainment of Sincerity is the Tao of Man. One who possesses Sincerity attains the Center without effort. Cf. the *Doctrine of the Mean*. LXI, *Good Faith*: The Spiritual Strength of Good Faith is likened to the Wind, a gentle breeze blowing over the Water of the Lake. XXV, *Freedom from Guile*: the Tao of Sincerity, of Innocence, causes each and every thing to be True to

its Nature, to its Life-Destiny, to Return to a state of Freedom from Guile. Each thing contains its own Truth. XXV/5: *Absolute Sincerity*, writes Magister Liu, brings a Return to Innocence, to Freedom from Guile. The Inner Child (the Alchemical Embryo) has been formed. XLI, *Decrease*: Few are capable of being Sincere in this endeavor. They may begin it, but they cannot bring it to a Conclusion. With Sincerity, every thought is True. Wherever the Heart-and-Mind is Sincere, wherever there is Good Faith, it can be seen in one's Actions.

Spontaneity, Suchness, *ziran*
Literally, the "so of itself." XXIV/5, *Return*: This is an easy, spontaneous Return, accomplished with nobility of Spirit (*dun*). It is simple, genuine, honest, and generous. *Dun* describes an essential spontaneous quality of the Tao. See *The Tao and the Power*, chapter 15: "How simple is the Tao, like the Uncarved Block!"

Springs, Triggers, Hinges, Pivots, *ji*
These are "that from which movement starts, like the trigger of a crossbow." They are the inklings of Change in the air. Words and Actions are Hinges of the Door, the Trigger of the True Gentleman's Crossbow. LX, *Notch*: The "subtlest Springs," the infinitesimally small "germs of Change," are the first inklings or stirrings, the faintest hints or suggestions of Movement in the environment. They are turning points. In *The Art of War*, in many ways a simplistic (and by no means always benign) strategic application of some of the basic ideas found in the *I Ching*, it is the Warrior Adept's awareness of the Springs that brings victory. Hexagram I, *Heaven*: This is the unique access the *I Ching* provides to the deep inner structure of the present moment, of the "now," the perception it brings of the moment's Inner Dynamic or Potential Energy. It does not bring *victory* as such. Instead it bestows both Spiritual and strategic insight, and so Strength or Power.

Steadfast, *zhen*
To be Steadfast (Legge translates it as Correct and Firm, Wilhelm as Persevering) is one of the key qualities advocated by the *I Ching*. It goes hand in hand with Self-Cultivation, Sincerity, and Good Faith. It is the Resolve to hold fast to the Truth, to the Tao. This is the positive mental attitude that dispels Regret. The word originally (in the Oracle text) meant Divination or Augury. XVI/2, *Elation*: "To abide quietly and firmly in one's station," writes Legge, "like a rock, unaffected by others, not misled by illusion, by greed, by cravings, not letting False externals harm Inner Truth, alert to the slightest signs of Change—this is to be Steadfast. This is Auspicious." LII, *Mountain*: Xie Lingyun's poem—"I cherish the Tao, / I will never abandon it. / My heart is one / With the trees of late autumn; / My eyes delight /In the buds of early spring. / I will remain Steadfast, / Waiting for my end, / Content to find peace in the natural order of things."

Stillness, *jing*
Tranquillity. One of the keys to Self-Cultivation. LII, *Mountain*: Richard Wilhelm—"It is always an experience to go up this mountain. You continue to see its cloudy top rise up out of the host of the other hills, and it seems as if it were revealing a secret every time: the secret of the connection between life and death in that great Stillness whose symbol is the Hexagram Mountain." Inner and Outer Stillness, writes Magister Liu, are connected. Through Stillness one Cultivates Energy. One discerns that which is good, and holds to it Steadfastly. Outer Stillness is Action that knows its proper time and place, it is True Movement. This too forms part of Stillness. *The Tao and the Power*, chapter 16: "The Return to the Root is Stillness, recognition of Life-Destiny." Quietness and Stillness represent Meditation, which, by keeping external things quiescent, quickens the Inner

World. XVIII/6, *Blight*: Xie Lingyun's poem—"Fain would I live in solitude, / Embrace Unity. / There, in that fusion / Of tranquillity and wisdom, / Inborn Nature will begin to heal."

Supreme Ultimate, *taiji*

The Unitary Pole, the Supreme Ridgepole or Pinnacle, the prime principle of the world, from which Yin and Yang (and therefore the entire system of Trigrams and Hexagrams, the Tao, and the whole of the Universe) are generated. For the Taoist Alchemist, it is Illumination, the Real Nature of things, the Elixir, the Light that lies within each human being, simultaneously the point of departure and the goal of the alchemical Work.

Tao, *dao*

"The Tao that can be spoken of is not the true Tao." These are the opening words of *The Tao and the Power*. The True Taoist is incognito. The word *Tao* was translated by the Jesuit Jean-Baptiste Régis as *Vis Operativa et Operandi, Via, Ratio, Lex*. The Tao is "the unnameable in union with which we are spontaneously on course." To adapt the words of Krishnamurti, it is "that extraordinary sense of reality, that creative being, which comes when we really understand ourselves." Major writes in *The Huainanzi* (page 872): "To say that it is the origin, totality, and animating impulse of all that is, ever was, and ever shall be is inadequate, for this would exclude what is not, never was, and never shall be. . . . The Way is ultimately ineffable and thus cannot be 'understood' cognitively. Even though it cannot be known intellectually, because the Way is fundamental to all Being, it can be experienced and embodied." XLII/5, *Increase*: Good Faith and Inner Strength prevail. This Yang Line is Centered and True, writes Magister Liu. The Great Tao is complete. With Good Faith and Kindness, one sees the Myriad Things as one great entity; one sees Self and Other as one great Family. It is like the Wind blowing. . . . Everything dances before it. LV/4, *Canopy*: The Darkness increases, writes Magister Liu. Cultivate Inner Light, go to meet the Lord of True Mind, though he may often be hard to see. The True Taoist often conceals his Treasure; he lives hidden in the crowd. But once met, he kindles Light in others. LV/6: The darkened, deserted house, writes Magister Liu, is ignorance of the Great Tao, conceit; it is self-satisfaction, vain embellishment of the façade. This gaudy shrine contains no Buddha. LVIII, *Joy*: This Joy is the Joy of Cultivating the Tao, writes Magister Liu. Aspiration is set on the Tao. Joy is in the Tao. To practice the Tao is Joy. This is Fortune. With Inner Joy (in the Lower Trigram) comes Outer Joy (in the Upper Trigram). If Inner Joy is False, so too will be Outer Joy. True Joy is long-lasting. False Joy is short-lived. This is the Profit of Steadfastness. The True Taoist finds no Joy in sensual pleasure or material wealth. His Joy is in the Tao and its Inner Strength, its Power. If the Tao itself is ineffable, it is hardly any easier to describe Men of the Tao. LIX, *Dispersal*: From *The Tao and the Power*, chapter 15—"In olden times Men of the Tao were wondrously subtle; / They were Mysteriously Connected, inscrutable, too deep to fathom. . . . Cautious they were, as if crossing a stream in winter; / Circumspect, as if sensing peril on every side. / They were respectful, like guests. / Theirs was a Dispersal, like ice melting. . . ." LXIII/6, *Gradual*: The Taoist must combine Action and Non-Action in a timely way, varying them according to the needs of the moment. The Taoist pays attention to both Emptiness and Substance, understanding both Inner Essence and Life-Destiny, the objective external Life-Situation. XXIX, *The Abyss*: Angus Graham commenting on Taoist Master Lie—"One whose mind is a pure mirror of his situation, unaware of himself and therefore making no distinction between Profit and Danger, will act with absolute assurance, and nothing will stand in his way. . . . Outside things can obstruct and injure us only if we are assertive instead of adaptable. . . . Possession of the Tao is thus a capacity for dealing effortlessly with external things."

True Gentleman, *junzi*

Also translated as the Superior Man. XXXII, *Endurance*: The True Gentleman stands firm; he does not change direction. Hexagram I, *Heaven*, On the Words: Neither oppressed by solitude, nor saddened by neglect, in Joy he Acts, in sorrow stands aside. He is never uprooted. XXXIII, *Retreat*: The True Gentleman distances himself from the Small Man, not in bitterness, but wishing to remain aloof. The True Gentleman, who practice the Tao, gathers his Vital Spirit, vast as the Heavens. He learns to live in the world without injuring Spirit. He dwells in the dust but is able to rise above the dust. XXXIV, *Great Might*: The True Gentleman does not tread where Ritual is absent. XLVII, *Confinement*: Only the True Gentleman can hold on to Fortune in Confinement. The True Gentleman fathoms Life-Destiny, holds fast to Aspiration. He is Steadfast; he perseveres in Self-Cultivation even in times of Confinement; he finds Joy even when material circumstances are hard, during times of illness, in old age, in the face of psychological obstacles. LII, *Mountain*: Ban Biao's poem—"The Man of True Discernment . . . / Whether Moving or Still / Whether curved or straight, / Is always in tune with Time. / He treads the path of Sincerity, / He can live in any place, / He fears not the wildest barbarian shore." LXI, *Good Faith*: The Yang Lines on each side, above and below the Void, including two in the Center of each Trigram, are the building blocks of Good Faith, of Inner Truth and Sincerity. Sincerity, Good Faith, Trust—these are all connected; they all flow from the Tao; they are the essential qualities of the True Gentleman.

True Nature, *xing*

This is True Human Nature or Essence. It is composed of the human spiritual faculties, which become clouded over by desire, by things, by sensory stimuli (activities of the Human Heart-and-Mind). The Complete Reality Taoist path consists in the "double real-ization" of True Nature and of Life-Destiny. These are two parts of one whole. They are rediscovered or recovered through a Return in Stillness to the Primordial Origin, to the Uncarved Block of the Tao. This mirrors the undifferentiated state of the Universe before it became divided into Yin and Yang. LIX, *Dispersal*: To see through what is False, not to be bound by conditioned ways of thinking and being—this is a Vast Dispersal. "Great cries are uttered" as Falsehood is removed, stripped away. This is the Tao of Dispersal, Mastery of Self, a return to what is proper, to kindness. The Lord of Heart-and-Mind is at one with the Principle of Nature. This is Dispersal of the False, and Completion of Reality.

Work, *gongfu*

I use this term for the Spiritual Process of Inner Alchemy, or Self-Cultivation. XLVI, *Ascent*: This Hexagram, comments Magister Liu, stresses gentle progress, a gradual Ascent into the realm of Truth, requiring long and patient Self-Cultivation. It requires proper teaching from a Master, a Great Man, whose words can open up a path leading upward to Wisdom, like an all-penetrating Wind. It is a journey toward the Light, step by step, day by day. LIII, *Gradual*: The Work of Self-Realization is not accomplished in a single morn-ing or evening. The sequence is a subtle one. The Work is of long duration. It requires order, and Gradual Progress.

Yielding, *rou*

This is Soft as opposed to Hard. It is a quality of Yin, and of Yin Lines, by contrast with Firm, which is a quality of Yang. It is characteristic of Water, and a quality much prized in Taoism. In interpreting Hexagram XXXI, *Resonance*, the Commentary on the Image understands the Upper Trigram, Lake, as an emblem of Yielding Humility, further understood as Emptiness of Self, the open, hollow mental space that receives and responds, while the Lower Trigram, Mountain, is Firm and initiates.

Yin and Yang

These have been the two fundamental and interconnected binary polarities, or planes, of Chinese thought ever since late Zhou times (c. fourth century BC). They do not feature in the core text of the Oracle, but are basic to any understanding of the *I Ching* as a Book of Wisdom, and feature prominently in the Great Treatise and all subsequent commentaries. The words themselves may originally have referred to the sunny or southern side (Yang) and the shady or northern side (Yin) of a mountain or valley. From this they came to be associated with a wide range of "modalities": Yang for Heaven, the Sun, the bright, hot and dry, Fire, day, the male, the penis, the pure and light; Yin for Earth, the Moon, Water, night, the female, the vagina, the opaque and heavy, the dark, cool, and moist. All phenomena (the Myriad Things), including humanity, and, of course, the Trigrams and Hexagrams, are made up of Yin and Yang. In the *I Ching*, Yang is the Firm, Undivided Line; Yin is the Yielding, Divided Line. In a certain sense (but we need to be careful of words with such precise Western connotations), Yang is positive and active, Yin is negative and passive. Yang is assertive, Yin is receptive. Yang is purposeful and planned, Yin is spontaneous and effortless. Yang begins, Yin completes. With the passage of the dynasties, and the evolution of schools of thought, there were more complex models of the cosmological relationship between Yin and Yang, the Tao, and the Supreme Ultimate, the *taiji* from which the Yin and Yang emerged (see the diagram on page xxxiii.) To comprehend the modalities of Yin and Yang is to comprehend the Tao. Yang is action and expansion, Yin rest and contraction. Yang is potentiality, Yin actualization. Yang initiates, Yin nurtures. The Taoist alchemists of the Complete Reality School such as Magister Liu Yiming often analyze the Hexagrams in terms of overcoming and eliminating negative, or False, Yin Energy and reinforcing positive, or True, Yang Energy. It is in the interaction or dynamic of these two that every event originates. Their workings affect everything within the Universe. When they interact in Harmony, when the situation is in Harmony with the Tao, all is well—this is Auspicious. This Truth operates at all levels, the political as well as the personal, the psychological as well as the sexual. The secret to all is Harmony, and the way to Harmony lies through Self-Cultivation. Yin and Yang are not opposites. They are interconnected, mutually complementary polarities. Each needs the Other. Each contains the seed of the Other. They are lines of force, whose Nature it is to cross and mingle. Neither can continue to exist at its extreme; at that point it reverses into its opposite. This is the cycle. Yang gives birth to Yin. Yin gives birth to Yang. True Yin (in the words of Magister Liu) is contained within Yang. And vice versa. The Yin of Winter is transformed into the Yang of Summer. This process continues in an endless continuum. Their interdependence illustrates the oneness of the Tao. XVIII/6, *Blight*: In the fusion of Yin and Yang, one returns to the highest realm. With the Tao, one becomes one with Truth, one becomes indestructible. Cf. the entry in this Glossary for Elixir. XXIX, *The Abyss*: In the Taoist sexual-alchemical scheme of things, the *Kan* Trigram (one Yang line surrounded by two Yin, Yang within Yin) represents the Female element (Water, Kidneys, White Tiger, Earthly Anima), while the *Li* Trigram (one Yin line surrounded by two Yang, Yin within Yang) represents the Male element (Fire, Heart, Green Dragon, Celestial Animus). This is also true of the two Hexagrams (XXIX and XXX) formed by doubling these two Trigrams. Their Harmony (the Harmony of *Li* and *Kan*) is seen both in sexual intercourse and in advanced meditation practice, where the Inner Yin and Inner Yang of the individual fuse into one whole. (See the illustration of the Taoist Adept page xix.) Its fruits can be seen in Hexagram LXIII, *Complete*, where *Li* sits under *Kan*. The empty center of male *Li* is True (i.e., truly fulfilled) Yin; its Outer Yang enfolds Inner Yin. The full center of female *Kan* is True Yang; its Outer Yin encloses Inner Yang. When *Kan* and *Li* enjoy intercourse, then True Yin is "garnered"; it "supplements" True Yang. This produces Pure Essential Yang. This is the Return to Primordial Undifferentiated Energy.

Acknowledgments

I have accumulated many debts since this translation began over twelve years ago. I must begin by thanking Caroline White, at the time senior editor with Viking Penguin in New York, who so impulsively commissioned it in the first place. I am sure neither she nor I had any idea what I was letting myself in for! Next, profound thanks and apologies are due to John Siciliano, who has waited so patiently and sympathetically for the completed manuscript to arrive. A True Gentleman! I have been most fortunate to have my manuscript worked on by an outstanding copy editor, Janet Fletcher, who seems to have read my innermost thoughts, and by two diligent and gentle-minded editorial assistants, Doug Clark and Emily Hartley.

Throughout the long-drawn-out process, my wife, Rachel May, has given me generously of her time and of her acute critical judgment. Her companionship and love have indeed been Auspicious, her readings insightful and meticulous. Without her this task would simply never have been finished. Over the years, until his death in July 2009, I benefited from the constant kindness of David Hawkes, who followed the progress of my work with humor, constantly reminding me that "no one really knows what it all means."

To Professor Jao Tsung-yi, Hong Kong's preeminent man of letters, painter, and calligrapher, now in his ninety-seventh year, I am indebted for his calligraphic frontispiece, which echoes the inscription done more than fifty years ago by Tung Tso-pin for the Wilhelm/Baynes version. Professor Liu Ts'un-yan, to whose memory this translation is dedicated, guided my studies from April 1977 until his death in August 2009. For over thirty years he illustrated in his unstinted friendship the ultimate quality of Good Faith. I wish to honor his memory with this book.

The project began in France, where my old friend Alain Ginesty shared many moments of enthusiasm concerning the *I Ching* and Chinese culture—not as an intellectual pursuit, but as a *mode de vivre*. The work continued in Australia and Hong Kong. Numerous friends have asked me to consult the text with them, and in those consultations I have witnessed the powerful working of Sincerity. Louis Lee and Jacqueline Leung, dependable friends, were clearly apprehensive that I might not live to see Completion, and they performed many a service in order to ensure that their worst fears were not realized! Steve Balogh, old-time friend and Sage from the Oxford of the 1960s, kept tabs on me faithfully and alerted me to possible oversights with many an intercontinental phone call. My sister Sally Pullinger gave me courage with her finely tuned ear for the voice of the Tao.

Anthony C. Yu has sustained me through the past three decades, with his gentle insistence on the timeless *zhiyin* bond, Knowing the Sound, true friendship. One learns the hard way to discriminate between true and false! Leo Ou-fan Lee has been an inspirational friend these past few years, with his free spirit of the *xiaoyao xuezhe*, a latter-day Scholar Gipsy. The mellow friendship of Jan Kiely and Izumi Nakayama provided the best kind of Resonance.

All the calligraphy in this book was done by my good friend Liao Hsintien, artist and inspirational teacher, of Taiwan's National University of the Arts.

Duncan Campbell generously took time off to read the final draft, and kindly gave me both general and detailed comments. Eugenie Edquist also read the draft. She gave encouragement when it was most needed, and shared her passion for the strange and unexpected. Many friends in Hong Kong have tolerated my obsession. The *Kunqu* artist Tang Yuen-ha has shown me, through her performances and written reflections, that the principles underlying the *I Ching* apply equally to the art of Chinese musical theater—and indeed to everything else. On one memorable occasion, the chief percussionist from her opera troupe, Zhang Peicai, explained to me the musical counterpoint of the Hexagrams, and demonstrated the art of "drumming" the *I Ching*. Edwin Kong, another close friend of many decades, has constantly raised my spirits with his ever-ready wit and gift for lateral thinking. My dear friend the poet P. K. Leung, who passed away in early 2013, a matter of weeks before this work-in-progress was sent to the publisher, was a latter-day Sage of the Bamboo Grove, who would certainly have thought of a good way of celebrating Incompletion!

Chung Ling has quietly followed my progress, with her gently concerned comments. I deeply regret not having accepted her invitation, many years ago, to visit her *I Ching* Master in the mountains near Kao-hsiung. Over the years, lengthy breakfasts in Hong Kong with Brother Nicholas Koss have provided welcome spiritual sustenance, as have dinners with my friend Soong Shukong, embodiment of the fine Chinese tradition of the maverick man of letters.

Professor Mun Kin Chok convinced me that there is genuine value in relating this ancient text to the dilemmas of the modern business world. His is a deeply reasoned conviction. It certainly Profited me to see this Great Man.

I thank Kent Anderson, staunch supporter during several years in Canberra, for the trust he showed in my sometimes idiosyncratic endeavors. He was Steadfast. His humane approach to the running of a university community is, alas, all too rare nowadays. My assistant in Hong Kong, Tse Ka-hung, otherwise known as PS, did wonders with the computer, and saved me from many a Danger.

Over the past few difficult months, I have received infinite love and precious infusions of Inner Strength from my wife, Rachel, and my four wonderful children, Emma, Luke, Daniel, and Laura, who have stood Steadfastly around me and protected me during many an Inauspicious moment. I owe much also to friends old and new, whose presence and messages have brought light into places of Darkness: Will Channing, René and Sarah Coppieters, Mimi and Doug Christie, Fan Shengyu (*shutong extraordinaire*), Pieter and Marianne Holstein, Nick Hordern, Willy Matthews, Keiron Pearce, Lihong Rambeau, Richard Rigby, Christina Sanderson (*chauffeur fidèle*), Sue and Graeme Ward.

Finally, anyone glancing at these pages will immediately become aware of the huge debt I owe to many generations of *I Ching* scholars, of many dynasties and nationalities.

Fontmarty, Hong Kong, Canberra, and Broulee
February 2002 – April 2014

Index

Finding Table for Hexagrams

UPPER TRIGRAM / LOWER TRIGRAM	Qian	Zhen	Kan	Gen
Qian	1	34	5	26
Zhen	25	51	3	27
Kan	6	40	29	4
Gen	33	62	39	52
Kun	12	16	8	23
Xun	44	32	48	18
Li	13	55	63	22
Dui	10	54	60	41

Kun	Xun	Li	Dui
11	9	14	43
24	42	21	17
7	59	64	47
15	53	56	31
2	20	35	45
46	57	50	28
36	37	30	49
19	61	38	58

 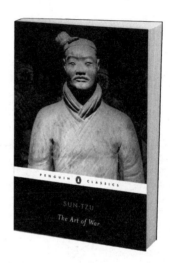

AVAILABLE FROM PENGUIN CLASSICS

One of the greatest novels of Chinese literature—also known as
The Dream of the Red Chamber—**in five volumes:**

The Golden Days: The Story of the Stone, Vol. 1

The Crab-Flower Club: The Story of the Stone, Vol. 2

The Warning Voice: The Story of the Stone, Vol. 3

The Debt of Tears: The Story of the Stone, Vol. 4

The Dreamer Wakes: The Story of the Stone, Vol. 5

PENGUIN CLASSICS